Lecture Notes in Computer Science　13630

Founding Editors

Gerhard Goos
Karlsruhe Institute of Technology, Karlsruhe, Germany

Juris Hartmanis
Cornell University, Ithaca, NY, USA

Editorial Board Members

Elisa Bertino
Purdue University, West Lafayette, IN, USA

Wen Gao
Peking University, Beijing, China

Bernhard Steffen
TU Dortmund University, Dortmund, Germany

Moti Yung
Columbia University, New York, NY, USA

More information about this series at https://link.springer.com/bookseries/558

Sankalp Khanna · Jian Cao · Quan Bai ·
Guandong Xu (Eds.)

PRICAI 2022:
Trends in
Artificial Intelligence

19th Pacific Rim International Conference on Artificial Intelligence
PRICAI 2022, Shanghai, China, November 10–13, 2022
Proceedings, Part II

 Springer

Editors
Sankalp Khanna (iD)
CSIRO Australian e-Health Research Centre
Brisbane, QLD, Australia

Quan Bai (iD)
University of Tasmania
Hobart, TAS, Australia

Jian Cao (iD)
Shanghai Jiao Tong University
Shanghai, China

Guandong Xu (iD)
University of Technology Sydney
Sydney, NSW, Australia

ISSN 0302-9743   ISSN 1611-3349 (electronic)
Lecture Notes in Computer Science
ISBN 978-3-031-20864-5   ISBN 978-3-031-20865-2 (eBook)
https://doi.org/10.1007/978-3-031-20865-2

© The Editor(s) (if applicable) and The Author(s), under exclusive license
to Springer Nature Switzerland AG 2022
This work is subject to copyright. All rights are reserved by the Publisher, whether the whole or part of the material is concerned, specifically the rights of translation, reprinting, reuse of illustrations, recitation, broadcasting, reproduction on microfilms or in any other physical way, and transmission or information storage and retrieval, electronic adaptation, computer software, or by similar or dissimilar methodology now known or hereafter developed.
The use of general descriptive names, registered names, trademarks, service marks, etc. in this publication does not imply, even in the absence of a specific statement, that such names are exempt from the relevant protective laws and regulations and therefore free for general use.
The publisher, the authors, and the editors are safe to assume that the advice and information in this book are believed to be true and accurate at the date of publication. Neither the publisher nor the authors or the editors give a warranty, expressed or implied, with respect to the material contained herein or for any errors or omissions that may have been made. The publisher remains neutral with regard to jurisdictional claims in published maps and institutional affiliations.

This Springer imprint is published by the registered company Springer Nature Switzerland AG
The registered company address is: Gewerbestrasse 11, 6330 Cham, Switzerland

Preface

These three-volume proceedings contain the papers presented at the 19th Pacific Rim International Conference on Artificial Intelligence (PRICAI 2022), held as a hybrid conference with both physical and online options during November 10–13, 2022, in Shanghai, China.

PRICAI, which was inaugurated in Tokyo in 1990, started out as a biennial international conference concentrating on artificial intelligence (AI) theories, technologies, and applications in the areas of social and economic importance for Pacific Rim countries. It provides a common forum for researchers and practitioners in various branches of AI to exchange new ideas and share experience and expertise. Since then, the conference has grown, both in participation and scope, to be a premier international AI event for all major Pacific Rim nations as well as countries from all around the world. In 2018, the PRICAI Steering Committee decided to hold PRICAI on an annual basis starting from 2019.

This year, we received an overwhelming number of valid submissions to the main track (403 submissions), the special track (18 submissions), and the industry track (11 submissions). This number was impressive considering the continuing COVID-19 pandemic situation around the globe. All submissions were reviewed and evaluated with the same highest quality standard through a double-blind review process.

Each paper received at least two reviews, with over 90% receiving three or more. During the review process, discussions among the Program Committee (PC) members in charge were carried out before recommendations were made, and, when necessary, additional reviews were sourced. Finally, the conference and program co-chairs read the reviews and comments and made a final calibration for differences among individual reviewer scores in light of the overall decisions. The entire Program Committee (including PC members, external reviewers, and co-chairs) expended tremendous effort to ensure fairness and consistency in the paper selection process.

Eventually, we accepted 91 regular papers and 39 short papers for oral presentation. This gives a regular paper acceptance rate of 21% and an overall acceptance rate of 30%.

The technical program consisted of three workshops and the main conference program. The workshops included the "Principle and practice of data and Knowledge Acquisition Workshop (PKAW 2022)," the "Decoding Models of Human Emotion Using Brain Signals Workshop", and the "The 1st International Workshop on Democracy and AI (DemocrAI2022)". The main program included an industry track and a special track on "Strong and General AI."

All regular and short papers were orally presented over four days in parallel and in topical program sessions. We were honored to have keynote presentations by four distinguished researchers in the field of AI whose contributions have crossed discipline boundaries: Toby Walsh (University of New South Wales, Australia), Qing Li (Hong Kong Polytechnic University, China), Jie Lu (University of Technology Sydney, Australia), and Yu Zheng (JD Technology, China). We were grateful to them for sharing their insights on their latest research with us.

The success of PRICAI 2022 would not be possible without the effort and support of numerous people from all over the world. First, we would like to thank the authors, PC members, and external reviewers for their time and efforts spent in making PRICAI 2022 a successful and enjoyable conference. We are also thankful to various fellow members of the conference committee, without whose support and hard work PRICAI 2021 could not have been successful:

- Advisory Board: Abdul Sattar, Beyong Kang, Takayuki Ito, Zhihua Zhou, Chengqi Zhang, and Fenrong Liu
- Special Track Chairs: Ji Zhang and Biao Wang
- Industry Chair: Hengshu Zhu
- Workshop Chairs: Ryuta Arisaka and Zehong Cao
- Tutorial Chairs: Weiwei Yuan and Rafik Hadfi
- Finance Chair: Shiyou Qian
- Local/Virtual Organizing Chairs: Shiyou Qian and Nengjun Zhu
- Publicity Chairs: Yi Yang and Mukesh Prasad
- Sponsorship Chairs: Dengji Zhao and Xiangfeng Luo
- Webmaster: Shiqing Wu

We gratefully acknowledge the organizational support of several institutions including the University of Tasmania (Australia), the University of Technology Sydney (Australia), Shanghai Jiao Tong University (China), CSIRO (Australia), Griffith University (Australia), Kyoto University (Japan), ShanghaiTech University (China), the University of South Australia (Australia), Nanjing University of Aeronautics and Astronautics (China), Shanghai University (China), Hefei University of Technology (China), the University of Southern Queensland (Australia), and the Shanghai Computer Society (China). Finally, we thank the team at Springer for their assistance in publishing the PRICAI 2022 proceedings as three volumes of its Lecture Notes in Artificial Intelligence series.

November 2022

Sankalp Khanna
Jian Cao
Quan Bai
Guandong Xu

Organization

PRICAI Steering Committee

Steering Committee

Hideyuki Nakashima (Chair)	Future University Hakodate, Japan
Zhi-Hua Zhou (Vice-chair)	Nanjing University, China
Abdul Sattar (Treasurer)	Griffith University, Australia
Sankalp Khanna (Secretary)	CSIRO Australian e-Health Research Centre, Australia
Quan Bai	University of Tasmania, Australia
Tru Hoang Cao	Ho Chi Minh City University of Technology, Vietnam
Xin Geng	Southeast University, China
Guido Governatori	Singapore Management University, Singapore
Takayuki Ito	Kyoto University, Japan
Fenrong Liu	Tsinghua University, China
Byeong Ho Kang	University of Tasmania, Australia
M. G. M. Khan	University of the South Pacific, Fiji
Dickson Lukose	Monash University, Australia
Abhaya Nayak	Macquarie University, Australia
Seong-Bae Park	Kyung Hee University, South Korea
Duc Nghia Pham	MIMOS Berhad, Malaysia
Alok Sharma	RIKEN, Japan, and University of the South Pacific, Fiji
Thanaruk Theeramunkong	Thammasat University, Thailand

Honorary Members

Randy Goebel	University of Alberta, Canada
Tu-Bao Ho	Japan Advanced Institute of Science and Technology, Japan
Mitsuru Ishizuka	University of Tokyo, Japan
Hiroshi Motoda	Osaka University, Japan
Geoff Webb	Monash University, Australia
Albert Yeap	Auckland University of Technology, New Zealand
Byoung-Tak Zhang	Seoul National University, South Korea
Chengqi Zhang	University of Technology Sydney, Australia

Conference Organizing Committee

General Chairs

Guandong Xu   University of Technology Sydney, Australia
Quan Bai   University of Tasmania, Australia

Program Chairs

Sankalp Khanna   CSIRO Australian e-Health Research Centre,
                                   Australia
Jian Cao   Shanghai Jiao Tong University, China

Special Track Chairs

Ji Zhang   University of Southern Queensland, Australia
Biao Wang   Zhejiang Lab, China

Industry Chair

Hengshu Zhu   Baidu Inc., China

Workshop Chairs

Ryuta Arisaka   Kyoto University, Japan
Zehong Cao   University of South Australia, Australia

Tutorial Chairs

Weiwei Yuan   Nanjing University of Aeronautics and
                                   Astronautics, China
Rafik Hadfi   Kyoto University, Japan

Local and Virtual Conference Chairs

Shiyou Qian   Shanghai Jiao Tong University, China
Nengjun Zhu   Shanghai University, China

Finance Chair

Shiyou Qian   Shanghai Jiao Tong University, China

Sponsorship Chairs

Dengji Zhao   ShanghaiTech University, China
Xiangfeng Luo   Shanghai University, China

Publicity Chairs

Yi Yang   Hefei University of Technology, China
Mukesh Prasad   University of Technology Sydney, Australia

Webmaster

Shiqing Wu   University of Tasmania, Australia

Advisory Board

Abdul Sattar   Griffith University, Australia
Byeong Kang   University of Tasmania, Australia
Takayuki Ito   Kyoto University, Japan
Zhihua Zhou   Nanjing University, China
Chengqi Zhang   University of Technology Sydney, Australia
Fenrong Liu   Tsinghua University, China

Program Committee

Eriko Aiba   University of Electro-Communications, China
Abdullah Alsuhaibani   University of Technology Sydney, Australia
Patricia Anthony   Lincoln University, New Zealand
Mohammad Arshi Saloot   MIMOS Berhad, Malaysia
Mohamed Jaward Bah   Zhejiang Lab, China
Quan Bai   University of Tasmania, Australia
Chutima Beokhaimook   Rangsit University, Thailand
Ateet Bhalla   Independent Technology Consultant, India
Chih How Bong   Universiti Malaysia Sarawak, Malaysia
Poonpong Boonbrahm   Walailak University, Thailand
Aida Brankovic   CSIRO Australian e-Health Research Centre,
                             Australia
Xiongcai Cai   University of New South Wales, Australia
Jian Cao   Shanghai Jiao Tong University, China
Jimmy Cao   University of South Australia, Australia
Tru Cao   University of Texas Health Science Center at
                             Houston, USA
Hutchatai Chanlekha   Kasetsart University, Thailand
Siqi Chen   Tianjin University, China
Songcan Chen   Nanjing University of Aeronautics and
                             Astronautics, China
Tony Chen   University of Adelaide, Australia
Wu Chen   Southwest University, China
Yakun Chen   University of Technology Sydney, Australia

Yingke Chen	Sichuan University, China
Wai Khuen Cheng	Universiti Tunku Abdul Rahman, Malaysia
Yihang Cheng	Tianjin University, China
Boonthida Chiraratanasopha	Yala Rajabhat University, Thailand
Dan Corbett	University of Sydney, Australia
Zhihong Cui	Shandong University, China
Célia da Costa Pereira	Université Côte d'Azur, France
Jirapun Daengdej	Assumption University, Thailand
Abdollah Dehzangi	Rutgers University, USA
Clare Dixon	University of Manchester, UK
Zheng Dong	Baidu Inc., China
Shyamala Doraisamy	Universiti Putra Malaysia, Malaysia
Tri Duong	University of Technology Sydney, Australia
Shanshan Feng	Shandong Normal University, China
Somchart Fugkeaw	Thammasat University, Thailand
Katsuhide Fujita	Tokyo University of Agriculture and Technology, Japan
Naoki Fukuta	Shizuoka University, China
Marcus Gallagher	University of Queensland, Australia
Dragan Gamberger	Rudjer Boskovic Institute, Croatia
Xiaoying Gao	Victoria University of Wellington, New Zealand
Xin Geng	Southeast University, China
Manolis Gergatsoulis	Ionian University, Greece
Alban Grastien	Australian National University, Australia
Charles Gretton	Australian National University, Australia
Jie Gui	University of Michigan, USA
Fikret Gurgen	Boğaziçi University, Turkey
Rafik Hadfi	Kyoto University, Japan
Songqiao Han	Shanghai University of Finance and Economics, China
Bavly Hanna	University of Technology Sydney, Australia
David Hason Rudd	University of Technology Sydney, Australia
Hamed Hassanzadeh	CSIRO Australian e-Health Research Centre, Australia
Tessai Hayama	Nagaoka University of Technology, Japan
Linlin Hou	Zhejiang Lab, China
Juhua Hu	University of Washington, USA
Liang Hu	University of Technology Sydney, Australia
Jiwei Huang	China University of Petroleum, Beijing, China
Xiaodi Huang	Charles Sturt University, Australia
Nguyen Duy Hung	Thammasat University, Thailand
Huan Huo	University of Technology Sydney, Australia

Van Nam Huynh	Japan Advanced Institute of Science and Technology (JAIST), Japan
Masashi Inoue	Tohoku Institute of Technology, Japan
Md Rafiqul Islam	University of Technology Sydney, Australia
Takayuki Ito	Kyoto University, Japan
Sanjay Jain	National University of Singapore, Singapore
Guifei Jiang	Nankai University, China
Ting Jiang	Zhejiang Lab, China
Yichuan Jiang	Southeast University, China
Nattagit Jiteurtragool	King Mongkut's University of Technology North Bangkok, Thailand
Hideaki Kanai	Japan Advanced Institute of Science and Technology (JAIST), Japan
Ryo Kanamori	Nagoya University, Japan
Natsuda Kaothanthong	Thammasat University, Thailand
Jessada Karnjana	National Electronics and Computer Technology Center, Thailand
C. Maria Keet	University of Cape Town, South Africa
Gabriele Kern-Isberner	Technische Universitaet Dortmund, Germany
Nor Khalid	Auckland University of Technology, New Zealand
Sankalp Khanna	CSIRO Australian e-Health Research Centre, Australia
Nichnan Kittiphattanabawon	Walailak University, Thailand
Sébastien Konieczny	CRIL - CNRS, France
Alfred Krzywicki	University of Adelaide, Australia
Li Kuang	Central South University, China
Young-Bin Kwon	Chung-Ang University, South Korea
Ho-Pun Lam	Data61, CSIRO, Australia
Nasith Laosen	Phuket Rajabhat University, Thailand
Siddique Latif	University of Southern Queensland, Australia
Roberto Legaspi	KDDI Research, Inc., Japan
Gang Li	Deakin University, Australia
Guangliang Li	Ocean University of China, China
Qian Li	Chinese Academy of Sciences, China
Tianrui Li	Southwest Jiaotong University, China
Weihua Li	Auckland University of Technology, New Zealand
Yicong Li	University of Technology Sydney, Australia
Zihao Li	University of Technology Sydney, Australia
Chanjuan Liu	Dalian University of Technology, China
Guanfeng Liu	Macquarie University, Australia
Hao Liu	HKUST(GZ), China
Kangzheng Liu	Huazhong University of Science and Technology, China

Tun Lu	Fudan University, China
Dickson Lukose	GCS Agile Pty. Ltd., Australia
Xiangfeng Luo	Shanghai University, China
Haiping Ma	Anhui University, China
Michael Maher	Reasoning Research Institute, Australia
Xinjun Mao	National University of Defense Technology, China
Eric Martin	University of New South Wales, Australia
Sanparith Marukatat	NECTEC, Thailand
Michael Mayo	University of Waikato, New Zealand
Qingxin Meng	Nottingham University Business School, China
Nor Liyana Mohd Shuib	Universiti Malaya, Malaysia
M. A. Hakim Newton	University of Newcastle, Australia
Phi Le Nguyen	Hanoi University of Science and Technology, Vietnam
Kouzou Ohara	Aoyama Gakuin University, Japan
Mehmet Orgun	Macquarie University, Australia
Maurice Pagnucco	University of New South Wales, Australia
Songwen Pei	University of Shanghai for Science and Technology, China
Laurent Perrussel	IRIT, Université de Toulouse, France
Bernhard Pfahringer	University of Waikato, New Zealand
Jantima Polpinij	Mahasarakham University, Thailand
Thadpong Pongthawornkamol	Kasikorn Business-Technology Group, Thailand
Mukesh Prasad	University of Technology, Sydney, Australia
Shiyou Qian	Shanghai Jiao Tong University, China
Chuan Qin	Baidu, China
Joel Quinqueton	LIRMM, France
Teeradaj Racharak	Japan Advanced Institute of Science and Technology, Japan
Jessica Rahman	Australian National University, Australia
Farid Razzak	New York University, USA
Fenghui Ren	University of Wollongong, Australia
Mark Reynolds	University of Western Australia, Australia
Vahid Riahi	CSIRO Australian e-Health Research Centre, Australia
Kazumi Saito	University of Shizuoka, Japan
Chiaki Sakama	Wakayama University, Japan
Nicolas Schwind	National Institute of Advanced Industrial Science and Technology (AIST), Japan
Lin Shang	Nanjing University, China
Alok Sharma	RIKEN, Japan

Dazhong Shen	University of Science and Technology of China, China
Chenwei Shi	Tsinghua University, China
Kaize Shi	University of Technology Sydney, Australia
Zhenwei Shi	Beihang University, China
Soo-Yong Shin	Sungkyunkwan University, South Korea
Yanfeng Shu	CSIRO, Australia
Chattrakul Sombattheera	Mahasarakham University, Thailand
Insu Song	James Cook University, Australia
Markus Stumptner	University of South Australia, Australia
Xing Su	Beijing University of Technology, China
Xin Sun	Catholic University of Lublin, Poland
Ying Sun	The Hong Kong University of Science and Technology (Guangzhou), China
Boontawee Suntisrivaraporn	DTAC, Thailand
Thepchai Supnithi	NECTEC, Thailand
David Taniar	Monash University, Australia
Xiaohui Tao	University of Southern Queensland, Australia
Yanyun Tao	Soochow University, China
Mingfei Teng	Rutgers University, USA
Michael Thielscher	University of New South Wales, Australia
Satoshi Tojo	Japan Advanced Institute of Science and Technology (JAIST), Japan
Shikui Tu	Shanghai Jiao Tong University, China
Miroslav Velev	Aries Design Automation, USA
Muriel Visani	Hanoi University of Science and Technology, Vietnam, and La Rochelle University, France
Nhi N. Y. Vo	Royal Melbourne Institute of Technology University, Vietnam
Biao Wang	Zhejiang Lab, China
Chao Wang	Guangzhou HKUST Fok Ying Tung Research Institute, China
Hao Wang	Nanyang Technological University, Singapore
Xiangmeng Wang	University of Technology, Sydney, Australia
Xinxhi Wang	Shanghai University, China
Zhen Wang	Zhejiang Lab, China
Xiao Wei	Shanghai University, China
Paul Weng	UM-SJTU Joint Institute, China
Yang Wenli	University of Tasmania, Australia
Wayne Wobcke	University of New South Wales, Australia
Sartra Wongthanavasu	Khon Kaen University, Thailand
Brendon J. Woodford	University of Otago, New Zealand

Hongyue Wu	Zhejiang University, China
Ou Wu	Tianjin University, China
Shiqing Wu	University of Technology Sydney, Australia
Xing Wu	Shanghai University, China
Xiaoyu Xia	University of Southern Queensland, Australia
Kaibo Xie	University of Amsterdam, The Netherlands
Dawei Xu	University of Technology Sydney, Australia
Guandong Xu	University of Technology Sydney, Australia
Ming Xu	Xi'an Jiaotong-Liverpool University, China
Shuxiang Xu	University of Tasmania, Australia
Zenghui Xu	Zhejiang Lab, China
Hui Xue	Southeast University, China
Kong Yan	Nanjing University of Information, Science and Technology, China
Bo Yang	University of Science and Technology of China, China
Chao Yang	University of Technology, Sydney, Australia
Haoran Yang	University of Technology Sydney, Australia
Wencheng Yang	University of Southern Queensland, Australia
Yang Yang	Nanjing University of Science and Technology, China
Yi Yang	Hefei University of Technology, China
Roland Yap	National University of Singapore, Singapore
Kenichi Yoshida	University of Tsukuba, Japan
Dianer Yu	University of Technology Sydney, Australia
Hang Yu	Shanghai University, China
Ting Yu	Zhejiang Lab, China
Weiwei Yuan	Nanjing University of Aeronautics and Astronautics, China
Takaya Yuizono	Japan Advanced Institute of Science and Technology (JAIST), Japan
Du Zhang	California State University, USA
Haijun Zhang	Harbin Institute of Technology Shenzhen Graduate School, China
Ji Zhang	University of Southern Queensland, Australia
Le Zhang	University of Science and Technology of China, China
Min-Ling Zhang	Southeast University, China
Qi Zhang	University of Science and Technology of China, China
Shichao Zhang	Guangxi Normal University, China
Wen Zhang	Beijing University of Technology, China
Xiaobo Zhang	Southwest Jiaotong University, China

Xuyun Zhang	Macquarie University, Australia
Yang Zhang	Zhejiang Lab, China
Zili Zhang	Deakin University, Australia
Dengji Zhao	ShanghaiTech University, China
Hongke Zhao	Tianjin University, China
Ruilin Zhao	Huazhong University of Science and Technology, China
Sirui Zhao	Southwest University of Science and Technology, China
Yanchang Zhao	CSIRO, Australia
Shuigeng Zhou	Fudan University, China
Chen Zhu	Baidu Talent Intelligence Center, China
Guohun Zhu	University of Queensland, Australia
Hengshu Zhu	Baidu Inc., China
Nengjun Zhu	Shanghai University, China
Xingquan Zhu	Florida Atlantic University, USA
Guobing Zou	Shanghai University, China

Additional Reviewers

Agyemang, Brighter
Arisaka, Ryuta
Bea, Khean Thye
Burgess, Doug
Cao, Zehong
Chalothorn, Tawunrat
Chandra, Abel
Chandra, Rohitash
Chen, Siqi
Clifton, Marshall
Colley, Rachael
Dawoud, Ahmed
Delobelle, Jérôme
Dinh, Thi Ha Ly
Duan, Jiaang
Duchatelle, Théo
Effendy, Suhendry
Everaere, Patricia
Feng, Shanshan
Feng, Xuening
Gao, Jianqi
Gao, Shang
Gao, Yi
Geng, Chuanxing

Haiyang, Xia
Han, Aiyang
Hang, Jun-Yi
He, Yifan
He, Zhengqi
Hu, Jianshu
Hu, Liang
Hu, Mengting
Hu, Yuxuan
Ishikawa, Yuichi
Jia, Binbin
Jiang, Shan
Jiang, Yunpeng
Jiang, Zhaohui
Khan, Naimat Ullah
Kliangkhlao, Mallika
Konishi, Tatsuya
Kumar, Shiu
Lai, Zhong Yuan
Le, Van An
Leow, Steven
Li, Jinpeng
Li, Li
Li, Pengbo

Li, Renjie
Li, Ruijun
Li, Shu
Lin, Shuxia
Liu, Xiaxue
Liu, Yuxin
Ma, Zhongchen
Malysiak, Kevin
Mayer, Wolfgang
Meng, Qiang
Mezza, Stefano
Mi, Yuxi
Miao, Ran
Ming, Zuheng
Mittelmann, Munyque
Muhammod, Rafsanjani
Ngo, Courtney
Nguyen, Mau Toan
Nguyen, Minh Hieu
Nguyen, Trong-Tung
Nguyen, Trung Thanh
Niu, Hao
Parker, Timothy
Pereira, Gean

Pho, Ngoc Dang Khoa
Pino Perez, Ramon
Polpinij, Jantima
Qian, Junqi
Raboanary, Toky Hajatiana
Rashid, Mahmood
Ren, Yixin
Riahi, Vahid
Rosenberg, Manou
Sahoh, Bukhoree
Selway, Matt
Sharma, Ronesh
Shi, Jingli
Shi, Kaize
Song, Baobao
Song, Zhihao
Sun, Qisong
Sun, Ruoxi
Takeda, Naoto
Tan, Hongwei
Tang, Huaying

Tang, Wei
Tao, Yanyun
Thao Nguyen, Truong
Tran, Kim Dung
Vo, Chau
Wang, Deng-Bao
Wang, Guodong
Wang, Hui
Wang, Mengyan
Wang, Xinyu
Wang, Zirui
Wanyana, Tezira
Wardah, Wafaa
Wu, Yao
Xia, Dawen
Xia, Yewei
Xiangru, Yu
Xie, Kaibo
Xu, Rongxin
Yang, Bo
Yang, Yang

Yang, Yikun
Yang, Zhichao
Yao, Naimeng
Ye, Tangwei
Yi, Fan
Yin, Ze
Yu, Guanbao
Yu, Yongxin
Yuan, Weiwei
Zang, Hao
Zhang, Chris
Zhang, Jiaqiang
Zhang, Qingyong
Zhang, Sixiao
Zhang, Tianyi
Zhang, Yao
Zhang, Yi-Fan
Zhao, Jianing
Zhou, Wei

Contents – Part II

Natural Language Processing

Neural Networks and Deep Learning

Knowledge Representation
and Reasoning

Moderately-Balanced Representation Learning for Treatment Effects with Orthogonality Information

Yiyan Huang[1], Cheuk Hang Leung[1], Shumin Ma[2], Qi Wu[1(✉)],
Dongdong Wang[3], and Zhixiang Huang[3]

[1] School of Data Science, City University of Hong Kong, Hong Kong, China
yiyhuang3-c@my.cityu.edu.hk, {chleung87,qiwu55}@cityu.edu.hk
[2] Guangdong Provincial Key Laboratory of Interdisciplinary Research
and Application for Data Science, BNU-HKBU United
International College, Zhuhai, China
shuminma@uic.edu.cn
[3] JD Digits, Beijing, China
{wangdongdong9,huangzhixiang}@jd.com

Abstract. Estimating the average treatment effect (ATE) from observational data is challenging due to selection bias. Existing works mainly tackle this challenge in two ways. Some researchers propose constructing a score function that satisfies the orthogonal condition, which guarantees that the established ATE estimator is "orthogonal" to be more robust. The others explore representation learning models to achieve a balanced representation between the treated and the controlled groups. However, existing studies fail to 1) discriminate treated units from controlled ones in the representation space to avoid the over-balanced issue; 2) fully utilize the "orthogonality information". In this paper, we propose a moderately-balanced representation learning (MBRL) framework based on recent covariates balanced representation learning methods and orthogonal machine learning theory. This framework protects the representation from being over-balanced via multi-task learning. Simultaneously, MBRL incorporates the noise orthogonality information in the training and validation stages to achieve a better ATE estimation. The comprehensive experiments on benchmark and simulated datasets show the superiority and robustness of our method on treatment effect estimations compared with existing state-of-the-art methods.

Keywords: Treatment effects · Causal inference · Representation learning

1 Introduction

Causal inference has drawn a lot of attention across various research areas including statistics [2,25], economics and finance [3,7,15] commercial social network

---

Y. Huang and C. H. Leung—Co-first authors are in alphabetical order.

© The Author(s), under exclusive license to Springer Nature Switzerland AG 2022
S. Khanna et al. (Eds.): PRICAI 2022, LNCS 13630, pp. 3–16, 2022.
https://doi.org/10.1007/978-3-031-20865-2_1

applications [5,10] and health care [8,12]. One of the main tasks of causal inference is to estimate the *average treatment effect* (ATE). For example, a biotech company must know to what extent a newly developed vaccine can reduce the probability of infection for the whole population. The classical method to acquire the ATE is to conduct randomized controlled trials (RCTs), where the treatment is randomly assigned to the population but not selectively. Then the effect of the vaccine (treatment) on the infection (outcome) is measured by the difference between the average infection rate of the vaccinated group (treated group) and that of the unvaccinated group (controlled group). RCTs are regarded as the golden standard for treatment effect estimation, but conducting RCTs is costly and time-consuming [9,21]. Thus, estimating the treatment effects in the observational study instead of RCTs becomes more and more tempting.

When it comes to estimating the ATE from the observational data, we need to handle the selection bias. The selection bias exists due to the non-random treatment assignment. The treatment assignment may be further influenced by the covariates that also directly affect the outcome. In the vaccine example, limited vaccines tend to be distributed to vulnerable individuals who are susceptible to infection. Such a non-random treatment assignment mechanism naturally results in a covariate shift phenomenon. That is, the covariates of the treated population can substantially differ from that of the controlled population.

Two classical methods are developed for adjusting the shifted covariates: inverse propensity weighting (IPW) and regression adjustment (see more details in [26]). IPW weights the instances based on the propensity scores to mimic the principle of RCTs to estimate ATE. Nevertheless, the IPW estimators are sensitive to the misspecification of the propensity score. Regression adjustment methods directly estimate the outcome model instead of propensity scores, whereas they would inevitably lead to biased ATE estimations due to overfitting and regularization bias [3]. Researchers improve classical methods from the perspectives of statistics and methodology.

The *orthogonal score function* proposed in [3] is a statistical correction by incorporating both the outcome model and the propensity score estimations. Since such a score function satisfies the *orthogonal condition*, the ATE estimator derived from the score function is consistent as long as one of the two underlying relations is correctly specified. This is also known as the *doubly robust* property. Recently, balanced representation learning techniques have attracted researchers' attention. The intuitive idea is to construct a pair of "twins" in the representation space by minimizing the imbalance between the distributions of the treated and controlled groups [23]. However, such methods mainly focus on the balance but overlook the discrimination between treated and controlled units. If the distributions of the treated and controlled groups in the representation space are too similar to be distinguished, it would be difficult to infer the ATE accurately. Such a trade-off plays a crucial role in identifying the treatment effects [23]. The importance of the undiscriminating problem is also emphasized by [10].

In this paper, with the tool of orthogonal machine learning, we propose a moderately-balanced representation learning (MBRL) framework to estimate the treatment effects. MBRL trains in a multi-task framework and stops on a perturbation error metric to obtain a moderately-balanced representation. The merits of MBRL include i) preserving predictive information for inferring individual outcomes; ii) designing a multi-task learning framework to achieve a moderately-balanced rather than over-balanced representation; iii) fully utilizing the orthogonality information during the training and validation stages to achieve superior treatment effect estimations.

2   Preliminaries

Potential Outcome Framework. Let $\mathbf{Z}$ be s-dimensional covariates such that $\mathbf{Z} \in \mathcal{Z} \subset \mathbb{R}^s$, where $\mathcal{Z}$ is the sample space of covariates. $D \in \{0,1\}$ denotes the treatment variable. $Y(0), Y(1)$ represent the potential outcomes for the treatment $D = 0$ and $D = 1$ respectively such that $Y(0), Y(1) \in \mathcal{Y} \subset \mathbb{R}$ with $\mathcal{Y}$ being the sample space of outcome. We denote $w = (\mathbf{z}, d, y)$ as the realizations of the random variables $W = (\mathbf{Z}, D, Y)$. If the observed treatment is d, then the factual outcome Y^F equals $Y(d)$. We suppose the observational dataset contains N individuals and the mth individual is observed as $(\mathbf{z}_m, d_m, y_m)$. The target quantity ATE τ is defined as $\tau := \mathbb{E}[Y(1) - Y(0)]$.

Identifying the treatment effects under the potential outcome framework [22] requires some fundamental assumptions: Strong Ignorability, Overlap, Consistency and Stable Unit Treatment Value Assumption (SUTVA). These assumptions guarantee that treatment effects can be inferred if we specify the relation $\mathbb{E}[Y \mid D, \mathbf{Z}]$, which is equivalent to estimating $g_0(D, \mathbf{Z})$ in the following interactive model when the treatment variable takes a binary value [3]:

$$
\begin{aligned}
Y &= g_0(D, \mathbf{Z}) + \xi, & \mathbb{E}[\xi \mid D, \mathbf{Z}] &= 0, \\
D &= m_0(\mathbf{Z}) + \nu, & \mathbb{E}[\nu \mid \mathbf{Z}] &= 0.
\end{aligned}
\tag{1}
$$

Here, g_0 and m_0 are the true *nuisance functions*. ξ and ν are the noise terms. $m_0(\mathbf{Z}) = \mathbb{E}[D \mid \mathbf{Z}]$ is the *propensity score*. Let i be an element of $\{0,1\}$. The true causal parameter θ_0^i is defined as $\theta_0^i := \mathbb{E}[Y(i)] = \mathbb{E}[g_0(i, \mathbf{Z})]$ for $i \in \{0,1\}$, and the true ATE τ is computed by $\tau = \theta_0^1 - \theta_0^0$. We denote the estimated (θ_0^i, g_0, m_0) as $(\hat{\theta}^i, \hat{g}, \hat{m})$, and then the estimated ATE is computed by $\hat{\tau} = \hat{\theta}^1 - \hat{\theta}^0$.

Orthogonal Estimators. We aim to estimate the true causal parameters θ_0^1 and θ_0^0 given N i.i.d. samples $\{W_m = (\mathbf{Z}_m, D_m, Y_m)\}_{m=1}^N$. The standard procedure to acquire the estimated causal parameters $\hat{\theta}^1$ and $\hat{\theta}^0$ is: 1) getting the estimated nuisance functions $\hat{\rho}$, e.g., $\hat{\rho} = (\hat{g}, \hat{m})$; 2) constructing a score function $\psi(W, \theta^i, \rho)$ such that we can derive the estimated causal parameter $\hat{\theta}^i$ by solving $\mathbb{E}[\psi(W, \theta^i, \hat{\rho})] = 0$, where θ^i is a causal parameter that lies in the causal parameter space. According to [3], the estimator $\hat{\theta}^i$ solved from $\mathbb{E}[\psi(W, \theta^i, \hat{\rho})] = 0$ is robust to the estimated nuisance functions $\hat{\rho}$ if the corresponding score function $\psi(W, \theta^i, \rho)$ satisfies the orthogonal condition that is stated in Definition 1.

Definition 1 (Orthogonal Condition). *Let* $W = (\mathbf{Z}, D, Y)$, $\rho_0 = (h_{0,1}, \ldots, h_{0,\gamma})$ *be the true nuisance functions and* θ_0 *be the true causal parameter with* θ *being a causal parameter that lies in the causal parameter space. A score function* $\psi(W, \theta, \rho)$ *is said to satisfy the orthogonal condition with respect to* $\rho = (h_1, \ldots, h_\gamma)$ *if*

$$\mathbb{E}\left[\partial_{h_i}\psi(W, \theta, \rho)\mid_{\rho=\rho_0, \theta=\theta_0} \mid \mathbf{Z}\right] = 0 \quad \forall 1 \leq i \leq \gamma.$$

Under the interactive model setup (1), the nuisance functions are (g, m), and the true ones are (g_0, m_0). In this case, the orthogonal condition guarantees that the estimator is consistent if either one of the two nuisance functions, but unnecessarily both, is accurately estimated. This is well known as the doubly robust property. In this paper, we introduce two orthogonal estimators $\hat{\theta}_1$ [3] and $\hat{\theta}_2$ [14] in Proposition 1, and we can estimate ATE by plugging the learned nuisance functions into the orthogonal estimators.

Proposition 1 (Orthogonal Estimators). *Let the nuisance functions be* $\rho = (g, m)$ *and the causal parameter be* θ^i *for* $i \in \{0, 1\}$, *the score functions* $\psi_1(W, \theta^i, \rho)$ *and* $\psi_2(W, \theta^i, \rho)$ *that satisfy the orthogonal condition (Definition 1) are:*

$$\psi_1(W, \theta^i, \rho) = \theta^i - g(i, \mathbf{Z}) - (Y - g(i, \mathbf{Z}))\frac{iD + (1-i)(1-D)}{im(\mathbf{Z}) + (1-i)(1-m(\mathbf{Z}))}; \quad (2)$$

$$\psi_2(W, \theta^i, \rho) = \theta^i - g(i, \mathbf{Z}) - (Y(i) - g(i, \mathbf{Z}))\frac{((D - m(\mathbf{Z})) - \mathbb{E}[\nu \mid \mathbf{Z}])^2}{\mathbb{E}[\nu^2 \mid \mathbf{Z}]}. \quad (3)$$

The corresponding orthogonal estimators are:

$$\hat{\theta}_1^i \quad solves \quad \frac{1}{N}\sum_{m=1}^{N}\psi_1(W_m, \theta^i, \hat{\rho}) = 0; \quad \hat{\theta}_2^i \quad solves \quad \frac{1}{N}\sum_{m=1}^{N}\psi_2(W_m, \theta^i, \hat{\rho}) = 0.$$

3   Method

In this section, we first introduce the orthogonality information in Sect. 3.1. Then we present the network structure, objective function and model selection criterion of the proposed MBRL method based on the orthogonality information in Sect. 3.2.

3.1   Orthogonality Information

Recall that the ATE estimators $\hat{\theta}_1^i$ and $\hat{\theta}_2^i$ are doubly robust since they are orthogonal estimators. Still, they could be non-orthogonal once the model setup (1) relaxes the restrictions on the noise terms ξ and ν since the score functions ψ_1 and ψ_2 might violate the orthogonal condition. Hence, we propose the *Noise Conditions*, which would enforce the learned nuisance functions adapted to orthogonal estimators.

Proposition 2 (Noise Conditions). *Under the interactive model setup* (1), *the conditions on the noise terms ξ and ν, i.e., $\mathbb{E}\left[\xi \mid D, \mathbf{Z}\right] = 0$ and $\mathbb{E}\left[\nu \mid \mathbf{Z}\right] = 0$, are sufficient conditions for ψ_1 and ψ_2 being orthogonal score functions ($\hat{\theta}_1^i$ and $\hat{\theta}_2^i$ being orthogonal estimators).*

Given the noise conditions, we can exploit an essential property, the *noise orthogonality* property.

Property 1 (Noise Orthogonality). Under the interactive model setup (1) and the noise conditions, we have $\mathbb{E}[(Y - g_0(D, \mathbf{Z}))(D - m_0(\mathbf{Z}))] = 0$.

The noise conditions are sufficient conditions for the estimators $\hat{\theta}_1^i$ and $\hat{\theta}_2^i$ being orthogonal, so noise conditions play an important role when we approximate the true nuisance functions (g_0, m_0) with estimated ones $(\hat{g}, \hat{m})$. Besides, under the noise conditions, the noise orthogonality can be utilized for our model selection. The decompositions similar to Noise Orthogonality also appeared in [3,11].

3.2   The Proposed Framework

We propose a moderately-balanced representation learning (MBRL) framework to obtain $(\hat{g}, \hat{m})$ to estimate ATE, and the MBRL architecture is illustrated in Fig. 1. The MBRL network maps the original covariates space to the representation space (i.e., $\Phi : \mathcal{Z} \rightarrow \mathcal{R}$) such that 1) the representation preserves predictive information for outcomes; 2) the map makes the distributional discrepancy between the treated group and the controlled group small enough; 3) the domain (treated or controlled) of each individual is well discriminated; 4) the orthogonality information is involved.

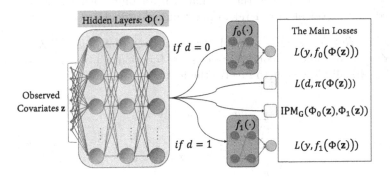

Fig. 1. The MBRL network architecture.

Learning Representation of Covariates. The distributions of the treated group and the controlled group are inherently disparate due to selection bias. Previous works handle this problem using a balanced representation learning method

[16,23], which forces the distributions of treatment and control groups to be similar enough in the representation space. Specifically, a representation is learned by minimizing the integral probability metrics (IPM), which measures the imbalance between the distributions of the treated population and the controlled population (see the details in [23]):

$$\mathcal{L}_{imb} = \text{IPM}_G(\{\Phi(\mathbf{z}_m)\}_{m:d_m=1}, \{\Phi(\mathbf{z}_m)\}_{m:d_m=0}). \tag{4}$$

The Prediction of Outcome and Treatment. MBRL predicts the outcome by the function $f : \{0,1\} \times \mathcal{R} \to \mathcal{Y}$, which is partitioned into two functions f_0 and f_1:

$$f(d_m, \Phi(\mathbf{z}_m)) = d_m f_1(\Phi(\mathbf{z}_m)) + (1 - d_m) f_0(\Phi(\mathbf{z}_m)). \tag{5}$$

f_1 and f_0 are the output functions that map the representation to the potential outcomes for $D = 1$ and $D = 0$, respectively. $f(d_m, \Phi(\mathbf{z}_m))$ is the predicted factual outcome and we aim to minimize the factual outcome loss $\mathcal{L}_{fo}$ such that

$$\mathcal{L}_{fo} = \frac{1}{N} \sum_{m=1}^{N} [y_m - f(d_m, \Phi(\mathbf{z}_m))]^2. \tag{6}$$

Here, $\hat{g}(d_m, \mathbf{z}_m) = f(d_m, \Phi(\mathbf{z}_m))$ is the estimated factual outcome of the mth unit. Aside from making a low-error prediction over factual outcomes with a small divergence between treated and controlled groups, the distinguishability of the treated units from the controlled ones is also non-negligible. Therefore, we propose to maximize the distinguishability loss $\mathcal{L}_{dis}$ (measured by log-likelihood) such that

$$\mathcal{L}_{dis} = \frac{1}{N} \sum_{m=1}^{N} \left[d_m \log \pi(\Phi(\mathbf{z}_m)) + (1 - d_m) \log(1 - \pi(\Phi(\mathbf{z}_m))) \right]. \tag{7}$$

Here, $\hat{m}(\mathbf{z}_m) = \pi(\Phi(\mathbf{z}_m))$ is the estimated probability of the mth unit being assigned the treatment $D = 1$ (aka the estimated propensity score).

The Noise Regularizations. Recall Proposition 2 that $\mathbb{E}[\xi \mid D, \mathbf{Z}] = 0$ and $\mathbb{E}[\nu \mid \mathbf{Z}] = 0$ are sufficient conditions for score functions ψ_1 and ψ_2 being orthogonal. Empirically, we want to involve the following constraints:

$$\frac{1}{N} \sum_{m=1}^{N} [y_m - f(d_m, \Phi(\mathbf{z}_m))] = 0,$$

$$\frac{1}{N} \sum_{m=1}^{N} [d_m - \pi(\Phi(\mathbf{z}_m))] = 0. \tag{8}$$

This motivates us to formalize Ω_y and Ω_d such that

$$\Omega_y = \epsilon_y \Big| \frac{1}{N} \sum_{m=1}^{N} [y_m - f(d_m, \Phi(\mathbf{z}_m))] \Big|,$$

$$\Omega_d = \epsilon_d \Big| \frac{1}{N} \sum_{m=1}^{N} [d_m - \pi(\Phi(\mathbf{z}_m))] \Big|. \tag{9}$$

The partial derivative of Ω_y w.r.t. ϵ_y (or Ω_d w.r.t. ϵ_d) equaling 0 forces the learned nuisance functions to satisfy Eqn. (8). Therefore, minimizing the noise regularizations Ω_y and Ω_d adapts the entire learning process to satisfy the orthogonal score function. This idea corresponds to the targeted regularizations (see more discussions in [11,24]).

Multi-task Learning and Perturbation Error. MBRL learns the nuisance functions through multi-task learning with following three tasks in each iteration:

$$\text{Task 1:} \quad \max_{\pi,\epsilon_d} \quad \mathcal{L}_{dis} - \lambda_1 \Omega_d$$

$$\text{Task 2:} \quad \min_{\Phi} \quad \mathcal{L}_{imb} \tag{10}$$

$$\text{Task 3:} \quad \min_{\Phi,f,\epsilon_y} \quad \mathcal{L}_{fo} + \lambda_2 \Omega_y$$

Instead of putting $\mathcal{L}_{imb}$ into Task 3 as a regularization, we let $\mathcal{L}_{imb}$ be one of the multiple tasks. To be specific, Task 1 updates π to produce the propensity scores, and Task 2 achieves a balance between $\{\Phi(\mathbf{z}_m)\}_{m:d_m=1}$ and $\{\Phi(\mathbf{z}_m)\}_{m:d_m=0}$. Additionally, MBRL incorporates a novel model selection criterion, the *Perturbation Error*, according to the noise orthogonality property. It takes advantage of the noise orthogonality information by perturbating the main evaluation metric. For example, if the final model is selected by the metric root-mean-square error ($RMSE = \sqrt{\frac{1}{N}\sum_{m=1}^{N}(y_m - \hat{y}_m)^2}$), then the perturbation error ϵ_p is defined as

$$\epsilon_p = RMSE + \beta|\frac{1}{N}\sum_{m=1}^{N}(y_m - \hat{y}_m)(d_m - \hat{d}_m)|.$$

Here, β is the perturbation coefficient which is a constant; $\hat{y}_m$ and $\hat{d}_m$ are the predicted values of $f(d_m, \Phi(\mathbf{z}_m))$ and $\pi(\Phi(\mathbf{z}_m))$, respectively. The final model is selected on the validation set based on the minimum ϵ_p. If either outcome or propensity score is well specified (i.e., representations are moderately-balanced instead of over-balanced), the second term in ϵ_p would be small.

4   Experiments

In this section, we conduct comprehensive experiments on benchmark datasets to evaluate the performance produced by MBRL and other prevalent causal inference methods. We further test the effectiveness of MBRL on simulated datasets with different levels of selection bias. All the experiments are run on Dell 7920 with 1×16-core Intel Xeon Gold 6250 3.90 GHz CPU and 3x NVIDIA Quadro RTX 6000 GPU.

4.1   Dataset Description

Since the ground truth of treatment effects are inaccessible for real-world data, it is difficult to evaluate the performance of causal inference methods for ATE estimation. Previous causal inference literatures assess their methods on two prevalent semi-synthetic datasets: IHDP and Twins.

IHDP. The IHDP dataset is a well-known benchmark dataset for causal inference introduced by [13]. It includes 747 samples with 25-dimensional covariates associated with the information of infants and their mothers, such as birth weight and mother's age. These covariates are collected from a real-world randomized experiment. Our aim is to study the treatment effect of the specialist visits (binary treatment) on the cognitive scores (continuous-valued outcome). The outcome is generated using the NPCI package [6], and the selection bias is created by removing a subset of the treated population. We use the same 1000 IHDP datasets as the ones used in [23], where each dataset is split by the ratio of 63%/27%/10% as training/validation/test sets.

Twins. The Twins dataset [19] collects twin births in the USA between 1989 and 1991 [1]. After the data processing, each unit has 30 covariates relevant to parents, pregnancy and birth [28]. The treatment $D = 1$ indicates the heavier twin while $D = 0$ indicates the lighter twin, and the outcome Y is a binary variable defined as the 1-year mortality. Similar to [28], we only select twins who have the same gender and both weigh less than $2\,\mathrm{kg}$, which finally gives 11440 pairs of twins whose mortality rate is 17.7% for the lighter twin, and 16.1% for the heavier twin. To create the selection bias, we selectively choose one of the two twins as the factual observation based on the covariates of mth individual: $D_m|\mathbf{Z}_m \sim \mathrm{Bernoulli}(\mathrm{Sigmoid}(\mathbf{w}^T\mathbf{Z}_m + n))$, where $\mathbf{w} \sim \mathcal{U}((-0.01, 0.01)^{30 \times 1})$ and $n \sim \mathcal{N}(0, 0.01)$. We repeat the data generating process for 100 times, and the generated 100 Twins datasets are all split by the ratio of 56%/24%/20% as training/validation/test sets.

4.2   Performance Measurement and Experimental Settings

Performance Measurement. Generally, the comparisons are based on the absolute error in ATE: $\epsilon_{ATE} = |\tau - \hat{\tau}|$. Additionally, we also test the performance of MBRL on individual treatment effect (ITE) estimations. For IHDP datasets, we adopt Precision in Estimation of Heterogeneous Effect (PEHE):

$$\epsilon_{PEHE} = \frac{1}{N} \sum_{m=1}^{N} \left([y_m(1) - y_m(0)] - [\hat{y}_m(1) - \hat{y}_m(0)]\right)^2.$$

For Twins datasets, we follow [19] to adopt Area Under ROC Curve (AUC).

Baseline Models. We compare our MBRL method with the following basline models: linear regression with the treatment as feature (**OLS/LR$_1$**), separate linear regression for each treatment group (**OLS/LR$_2$**), k-nearest neighbor (**k-NN**), bayesian additive regression trees (**BART**) [4], causal forest (**CF**) [25], balancing linear regression (**BLR**) [16], balancing neural network (**BNN**) [16], treatment-agnostic representation network (**TARNet**) [23], counterfactual regression with Wasserstein distance (**CFR-WASS**) [23], causal effect variational autoencoders (**CEVAE**) [19], local similarity preserved individual treatment effect (**SITE**) [27], generative adversarial networks for inference of treatment effect (**GANITE**) [28] and (**Dragonnet**) [24].

Experimental Details. In our experiments, IPM$_\mathcal{G}$ is chosen as the Wasserstein distance. Let the empirical distribution of representation be $P(\Phi(\mathbf{Z})) = P(\Phi(\mathbf{Z}) \mid D = 1)$ for the treated group and $Q(\Phi(\mathbf{Z})) = Q(\Phi(\mathbf{Z}) \mid D = 0)$ for the controlled group. Assuming that $\mathcal{G}$ is defined as the functional space of a family of 1-Lipschitz functions, we obtain the 1-Wasserstein distance for IPM$_\mathcal{G}$ [23]:

$$Wass(P, Q) = \inf_{k \in \mathcal{K}} \int_{\mathbf{h} \in \{\Phi(\mathbf{Z}_m)\}_{m: D_m = 1}} \|k(\mathbf{h}) - \mathbf{h}\| P(\mathbf{h}) d\mathbf{h}.$$

Here, $\mathcal{K} = \{k \mid k : Q(k(\Phi(\mathbf{Z}))) = P(\Phi(\mathbf{Z}))\}$ defines the set of push-forward functions that transform the representation distribution of the treated group $P(\Phi(\mathbf{Z}))$ to that of the controlled group $Q(\Phi(\mathbf{Z}))$.

Table 1. Performance comparisons and ablation study with mean $\pm$ standard error on 1000 **IHDP** datasets. ϵ_{ATE}: Lower is better. $\sqrt{\epsilon_{PEHE}}$: Lower is better.

Method	In-sample		Out-of-sample	
	$\sqrt{\epsilon_{PEHE}}$	ϵ_{ATE}	$\sqrt{\epsilon_{PEHE}}$	ϵ_{ATE}
OLS/LR$_1$	$5.8 \pm .3$	$.73 \pm .04$	$5.8 \pm .3$	$.94 \pm .06$
OLS/LR$_2$	$2.4 \pm .1$	$.14 \pm .01$	$2.5 \pm .1$	$.31 \pm .02$
k-NN	$2.1 \pm .1$	$.14 \pm .01$	$4.1 \pm .2$	$.79 \pm .05$
BART	$2.1 \pm .1$	$.23 \pm .01$	$2.3 \pm .1$	$.34 \pm .02$
CF	$3.8 \pm .2$	$.18 \pm .01$	$3.8 \pm .2$	$.40 \pm .03$
CEVAE	$2.7 \pm .1$	$.34 \pm .01$	$2.6 \pm .1$	$.46 \pm .02$
SITE	$.69 \pm .0$	$.22 \pm .01$	$.75 \pm .0$	$.24 \pm .01$
GANITE	$1.9 \pm .4$	$.43 \pm .05$	$2.4 \pm .4$	$.49 \pm .05$
BLR	$5.8 \pm .3$	$.72 \pm .04$	$5.8 \pm .3$	$.93 \pm .05$
BNN	$2.2 \pm .1$	$.37 \pm .03$	$2.1 \pm .1$	$.42 \pm .03$
TARNet	$.88 \pm .0$	$.26 \pm .01$	$.95 \pm .0$	$.28 \pm .01$
CFR-WASS	$.71 \pm .0$	$.25 \pm .01$	$.76 \pm .0$	$.27 \pm .01$
Dragonnet	$1.3 \pm .4$	$.14 \pm .01$	$1.3 \pm .5$	$.20 \pm .05$
MBRL	$\mathbf{.52 \pm .0}$	$.12 \pm .01$	$\mathbf{.57 \pm .0}$	$\mathbf{.13 \pm .01}$
MBRL + $\hat{\theta}_1^i$	$\mathbf{.52 \pm .0}$	$.10 \pm .00$	$\mathbf{.57 \pm .0}$	$.17 \pm .01$
MBRL + $\hat{\theta}_2^i$	$\mathbf{.52 \pm .0}$	$.11 \pm .00$	$\mathbf{.57 \pm .0}$	$.20 \pm .01$

In addition, we adopt ELU activation function and set 4 fully connected layers with 200 units for both the representation encoder network $\Phi(\cdot)$ and the discriminator $\pi(\cdot)$, and 3 fully connected layers with 100 units for the outcome prediction networks $f_0(\cdot)$ and $f_1(\cdot)$. The optimizer is chosen as Adam [17], and the learning rate for the optimizer is set to be $1e^{-3}$. We set (batch size, epoch) to be $(100, 1000)/(1000, 250)$ for IHDP/Twins experiments, and the hyper parameters (λ_1, λ_2) to be $(0.01, 0.01)/(0.1, 0.1)$ for IHDP/Twins experiments. The final model early stops on the metric ϵ_p, and we choose β in ϵ_p as 0.1 and 100 for IHDP experiments and Twins experiments, respectively.

For the baseline models, we follow the same settings of hyperparameters as in their published paper and code. For our MBRL network, the optimal hyperparameters are chosen in the same way as [23]. The searching ranges are reported in Table 4.

4.3   Results Analysis

Table 1 and Table 2 report part of the performances of baseline methods and MBRL on IHDP and Twins datasets. We present the average values and standard errors of ϵ_{ATE}, ϵ_{PEHE} and AUC (mean ± std). The lower ϵ_{ATE} and ϵ_{PEHE} or the higher AUC, the better. Bold indicates the best method for each dataset.

As stated in Table 1 and Table 2, we have the following observations. 1) MBRL achieves significant improvements in both ITE and ATE estimations across all datasets compared to the baseline models. 2) The advanced representation learning methods that focus on estimating ITE (such as SITE, TARNet and CFR-WASS) show their inapplicability to ATE estimations. By contrast, MBRL not only significantly outperforms these representation learning methods in ITE estimations but also remains among the best ATE results. 3) The state-of-the-art ATE estimation method, Dragonnet, achieves superior ATE estimations across all the baseline models but yields a substantial error in ITE estimations. Although Dragonnet shares a similar basic network architecture to MBRL, MBRL can obtain a substantially lower ϵ_{ATE} than Dragonnet owing to

Table 2. Performance comparisons with mean ± standard error on 100 **Twins** datasets. ϵ_{ATE}: Lower is better. AUC: Higher is better.

Method	In-sample		Out-of-sample	
	AUC	ϵ_{ATE}	AUC	ϵ_{ATE}
OLS/LR$_1$	.660 ± .005	.004 ± .003	.500 ± .028	.007 ± .006
OLS/LR$_2$	.660 ± .004	.004 ± .003	.500 ± .016	.007 ± .006
k-NN	.609 ± .010	**.003 ± .002**	.492 ± .012	**.005 ± .004**
BART	.506 ± .014	.121 ± .024	.500 ± .011	.127 ± .024
CEVAE	.845 ± .003	.022 ± .002	.841 ± .004	.032 ± .003
SITE	.862 ± .002	.016 ± .001	.853 ± .006	.020 ± .002
BLR	.611 ± .009	.006 ± .004	.510 ± .018	.033 ± .009
BNN	.690 ± .008	.006 ± .003	.676 ± .008	.020 ± .007
TARNet	.849 ± .002	.011 ± .002	.840 ± .006	.015 ± .002
CFR-WASS	.850 ± .002	.011 ± .002	.842 ± .005	.028 ± .003
MBRL	**.879 ± .000**	**.003 ± .000**	**.874 ± .001**	.007 ± .001
MBRL + $\hat{\theta}_1^i$	**.879 ± .000**	**.003 ± .000**	**.874 ± .001**	.008 ± .000
MBRL + $\hat{\theta}_2^i$	**.879 ± .000**	**.003 ± .000**	**.874 ± .001**	.006 ± .001

the multi-task learning framework and the utilization for orthogonality information. These observations indicate that the proposed MBRL method is extremely
effective for estimating treatment effects.

We further conduct an ablation study on IHDP datasets to test if orthogonality information is practical in real applications. The relevant results are
reported in Table 3. We let MBRL* denote MBRL without perturbation error
ϵ_p, and MBRL** denote MBRL without any orthogonality information (ϵ_p, Ω_d
and Ω_y). We find that incorporating orthogonality information will enhance the
power of estimating treatment effects, whether with or without orthogonal estimators. This enhancement is pronounced especially when orthogonal estimators
are plugged in for in-sample data.

4.4   Simulation Study

In this part, we mainly investigate two questions. Q1. Does MBRL perform more
stably to the level of selection bias than the state-of-the-art model Dragonnet?
Q2. Can the noise orthogonality information, the perturbation error ϵ_p, improve
ATE estimations regardless of different models/estimators/selection bias levels?

We generate 2500 treated samples whose covariates $\mathbf{Z}^1 \sim \mathcal{N}(\boldsymbol{\mu}^1, 0.5 \times \Sigma\Sigma^T)$,
and 5000 controlled whose covariates $\mathbf{Z}^0 \sim \mathcal{N}(\boldsymbol{\mu}^0, 0.5 \times \Sigma\Sigma^T)$, where $\boldsymbol{\mu}^1$ and
$\boldsymbol{\mu}^0$ are both 10-dimensional vector and $\Sigma \sim \mathcal{U}((-1,1)^{10\times10})$. The level of selection bias, measured by KL divergence of $\boldsymbol{\mu}^1$ with respect to $\boldsymbol{\mu}^0$, would vary
by fixing $\boldsymbol{\mu}^0$ and adjusting $\boldsymbol{\mu}^1$. The potential outcomes of mth individual are
generated as $Y(1) \mid \mathbf{Z}_m \sim (\mathbf{w}_1^T \mathbf{Z}_m + n_1)$, $Y(0) \mid \mathbf{Z}_m \sim (\mathbf{w}_0^T \mathbf{Z}_m + n_0)$, where
$\mathbf{w}_1 \sim \mathcal{U}((-1,1)^{10\times1})$, $\mathbf{w}_0 \sim \mathcal{U}((-1,1)^{10\times1})$, $n_1 \sim \mathcal{N}(0,0.1)$, $n_0 \sim \mathcal{N}(0,0.1)$. By
adjusting $\boldsymbol{\mu}^1$ and fixing $\boldsymbol{\mu}^0$, we obtain five datasets with different levels of KL
divergence in $\{0,\ 62.85,\ 141.41,\ 565.63,\ 769.89\}$. We run experiments on each
dataset 100 times and draw box plots with regard to ϵ_{ATE} on the test set in
Fig. 2.

In Fig. 2(a), we first find that MBRL shows stronger robustness and achieves
significantly better ATE estimations with regard to different selection bias levels

Table 3. Ablation study on IHDP
datasets.

Method	In-sample		Out-of-sample	
	$\sqrt{\epsilon_{PEHE}}$	ϵ_{ATE}	$\sqrt{\epsilon_{PEHE}}$	ϵ_{ATE}
MBRL**	.523 ± .006	.129 ± .005	.568 ± .009	.141 ± .006
MBRL*	.522 ± .006	.128 ± .005	.567 ± .009	.139 ± .006
MBRL	.522 ± .007	.121 ± .005	.565 ± .008	.133 ± .005
MBRL** + θ_1^i	.523 ± .006	.101 ± .004	.568 ± .009	.171 ± .007
MBRL* + θ_1^i	.523 ± .006	.102 ± .004	.567 ± .009	.170 ± .007
MBRL + θ_1^i	.522 ± .007	.102 ± .004	.565 ± .008	.166 ± .007
MBRL** + θ_2^i	.523 ± .006	.122 ± .005	.568 ± .009	.210 ± .008
MBRL* + θ_2^i	.523 ± .006	.121 ± .005	.567 ± .009	.208 ± .008
MBRL + θ_2^i	.522 ± .007	.114 ± .005	.565 ± .008	.204 ± .008

Table 4. The searching ranges of
hyperparameters.

Hyperparameters	IHDP	Twins
λ_1, λ_2	0.01, 0.1, 1	0.01, 0.1, 1
Depth of Φ	2, 3, 4	2, 3, 4
Dim of Φ	100, 200	100, 200
Depth of π	2, 3, 4	2, 3, 4
Dim of π	100, 200	100, 200
Depth of f_0, f_1	2, 3, 4	2, 3, 4
Dim of f_0, f_1	100, 200	100, 200
Batch size	100, 300	500, 1000
Epoch	500, 1000	250, 500

compared with Dragonnet. In addition, it is noticable that choosing the perturbation error ϵ_p as the model selection metric would yield smaller ϵ_{ATE} for any model (Dragonnet or MBRL). Particularly, ϵ_p corrects more errors for MBRL than Dragonnet, which indicates that ϵ_p works better if a model utilizes the orthogonality information in the training stage. In Fig. 2(b), we have two main observations: i) the criterion ϵ_p improves ATE estimations for all estimators across different selection bias levels; ii) the improvement brought by ϵ_p becomes more substantial when selection bias increases.

5 Related Work

Representation Learning. Our work has a strong connection with the balanced representation learning methods proposed in [16,23], where they mainly focus on minimizing the imbalance between the different treatment groups in the representation space but overlook maximizing the discrimination of each unit's treatment domain. IGNITE framework is proposed in [10] to infer individual treatment effects from networked data, where they achieve a balanced representation that captures patterns of hidden confounders predictive of treatment assignments. This inspires us to study treatment effects by training a moderately-balanced representation via multi-task learning. Other works relevant to representation learning include [18,19,24,27,28] and references therein.

Orthogonal Score Function. [3] develop the theory of double/debiased machine learning (DML) from [20]. They define the notion of orthogonal condition, which allows their DML estimator to be doubly robust. Based on the theory of [3], another orthogonal estimator is proposed by [14], aiming to overcome the high

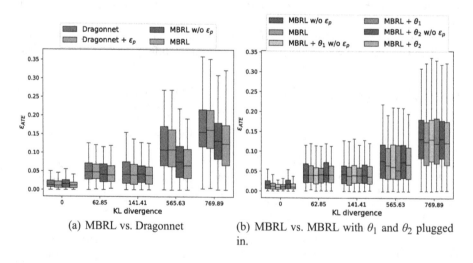

(a) MBRL vs. Dragonnet

(b) MBRL vs. MBRL with θ_1 and θ_2 plugged in.

Fig. 2. Comparisons between models with and without ϵ_p w.r.t. varying levels of selection bias.

variance issue suffered by DML due to the misspecified propensity score. Despite the success of orthogonal estimators, the establishment of them requires the noise conditions to guarantee the corresponding score functions satisfying the orthogonal condition. None of the existing literature emphasizes the critical role of noise conditions or utilizes the orthogonality information for the model selection.

6 Conclusion

This paper proposes an effective representation learning method, MBRL, to study the treatment effects. Specifically, MBRL avoids the over-balanced issue by leveraging treatment domains of the representations via multi-task learning. MBRL further takes advantage of the orthogonality information and involves it in the training and validation stages. The extensive experiments show that 1) MBRL has strong predictability for the potential outcomes, distinguishability for the treatment assignment, applicability to orthogonal estimators, and robustness to the selection bias; 2) MRBL achieves substantial improvements on treatment effect estimations compared with existing state-of-the-art methods.

Acknowledgement. Qi Wu acknowledges the support from the Hong Kong Research Grants Council [General Research Fund 14206117, 11219420, and 11200219], CityU SRG-Fd fund 7005300, and the support from the CityU-JD Digits Laboratory in Financial Technology and Engineering, HK Institute of Data Science. The work described in this paper was partially supported by the InnoHK initiative, The Government of the HKSAR, and the Laboratory for AI-Powered Financial Technologies.

References

1. Almond, D., Chay, K.Y., Lee, D.S.: The costs of low birth weight. Q. J. Econ. **120**(3), 1031–1083 (2005)
2. Athey, S., Wager, S.: Estimating treatment effects with causal forests: an application. Observat. Stud. **5**(2), 37–51 (2019)
3. Chernozhukov, V., et al.: Double/debiased machine learning for treatment and structural parameters. Econ. J. **21**(1), C1–C68 (2018)
4. Chipman, H.A., George, E.I., McCulloch, R.E.: Bart: Bayesian additive regression trees. Ann. Appl. Stat. **4**(1), 266–298 (2010)
5. Chu, Z., Rathbun, S.L., Li, S.: Graph infomax adversarial learning for treatment effect estimation with networked observational data. In: KDD, pp. 176–184 (2021). https://doi.org/10.1145/3447548.3467302
6. Dorie, V.: Nonparametric methods for causal inference. https://github.com/vdorie/npci (2021)
7. Farrell, M.H.: Robust inference on average treatment effects with possibly more covariates than observations. J. Econ. **189**(1), 1–23 (2015)
8. Glass, T.A., Goodman, S.N., Hernán, M.A., Samet, J.M.: Causal inference in public health. Ann. Rev. Public Health **34**, 61–75 (2013)
9. Guo, R., Cheng, L., Li, J., Hahn, P.R., Liu, H.: A survey of learning causality with data: problems and methods. ACM Comput. Surv. (CSUR) **53**(4), 1–37 (2020)

10. Guo, R., Li, J., Li, Y., Candan, K.S., Raglin, A., Liu, H.: Ignite: a minimax game toward learning individual treatment effects from networked observational data. In: IJCAI, pp. 4534–4540 (2020)
11. Hatt, T., Feuerriegel, S.: Estimating Average Treatment Effects via Orthogonal Regularization, pp. 680–689. Association for Computing Machinery, New York, NY, USA (2021). https://doi.org/10.1145/3459637.3482339
12. Hill, J., Su, Y.S.: Assessing lack of common support in causal inference using Bayesian nonparametrics: implications for evaluating the effect of breastfeeding on children's cognitive outcomes. The Annals of Applied Statistics, pp. 1386–1420 (2013)
13. Hill, J.L.: Bayesian nonparametric modeling for causal inference. J. Comput. Graph. Stat. **20**(1), 217–240 (2011)
14. Huang, Y., et al.: Robust causal learning for the estimation of average treatment effects. In: 2022 International Joint Conference on Neural Networks (IJCNN 2022). IEEE (2022)
15. Huang, Y., et al.: The causal learning of retail delinquency. In: Proceedings of the AAAI Conference on Artificial Intelligence, vol. 35, pp. 204–212 (2021)
16. Johansson, F., Shalit, U., Sontag, D.: Learning representations for counterfactual inference. In: International Conference on Machine Learning, pp. 3020–3029. PMLR (2016)
17. Kingma, D.P., Ba, J.: Adam: a method for stochastic optimization. arXiv preprint arXiv:1412.6980 (2014)
18. Li, S., Fu, Y.: Matching on balanced nonlinear representations for treatment effects estimation. In: NIPS (2017)
19. Louizos, C., Shalit, U., Mooij, J., Sontag, D., Zemel, R., Welling, M.: Causal effect inference with deep latent-variable models. In: Proceedings of the 31st International Conference on Neural Information Processing Systems, pp. 6449–6459 (2017)
20. Neyman, J.: C (α) tests and their use. Sankhyā Indian J. Stat. Ser. A, 1–21 (1979)
21. Pearl, J.: Causal inference in statistics: an overview. Stat. Surv. **3**, 96–146 (2009)
22. Rubin, D.B.: Causal inference using potential outcomes: design, modeling, decisions. J. Am. Stat. Assoc. **100**(469), 322–331 (2005)
23. Shalit, U., Johansson, F.D., Sontag, D.: Estimating individual treatment effect: generalization bounds and algorithms. In: International Conference on Machine Learning, pp. 3076–3085. PMLR (2017)
24. Shi, C., Blei, D., Veitch, V.: Adapting neural networks for the estimation of treatment effects. In: Advances in Neural Information Processing Systems, pp. 2503–2513 (2019)
25. Wager, S., Athey, S.: Estimation and inference of heterogeneous treatment effects using random forests. J. Am. Stat. Assoc. **113**(523), 1228–1242 (2018)
26. Yao, L., Chu, Z., Li, S., Li, Y., Gao, J., Zhang, A.: A survey on causal inference. ACM Trans. Knowl. Discov. Data **15**(5), 1–46 (2021). https://doi.org/10.1145/3444944
27. Yao, L., Li, S., Li, Y., Huai, M., Gao, J., Zhang, A.: Representation learning for treatment effect estimation from observational data. In: Advances in Neural Information Processing Systems 31 (2018)
28. Yoon, J., Jordon, J., Van Der Schaar, M.: GANITE: estimation of individualized treatment effects using generative adversarial nets. In: International Conference on Learning Representations (2018)

Source-Free Implicit Semantic Augmentation for Domain Adaptation

Zheyuan Zhang and Zili Zhang[✉]

College of Computer and Information Science, Southwest University,
Chongqing 400715, China
zhangzl@swu.edu.cn

Abstract. Unsupervised Domain Adaptation (UDA) challenges the problem of alleviating the effect of domain shift. Common UDA methods all require labelled source samples. However, in some real application scenarios, such as Federated Learning, the source data is inaccessible due to data privacy or intellectual property, and only a pre-trained source model and target data without labels are accessible. This challenging problem is called Source-Free Domain Adaptation (SFDA). To address this, we introduce a generation encoder to generate source prototypes depending on the hidden knowledge from the pre-trained source classifier. The generated source prototypes can describe the distribution of source samples in the feature space to a certain extent to solve the Source-Free problem. We also propose Source-Free Implicit Semantic Augmentation (SFISA) for adaptation. SFISA consists of two main stages: source and target class prototypes generation and Source-Free semantic augmentation adaptation based on generated class prototypes. Extensive experiments on the UDA benchmarks demonstrate the efficacy of our generation encoder and augmentation method SFISA.

Keywords: Source-free domain adaptation · Prototype generation · Implicit semantic augmentation

1 Introduction

On a variety of computer vision tasks, Deep Neural Networks (DNNs) have shown exceptional performance [8,9,16]. The success of DNNs depends on a huge amount of labelled data. Hence, it is necessary to utilize prior related labelled datasets to avoid data labelling, which is time-consuming and expensive. Many efforts to develop Unsupervised Domain Adaptation (UDA) methods have been made to transfer knowledge from a labelled source domain to a related, unlabelled target domain. UDA methods can be mainly divided into three branches: (1) methods based on domain discrepancy minimization [6,12,20,21]; (2) methods based on adversarial learning [7,25]; (3) methods based on classifier adaptation [2,5,13,15,19,32]. However, sometimes only the source pre-trained model is accessible in real-world application scenes due to data privacy. This situation

© The Author(s), under exclusive license to Springer Nature Switzerland AG 2022
S. Khanna et al. (Eds.): PRICAI 2022, LNCS 13630, pp. 17–31, 2022.
https://doi.org/10.1007/978-3-031-20865-2_2

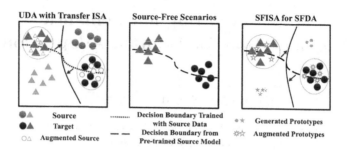

Fig. 1. Motivation of SFISA. In Source-Free domain adaptation scenarios, SFISA is able to augment generated source class prototypes towards target semantics in order to effectively adapt the pre-trained classifier from source domain to target domain.

leads that common UDA methods fail due to the lack of source data (Source-Free Scenarios in Fig. 1). Therefore, this paper concentrates on this more practical task called Source-Free Domain Adaptation (SFDA). SFDA aims to adapt a pre-trained source model to a target domain without source data. Existing SFDA methods are concentrated on refining the pre-trained source model by using target pseudo-labelling training [10,17] or by generating target-style samples [14]. The shortcomings of these methods are: (1) pseudo-labelling may lead to noisy labels due to the domain shifts, and (2) generating target-style samples may be difficult due to the training difficulties of Generative Adversarial Networks.

Our Source-Free Implicit Semantic Augmentation (SFISA) is proposed to address these problems (SFISA for SFDA in Fig. 1). Specifically, SFISA comprises two stages: (1) Class Prototype Generation: We use pre-trained models to mine hidden knowledge from the source domain, and propose discriminant consistency to generate reliable target class prototypes. (2) Source-Free Semantic Augmentation Adaptation: The semantic bias between domains for each class is firstly calculated. Then, to capture the target intra-class semantic variations, SFISA calculates intra-class covariance. Finally, SFISA uses a multivariate normal distribution to sample semantic transformation directions for source prototype augmentation to guide source augmented prototypes towards the target domain. Extensive experiments on UDA benchmarks datasets demonstrate the effectiveness of SFISA. The following are the primary contributions of this paper:

- In SFISA, a novel class prototype generation strategy for SFDA is proposed. Our generation strategy makes the generated source prototypes more compact and discriminative and the generated target prototypes more reliable.
- In SFISA, an implicit semantic augmentation adaptation method in the Source-Free scenario for classifier adaptation is also proposed. This method enables that source prototype features can be augmented towards target implicitly.

The rest of the paper is organized as follows: Sect. 2 provides the related work; Sect. 3 describes the proposed method; Sect. 4 presents the results of applying the method in different benchmarks; Sect. 5 presents the conclusions.

2   Related Work

Our method is closely related to Unsupervised Domain Adaptation and Source-Free Domain Adaptation. In this section, we give a brief review of these two aspects.

2.1   Unsupervised Domain Adaptation (UDA)

UDA is to transfer knowledge from a label-rich source domain to a label-scarce domain. UDA methods can be mainly divided into three categories: (1) UDA based on adversarial Learning: With adversarial manners, UDA methods based on adversarial training make models learn domain-invariant features, which reduce the discrepancy between two domains. For instance, Domain Adversarial Neural Network (DANN) [7] and Multi-Adversarial Domain Adaptation (MADA) [25] introduce a domain discriminator or multi-mode discriminators to make the features of two domains indistinguishable. (2) UDA based on Statistical Moments Alignment (SMA): SMA concentrates on mitigating the domain difference by minimizing statistical discrepancy. To name a few, maximum mean discrepancy (MMD) [20,21] minimizes the domain discrepancy by measuring statistical metrics. Depending on contrastive learning, CAN [12] and CoSCA [6] are able to maximize intra-class discrepancy and minimize inter-class discrepancy. (3) UDA based on Classifier Adaptation: Classifier Adaptation (CA) is also an indispensable part of UDA. This is because the classifier sharing between domains is quite restrictive. Some CA methods augment training samples towards target style to adapt the classifier [2,5,19]. Another typical line of works concentrate on mitigating the classifier perturbation or achieving joint distribution alignment by constructing task-specific classifiers, such as [13,32].

These methods all require source domain labelled samples. However, source data may be inaccessible in practice due to data privacy, which makes these methods fail in Source-Free scenarios.

2.2   Source-Free Domain Adaptation (SFDA)

Source-Free Domain Adaptation (SFDA) aims to only utilize a pre-trained source model to transfer knowledge to target domain without using data from the source domain. Some existing methods adopt a self-training strategy to refine the pre-trained model either by generating pseudo-labels as SHOT [17] and NRC [31] or by generating samples with target domain style as MA [14]. However, the pseudo-labels can be quite noisy owing to the domain discrepancy, which is ignored by these methods. Moreover, it is tricky to train a Generative Adversarial Networks (GANs) to generate images with target style. BAIT [30] utilizes pre-trained source classifiers as anchors to align domains on class level.

Compared with the above methods, our SFISA generates source class prototypes to implement classifier adaptation rather than generating images with target style. Meanwhile, SFISA further alleviates the negative transfer effect by implementing weighted contrastive alignment and maintaining diversity-discriminability.

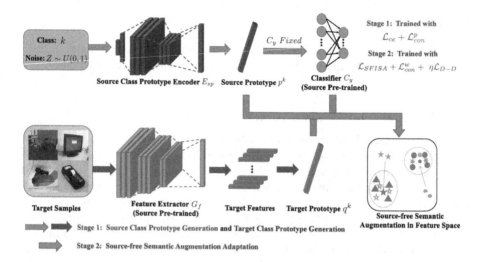

Fig. 2. Overview of our SFISA. SFISA consists of two stages: (1) **Class Prototype Generation:** Source class prototypes are generated depending on the hidden knowledge from C_y by $\mathcal{L}_{ce} + \mathcal{L}_{con}^p$ and target class prototypes are generated based on the pseudo-labelling strategies. (2) **Source-Free Semantic Augmentation Adaptation:** This adpatation is based on the generated prototypes by $\mathcal{L}_{SFISA} + \mathcal{L}_{con}^w + \eta\mathcal{L}_{D-D}$.

3 Method

The preliminaries of Source-Free Domain Adaptation (SFDA) are: Consider a source domain $\hat{D}_s$ only with a pre-trained source model M_s consisting of feature extractor G_f and classifier G_y and a target domain $\hat{D}_t$ with n_t unlabelled target examples. SFDA assumes a shared label space Y ($|Y| = K$) between $\hat{D}_s$ and $\hat{D}_t$.

The ultimate objective of SFDA is to adapt the source pre-trained model to the target domain only with the unlabelled target examples. Due to the shortage of source labelled data, the SFDA task is quite challenging because it is hard to tackle this task by using conventional Domain Adaptation methods.

3.1 Overall Scheme

Our SFISA comprises two stages (shown in Fig. 2): In stage one, the Source Class Prototype Encoder E_{sp} is trained to generate source class prototypes $\mathbf{p^k}$ depending on the hidden knowledge from G_y. The loss function $\mathcal{L}_{E_{sp}} + \mathcal{L}_{con}^p$ makes the generated source prototypes compact and discriminative. We also propose discriminant consistency to generate dependable target prototypes $\mathbf{q^k}$.

In stage two, Source-Free Semantic Augmentation Adaptation is implemented based on the generated $\mathbf{p^k}$ and $\mathbf{q^k}$ through the loss $\mathcal{L}_{SFISA}$. Contrastive class-wise alignment and diversity-discriminability maintaining are also conducted to reduce the pseudo-labelling noises, and the loss functions are $\mathcal{L}_{con}^w$

Algorithm 1. Training of SFISA

Input: $M_s, \hat{D}_t$; Source Class Prototype Encoder E_{sp}; Parameters τ, η

for $t = 1$ to T **do**

    Generate the k-th source prototypes $\mathbf{p}^k$ based on E_{sp};

    Compute $\mathcal{L}_{E_{sp}}$ and $\mathcal{L}^p_{con}$ according to Eq. 3 and Eq. 4 ;

    The loss $(\mathcal{L}_{ce} + \mathcal{L}^p_{con})$.backward() to train E_{sp};

end for

for $r = 1$ to R **do**

    Source prototypes are generated based on **fixed** E_{sp};

    Get the features of target data based on G_f;

    Obtain each class's target prototype based on Eq. 7 and Eq. 12;

    Compute $\mathcal{L}_{SFISA}, \mathcal{L}^w_{con}, \mathcal{L}_{D-D}$ based on Eq. 16, Eq. 9 and Eq. 17;

    loss.backward() (loss = $\mathcal{L}_{SFISA} + \mathcal{L}^w_{con} + \mathcal{L}_{D-D}$).

end for

Output: G_f and G_y.

---

and $\mathcal{L}_{D-D}$ respectively. The overall procedure of SFISA can be roughly formulated as:

$$\min_{\theta_E} \mathcal{L}_{E_{sp}}(\theta_E) + \mathcal{L}^p_{con}(\theta_E) \ (\textbf{Stage1}), \tag{1}$$

$$\min_{\{\theta_{G_f}, \theta_{G_y}\}} \mathcal{L}_{SFISA}(\theta_{G_y}) + \mathcal{L}^w_{con}(\theta_{G_f}) + \eta \mathcal{L}_{D-D}(\theta_{G_f}, \theta_{G_y}) \ (\textbf{Stage2}), \tag{2}$$

where θ_E, θ_{G_f} and θ_{G_y} denotes the parameters of E_{sp}, G_f and G_y. The overall scheme of SFISA is summarized as the algorithm flowchart Algorithm 1.

3.2 Source Class Prototype Generation

The lack of data from source domain is the reason why Source-Free Domain Adaptation (SFDA) is so challenging. Inspired by [26,29], a Source Class Prototype Encoder E_{sp} is designed to generate class prototype for each class. We utilize the pre-trained source classifier G_y to train E_{sp} (The parameters of G_y is **fixed** during training). Given a noise complying with uniform distribution $Z \sim U(0,1)$, the element-wise result of the noise Z and the k-th class embedding $Embed^k$ is the input of E_{sp} to generate the k-th class prototype $\mathbf{p}^k = E_{sp}(Z \odot Embed^k)$ firstly. Then the generated k-th class prototype can be judged whether this prototype belongs to class k and E_{sp} can be trained via the loss:

$$\mathcal{L}_{E_{sp}} = -\sum_{k=1}^{K} y_k \log G_y(E_{sp}(Z \odot Embed^k)). \tag{3}$$

In this way, E_{sp} is able to generate source class prototypes for each class. Considering the generated feature class prototypes from the same class should be **compact**, we impose a contrastive loss function motivated by simCLR and

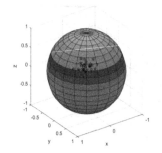 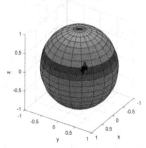

Prototype Generation without Contrastive Loss   **Prototype Generation with Contrastive Loss**

Fig. 3. The procedure of Source Class Prototype Generation. These two pictures illustrate the distribution of a certain class of source prototypes (red dots) generated in the feature space using and not using the contrastive loss $\mathcal{L}_{con}^p$. The contrastive loss $\mathcal{L}_{con}^p$ encourages the generated prototypes from the same class more compact. (Color figure online)

InfoNCE [23]. Implementing this loss can make the prototypes more discriminative. The prototype contrastive loss is formalized as:

$$\mathcal{L}_{con}^p = -\log \frac{\exp\left(\phi\left(\mathbf{p}, \mathbf{p}^+\right)/\tau\right)}{\exp\left(\phi\left(\mathbf{p}, \mathbf{p}^+\right)/\tau\right) + \sum_{j=1}^{K-1} \exp\left(\phi\left(\mathbf{p}, \mathbf{p}_j'\right)/\tau\right)}, \qquad (4)$$

where $\mathbf{p}$ represents the anchor prototype from any class. For every anchor prototype, the positive pair $\mathbf{p}^+$ is sampled from the same class to the anchor $\mathbf{p}$, and $K-1$ negative pairs $\mathbf{p}_j'$ which have different classes from the anchor are also sampled. For each class, as least two class prototypes are sampled to implement the contrastive loss. ϕ is the measurement criterion of prototype similarity and we use cosine similarity $\cos(a,b) = \frac{a \bullet b}{\|a\|_2 \times \|b\|_2}$ as the criterion. τ is the factor which controls the contrastive training intensity.

Overall, E_{sp} is trained with the sum of $\mathcal{L}_{E_{sp}}$ and $\mathcal{L}_{con}^p$, which makes the source class prototypes more compact and representative as the Fig. 3 shows.

3.3   Target Class Prototype Generation Based on Pseudo-labelling Strategy

Pseudo-labelling Strategy for Target Domain Samples. Considering the data structure especially the diversity among predictions of unlabelled target data is different from the source data, a strategy which can exploit the structure of the target data should be used [18]. In SFISA, we generate pseudo-labels based on the clustering strategy proposed by Liang [17]. The initial centroid for each class in the target domain is attained by:

$$c_k^{(0)} = \frac{\sum_{x_t \in \mathcal{X}_t} \delta_k\left(G_y\left(G_f\left(x_t\right)\right)\right) G_f\left(x_t\right)}{\sum_{x_t \in \mathcal{X}_t} \delta_k\left(G_y\left(G_f\left(x_t\right)\right)\right)}, \qquad (5)$$

where $\delta_k(a) = \frac{\exp(a_k)}{\sum_i \exp(a_i)}$ represents the k-th element in the softmax output of the vector a. These class centroids can reliably characterize the distribution of different categories and the diversity of data structure in the target domain. After that, the initial pseudo-labels are obtained by the nearest centroid strategy:

$$\hat{y}_t = \arg\min_k D_f\left(G_f(x_t), c_k^{(0)}\right), \tag{6}$$

where D_f is the cosine distance. Finally, the final centroids are computed based on the pseudo-labels generated in Eq. 6 and the final pseudo-labels are obtained:

$$c_k^{(1)} = \frac{\sum_{x_t \in \mathcal{X}_t} \mathbb{I}(\hat{y}_t = k) G_f(x_t)}{\sum_{x_t \in \mathcal{X}_t} \mathbb{I}(\hat{y}_t = k)}, \quad \hat{y}_t = \arg\min_k D_f\left(G_f(x_t), c_k^{(1)}\right). \tag{7}$$

Class Prototype Generation for Target Data. To make the target prototypes more reliable and the direction of Source-Free implicit semantic augmentation more clear, class-wise contrastive alignment is conducted to make the target features $\mathbf{f}_t = G_f(x_t)$ more compact in the feature space and closer to the source prototypes. Reliable samples are generally closer to the class centroid. Each contrastive confidence weight is computed by:

$$w_i = \frac{\exp\left(\phi\left(G_f(x_t^i), \mathbf{c}_{\hat{y}_t^i}^{(1)}\right)/\tau\right)}{\sum_{k=1}^K \exp\left(\phi\left(G_f(x_t^i), \mathbf{c}_k^{(1)}\right)/\tau\right)}. \tag{8}$$

To avoid the collapsing problems [11], we depend on a trainable nonlinear projector C_{pro} to design the contrastive criterion. ϕ is cosine similarity criterion based on the projection ($\phi(a,b) = \cos(C_{pro}(a), C_{pro}(b))$). The features closer to the corresponding centroid will have higher weight. Then the contrastive class-wise alignment is conducted. In this alignment, $\mathbf{f}_t^i$ represents the feature of the target samples x_t^i and the criterion of the indicator function $\mathbb{I}$ is whether $j \neq \hat{y}_t^i$:

$$\mathcal{L}_{con}^w = -w_i \log \frac{\exp\left(\phi\left(\mathbf{f}_t^i, \mathbf{p}^{\hat{y}_t^i}\right)/\tau\right)}{\exp\left(\phi\left(\mathbf{f}_t^i, \mathbf{p}^{\hat{y}_t^i}\right)/\tau\right) + \sum_{j=1}^K \mathbb{I}\exp\left(\phi\left(\mathbf{f}_t^i, \mathbf{p}^j\right)/\tau\right)}. \tag{9}$$

Due to the noises in pseudo-labelling, the target domain's class prototypes $\mathbf{q}^k$ should be generated according to the confidence of target samples annotated as class $\mathbf{k}$. In SFISA, we propose Discriminant Consistency (DC) to weight the target domain samples. More specifically, DC refers to the classifier's discrimination similarity between the target samples and these samples after data augmentation. If the classifier provides two quite different class predictions for a target sample, the approximated discrimination similarity will obtain one small value. Jensen-Shannon divergence is used to measure the discrimination similarity of predictions ($\overline{P}$ is the prediction probability of the augmented samples):

$$JS(P\|\overline{P}) = \frac{1}{2}\sum p(x)\log\left(\frac{2\,p(x)}{p(x) + \overline{p}(x)}\right) + \frac{1}{2}\sum \overline{p}(x)\log\left(\frac{2\,\overline{p}(x)}{p(x) + \overline{p}(x)}\right). \tag{10}$$

When generating the target class prototype $\mathbf{q^k}$, we hope that samples with higher discriminative consistency (smaller $JS(P\|\overline{P})$) have greater weight. The generated weight of target sample t_i judged as class k is:

$$gw_i = \frac{n_t^k \left(1 + \exp\left(-JS\left(P_i\|\overline{P_i}\right)\right)\right)}{\sum_{i'=1}^{n_t} \mathbb{I}(\hat{y}_t^{i'} = k)\left(1 + \exp\left(-JS\left(P_{i'}\|\overline{P_{i'}}\right)\right)\right)}, \qquad (11)$$

where n_t^k is the number of target samples judged as class k. Overall, for each class k, the calculation of target class prototype can be formulated as:

$$\mathbf{q^k} = \frac{\sum_{i=1}^{n_t} \mathbb{I}(\hat{y}_t^i = k)\ gw_i\ G_f(x_t^i)}{\sum_{i=1}^{n_t} \mathbb{I}(\hat{y}_t^i = k)\ gw_i}, \qquad (12)$$

3.4   Source-Free Semantic Augmentation Adaptation Based on Generated Class Prototypes

Transferable Semantic Augmentation (TSA) [15] has been proven effective in enhancing the adaptation ability. To address this issue, our SFISA uses generated class prototype to obtain inter-domain class difference. In the k-th class, the inter-domain class difference $\Delta\mu^k = \mathbf{q^k} - \mathbf{p^k}$ can be exploited as the overall semantic bias. Meanwhile, the k-th target intra-class feature covariance Σ_t^k is paid attention to capture semantic variations in the target domain. The semantic transformation directions from gaussian distribution are sampled as $N(\lambda\Delta\mu^k, \lambda\Sigma_t^k)(\lambda = \lambda_0 \times (t/T))$, where T and t are the maximum and current iterations respectively, and λ_0 is the hyper-parameter to control the augmentation strength.

After the construction of K sampling distributions, the k-th generated source class prototype $\mathbf{p^k}$ can conduct different target semantic transformations along the random directions sampled from the distribution $N(\lambda\Delta\mu^k, \lambda\Sigma_t^k)$ to generate the augmented prototype $\overline{\mathbf{p^k}} \sim N(\mathbf{p^k} + \lambda\Delta\mu^k, \lambda\Sigma_t^k)$. We can augment generated prototypes from each class for M times naively:

$$\mathcal{L}_{sf}(\mathbf{W}, b) = \frac{1}{M}\sum_{m=1}^{M}\frac{1}{K}\sum_{k=1}^{K} -\log\left(\frac{e^{w_k^\top \overline{\mathbf{p^k}} + b_k}}{\sum_{k'=1}^{K} e^{w_{k'}^\top \overline{\mathbf{p^k}} + b_{k'}}}\right), \qquad (13)$$

where $\mathbf{W} = [w_1, w_2, \ldots, w_K]^\top \in \mathbb{R}^{K \times F}$ and $b = [b_1, b_2, \ldots, b_K]^\top \in \mathbb{R}^K$ are the weight matrix and bias vector of the pre-trained classifier G_y respectively. To achieve our desired performance, we implicitly generate infinite augmented source class prototypes. The upper-bound of the augmentation loss can be derived according to the Law of Large Numbers. To be specific, in the case of M $\to +\infty$, the expected transferable semantic augmentation loss over the augmented source class prototype can be formulated as:

$$\lim_{M \to +\infty} \mathcal{L}_{sf} = \frac{1}{K} \sum_{k=1}^{K} \mathbb{E}_{\overline{\mathbf{p}^k}} \left[-\log \left(\frac{e^{\mathbf{w}_k^\top \overline{\mathbf{p}^k} + b_k}}{\sum_{k'=1}^{K} e^{\mathbf{w}_{k'}^\top \overline{\mathbf{p}^k} + b_{k'}}} \right) \right]$$

$$= \frac{1}{K} \sum_{k=1}^{K} \mathbb{E}_{\overline{\mathbf{p}^k}} \left[\log \left(\sum_{k'=1}^{K} e^{\left(\mathbf{w}_{k'}^\top - \mathbf{w}_k^\top \right) \overline{\mathbf{p}^k} + (b_{k'} - b_k)} \right) \right]. \tag{14}$$

According to Jensen's inequality [22], it is obvious that $\mathbb{E}[\log(X)] \leq \log(\mathbb{E}[X])$. In this way, the upper bound of $\lim_{M \to +\infty} \mathcal{L}_{sf}$ is derived as:

$$\lim_{M \to +\infty} \mathcal{L}_{sf} \leq \frac{1}{K} \sum_{k=1}^{K} \log \left(\mathbb{E}_{\overline{\mathbf{p}^k}} \left[\sum_{k'=1}^{K} e^{\left(\mathbf{w}_{k'}^\top - \mathbf{w}_k^\top \right) \overline{\mathbf{p}^k} + (b_{k'} - b_k)} \right] \right)$$

$$= \frac{1}{K} \sum_{k=1}^{K} \log \left(\sum_{k'=1}^{K} \mathbb{E}_{\overline{\mathbf{p}^k}} \left[e^{\left(\mathbf{w}_{k'}^\top - \mathbf{w}_k^\top \right) \overline{\mathbf{p}^k} + (b_{k'} - b_k)} \right] \right). \tag{15}$$

Due to $\overline{\mathbf{p}^k} \sim N(\mathbf{p}^k + \lambda \Delta \mu^k, \lambda \Sigma_t^k)$, we can derive that $\left(\mathbf{w}_{k'}^\top - \mathbf{w}_k^\top \right) \overline{\mathbf{p}^k} + (b_{k'} - b_k) \sim N \left(\left(\mathbf{w}_{k'}^\top - \mathbf{w}_k^\top \right) (\mathbf{p}^k + \lambda \Delta \mu^k) + (b_{k'} - b_k), \sigma_k^{k'} \right)$, where $\sigma_k^{k'} = \lambda \left(\mathbf{w}_{k'}^\top - \mathbf{w}_k^\top \right) \Sigma_t^k (\mathbf{w}_{k'} - \mathbf{w}_k)$. Leveraging the moment generating function $\mathbb{E} \left[e^{aX} \right] = e^{a\mu + \frac{1}{2} a^2 \sigma}$, where X complies with the Gaussian distribution $N(\mu, \sigma)$, we can obtain that:

$$\lim_{M \to +\infty} \mathcal{L}_{sf} \leq \mathcal{L}_{SFISA} = -\frac{1}{K} \sum_{k=1}^{K} \log \frac{e^{Z_k^k}}{\sum_{k'=1}^{K} e^{Z_k^{k'}}}, \tag{16}$$

where $Z_k^{k'} = \hat{y}_k^{k'} + \lambda \left(\mathbf{w}_{k'}^\top - \mathbf{w}_k^\top \right) \Delta \mu^k + \frac{\sigma_k^{k'}}{2}$. $\hat{y}_k^{k'}$ denotes the k'-th element of logits output of $\mathbf{p}^k$.

By optimizing the upper bound loss function $\mathcal{L}_{SFISA}$ of $\lim_{M \to +\infty} \mathcal{L}_{sf}$ using cross entropy loss, Source-Free semantic augmentation adaptation based on generated class prototypes can be implemented to train the classifier.

3.5 Diversity and Discriminability Analysis During Source-Free Adaptation

In Domain Adaptation, maintaining the diversity and discriminability of prediction is quite important. Due to the target label insufficiency, the domain adaptation performance degrades on the decision boundary with high data density dramatically [3,4]. The Shannon Entropy Minimization (SEM) is used to promote the discriminability of each target sample. However, the side effect of using SEM is that the diversity of overall data prediction will be impaired: SEM pushes the sample to nearby examples far from the decision boundary. Since the distribution of the data mostly follows the long-tailed distribution, examples from minority categories are prone to be pushed into majority categories. To alleviate the side effect caused by SEM, the maximization of average prediction entropy $\max(\sum_{k=1}^{K} -\hat{P}^k \log \hat{P}^k)$ is implemented to maintain the diversity of overall data prediction $(\hat{P} = \frac{1}{n_t} \sum_{i=1}^{n_t} P_i)$. The objective loss function is formalized as:

$$\mathcal{L}_{D-D} = \sum_{k=1}^{K} \hat{P}^k \log \hat{P}^k - \frac{1}{n_t} \sum_{i=1}^{n_t} \sum_{k=1}^{K} P_i^k \log P_i^k. \tag{17}$$

3.6   Theoretical Insight

Let $\mathcal{H}$ denote a classification hypothesis space which VC dimension is d [1], the upper bound of the classification error on target domain can be defined as:

$$\epsilon_t(h) \leq \hat{\epsilon}_s(h) + d_{\mathcal{H}}\left(\hat{D}_s, \hat{D}_t\right) + \lambda^* + \sqrt{\frac{4}{m}\left(d \log \frac{2em}{d} + \log \frac{4}{\delta}\right)}, \tag{18}$$

where $\hat{\epsilon}_s(h)$ is the generalization classification error on source domain, e is the natural base, $\lambda^* = \epsilon_s(h^*) + \epsilon_t(h^*)$ represents the ideal joint error of an ideal joint hypothesis.

In our SFISA, $\hat{\epsilon}_s$ is well bounded because the source pre-trained model has already been trained in the source domain. The contrastive adaptation of target domain samples to source domain prototypes can effectively bound the distribution difference $d_{\mathcal{H}}\left(\hat{D}_s, \hat{D}_t\right)$. Furthermore, the constructed multivariate distribution's transformation directions enable the pre-trained classifier to jointly minimize $\epsilon_s(h^*)$ and $\epsilon_t(h^*)$ of the joint error λ^*. To summarize, our SFISA enhances the adaptation ability dramatically because it complies with the transfer learning theory based on $\mathcal{H}$-divergence well.

4   Experiments

4.1   Datasets

Office-31 [27] is one of the most popular benchmark in visual Source-Free Domain Adaptation field, which consists of 3 different domains: Amazon (**A**), Webcam (**W**), and DSLR (**D**), our SFISA is evaluated on 6 transfer tasks. **Office-Home** [28] is a more challenging benchmark which consists of images from 4 different domains: Artistic (**Ar**) images, Clip Art (**Cl**), Product (**Pr**) images, and Real-World (**Rw**) images, 8 transfer tasks are selected for evaluation.

4.2   Implementation Details

SFISA is implemented based on PyTorch. ResNet-50 [9] is adopted as the backbone network pre-trained on ImageNet. For every transfer task, the source pre-trained model is trained based on label smoothing strategy [24]. The learning rate of mini-batch SGD optimizer and the training epochs are set as 10^{-3} and 400. For other hyper-parameters, batch size, τ, η, λ_0 and the dimension of source prototype generation noise Z are set as 64, 0.07, 0.1, 0.15 and 100.

Table 1. Accuracy (%) for unsupervised domain adaptation on **Office-31** [27] based on ResNet-50.

Method \ Tasks	Source-Free	A→W	A→D	D→W	W→D	D→A	W→A	AVG
ResNet-50 [9]	✗	68.4	68.9	96.7	99.3	62.5	60.7	76.1
BNM [3]	✗	94.0	92.2	98.5	100	74.9	75.3	89.2
ATDOC [18]	✗	94.0	92.2	98.5	100	74.9	75.3	89.2
TSA [15]	✗	96.0	95.4	98.7	100	76.7	76.8	90.6
SHOT [17]	✔	90.9	93.1	98.8	99.9	74.5	74.8	88.7
BAIT [30]	✔	**94.6**	92.0	98.1	**100**	74.6	**75.2**	89.1
NRC [31]	✔	90.8	**96.0**	**99.0**	100	75.3	75.0	89.4
SFISA(ours)	✔	94.1	94.2	98.7	**100**	**75.5**	75.0	**89.6**

4.3   Results

Our SFISA is compared with the state-of-the-art methods. The classification accuracies on the dataset **Office-31** based on the ResNet are shown in Table 1. SFISA achieves the best performance on average accuracy compared with all of the state-of-the-art methods. In addition, our SFISA shows superiority on the tasks W→D and D→A and outperforms SHOT [17] by a notable margin of 0.9%. This demonstrates that our method can effectively adapt the classifier by implicitly generating prototypes towards target semantics. From Table 2, our

Table 2. Accuracy (%) for unsupervised domain adaptation on **Office-Home** [27] based on ResNet-50.

Method \ Tasks	Source-Free	Ar→Cl	Ar→Pr	Ar→Rw	Pr→Ar	Pr→Cl	Pr→Rw	Rw→Ar	Rw→Cl	AVG
ResNet-50 [9]	✗	34.9	50.0	58.0	38.5	31.2	60.4	53.9	41.2	46.0
BNM [3]	✗	56.7	77.5	81.0	65.3	55.1	82.0	73.6	57.0	68.5
ATDOC [18]	✗	58.3	78.8	82.3	67.1	56.0	82.7	72.0	58.2	69.4
TSA [15]	✗	57.6	75.8	80.7	66.7	55.7	81.2	75.7	61.9	69.5
SHOT [17]	✔	56.9	78.1	81.0	67.0	54.6	81.8	73.4	58.1	68.9
BAIT [30]	✔	57.4	77.5	**82.4**	**67.1**	55.5	81.9	**73.9**	59.5	**69.4**
NRC [31]	✔	57.7	**80.3**	82.0	65.3	56.4	**83.0**	71.0	58.6	69.3
SFISA(ours)	✔	**58.3**	78.6	79.9	65.4	**57.3**	81.4	71.7	**62.4**	69.4

SFISA outperforms almost all of the state-of-the-art methods on the more challenging dataset benchmark **Office-Home**. Moreover, our SFISA is able to surpass some baseline methods requiring source data, which further demonstrates the effectiveness of SFISA.

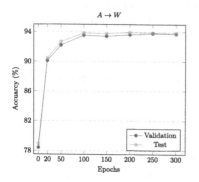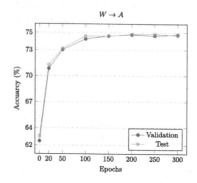

Fig. 4. Optimization accuracy curves of SFISA on benchmark **Office-31**(A→W and W→A).

4.4   Robustness Analysis

The robustness of our SFISA on the tasks A→W and W→A based on the benchmark **Office-Home** is studied. Figure 4 shows that our SFISA converges well in terms of accuracy in the training phase. Training for 20 epochs increases the accuracy by about 12% in the A→W task and 8% in the W→A task, which demonstrates the efficiency of our method. Besides, the curve on the Validation set means our pseudo-labelling strategy can alleviate pseudo-labelling noise effectively.

4.5   Ablation Study

A series of ablation studies on **Office-Home** are implemented to evaluate the effectiveness of each module proposed in SFISA. Firstly, the importance of $\mathcal{L}_{con}^{p}$ and our proposed Discriminant Consistency (DC) in the class prototype generation stage are studied. $\mathcal{L}_{con}^{p}$ makes the source inter-class prototypes separated (*i.e.*, larger inter-class distance) and intra-class prototypes compact (*i.e.*, smaller intra-class distance), which makes the enhancement from 67.9% to 68.7% and 68.8% to 69.4% shown in Table 3. DC makes SFISA improve slightly in performance. Then we investigate the losses of Source-Free semantic augmentation adaptation and show the quantitative results of the model that has been optimized using various loss combinations which are also shown in Table 3. Combining all the three losses ($\mathcal{L}_{con}^{w}$, $\mathcal{L}_{D-D}$ and $\mathcal{L}_{SFISA}$), the best performance is obtained.

Table 3. Ablation Studies for the losses($\mathcal{L}^p_{con}$, $\mathcal{L}^w_{con}$, $\mathcal{L}_{D-D}$, $\mathcal{L}_{SFISA}$) on **Office-Home** based on **ResNet-50**. These studies include average accuracies, inter-class distance and intra-class distance (based on cosine distance).

ResNet-50 [9]	$\mathcal{L}^p_{con}$	$\mathcal{L}^w_{con}$	$\mathcal{L}_{D-D}$	$\mathcal{L}_{SFISA}$	DC	AVG
✔						46.0
✔			✔	✔	✔	67.9
✔		✔	✔	✔	✔	68.8
✔	✔		✔	✔	✔	68.7
✔	✔	✔	✔	✔		69.2
✔	✔	✔	✔	✔	✔	69.4

loss combination	Intra-class Distance	Inter-class Distance
$\mathcal{L}_{E_{sp}}$	$2.41 \times e^{-3}$	0.421
$\mathcal{L}_{E_{sp}} + \mathcal{L}^p_{con}$	$1.05 \times e^{-5}$	0.592

5   Conclusions

This paper proposed a prototype generation strategy and an implicit semantic augmentation adaptation approach (SFISA) in Source-Free Domain Adaptation (SFDA) scenario. Common SFDA methods always suffer from the label noise of the target pseudo-labeled samples and domain discrepancies which are hard to be calculated. To alleviate the negative effect of the label noise, a reliable pseudo-labelling strategy and Discriminant Consistency are adopted. In order to calculate and minimize the domain discrepancies precisely, the class prototype generation strategy is proposed to address the lack of source data and generate reliable source and target prototypes. Based on these generated prototypes, Source-Free semantic augmentation adaptation adapts the classifier through implicitly generating source prototypes towards target semantics. Comprehensive experiments on several cross-domain benchmark tasks have demonstrated the efficacy and versatility of SFISA.

References

1. Ben-David, S., Blitzer, J., Crammer, K., Kulesza, A., Pereira, F., Vaughan, J.W.: A theory of learning from different domains. Mach. Learn. **79**(1), 151–175 (2009). https://doi.org/10.1007/s10994-009-5152-4
2. Choi, J., Kim, T., Kim, C.: Self-ensembling with GAN-based data augmentation for domain adaptation in semantic segmentation. In: ICCV, pp. 6829–6839 (2019)
3. Cui, S., Wang, S., Zhuo, J., Li, L., Huang, Q., Tian, Q.: Towards discriminability and diversity: batch nuclear-norm maximization under label insufficient situations. In: CVPR, pp. 3940–3949 (2020)
4. Cui, S., Wang, S., Zhuo, J., Li, L., Huang, Q., Tian, Q.: Fast batch nuclear-norm maximization and minimization for robust domain adaptation. CoRR (2021)

5. Cui, S., Wang, S., Zhuo, J., Su, C., Huang, Q., Tian, Q.: Gradually vanishing bridge for adversarial domain adaptation. In: CVPR, pp. 12452–12461 (2020)
6. Dai, S., Cheng, Y., Zhang, Y., Gan, Z., Liu, J., Carin, L.: Contrastively smoothed class alignment for unsupervised domain adaptation. In: ACCV, pp. 268–283 (2020)
7. Ganin, Y., Lempitsky, V.S.: Unsupervised domain adaptation by backpropagation. In: ICML, pp. 1180–1189 (2015)
8. Gu, J., Dong, C.: Interpreting super-resolution networks with local attribution maps. In: CVPR, pp. 9199–9208 (2021)
9. He, K., Zhang, X., Ren, S., Sun, J.: Deep residual learning for image recognition. In: CVPR, pp. 770–778 (2016)
10. Huang, J., Guan, D., Xiao, A., Lu, S.: Model adaptation: historical contrastive learning for unsupervised domain adaptation without source data. In: NeurIPS, pp. 3635–3649 (2021)
11. Jing, L., Vincent, P., LeCun, Y., Tian, Y.: Understanding dimensional collapse in contrastive self-supervised learning. CoRR (2021)
12. Kang, G., Jiang, L., Yang, Y., Hauptmann, A.G.: Contrastive adaptation network for unsupervised domain adaptation. In: CVPR, pp. 4893–4902 (2019)
13. Lee, C., Batra, T., Baig, M.H., Ulbricht, D.: Sliced wasserstein discrepancy for unsupervised domain adaptation. In: CVPR, pp. 10285–10295 (2019)
14. Li, R., Jiao, Q., Cao, W., Wong, H., Wu, S.: Model adaptation: unsupervised domain adaptation without source data. In: CVPR, pp. 9638–9647 (2020)
15. Li, S., Xie, M., Gong, K., Liu, C.H., Wang, Y., Li, W.: Transferable semantic augmentation for domain adaptation. In: CVPR, pp. 11516–11525 (2021)
16. Li, X., et al.: PointFlow: flowing semantics through points for aerial image segmentation. In: CVPR, pp. 4217–4226 (2021)
17. Liang, J., Hu, D., Feng, J.: Do we really need to access the source data? Source hypothesis transfer for unsupervised domain adaptation. In: ICML, pp. 6028–6039 (2020)
18. Liang, J., Hu, D., Feng, J.: Domain adaptation with auxiliary target domain-oriented classifier. In: CVPR, pp. 16632–16642 (2021)
19. Liu, H., Long, M., Wang, J., Jordan, M.I.: Transferable adversarial training: a general approach to adapting deep classifiers. In: ICML, pp. 4013–4022 (2019)
20. Long, M., Cao, Y., Wang, J., Jordan, M.I.: Learning transferable features with deep adaptation networks. In: ICML, pp. 97–105 (2015)
21. Long, M., Zhu, H., Wang, J., Jordan, M.I.: Deep transfer learning with joint adaptation networks. In: ICML, pp. 2208–2217 (2017)
22. McShane, E.J.: Jensen's inequality. BAMS, pp. 521–527 (1937)
23. Mei, H., Wan, T., Eisner, J.: Noise-contrastive estimation for multivariate point processes. In: NeurIPS, pp. 5204–5214 (2020)
24. Müller, R., Kornblith, S., Hinton, G.E.: When does label smoothing help? In: NeurIPS, pp. 4696–4705 (2019)
25. Pei, Z., Cao, Z., Long, M., Wang, J.: Multi-adversarial domain adaptation. In: AAAI, pp. 3934–3941 (2018)
26. Qiu, Z., et al.: Source-free domain adaptation via avatar prototype generation and adaptation. In: IJCAI, pp. 2921–2927 (2021)
27. Saenko, K., Kulis, B., Fritz, M., Darrell, T.: Adapting visual category models to new domains. In: ECCV, pp. 213–226 (2010)
28. Venkateswara, H., Eusebio, J., Chakraborty, S., Panchanathan, S.: Deep hashing network for unsupervised domain adaptation. In: CVPR, pp. 5385–5394 (2017)
29. Xu, S., et al.: Generative low-bitwidth data free quantization. In: ECCV, pp. 1–17 (2020)

30. Yang, S., Wang, Y., van de Weijer, J., Herranz, L., Jui, S.: Unsupervised domain adaptation without source data by casting a BAIT. CoRR (2020)
31. Yang, S., Wang, Y., van de Weijer, J., Herranz, L., Jui, S.: Exploiting the intrinsic neighborhood structure for source-free domain adaptation. In: NeurIPS, pp. 29393–29405 (2021)
32. Zhang, Y., Tang, H., Jia, K., Tan, M.: Domain-symmetric networks for adversarial domain adaptation. In: CVPR, pp. 5031–5040 (2019)

Role-Oriented Network Embedding Method Based on Local Structural Feature and Commonality

Liang Ge[✉], Xiaofeng Ye, Yixuan Jia, and Qinhong Li

College of Computer Science, Chongqing University, Chongqing 400030, China
{geliang,yexiaofeng,jiayixuan,qinhong}@cqu.edu.cn

Abstract. Role-oriented network embedding has become a powerful technique for solving real-world problems, because it can capture the structures of nodes and make node embeddings better reflect the functions or behaviors of entities in the network. At present, various role-oriented network embedding methods have been proposed. However, most of the methods ignore degree distribution and the commonalities among local structures, resulting in insufficient information of node embeddings, and some methods that preserve commonality always have high time complexity. To address the above challenges, we propose a novel model ReVaC from two aspects of extracting higher-quality local structural features and strengthening the commonalities among local structures in node embeddings. In detail, the degree distribution from node's 1-hop egonet is incorporated into the extraction process of local structural features to improve traditional ReFeX firstly, and the Variational Auto-Encoder is used to map those features to the local structural embedding space. Then, in the embedding space, we cluster nodes to model the commonalities among local structures. Finally, local structural embeddings and commonalities are fused to get node embeddings. We conduct extensive comparative experiments on real-word networks, and results show that ReVaC has better performance than other state-of-the-art approaches and adapts well to network scale.

Keywords: Role-oriented network embedding · Degree distribution · Local structural commonality

1 Introduction

In almost all networks, nodes tend to have one or more functions that largely determine their structural identity in the system. When considering the problem of learning a representation that captures the structural identity of nodes in a network, even if two nodes do not share the connection or are even far apart, but they have similar functions or occupy similar positions (similar structures) in the

© The Author(s), under exclusive license to Springer Nature Switzerland AG 2022
S. Khanna et al. (Eds.): PRICAI 2022, LNCS 13630, pp. 32–44, 2022.
https://doi.org/10.1007/978-3-031-20865-2_3

network, then their potential representations should be close to each other. Obviously, community-oriented embedding methods can't handle such case, those are all based on the connection of nodes. The structure-based network embedding methods emerge as the times require. They encode local structural features into vectors to capture structural similarity and obtain role-oriented embedding representations, so are also called role-oriented embedding methods.

At present, role-oriented network embedding has gradually become one of the most important research hotspots. It still faces the following challenges: (1)the key to learning role-oriented network embedding is to extract high-quality local structural features, degree distribution is a very good local structural feature. According to the paper [1], it is shown that degree distribution, generalized to include the distribution in its k-hop neighborhood, may indeed be a good indicator of the structural position or role in the network. It excels in the evaluation of automorphic and regular equivalence, and achieves superior results in various experiments on real networks. However, this useful structural information is not well utilized. Few methods take advantage of it, and operations based on it are limited. For example, struc2vec [2] and XNetMF [3] determine their similarity only by computing distances between k-order degree sequences or degree vectors. (2)Some approaches only preserve the local structural features of nodes as much as possible into embeddings, ignoring the commonalities among local structures. The commonality of a class of similar local structures can be regarded as the feature a structural role, and ignoring it means losing part of the characteristics of the role, which is unfriendly to role-oriented embedding. However, the approach that retains commonalities needs to calculate structural similarities, which often has high time complexity and is not suitable for large datasets.

In order to meet the above challenges, we propose our model ReVaC from two aspects of extracting higher-quality local structural features and strengthening the commonalities among local structures. The model consists of three parts: local structural feature extraction, commonality modeling and fusion encoding. Firstly, we improve the traditional ReFeX [4] by incorporating degree distributions from nodes' 1-hop egonet into their initial features and leveraging iterative process to obtain local structural features. At the same time, to avoid the over-fitting caused by the high-order iteration, the Variational Auto-Encoder is regarded as the operator to map those features to a local structural embedding space. Secondly, in the embedding space, we model the commonalities among local structures. That is, nodes with similar local structures are captured by clustering, and then the common feature of nodes in the same cluster is modeled as the commonality of such similar nodes. Finally, to enrich the structural information of nodes and make the structural roles and embedding distances of nodes highly correlated, local structural embeddings and commonalities are fused to obtain node embeddings. Our main contributions can be summarized as follows:

– The traditional ReFeX is improved to incorporate degree distributions of nodes into their initial features, and iterate new initial features to obtain higher-quality local structural features.

– We propose to explicitly model the commonalities among local structures by clustering in the local structural embedding space, and fuse them with local structure embeddings. That enriches the information of node embeddings and improves the expressive ability of node embeddings.
– We conduct several extensive experiments on real-world networks via our model ReVaC, and compare the results with other state-of-the-art methods. The results demonstrate the superiority of our model, and prove that our model scales well with network size.

2   Related Work

Obtaining high-quality structural features is the key to learning role-oriented embeddings, and current methods are diverse. ReFeX [4] (Recursive Feature eXtraction) extracts local and egonet features and aggregates the features of neighbors recursively. As an effective method to capture structural features, ReFeX is widely used in many other role-oriented embedding methods. For example, RolX [5] and GLRD [6] leverage the structural features extracted by ReFeX and uses matrix factorization to get low-dimension node representation. In RESD [7] and RDAA [8], ReFeX is proposed to extract structural features and utilizes encoder framework to map the network to the latent space. The key idea of GAS [9] is to extract some key structural features based on ReFeX as the guidance information to train the model. There are other methods directly based on degree features, such as SIR-GN [10] encodes the degree of each node as a one-hot vector. RoINE [11] also concatenates the degree of a node and the sum of its immediate neighbors' degree as structural feature. Besides, HONE [12] generates the high-order network embeddings by decompose a set of motif-based matrices. GraphWave [13] is based on heat-wavelet diffusion patterns, it treats graph diffusion kernels as probability distributions over networks. DRNE [14] is designed to leverage a layer-normalized LSTM to process the sequences of nodes' degree-based direct neighbors, which are treated as structural features. Gralsp [15] captures structural patterns by generating w anonymous random walks starting from one node with length L.

Structural properties also are contained in pair-wise similarities, and there are various ways to calculate them. XNetMF [3] take advantages of Singular Value Decomposition to encode the similarities based on the K-order degree vector and attribute vector as embeddings. Struc2vec [2] constructs a hierarchy of complete graphs by transforming similarities of the k-order ordered degree sequences to weights of edges. SEGK [16] decomposes the similarity matrix computed by graph kernels. REACT [17] aims to obtain node representations by applying non-negative matrix database on RoleSim [18] similarity matrix and adjacency matrix, respectively. Struc2gauss [19] generates structural contexts based on the RoleSim similarity matrix, and learns node representations in the space of Gaussian distributions. SPaE [20] computes cosine similarity between the standardized Graphlet Degree Vectors of nodes, and generates role-based embeddings via

Laplacian eigenmaps method. Role2vec [21] also recommends Motif-based features, such as mapping nodes to multiple disjoint roles based on Graphlet degree vectors.

To sum up the above, we have to admit that degree, degree-based sequences, and related degree vectors are recognized good indicators of structures, and most methods directly or indirectly utilize them. However, it is obvious that only a few methods involve degree distribution in the process of constructing feature matrix, and their operations on it are too limited.

3   Methodology

In this section, we declare the concepts used in this paper, and then introduce our framework ReVaC in detail.

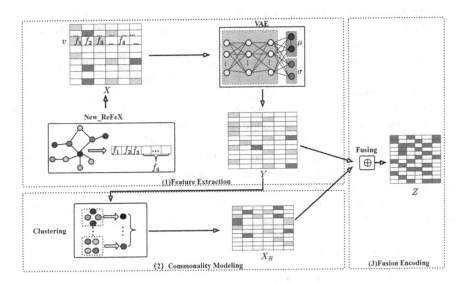

Fig. 1. An overview of the proposed ReVaC: (1) extract local structural features X with improved ReFeX and map them to local structural embedding space Y by the VAE, (2) explicitly model the commonalities among local structures in the space by clustering and obtain the common features X_R, (3) fuse local structure embeddings Y and common features X_R to obtain the final node embeddings Z.

3.1   Notions

A network is represented by an undirected unweighted graph $G = (V, E)$, where $V = \{v_1, ..., v_n\}$ is the set of nodes and E is the set of edges. For each node $v \in V$, the set of node v's neighbors is defined as $N(v)$, d(v) denotes the degree of node v. The 1-hop egonet of node v is defined as $G_v = \{V(g_v), E(g_v)\}$, where

$V(g_v) = \{v\} \bigcup \{u \in V | (v,u) \in E\}$ and $E(g_v)$ is the set of edges in the 1-hop egonet of v. D_v represents the degree distribution from the 1-hop egonet of node v. The extracted features of nodes are denoted as $X \in R^{n \times f}$, where f is the dimension of features. $Y \in R^{n \times d}$ are the local structural embeddings. $X_R \in R^{k \times d}$ are the common features of similar local structures, where k is the number of node structure roles. $Z \in R^{n \times d}$ represent the final node embeddings, where d is the dimension of embedding.

3.2   Model

In this section, we introduce the proposed method ReVaC. The framework is shown in Fig. 1. The ReVaC consists of three parts: (1) local structural feature extraction, (2) commonality modeling, (3) fusion encoding.

Feature Extraction. ReFeX is an effective method to capture structural features, which firstly computes initial features and then aggregates neighbors' initial features with sum- and mean-aggregator recursively to get local structural features. The initial feature of the traditional ReFeX is mostly composed of node degree and egonet-based information. It is still hard to be applied to discover node roles and complex tasks as simple statistical is preserved. Recent research [2] shows that node's degree distribution may indeed be a good indicator of the structural position or role of the node in the network and degree distributions of higher-order local neighborhoods are also sufficiently expressive structural descriptors. The 1-hop egonet of node is the smallest local structure, degree distribution from it can intuitively reflect connection pattern. So, we draw on the experience of ReFeX to incorporate degree distribution features from 1-hop egonet of nodes into initial features to help to enrich local domain information and participate in recursive process to capture higher-quality local structural features.

For each node v, the initial features extracted in this paper are as follows:

- (1) The degree of v: $f_1 = |N(v)|$
- (2) The sum of node's degree in the 1-hop egonet of v: $f_2 = \sum_{u \in V(g_v)} d(u)$
- (3) The number of edges from the 1-hop egonet of v: $f_3 = |E(g_v)|$
- (4) The degree distribution in the 1-hop egonet of v: $f_4 = D_v$

We represent D_v with the degree distribution of node v's 1-hop neighbors. To prevent one high-degree node from inflating the length of these vectors and make their entries more robust, we bin nodes together into $b = [log(d_{max} + 1)]$ logarithmically scaled buckets, where d_{max} is the maximum degree in the original graph. So that the i-th item of the degree distribution vector D_v of node v is the number of nodes that satisfy $[log(d(u) + 1)] = i, u \in V(g_v)$. Namely, $D_v^i = |\{u \in V(g_v)|[log(d(u) + 1)] = i\}|$, where the dimension of D_v is b. And then, based on the initial features, an iterative process similar to traditional ReFeX is used to obtain local structural features, so we call the above process as New_ReFeX, and the features are denoted as: $X = New\_ReFeX(f_1, f_2, f_3, f_4)$.

At the same time, we also noticed that with the increase of the number of iterations, each node can meet fairly high-order neighbors, which may cause over-fitting. For this reason, the Variational Auto-Encoder is acted as the operator to encode local structural features to get more compact and robust local structural embeddings. Specifically, the structural feature reconstruction loss of VAE is defined as follows:

$$L_{VAE} = ||X - \hat{X}||_2^2 = \sum_{v=1}^{n} ||X_v - \hat{X}_v||_2^2 \tag{1}$$

At the same time, to prevent over-fitting and better preserve key local structural information, referring to RESD, we add a degree-based regularizer, as follows:

$$L_{reg} = \sum_{v=1}^{n} (log(d(v) + 1) - MLP(Y_v))^2 \tag{2}$$

where $MLP(\cdot)$ is also a Multi-Layer perceptron model with rectified linear unit activation $ReLU(\cdot)$.

We train our model ReVaC by jointly minimizing the loss of feature reconstruction and degree-regularized constraint as follows:

$$L = L_{VAE} + \alpha L_{reg} \tag{3}$$

where α is the weight of the degree-based regularize. Through the above process, we get the local structural embeddings, we define: $Y = VAE(X)$.

Commonality Modeling. When looking at the similarity from a global perspective, the local structural information extracted are preserved as much as possible in the local structural embeddings in the above process, while commonalities among local structures are ignored. The similar local structures always correspond to the same structural role, so the commonality can be regardes as a common feature of a class of similar local structures, and can also be regarded as the feature of a structural role. If commonalities preserved in node embeddings, there is no doubt that we have captured different structural roles to which the nodes belongs, which helps to make nodes with similar local structures have similar embeddings. However, most of the current role-oriented methods ignore commonalities, and some methods that preserve commonalities tend to have high time and space complexity.

To solve the above problem, we propose to explicitly model commonalities among local structures. We were inspired by two things: (1) Clustering algorithms can cluster nodes with similar local structures. So we find the nodes with the same structural role by clustering in the embedding space. (2) Clusters describe the main structural roles that exist in the local structural embedding space, we can model their commonalities according to the set of nodes in the cluster. So in the commonality modeling part of ReVaC, the details are as follows: we use K-Means clustering based on Euclidean distance in the local structural embedding space to make nodes with similar local structures have the same cluster label. The cluster label of the i cluster is denoted i, and all nodes in this cluster form the node set R_i. Because the centroid of a cluster is the mean of the local structural embeddings of all nodes in the cluster, it represents the common feature of the cluster to a certain extent. Thus, the centroid of a cluster can be modeled as the commonality among a class of similar local structures. That is for the node v, the label i of its cluster is obtained by K-means algorithm, and then the cluster center is modeled as a commonality with a similar local structures to v, and its feature is denoted as:

$$X_{R_i} = \frac{\sum_{u \in R_i} Y_u}{|\{u | u \in R_i\}|} \quad (4)$$

where Y_u is the local structural embedding of node u and R_i denotes the set of nodes of cluster i.

For the K-mean algorithm, since the degree of real network always follows the power-law distribution, so we set K as the logarithm of the maximum degree in the network, $K = [log(d_{max}+1)]$, that is, assuming the number of potential main structural roles in the network is K. Then, we finally get the features of all structural roles via modeling, which are defined as follows: $X_R = clustering(Y, K)$

Fusion Encoding. The key idea of our algorithm is to strengthen the structural role features of nodes on the basis of preserving local structural information, that is, to explicitly preserve commonalities among local structures in node embeddings. In detail, the modeled commonalities and the local structural embeddings of nodes are fused to get node embeddings. For node v, its node embedding is defined as follows:

$$Z_v = \beta * Y_v + \gamma * X_{R_i} \quad (5)$$

where Y_v is the local structural embedding of node v, and X_{R_i} is the common feature of similar local structures of the i-th cluster which v belongs. And β and γ are hyperparameters. We think the local structural embedding and common feature of node to be equally important, so both β and γ are set to 0.5. The above is the whole process of the algorithm.

3.3   Complexity Analysis

Given a network G, let n denote the number of nodes, e denote the number of edges, m denote the feature aggregation number of New_ReFeX, f be the dimension of extracted feature matrix X, d represent the dimension of local structural embedding Y. For the local structural feature extraction part, firstly, it takes $O(n+f \cdot m \cdot (e+nf))$ to iteratively capture the local structural features of nodes by improving the traditional ReFeX method, and then map the extracted features to the local structural embedding space through the VAE, which requires $O(nf^2 d + nd^2)$. Therefore, the time complexity of this part is $O(n + f \cdot bin \cdot (e + nf) + nf^2 d + nd^2$. For the commonality modeling part, the time complexity of

K-Means clustering is $O(nkt)$, where k is the number of cluster centroids and t is the number of clustering iterations. At last, for the fusion encoding part, fusing local structural embeddings and commonalities to get node embeddings takes $O(n)$. To sum up, the whole computation of ReVaC is $O(2n + ktn + f^2 \cdot bin \cdot n + f \cdot bin \cdot e + f^2 dn + d^2 n)$. Since k, t, bin are always very small and $k < f < d \ll n$, our model has an advantage over other methods for large-scale networks, such as the complexity of struc2vec is $O(n^3)$.

Table 1. Detailed statistic of the datasets, including the number of nodes, edges, categories, and nodes in each category.

Dataset	Nodes	Edegs	Classes	Category0	Category1	Category2	Category3
Brazil	131	1074	4	32	32	32	35
Europe	399	5995	4	99	99	99	102
USA	1190	13599	4	297	297	297	299
Actor	7779	26733	4	1782	1787	1798	1797
Film	27312	122706	4	10101	2378	3725	11108

4   Experiments

In this section, to evaluate the effectiveness of our model, we select three tasks for the evaluation including (1)the visualization experiment by plotting the node representations in a 2-D space to observe the relationships between node embeddings and their roles, (2)the classification experiment based on the ground-truth labels of datasets by comparing the Micro-F1 and Macro-F1 scores, (3)the top-k similarity search experiment to see if nodes in the same role are mapped into close position in the embedding space.

4.1   Datasets

We conduct experiments on several real-world networks with unweighted undirected edges. The datasets we use are listed as follows and the statistics are shown in Table 1:

(1) Air-traffic networks [15]: there are three networks, consisting of American, Brazilian, and Europe air-traffic networks (Brazil, Europe, and USA for short). In these networks, nodes represent airports and edges represent the existed flights between airports.
(2) Actor co-occurrence network [22]: In Actor network, nodes represent actors and are labeled based on their influences which are measured via the number of words in their Wiki pages.
(3) English-language film network [23]: it is a film-director-actor-writer-network (Film for short). And edges denote whether two nodes appear in the same Wiki page.

4.2   Baseline

We evaluate the effectiveness of the ReVaC by comparing it with widely used role-oriented embedding algorithms. We choose eight state-of-the-art methods including struc2vec [2], ReFeX [4], RolX [5], RESD [7], RDAA [8], GraphWave [13], SEGK [16], role2vec [21]. In addition, the results of New_ReFeX on those datasets are also demonstrated in subsequent experiments.

4.3   Experiment Settings

All embedding methods using ReFeX set the number of feature aggregations to 3, the number of bins to 4, as does New_ReFeX. The number of hidden layers of the encoder and decoder are all set to 2. We apply Adam SGD optimizer with the learning rate of 0.001 and set the $L2$ regularization with weight of 0.001 to avoid over-fitting. In our later experiments, if not stated specifically, α is set to 0.3, β and γ are both set to 0.5. The dimension of node embedding is set to 128 for all methods, except ReFeX and New_ReFeX.

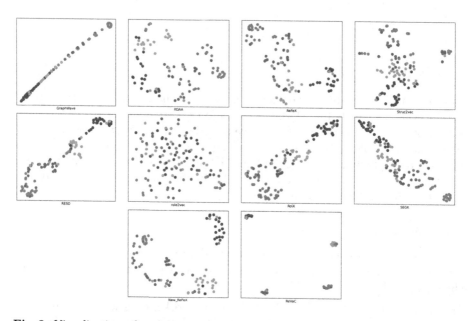

Fig. 2. Visualization of node representations on Brazil network in two-dimensional space. The label is mapped into color of point.

4.4   Visualization

In this section, we visualize the learned embeddings, which can directly reflect the performance of different methods. The Brazil network is selected, and we apply t-SNE to reduce the dimension of embeddings to 2 for visualization. Each node is represented as a point and the color indicates its role label. Ideally, points in the same color should be close together, and those in different colors should be farther away from each other. As shown in Fig. 2, we observe that role2vec cannot extract role information well as the points in different colors are mixed up. Graphwave may be over-fitting to one specific structure characteristic as the points are almost lined up. The other methods achieve that points in the same color are clustered in varying degrees, such as RDAA, RESD, RolX, SEGK, struc2vec. We note that the New_ReFeX extracts higher quality features than ReFeX as expected, because points in the same color are closer and points in different colors are further apart. Obviously, the ReVaC divides the points with different colors into different clusters, and the clusters in different colors are far apart.

Table 2. Node classification average F1-micro score(F1 for short) and F1-macro score(F2 for short) on different networks. For each column, we mark the values with significant advantages, i.e. the top results of these methods. OM means that it cannot be calculated in fixed memory, and OT means that the result cannot be calculated within 12 h.

Method	Brazil		Europe		USA		Actor		Film	
	F1	F2	F1	F2	F1	F2	F1	F2	F1	F2
GraphWave	0.762	0.757	0.521	0.490	0.523	0.472	0.477	0.448	OM	OM
RDAA	0.790	0.783	0.462	0.436	0.610	0.597	0.473	0.456	0.509	0.406
ReFeX	0.763	0.758	0.567	0.555	0.630	0.625	0.479	0.460	0.513	0.409
New_ReFeX	0.786	0.782	0.572	0.563	0.641	0.635	0.480	0.461	0.539	0.411
RESD	0.791	0.787	0.557	0.545	0.631	0.622	0.471	0.458	0.477	0.375
role2vec	0.323	0.312	0.350	0.348	0.422	0.418	0.311	0.304	0.338	0.302
RolX	0.796	0.793	0.551	0.528	0.627	0.618	0.467	0.452	0.487	0.383
SEGK	0.733	0.726	0.536	0.524	0.615	0.606	OT	OT	OT	OT
struc2vec	0.742	0.737	0.578	0.560	0.647	0.644	OT	OT	OT	OT
ReVaC	**0.835**	**0.831**	**0.582**	**0.563**	**0.660**	**0.654**	**0.481**	**0.463**	**0.526**	**0.401**

4.5   Role-Oriented Node Classification

We conduct the task of role-based node classification on five real-world networks to quantitatively evaluate role-oriented embedding methods. To be specific, for each dataset, a linear logistic regression classifier trained and tested using embeddings generated by each base-line and our model. We randomly sample 70% node embeddings as the training set and the other embeddings are used as the test set with 20 random runs. The performance on the Micro-F1(F1 for short) and Macro-F1(F2 for short) is shown in Table 2, for each column, we label the values of methods with significant advantages.

We have following observations: (1) Role2vec gets the worst performance. RESD achieves competitive results on this task. Struc2vec shows superiority on small networks, like USA, Europe, while struc2vec and SEGK have high computational complexity. (2) As expected, the classification results of New_-ReFeX on multiple datasets are better than that of ReFeX, where New_ReFeX outperforms others on Actor and gets the highest score on Film. This further illustrates that the New_ReFeX extracts higher quality local structural features and performs well on large datasets. (3) In general, Our ReVaC overperforms all of the baselines on all the datasets, which verifies the correctness of the idea extracting degree distribution features and strengthening the commonalities among local structures in node embeddings. ReVaC is a state-of-the-art method for role-oriented network representation learning.

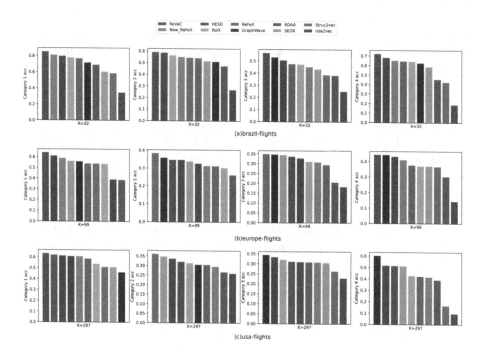

Fig. 3. Accurate values of Top-k similarity search for different embedding methods on three datestes.

4.6 Top-k Similarity Search

In this section we demonstrate the effectiveness of our model in finding the top-k nodes that are most structurally similar to the query node. We apply the top-k similarity search task on the three air-traffic datasets, respectively. In specific, we find the k most similar nodes for the central node by computing the euclidean distance. Then we count the nodes with the same label as the central node among the K nodes and calculate the accurate value of top-k. We expect that the embedding distance of nodes with similar local structures is closer, and the number of nodes with the same label in the K nodes is greater, that is, the larger the accurate value, the better. Referring to Table 1, the number of nodes in different categories of the three air-traffic datasets is different, so we set K = 32, K = 97, K = 297. Figure 3 shows the performance of top-k search on four categories of three datasets by different embedding methods.

We can come to this conclusion gradually through the following observations: (1)none of the compared methods can produce top results on all categories across the three air traffic networks. Some methods have very high accuracy in one category but low accuracy in other categories, which leads to poor overall performance of embedding methods, such as the performance of role2vec and struc2vec on the USA network. (2)our model achieves excellent and stable results. Firstly, the accuracy of the ReVaC on all four categories on the Brazil network is significantly higher than other baseline methods. Secondly, on Europe and USA networks, although the accuracy of ReVaC on all four categories is not better than that of other methods, the average accuracy of those is significantly higher.

5   Conclusion

In this paper, aiming at the challenges of the existing role-oriented network embedding methods, we propose solutions from two aspects. On the one hand, we incorporate degree distributions of nodes into the extraction of local structural features to improve the traditional ReFeX, and then we use the Variational Auto-Encoder as an operator to obtain noise-reduced and more robust local structural embeddings. On the other hand, in the local structural embedding space, we exploit a clustering algorithm to model the common features among similar local structures and fuse them into the local structural embeddings. This makes it possible to strengthen the commonality of local structural roles on the basis of keeping local structural features, so as to achieve the purpose of enriching structural information and improving the expression power of node embedding. At the same time, we also introduce the framework of the model, carried out theoretical analysis and experiments. Extensive experiments confirm the effectiveness of ReVaC, and also demonstrate that our framework can adapt well to network scale and dimensions.

References

1. Jin, J., Heimann, M., Jin, D., Koutra, D.: Toward understanding and evaluating structural node embeddings. ACM Trans. Knowl. Discov. Data **16**(3), 1–32 (2022)
2. Ribeiro, L., Saverese, P., Figueiredo, D.: struc2vec: Learning node representations from structural identity, vol. 129685, pp. 385–394. ACM (2017)
3. Heimann, M., Shen, H., Safavi, T., Koutra, D.: Regal: representation learning-based graph alignment, pp. 117–126. ACM (2018)

4. Henderson, K., Gallagher, B., Li, L., Akoglu, L., Eliassi-Rad, T., Tong, H., Faloutsos, C.: It's who you know: graph mining using recursive structural features, pp. 663–671. ACM (2011)

5. Henderson, K., et al.: Rolx: structural role extraction mining in large graphs, pp. 1231–1239. ACM (2012)

6. Gilpin, S., Eliassi-Rad, T., Davidson, I.: Guided learning for role discovery (glrd): framework, algorithms, and applications. vol. 128815, pp. 113–121. ACM (2013)

7. Zhang, W., Guo, X., Wang, W., Tian, Q., Pan, L., Jiao, P.: Role-based network embedding via structural features reconstruction with degree-regularized constraint. Knowl.-Based Syst. **218**, 106872 (2021)

8. Jiao, P., Tian, Q., Zhang, W., Guo, X., Jin, D., Wu, H.: Role discovery-guided network embedding based on autoencoder and attention mechanism. IEEE Trans. Cybern. **PP**, 1–14 (2021)

9. Guo, X., Zhang, W., Wang, W., Yu, Y., Wang, Y., Jiao, P.: Role-oriented graph auto-encoder guided by structural information **12113**, 466–481 (2020)

10. Joaristi, M., Serra, E.: Sir-gn: a fast structural iterative representation learning approach for graph nodes. ACM Trans. Knowl. Discov. Data **15**(6), 1–39 (2021)

11. Liang, Q., et al.: Rolne: improving the quality of network embedding with structural role proximity, vol. 12342, pp. 16–28 (2020)

12. Rossi, R., Ahmed, N., Koh, E., Kim, S., Rao, A., Abbasi-Yadkori, Y.: A structural graph representation learning framework, pp. 483–491. ACM (2020)

13. Donnat, C., Zitnik, M., Hallac, D., Leskovec, J.: Learning structural node embeddings via diffusion wavelets, pp. 1320–1329. ACM (2018;2017;)

14. Tu, K., Cui, P., Wang, X., Yu, P., Zhu, W.: Deep recursive network embedding with regular equivalence, pp. 2357–2366. ACM (2018)

15. Jin, Y., Song, G., Shi, C.: Gralsp: graph neural networks with local structural patterns, pp. 4361–4368 (2020)

16. Nikolentzos, G., Vazirgiannis, M.: Learning structural node representations using graph kernels. IEEE Trans. Knowl. Data Eng. **33**(5), 2045–2056 (2021, 2019)

17. Pei, Y., Fletcher, G., Pechenizkiy, M.: Joint role and community detection in networks via l2,1 norm regularized nonnegative matrix tri-factorization, pp. 168–175. ACM (2019)

18. Jin, R., Lee, V., Hong, H.: Axiomatic ranking of network role similarity, pp. 922–930. ACM (2011)

19. Pei, Y., Du, X., Zhang, J., Fletcher, G., Pechenizkiy, M.: struc2gauss: structural role preserving network embedding via gaussian embedding. Data Min. Knowl. Disc. **34**(4), 1072–1103 (2020)

20. Shi, B., Zhou, C., Qiu, H., Xu, X., Liu, J.: Unifying structural proximity and equivalence for network embedding. IEEE access **7**, 106124–106138 (2019)

21. Ahmed, N.K., et al.: Role-based graph embeddings. IEEE Trans. Knowl. Data Eng. **34**(5), 2401–2415 (2022, 2020)

22. Rossi, R.A., Ahmed, N.K.: The network data repository with interactive graph analytics and visualization. **6**, 4292–4293 (2015)

23. Leskovec, J., Huttenlocher, D., Kleinberg, J.: Predicting positive and negative links in online social networks, pp. 641–650. ACM (2010)

Dynamic Refining Knowledge Distillation Based on Attention Mechanism

Xuan Peng and Fang Liu[✉]

School of Electronic Science, National University of Defense Technology,
Changsha, China
smartlf@sina.com

Abstract. Knowledge distillation is an effective strategy to compress large pre-trained Convolutional Neural Networks (CNNs) into models suitable for mobile and embedded devices. In order to transfer better quality knowledge to students, several recent approaches have demonstrated the benefits of introducing attention mechanisms. However, the existing methods suffer from the problems that the teachers are very rigid in their teaching and the application scenarios are limited. In face of such problems, a dynamic refining knowledge distillation is proposed in this paper based on attention mechanism guided by the knowledge extraction (KE) block whose parameters can be updated. With the help of the KE block, the teacher can gradually guide students to achieve the optimal performance through a question-and-answer format, which is a dynamic selection process. Furthermore, we are able to select teacher networks and student networks more flexibly with the help of channel aggregation and refining factor r. Experimental results on the CIFAR dataset show the advantages of our method for training small models and having richer application scenarios compared to other knowledge distillation methods.

Keywords: Network compression · Knowledge distillation · Dynamic refining · Attention mechanism

1 Introduction

Convolutional neural networks (CNNs) have achieved impressive success in computer vision tasks such as image classification [4,23], object detection [14,16], and semantic segmentation [21,24]. However, the advantages of performance are driven at the cost of training and deploying resource intensive networks with millions of parameters. As application scenarios shift toward mobile and embedded devices, the computational cost, memory consumption, and power consumption of large CNNs prevent them from being deployed to these devices, which drives research on model compression. Several directions such as model pruning [10,11,20], model quantization [12], and knowledge distillation [5,9,15,17,22] are proposed to enable the model to be deployed in resource-constrained scenarios.

© The Author(s), under exclusive license to Springer Nature Switzerland AG 2022
S. Khanna et al. (Eds.): PRICAI 2022, LNCS 13630, pp. 45–58, 2022.
https://doi.org/10.1007/978-3-031-20865-2_4

Among them, knowledge distillation aims to compress a network by using the knowledge of a larger network or its ensemble (teacher) as a supervision to train a compact network (student) [19]. Different from other compression methods, it can compress the network regardless of the structural differences between teachers and students.

Attention plays a critical role in the human visual experience. In computer vision, methods of focusing attention on the most important regions of an image and ignoring irrelevant parts are called attention mechanisms [3]. In a vision system, the attention mechanism can be considered as a dynamic selection process, which is implemented by adaptively weighting the features according to the importance of the input. [22] first introduced spatial attention in knowledge distillation (AT), which transfers spatial attention maps to students as knowledge. [17] introduced channel attention in knowledge distillation (KDPA) through borrowing the squeezing operation of Squeeze-and-Excitation Networks proposed by [6]. These methods have yielded good results, but there are still some problems.

For example, firstly, teachers are too rigid in teaching students as they only give steps on how to solve a problem, which is more like students learning on their own through reference answers. However, this is not enough, because a real teacher usually guides his students' learning through a question-and-answer format. More interaction should be generated between the teacher and the students. Secondly, the choice of teacher-student combinations is restricted. AT must ensure that the spatial dimensions $W \times H$ of the blocks corresponding to the teacher and student networks are equal, while KDPA needs to ensure that the channel dimension C of the blocks corresponding to the teacher and student networks is equal.

In order to address these issues, we propose a dynamic refining knowledge distillation based on attention mechanism named DRKD, which introduces the KE block whose parameters can be updated. During training, a complete question and answer session is composed of one forward and one backward propagation. The forward propagation means that the teacher and the student give their answers separately to the same problem. During the back propagation, the parameters of both the KE block and the student are updated. The process of the student's parameters being updated indicates that the student is correcting the answer based on the teacher's response, and the parameters of the KE block being updated means that the teacher is recalibrating the answer based on the student's feedback. After many question and answer sessions, the teacher gradually guides the students to find the best answer. Moreover, with the help of the channel encoding and the channel refining, the choice of teacher-student combinations can be more flexible regardless of the dimensional differences in the feature maps of the corresponding blocks between teachers and students. In short, the contributions of this paper can be summarized as follows:

1) We propose a novel knowledge distillation method named DRKD. By introducing the KE block with parameters that can be updated, our approach is able to dynamically adjust the knowledge transferred to students based on

their feedback. The approach emulates the human knowledge transfer approach driven by questions.

2) Our proposed method effectively mitigates the problem that many excellent knowledge distillation methods cannot be used in most teacher-student combinations, which greatly enriches the application scenarios of the algorithm.

3) We experimentally demonstrate that our approach provides significant improvements in the training of small models and shows flexibility in the selection of teacher-student combinations.

2 Related Work

Knowledge Distillation. Many studies have been conducted since [5] proposed the first knowledge distillation based on the soften class probabilities. [15] first introduced the knowledge of the hidden layer to improve knowledge distillation, which suggests that the knowledge of the hidden layer also has an important impact on students during the process of knowledge transfer. Inspired by this, various other methods have been proposed to indirectly match the feature activation values of teacher and student networks. [9] proposed knowledge distillation combined with singular value decomposition (SVD) to effectively remove the spatial redundancy in the feature map by reducing the spatial dimension of the feature maps. [8] introduced the so-called "factors", which uses convolutional operations to paraphrase teacher's knowledge and to translate it for the student. [7] utilized the outputs of the hint layer of teacher to supervise student, which reduces the performance gap between teacher and student. [22] proposed to use the sum of absolute values of a feature as the attention map to implement knowledge distillation. [17] used the channel attention mechanism to highlight the expressive feature in the middle layer.

Channel Attention Mechanism. In deep neural networks, different channels in different feature maps usually possess different features [1]. Channel attention adaptively adjusts the weights of each channel, which can be seen as a feature selection process to determine what should be paid attention to [3]. [6] first proposed the concept of channel attention and presented SENet, which can capture channel-wise relationships and improve representation ability. Inspired by this, many SENet-based channel attention studies began to emerge. [2] proposed a global second-order pooling block to solve the problem of SENet's difficulty in capturing higher-order statistics. [18] proposed the efficient channel attention block which uses a 1D convolution to determine the interaction between channels. It tackles the issue that SENet cannot directly model the correspondence between weight vectors and inputs. Only using the global average pooling in the squeeze module limits representation ability. To obtain a more powerful representation ability, [13] rethought global information captured from the viewpoint of compression and analysed global average pooling in the frequency domain.

3   Methodology

The core idea of our proposed approach is how to dynamically extract the knowledge transferred to students. This section is divided into three parts to present our proposed method. Section 3.1 presents the general structure of DRKD. Sect. 3.2 introduces the specific details of implementing the KE block. Finally, we define the loss terms in Sect. 3.3 based on the carefully designed distilled knowledge.

3.1   Overall Structure of DRKD

The structure of the DRKD is shown in Fig. 1. Most existing neural networks are composed of several blocks. For example, WideResNet (WRN) consists of three blocks and ResNet consists of four blocks. Each block contains many convolutional layers, batch normalization layers and activation layers. In this paper, the dynamic refining process is implemented by introducing a pair of the KE blocks at the output of the corresponding blocks in the teacher and student networks. The refining process does not mean to extract specific knowledge, but rather to dynamically adjust the knowledge transferred to students based on their feedback. And this process is more similar to the dynamic selection process of the attention mechanism.

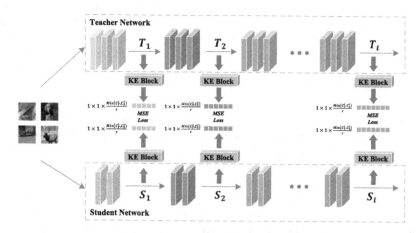

Fig. 1. Schematic diagram of the overall structure of the algorithm. T_i and S_i denote the output feature maps of the i-th block of the teacher and student networks, respectively. C_T^i and C_S^i denote the number of channels of the feature map of the i-th block of the teacher and student networks, respectively.

In details, the feature map of i-th block of the teacher network is written as $T_i = \left\{ f_{T_i}^1, f_{T_i}^2, \cdots, f_{T_i}^{C_T^i} \right\}$, C_T^i denotes the number of channels of the T_i, and the feature map of all blocks of the teacher network can be described as $T =$

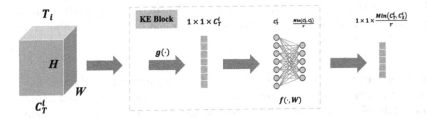

Fig. 2. Schematic diagram of the structure of the KE block, which is divided into two steps: $g(\cdot)$ and $f(\cdot, W)$. Where $W \in R^{C_T^i \times \frac{Min(C_T^i, C_S^i)}{r}}$, which is determined by the number of channels of the i-th block feature map of the teacher and student networks.

$\{T_1, T_2, \cdots, T_N\}$, N denotes the number of the entire network block. The feature map of i-th block of the student network is written as $S_i = \left\{ f_{S_i}^1, f_{S_i}^2, \cdots, f_{S_i}^{C_S^i} \right\}$, C_S^i denotes the number of channels of the S_i, and the feature map of all blocks of the student network can be described as $S = \{S_1, S_2, \cdots, S_N\}$, N denotes the number of the entire network block.

3.2   KE Blocks

Figure 2 shows the specific structure of the KE block with T_i as the input example. The KE block is implemented on the features of each block through two steps: channel encoding and channel refining.

Channel Encoding. In order to tackle the issue of spatial dimension mismatch between corresponding blocks of the teacher and student networks, it is a feasible approach that encodes the global spatial information of each channel into a channel descriptor. The study by [6] also showed that features T_i or S_i in the hidden layer can be interpreted as a collection of the local descriptors whose statistics are expressive for the whole image. Many aggregation strategies can be used to achieve channel aggregation. Considering the computational complexity, the simplest global average pooling is chosen. The statistics $Z_{T_i} \in \mathbb{R}^{C_T^i}$ and $Z_{S_i} \in \mathbb{R}^{C_S^i}$ are generated by shrinking T_i and S_i through spatial dimensions, respectively. The k-th element of Z_{T_i} and the m-th element of Z_{S_i} are calculated by:

$$Z_{T_i}^k = g\left(f_{T_i}^k\right) = \frac{1}{H_{T_i} \times W_{T_i}} \sum_{x=1}^{H_{T_i}} \sum_{y=1}^{W_{T_i}} f_{T_i}^k(x, y) \tag{1}$$

$$Z_{S_i}^m = g\left(f_{S_i}^m\right) = \frac{1}{H_{S_i} \times W_{S_i}} \sum_{x=1}^{H_{S_i}} \sum_{y=1}^{W_{S_i}} f_{S_i}^m(x, y) \tag{2}$$

where $Z_{T_i}^k$ denotes the k-th element of the channel descriptor vector of the i-th block of the teacher network, $f_{T_i}^k$ denotes the k-th channel feature map of the

i-th block of the teacher network, and $H_{T_i} \times W_{T_i}$ denotes the spatial dimension of the i-th block of the teacher network. The student network is as above. Where $1 \leq k \leq C_T^i$, $1 \leq m \leq C_S^i$.

Channel Refining. Related studies [10,11] have shown that there is a certain degree of redundancy in the numerous channels in the convolutional neural networks. Therefore, in order to take advantage of the information aggregated in the channel encoding operation, we follow it with a second operation which aims to dynamically refine the knowledge transferred to the students based on their feedback. To fulfil this objective, the function must satisfy two criteria: first, its parameters must be updatable since we need to ensure that knowledge transfer is a dynamic selection process, and second, its input must be 1D tensor as the output of the channel encoding is 1D tensor. Besides, the function must also act as a dimensionality reduction, considering the problem of channel dimension mismatch between teachers and students. Therefore, the fully connected layer is the only choice:

$$V_{T_i} = f\left(Z_{T_i}, W_{T_i}\right) = \sigma\left(W_{T_i} Z_{T_i}\right) \tag{3}$$

$$V_{S_i} = f\left(Z_{S_i}, W_{S_i}\right) = \sigma\left(W_{S_i} Z_{S_i}\right) \tag{4}$$

where $W_{T_i} \in \mathbb{R}^{\frac{Min\left(C_T^i, C_S^i\right)}{r} \times C_T^i}$, $W_{S_i} \in \mathbb{R}^{\frac{Min\left(C_T^i, C_S^i\right)}{r} \times C_S^i}$ and σ refers to sigmoid activation function. The r is a hyperparameter which plays a crucial role in our proposed algorithm. With the help of r, the problem of mismatching the number of channels in the corresponding blocks of the teacher and student networks can be solved. And r is usually set to an integer value, $1 \leq r \leq Min\left(C_T^i, C_S^i\right)$. As r increases, the total amount of knowledge transferred from the teacher to the students is decreasing, with a greater tendency to filter for high-priority features. The balance between quality and quantity is very important in the knowledge transfer process. The degree of dynamic refining can be adjusted according to the actual situation with the help of r (the choice of this hyperparameter is discussed in Sect. 4.4).

3.3 Loss Function

The loss function of our proposed method consists of two components. One is a cross-entropy loss based on the ground-truth labels and the predicted labels of the student network, and the other is a dynamic refining (DR) loss based on the middle layer features of the network.

At the beginning of training, the ground-truth loss plays an important role in improving the convergence speed of the student network. The loss is calculated by:

$$\mathcal{L}_{cross} = \mathcal{H}_{cross}(y, \hat{y}) \tag{5}$$

where y denotes the ground-truth label, $\hat{y}$ denotes the predicted label of the student network, and $\mathcal{H}_{cross}$ denotes the cross-entropy function.

During network training, the DR loss acts as a regularization term and helps improve robust. The loss is calculated by:

$$\mathcal{L}_{DR} = \sum_{i=1}^{N} \frac{1}{\lambda_i} \|V_{T_i} - V_{S_i}\|_2^2, \lambda_i = \frac{Min\left(C_T^i, C_S^i\right)}{r} \tag{6}$$

where $V_T = \{V_{T_1}, V_{T_2}, \cdots, V_{T_N}\}$ represents the knowledge transferred from the teacher to the student. The r is usually set to an integer value and $1 \leq r \leq Min\left(C_T^i, C_S^i\right)$.

Objective function:

$$\mathcal{L}_{Total} = \mathcal{L}_{cross} + \alpha \mathcal{L}_{DR} \tag{7}$$

where the α is a hyperparameter that adjusts the proportion of the DR loss term in the final objective function.

4 Experiments

In this section, WideResNet (WRN) and ResNet will be used as our deep neural network models and experimented on the CIFAR datasets. The CIFAR dataset contains CIFAR-10 and CIFAR-100, consisting of 60,000 RGB images of 32×32 pixels. The ratio of both training set and test set is $5 : 1$.

4.1 Experiments on Benchmark Datasets

The performance of the algorithm will be proved in two aspects: different network architectures and different number of channels. Therefore, three teacher-student combinations will be chosen, which are the [ResNet34, ResNet18], the [WRN-28-2, WRN-16-2] and the [WRN-10-5, WRN-16-1]. In WRN-n-k, n denotes the depth of the network, and k denotes that the number of channels of the network is k times the number of base channels. During training, the teacher network is untrainable and the student network is used with stochastic gradient descent (SGD) as the optimizer, with momentum set to 0.9 and weight decay set to 5e-4. The initial value of the learning rate is set to 1e-1 and all learning rates are multiplied by 0.7 every 10 epochs. When the [ResNet34, ResNet18] is trained, the best received results are at $\alpha = 1.0, r = 1$. When the [WRN-28-2, WRN-16-2] is trained, the best received results are at $\alpha = 1.0, r = 2$. When the [WRN-10-5, WRN-16-1] is trained, the best received results are at $\alpha = 1.0, r = 16$.

Table 1 and Table 2 show the performance of DR on the CIFAR-10 and CIFAR-100, respectively. In the tables, the compression ratio is calculated as $\frac{T_{params} - S_{params}}{T_{params}}$. Among them, T_{params} denotes the parameters of the teacher, and S_{params} denotes the parameters of the student. When the experiment is conducted on the ResNet, ResNet34 is selected as the teacher network and ResNet18 is chosen as the student network. Compared with the student baseline, the accuracy of the student trained by DR on the CIFAR-10 and CIFAR-100 is improved by 1.99% and 3.29%, separately. When the experiment is carried out on the

Table 1. The performance of DR algorithm on CIFAR-10

Teacher	Student	Compression Ratio	FLOPs	Student Baseline	DR	Teacher Baseline
ResNet34, 21.28M	ResNet18, 11.17M	47.51%	0.56 G	94.10%	**96.09%**	94.21%
WRN-28-2, 1.47M	WRN-16-2, 0.69M	53.06%	0.13 G	92.80%	**95.70%**	93.89%
WRS-10-5, 1.90M	WRN-16-1, 0.08M	95.68%	0.01 G	90.19%	**93.36%**	92.05%

Table 2. The performance of DR algorithm on CIFAR-100

Teacher	Student	Compression Ratio	FLOPs	Student Baseline	DR	Teacher Baseline
ResNet34, 21.28M	ResNet18, 11.17M	47.51%	0.56G	76.01%	**79.30%**	76.71%
WRN-28-2, 1.47M	WRN-16-2, 0.69M	53.06%	0.13G	70.79%	**75.39%**	72.50%
WRS-10-5, 1.90M	WRN-16-1, 0.08M	95.68%	0.01G	64.92%	**71.09%**	70.09%

WideResNet, two teacher-student combinations are selected in terms of whether the number of channels matches. One is the [WRN-28-2, WRN-16-2], in which the accuracy of the student trained by DR on the CIFAR-10 and CIFAR-100 is improved by 2.90% and 4.60%, respectively, compared with the student baseline. The other is the [WRN-10-5, WRN-16-1], in which the accuracy of the student trained by DR on the CIFAR-10 and CIFAR-100 is improved by 3.17% and 6.17%, separately, compared with the student baseline.

From these experiments, it can be seen that DR can significantly improve the performance of the student. As the capacity of the student network gradually decreases, the performance improvement of the students trained by DR gradually becomes larger and the value of the refining factor r increases. Among them, the improvement is more obvious on the CIFAR-100. These show that our method works very well when small models are trained since the lower capacity student network is transferred with higher quality knowledge, reflecting the adjustment effect of r on the balance between quantity and quality. Furthermore, the students even outperform the teachers due to the added ground-truth loss.

4.2 Comparison with Other Methods

In order to demonstrate the effectiveness of our proposed DR more extensively, it is used to compare with other typical knowledge distillation methods. WideRes-Net is widely used in various knowledge distillation methods for training on the CIFAR. Therefore, WRN-28-2 is chosen as the teacher and WRN-16-2 is selected as the student to perform experiments on the CIFAR. Table 3 shows the performance of DR compared with other typical knowledge distillation algorithms. The accuracy's improvement in the table refers to the comparison with the student baseline, which is obtained by training with a standard back-propagation algorithm. Here the teacher baseline corresponds to the last column of Table 1 and Table 2 and the student baseline corresponds to column 5 of Table 1 and Table 2.

Table 3. Comparison of DR and other typical algorithms on CIFAR

Algorithm	Parameters	FLOPs	CIFAR-10	CIFAR-100
Teacher	1.47 M	0.21 G	+1.09%	+1.71%
KD	0.69 M	0.13 G	+0.74%	+1.52%
AT	0.69 M	0.13 G	+1.17%	+1.66%
KDPA	0.69 M	0.13 G	+1.75%	+2.32%
DRKD (our)	0.69 M	0.13 G	**+2.90%**	**+4.60%**

From these experiments, it can be found that the accuracy of the student trained by DR is improved by 2.90% and 4.60% on the CIFAR-10 and CIFAR-100, respectively, compared to the student baseline. Compared to the teacher baseline, the improvement is 1.81% and 2.89% separately. It performs the best of all methods. And this improvement is even more evident on the CIFAR-100, which again demonstrates the advantage of our approach to train small models. This is because the capacity of the student network is small compared to the task complexity of the CIFAR-100. Our method is more advantageous in dealing with the problem that small capacity networks are difficult to train.

4.3 Ablation Experiments

In this section, a series of experiments based on the teacher-student combination [WRN-28-2, WRN-16-2] are employed to investigate the effect of the hyperparameter α and each block in the network on the algorithm.

First, the effect of each block in the network on the algorithm is studied. WideResNet has three blocks. θ is used to indicate that some blocks of the network are not involved in the loss calculation. For example, $\theta = 001$ means to only calculate the loss for the third block, and so on. When studying the importance of each block, hold other hyperparameters constant and let $\alpha = 1$,

$r = 2$. As shown in Table 4, the student obtains the optimal result when all blocks of the teacher and the student are involved in the loss calculation. From these experiments, it can be found that distillation is not very effective when the knowledge is transferred for only one block, suggesting that the shallow information of the network also plays an important role in guiding students.

Table 4. The effect of each block in the network on the performance of the DR algorithm

θ	CIFAR-10	CIFAR-100
001	93.75%	74.22%
010	95.31%	74.61%
011	94.14%	74.61%
100	94.53%	75.00%
101	94.14%	74.22%
110	94.14%	74.22%
111	**95.70%**	**75.39%**

Second, the importance of the DR loss term is investigated. The α is used to adjust the DR loss term as a percentage of the total loss. When exploring the effect of α on the algorithm, keep other hyperparameters unchanged and let $r = 2$, $\theta = 111$. Table 5 shows how the accuracy of the student network on the CIFAR changes when the DR loss term increases as a percentage of the total loss, and the student obtains the best results when $\alpha = 1$. At first, the accuracy of the student network increases as α becomes larger, but starts to decrease after reaching a certain threshold. Moreover, the algorithm is more sensitive to the value of α before reaching the threshold, because its small changes can lead to large fluctuations in accuracy. From these experiments, it can be found that a balance should be maintained between the DR loss term and the ground-truth loss term. It still helps to improve student's performance when the DR loss is small. But when the DR loss is too large, the degradation of the students' performance is very dramatic as the ground-truth loss term hardly works.

Table 5. The effect of α on the performance of the DR algorithm

α	CIFAR-10	CIFAR-100
0.1	94.53%	73.83%
0.5	94.92%	74.22%
0.7	95.31%	74.61%
1	**95.70%**	**75.39%**
2	94.92%	73.83%
4	95.31%	75.00%
6	94.53%	74.22%
8	94.53%	73.44%
30	93.75%	72.67%

4.4   Refining Factor

The refining factor r is an important hyperparameter that can be used to control the balance between the quantity and the quality of knowledge transferred to students. In this paper, the quantity of knowledge is simply measured by the number of channels. To investigate this relationship, the experiment has been conducted based on whether the number of teacher-student channels matches.

Table 6. Performance of the teacher-student combinations [ResNet34, ResNet18] and [WRN-28-2, WRN-16-2] on CIFAR when the refining factor r takes different values.

Teacher-Student	r	Compression ratio	FLOPs	CIFAR-10	CIFAR-100
[ResNet34, ResNet18]	1	47.51%	0.56 G	**96.09%**	**79.30%**
	2	47.51%	0.56 G	95.70%	78.91%
	4	47.51%	0.56 G	95.70%	78.91%
	8	47.51%	0.56 G	95.31%	78.91%
	16	47.51%	0.56 G	95.31%	77.73%
	32	47.51%	0.56 G	94.53%	75.39%
[WRN-28-2, WRN-16-2]	1	53.06%	0.13 G	93.75%	74.22%
	2	53.06%	0.13 G	**95.70%**	**75.39%**
	4	53.06%	0.13 G	94.92%	73.43%
	8	53.06%	0.13 G	94.53%	75.00%
	16	53.06%	0.13 G	94.53%	73.44%
	32	53.06%	0.13 G	94.14%	73.05%

Table 7. Multiple teacher-student combinations with mismatched channel numbers

Student	Teacher	Compression Ratio	k
WRN-16-1	WRN-10-2	75.00%	2
	WRN-10-3	88.41%	3
	WRN-10-4	93.44%	4
	WRN-10-5	95.68%	5

When the Number of Channels in the Teacher-Student Combination Matches. Considering $C_T^i = C_S^i$, experiments have been performed based on teacher-student combinations [ResNet34, ResNet18] and [WRN-28-2, WRN-16-2] for a range of different r values. When studying the effect of r on the algorithm, hold the other hyperparameters constant and let $\alpha = 1$, $\theta = 111$.

The top half of Table 6 shows that the best results are obtained from the teacher-student combination [ResNet34, ResNet18] with the refining factor $r = 1$, meaning that the KE block is still beneficial for improving student's performance even without refining channel features. The bottom half of Table 6 shows that the teacher-student combination [WRN-28-2, WRN-16-2] obtains the optimal results with the refining factor $r = 2$. In summary, when the total amount of knowledge is equal, the knowledge of the high-capacity teacher network can be transferred to students without refining, on the contrary, the low-capacity teacher network needs to further improve the quality of knowledge.

When the Number of Channels in the Teacher-Student Combination Does Not Match. Considering $C_T^i \neq C_S^i$, experiments have been conducted based on Table 7 for a range of different r values, where k denotes the ratio of the number of teacher and student channels. When exploring the effect of r on the algorithm, keep the other hyperparameters constant and let $\alpha = 1$, $\theta = 111$.

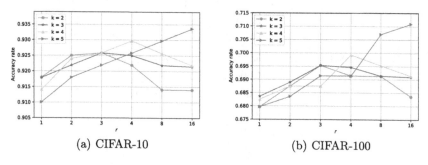

(a) CIFAR-10   (b) CIFAR-100

Fig. 3. On the CIFAR-10, the student gets the highest accuracy rate of 92.58% at $r = 3$ when $k = 2$, 92.58% at $r = 3$ when $k = 3$, 92.97% at $r = 4$ when $k = 4$ and 93.36% at $r = 16$ when $k = 5$. On the CIFAR-100, the student gets the highest accuracy rate of 69.53% at $r = 3$ when $k = 2$, 69.53% at $r = 3$ when $k = 3$, 69.92% at $r = 4$ when $k = 4$ and 71.09% at $r = 16$ when $k = 5$.

Figure 3(a) and Fig. 3(b) show the variation in student's accuracy for different student-teacher combinations for different r values on the CIFAR-10 and CIFAR-100, respectively. From these experiments, it can be found that as the ratio of the number of channels between teachers and students increases, the refining factor r for obtaining the best performance increases as well. However, the refining factor cannot always be increased because of the limitations of the student network. In general, when the total amount of knowledge is not equal, the larger the total amount is, the more the teacher network needs to further improve the quality of the knowledge transferred to the students. This is also consistent with our conventional perception that the larger the total amount is, the more redundancy exists. But the refining factor r cannot be increased all the time and its maximum value is $Min\left(C_T^i, C_S^i\right)$ limited by the teacher and student network architecture.

5 Conclusion

In this paper, we propose a knowledge distillation method based on attention mechanism named DRKD, which aims to dynamically select the knowledge transferred to students. This provides a novel way of thinking, where the teacher gradually guides the students to get the best answer through a question-and-answer format as a real teacher teaches the students, rather than simply instilling them with knowledge. In addition, our proposed approach deeply explores the balanced relationship between the quantity and the quality of knowledge transferred from the teacher to the student, not only laying the theoretical foundation for achieving stronger compression for small model optimization, but also improving the versatility of knowledge distillation methods for multi-structural combination situations. Finally, we testify the effectiveness of this approach and the flexibility in selecting teacher-student combinations on the CIFAR-10 and CIFAR-100.

References

1. Chen, L., et al.: Sca-cnn: spatial and channel-wise attention in convolutional networks for image captioning. In: 2017 IEEE Conference on Computer Vision and Pattern Recognition (CVPR), pp. 6298–6306 (2017)
2. Gao, Z., Xie, J., Wang, Q., Li, P.: Global second-order pooling convolutional networks. In: 2019 IEEE/CVF Conference on Computer Vision and Pattern Recognition (CVPR), pp. 3019–3028 (2019)
3. Guo, M.H., et al.: Attention mechanisms in computer vision: a survey. Computational Visual Media, pp. 1–38 (2022)
4. He, K., Zhang, X., Ren, S., Sun, J.: Deep residual learning for image recognition. In: 2016 IEEE Conference on Computer Vision and Pattern Recognition (CVPR), pp. 770–778 (2016). https://doi.org/10.1109/CVPR.2016.90
5. Hinton, G., Vinyals, O., Dean, J., et al.: Distilling the knowledge in a neural network. arXiv preprint arXiv:1503.02531 2(7) (2015)
6. Hu, J., Shen, L., Sun, G.: Squeeze-and-excitation networks. In: 2018 IEEE/CVF Conference on Computer Vision and Pattern Recognition, pp. 7132–7141 (2018)
7. Jin, X., et al.: Knowledge distillation via route constrained optimization. In: Proceedings of the IEEE/CVF International Conference on Computer Vision, pp. 1345–1354 (2019)
8. Kim, J., Park, S., Kwak, N.: Paraphrasing complex network: network compression via factor transfer. In: Advances in Neural Information Processing Systems 31 (2018)
9. Lee, S.H., Kim, D.H., Song, B.C.: Self-supervised knowledge distillation using singular value decomposition. In: Ferrari, V., Hebert, M., Sminchisescu, C., Weiss, Y. (eds.) ECCV 2018. LNCS, vol. 11210, pp. 339–354. Springer, Cham (2018). https://doi.org/10.1007/978-3-030-01231-1_21
10. Li, Y., et al.: Towards compact cnns via collaborative compression. In: Proceedings of the IEEE/CVF Conference on Computer Vision and Pattern Recognition, pp. 6438–6447 (2021)
11. Liu, L., et al.: Group fisher pruning for practical network compression. In: International Conference on Machine Learning, pp. 7021–7032. PMLR (2021)

12. Liu, Z., Wang, Y., Han, K., Zhang, W., Ma, S., Gao, W.: Post-training quantization for vision transformer. In: Advances in Neural Information Processing Systems 34 (2021)
13. Qin, Z., Zhang, P., Wu, F., Li, X.: Fcanet: frequency channel attention networks. In: 2021 IEEE/CVF International Conference on Computer Vision (ICCV), pp. 763–772 (2021)
14. Redmon, J., Farhadi, A.: Yolov3: An incremental improvement. CoRR abs/1804.02767 (2018)
15. Romero, A., Ballas, N., Kahou, S.E., Chassang, A., Gatta, C., Bengio, Y.: Fitnets: hints for thin deep nets. arXiv preprint arXiv:1412.6550 (2014)
16. Tan, M., Pang, R., Le, Q.V.: Efficientdet: scalable and efficient object detection. In: Proceedings of the IEEE/CVF Conference on Computer Vision and Pattern Recognition, pp. 10781–10790 (2020)
17. Tang, J., Liu, M., Jiang, N., Yu, W., Yang, C., Zhou, J.: Knowledge distillation based on positive-unlabeled classification and attention mechanism. In: 2021 IEEE International Symposium on Circuits and Systems (ISCAS), pp. 1–5. IEEE (2021)
18. Wang, Q., Wu, B., Zhu, P., Li, P., Zuo, W., Hu, Q.: Eca-net: efficient channel attention for deep convolutional neural networks. In: 2020 IEEE/CVF Conference on Computer Vision and Pattern Recognition (CVPR), pp. 11531–11539 (2020)
19. Wang, X., Fu, T., Liao, S., Wang, S., Lei, Z., Mei, T.: Exclusivity-consistency regularized knowledge distillation for face recognition. In: Vedaldi, A., Bischof, H., Brox, T., Frahm, J.-M. (eds.) ECCV 2020. LNCS, vol. 12369, pp. 325–342. Springer, Cham (2020). https://doi.org/10.1007/978-3-030-58586-0_20
20. Wang, Z., Li, C., Wang, X.: Convolutional neural network pruning with structural redundancy reduction. In: Proceedings of the IEEE/CVF Conference on Computer Vision and Pattern Recognition, pp. 14913–14922 (2021)
21. Yu, F., Koltun, V.: Multi-scale context aggregation by dilated convolutions. arXiv preprint arXiv:1511.07122 (2015)
22. Zagoruyko, S., Komodakis, N.: Paying more attention to attention: improving the performance of convolutional neural networks via attention transfer. arXiv preprint arXiv:1612.03928 (2016)
23. Zagoruyko, S., Komodakis, N.: Wide residual networks. In: Proceedings of the British Machine Vision Conference (BMVC), pp. 87.1-87.12. BMVA Press (2016)
24. Zheng, S., et al.: Rethinking semantic segmentation from a sequence-to-sequence perspective with transformers. In: Proceedings of the IEEE/CVF Conference on Computer Vision and Pattern Recognition, pp. 6881–6890 (2021)

Entity Representation by Neighboring Relations Topology for Inductive Relation Prediction

Zhigui Chen, Hang Yu$^{(\boxtimes)}$, Jinpeng Li, and Xiangfeng Luo

School of Computer Engineering and Science, Shanghai University,
Shanghai 200444, China
{chenzhigui,yuhang,lijinpeng,luoxf}@shu.edu.cn

Abstract. Inductive relation prediction is to predict relations between unseen entities. The current methods implicitly learn the logical rules in the knowledge graph through the local subgraph structures, and obtain the latent semantic representation of the predicted triples. However, existing methods lack relation information of neighboring triples due to the incompleteness of the knowledge graph, and the representation of entities does not consider the connection structures between relations which contain different semantic information. To address these challenges, we propose a novel entity representation by Neighboring Relations Topology Graph (NRTG) for inductive relation prediction. Specifically, we divide connection structures between relations into several *topological patterns*, and design a module to extract relations of all neighboring triples for constructing Neighboring Relations Topology Graph (NRTG). In NRTG, the nodes represent the relations and the edges represent the *topological patterns*. Afterward, we design an information aggregation module to encode the NRTG as the entity representation, and then use the scoring network to predict relations between unseen entities. Experiments demonstrate that our model can effectively capture relation information of neighboring triples and semantic information of connection structures between relations. Moreover, it outperforms existing methods on benchmark datasets for the inductive relation prediction task.

Keywords: Knowledge graph · Knowledge graph completion · Inductive relation prediction

1 Introduction

Nowadays, knowledge graphs play a very important role in natural language processing [27], recommendation systems [21] and question answering [8]. However, the existing knowledge graphs are incomplete, so the relation prediction task is required for reasoning and completion. The relation prediction on the knowledge graph is divided into transductive and inductive. Transductive relation prediction [1,3,16] learns and operates on latent representations (i.e., embeddings) of

© The Author(s), under exclusive license to Springer Nature Switzerland AG 2022
S. Khanna et al. (Eds.): PRICAI 2022, LNCS 13630, pp. 59–72, 2022.
https://doi.org/10.1007/978-3-031-20865-2_5

entities and relations in a knowledge graph. However, this method can only make relation predictions for entities that appear in the training set, and cannot represent unseen entities. On the contrary, inductive relation prediction [6,17,19] is entity-independent, and this approach can make relation prediction for entities that are not present in the training set. For the real world, existing knowledge graphs cannot cover all entities, so the problem of relation prediction for unseen entities has been paid more and more attention by researchers.

Existing models of inductive relation prediction mainly predict missing relations by learning logical rules in knowledge graphs. At present, there are mainly two types of methods for learning logic rules. Rule-based learning explicitly mines logical rules based on co-occurrence patterns of relations. Inductive relation prediction by local subgraph structures, such as GraIL [17], implicitly learns the logical rules in subgraph based on Graph Neural Networks (GNN) [7,12,14]. More recently, TACT [2] classifies relation pairs in subgraphs into several patterns, and incorporates these messages into the representation of relations.

Although subgraph-based models have shown inductive learning capability in validating unseen nodes, there are some disadvantages. First, many inference paths are disconnected due to the incompleteness of the knowledge graphs. Therefore, the subgraph will miss a lot of neighboring relation information. Taking Fig. 1 as an example, for entity "GSW", neighboring relations "coach_of" and "belong_to" are not connected to the tail node so the representation of "GSW" lacks these relation information. Moreover, existing methods do not take into account connection structures between relations in entity representation. For example, in Fig. 1, the relation "part_of" has three connection structures such as "parallel", "tail-to-head" and "tail-to-tail" with predicted relation "located_in" and these connection structures have different effects on the representation of "GSW". In this way, the representations of nodes "GSW" and "Californla" with topology information are obtained, respectively. Then, combine the embedding of "located_in" into the scoring function to get the likelihood of this triple.

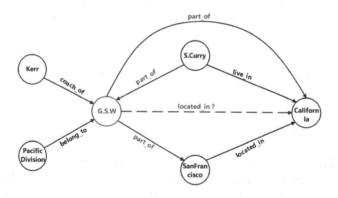

Fig. 1. An example in knowledge graphs.

To address these disadvantages, we propose a novel entity representation by Neighboring Relations Topology Graph (NRTG) for inductive relation prediction. Specifically, the NRTG extracts all neighboring triples and then divides the connection structures between relations into six topological patterns. Therefore, our method can capture relation information of neighboring triples and connection structures between relations by NRTG.

For predicted triples, our model consists of the following stages: (1) constructing NRTG via relations topology module. (2) getting head and tail entity representations of predicted triple via information aggregation module based on GNN [7]. (3) inputting head and tail entity representations and embedding the predicted relation into the scoring network to obtain the predicted triples score.

Our contributions are as follows. First of all, we propose a novel framework that uses two graph structures to represent the head and tail entities of predicted triples separately. This framework can more completely mine the logical information implied by the head and tail entities in the knowledge graph. Secondly, we design Neighboring Relations Topology Graph (NRTG) to capture the semantic information of connection structures among relations. Finally, it significantly outperforms existing inductive relation prediction methods on benchmark datasets.

The remainder of this article is structured as follows. Related works are introduced in Sect. 2. The specific details of our method are introduced in Sect. 3. The experiments used to analyze and verify the effectiveness of our method in Sect. 4. Section 5 concludes this article and proposes future works.

2   Related Work

At present, there are two main methods for relation prediction on knowledge graphs. One is the rule learning-based methods, and the other is the embedding-based reasoning methods:

Rule Learning-Based Methods. Rule-based methods [4] learn logical rules by relational co-occurrence patterns of knowledge graphs. Because these logic rules are independent of entities, these methods can predict relations between unseen entities. Despite the fact that these methods are inherently inductive, these methods are difficult to scale to large datasets. Recently, NeuralLP [23] proposed an end-to-end framework to address scalability issues. Based on NeuralLP, DRUM [13] can mine more correct logic rules. However, These logical rules cannot learn the complex topological structure between relations.

Embedding-Based Methods. Most of the existing methods are embedding-based methods such as TransE [1], ConvE [3], ComplEx [20] and RotatE [16], which is to learn a low-dimensional embedding vector for each entity and relation in a knowledge graph. In recent years, more and more researchers have applied graph neural networks (GNN) [7,12,14] to relation prediction, as knowledge graphs naturally have graph structures. Schlichtkrull et al. [15] propose a relational graph neural network that considers the connected relations to represent entities. Afterward, GAT [11] proposes a graph neural network based on an attention mechanism to teaches the representation of entities, which effectively learn the knowledge of neighboring triples. More recently, Zhang et al. [26] proposed a relational graph neural network with hierarchical attention to effectively utilize the neighborhood information of entities in knowledge graphs.

To predict the relation between unseen entities, GraIL [17] reasons via entity-independent local subgraph structures. On the basis of GraIL, TACT [2] considers semantic correlations between relations, and models correlation coefficients of the different semantic correlations into relation representation. Moreover, there are some neural networks [24, 25] that learn topology.

However, these methods have limitations. The incompleteness of the graph can lead to insufficient learning of neighboring relations. Furthermore, these methods are too simplistic to model entity representations since these methods do not take into account the topological structure between neighboring relations and predicted relations.

3   Methods

In this section, we introduce our proposed model. The task of our model is inductive relation prediction, which predicts the relation between unseen entities. For inductive relation prediction, we need to represent entities that have not been seen in the training set. Therefore, our model uses two Neighboring Relations Topology Graphs (NRTGs), in which the nodes represent the relations and the edges represent the connection structures between relations, to represent the head and tail entity respectively. Then our model scores the predicted triple through head representation, tail entity representation and embedding of predicted relation. Our model consists of the following parts: (1) Relations topology module. (2) Information aggregation module based on GNN [7]. (3) Scoring network and Loss function. Figure 2 gives an overview of our model.

3.1   Relations Topology Module

In order to solve the problems that the existing model does not capture the complete neighboring relations and does not consider connection structures between relations, we design this module to fully mine the implicit logical rules of predicted triple in knowledge graphs in two aspects: neighboring relations extraction and Neighboring Relations Topology Graph (NRTG).

Neighboring Relations Extraction. For existing subgraph-based methods, they assume that the paths connecting the head and tail entity contain the logical information that could represent the predicted triple. Differing from the existing subgraph-based models, we assume that the relations of all neighboring triples imply the logical rules of relation prediction. Because the knowledge graph is incomplete, many reasoning paths are disconnected. Therefore, neighboring relations that do not exist on the reasoning path can also provide a basis for relation prediction. Furthermore, we extract two subgraphs from the knowledge graph to represent the head and tail entity of the predicted triple,

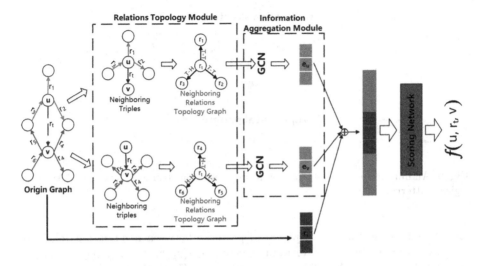

Fig. 2. An overview of our model. The framework consists of two modules. The blue vector represents the initial predicted relation embedding. We use a scoring network to score a triple. (Color figure online)

respectively. Compared with using an enclosing subgraph to represent triples, our method can better emphasize the logical information implied by entities.

In this module, we extract all n-hop neighboring triples of the head and tail entity, respectively. For example, given a predicted triplet (u, r_t, v), we iteratively obtain the n-hop neighboring triples of the node u and node v through the breadth-first search(BFS) algorithm. Let $\mathcal{N}_n(u)$ and $\mathcal{N}_n(v)$ be set of triples in the n-hop neighborhood of node u and node v in the KG. For existing subgraph-based methods, they compute the enclosing subgraph by taking the intersection, $\mathcal{N}_n(u) \cap \mathcal{N}_n(v)$, of these k-hop neighborhood sets. However, these models will lack many neighboring triples. Therefore, we respectively use $\mathcal{N}_n(u)$ and $\mathcal{N}_n(v)$ to represent node u and node v, which can fully capture the logical rules implied by the neighboring triples of the head and tail entity.

Neighboring Relations Topology Graph. Since the n-hop neighboring triples extracted from the KG do not consider the connection structures between relations, we design the Neighboring Relations Topology Graph (NRTG) to address this problem. Inspired by TACT [2], to model the connection structures between relations of neighboring triples, we categorize relation pairs, consisting of neighboring and predicted relations, into six topological patterns. As illustrated in Fig. 3, there are six connection structures for connected relations in the knowledge graph, namely "head-to-tail", "tail-to-tail", "head-to-head", "tail-to-head", "parallel", and "loop". The connection structures are called topological patterns and they are named "H-T", "T-T", "H-H", "T-H", "PARA" and "LOOP" respectively.

Based on the definition of different topological patterns, we can convert the n-hop neighboring triples to NRTG, where the nodes represent the relations

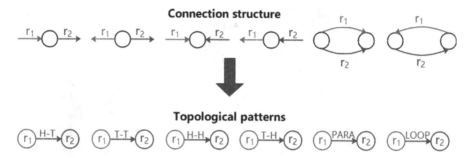

Fig. 3. An illustration of the transition from connection structure between relations to logical patterns.

and the edges indicate the topological patterns between neighboring relations and predicted relations. For example, the triples (e_1, r_1, e_2) and (e_2, r_2, e_3) are connected by e_2, and their topological pattern is "H-T". So, we construct a new triple $(r_1, H - T, r_2)$ in NRTG. For n-hop neighboring triples of head and tail entity, $\mathcal{N}_n(u)$ and $\mathcal{N}_n(v)$, we can convert the n-hop neighboring triples of entity u and entity v into NRTG in this way, respectively.

In this module, we extract the n-hop neighboring triples of the head and tail entity, respectively, and then convert the neighboring triples into NRTGs. As we can see, the NRTGs not only contain neighboring relations of the entities, but also take into account the connection structures between relations. Therefore, entity representation by NRTG can better mine the logical rules implied by entities predicted in KG. The detailed procedure is presented in Algorithm 1.

3.2   Information Aggregation Module

Based on the Neighboring Relations Topology Graphs (NRTGs) of the head and tail entity, we design a module to aggregate neighboring relations and topological patterns between relations in NRTGs as entity representations. Specifically, the information aggregation module is based on Relational Graph Convolutional Network (R-GCN) [15], and uses a message passing mechanism [5] in graph neural networks to update node representations. Finally, we use the average pooling of all the latent node representations to represent head, and tail entities of the predicted triple, respectively. As we can see, the entity representation contains the neighboring relations and topological patterns through this module. In this module, the message passing mechanism of node update is mainly divided into message function and aggregation function.

Message Function. The purpose of the message function is to pass the information to update the node in the NRTG. For each target node, it may receive messages from multiple nodes. Inspired by R-GCN [15], we define the message function of the k-th layer as:

Algorithm 1. Neighboring Relations Topology Graph Construction

---

Input: Origin graph $\mathcal{G}$, predicted triple (u, r_t, v), hop of neighboring n

Output: neighboring relations topology graph of head entity $\mathcal{G}_u$, neighboring relations topology graph of tail entity $\mathcal{G}_v$

1: $\mathcal{N}_0(u) \longleftarrow \{u\}$, $\mathcal{N}_0(v) \longleftarrow \{v\}$
2: **for** each triple (s, r, t) in $\mathcal{G}$ **do**
3:     **for** $i \longleftarrow 1$ to n **do**
4:         **if** (s, r, t) connect with $\mathcal{N}_{i-1}(u)$ **then**
5:             $\mathcal{N}_i(u) \longleftarrow \mathcal{N}_{i-1}(u) \cup (s, r, t)$
6:         **end if**
7:         **if** (s, r, t) connect with $\mathcal{N}_{i-1}(v)$ **then**
8:             $\mathcal{N}_i(v) \longleftarrow \mathcal{N}_{i-1}(v) \cup (s, r, t)$
9:         **end if**
10:    **end for**
11: **end for**
12: $\mathcal{G}_u \longleftarrow \{\}$, $\mathcal{G}_v \longleftarrow \{\}$
13: **for** each triple (s, r, t) in $\mathcal{N}_n(u)$ **do**
14:     **if** (s, r, t) connect with (u_i, r_t, v_i) **then**
15:         Get pattern between (s, r, t) and (u, r_t, v) via the definition of topological patterns
16:         $\mathcal{G}_u \longleftarrow \mathcal{G}_u \cup (r_t, pattern, r)$
17:     **end if**
18: **end for**
19: **for** each triple (s, r, t) in $\mathcal{N}_n(v)$ **do**
20:     **if** (s, r, t) connect with (u_i, r_t, v_i) **then**
21:         Get pattern between (s, r, t) and (u, r_t, v) via the definition of topological patterns
22:         $\mathcal{G}_v \longleftarrow \mathcal{G}_v \cup (r_t, pattern, r)$
23:     **end if**
24: **end for**
25: **return** $\mathcal{G}_u, \mathcal{G}_v$

$$m_t^k = \sum_{p=1}^{P} \sum_{s \in \mathcal{N}_r} a_{t,s}^k W_p^k n_s^{k-1}, \tag{1}$$

where $\mathcal{N}_r$ is the neighboring relations of predicted triple and P is the topological patterns between relations. n_s^{k-1} represent the node representation of the last layer, and it is represented as the embedding of relation when in the input layer. W_p^k represents the transformation matrix of the topological pattern p of the relation pair at the k-th layer. $a_{t,s}^k$ is the edge attention weight at the k-th layer corresponding to the edge connecting nodes s and t via topological patterns. The attention weights of the k-th layer are as follows:

$$a_{t,s}^k = \sigma \left(W_1^a \cdot ReLU \left(W_2^a \left[n_s^{k-1} \oplus n_t^{k-1} \oplus n_p^a \right] \right) \right). \tag{2}$$

Here W_1^a and W_2^a are the weight parameters in the attention mechanism, respectively. n_p^a is the attention vector of topological pattern p. $\sigma(\cdot)$ and $Relu(\cdot)$ are the activation functions.

Aggregation Function. The purpose of the aggregation function is to update the representation of the node according to the neighboring message. After obtaining the message vector m_t^k, we update the nodes in the NRTG. The aggregation function of the k-th layer is:

$$n_t^k = \sigma\left(W_0^k n_t^{k-1} + m_t^k\right), \tag{3}$$

where W_0^k is the weight parameters.

We acquire the node representations of the NRTG through the message function and aggregation function. Finally, the representation of the entity is obtained by average pooling of all the latent node representations in the NRTG:

$$e^k = \frac{1}{|\mathcal{V}|} \sum_{i \in \mathcal{V}} n_i^k, \tag{4}$$

where $\mathcal{V}$ denotes the set of vertices in the graph.

In this module, based on two NRTGs, we adopt two identical R-GCN [15] to get the representation of head and tail entities, respectively.

3.3   Scoring Network and Loss Function

Scoring Network. The final step in our framework is to score the likelihood of predicted triples. For the predicted triple (u, r_t, v), the representations of entity u and entity v is obtained by the information aggregation module, and then we design a scoring network to output scores. The scoring function is defined as:

$$f(u, r_t, v) = W^T[e_u^k \oplus v_{r_t} \oplus e_v^u]. \tag{5}$$

In the scoring network, we obtain the scoring by a linear layer.

Loss Function. For each triple in the training graph, we sample a negative triple by replacing the head (or tail) entity. Afterward, we train our model to score positive triplets higher than the negative by using noise-contrastive hinge loss [1]. The specific loss function is as follows:

$$\mathcal{L} = \sum_{i=1}^{|\varepsilon|} \max\left(0, f\left(u_i', r_t', v_i'\right) - f\left(u, r_t, v\right) + \gamma\right), \tag{6}$$

where γ is the margin hyperparameter; ε is the set of all triplets in the neighboring relations topology graph. (u_i', r_t', v_i') denotes the i-th negative triple of the ground-truth triple (u, r_t, v).

Table 1. Statistics of inductive benchmarks. We use #E and #R and #TR to denote the number of entities, relations, and triples, respectively.

		WN18RR			FB15k-237			NELL-995		
		#R	#E	#TR	#R	#E	#TR	#R	#E	#TR
v1	Train	9	2746	6678	183	2000	5226	14	10915	5540
	Test	9	922	1991	146	1500	2404	14	225	1034
v2	Train	10	6954	18968	203	3000	12085	88	2564	10109
	Test	10	2923	4863	176	2000	5092	79	4937	5521
v3	Train	11	12078	32150	218	4000	22394	142	4647	20117
	Test	11	5084	7470	187	3000	9137	122	4921	9668
v4	Train	9	3861	9842	222	5000	33916	77	2092	9289
	Test	9	7208	15157	204	3500	14554	61	3294	8520

4 Experiments

In this section, there are the following parts. First, we introduce the experimental setup, such as datasets, training protocol, and evaluation protocol. Second, we compare our model with other approaches on several benchmark datasets. Third, we show the results of ablation studies to verify the effectiveness of our method. At last, we do some experiments to analyze the effect of hops on our model.

4.1 Experimental Setup

Datasets. In order to facilitate inductive testing, the test set needs to contain entities not seen in the training set. Therefore, we use some benchmark datasets for inductive relation prediction proposed in GraIL [17], which are derived from WN18RR [3], FB15k-237 [18], and NELL995 [22]. Specifically, each dataset consists of a pair of graphs: train-graph and ind-test-graph. We randomly select 10% of the edges/tuples in ind-test-graph as test edges. Details of the datasets are summarized in Table 1. The distribution of the six topological patterns in WN18RR and FB15k-237 is relatively uniform, and there are enough training examples. NELL-995 is a dataset with very sparse relationships, in which "PAPR" and "LOOP" are relatively rare. Furthermore, the same relational pairs have different topological patterns in each dataset.

 Training Protocol. During training, we set the batch size to 32 and set the epoch to 100. We set the size of relations embedding to 32. In order to represent the entity, we convert 2-hop (or 3-hop) neighboring triples to Neighboring Relations Topology Graph (NRTG) and then use one-layer R-GCN [15] to represent an entity. We use Adam [9] to optimize all the parameters with an initial learning rate set at 0.01.

 Evaluation Protocol. In the relation prediction task, the aim is to predict a triple (u, r_t, v) with u or v missing. We use the area under the precision-recall curve (AUC-PR) and Hits@10 to evaluate our models. To calculate the

Table 2. AUC-PR results on the inductive benchmark datasets extracted from WN18RR, FB15k-237 and NELL-995. The best score is in **bold** and second best score is <u>underlined</u>.

	WN18RR				FB15k-237				NELL-995			
	v1	v2	v3	v4	v1	v2	v3	v4	v1	v2	v3	v4
Neural-LP	86.02	83.78	62.90	82.06	69.64	76.55	73.95	75.74	64.66	83.61	87.58	85.69
DRUM	86.02	84.05	63.20	82.06	69.71	76.44	74.03	76.20	59.86	83.99	87.71	85.94
RuleN	90.26	89.01	76.46	85.75	75.24	88.70	91.24	91.79	84.99	88.40	87.20	80.52
GraIL	94.32	94.18	85.80	92.72	84.69	90.57	91.68	<u>94.46</u>	**86.05**	92.62	**93.34**	**87.50**
TACT	<u>95.79</u>	<u>95.05</u>	<u>85.58</u>	**96.60**	<u>85.67</u>	<u>91.77</u>	<u>93.29</u>	92.24	79.60	**94.40**	92.66	80.22
Our work	**97.35**	**96.55**	**89.86**	<u>96.15</u>	**90.79**	**95.32**	**95.40**	**95.83**	<u>81.84</u>	<u>92.90</u>	<u>92.84</u>	<u>85.80</u>

Table 3. H@10 results on the inductive benchmark datasets extracted from WN18RR, FB15k-237, and NELL-995.The best score is in **bold** and second best score is <u>underlined</u>.

	WN18RR				FB15k-237				NELL-995			
	v1	v2	v3	v4	v1	v2	v3	v4	v1	v2	v3	v4
Neural-LP	74.37	68.93	46.18	67.13	52.92	58.94	52.90	55.88	40.78	78.73	82.71	80.58
DRUM	74.37	68.93	46.18	67.13	52.92	58.73	52.90	55.88	19.42	78.55	82.71	80.58
RuleN	80.85	78.23	53.39	71.59	49.76	77.82	87.69	85.60	53.50	81.75	77.26	61.35
GraIL	82.45	78.68	58.43	73.41	64.15	81.80	82.83	89.29	**59.50**	**93.25**	<u>91.41</u>	**87.50**
TACT	<u>84.04</u>	<u>81.63</u>	<u>58.59</u>	<u>76.34</u>	<u>64.39</u>	<u>82.11</u>	<u>84.04</u>	<u>90.58</u>	57.50	<u>92.96</u>	**93.32**	74.07
Our work	**90.69**	**86.39**	**74.71**	**84.07**	**81.95**	**93.20**	**94.45**	**95.11**	<u>59.00</u>	91.80	89.80	<u>81.25</u>

AUC-PR, we replace the head or tail entity with a random entity to sample the negative triple, and then score the positive triples with an equal number of negative triples. To evaluate Hits@10, We select the top 10 triples among the 50 negative triples, and then calculate the proportion of correct triples.

4.2   Results and Analysis

We validate the models on classification metrics (AUC-PR) and ranking metrics (Hit@10), respectively. Then, we compare our method to several state-of-the-art methods on these metrics, such as NeuralLP [23], DRUM [13], RuleN [10], GraIL [17] and TACT [2].

Table 2 shows the mean AUC-PR results, averaged over 5 runs. The results show that our model achieves improvements on WN18RR and FB-237. Especially on the FB-237, the accuracy is improved by an average of 5%. Competitive results are achieved on the NELL-995. Table 3 shows the mean Hit@10 results, averaged over 5 runs. Our model achieves the state-of-the-art results on WN18RR and FB-237, and also competitive results on NELL-995.

As we can see, our model achieves huge improvements on all metrics on WN18RR and FB237. Therefore, our model successfully captures neighboring relations as well as the topological patterns between relations in entity rep-

Table 4. Ablation results the inductive benchmark datasets extracted from WN18RR, FB15k-237, and NELL-995. The best score is in **bold**

	WN18RR				FB15k-237				NELL-995			
	v1		v4		v1		v4		v1		v4	
	MRR	Hit@10	MRR	Hit@10	MRR	Hit@10	MRR	Hit@10	MRR	Hit@10	MRR	Hit@10
Our work w/o NR	76.70	84.30	72.07	80.40	35.03	50.73	40.27	59.41	35.16	56.50	54.05	73.59
Our work w/o TP	69.71	85.37	71.52	77.92	34.45	70.73	55.52	90.66	41.17	49.50	25.93	63.67
Our work	**81.22**	**90.69**	**78.95**	**84.07**	**58.49**	**81.95**	**74.15**	**95.11**	**53.98**	**59.00**	**54.68**	**81.25**

resentation. Meanwhile, the improvement is particularly significant on FB237, which indicates that our method can better model complex topological structures between relations. Possible reasons why there is no improvement on NELL-995 are: compared to the other two datasets, the relational connection structures of the NELL-995 dataset are relatively sparse, which makes it difficult for our method to learn the topological patterns.

4.3 Ablation Study

In this part, we conduct ablation experiments to verify the effectiveness of our model. We mainly emphasize the effectiveness of our method by two experiments respectively: (1) Our work w/o NR (2) Our work w/o TP.

Our Work w/o NR. In order to learn the logical rules between the target nodes of predicted triples, the existing methods extract paths of head and tail nodes. However, these methods have obvious drawbacks: the incompleteness of the knowledge graph leads to missing paths that disconnect with target nodes, so the model lacks many useful neighboring relations. To verify the effectiveness of neighboring relations extraction in the relations topology module, we perform an ablation experiment with the subgraph construction method proposed by GraIL [17] instead of our method. We called this ablation experiment "Our work w/o NR".

Our Work w/o TP. In the relations topology module, we classify the connection structures between neighboring relations and predicted relations into six topological patterns, and use the information aggregation module based on R-GCN [15] to represent head and tail entities. To verify that we capture the topological patterns between neighboring relations and predicted relation in the entity representation, we set all topological patterns between relations to 1. We called this ablation experiment "Our work w/o TP".

Table 4 shows the performance of our method on three datasets. Results show that our model performs better than the two ablated models on three datasets. Experiments demonstrate that our method can more completely capture the relational logic rules for predicting triples, and better represent entities.

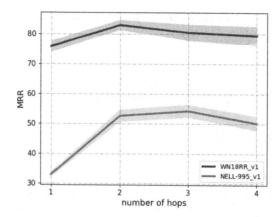

Fig. 4. The effect of different hops on MRR

4.4 Performance with Different Number of Hops

In this part, on WN18RR_v1 and NELL-995_v1, we extract the 1-hop, 2-hop, 3-hop and 4-hop neighboring triples of the head and tail entities respectively to construct NRTGs for inductive relation prediction. And we report the mean MRR, averaged over 5 runs. In Fig. 4, the performance of the model improves with the increase of the number of hops at the beginning, but after reaching 2 or 3 hops, the performance of the model does not improve, or even declines. The results show that the more hops, the more complete the logical information in the knowledge graph can be learned. However, the more hops will add a lot of noise information, which will reduce the performance of the model. Furthermore, with the number of hops increases, the fluctuation of the MRR value will also increase. Experiments demonstrate that our model can best learn the logical information implicit in the knowledge topology through the 2-hop (or 3-hop) NRTG.

5   Conclusion

We propose a novel entity representation method for inductive relation prediction. This entity representation method is based on a Neighboring Relations Topology Graph (NRTG), in which the nodes represent relations and the edges represent topological patterns between relations. The NRTG not only implies the logical rules of neighbor, but also is entity-independent. Thus, our model is able to make relation predictions in an inductive setting. Experiments demonstrate that our method significantly outperforms several existing state-of-the-art methods on benchmark datasets for the inductive link prediction task. In the future, we plan to extend our model further to capture the implicit logical rules in Few-shot Relations.

References

1. Bordes, A., et al.: Translating embeddings for modeling multi-relational data. In: Advances in Neural Information Processing Systems 26 (2013)
2. Chen, J., et al.: Topology-aware correlations between relations for inductive link prediction in knowledge graphs. In: Proceedings of the AAAI Conference on Artificial Intelligence, vol. 35. 7, pp. 6271–6278 (2021)
3. Dettmers, T., et al.: Convolutional 2d knowledge graph embeddings. In: Proceedings of the AAAI Conference on Artificial Intelligence, vol. 32, January 2018
4. Galárraga, L.A., et al.: AMIE: association rule mining under in-complete evidence in ontological knowledge bases. In: Proceedings of the 22nd international conference on World Wide Web, pp. 413–422 (2013)
5. Gilmer, J., et al.: Neural message passing for quantum chemistry. In: International Conference on Machine Learning. PMLR. 2017, pp. 1263–1272
6. Hamaguchi, T., et al.: Knowledge transfer for out-of-knowledge-base entities: a graph neural network approach. In: arXiv preprint arXiv:1706.05674 (2017)
7. Hamilton, W.L., Ying, R., Leskovec, J.: Representation learning on graphs: methods and applications. In: arXiv preprint arXiv:1709.05584 (2017)
8. Huang, X., et al.: Knowledge graph embedding based question answering. In: Proceedings of the Twelfth ACM International Conference on Web Search and Data Mining, pp. 105–113 (2019)
9. Kingma, D.P., Ba, J.: Adam: a method for stochastic op- timization. In: arXiv preprint arXiv:1412.6980 (2014)
10. Meilicke, C., et al.: Fine-grained evaluation of rule-and embedding-based systems for knowledge graph completion. In: International Semantic Web Conference, pp. 3–20. Springer (2018)
11. Nathani, D., et al.: Learning attention-based embeddings for relation prediction in knowledge graphs. In: arXiv preprint arXiv:1906.01195 (2019)
12. Nguyen, D.Q., et al.: A novel embedding model for knowledge base completion based on convolutional neural network. In: arXiv preprint arXiv:1712.02121 (2017)
13. Sadeghian, A., et al.: Drum: end-to-end di erentiable rule mining on knowledge graphs. In: Advances in Neural Information Processing Systems 32 (2019)
14. Scarselli, F., et al.: The graph neural network model. IEEE Trans. Neural Networks **20**(1), 61–80 (2008)
15. Schlichtkrull, M., et al.: Modeling relational data with graph convolutional networks. In: European Semantic Web Conference, pp. 593–607. Springer (2018)
16. Sun, Z., et al.: Rotate: knowledge graph embedding by relational rotation in complex space. In: arXiv preprint arXiv:1902.10197 (2019)
17. Teru, K., Denis, E., Hamilton, W.: Inductive relation pre- diction by subgraph reasoning. In: International Conference on Machine Learning. PMLR, pp. 9448–9457 (2020)
18. Toutanova, K., et al.: Representing text for joint embedding of text and knowledge bases. In: Proceedings of the 2015 Conference on Empirical Methods in Natural Language Processing, pp. 1499–1509 (2015)
19. Tran, H.D., et al.: Towards nonmonotonic relational learning from knowledge graphs. In: International Conference on Inductive Logic Pro- gramming, pp. 94–107. Springer (2016)
20. Trouillon, T., et al.: Knowledge graph completion via complex tensor factorization. In: arXiv preprint arXiv:1702.06879 (2017)

21. Wang, H., et al.: Ripplenet: propagating user preferences on the knowledge graph for recommender systems. In: Proceedings of the 27th ACM International Conference on Information and Knowledge Management, pp. 417–426 (2018)
22. Xiong, W., Hoang, T., Wang, Y.: Deeppath: a reinforcement learning method for knowledge graph reasoning. In: arXiv preprint arXiv:1707.06690 (2017)
23. Yang, F., Yang, Z., Cohen, W.W.: Di erentiable learning of logical rules for knowledge base reasoning. In: Advances in Neural Information Processing Systems 30 (2017)
24. Yu, H., Lu, J., Zhang, G.: Online topology learning by a gaussian membership-based self-organizing incremental neural network. In: IEEE Trans. Neural Networks Learn. Syst. 31(10), 3947–3961 (2019)
25. Yu, H., Lu, J., Zhang, G.: Topology learning-based Fuzzy random neural network for streaming data regression. IEEE Trans, Fuzzy Syst (2020)
26. Zhang, Z., et al.: Relational graph neural network with hierarchical at- tention for knowledge graph completion. In: Proceedings of the AAAI Conference on Artificial Intelligence, vol. 34(05), 9612–9619 (2020)
27. Zhang, Z., et al.: ERNIE: enhanced language representation with informative entities. In: arXiv preprint arXiv:1905.07129 (2019)

Entity Similarity-Based Negative Sampling for Knowledge Graph Embedding

Naimeng Yao[1]($\boxtimes$) (iD), Qing Liu[2] (iD), Xiang Li[1] (iD), Yi Yang[3] (iD), and Quan Bai[1] (iD)

[1] The University of Tasmania, Hobart, Australia
{naimeng.yao,x.li,quan.bai}@utas.edu.au
[2] Data61, CSIRO, Hobart, Australia
q.liu@data61.csiro.au
[3] Hefei University of Technology, Hefei, China
yyang@hfut.edu.cn

Abstract. Knowledge graph embedding (KGE) models optimize loss functions to maximize the total plausibility of positive triples and minimize the plausibility of negative triples. Negative samples are essential in KGE training since they are not as observable as positive samples. Currently, most negative sampling methods apply different techniques to keep track of negative samples with high scores that are regarded as quality negative samples. While, we found entities with similar semantic contexts are easier to be deceptive and misclassified, contributing to quality negative samples. This is not considered in most negative sampling approaches. Besides, the unequal effectiveness of quality negative samples in different loss functions is usually ignored. In this paper, we propose an Entity Similarity-based Negative Sampling framework (ESNS). The framework takes semantic similarities among entities into consideration with a shift-based logistic loss function. Comprehensive experiments on the five benchmark datasets have been conducted, and the experimental results demonstrate that ESNS outperforms the state-of-the-art negative sampling methods in the link prediction task.

Keywords: Knowledge graph · Knowledge graph embedding · Negative sampling · Knowledge graph completion

1 Introduction

A knowledge graph (KG) is a structured graph with facts where entities as nodes and relations between entities as edges. A fact in a knowledge graph is usually represented by a triple (h, r, t), where h, r and t are the head entity, the relation, and the tail entity, respectively. Figure 1 shows a small KG with several facts in the form of discrete triples, i.e., $(JerryYang, Nationality, USA)$. Large-scale KGs, such as Google Knowledge Vault [6], Freebase [3], and DBpedia [2], have served many real-world applications including question answering [8], recommendation [28], structured search [32], and etc.

© The Author(s), under exclusive license to Springer Nature Switzerland AG 2022
S. Khanna et al. (Eds.): PRICAI 2022, LNCS 13630, pp. 73–87, 2022.
https://doi.org/10.1007/978-3-031-20865-2_6

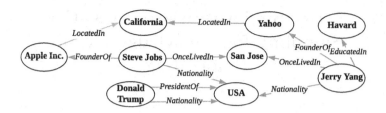

Fig. 1. Entities, relations and facts in a knowledge graph.

Since triples in a KG are hard to be manipulated, knowledge graph embedding (KGE) methods are proposed to provide better generalization ability and inference efficiency [9] for large-scale KGs. These methods [4,9,12,16,25,33] encode entities and relations into a low-dimensional vector space while preserving KG structures. A KGE model has a model-specific score function that is designed to model complex interactions among entities and relations. A score function tends to endow positive triples with high scores and negative samples with low scores when optimizing a loss function.

While many works focus on designing score functions to improve the performance of KGE, negative sampling methods have not received much attention. Negative triples are constructed mainly by replacing either head or tail entities from positive triples with entities sampled from entity sets. For a triple (h, r, t), its negative samples are denoted as $(\bar{h}, r, \bar{t}) = (\bar{h}, r, t) \cup (h, r, \bar{t})$, $\bar{h}, \bar{t} \in \mathcal{E}$, where $\mathcal{E}$ is the entity set. Generally, the quality of negative samples is measured by the scoring function. Negative samples with high quality are those with high scores and annotated as quality negative samples. It has been observed that quality negative samples are rare but important, and the distribution of negative samples varies during the KGE training process [34]. However, why some negative samples have high scores are rarely studied, which hinders the improvement of KGE performance. To the best of our knowledge, we are the first to analyze the underlying characteristics of quality negative samples and propose a simple but effective method accordingly. Furthermore, in the past, negative sampling methods are studied independently to loss functions. Our experimental analysis reveals that the pairwise hinge loss function impedes discriminating quality negative samples from other positive samples and deteriorates the effectiveness of the quality negative samples. In the paper, we analyze the contribution of semantically similar entities to quality negative samples and propose an Entity Similarity-based Negative Sampling (ESNS) framework. The contributions of the paper are:

- We analyze the link between entity similarity and quality negative triples and find that similarity-based negative samples significantly contribute to quality negative samples.
- We propose a simple but effective ESNS that identifies quality negative samples, captures the dynamic distribution and reduces false negatives.

- We design a shift-based pointwise logistic loss function for quality negative sampling methods. It works effectively with both translational distance-based KGE models and semantic matching KGE models.
- Comprehensive experiments conducted on the five benchmark knowledge graphs demonstrate that our method is more efficient and effective than the state-of-the-art negative sampling methods.

2   Related Work

The negative sampling methods can be categorized into random sampling, static sampling, and dynamic sampling. As random sampling methods, Uniform negative sampling [4] and Bernoulli sampling [30] have been used in many KGE models for high efficiency and simplicity. Static sampling methods [11,14,15,31] analyze some statistic features of knowledge graphs and get better performance than random sampling methods. But the above-mentioned methods suffer from the vanishing gradient problem because they ignore changes in negative sample distribution in the training process [34]. Most dynamic sampling methods feature capturing the distribution of negative samples [1,5,7,17,23,26,34] and generating negative samples from a list of candidates according to the probability distribution of their scores computed by model-specific scoring functions. Among them, GAN-based approaches [5,7,17,26] use reinforcement learning to effectively generate quality negative samples, but it introduces high computational complexity. NSCaching [34] maintains quality samples with high scores in head/tail caches indexed by $(r, t)/(r, h)$ to avoid vanishing gradient, but false negative samples (not observed positive samples but regarded as negative samples) are easily stuck in caches. Self-Adv [23] is an effective self-adversarial negative sampling technique incorporated in RotatE model but does not have consistent performances on other KGE models. SANS [1] improves from Self-Adv by applying random walk to identify negatives but ignores that non-semantic similar neighbors do not necessarily contribute to quality negative samples. Unlike the above-mentioned methods, ANS [21] captures dynamic entity embeddings rather than negative sample distribution. It suffers from the typical problems of K-means clustering methods, including the hard-choice of cluster centers and the dilemma of defining K for datasets with different distributions. Although there is no clear definition, negative samples with high scores computed by KGE model-specific score functions are regarded as quality negative samples in general. This is because negative samples with low scores cannot contribute to the loss function and result in the vanishing gradient problem.

Two widely used loss functions into which negative samples are fed are pairwise hinge loss function (PH) and pointwise logistic loss function (PL). The former is usually adopted by translational distance-based models [4,9,16,23,30]:

$$L = \sum_{(h,r,t)\in\mathcal{F}} [\gamma - f(\mathbf{h}, \mathbf{r}, \mathbf{t}) + f(\overline{\mathbf{h}}, \mathbf{r}, \overline{\mathbf{t}})]_+ \tag{1}$$

, where f is the scoring function, $\mathbf{h}$, $\mathbf{r}$ and $\mathbf{t}$ are embeddings of h, r and t. $\mathcal{F}$ is the set of facts, γ is the margin between positive and negative samples, and

$[x]_+ = max(0, x)$ is the hinge function. The latter is introduced in [25] and usually used by semantic matching models [10, 27, 34]:

$$L = -\sum_{(h,r,t)\in\mathcal{F}} \log \sigma(f(\mathbf{h}, \mathbf{r}, \mathbf{t})) - \sum_{(\overline{h},r,\overline{t})\notin\mathcal{F}} \log \sigma(-f(\overline{\mathbf{h}}, \mathbf{r}, \overline{\mathbf{t}})) \quad (2)$$

, where $\sigma(x) = \frac{1}{1+\exp(-x)}$ is a sigmoid function. Recent studies [20, 22, 35] explore the influence of loss functions in KGE model training, but they only consider general negative samples. The effectiveness of quality negative samples with different loss functions in training is first discussed in this paper.

3   Entity Similarity-Based Negative Sampling Framework

In this section, we introduce the intuition behind our method and define the concepts of Entity Context and Entity Similarity. Then, we analyze the contributions of Entity Similarity to quality negative samples and introduce our proposed ESNS framework.

3.1   Problem Definition

Our general intuition is that a negative sample $(\overline{h}, r, t)$ is hard to be discriminated against a positive sample (h, r, t), when the negative entity $\overline{h}$ is similar to the replaced entity h in terms of the contexts in a knowledge graph. For example, in Fig. 1, given a positive triple (*Steve Jobs, FounderOf, Apple Inc.*), (*Jerry Yang, FounderOf, Apple Inc.*) could be a quality negative sample because *Steve* and *Jerry* share similar context $\{$(*FounderOf, Apple Inc.*), (*OnceLivedIn, San Jose*), (*Nationality, USA*)$\}$. It is harder to be discriminated than (*Havard, FounderOf, Apple Inc.*), (*Yahoo, FounderOf, Apple Inc.*) etc. Next, we formally define the concept of Entity Context and Entity Similarity in a knowledge graph.

Definition 1 (Head/Tail Entity Context).   *Given an entity e, its head context $C_h(e)$ and tail context $C_t(e)$ are a set of 2-tuples, where $C_h(e) = \{(r,t)|(e,r,t) \in \mathcal{F}\}$ and $C_t(e) = \{(r,h)|(h,r,e) \in \mathcal{F}\}$ and $\mathcal{F}$ is the set of observed facts.*

Definition 2 (Head/Tail Entity Similarity).   *The entity similarity S between two entities e_i and e_j is the number of shared head/tail context when e_i is a head/tail entity, respectively.*

$$S_h(e_i, e_j) = |C_h(e_i) \cap C_h(e_j)|, S_t(e_i, e_j) = |C_t(e_i) \cap C_t(e_j)| \quad (3)$$

Entity Context captures an entity's structural and semantic contexts in a KG. Entity Similarity computes the contextual similarity between two entities. In Fig. 1, *Steve Jobs* shares the head contexts with *Jerry Yang* and *Donald Trump*, given S_h(*Steve Jobs, Jerry Yang*) $= 2$((*OnceLivedIn, San Jose*), (*Nationality, USA*)) and S_h(*Steve Jobs, Donald Trump*) $= 1$((*Nationality, USA*)). For all the other entities, S_h(*Steve Jobs, ** $) = 0$. It indicates that using *Jerry Yang* or *Donald Trump* to replace *Steve Jobs* as a negative sample would be more likely to be a quality negative sample compared with the other entities.

3.2   The Analysis of Quality Negative Samples

To verify our assumption, we experimentally analyze and compare the distribution of similarity-based negative samples (SNS, solid curve in Fig. 2) and that of non-similar negative samples (NNS, dotted curve in Fig. 2), respectively. TransD model and YAGO3-10 data (see Sect. 4.1) are used to show the analysis.

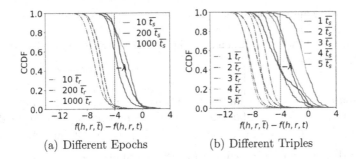

(a) Different Epochs   (b) Different Triples

Fig. 2. Distribution of NS on YAGO3-10 trained by TransD. The black dashed line indicates the minus margin λ in the PH loss function. (Color figure online)

SNS vs. NNS: We randomly pick one triple (h, r, t) and classify t's all possible negative samples into 2 groups by fixing h and r: (a) $\{(h, r, \bar{t}_s)\}$, in which entities $\bar{t}_s$s share similar context with t $(S_t(t, \bar{t}_s) > 0)$, and (b) $\{(h, r, \bar{t}_r)\}$ includes the rest of the negative samples $(S_t(t, \bar{t}_r) = 0)$. Figure 2 uses the complementary cumulative distribution function (CCDF) $F_d(x) = P(d \geq x)$ to show the proportion of negatives that satisfy $d \geq x$. $d(h, r, \bar{t}) = f(h, r, \bar{t}) - f(h, r, t)$ is the minus distance between the positive sample's and its negative samples' scores. When d is smaller than a minus margin -λ ($\lambda > 0$), the distance between positive and negative samples is large enough, and the negative sample contributes a zero gradient to the loss function. Hence, quality negative samples (QNS) are those with $d > -\lambda$. Figure 2(a) shows distributions of negative triples from two groups over epochs 10, 200 and 1000. The distribution of SNS and QNS changes in different epochs. Most of SNS have $d > -\lambda$ and only a few QNS have $d > -\lambda$, which means most of SNS could be potential QNS $(d > -\lambda)$, but rare NNS could be potential QNS $(d > -\lambda)$. Figure 2(b) shows the results from 5 randomly picked triples at epoch 200. The proportions of QNS in SNS are always far larger than the proportions of QNS in NNS of these triples. This confirms that SNS can contribute to QNS far more than NNS.

SNS vs. QNS: We further investigate the contribution of SNS to QNS. First, we randomly pick 30 positive triples and compute all their quality negative samples that contribute to a loss function at discrete epochs 50 and 1000. Figure 3(a) shows the number of QNS and the number of SNS for each triple, respectively. Most of the QNS are contributed by SNS. Figure 3(b) shows the proportion of positive triples that satisfy $|SNS|/|QNS| > x$ from 2000 triples randomly picked from YAGO3-10. For 80% of the positive triples, more than 50% of QNS

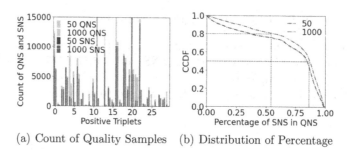

(a) Count of Quality Samples   (b) Distribution of Percentage

Fig. 3. Statistics of the contribution of similarity-based NS to the quality NS at epoch 50 and 1000, respectively.

are contributed by SNS. For half of the positive triples, more than 80% of QNS is contributed by SNS. Similar results can be found at any epoch on different models. By the above analysis, we summarize our key observations as follows:

Ob1: The distribution of NS changes in the training process as in the previous study [34].

Ob2: For most of NNS (dotted curve) in group (b), the distances are smaller than the minus margin ($d < -\lambda = -4$). It means that the gradient of these NNS will vanish to zero. Only a few NNS ($d > -\lambda$) contribute to the loss function.

Ob3: Compared with NNS, most of but not every SNS in group (a) have distances larger than the minus margin. It means that SNS have higher probabilities with large scores and thus be able to contribute to a loss function.

Ob4: Among all QNS ($d > -\lambda$), the SNS has a higher probability with larger scores than NNS.

These comparisons further suggest that SNS should be considered as quality negative sample candidates during KGE training since the observations mentioned above can be found through all the epochs and triples. Next, we present our simple but effective ESNS method.

3.3 ESNS Negative Sampling Method

Recall that there are several challenges in generating quality negative samples: (a) How to model the dynamic distribution, given the negative samples' distribution changes in the training process; (b) How to balance the exploration and exploitation? Quality negative samples are contributed by not only some similarity-based samples but also other negative samples, although the amount is very small. We need to ensure that all possible quality negative samples are explored. Meanwhile, sampling the negative triples with large scores is more effective than those with small scores; and (c) How to avoid false negatives that may have very high scores? A negative sampling method needs to be carefully designed to overcome these challenges. Next, we describe how entity similarity is obtained from a KG. Then we describe our negative sampling method.

Algorithm 1: KGE Training Process

Input : training KG $\mathcal{F} = \{(h, r, t)\}$, $h, t \in \mathcal{E}$ (entity set), $r \in \mathcal{R}$ (relation set), $EII_{h/t}^k$, score function f, sampling size N, quality candidate set size N_1, training epoch T, mini-batch size m

Output : the KGE model

1   Initialize the embedding of KGE;
2   **foreach** $epoch \in [1, T]$ **do**
3   Sample a mini-batch $\mathcal{F}_{batch} \in \mathcal{F}$ with size m;
4   **foreach** $p = (h, r, t) \in \mathcal{F}_{batch}$ **do**
        `// negative sampling`
5         $e \leftarrow Bernoulli(h, t)$;
6         $\mathcal{U} \leftarrow uniformSampleSet(\mathcal{E}, N)$;
7         $\mathcal{Q} \leftarrow getQualityCandidates(e, \mathcal{U}, N_1, EII_{h/t}^k)$;
8         $e^{ns} \leftarrow getEntityWithHighestScore(\mathcal{Q}, f)$;
9         $\bar{p} \leftarrow generateNegativeTriple(e^{ns}, p)$;
10        $\mathcal{P} \leftarrow \mathcal{P} \cup (p, \bar{p})$;
11   Compute the loss function Equation (4) using $\mathcal{P}$;
12   Update the parameters of KGE;
13 **return** KGE

Inverted Index $EII_{h/t}$. Instead of using head-cache $\mathcal{H}$ (indexed by (r, t)) and tail-cache $\mathcal{T}$ (indexed by (r, h)) to store negative candidates with large scores as NSCaching does, an entity inverted index $EII_{h/t}$ that stores the head/tail entity similarity is proposed. Every entity has a unique identifier in a KG. Each row i in $EII_{h/t}$, representing entity e_i, stores a list of 2-tuple $\{(j, S(e_i, e_j))\}$ that are e_i's similar entities e_js and their corresponding entity similarity S. These e_js act as quality negative candidates for e_i in the training process. Parameter k is defined to control the number of similar entities for each entity stored in $EII_{h/t}$.

Negative Sampling Method. Algorithm 1 shows the general framework of KGE training with ESNS (Line 5–11) as the negative sampling method. For each positive triple p in a mini-batch (Line 4), Bernoulli is applied to decide if head h or tail t should be replaced to construct p's negative triple (Line 5). From Observations 2 and 3, we know that quality negatives are contributed by both similar and non-similar entities. By uniformly sampling N entities from $\mathcal{E}$ (Line 6), we construct a small candidate set $\mathcal{U}$ that follows the same distribution as $\mathcal{E}$ has. This step ensures that all possible negatives, including both similar and non-similar entities are explored.

Recall that e's similar entities e_s stored in $EII_{h/t}^k$ have higher probabilities with large scores (Observation 3). For $\forall e_s \in \mathcal{U}$, we retrieve the top N_1 similar entities from $EII_{h/t}^k$ and put them in $\mathcal{Q}$ (Line 7). Non-similar entities in $\mathcal{U}$ are randomly selected for $\mathcal{Q}$ if the number of similar entities is less than N_1. In other words, e's quality negative candidates can be dynamically identified because they have higher probabilities with large scores (Observation 4). Entity e^{ns} in $\mathcal{Q}$ with the highest score f is selected (Line 8) to construct p's negative triple $\overline{p}$ (Line 9). All the quality negative triples $\overline{p}$ in $\mathcal{F}_{batch}$ are collected (Line 10). Then the loss function is computed (Line 11).

ESNS Loss Function. We take the loss function in RotatE [23] as a base form and propose a shift-based logistic loss function that requires only 1 negative sample for each positive because our similarity-based sampling method is able to target quality negatives very effectively. The introduced shift-based pointwise logistic loss function (SPL)(Line 11) is as follows:

$$L_s = -\sum_{(h,r,t)\in\mathcal{F}} \log\sigma(\kappa + f(\mathbf{h},\mathbf{r},\mathbf{t})) - \sum_{(\overline{h},r,\overline{t})\notin\mathcal{F}} \log\sigma(-(\kappa + f(\overline{\mathbf{h}},\mathbf{r},\overline{\mathbf{t}}))) \tag{4}$$

, where κ is a configurable shift. When $\kappa = 0$, Equation (4) is equal to typical pointwise logistic loss function used in semantic matching models. When $\kappa > 0$, it replaces the PH loss function for translational distance-based models in ESNS. The range of x in $\sigma(x)$ needs to be close 0 (approaching from the positive and negative sides) to conform to the principle of cross-entropy loss. In translational distance-based models, the range of scores is $(-\infty, 0)$, so a shift is needed to adjust its range.

The proposed method distinguishes itself from the state-of-the-art negative sampling methods from 3 perspectives: First, by constructing a quality negative candidate set based on entity similarity, ESNS can effectively target rare but quality negatives without applying either complex GAN or caching techniques. Second, given a positive triple p, most existing methods choose $\overline{p}$ following a score probability distribution to avoid false negatives. In ESNS, the sample with the highest score is selected as $\overline{p}$. Because the 2-step selection process involves uniform sampling and similarity-based filtering, the probability (a false negative $\overline{p}$ is selected) is very low. Third, ESNS aborts PH loss function on translational distance-based models. PH loss function maximizes the distance between the scores from the positive triple and its corresponding negative sample by a margin γ. It favors the difference but ignore $f(\overline{h},r,t)/f(h,r,\overline{t})$ may still higher than other $f(*,r,t)/f(h,r,*)$, because the latter are not always equally high [35]. This situation gets worse when facing quality negative samples for their high scores. NSCaching uses head/tail caches indexed by $(r,t)/(r,h)$ and enables positive samples $(*,r,t)/(h,r,*)$ share quality negative samples, which ensure $f(h,r,\overline{t})/f(\overline{h},r,t)$ are smaller than $f(h,r,*)$ $(f(*,r,t))$. Since caching incurs false negative samples, we introduce a shift-based pointwise logistic loss function to ensure that quality negative samples have lower scores compared with all positive samples and avoid false negative samples. These three changes not only eliminate the cache maintenance cost, lead to fast convergence, but also diminish the cache-induced false negatives. The experimental results confirm the strength of our approach.

4 Experiments

4.1 Experimental Setup

Datasets. We evaluate our proposed method on five benchmark knowledge graphs that have been widely used for KGE evaluation [4, 12, 23, 30, 33]. FB15K and WN18 are subsets of FreeBase [3] and WordNet [19], respectively. FB15K237 [24] and WN18RR [29] remove duplicated and inverse relations from FB15K and WN18. YAGO3-10 is a subset of YAGO3 [18]. The statistics of the datasets are shown in Table 1.

Table 1. Statistics of the datasets

Dataset	Ent.	Rel.	Train	Valid	Test
WN18	40,943	18	141,442	5,000	5,000
WN18RR	40,943	11	86,835	3,034	3,134
FB15K	14,951	1,345	483,142	50,000	59,071
FB15K237	14,541	237	272,115	17,535	20,466
YAGO3-10	123,182	37	1,079,040	5000	5000

Baselines. We compare ESNS with the following state-of-the-art negative sampling methods. Uniform [4] and Bernoulli [30] are two basic random sampling schemes. KBGAN [5] uses one KGE model as a negative sample generator that continuously generates quality negative samples to train the other KGE model in the discriminator. NKSGAN [17] obtains its generator by applying the attention mechanism to the neighborhood aggregator. NSCaching [34] introduces caches to track negative triples with large scores. ANS [21] is a present entity similarity-based negative sampling method. Self-Adv [23] has multiple negative samples for each positive sample, which is different from the previous methods. Performances are tested on three representative translational distance-based models (TransE [4], TransD [9], and RotatE [23]) and three representative semantic matching models (DistMult [33], ComplEx [25] and SimplE [12]).

Evaluation Metrics. Link prediction is to predict the missing entity h (or t) in a positive triple (h, r, t). In the task, we measure the rank of the missing entity h (or t) among all the entity sets. Two standard metrics are used: (1) Mean Reciprocal Rank (MRR), which computes the average of reciprocal ranks, and (2) Hit@10, which calculates the percentage of ranks within the top 10. To be consistent, the performance is reported in a "Filtered" setting so that all the corrupted triples that exist in the train, valid and test set are filtered out.

Hyper-parameter Settings. We use the Adam method [13] as the optimizer in training and adopt its default setting except for the learning rate and weight decay. $EII_{h/t}^k$ index column size $k = 1000$ for ESNS. The candidate size $N = 100$ and $N_1 = 50$ are set for ESNS, ANS, KBGAN, and $N_2 = 50$, $N_1 = 50$ are set for NKSGAN and NSCaching. For Self-Adv, $N_1 = 50$ negative samples per positive sample are fed into models. Grid search to select hyper-parameters for others negative sampling approaches is defined as follows: the hidden dimension d in $\{50, 100, 200\}$, batch size b in $\{512, 1024, 2048\}$, learning rate $lr \in \{0.00005, 0.0001, 0.0005, 0.001, 0.01\}$, the regularization factor $\mu \in \{0.1, 0.01, 0.001\}$, the shift value $\kappa \in [5 \cdots 25]$ and $\kappa = 0$ for translational-based and semantic matching models. The hyper-parameters are fine-tuned on the validation data sets. The results are evaluated within 1000 epochs, and the early-stop process presents every 100 epochs.

4.2   Main Results

Table 2 summarizes the main comparison results. In the RotatE, DistMult, ComplEx and SimiplE models, we used the same SLP loss function in negative sampling methods. ESNS outperforms other state-of-the-art negative sampling methods and achieves the highest MRR, which is mainly influenced by the top 1 ranking. ESNS also wins in the overall performance on Hit@10, which evaluate the general top rankings of correct entities. On YAGO3-10, ESNS has the biggest improvements compared with others because each entity in YAGO3-10 has at least ten relations and rich contexts. To conclude, the performance of ESNS rises when rich entity contexts are contained in the KG.

NSCaching has comparable performance on most datasets. Self-Adv has the best Hit@10 result on translational-based models on FB15K and FB15K237. For datasets with smaller entity sets, it effectively benefits the general top ranking because of multiple samples. Self-Adv does not have consistently good performances on all KGE models, especially on semantic matching models. NKSGAN has better MRR and Hit@10 results than KBGAN on most models and datasets by aggregating neighborhood information in the generator, but its performance is still inferior. The performance of ANS is worse than other negative sampling methods on most models and datasets. This is because ANS ignores the dynamic distribution of negative samples and only considers the dynamic of entity embeddings. Limited by length, we only present Hit@10 results here, but Hit@1 and Hit@3 results from ESNS are pervasively better than other negative sampling methods.

On TransE and TransD models, ESNS applies SPL loss function and others apply PH loss function. Self-Adv, NSCaching and ESNS have shown the most evident improvements to other models. Self-adv, NSCaching and ESNS overcome the drawback of PH by multiple sampling, caching and applying SPL, respectively. The results indicate that changing the loss function brings the greatest improvement.

We also investigate the MRR and Hit@10 convergence trend from different negative sampling algorithms. MRR and Hit@10 of ESNS increase much faster and are more stable than other methods. Due to limited space, results are not presented.

Table 2. MRR and Hit@10 comparison. Results marked with − are cited from their original papers.

Dataset	Model	Translational Distance-based Models						Semantic Matching Models					
		TransE		TransD		RotatE		DistMult		ComplEx		SimplE	
	Metric	MRR	H@10	MRR	H@10	MRR	H@10	MRR	H@10	MRR	H@10	MRR	H@10
YAGO3-10	ESNS	**.457**	**65.7**	**.466**	**66.3**	**.469**	64.8	**.455**	61.8	**.450**	60.1	**.462**	61.0
	Uniform	.233	47.0	.202	46.3	.338	52.0	.150	31.3	.170	34.0	.172	35.9
	Bernoulli	.180	33.9	.176	34.2	.372	58.0	.266	43.9	.281	45.6	.255	43.2
	NKSGAN	.317	54.0	.327	55.0	.400	59.0	.453	60.1	.384	57.6	.448	59.9
	KBGAN	.228	56.6	.239	56.3	.395	58.5	.371	53.0	.377	53.5	.364	55.8
	Self-Adv	.403	61.7	.454	65.4	.464	64.5	.422	57.8	.403	57.9	.425	60.4
	NSCaching	.307⁻	50.7⁻	.315⁻	52.7⁻	.423	59.5	.403⁻	56.6⁻	.405⁻	57.8⁻	.419⁻	56.5⁻
	ANS	.239	57.9	.172	49.7	.383	55.2	.113	24.9	.249	43.6	.244	37.5
WN18	ESNS	**.801**	**95.4**	**.816**	**95.4**	**.950**	**96.0**	**.834**	**94.5**	**.943**	**95.2**	**.943**	**95.3**
	Uniform	.642	93.9	.519	92.5	.928	94.4	.791	92.8	.842	86.6	.849	89.3
	NSCaching	.782⁻	94.6⁻	.799⁻	95.2⁻	.944	95.3	.831⁻	93.7⁻	.936⁻	94.0⁻	.942⁻	94.8⁻
	NKSGAN	.783	95.2	.811	95.4	.934	95.7	.821	94.5	.928	95.2	.942	95.0
	KBGAN	.710⁻	94.9⁻	.779⁻	94.8⁻	.937	95.3	.791	94.5	.933	94.5	.941	95.0
	Bernoulli	.432	93.9	.409	92.4	.926	95.3	.782	94.5	.923	94.1	.921	94.8
	Self-Adv	.785	95.3	.809	95.3	.948	95.9	.813	94.3	.938	95.0	.938	94.9
	NSCaching	.782⁻	94.6⁻	.799⁻	95.2⁻	.944	95.3	.831⁻	93.7⁻	.936⁻	94.0⁻	.942⁻	94.8⁻
	ANS	.475	94.7	.485	94.9	.947	95.6	.790	94.1	.931	94.9	.924	94.7
WN18RR	ESNS	**.227**	**52.1**	**.225**	50.9	**.481**	57.5	**.424**	48.8	**.450**	51.2	**.442**	**49.0**
	Uniform	.199	46.3	.203	47.5	.471	55.3	.412	46.3	.429	47.8	.426	48.1
	Bernoulli	.176	44.1	.174	45.1	.447	54.7	.396	43.7	.405	44.1	.433	48.1
	NKSGAN	.212	49.0	.214	49.9	.451	55.4	.392	42.8	.406	45.6	.432	47.8
	KBGAN	.213⁻	48.1⁻	.215⁻	47.2⁻	.467	56.0	.389	42.2	.402	44.9	.435	48.2
	Self-Adv	.217	51.2	.214	49.9	.472	55.8	.416	46.3	.435	49.3	.414	45.9
	NSCaching	.200⁻	47.8⁻	.201⁻	48.4⁻	.466	54.1	.413⁻	45.5⁻	.446⁻	50.9⁻	.436⁻	47.4⁻
	ANS	.206	46.5	.199	45.8	.456	53.3	.383	43.3	.402	44.4	.400	44.2
FB15K	ESNS	**.655**	82.8	**.655**	82.4	**.765**	86.4	**.776**	**84.9**	**.808**	86.4	**.808**	**87.0**
	Uniform	.508	76.3	.466	75.8	.634	85.0	.507	76.5	.612	79.8	.599	79.3
	Bernoulli	.481	73.5	.465	73.2	.596	80.2	.511	76.9	.615	80.9	.614	79.1
	NKSGAN	.459	70.2	.474	71.7	.726	85.1	.759	84.3	.758	84.2	.764	84.4
	KBGAN	.458	70.2	.434	70.4	.717	83.7	.666	80.9	.723	82.3	.729	82.8
	Self-Adv	.647	**83.7**	.633	**84.1**	.743	**87.1**	.726	84.1	.773	85.8	.768	86.0
	NSCaching	.639⁻	81.0⁻	.641⁻	81.3⁻	.705	84.1	.745⁻	83.9⁻	.800⁻	86.3⁻	.803⁻	86.9⁻
	ANS	.449	74.1	.372	72.3	.647	81.6	.244	45.5	.347	64.1	.420	66.8
FB15K237	ESNS	**.308**	48.4	**.314**	49.4	**.315**	49.6	**.296**	46.5	**.303**	47.1	**.297**	**46.7**
	Uniform	.278	47.5	.253	45.0	.279	46.5	.213	38.3	.214	38.7	.225	38.0
	Bernoulli	.291	47.2	.286	47.4	.258	43.5	.262	43.0	.268	44.2	.225	37.3
	NKSGAN	.280	46.2	.281	46.7	.314	49.6	.267	43.0	.269	44.0	.276	44.3
	KBGAN	.278⁻	45.3⁻	.278⁻	45.8⁻	.306	48.1	.259	41.6	.247	40.8	.274	45.8
	Self-Adv	.307	**49.9**	.309	**50.8**	.314	**50.8**	.215	39.5	.211	39.5	.218	40.0
	NSCaching	.299⁻	47.6⁻	.286⁻	47.9⁻	.315	50.5	.288⁻	45.8⁻	.302⁻	48.1⁻	.272⁻	43.9⁻
	ANS	.219	40.4	.208	39.7	.284	47.7	.230	36.0	.232	35.5	.230	35.0

4.3 SPL Loss Function

Visualization of PH's Drawback. Recall that the PH loss function results in overlaps between quality negative samples and positive samples' scores. Here, we visualize this problem. We analyze the score distribution of 2000 randomly selected positive samples and their corresponding 2000 randomly selected quality negative samples. They are trained by TransD model with PH and SPL, respectively. Figure 4(a) shows the overlaps between distributions of positive samples' scores and negative samples' scores with PH. Within 2000 negative samples, about 7% of quality negative samples (PH, blue dashed line) lie in the right of the lowest value of positive scores (vertical blue dashed line). This means that the distribution of negative samples overlaps with the distribution of positive samples, and quality negative samples are mixed with positive samples. In practice, one positive sample has far larger than 1 quality negative samples, and the number of quality negative samples mixed with positive samples can be quite huge. PH cannot help the model clearly separate quality negative samples from positive samples. By contrast, with the SLP, a clear distance between positive triples and quality negative samples exists. The reason for this difference is the distribution of positive samples' scores in PH has a wider range, and quality negative samples are always mixed with those relatively low score positive samples.

False Negative Samples of Caching. NSCaching establishes head and tail caches and mitigates the overlaps between quality negative samples and positive samples, but it suffers the false negative sample problem. During training, the ratio of false negatives (positive samples in the train, valid and test sets) in all negatives keeps increasing in NSCaching due to using caches (Fig. 4(b)). Caches preserve negative samples with high scores and some false negatives mixed with them can be trapped and accumulated. In contrast, ESNS does not use caches and explores new samples in each epoch. When a false negative sample is sampled, it will be released immediately in the next epoch.

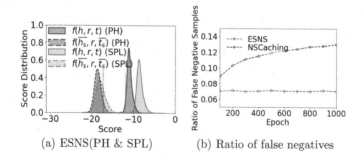

(a) ESNS(PH & SPL)   (b) Ratio of false negatives

Fig. 4. The ratio of false negatives in NSCaching and ESNS in Fig. 4(b). PH and SPL Loss function using TransD on YAGO3-10 in Fig. 4(a). The dash lines indicate the minimum positive score in the corresponding distributions. $\{(\overline{h}_s, s, \overline{t}_s)\}$ are quality samples generated in ESNS and NSCaching.

We also compared the results between NSCaching (SPL) and ESNS (SPL). As shown in Table 3, NSCaching (SPL) could perform better than NSCaching (PH) but still worse than ESNS (SPL). It is interesting that uniform, as a non-quality sampling method, has inconsistent performance with SPL compared to PH on different datasets. Hence, SPL is not always better than PH without considering quality negative samples. The above results prove that ESNS (SPL) achieves the best performance because the entity similarity sampling method is effective, and SPL does not inhibit its strengths. Due to space limitations, we only present results on three datasets, and similar results can be found on the other datasets.

Table 3. Applying different loss functions using TransE and TransD on different datasets

Dataset	FB15K237				WN18RR				YAGO3-10			
model	TransE		TransD		TransE		TransD		TransE		TransD	
metrics	MRR	H@10	MRR	H@10	MRR	H@10	MRR	H@10	MRR	H@10	MRR	H@10
Uniform(PH)	.278	47.5	.253	45.0	.199	46.3	.203	47.5	.233	47.0	.202	46.3
Uniform(SPL)	.243	41.3	.240	41.1	.220	51.5	.205	48.1	.187	34.5	.172	33.5
NSCaching(PH)	$.299^-$	47.6^-	$.286^-$	47.9^-	$.200^-$	47.8^-	$.201^-$	48.4^-	$.307^-$	50.7^-	$.315^-$	52.7^-
NSCaching(SPL)	.301	48.0	.311	49.4	.221	52.0	.216	50.0	.434	62.4	.452	64.9
ESNS(SPL)	**.308**	**48.4**	**.314**	**49.4**	**.227**	**52.1**	**.225**	**50.9**	**.457**	**65.7**	**.466**	**66.3**

5   Conclusion

In this paper, we investigate the characteristics of quality negative samples and propose a simple ESNS framework. A shift-based pointwise logistic loss function is designed to benefit the effectiveness of quality negative samples in training. We perform a large-scale evaluation to comprehensively validate our method on benchmark knowledge graphs, demonstrating that ESNS outperforms the state-of-the-art. Future studies will focus on applying ESNS to neural network KGE models.

References

1. Ahrabian, K., Feizi, A., Salehi, Y., Hamilton, W.L., Bose, A.J.: Structure aware negative sampling in knowledge graphs. In: Proceedings of the 2020 Conference on Empirical Methods in Natural Language Processing (EMNLP) (2020)
2. Auer, S., Bizer, C., Kobilarov, G., Lehmann, J., Cyganiak, R., Ives, Z.: DBpedia: a nucleus for a web of open data. In: Aberer, K., et al. (eds.) ASWC/ISWC -2007. LNCS, vol. 4825, pp. 722–735. Springer, Heidelberg (2007). https://doi.org/10.1007/978-3-540-76298-0_52
3. Bollacker, K., Evans, C., Paritosh, P., Sturge, T., Taylor, J.: Freebase: a collaboratively created graph database for structuring human knowledge. In: Proceedings of the 2008 ACM SIGMOD International Conference on Management of Data, pp. 1247–1250 (2008)

4. Bordes, A., Usunier, N., Garcia-Duran, A., Weston, J., Yakhnenko, O.: Translating embeddings for modeling multi-relational data. In: Proceedings of the 26th International Conference on Advances Neural Information Processing System, pp. 2787–2795 (2013)

5. Cai, L., Wang, W.Y.: Kbgan: Adversarial learning for knowledge graph embeddings. CoRR (2017)

6. Dong, X., et al.: Knowledge vault: A web-scale approach to probabilistic knowledge fusion. In: Proceedings of the 20th ACM SIGKDD International Conference on Knowledge Discovery and Data Mining, pp. 601–610 (2014)

7. Hu, K., Liu, H., Hao, T.: A Knowledge selective adversarial network for link prediction in knowledge graph. In: Tang, J., Kan, M.-Y., Zhao, D., Li, S., Zan, H. (eds.) NLPCC 2019. LNCS (LNAI), vol. 11838, pp. 171–183. Springer, Cham (2019). https://doi.org/10.1007/978-3-030-32233-5_14

8. Huang, X., Zhang, J., Li, D., Li, P.: Knowledge graph embedding based question answering. In: Proceedings of the Twelfth ACM International Conference on Web Search and Data Mining, pp. 105–113 (2019)

9. Ji, G., He, S., Xu, L., Liu, K., Zhao, J.: Knowledge graph embedding via dynamic mapping matrix. In: Proceedings of the 53rd Annual Meeting of the Association for Computational Linguistics and the 7th International Joint Conference on Natural Language Processing (volume 1: Long papers), pp. 687–696 (2015)

10. Ji, S., Pan, S., Cambria, E., Marttinen, P., Yu, P.S.: A survey on knowledge graphs: representation, acquisition and applications. CoRR (2020)

11. Kanojia, V., Maeda, H., Togashi, R., Fujita, S.: Enhancing knowledge graph embedding with probabilistic negative sampling. In: Proceedings of the 26th International Conference on World Wide Web Companion, pp. 801–802 (2017)

12. Kazemi, S.M., Poole, D.: Simple embedding for link prediction in knowledge graphs. In: Proceedings of the 32nd International Conference on Neural Information Processing System (2018)

13. Kingma, D.P., Ba, J.: Adam: A method for stochastic optimization. Technical report (2014)

14. Kotnis, B., Nastase, V.: Analysis of the impact of negative sampling on link prediction in knowledge graphs. CoRR (2017)

15. Krompaß, D., Baier, S., Tresp, V.: Type-constrained representation learning in knowledge graphs. In: Arenas, M., et al. (eds.) ISWC 2015. LNCS, vol. 9366, pp. 640–655. Springer, Cham (2015). https://doi.org/10.1007/978-3-319-25007-6_37

16. Lin, Y., Liu, Z., Sun, M., Liu, Y., Zhu, X.: Learning entity and relation embeddings for knowledge graph completion. In: Bonet, B., Koenig, S. (eds.) Proceedings of the Twenty-Ninth AAAI Conference on Artificial Intelligence, 25–30 January 2015, Austin, Texas, USA, pp. 2181–2187. AAAI Press (2015)

17. Liu, H., Hu, K., Wang, F.L., Hao, T.: Aggregating neighborhood information for negative sampling for knowledge graph embedding. Neural Comput. Appl. **32**(23), 17637–17653 (2020)

18. Mahdisoltani, F., Biega, J., Suchanek, F.: Yago3: A knowledge base from multilingual wikipedias. In: 7th Biennial Conference on Innovative Data Systems Research. CIDR Conference (2014)

19. Miller, G.A.: WordNet: a lexical database for English. Commun. ACM **38**(11), 39–41 (1995)

20. Mohamed, S.K., Muñoz, E., Novacek, V.: On training knowledge graph embedding models. Information **12**(4), 147 (2021)

21. Qin, S., Rao, G., Bin, C., Chang, L., Gu, T., Xuan, W.: Knowledge graph embedding based on adaptive negative sampling. In: Cheng, X., Jing, W., Song, X., Lu, Z. (eds.) ICPCSEE 2019. CCIS, vol. 1058, pp. 551–563. Springer, Singapore (2019). https://doi.org/10.1007/978-981-15-0118-0_42

22. Ruffinelli, D., Broscheit, S., Gemulla, R.: You can teach an old dog new tricks! on training knowledge graph embeddings. In: International Conference on Learning Representations (2019)

23. Sun, Z., Deng, Z.H., Nie, J.Y., Tang, J.: RotatE: knowledge graph embedding by relational rotation in complex space. In: International Conference on Learning Representations (2019)

24. Toutanova, K., Chen, D.: Observed versus latent features for knowledge base and text inference. In: Proceedings of the 3rd Workshop on Continuous Vector Space Models and their Compositionality, pp. 57–66 (2015)

25. Trouillon, T., Welbl, J., Riedel, S., Gaussier, É., Bouchard, G.: Complex embeddings for simple link prediction. In: International Conference on Machine Learning (ICML) (2016)

26. Wang, P., Li, S., et al.: Incorporating GAN for negative sampling in knowledge representation learning. CoRR (2018)

27. Wang, Q., Mao, Z., Wang, B., Guo, L.: Knowledge graph embedding: A survey of approaches and applications. IEEE Trans. Knowl. Data Eng. **29**(12), 2724–2743 (2017)

28. Wang, X., He, X., Cao, Y., Liu, M., Chua, T.S.: KGAT: Knowledge graph attention network for recommendation. In: Proceedings of the 25th ACM SIGKDD International Conference on Knowledge Discovery & Data Mining, pp. 950–958 (2019)

29. Wang, Y., Ruffinelli, D., Gemulla, R., Broscheit, S., Meilicke, C.: On evaluating embedding models for knowledge base completion. In: Proceedings of the 4th Workshop on Representation Learning for NLP (RepL4NLP-2019) (2019)

30. Wang, Z., Zhang, J., Feng, J., Chen, Z.: Knowledge graph embedding by translating on hyperplanes. In: Aaai. vol. 14, pp. 1112–1119. Citeseer (2014)

31. Xie, Q., Ma, X., Dai, Z., Hovy, E.: An interpretable knowledge transfer model for knowledge base completion. CoRR (2017)

32. Xiong, C., Power, R., Callan, J.: Explicit semantic ranking for academic search via knowledge graph embedding. In: Proceedings of the 26th International Conference on World Wide Web, pp. 1271–1279 (2017)

33. Yang, B., Yih, W., He, X., Gao, J., Deng, L.: Embedding entities and relations for learning and inference in knowledge bases. In: Bengio, Y., LeCun, Y. (eds.) 3rd International Conference on Learning Representations, ICLR 2015, San Diego, CA, USA, 7–9 May 2015, Conference Track Proceedings (2015)

34. Zhang, Y., Yao, Q., Shao, Y., Chen, L.: Nscaching: simple and efficient negative sampling for knowledge graph embedding. In: 2019 IEEE 35th International Conference on Data Engineering (ICDE), pp. 614–625. IEEE (2019)

35. Zhou, X., Zhu, Q., Liu, P., Guo, L.: Learning knowledge embeddings by combining limit-based scoring loss. In: Proceedings of the 2017 ACM on Conference on Information and Knowledge Management, pp. 1009–1018 (2017)

Label Enhancement Using Inter-example Correlation Information

Chong Li, Chao Tan[✉], Qin Qin, and Genlin Ji

School of Computer and Electronic Information/School of Artificial Intelligence,
Nanjing Normal University, Nanjing, China
tutu_tanchao@163.com

Abstract. Label distribution learning (LDL) to characterize the importance of different labels by label distribution has achieved good results in many application fields. LDL can learn more semantic information from the data than multi-label learning, however, most of the data in practical applications are single-label annotated or multi-label annotated, lacking the complete label distribution information suitable for label distribution learning. Thus, label enhancement (LE) is proposed to recover the label distributions from the logical labels. In this paper, we propose a new label enhancement method using inter-example correlation information that can automatically learn label correlations from data and jointly learn model and label correlations in a unified learning framework. Moreover, we also exploit the feature correlations constraining the model in the proposed method, which solves the problem that existing label enhancement algorithms cannot fully utilize the label information to improve the model performance. The experimental results on several real-world data sets validate the effectiveness of our method.

Keywords: Label enhancement · Label distribution learning · Label correlation · Feature correlation · Low rank

1 Introduction

In label distribution learning, a example is often associated with multiple semantic labels at the same time, and each label has a different degree of description of the example. Compared with the traditional multi-label learning framework, which assumes that all labels related to the example are equally important, the label distribution learning is more effective in handling the semantic information of training examples, and thus has received more and more attention. It has been successfully applied in various fields such as image and video annotation [12], Facial Age Estimation [16], head pose estimation [6], facial expression recognition [3], and Crowd Counting [20]. However, the process of labeling examples requires a lot of labor, material, and time, and it is difficult to standardize the label classification criteria, which makes traditional labeled distribution learning models fail to achieve good generalization performance.

© The Author(s), under exclusive license to Springer Nature Switzerland AG 2022
S. Khanna et al. (Eds.): PRICAI 2022, LNCS 13630, pp. 88–101, 2022.
https://doi.org/10.1007/978-3-031-20865-2_7

Fortunately, there are already a large number of logical label data sets in the field of multi label learning, and Xu et al. [17] proposed a method that exploits the topological information of the feature space and the correlation between the labels aimed at recovering the hidden label distribution values from the logical labels of the dataset, called the label enhancement (LE) learning paradigm. Xu et al. [17] proposed the graph Laplacian (GLLE) label enhancement algorithm. The method is based on the smoothness assumption [23] to construct a local correlation matrix to mine the hidden topological information among examples. Tang et al. [14] proposed Label Enhancement with example Correlations via low-rank representation (LESC) algorithm. LESC first applies a low rank constraint to the training set to obtain the feature representation with the global relationship of all examples,, and then smoothly transfers the constructed low-rank representation of the examples into the label space, using the low-rank representation of the feature space to represent the low-rank representation of the label space. Both of the above methods mine the topological information implied by the examples in the feature space, but neither of them exploits the correlation information implied by the label space. Zhu et al. [22] proposed the privileged label enhancement method with multi-label learning (PLEML). The method is divided into two steps, first generating the auxiliary label distribution for label enhancement using the multi-label learning model, and then using the RSVM+ model as the final prediction model, which is a support vector machine discriminative model implementing the LUPI (learning with privileged information) paradigm [15]. Although this method first generates the auxiliary label distribution using the correlation of labels in the label space, the algorithm is divided into two steps, which results in some loss of label information, and PLEML does not take full advanlabele of the correlation between examples in the feature space. Therefore, the effect of this method is suboptimal.

In view of this, this paper proposes a label enhancement method using inter-example correlation information, Both feature correlation and label correlation are used to enhance the generalization ability. Firstly, we construct a label correlation matrix which generally captures richer information regarding label dependence than the original label matrix to convert the existing logical labels into auxiliary label distributions. Note that, In this paper, instead of specifying any label correlation matrix, label correlation matrix S is learned directly, the matrix S is integrated in the objective function to enhance the prediction of label assignments. Secondly, in real-world tasks, label correlations are naturally local, where a label correlation may be shared by only a subset of instances rather than all the instances [9], so a low rank structure is adopted to capture the local label correlations. Furthermore, like the previous work of Xu et al. [17]. We construct a local correlation matrix to mine the correlations between examples. With these components, we are able to expand the forms of label correlations and achieve a novel Label Enhancement method that captures more complex and flexible dependencies among labels. Extensive experiments have shown that the proposed LEEC algorithm is stable to obtain remarkable performance as we expect. In summary, The major contributions of this paper are:

- A novel algorithm is proposed to exploit both feature correlation and label correlation for label enhancement.
- By introducing a label correlation matrix in the label space while imposing a low-rank constraint on it, richer label information than the original logical label matrix is captured.
- Comprehensive experiments conducted on 12 real world datasets show excellent power and generation compared with several state-of-the-art methods.

2   Related Work

label enhancement algorithms can be broadly classified into two categories: label enhancement algorithms based on '*fuzzy theory*' and label enhancement algorithms based on '*graph model*'. Fuzzy theory-based label enhancement methods are usually based on fuzzy mathematical ideas to construct fuzzy affiliation of each class of label by fuzzy operations or fuzzy clustering to convert logical label into numerical label. Such as the fuzzy clustering-based label enhancement algorithm FCM [5] and the kernel-based label enhancement algorithm KM [10]. label enhancement based on fuzzy clustering [5] transforms the affiliation of each example x_i to a cluster in the training set S by the fuzzy C-means clustering algorithm (FCM) [5] The affiliation of the examples generated during the clustering process to each cluster and the fuzzy operations, through the association matrix of categories and clusters into the affiliation of each example x_i to the category D_i, thus obtaining the labeled distribution training set $\mathcal{E} = \{(x_i, D_i)|1 \leq i \leq n\}$.

The graph model-based label enhancement algorithm uses a graph model to represent the topological relationships between examples, and enhances logical labels into label distributions by establishing the relationship between instance correlations and label correlations. Typical graph-based label enhancement methods include label propagation-based LE algorithm (LP) [11], manifold learning-based LE algorithm (ML) [8], and graph laplacian-based label enhancement algorithm (GLLE) [17].

2.1   Label Propagation Based LE Algorithm (LP)

LP first constructs a symmetric similairy matrix $W = (w_{ij})_{n \times n}$ based on the inter-example correlation, whose elements can be calculated by the following equation:

$$w_{ij} = \begin{cases} \exp(-\frac{||x_i - x_j||^2}{2\sigma^2}) & \text{if } i \neq j \\ 0 & \text{if } i = j \end{cases}, \tag{1}$$

The label propagation matrix P is calculated from the similairy matrix W :

$$P = Q^{-\frac{1}{2}} W Q^{-\frac{1}{2}}, \tag{2}$$

where $Q = diag(d_1, d_2, \cdots, d_m)$ with the elements $d_i = \sum_{j=1}^{n} w_{ij}$. Assuming that the descriptive degrees of all labels for all examples form a label distribution matrix $\boldsymbol{F}$, LP uses an iterative method to continuously update $\boldsymbol{F}$. The initial value of $\boldsymbol{F}^0 = \phi = [\phi_{ij}]_{n \times c}$ consists of the logical labels for example $\boldsymbol{x}_i$, i.e. $\forall_{i=1}^n \forall_{j=1}^c : \phi_{ij} = l_{\boldsymbol{x}_i}^{y_j}$. The label distribution matrix $\boldsymbol{F}$ is updated using the following formula

$$\boldsymbol{F}^{(t)} = \alpha \boldsymbol{P} \boldsymbol{F}^{(t-1)} + (1-\alpha)\Phi, \tag{3}$$

where α is the balancing parameter that controls the initial logical label and the degree of influence of label propagation on the final description. After iteration, eventually $\boldsymbol{F}$ converges to $\boldsymbol{F}^* = (1-\alpha)(\boldsymbol{I} - \alpha \boldsymbol{P})^{-1}\Phi$. Since the label propagation is influenced by the weights on the path, it will naturally form the difference in the descriptive degree of different labels, and when the label propagation converges, the original logical labels of each example can be enhanced to the label distribution.

2.2 The LE Algorithm Based on Manifold Learning (ML)

The label enhancement algorithm based on manifold learning [8] assumes that the data are distributed on some manifold space in both feature space and label space. According to the smoothness assumption [23], the points close to each other are more likely to share a label. Thus, the topological relationship of the feature space manifold can be used to guide the construction of the label space manifold, based on which the logical labels of the examples are enhanced to label distributions. Specifically, assuming that any example $\boldsymbol{x}_i$ can be reconstructed by a linear combination of its k incoming neighbors, the reconstructed weight matrix $\boldsymbol{W}$ can be obtained by minimizing the following equation:

$$\Theta(\boldsymbol{W}) = \sum_{i=1}^n ||\boldsymbol{x}_i - \sum_{j \neq i} w_{ij} \boldsymbol{x}_j||^2, \tag{4}$$

where $\sum_{j=1}^n w_{ij} = 1$. If $\boldsymbol{x}_j$ is not a k - nearest neighbor of $\boldsymbol{x}_i$, then $w_{ij} = 0$. By the smoothness assumption [23], the topological structural information in the feature space can be transferred to the label space. i.e., the local linear reconstruction matrix obtained in the feature space is used to replace the unknown linear reconstruction matrix in the label space. So the label distribution of the example can be obtained by minimizing the following equation:

$$\Psi(\boldsymbol{d}) = \sum_{i=1}^n ||\boldsymbol{d}_i - \sum_{j \neq i} w_{ij} \boldsymbol{d}_j||^2,$$

$$d_{\boldsymbol{x}_i}^{y_l} l_{\boldsymbol{x}_i}^{y_l} > \lambda, \forall 1 \leq i \leq n, 1 \leq j \leq c. \tag{5}$$

where $\lambda > 0$. The label distributions are generated with the optimization by using a constrained quadratic programming process. Finally, $\boldsymbol{d}_i$ can be normalize via the softmax normalization.

2.3 Privileged Label Enhancement Method with Multi-label Learning (PLEML)

Zhu [22] propose a privileged label enhancement method with multi-label learning (PLEML). Firstly, author apply a multi-label learning model to generate auxiliary information for LE. The auxiliary information $Y^* = [y_1^*, y_2^*, \cdots, y_n^*]$ can be obtained by the following formula:

$$Y^* = X\bar{W}, \tag{6}$$

and $\bar{W}$ can be obtained by:

$$\bar{W} = \arg\min_{\bar{W}} L(\bar{W}) + \lambda_1 \Omega(\bar{W}) + \lambda_2 Z(\bar{W}), \tag{7}$$

where $L(\bar{W}) = \frac{1}{2}||Y^* - Y||_F^2$ is the loss function defined on the training data and Y denote the logical value of the training set, $\Omega(\bar{W}) = ||\bar{W}||_F^2$ is a regularizer to control the complexity of the output model, $Z(\bar{W}) = ||Y^*||_{tr}$ is a low-rank regularizer to implicitly exploit the correlation of the labels., and λ_1 and λ_2 are two parameters to balance the three terms. When the auxiliary label distribution Y^* that can capture the injective relationship between the feature space and the label space is obtained by the multi-label learning model, PLEML use LUPI (learning with privileged information) paradigm [15] which is supplied by a teacher about instances at the training stage to make reasonable use of additional information. Finally, PLEML use the RSVM+ model as the final prediction model, and use feature information and privileged information to obtain the final label distribution value.

3 Methodology

3.1 Formulation of Label Enhancement

The main notations used in this paper are listed as follows. Let $X = [x_1; x_2; \cdots; x_n] \in \mathbb{R}^{n \times d}$ denote the feature matrix and $L = [l_1; l_2; \cdots; l_n] \in \mathbb{R}^{n \times c}$ denote the logical label matric, where n denotes the number of instances, d denotes the dimension of the feature and c is the number of all possible labels. Let $D = [d_1; d_2; \cdots; d_n] \in \mathbb{R}^{n \times c}$ denotes the label distribution matrix, where $d_i = [d_{x_i}^{y_1}, d_{x_i}^{y_2}, \cdots, d_{x_i}^{y_c}]$ is the label distribution associated with x_i, $d_{x_i}^{y_j}$ is used to indicate the importance of label y_j to instance x_i, which satisfies $d_{x_i}^{y_j} \in [0, 1]$ and $\sum_{j=1}^{c} d_{x_i}^{y_j} = 1$. Given the training set $\mathcal{S} = \{(x_i, l_i)|1 \leq i \leq n\}$, the label enhancement is the process of transforming the logical label vector l_i of each example x_i into the corresponding label distribution d_i, thus obtaining the training set of label distribution $\mathcal{E} = \{(x_i, d_i)|1 \leq i \leq n\}$.

3.2 The LEEC Algorithm

To solve the problem we discussed Previously, consider the following label enhancement framework:

$$\hat{W} = \min_{\hat{W}} L(\hat{W}) + \Omega(\hat{W}), \tag{8}$$

where $L(.)$ is a loss function, the regularization term $\Omega(\hat{W})$ is used to capture the specific structures of features and labels with various norms. Apparently, we need to induce the minimization of the formula to get an optimal $\hat{W}$. Assuming that the feature space and the label space are linearly related, we consider using a linear model for prediction, the output model can be represented by the following equation:

$$\hat{D} = XW, \tag{9}$$

where $\hat{D}$ is the predicted label distribution, and W is the weight matrix. For easy computation, We use the square of the Euclidean distance as the loss function and constrain the parameter $\hat{W}$ at the same time:

$$L(\hat{W}) = \min_{\hat{W}} \frac{1}{2}||X\hat{W} - Y||^2 + \lambda_1||\hat{W}||_F^2. \tag{10}$$

In the previously proposed label enhancement algorithms, the models directly approximate the logical labels. Although this is simple, it loses some semantic information to a certain extent. Motivated by the idea of [21], if we can restore partial label information and let the model approach a certain auxiliary label distribution instead of logical labels, there is no doubt that the representation ability of the model can be greatly improved. For the above considerations, we introduce the label correlation matrix S. In particular, given the observed logical label matrix Y, the reconstructed label j-th of example i-th can be calculated as a liner aggregation of the existing logical labels of example i-th, that is, $\hat{y}_{j,i} = l_i S_{:,j}$, where $S_{:,j}$ denotes the j-th column of label correlation matrix S. The reconstructed labels of example x_i can be built for all logical label with $\hat{y}_{:,i} = l_i S$. Considering all examples simultaneously, the final formulation can be written as $\hat{Y} = YS$, where $S \in \mathbb{R}^{c \times c}$ is a linear aggregation coefficient matrix reflecting the correlation of labels and it's element s_{ij} represents the correlation among the i-th label and j-th label. A simple example is shown in Fig. 1, we assume that the face expression image in Fig. 1 has four labels, which are 'Sad','Anger','Disgust' and 'Fear'. Taking the label 'Anger' for example, we can obtain that the relative importance of 'Anger' is changed from 0 to 0.8 (It needs to be normalized) for the high correlation of label 'Anger' with the labels 'Sad' and 'Disgust' shown in matrix S, i.e., the reconstructed distribution $l_i S$ can provide more information and assign a new relevance of a label to a particular instance based on the global label correlations. To exploit the dependence among labels, Eq. (10) can be rewritten as Eq. (11):

$$\min_{\hat{W},S} \frac{1}{2}||X\hat{W} - YS||^2 + \lambda_1||\hat{W}||_F^2 + \lambda_2||Y - YS||_F^2. \tag{11}$$

In real-world tasks, label correlations are naturally local, where a label correlation may be shared by only a subset of instances rather than all the instances [9], so a low rank structure is adopted to capture the local label correlations based on the intuition that a subset of labels can be closely related to each other

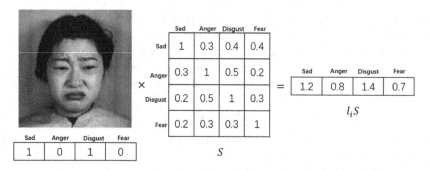

Fig. 1. Illustration of label correlations. $l_i S$ is the reconstructed label distribution which is obtained by multiplying the logical label l_i with the label correlation matrix S.

with similar semantic contexts, while being independent of the rest.

$$\min_{\hat{W},S} \frac{1}{2}||X\hat{W} - YS||^2 + \lambda_1||\hat{W}||_F^2 + \lambda_2||Y - YS||_F^2 \tag{12}$$
$$+ \lambda_3||S||_*,$$

where λ_1, λ_2 and λ_3 are balance factors. Considering that the low-rank function is difficult to optimize, we use the nuclear norm $||\cdot||_*$ as a convex approximation of the low-rank function.

Also, as in the GLLE [17] work, we introduce sample correlation and thus further constrain the parameter $\hat{W}$. Specifically, We constructs a local correlation matrix A to exploit the topological information in the feature space, and the elements of the local correlation matrix A can be calculated by the following equation:

$$a_{ij} = \begin{cases} \exp(-\frac{||x_i - x_j||^2}{2\sigma^2}) & if \ x_i \in N(i) \\ 0 & \text{otherwise} \end{cases}, \tag{13}$$

where $N(i)$ means the set of $x_i's$ K-nearest neighbors, and $\sigma \geq 0$ is the width parameter for correlation calculation. Then under the assumption of smoothness [23] the labels of the examples with similar features are also likely to correlation, the topological information in the feature space is passed to the label space, i.e., the following equation needs to be minimized:

$$\Omega(\hat{W}) = \sum_{i,j} a_{ij}||d_i - d_j||^2$$
$$= tr(DGD^\top) \tag{14}$$
$$= tr(X\hat{W}G\hat{W}^\top X^\top),$$

where $G = A - \hat{A}$ is the graph Laplacian and $\hat{A}$ is the diagonal matrix whose elements are $\hat{A}_{ij} = \sum_{j=1}^n a_{ij}$. Formulating the LE problem into an optimization framework over Eq. (12) and Eq. (14), the following optimization problem is obtained:

$$\min_{\hat{W},S} \frac{1}{2}||X\hat{W} - YS||^2 + \lambda_1||\hat{W}||_F^2 + \lambda_2||Y - YS||_F^2$$
$$+ \lambda_3||S||_* + \lambda_4 tr(X\hat{W}G\hat{W}^\top X^\top). \tag{15}$$

3.3 Optimization

Since the optimization problem in Eq. (15) is convex, it can be optimized by using ADMM [1]. Here, we introduce an auxiliary variable Z to make the objective function separable for the two non-smooth regularization terms in Eq. (15):

$$\min_{\hat{W},S} \frac{1}{2}||X\hat{W} - YS||^2 + \lambda_1||\hat{W}||_F^2 + \lambda_2||Y - YS||_F^2$$
$$+ \lambda_3||Z||_* + \lambda_4 tr(X\hat{W}G\hat{W}^\top X^\top), \tag{16}$$
$$s.t. \quad S - Z = 0.$$

The augmented Lagrangian function of Eq. (16) is:

$$\min_{\hat{W},S,Z} \frac{1}{2}||X\hat{W} - YS||^2 + \lambda_1||\hat{W}||_F^2 + \lambda_2||Y - YS||_F^2$$
$$+ \lambda_3||Z||_* + \lambda_4 tr(X\hat{W}G\hat{W}^\top X^\top) \tag{17}$$
$$+ <\Lambda, S - Z> +\frac{\rho}{2}||S - Z||_F^2,$$

where Λ is the Lagrange multiplier, ρ is the penalty parameter, and $< \cdot, \cdot >$ is the Frobenius dot-product. The optimization problem of Eq. (17) can be solved using the alternating solution method.

To solve for $\hat{W}$, Eq. (17) can be reduced to the following alternative methods:

$$\hat{W} = \arg\min_{\hat{W}} \frac{1}{2}||X\hat{W} - YS||^2 + \lambda_1||\hat{W}||_F^2$$
$$+ \lambda_4 tr(X\hat{W}G\hat{W}^\top X^\top), \tag{18}$$

In the same way, S can be solved by optimizing the following sub-problem,

$$S = \arg\min_{S} \frac{1}{2}||X\hat{W} - YS||^2 + \lambda_2||Y - YS||_F^2$$
$$+ <\Lambda, S - Z> +\frac{\rho}{2}||S - Z||_F^2, \tag{19}$$

Both Eq. (18) and Eq. (19) can be solved by the limited-memory quasi-Newton method effectively [19]. The basic idea is to avoid explicit calculation of the inverse Hessian matrix, which is required in the Newton method. For the optimization of Eq. (18) and Eq. (19), the computation of L-BFGS is mainly related to the first-order gradient, which can be obtained by

$$\nabla\hat{W} = X^\top(X\hat{W} - YS) + 2\lambda_1\hat{W} + \lambda_4 X^\top X\hat{W}(G + G^\top), \tag{20}$$

$$\nabla S = - Y^\top (X\hat{W} - YS) - 2\lambda_2 Y^\top (Y - YS) + Z \\ + \rho(S - Z),$$ (21)

Similarly, Z can be obtained by solving the problems as follows:

$$Z = \arg\min_{Z} ||Z||_* + < \Lambda, S - Z > + \frac{\rho}{2}||S - Z||_F^2,$$ (22)

Equation (22) have a closed solution [2]. The multiplier Λ can be updated directly by

$$\Lambda = \Lambda + \rho(S - Z).$$ (23)

4 Experiments

4.1 DataSets

There are 12 real-world label distribution datasets in our experiments, including two facial expression datasets SJAFFE [13] and SBU_3DFE [18], ten biological experiments datasets Yeast [4]. Some basic statistics about these 12 datasets are given in Table 1.

Table 1. 12 multi-label datasets with known ground-truth label distributions from used in LDL experiments

No	Dataset	Examples	Features	Labels
1	SJAFFE	213	243	9
2	SBU_3DFE	2500	243	6
3	Yeast_spoem	2465	24	2
4	Yeast_alpha	2465	24	18
5	Yeast_cdc	2465	24	15
6	Yeast_cold	2465	24	4
7	Yeast_diau	2465	24	7
8	Yeast_dtt	2465	24	4
9	Yeast_elu	2465	24	14
10	Yeast_heat	2465	24	6
11	Yeast_spo	2465	24	6
12	Yeast_spo5	2465	24	3

4.2 Evaluation Measures

To measure the distance or similairy between the recovered label distributions and the ground-truth label distributions, according to Geng's suggestion [7], six LDL measures are adopted, i.e., Chebyshev distance (Cheb), Clark distance (Clark), Canberra metric (Canber), Kullback-Leibler divergence (KL), Cosine coefficient (Cosine) and Intersection similarity (Intersec). The former four are distance measures and the last two are similarity measures. For Cheb, Clark, Canberra and KL, the smaller the value, the better the generalization performance. For Cosine and Intersec, the larger the value, the better the performance.

Table 2. Comparison results of label enhancement methods on real-world datasets. The best performance on each measure is marked in bold.

Data	Algorithm	Yeast-alpha	Yeast-cdc	Yeast-cold	Yeast-diau	Yeast-dtt	Yeast-elu	Yeast-heat	Yeast-spo	Yeast-spo5	Yeast-spoem	SBU_3DFE	SJAFFE	Avg_Rank
Cheb↓	LP	0.0400(6)	0.0420(5)	0.1370(6)	0.0990(5)	0.1280(6)	0.0440(5)	0.0860(5)	0.0900(5)	0.1140(5)	0.1630(6)	0.1230(2.5)	0.1070(5)	5.1250
	ML	0.0387(5)	0.0475(6)	0.1207(5)	0.2011(6)	0.1073(5)	0.0499(6)	0.0915(6)	0.0953(6)	0.1514(6)	0.1319(5)	0.1868(6)	0.2188(6)	5.6667
	GLLE	0.0192(4)	0.0217(4)	0.0650(4)	0.0530(4)	0.0518(4)	0.0221(4)	0.0478(4)	0.0608(3)	0.0980(4)	0.0870(2.5)	0.1230(2.5)	0.0845(2)	3.5000
	PLEML	0.0137(2)	0.0167(2)	0.0540(2)	0.0415(2)	0.0372(2)	0.0165(2)	0.0433(2)	0.0603(2)	**0.0921(1)**	0.1170(4)	**0.1228(1)**	0.0885(4)	2.1667
	LESC	0.0169(3)	0.0198(3)	0.0572(3)	0.0419(3)	0.0466(3)	0.0208(3)	0.0466(3)	0.0609(4)	0.0933(3)	0.0870(2.5)	0.1231(4)	**0.0692(1)**	2.9583
	LEEC	**0.0135(1)**	**0.0163(1)**	**0.0514(1)**	**0.0383(1)**	**0.0361(1)**	**0.0162(1)**	**0.0425(1)**	**0.0587(1)**	0.0923(2)	**0.0856(1)**	0.1265(5)	0.0869(3)	**1.5833**
Clark↓	LP	0.4322(5)	0.3803(5)	0.1805(5)	0.2841(4)	0.1902(5)	0.3642(5)	0.2144(5)	0.5585(6)	0.2741(5)	0.2718(6)	0.5810(5)	0.3140(3)	4.9167
	ML	0.6025(6)	0.5593(6)	0.3224(6)	0.7276(6)	0.2953(6)	0.5340(6)	0.3823(6)	0.4030(5)	0.3015(6)	0.2036(5)	0.7861(6)	0.8055(6)	5.8333
	GLLE	0.3304(4)	0.3018(4)	0.1738(4)	0.2964(5)	0.1413(4)	0.2845(4)	0.2082(4)	0.2618(4)	0.1943(4)	0.1321(3)	0.3818(4)	0.36334(4)	4.0000
	PLEML	0.2147(2)	0.2191(2)	0.1465(2)	0.2222(2)	0.1012(2)	0.2042(2)	0.1871(2)	0.2558(2)	0.1855(2)	0.1757(4)	0.3689(2)	0.3775(5)	2.4167
	LESC	0.2823(3)	0.2727(3)	0.1552(3)	0.2302(3)	0.1278(3)	0.2617(3)	0.2037(3)	0.2596(3)	0.1871(3)	0.1295(2)	0.3785(3)	**0.2763(1)**	2.7500
	LEEC	**0.2097(1)**	**0.2148(1)**	**0.1397(1)**	**0.2050(1)**	**0.0986(1)**	**0.1986(1)**	**0.1828(1)**	**0.2494(1)**	**0.1851(1)**	**0.1273(1)**	**0.3665(1)**	0.2997(2)	**1.0833**
Canber↓	LP	1.7068(5)	1.3532(5)	0.3241(5)	0.6425(4)	0.3560(5)	1.2612(5)	0.4706(5)	1.2341(6)	0.4013(5)	0.3655(6)	1.2463(5)	1.0708(5)	5.0833
	ML	2.0181(6)	1.7591(6)	0.5598(6)	1.6538(6)	0.5070(6)	1.6263(6)	0.7826(6)	0.8440(5)	0.4664(6)	0.2800(5)	1.6593(6)	1.6894(6)	5.8333
	GLLE	1.1135(4)	0.9442(4)	0.3016(4)	0.6734(5)	0.2458(5)	0.8692(4)	0.4203(4)	0.5422(4)	0.3018(4)	0.1840(4)	0.8409(4)	0.7518(3)	4.0000
	PLEML	0.6981(2)	0.6545(2)	0.2527(2)	0.4772(2)	0.1747(2)	0.6014(2)	0.3741(2)	0.5281(2)	**0.2849(1)**	0.1837(3)	**0.7866(1)**	**0.5606(1)**	2.0833
	LESC	0.9514(3)	0.8405(3)	0.2680(3)	0.5021(3)	0.2229(3)	0.7906(3)	0.4110(3)	0.5329(3)	0.2884(3)	0.1801(2)	0.8039(3)	0.5996(2)	2.7500
	LEEC	**0.6780(1)**	**0.6393(1)**	**0.2403(1)**	**0.4363(1)**	**0.1696(1)**	**0.5808(1)**	**0.3637(1)**	**0.5137(1)**	0.2857(2)	**0.1772(1)**	0.7953(2)	0.5996(2)	**1.2500**
KL↓	LP	0.1210(6)	0.1110(6)	0.1030(5)	0.1270(5)	0.1080(6)	0.1090(6)	0.0890(6)	0.0840(5)	0.0420(5)	0.0670(5)	0.1050(5)	0.0770(5)	5.4167
	ML	0.0550(5)	0.0609(5)	0.5560(6)	0.1934(6)	0.0648(5)	0.0567(5)	0.0656(5)	0.5320(6)	0.0811(6)	0.5030(6)	0.2489(6)	0.2513(6)	5.5833
	GLLE	0.0130(4)	0.0140(4)	0.0190(4)	0.0270(4)	0.0130(4)	0.0130(4)	0.0170(4)	0.0290(4)	0.0340(4)	0.0270(2.5)	0.0690(3)	0.0500(4)	3.7692
	PLEML	0.0057(2)	0.0073(2)	0.0135(2)	0.0158(2)	0.0066(2)	0.0064(2)	0.0134(2)	0.0271(2)	**0.0299(1.5)**	0.0310(4)	**0.0659(1)**	0.0494(3)	2.1250
	LESC	0.0080(3)	0.0100(3)	0.0150(3)	0.0170(3)	0.0100(3)	0.0090(3)	0.0155(3)	0.0280(3)	0.0310(3)	0.0270(2.5)	0.0692(4)	**0.0290(1)**	2.8750
	LEEC	**0.0055(1)**	**0.0070(1)**	**0.0122(1)**	**0.0136(1)**	**0.0063(1)**	**0.0061(1)**	**0.0128(1)**	**0.0253(1)**	**0.0299(1.5)**	**0.0246(1)**	0.0682(2)	0.0354(2)	**1.2083**
Cosine↑	LP	0.9814(5)	0.9828(5)	0.9847(4)	0.9805(4)	0.9835(5)	0.9829(5)	0.9861(3)	0.9386(5)	0.9686(5)	0.9503(5)	0.9220(5)	0.9410(5)	4.6667
	ML	0.9530(6)	0.9468(6)	0.9429(6)	0.8427(6)	0.9515(6)	0.9489(6)	0.9454(6)	0.8397(6)	0.9359(6)	0.8530(6)	0.8435(6)	0.8231(6)	6.0000
	GLLE	0.9876(4)	0.9875(4)	0.9827(5)	0.9750(5)	0.9884(4)	0.9879(4)	0.9845(5)	0.9747(3)	0.9713(4)	0.9780(2.5)	0.9594(4)	0.9594(3)	3.9583
	PLEML	0.9944(2)	0.9930(2)	0.9873(2)	0.9854(2)	0.9937(2)	0.9937(2)	0.9872(2)	0.9747(3)	**0.9736(1)**	0.9620(4)	**0.9344(1)**	0.9576(4)	2.2500
	LESC	0.9905(3)	0.9896(3)	0.9859(3)	0.9844(3)	0.9901(3)	0.9896(3)	0.9851(4)	0.9747(3)	0.9732(3)	0.9780(2.5)	0.9319(3)	**0.9731(1)**	2.8750
	LEEC	**0.9946(1)**	**0.9933(1)**	**0.9885(1)**	**0.9876(1)**	**0.9940(1)**	**0.9941(1)**	**0.9878(1)**	**0.9763(1)**	0.9735(2)	**0.9791(1)**	0.9327(2)	0.9656(2)	**1.2500**
Intersec↑	LP	0.9074(5)	0.9122(5)	0.9213(5)	0.9128(4)	0.9134(5)	0.9120(5)	0.9237(5)	0.8184(5)	0.8855(5)	0.8367(5)	0.8096(5)	0.8361(5)	4.9167
	ML	0.8898(6)	0.8836(6)	0.8646(6)	0.7557(6)	0.8779(6)	0.8839(6)	0.8718(6)	0.7614(6)	0.7486(6)	0.7681(6)	0.7414(6)	0.7251(6)	6.0000
	GLLE	0.9386(4)	0.9376(4)	0.9250(4)	0.9052(5)	0.9393(4)	0.9383(4)	0.9310(4)	0.9105(4)	0.9020(4)	0.9109(3.5)	0.8531(4)	0.8737(3)	3.9583
	PLEML	0.9615(2)	0.9569(2)	0.9376(2)	0.9335(2)	0.9570(2)	0.9575(2)	0.9385(2)	0.9130(2)	**0.9079(1)**	0.9109(3.5)	**0.8570(1)**	0.8718(4)	2.1250
	LESC	0.9473(3)	0.9445(3)	0.9338(3)	0.9301(3)	0.9448(3)	0.9439(3)	0.9324(3)	0.9121(3)	0.9067(3)	0.9130(2)	0.8542(3)	**0.9050 (1)**	2.7500
	LEEC	**0.9626(1)**	**0.9579(1)**	**0.9408(1)**	**0.9396(1)**	**0.9582(1)**	**0.9590(1)**	**0.9403(1)**	**0.9154(1)**	0.9077(2)	**0.9144(1)**	0.8568(2)	0.8977(2)	**1.2500**

4.3   Experimental Setting

The experiment is divided into two parts. In the first part, we first recover the label distribution from the logical labels by the LE algorithm, and then we compare the recovered label distribution with the ground-truth label distribution. In the second part, to further test the effectiveness of the LE algorithm, we trained LDL models using the recovered label distributions from the first part of the experiments, and then tested the trained LDL models on a new test dataset and compared the label distribution predictions with those made by the models trained directly on the ground-truth label distributions. Ten-fold cross-validation was performed for each algorithm. Note that due to the lack of datasets with both logical labels and label distributions, logical labels must be binarized from the ground-truth label distribution in the LDL training set in order to implement the LE algorithm and measure the similarity between the recovered label distribution and the ground-truth label distribution. To ensure consistent evaluation, we uniformly binarized the logical labels by the way in GLLE.

The performance of LEEC is compared against five label enhancement learning algorithms, including ML [8], LP [11], GLLE [17], PLEML [22], and LESC [14]. For the comparison algorithms, parameter configurations suggested in corresponding literatures are used, The number of neighbors K for ML is set to $c + 1$. For GLLE, the parameter λ is chosen among $\{10^{-2}, 10^{-1}, \cdots, 10^2\}$ and the number of neighbors k is set to $c + 1$. The kernel function in GLLE is Gaussian kernel. The parameter α in LP is set to 0.5. In LESC algorithm, the parameters λ_1 and λ_2 are selected among $\{10^{-4}, 10^{-3}, \cdots, 10\}$. For PLEML, the values of the parameters λ_1 and λ_2 are selected among $\{2^{-4}, 2^{-3}, \cdots, 2^8\}$, and $\gamma = 0.1$, $C = 0.1$. In LEEC, the parameters λ_1 and λ_4 are selected among $\{10^{-8}, 10^{-3}, 10^{-2}\}$, $\{10^{-3}, 10^{-2}, 10^{-1}\}$ respectively, and $\lambda_2 = 10$, $\lambda_3 = 10^{-3}$. Besides, ρ is simply set as 1.

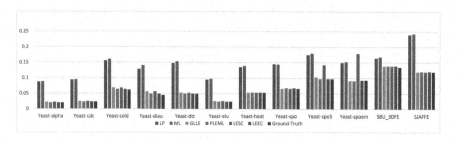

Fig. 2. Comparison of the LDL after the LE pre-process against the direct LDL measured by Cheb ↓.

4.4   Experimental Results

Table 2 tabulate the results of the six LE algorithms on all the datasets, and the best performance on each dataset is highlighted by boldface.To exhibit the mean accuracy of the recovered label distribution, the average rank of every algorithm among all datasets is also listed. For each evaluation metric, ↓ indicates the smaller the better while ↑ indicates the larger the better. For the second step of experiments, due to page limitation and refer to [17], we only show the effect on the two evaluation measures of Chebyshev and Cosine in Fig. 2 and Fig. 3, respectively. The results of other measures are similar.

From Table 2, we can see that LEEC significantly outperforms LP, ML, GLLE, PLEML and LESC on the most measures. Compared with the PLEML algorithm, LEEC performs slightly worse on the SBU_3DFE and Yeast-spo5 datasets on all the measures, and LEEC performed slightly worse on the SJAFFE dataset comd with the LESC algorithm. However, in other cases, the LEEC algorithm outperforms the rest of the LE algorithms. From Fig. 2 and Fig. 3, we can

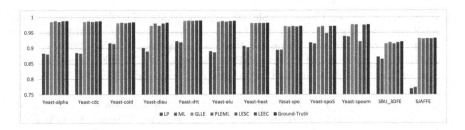

Fig. 3. Comparison of the LDL after the LE pre-process against the direct LDL measured by Cosine ↑ .

find that the LEEC algorithm achieves good performance on most of the datasets and does not falling behind the existing state-of-the-art LE algorithms in terms of Cheb and Cosine. It is worth mentioning that the effectiveness of LDL using the label distributions recovered by the GLLE and PLEML algorithms is even better than that of LDL using the Ground-Truth label distributions directly after the LE pre-process. A reasonable explanation for this is that since the Yeast-spoem dataset contains only two labels, a large amount of label information is lost after the binarization operation, which makes it difficult for the LE algorithm to recover a reasonable label distribution.

5   Conclusion

In this paper, we propose a new label enhancement algorithm LEEC, which exploits both feature correlation and label correlation, mainly to solve the problem that existing label enhancement algorithms cannot make full use of label information to improve model performance. Unlike existing methods, LEEC mines the hidden label information simultaneously with the model training, making the best possible use of the label information. Extensive experimental results on 12 datasets show that the algorithm outperforms several existing algorithms in recovering label distribution and LDL prediction after LE preprocessing of logical labels.

Acknowledgements. This work is supported by National Natural Science Foundation of China (41971343, 61702270), the Project funded by China Postdoctoral Science Foundation under Grant. 2017M621592.

References

1. Boyd, S., Parikh, N., Chu, E., Peleato, B., Eckstein, J., et al.: Distributed optimization and statistical learning via the alternating direction method of multipliers. Found. Trends Mach. Learn. **3**(1), 1–122 (2011)
2. Cai, J.F., Candès, E.J., Shen, Z.: A singular value thresholding algorithm for matrix completion. SIAM J. Optim. **20**(4), 1956–1982 (2010)

3. Chen, S., Wang, J., Chen, Y., Shi, Z., Rui, Y.: Label distribution learning on auxiliary label space graphs for facial expression recognition. In: 2020 IEEE/CVF Conference on Computer Vision and Pattern Recognition (CVPR) (2020)
4. Eisen, M.B., Spellman, P.T., Brown, P.O., Botstein, D.: Cluster analysis and display of genome-wide expression patterns. Proc. Natl. Acad. Sci. **95**(25), 14863–14868 (1998)
5. El Gayar, N., Schwenker, F., Palm, G.: A study of the robustness of KNN classifiers trained using soft labels. In: Schwenker, F., Marinai, S. (eds.) ANNPR 2006. LNCS (LNAI), vol. 4087, pp. 67–80. Springer, Heidelberg (2006). https://doi.org/10.1007/11829898_7
6. Geng, X., Qian, X., Huo, Z., Zhang, Y.: Head pose estimation based on multivariate label distribution. IEEE Trans. Softw. Eng. (99) (2020)
7. Geng, X.: Label distribution learning. IEEE Trans. Knowl. Data Eng. **28**(7), 1734–1748 (2016)
8. Hou, P., Geng, X., Zhang, M.L.: Multi-label manifold learning. In: Proceedings of the AAAI Conference on Artificial Intelligence, vol. 30 (2016)
9. Huang, S.J., Zhou, Z.H.: Multi-label learning by exploiting label correlations locally. In: Proceedings of the AAAI Conference on Artificial Intelligence, vol. 26, pp. 949–955 (2012)
10. Jiang, X., Yi, Z., Lv, J.C.: Fuzzy SVM with a new fuzzy membership function. Neural Comput. Appl. **15**(3), 268–276 (2006)
11. Li, Y.K., Zhang, M.L., Geng, X.: Leveraging implicit relative labeling-importance information for effective multi-label learning. In: 2015 IEEE International Conference on Data Mining, pp. 251–260. IEEE (2015)
12. Ling, M., Geng, X.: Soft video parsing by label distribution learning. Front. Comput. Sci. **13**, 302–317 (2019)
13. Lyons, M., Akamatsu, S., Kamachi, M., Gyoba, J.: Coding facial expressions with Gabor wavelets. In: Proceedings Third IEEE International Conference on Automatic Face and Gesture Recognition, pp. 200–205. IEEE (1998)
14. Tang, H., Zhu, J., Zheng, Q., Wang, J., Pang, S., Li, Z.: Label enhancement with sample correlations via low-rank representation. In: Proceedings of the AAAI Conference on Artificial Intelligence, vol. 34, pp. 5932–5939 (2020)
15. Vapnik, V., Vashist, A.: A new learning paradigm: learning using privileged information. Neural Netw. **22**(5–6), 544–557 (2009)
16. Xin, G., Qin, W., Yu, X.: Facial age estimation by adaptive label distribution learning. In: 22nd International Conference on Pattern Recognition (2014)
17. Xu, N., Tao, A., Geng, X.: Label enhancement for label distribution learning. In: Proceedings of the 27th International Joint Conference on Artificial Intelligence, pp. 2926–2932 (2018)
18. Yin, L., Wei, X., Sun, Y., Wang, J., Rosato, M.J.: A 3D facial expression database for facial behavior research. In: 7th International Conference on Automatic Face and Gesture Recognition (FGR06), pp. 211–216. IEEE (2006)
19. Yuan, Y.x.: A modified BFGS algorithm for unconstrained optimization. IMA J. Num. Anal. **11**(3), 325–332 (1991)
20. Zhang, Z., Wang, M., Geng, X.: Crowd counting in public video surveillance by label distribution learning. Neurocomputing **166** (2015)
21. Zhao, F., Xiao, M., Guo, Y.: Predictive collaborative filtering with side information. In: Proceedings of the Twenty-Fifth International Joint Conference on Artificial Intelligence (IJCAI), pp. 2385–2391 (2016)

22. Zhu, W., Jia, X., Li, W.: Privileged label enhancement with multi-label learning. In: Proceedings of the Twenty-Ninth International Conference on International Joint Conferences on Artificial Intelligence, pp. 2376–2382 (2021)
23. Zhu, X.: Semi-supervised Learning with Graphs. Carnegie Mellon University (2005)

Link Prediction via Fused Attribute Features Activation with Graph Convolutional Network

Yayao Zuo$^{(\boxtimes)}$, Yang Zhou, Biao Yi, Minghao Zhan, and Kun Chen

Guangdong University of Technology, Guangzhou, China
yyzuo@gdut.edu.cn

Abstract. Link prediction is an effective method to guarantee the integrity of the knowledge graph, aiming to predict the missing part of the triple. So far most of the existing researches have been propo-seed to embed entities and relations into a vector space or inferred the paths between entities in a knowledge graph. However, most of the previous works merely take account of the single path or first-order information, ignoring the relation between the entities and their attributes. Motivated by this, for a better representation of entities and relations, we in this article exploit the characteristics of the attribute to enrich the information of entities cooperated with a graph neural network. In our method the edges connected by a node are regarded as its contextual information, which will be extracted as an attribute feature. Then the message propagation network is utilized to generate the node and edge representions, after which an aggregation function is applied to integrate node attributes, node representation as well as edge representation to realize link prediction. Experiments on the same datasets show that our model outperforms the baselines in multiple metrics including MRR and Hits@N. At the same time, ablation experiments validate a strong expandability of the node attribute feature learning method we propose, which enables the model to accelerate the convergence of training and improve the performance on the link prediction task.

Keywords: Knowledge graph · Graph convolutional neural network · Link prediction · Attribute activation · Node attribute characteristics

1 Introduction

The essence of knowledge graph (KG) is a semantic network, in which its nodes represent the entities in reality and its edges imply various semantic relations between entities. However, most of the existing knowledge graphs are incomplete. As for those incomplete KGs, it is necessary to complete their missing knowledge to guarantee a better knowledge service for downstream tasks, such as question answering systems [2], recommendation systems [5,24], and information retrieval [10].

© The Author(s), under exclusive license to Springer Nature Switzerland AG 2022
S. Khanna et al. (Eds.): PRICAI 2022, LNCS 13630, pp. 102–113, 2022.
https://doi.org/10.1007/978-3-031-20865-2_8

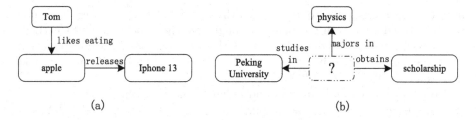

Fig. 1. Node attribute examples

For the missing knowledge, early approaches usually apply a simple vector operation in link prediction. In 2013, Bordes [1] proposed the TransE to obtain the representation of entities and relations in a low-dimensional vector space, with the assumption that the head entity plus the relation equals to the tail entity. Owing to the limitations in dealing with complex relations, researchers later proposed some variants based on TransE including TransH [21], TransR [12] and TransD [8] to enhance the representation of relations and entities. Although Trans models are easily extended to a large-scale multi-relational knowledge graph, there still exists a weakness in feature learning and interpretability. In order to solve the shortcomings mentioned above, researchers put forward a deep learning model based on Convolutional Neural Networks [13]. ConvE [3] stacks and splices the head entity and relation vector, and then converts them into a two-dimensional tensor, which is finally applied to a convolution operation to predict the missing tail entity. Based on ConvE, ConvKB [15] proposes converting the stacking and splicing of triples into one-dimensional vectors for one-dimensional convolution, and distinguish whether the triples exist in the knowledge graph based on the score.

Subsequently, scholars proposed Graph Neural Networks(GNN) based on convolutional neural networks to specialize in graph data. RGCN [11] employs GCN to deal with the impact of different relations on nodes in the graph structure. It applies an encoder model in the relation graph to accumulate information in multiple steps for link prediction inferring. Vashishth [20] proposed a novel graph convolutional framework CompGCN, which embeds nodes and relations into a uniform vector space, and updates node information through a propagation mechanism. While methods based on graph convolutional neural network have achieved remarkable improvement in link prediction, they merely explore the vector representation of entities and relations themselves, and do not make full use of other characteristics of the nodes.

In the task of relation classification [7,14], the type information of entities has been proven to play an important role in improving the representation of an entity. Inspired by their researches, we introduce attribute information to enrich the representation of a node in KGs. We assume the attribute information of any node is closely related to the edges it connects to. The attribute of a missing link can be inferred from the existing links which connect to it. As shown in Fig. 1, for the node "apple" with multiple meanings, its meaning is distinguished from the edges connected to it. Through the edge labeled as "releases", the node can be defined as a "tech company"; through the edge labeled as "likes eating", it can be defined as "fruit" instead. Similarly, for the node "?", if the connected edges including "studies in", "majors in" and "obtains" has been known, we can infer the type of "?" should be "student".

To explore latent information and enhance the representation of nodes in the knowledge graph, this paper proposes a link prediction model AAGCN (Attribute Activate Graph Convolutional Network) based on a node attribute activation. We define an attribute feature of a node by all edges it connects to. AAGCN takes the edge connected by the node as a feature of itself, and then puts it into a graph convolutional network for capturing the node attribute characteristics. In the next step, it applies the message propagation neural network [4] (MPNN) to aggregate neighbor information and obtains the characteristics of a node and relation. Finally, it integrates the representations of node, relation and node attribute characteristics to realize link prediction, which solves the weakness of an incomprehensive representation exposed to previous GNN models.

The main contributions of this paper are as follows:

1. To enhance the expression of each node in the knowledge graph, an attribute information learning method based on node attribute activation is proposed in this article.
2. This paper proposes an AAGCN model that integrates multi-relation information in graph convolutional networks and converts the connected relations of the nodes into attribute characteristics. It employs the embedding technique of the knowledge graph to embed nodes, relations, and node attributes into a vector space, which learns the obtained vectors by a convolution operation to predict the missing entities and relations.
3. Experiments on the benchmark datasets validate the effectivess of our proposed model and show that our model is able to accelerate the convergence of training and improve performance on the link prediction task.

2   Related Work

Knowledge representation learning is also known as knowledge graph embedding. Its target is to embed the entities and relations in the knowledge graph to a low-dimensional vector space. Knowledge graph is a network composed of relations and entities, usually represented by triples (h,r,t), where h,t and r respectively represents head entity, tail entity and relation. Knowledge representation learning is to explore the vector representation of triples (h,r,t).

Early knowledge representation methods mainly pay attention to the structure of triples for realizing the representation learning of entities and relations in the knowledge graph, such as TransE [1], TransH [21] and TransR [12]. These methods based on translational model explain a relation as a translation from a head entity to a tail. However, weakness in multiple relations learning and a poor interpretability of these methods restrain their performance on knowledge graph embedding. Later, DistMult [22] and ComplEx [19] are proposed based on the semantics model. DistMult [22] uses a diagonal matrix to represent each relation in KG but it fails to model antisymmetric relations. By contrast, ComplEx [19] introduces a complex space and utilizes complex vectors to represent antisymmetric relations. In recent years, a great success in neural networks on graph embedding has drawn much attention to KG embedding research. ConvE [3] uses a convolutional neural network to exploit potential feature information from entities and relations, and then applies these extracted features to estimate the confidence of triples. WGCN [18] learns the information from neighbors in an adaptive way for capturing the entity characteristics relevant to its relation, thus the information of neighbors is shared with all nodes when they are embedded in the same vector space.

The models mentioned above have made achievements in the task of knowledge representation, but a node is composed of multiple attributes which exactly help the model better understand the representation of the node. Aware of the importance of node attributes, our model defines an attribute feature for a node and activates it. We utilize GCN to learn the edges in KGs, which are defined as attributes of nodes in our assumption.

3 AAGCN Model

In this section, we introduce our proposed AAGCN model. We will first define the problem formulation of knowledge graph and then illustrate the component of AAGCN in detail. The framework of AAGCN is shown in Fig. 2.

3.1 Problem Formulation

A knowledge graph can be defined as a directed graph $\mathcal{G} = (\mathcal{V}, \mathcal{R}, \mathcal{E}, \mathcal{X}, \mathcal{Z})$, where $\mathcal{V}$ and $\mathcal{R}$ are the sets of nodes and edges in the graph. $\mathcal{E}$ denotes the sets of triples in the form of (u, v, r), where u, v, r respectively represents the head entity, tail entity and the relation between them. $\mathcal{X} \in \mathbb{R}^{|\mathcal{V}| \times d_0}$ is the random initialized characteristic of all nodes in $\mathcal{V}$, where d_0 is the initial dimension of the feature. $\mathcal{Z} \in \mathbb{R}^{|\mathcal{R}| \times d_0}$ denotes the characteristic of all relations in $\mathcal{R}$. For the triples (u, v, r) in the knowledge graph, there exists a reverse relation r^{-1} and a reverse triple (v, u, r^{-1}), thus we extend $\mathcal{R}$ and $\mathcal{E}$ to $\mathcal{R}'$ and $\mathcal{E}'$, where $\mathcal{R}' = \mathcal{R} \cup \{r^{-1} | r \in \mathcal{R}\} \cup r_{self}$, r_{self} denotes a self-loop relation of the nodes, and $\mathcal{E}' = \mathcal{E} \cup \{(v, u, r^{-1}) | (u, v, r) \in \mathcal{E}\} \cup \{(u, u, r_{self}) | u \in \mathcal{V}\}$, then the $\mathcal{Z}$ is also extended to $\mathcal{Z}' \in \mathbb{R}^{(|\mathcal{R}| \times 2 + 1) \times d_0}$.

3.2 Node Attribute Activation

In the knowledge graph, for any node, its representation is closely related to the edges it connects with. AAGCN regards the edge connected with the node as a context feature. For any edge $j \in \mathcal{R}$ in $\mathcal{G}$, we regard j as a feature $s_i[j]$ of the node $i \in \mathcal{V}$ which it connects with. For all nodes in the knowledge graph, we define a feature matrix $S = \{s_1, s_2, ..., s_{|\mathcal{V}|}\}$, where s_i denotes the feature vector of node i, $|\mathcal{V}|$ is the number of nodes in KG. The feature activation operation of each node is shown in (1), where $*$ represents any node in the $\mathcal{V}$ set. $s_i[j]$ indicates whether the node i is connected to the relation j in the knowledge graph. If connected, the features j of node i will be activated and $s_i[j] = 1$.

$$s_i[j] = \begin{cases} 1, if(i, *, j) \in \mathcal{E} \wedge i \in \mathcal{V} \wedge j \in \mathcal{R}' \\ 0 \quad other \end{cases} \tag{1}$$

After obtaining the feature matrix S, the initial feature is input into the graph convolutional neural network for further learning to capture the attribute characteristics of the node. It uses forward propagation as:

$$Y^{(k+1)} = \sigma(\tilde{D}^{-\frac{1}{2}} \tilde{A} \tilde{D}^{-\frac{1}{2}} Y^{(k)} W^{(k)}) \tag{2}$$

where $\tilde{D}^{-\frac{1}{2}} \tilde{A} \tilde{D}^{-\frac{1}{2}}$ uses the adjacency matrix of the graph to obtain the Laplacian matrix. $Y^{(l)}$ is the feature vector of the k layer. When $k = 0$, $Y^{(0)} = S$, and $W^{(l)}$ represents the adjustable weight parameter of the k layer. $\sigma(\cdot)$ denotes the sigmoid function. After learning an k-layer neural network, attribute characteristics of all nodes are represented as $Y^{(k+1)} = \{a_1^{k+1}, a_2^{k+1}, ..., a_{|\mathcal{V}|}^{k+1}\}$, where a_v^{k+1} denotes the attribute characteristics of node v.

3.3 Relation Features

To prevent the overfitting in rare relations as the number of relations increases, our model does not take a random initialization for all relation vectors, but uses the basis-decomposition method [17] for relation initialization. All the relations in the knowledge graph can be defined as a weighted summation of a set of learnable basis vectors $\{v_1, v_2, ..., v_B\}$. Each relation $r \in \mathcal{R}$ is defined as followed:

$$z_r = \sum_{b=1}^{B} \alpha_{br} v_b, \tag{3}$$

where $\alpha_{br} \in \mathbb{R}$ refers to the weight of each basis vector v_b for the relation r. After obtaining the representation z_r of the relation, z_r is sent to a fully connected layer to extract high-level features:

$$h_r^{l+1} = W_{rel}^l h_r^l \tag{4}$$

where W_{rel}^l represents the learnable weight parameter of the lth layer, h_r^{l+1} refers to the relation feature after propagation in a l layer neural network and $h_r^0 = z_r$.

3.4 Node Features

In our model, we use CompGCN [20] to update the embedding of the node, and its aggregation function is defined as

$$h_v = f\left(\sum_{(u,r) \in \mathcal{N}(v)} W_{\lambda(r)} \phi(x_u, z_r) \right) \tag{5}$$

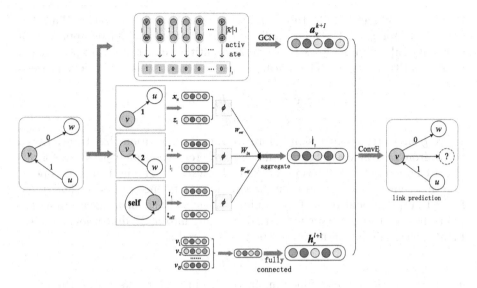

Fig. 2. Link prediction model based on node attribute activation

For the node v, there are three kinds of relations related to it. When v is the head node, it is interpreted as active relation r_{out}; when v is the tail node, it is called the passive relation r_{in}. At the same time, v will also have a self-relation r_{self} with itself. Hence, when aggregating neighbor nodes, according to the different kinds of relation with neighbor nodes, we have different weight parameter matrices for relation as shown in (6).

$$W_{\lambda(r)} = \begin{cases} W_{out}, r = r_{out} \\ W_{in}, r = r_{in} \\ W_{self}, r = r_{self} \end{cases} \tag{6}$$

For any neighbor node of v, we integrate its neighbor node u and relation r by utilizing the ϕ function, and then select different weight parameter matrices $W_{\lambda(r)}$ for different relations according to its type, and finally obtain the information of neighbor node u after a matrix multiplication. Among them, ϕ denotes the Circular- correlarion [16] operation. After the information aggregation of all neighboring nodes, the vector of v represented as h_v is obtained. After a learning for an l-layer graph neural network, the v can be represented as h_v^{l+1} and its update equation is as follows in (7):

$$h_v^{l+1} = f \left(\sum_{(u,r) \in \mathcal{N}(v)} W_{\lambda(r)} \phi(h_u^l, h_r^l) \right) \tag{7}$$

3.5   Features Integration

In the stage of features integration, we have obtained the node representation h_v^{l+1}, edge representation h_r^{l+1} and attribution representation a_v^{k+1}. Our next step is to combine these features through a concatenation operation that generates a vector $\boldsymbol{g}$ for the final prediction task. Later, $\boldsymbol{g}$ would be applied in a convolutional neural network that leverages entities and relations to predict the missing entity in a triple. The concatenation and convolution operations proceed as follows:

$$\boldsymbol{g} = concat(\boldsymbol{h}_v^{l+1}, \boldsymbol{h}_r^{l+1}, \boldsymbol{a}_v^{k+1}), \tag{8}$$

$$\psi_u(\boldsymbol{g}) = (vec(\bar{\boldsymbol{g}} * \omega))\boldsymbol{W}, \tag{9}$$

where $\bar{g}$ indicates a conversion before convolution operation that transforms a vector from one-dimension to two-dimension. ω represents multiple filters for different characteristics extractions of the nodes. $vec()$ is another transition operation that converts the output from three-dimension to one-dimension. The transformed output would be sent to a fully connected layer for a linear transition where it would map the one-dimensional input into a $|\mathcal{V}|$-dimensional vector. Finally, each missing entity for prediction is scored as:

$$p = \sigma(\psi_u(\boldsymbol{g})) \tag{10}$$

$\sigma(\cdot)$ refers to the sigmoid function. In the training state, we utilize the cross-entropy loss to optimize our model:

$$\mathcal{L}(p, t) = -\frac{1}{N} \sum_i (t_i \cdot \log(p_i) + (1 - t_i) \cdot \log(1 - p_i)) \tag{11}$$

where p_i and t_i respectively denotes the score and label of the node i.

4   Experiments

4.1   Experimental Settings

Table 1. Statistic of datasets.

Dataset	Rels	Ents	Train	Valid	Test
WN18RR	1345	14,951	483,142	50,000	59,071
FB15K-237	237	14,541	272,115	17,535	20,466
NELL-955	200	75,492	149,678	543	3,992

Datasets and Evaluation Metrics. In this article, we choose FB15k-237 and NELL-995 in the comparative experiment. As for ablation experiment, we choose FB15k-237 with more complex relations and WN18RR composed of simple relations for comparison. The number of entities and relations in the datasets and the number of triples in the training set, test set and validation set are shown in Table 1. We adopt Mean Reciprocal Ranks(MRR) and Hits@1/3/10 to measure the performance of AAGCN. For the facts in dataset, if entity h has a relation r, the model will generate a reverse relation r^{-1} associated with h. Therefore, the number of triples in the dataset after processing will be twice as the initial data.

Parameter Settings and Baselines. GCN Layer1 is set to 1 and GCN Layerk is set to 2. The batch size is set to 256. The dropout rate is set to 0.1. We use the Adam optimizer to update the weights with a learning rate of 0.001. We choose the following methods as baselines for comparison with AAGCN, including DistMult [22], ComplEx [19], ConvE [3], ConvR [9], and CompGCN [20].

Table 2. Comparatie experiment results

	FB15k-237				NELL-955			
	MRR	H@10	H@3	H@1	MRR	H@10	H@3	H@1
DisMult	0.241	0.419	0.263	0.155	0.410	0.512	0.444	0.353
ComplEx	0.247	0.428	0.275	0.158	0.408	0.514	0.453	0.345
ConvE	0.318	0.493	0.349	0.230	0.415	0.527	0.461	0.346
ConvR	0.350	0.528	0.385	0.261	–	–	–	–
CompGCN	0.355	0.535	0.390	0.264	0.429	0.542	0.477	0.361
AAGCN	**0.357**	**0.538**	**0.391**	**0.267**	**0.431**	**0.542**	0.467	**0.367**

4.2 Results and Discussion

Table 2 shows the overall experiments result of AAGCN against baseline methods. On FB15k-237, AAGCN outperforms all baseline methods in four metrics including MRR, H@10, H@3, and H@1. At the same time, on NELL-995, AAGCN ranks first in three metrics referred to MRR, H@10, and H@1. Experiments show that AAGCN effectively exploit the characteristics of multiple relations in the knowledge graph to learn attribute information. Combined with the graph convolutional network for information update, the added attribute features strengthen the representation of a node, thus improve the performance on link prediction.

On the NELL-995 data set, the convergence process of the MRR metric on validation sets in the first 150 epochs is shown in Fig. 3. It is clear that ComplEx converges faster than other counterparts as it approximately converges in the 100th epoch. On the contrary, the MRR metric of ConvE increases slowly and its convergence period exceeds 150 epochs. As for CompGCN and AAGCN, we observe that their fitting process is similar with each other. But when the MMR metric keeps the same in the validation sets, we find that in the test sets the metric of AAGCN is higher than that of CompGCN, which illustrates AAGCN has better performance on generalization than CompGCN.

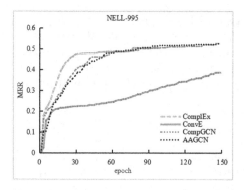

Fig. 3. MRR of different benchmark models in the learning process

4.3   Ablation Experiment

To evaluate the validity and extensibility of the node attribute features in AAGCN model, we conduct an ablation experiment to explore the impact of the node attribute features on the link prediction task.

Table 3. Ablation experiment results

	FB15k-237		WN18RR	
	ConvE	ConvE+Attr	ConvE	ConvE+Attr
MRR	0.318	**0.321**	0.423	**0.435**
H@10	0.493	**0.494**	0.488	**0.504**
H@3	0.349	**0.355**	0.431	**0.445**
H@1	0.230	**0.234**	0.393	**0.402**

In the experiment, node attribute characteristics are added to the ConvE model. Considering the influence of the complexity of relations on attribute features learning, we choose FB15k-237 and WN18RR for our ablation experiment. The parameters of ConvE keep consistent during the experiment. As illustrated in Table 3, compared to the original model, the variant model that adds attribute features has improved on MRR and H@N metrics. Besides we conclude their convergence performance on the two data sets as shown in Fig. 4. On WN18RR, ConvE begins to learn quickly at the 50th epoch, then it becomes stable at the 100th epoch, and finally converges at the 400th epoch. As for the variant, it is in a fast learning phase during the 25th epoch and the 50th epoch, after which it becomes stable and finally converges at the 200th epoch. As for convergence performance on FB15K-237, there is no significant difference between the two models, but ConvE is slightly faster than the variant in learning.

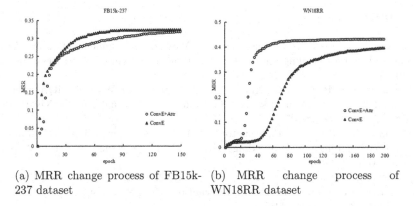

(a) MRR change process of FB15k-237 dataset   (b) MRR change process of WN18RR dataset

Fig. 4. MRR value change process in the ablation experiment

Therefore, in a knowledge graph with simple relations, the attribute information of the node can quickly capture the attribute characteristics according to the relations, thus promoting the representation learning for the entire model and accelerating its convergence. But in a knowledge graph with more complex relations, the variety of relations restrains the nodes from a quick learning for their characteristics of attribute. Compared with the original model, the learning speed of the variant decreases moderately, but they converge almost at the same time. In general, the variant model adding attribute features performs better on the link prediction task.

5 Conclusion

This paper proposes a knowledge graph embedding method AAGCN that integrates the characteristics of node attributes with relations. The model exploits the relations between nodes as their contextual information and utilizes an activation function to transform those contextual information into node attributes. It combines the graph neural network to aggregate neighbor information and takes a convolutional neural network as a feature extractor to perform the link prediction task. Experiments show that the AAGCN model is superior to other existing models in multiple metrics on the two benchmark datasets. At the same time, through ablation experiments, node attribute features are proven to enhance the representations of nodes. The attribute feature learning method has strong extensibility, and is able to accelerate the learning of the model on simple relational datasets.

Acknowledgements. The research is supported by The Natural Science Foundation of Guangdong Province (No. 2018A030313934).

References

1. Bordes, A., Usunier, N., Garcia-Duran, A., Weston, J., Yakhnenko, O.: Translating embeddings for modeling multi-relational data. Adv. Neural Inf. Process. Syst. **26** (2013)
2. Chen, W., Zha, H., Chen, Z., Xiong, W., Wang, H., Wang, W.: HybridQA: a dataset of multi-hop question answering over tabular and textual data. arXiv preprint arXiv:2004.07347 (2020)
3. Dettmers, T., Minervini, P., Stenetorp, P., Riedel, S.: Convolutional 2D knowledge graph embeddings. In: Proceedings of the AAAI Conference on Artificial Intelligence, vol. 32 (2018)
4. Gilmer, J., Schoenholz, S.S., Riley, P.F., Vinyals, O., Dahl, G.E.: Neural message passing for quantum chemistry. In: International Conference on Machine Learning, pp. 1263–1272. PMLR (2017)
5. Guo, Q., et al.: A survey on knowledge graph-based recommender systems. IEEE Trans. Knowl. Data Eng. **34**, 3549–3568 (2020)
6. Hamilton, W., Ying, Z., Leskovec, J.: Inductive representation learning on large graphs. In: Proceedings of the 31st International Conference on Neural Information Processing Systems (2017)
7. Han, X., Wang, L.: A novel document-level relation extraction method based on BERT and entity information. IEEE Access **8**, 96912–96919 (2020)
8. Ji, G., He, S., Xu, L., Liu, K., Zhao, J.: Knowledge graph embedding via dynamic mapping matrix. In: Proceedings of the 53rd Annual Meeting of the Association for Computational Linguistics and the 7th International Joint Conference on Natural Language Processing (volume 1: Long papers), pp. 687–696 (2015)
9. Jiang, X., Wang, Q., Wang, B.: Adaptive convolution for multi-relational learning. In: Proceedings of the 2019 Conference of the North American Chapter of the Association for Computational Linguistics: Human Language Technologies, Volume 1 (Long and Short Papers), pp. 978–987 (2019)
10. Kaur, P., Pannu, H.S., Malhi, A.K.: Comparative analysis on cross-modal information retrieval: a review. Comput. Sci. Rev. **39**, 100336 (2021)
11. Kipf, T.N., Welling, M.: Semi-supervised classification with graph convolutional networks. arXiv preprint arXiv:1609.02907 (2016)
12. Lin, Y., Liu, Z., Sun, M., Liu, Y., Zhu, X.: Learning entity and relation embeddings for knowledge graph completion. In: Twenty-Ninth AAAI Conference on Artificial Intelligence (2015)
13. Lu, J., Tan, L., Jiang, H.: Review on convolutional neural network (CNN) applied to plant leaf disease classification. Agriculture **11**(8), 707 (2021)
14. Lyu, S., Chen, H.: Relation classification with entity type restriction. In: Findings of the Association for Computational Linguistics: ACL-IJCNLP 2021, pp. 390–395 (2021)
15. Nguyen, D.Q., Nguyen, T.D., Nguyen, D.Q., Phung, D.: A novel embedding model for knowledge base completion based on convolutional neural network. arXiv preprint arXiv:1712.02121 (2017)
16. Nickel, M., Rosasco, L., Poggio, T.: Holographic embeddings of knowledge graphs. In: Proceedings of the AAAI Conference on Artificial Intelligence, vol. 30 (2016)
17. Schlichtkrull, M., Kipf, T.N., Bloem, P., van den Berg, R., Titov, I., Welling, M.: Modeling relational data with graph convolutional networks. In: Gangemi, A., et al. (eds.) ESWC 2018. LNCS, vol. 10843, pp. 593–607. Springer, Cham (2018). https://doi.org/10.1007/978-3-319-93417-4_38

18. Shang, C., Tang, Y., Huang, J., Bi, J., He, X., Zhou, B.: End-to-end structure-aware convolutional networks for knowledge base completion. In: Proceedings of the AAAI Conference on Artificial Intelligence, vol. 33, pp. 3060–3067 (2019)
19. Trouillon, T., Welbl, J., Riedel, S., Gaussier, É., Bouchard, G.: Complex embeddings for simple link prediction. In: International Conference on Machine Learning, pp. 2071–2080. PMLR (2016)
20. Vashishth, S., Sanyal, S., Nitin, V., Talukdar, P.: Composition-based multi-relational graph convolutional networks. arXiv preprint arXiv:1911.03082 (2019)
21. Wang, Z., Zhang, J., Feng, J., Chen, Z.: Knowledge graph embedding by translating on hyperplanes. In: Proceedings of the AAAI Conference on Artificial Intelligence. vol. 28 (2014)
22. Yang, B., Yih, W.t., He, X., Gao, J., Deng, L.: Embedding entities and relations for learning and inference in knowledge bases. arXiv preprint arXiv:1412.6575 (2014)
23. Zhou, J.: Embedding entities and relations for learning and inference in knowledge bases. arXiv preprint arXiv:1412.6575 (2014)
24. Zhou, S., et al.: Interactive recommender system via knowledge graph-enhanced reinforcement learning. In: Proceedings of the 43rd International ACM SIGIR Conference on Research and Development in Information Retrieval, pp. 179–188 (2020)

Multi-subspace Attention Graph Pooling

Yanwen Guo[1] and Yu Cao[2(✉)]

[1] Faculty of Engineering, The Hong Kong Polytechnic University, Hong Kong, China
[2] School of Computer Science, The University of Sydney, Sydney, NSW, Australia
ycao8647@uni.sydney.edu.au

Abstract. To effectively learn from different perspectives of a graph, we propose a new pooling mechanism based on joint attention scores of different representation subspaces of the graph, which we refer to as multi-head attention graph pooling. Instead of performing a single attention function over a graph, we propose to perform multiple attention functions that leverage information from different representation subspaces of both node features and graph topology. Each attention function is trained to attend to information from different representation subspaces, while the aggregation of attentions can exchange information globally on the entire graph. The results in graph classification experiments demonstrate that our method is comparable and often surpasses current state-of-the-art baselines on the benchmark datasets with fewer parameters (We release our code at https://github.com/caoyu-noob/MAGPool).

Keywords: Graph pooling · Graph neural network · Multi-subspace · Graph classification · Attention

1 Introduction

Large amounts of structured data exist in the non-Euclidean domain, such as social networks and biological networks, and these data can be represented by nodes and edges within graphs [8,12]. Recently, with the rapid development of graph neural networks (GNNs) [5,20], the recognition abilities of graph-structured data have improved dramatically. The general approach to realize this is regarding the underlying graph as a computation graph, learning neural network primitives that generate individual node embeddings by passing, transforming, and aggregating node features across the graph [15]. The generated node embeddings can then be used as input to any differentiable prediction layer for node classification [17] or link prediction [27], where the whole model is trained in an end-to-end fashion.

One core challenge of GNNs is how to develop graph pooling (downsampling) architectures. In CNNs, the pooling layers exploit the shift-invariance (also known as stationary) property and compositionality of grid-structured data, resulting in a satisfactory performance with fewer parameters. Thus recent studies apply pooling operation to graphs to attain scaled-down ones via GNNs. Defferrard et al. [9] and Rhee et al. [23] adopted the pooling methods considering

© The Author(s), under exclusive license to Springer Nature Switzerland AG 2022
S. Khanna et al. (Eds.): PRICAI 2022, LNCS 13630, pp. 114–126, 2022.
https://doi.org/10.1007/978-3-031-20865-2_9

only the graph topology. Some improvements were proposed by utilizing node features to obtain a smaller graph representation [7, 15, 36]. Recently, several innovative methods learn hierarchical representations of graphs [2, 6, 14, 35], or introduce self-attention that involves both node features and graph topology [21].

Different feature sets may characterize independent information dissimilarly. However, current graph pooling methods neglect such diverse representation subspaces and only focus on the global feature, which cannot well characterize complex linkage among graph nodes [18]. Since recent works already showed impressive results using the subspace of features for natural language [29] and computer vision tasks [13, 37], leveraging information from different views. Therefore, it also has a great potential for graph neural network modeling.

In this paper, we propose a new graph pooling method, referred to as **Multi-subspace Attention Graph Pooling** (MAGPool), leveraging information from different representation subspaces of both node features and graph topology. Similar to SAGPool [21], the attention mechanism is exploited to distinguish the nodes that should be retained from those being dropped. However, the key difference is that multiple representation subspaces of a graph are considered and the model learns various attention functions. Each attention function is trained to attend to information from the corresponding subspace, obtaining the attention score that is able to fully reflect the different perspectives of a graph. Both node features and graph topology are considered in multi-subspace attention since different graph convolutions are utilized to obtain the attention scores. Moreover, we investigate a series of aggregation mechanisms of attention that is able to exchange information globally across the entire graph.

Our main contribution is the multi-attention for graph pooling to drop and retain nodes. We also introduce a refined attention aggregation mechanism to generate node ranking scores. Experiments on 7 benchmark graph classification datasets show that our model outperforms strong baselines under the global pooling architecture, while it also works better for the hierarchical pooling architecture under most conditions and retains comparable under the rest. Besides, our model requires fewer parameters than other trainable methods, benefiting from the smaller cost of each sub-module from multiple subspaces.

2   Related Work

Graph Neural Networks. GNNs have been applied to a wide range of tasks, such as link prediction [26], graph classification [7] and so on. A wide variety kinds of GNN models have been proposed to handle these tasks, including models inspired by recurrent neural networks [16, 22, 25], convolutional neural networks [3, 5, 9, 20] and loopy belief propagation [7]. Graph Convolutional Networks (GCNs) are the most common ones, using central node to aggregate features directly from adjacent nodes via sampling, aggregation or attention mechanism [1, 17, 30].

Feature Subspace. Multi-head attention is investigated in NLP [29, 32], which splits the input information into subspaces using linear transformation and each of them poses various importance to the input. A similar idea is also used in multi-view clustering converting raw feature into multiple perspectives [13,37].

Graph Pooling. Similar to pooling layers in CNNs, graph pooling methods also aim to obtain coarsened graph features as well as stacking deep layers, but both node features and topology of the graph need to be considered. Graph pooling methods can be defined as **topology-based**, **global**, or **hierarchical**.

In **topology-based pooling**, only the topological structure is considered while node features are neglected. Related works include Graclus [10] that implements equivalent spectral clustering based on a weighted kernel k-means objective. Then the obtained graphs can be combined with GNNs [9,23].

Global pooling methods use summation or neural networks to pool all node representations after information propagation. Gilmer et al. [15] and Set2Set [31] utilize GNNs as message passing schemes to obtain the entire graph representations. SortPool [36] sorts node features based on their graph structural importance, where the sorted results are used for downstream tasks.

In **hierarchical pooling**, models capture multi-rank information from feature- or topology-based node assignments. DiffPool [35] employs a learnable soft assignment matrix in each layer along with GNN for clustering. MinCut-Pool [2] further extends this as a K-way normalized MinCUT problem by introducing a new auxiliary objective. gPool [14] adaptively selects partial nodes to form a smaller graph based on their ranking scores from on a trainable projection vector without taking graph topology into account. SAGPool [21] makes up for this deficiency through a node selection based on scores from GNN self-attention.

Different from previous works, we seek to learn different representation subspaces of both nodes and the graph topology via multiple attention modules.

3   Methodology

In this section, we describe the multi-subspace attention graph pooling whose framework is shown in Fig. 1. The most distinguishable property is that attention weights on different perspectives of graphs attend to produce the mask. Additionally, instead of a fixed pooling operation, our method involves an aggregation function, such as max and mean, to enable additional flexibility in designing a method and can thus adapt to the problem at hand.

3.1   Preliminaries

Graph. We present a graph G as $(X, \tilde{A})$, where $X \in \mathbb{R}^{n \times d}$ is the node features with feature dimension d, and $\tilde{A} \in \{0,1\}^{n \times n}$ is the adjacency matrix.

Graph Neural Networks (GNNs). We consider GNNs that have the following "message-passing" framework for node embeddings after after l iterations:

$$X^l = m(\tilde{A}, X^{l-1}; \theta^{(l)}), \tag{1}$$

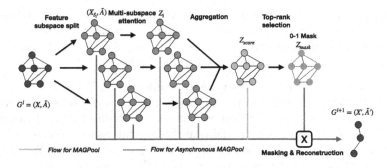

Fig. 1. The framework of **M**ulti-subspace **A**ttention **G**raph **Pool**ing (MAGPool). The flow of MAGPool is indicated by yellow lines, while red lines for its variant, Asynchronous MAGPool. The input will be split into feature subspaces during pooling.

where m is the message propagation function, which depends on the adjacency matrix $\tilde{A}$), trainable parameters $\theta^{(l)}$, and the node embeddings X^{l-1} from the previous iteration. The function m can be implemented in different ways.

Attention. Following [21], self-attention score Z is based on the graph convolution network (GCN) of [20] and can be calculated as follows,

$$Z = \text{Att}(X, \tilde{A}) = \sigma(\tilde{D}^{-\frac{1}{2}} \tilde{A} \tilde{D}^{-\frac{1}{2}} X \theta), \tag{2}$$

where σ is an activation function (e.g. softmax), $\tilde{D} \in \mathbb{R}^{n \times n}$ is the graph degree matrix, and $\theta \in \mathbb{R}^{d \times 1}$ is the trainable parameter of a single layer.

3.2   Pooling via Multi-subspace Attention

We define our attention pooling blocks based on exploiting node features of a graph. Rather than treating the graph integrally, we use different parts of node features and graph topology to concurrently affect the pooling process. , leveraging information from various representation subspaces. For this purpose, we adopt independent attention modules to better reflect each subspace, whose features are combined in node ranking to determine the retained nodes in pooling. Finally, node embeddings are recovered for the following processing.

Multi-subspace Attention. Given a graph $G^l = (X, \tilde{A})$ obtained from the lth layer, which presents a set of d-dimensional vectors from n nodes, we first define two kinds of subspace splitting strategies as follows.

1) Raw Split (raw): Each feature subspace X_{S_i} only contains partial of original feature values between a_i-th to b_i-th dimension, while $\tilde{A}_{S_i}$ is the same as $\tilde{A}$.

$$X_{S_i}^l = X^l[:, a_i : b_i] \in \mathbb{R}^{n \times (b_i - a_i)} \ (0 \le a_i < b_i \le d), \tag{3}$$

where $[:, a_i : b_i]$ means only values in the second dimension whose indices are among the interval $[a_i, b_i)$ are retained. Simply, a general way to determine a_i and b_i is evenly splitting, where we can define a_i as $d/H*(i-1)$ and b_i as $d/H*i$, $i \in \{1, 2, \cdots, H\}$, and H is the total subspace number.

2) Transform Split (transform): A trainable matrix $W_i^t \in \mathbb{R}^{d \times d_{S_i}}$ can be used to transform the original node features into corresponding subspace via $X_{S_i} = XW_i^t$, where d_{S_i} is the desired feature dimension of the i-th subspace. And the adjacency matrix also remains unchanged for each subspace.

Based on each of above ways, we construct H subspace graphs $\{(X_{S_1}, \tilde{A}), \cdots, (X_{S_H}, \tilde{A})\}$, which cover the entire feature space. Each subspace graph shares the same structure as G but has different feature subsets X_{S_i}.

As shown in Fig. 1, each subspace graph is processed independently. For $(X_{S_i}, \tilde{A})$, we calculate its attention results $Z_i \in \mathbb{R}^{n \times d_{S_i}}$ by

$$Z_i = Z_i' \odot X_{S_i}, Z_i' = \text{Att}_i(X_{S_i}, \tilde{A}) \in \mathbb{R}^{n \times 1}. \tag{4}$$

Here $\odot$ is broadcast element-wise product. Att_i is the attention function that takes a portion of node features and performs GCN-based self-attention to obtain the weights. Therefore, we have a series of attention output results $Z_{multi} = \{Z_1, \cdots, Z_H\}$ and each of them only contains partial information of X,

Node Ranking. In order to coarsen the graph, we need to retain some nodes while abandoning the rest based on ranking scores from Z_{multi}. A common approach to combine multiple values is applying an aggregation function f_{agg} such as dimension-wise average or maximization, which can be described as

$$Z_{agg} = f_{agg}(Z_{multi}) \in \mathbb{R}^{n \times d_{S_i}}. \tag{5}$$

Then we can obtain the importance scores $Z_{score} \in \mathbb{R}^{n \times 1}$ for all nodes via another GCN-based attention Att_{score} from Z_{agg}, based on both graph features and topology. The indices of retained nodes in the graph can be determined by

$$idx = \text{TOP-RANK}(Z_{score}, \lceil \rho n \rceil), Z_{score} = \text{Att}_{score}(Z_{agg}, \tilde{A}). \tag{6}$$

Here, TOP-RANK is the function that returns the indices of the top $\lceil \rho n \rceil$ values in Z_{score}, denoting the related node indices. ρ is a parameter for pooling ratio.

Graph Pooling. It is straightforward to use the global ranking score Z_{score} as the attention mask Z_{mask} on each subspace, (yellow lines in Fig. 1). This offers nodes with their importance as well as makes the procedure differentiable.

$$Z_{mask} = Z_{score}[idx, :] \in \mathbb{R}^{\rho n \times 1}, X_{S_i}' = X_{S_i}[idx, :] \odot Z_{mask}, \tilde{A}' = \tilde{A}[idx, idx], \tag{7}$$

where $[idx, :]$ means row-wise (node-wise) indexing on the matrix using idx, while $[idx, idx]$ is indexing on both dimensions.

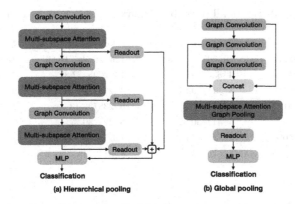

Fig. 2. Applications of MAGPool: (a)hierarchical pooling, and (b)global pooling.

We also propose another pooling variant, **Asynchronous MAGPool** (AMAGPool). The mask for each subspace is obtained independently based on the corresponding sub-attention results in Eq. 4, indicated as the red lines in Fig. 1.

$$Z_{i|mask} = Z_i[idx, :] \in \mathbb{R}^{\rho n \times d_{S_i}}. \tag{8}$$

Then the masking process is similar to Eq. 7, but it poses a fine-grained importance for each subspace than the former one.

Node Reconstruction. After getting the node features in different subspaces of a coarsened graph, we need to recovered them into the original feature space for the following procedures. In **raw** splitting, they can be simply concatenated in the feature dimension, like $X' = [X'_{S_1}; \cdots ; X'_{S_H}]$. While another linear transformation is applied for each subspace under **trans** splitting, and then added together $X' = \sum_{i=1}^{H} X'_{S_i} W_i^r$, where $W_i^r \in \mathbb{R}^{d_{S_i} \times d}$ is learnable. Note that d_{S_i} satisfy $d = \sum_{i=1}^{H} d_{S_i}$ to ensure that the reconstruction can be processed.

3.3 Deep Neural Networks with Pooling

We consider two common architectures for graph classification utilizing the proposed pooling method: hierarchical pooling architecture and global pooling architecture.

Hierarchical Pooling Architecture. We implement the hierarchical pooling architecture based on [6]. As shown in Fig. 2(a), there are three graph convolutional network (GCN) layers and each one is followed by a multi-subspace attention graph pooling layer. The subspace splitting is applied before each GCN layer, making it also in a multi-subspace pattern. Besides, there is a readout layer for the node feature vector X'_i of the ith node from each block to obtain a fixed-dimension feature, which is defined as

$$F = \text{concat}(\frac{1}{\rho n} \sum_{i=1}^{\rho n} X'_i \ , \ \max_{i=1}^{\rho n} X'_i) \in \mathbb{R}^{2d}, \tag{9}$$

Table 1. Statistics of all seven benchmark datasets in our experiments.

Dataset	Graph num	Range/Avg. node num	Range/Avg. edge num	|Class|	Node label
DD	1178	30~5478/284.32	126~28.5k/715.66	2	√
PROTEINS	1113	4~620/39.06	10~2098/72.82	2	√
NCI1	4110	3~111/29.87	4~238/32.30	2	√
NCI109	4127	4~111/29.68	6~238/32.13	2	√
MUTAGENICITY	4337	4~417/30.32	6~224/30.77	2	√
COLLAB	5000	31~491/74.49	120~80.2k/2457.78	3	×
REDDIT-BINARY	2000	5~3781/429.63	8~8142/497.75	2	×

Finally, summation is applied over outputs of all readout layers to generate an entire graph representation that is passed to the MLP for classification.

Global Pooling Architecture. We implement the global pooling architecture based on [36]. As shown in Fig. 2(b), there are three GCN layers, with a multi-subspace attention graph pooling layer at the end of them. The node embeddings from three GCN layers are concatenated together into a new node representations $X' \in \mathbb{R}^{n \times 3d}$, and fed to the pooling layer. There is also a readout operation employed as described in Eq. 9, resulting in the input of MLP with shape $\mathbb{R}^{6d}$.

4   Experiments and Analysis

4.1   Datasets and Baselines

We focus on graph classification problems to validate the effectiveness of our proposed approach. The following seven graph classification datasets are considered, and their statistics are shown in Table 1.

DD [11,28] is made up of non-redundant protein structures, in which nodes indicate types of amino acid while edges reflect whether the distances are within 6 Ångstorm. A graph label denotes whether it is enzymatic or non-enzymatic.

PROTEINS [4,11] is another protein structure dataset, where graphs are the secondary structures from DD and labels still indicate enzyme or non-enzyme.

NCI1 and **NCI109** [33] are datasets of chemical compounds for classifying the activity against cancers. Nodes represent atoms, while edges for chemical bonds.

Mutagenicity [24] contains different molecular structure graphs for mutagenicity classification. Nodes and edges have the same meaning as NCI1.

COLLAB and **REDDIT-BINARY** [34] are both social network datasets, where the first one reflects collaboration of researchers and the second one for comment relations between Reddit users. The graph labels reflect the research areas or discussion subreddit, and no node label is provided.

Methods under two architectures, global and hierarchical, are included.

AvgPool is a baseline global method that simply averages representation of all nodes as the input of a classification MLP.

DGCNN [36] is a global method which stacks GNN for several layers and uses the combined output from layers as the gist for final sorting to retain nodes.

DiffPool [35] is a hierarchical method. It maps the original nodes to a set of clusters via a learnable assignment matrix. It stacks GNN layers and pooling layers iteratively to form multiple representations. In the reference implementation, the cluster size is set to 25% of the maximum number of nodes.

gPool [14] is a hierarchical method. It adaptively selects some nodes to form a smaller graph based on a trainable projection vector. But it does not take graph topology into account. In the hierarchical pooling setting, MAGPool has the same K number of output nodes as gPool.

SAGPool [21] can be used for both global and hierarchical pooling. It uses a GCN self-attention to distinguish between the nodes that should be dropped or retained, involving both node features and graph topology.

Table 2. The average accuracy and standard deviation of 10-fold validation experiments with 20 random seeds on 7 datasets. (Upper/lower part: global/hierarchical pooling architecture. The best two results of each architecture are in **bold font**. Subscript g: global architecture, h: hierarchical architecture, $*$: transform subspace splitting.)

Models	DD	PROTEINS	NCI1	NCI109	MUTAGEN	COLLAB	REDDIT
AvgPool	71.8±3.4	71.3±3.1	71.1±3.2	69.2±2.9	**78.7±2.6**	67.6±2.1	79.1±6.9
DGCNN	73.4±3.7	72.7±2.9	**74.0±3.1**	**73.6±2.3**	74.5±2.8	65.7±2.4	77.9±4.4
SAGPool$_g$	75.9±3.1	73.0±2.9	73.2±3.3	**73.1±2.1**	76.1±2.2	67.7±2.0	82.6±4.0
MAGPool$_g$	**77.6±3.1**	**75.2±2.8**	**73.8±3.0**	71.7±2.4	**79.2±2.2**	69.6±1.9	**84.8±3.6**
AMAGPool$_g$	74.8±4.0	75.0±3.1	71.8±3.7	69.32±2.8	76.7±3.0	**69.7±2.4**	81.7±4.2
MAGPool$_g$*	**78.8±2.9**	**75.3±3.0**	70.9±4.2	66.5±5.2	76.3±3.4	68.5±2.0	**83.1±4.2**
AMAGPool$_g$*	72.7±3.8	73.9±3.4	63.3±2.1	64.6±2.0	70.2±5.4	66.3±2.2	80.4±5.0
DiffPool	**78.3±3.0**	70.7±3.2	65.2±2.9	64.5±2.4	**77.2±2.9**	**73.5±1.6**	**85.9±2.9**
gPool	74.3±3.9	72.7±3.5	68.0±4.1	67.1±3.6	71.9±3.1	72.3±2.0	80.4±4.9
SAGPool$_h$	76.8±3.2	73.7±3.1	**70.3±3.6**	**69.8±2.8**	74.5±2.5	69.1±1.7	84.9±3.4
MAGPool$_h$	**77.7±3.2**	75.4±2.9	**71.4±4.0**	**67.5±5.4**	**77.7±2.5**	71.9±1.7	**86.7±3.2**
AMAGPool$_h$	76.4±3.8	**75.6±3.1**	69.2±4.7	66.1±5.3	75.2±2.8	68.8±2.2	83.9±3.8
MAGPool$_h$*	74.6±4.0	75.3±3.3	63.6±2.3	64.5±1.5	74.2±4.2	**72.6±1.9**	85.8±4.1
AMAGPool$_h$*	72.7±3.6	75.2±3.0	63.4±2.3	64.6±1.9	72.5±3.7	69.5±1.9	80.9±4.5

4.2 Setup

We evaluate all methods on the above seven benchmark datasets. MAGPool and its variant AMAGPool are applied in both global and hierarchical architecture. Two subspace splitting methods, **raw** and **transform** are also applied.

Similar to previous work, to better show the training stability of models, we employ 10-fold cross-validation. And each 10-fold experiment is run 20 times using different seeds. Adam optimizer [19] is used to train the model with batch size as 128 for maximum $2k$ epochs. An early stopping strategy is also employed on the validation set when loss does not decrease for 50 epochs. The hyperparameters were determined via grid search, where the learning rate is 5e-4, the GCN has 3 layers whose hidden state size d is 128, the head number H is 4 and the keep ratio ρ in pooling is 0.5, while the aggregation function f_{agg} is Max.

4.3   Main Results

The average accuracy and standard deviation on 7 datasets are shown in Table 2. Obviously, our proposed method outperforms baselines on most datasets using the same architecture. Among the variants of our method, MAGPool is the most stable one, using raw subspace split and single masks for different subspaces. It means that the local subgraph masks are not as effective as overall scores, because they obtain more comprehensive information about the entire graph. The **transform** subspace splitting is weaker than **raw** unless it is used in graphs with dense connections, e.g. COLLAB, as the extra trainable matrices may introduce more uncertainty which cannot be well-trained via simple samples.

Table 3. Average accuracy of ablation study on two datasets.

Variants	DD		PROTEINS	
	Global	Hiera	Global	Hiera
MAGPool	77.54	77.71	75.16	75.38
-no-att	77.07	76.78	74.78	74.65
-mlp-att	76.43	76.75	74.50	74.44
-no-score	76.85	77.05	73.48	73.85
-mlp-score	77.12	77.28	73.93	73.63
-no-filter	76.82	76.37	**75.05**	**75.42**
-no-inter	–	74.25	–	74.40

Table 4. The average accuracy of global and hierarchical MAGPool on two datasets when using different aggregation functions.

Agg. Variants	DD		PROTEINS	
	Global	Hiera	Global	Hiera
Max	77.54	**77.71**	75.16	**75.38**
Avg	**77.90**	77.52	**75.27**	75.12
Min	77.06	77.30	74.62	74.87
Linear	76.93	77.46	74.64	74.93

Despite being a powerful baseline, SAGPool does not consider subspaces nor a refined approach for ranking scores, limiting its performance. DiffPool is another competitive baseline for complicated graphs such as DD and COLLAB as it realizes clustering via more parameters. But MAGPool shows comparable performance under these conditions with significantly higher accuracy on simpler graphs. Generally speaking, the global architecture tends to perform on smaller graphs, like **PROTEINS, NCI1, NCI109**, even the most intuitive AvgPool. As the average of a few nodes is efficient enough to represent the graph. On the contrary, the hierarchical architecture is stronger on complicated samples from **DD, COLLAB**, indicating more refined features are essential for such graphs.

4.4   Ablation Study

In order to demonstrate the contribution of each component, ablation study is conducted on **DD** and **PROTEINS**, involving both large-scale and small-scale graphs. The results are shown in Table 3, where the base model is MAGPool with global or hierarchical (HIERA) architectures. *-no-att* means no attention nor mask will be applied in Eq. 4, *-mlp-att* means an MLP is used in function Att_i instead of GCN. Similarly, the score function is removed from Eq. 6 and Z_{agg} is directly used for ranking in *-no-score*, and *-mlp-score* denotes using an MLP in Eq. 6. All nodes will be remained in pooling under *-no-filter*, and *-no-inter* indicates that no intermediate readout layers is included and only the output from the final layer is used for prediction (not applicable for global pooling).

According to the results, removing attention or scoring function both affect performance. Using MLP to replace GCN also degenerates the accuracy since no edge information is involved. *-no-filter* has a very slight influence on PROTEINS, proving that coarsening small graphs is not so necessary as larger ones. Shortcut connections from intermediate layers are also verified to be essential since accuracy sees a noticeable drop under *-no-inter* (Figs. 3 and 4).

4.5   More Analysis

Effect of Aggregation Functions. We evaluate different aggregation functions f_{agg} used in Eq. 5, including Max (default), Avg, Min and Linear. Linear means using a trainable linear function to fuse Z_{multi}. Based on Table 4, we can found that Max is the best aggregation function for general usage. Avg is a bit superior to Max under global architecture while a bit worse for hierarchical pooling. Min and Linear result in performance degeneration compared to Max, despite the latter one introduces extra parameters.

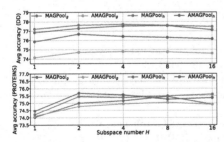

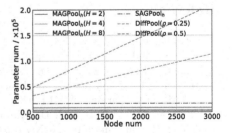

Fig. 3. The accuracy of hierarchical/global MAGPool/AMAGPool varies with subspace number H on two datasets (Upper: DD, lower: PROTEINS)

Fig. 4. Parameter quantities of methods vary with input node numbers. (ρ: the node preservation ratio.)

Influence of Subspace Number H. We further test different subspace numbers with fixed whole hidden dimension $d = 128$, whose results are illustrated in Fig. 4.4. Obviously, there is a noticeable promotion when increasing H from 1 to 2, proving that subspaces splitting benefits information extraction. But the performance seems to be saturated when further increasing H after 4, even sees drops when $H = 16$. It means more subspace may not result in a better effect as smaller feature dimensions cannot ensure comprehensive representation.

Model Complexity Analysis. Our proposed MAGPool has relatively lower complexity, benefiting from the subspace splitting. The parameter quantities of a single pooling in different methods are shown in Fig. 4.4. Compared to DiffPool, the scale of MAGPool are graph-invariant, while the assignment matrix S^l in DiffPool is $\mathbb{R}^{n_l \times n_{l+1}}$, depending on the node numbers. Although SAGPool$_h$ also has a constant parameter number, it still has more parameters than MAGPool$_h$. In addition, MAGPool is also faster, as multi-subspace results in fewer matrix operations and makes parallel computing possible. According to our experiments, the speed of MAGPool$_h$ is **3.08× the speed of** SAGPool and **8.71× the speed of** DiffPool in average on 7 datasets using one P40 GPU.

5   Conclusion

In this paper, we proposed a novel graph pooling method, MAGPool. MAGPool has multiple attention modules that are trained to leverage representations from different subspaces of a graph, capturing complex linkage forming mechanisms, and thereby improving performance. Experimental results demonstrate that our method is comparable and often surpasses strong baselines on several graph classification benchmarks, using fewer parameters and less computation time.

References

1. Bahdanau, D., Cho, K., Bengio, Y.: Neural machine translation by jointly learning to align and translate. arXiv preprint arXiv:1409.0473 (2014)
2. Bianchi, F.M., Grattarola, D., Alippi, C.: Spectral clustering with graph neural networks for graph pooling. In: Proceedings of the 37th International Conference on Machine Learning, ACM (2020)
3. Bianchi, F.M., Grattarola, D., Alippi, C., Livi, L.: Graph neural networks with convolutional arma filters. arXiv preprint arXiv:1901.01343 (2019)
4. Borgwardt, K.M., Ong, C.S., Schönauer, S., Vishwanathan, S., Smola, A.J., Kriegel, H.P.: Protein function prediction via graph kernels. Bioinformatics **21**(suppl_1), i47–i56 (2005)
5. Bruna, J., Zaremba, W., Szlam, A., LeCun, Y.: Spectral networks and locally connected networks on graphs. arXiv preprint arXiv:1312.6203 (2013)
6. Cangea, C., Veličković, P., Jovanović, N., Kipf, T., Liò, P.: Towards sparse hierarchical graph classifiers. arXiv preprint arXiv:1811.01287 (2018)

7. Dai, H., Dai, B., Song, L.: Discriminative embeddings of latent variable models for structured data. In: International Conference on Machine Learning, pp. 2702–2711 (2016)
8. Davidson, E.H., et al.: A genomic regulatory network for development. Science **295**(5560), 1669–1678 (2002)
9. Defferrard, M., Bresson, X., Vandergheynst, P.: Convolutional neural networks on graphs with fast localized spectral filtering. In: Advances in Neural Information Processing Systems, pp. 3844–3852 (2016)
10. Dhillon, I.S., Guan, Y., Kulis, B.: Weighted graph cuts without eigenvectors a multilevel approach. IEEE Trans. Pattern Anal. Mach. Intell. **29**(11), 1944–1957 (2007)
11. Dobson, P.D., Doig, A.J.: Distinguishing enzyme structures from non-enzymes without alignments. J. Mol. Biol. **330**(4), 771–783 (2003)
12. Duvenaud, D.K., et al.: Convolutional networks on graphs for learning molecular fingerprints. In: Advances in Neural Information Processing Systems, pp. 2224–2232 (2015)
13. Gao, H., Nie, F., Li, X., Huang, H.: Multi-view subspace clustering. In: Proceedings of the IEEE International Conference on Computer Vision, pp. 4238–4246 (2015)
14. Gao, H., Ji, S.: Graph u-nets. arXiv preprint arXiv:1905.05178 (2019)
15. Gilmer, J., Schoenholz, S.S., Riley, P.F., Vinyals, O., Dahl, G.E.: Neural message passing for quantum chemistry. In: Proceedings of the 34th International Conference on Machine Learning, vol. 70, pp. 1263–1272. JMLR. org (2017)
16. Graves, A., Mohamed, A.R., Hinton, G.: Speech recognition with deep recurrent neural networks. In: 2013 IEEE International Conference on Acoustics, Speech and Signal Processing, pp. 6645–6649. IEEE (2013)
17. Hamilton, W., Ying, Z., Leskovec, J.: Inductive representation learning on large graphs. In: Advances in Neural Information Processing Systems, pp. 1024–1034 (2017)
18. Jackson, M.O.: Social and Economic Networks. Princeton University Press, Princeton (2010)
19. Kingma, D.P., Ba, J.: Adam: a method for stochastic optimization. arXiv preprint arXiv:1412.6980 (2014)
20. Kipf, T.N., Welling, M.: Semi-supervised classification with graph convolutional networks. arXiv preprint arXiv:1609.02907 (2016)
21. Lee, J., Lee, I., Kang, J.: Self-attention graph pooling. arXiv preprint arXiv: 1904.08082(2019)
22. Li, Y., Tarlow, D., Brockschmidt, M., Zemel, R.: Gated graph sequence neural networks. arXiv preprint arXiv:1511.05493 (2015)
23. Rhee, S., Seo, S., Kim, S.: Hybrid approach of relation network and localized graph convolutional filtering for breast cancer subtype classification. arXiv preprint arXiv:1711.05859 (2017)
24. Riesen, K., Bunke, H.: IAM graph database repository for graph based pattern recognition and machine learning. In: da Vitoria Lobo, N., et al. (eds.) SSPR /SPR 2008. LNCS, vol. 5342, pp. 287–297. Springer, Heidelberg (2008). https://doi.org/10.1007/978-3-540-89689-0_33
25. Scarselli, F., Gori, M., Tsoi, A.C., Hagenbuchner, M., Monfardini, G.: The graph neural network model. IEEE Trans. Neural Netw. **20**(1), 61–80 (2008)
26. Schlichtkrull, M., Kipf, T.N., Bloem, P., van den Berg, R., Titov, I., Welling, M.: Modeling relational data with graph convolutional networks. In: Gangemi, A., et al. (eds.) ESWC 2018. LNCS, vol. 10843, pp. 593–607. Springer, Cham (2018). https://doi.org/10.1007/978-3-319-93417-4_38

27. Schütt, K., Kindermans, P.J., Felix, H.E.S., Chmiela, S., Tkatchenko, A., Müller, K.R.: Schnet: a continuous-filter convolutional neural network for modeling quantum interactions. In: Advances in Neural Information Processing Systems, pp. 991–1001 (2017)
28. Shervashidze, N., Schweitzer, P., Leeuwen, E.J.V., Mehlhorn, K., Borgwardt, K.M.: Weisfeiler-Lehman graph kernels. J. Mach. Learn. Rese. **12**, 2539–2561 (2011)
29. Vaswani, A., et al.: Attention is all you need. In: Advances in Neural Information Processing Systems, pp. 5998–6008 (2017)
30. Veličković, P., Cucurull, G., Casanova, A., Romero, A., Lio, P., Bengio, Y.: Graph attention networks. arXiv preprint arXiv:1710.10903 (2017)
31. Vinyals, O., Bengio, S., Kudlur, M.: Order matters: sequence to sequence for sets. arXiv preprint arXiv:1511.06391 (2015)
32. Voita, E., Talbot, D., Moiseev, F., Sennrich, R., Titov, I.: Analyzing multi-head self-attention: specialized heads do the heavy lifting, the rest can be pruned. In: Proceedings of the 57th Annual Meeting of the Association for Computational Linguistics, pp. 5797–5808 (2019)
33. Wale, N., Watson, I.A., Karypis, G.: Comparison of descriptor spaces for chemical compound retrieval and classification. Knowl. Inf. Syst **14**(3), 347–375 (2008)
34. Yanardag, P., Vishwanathan, S.: Deep graph kernels. In: Proceedings of the 21th ACM SIGKDD International Conference on Knowledge Discovery and Data Mining, pp. 1365–1374. ACM (2015)
35. Ying, Z., You, J., Morris, C., Ren, X., Hamilton, W., Leskovec, J.: Hierarchical graph representation learning with differentiable pooling. In: Advances in Neural Information Processing Systems, pp. 4800–4810 (2018)
36. Zhang, M., Cui, Z., Neumann, M., Chen, Y.: An end-to-end deep learning architecture for graph classification. In: Thirty-Second AAAI Conference on Artificial Intelligence (2018)
37. Zhao, H., Ding, Z.: Multi-view clustering via deep matrix factorization. In: AAAI (2017)

Learning Temporal and Spatial Embedding for Temporal Knowledge Graph Reasoning

Yayao Zuo[✉], Yang Zhou, Zhengwei Liu, Jiayang Wu, and Minghao Zhan

Guangdong University of Technology, Guangzhou, China
yyzuo@gdut.edu.cn

Abstract. Temporal knowledge graphs store a large number of temporal facts that simulate the dynamic interactions of entities along the timeline. Since existing temporal knowledge graphs often suffer from incompleteness, it is crucial to build time-aware representation learning models that help to infer the missing temporal facts. However, most of the existing models for temporal knowledge graph reasoning focus on mining temporal associations between entities, and do not fully exploit spatial information contained in entities. To this end, we propose spatial-temporal network(ST-Net), a new representation learning model for temporal knowledge graphs, which has both temporal and spatial awareness capabilities. Specifically, ST-Net enriches the hidden features of entities by simultaneously fusing their temporal and spatial information. At the same time, we introduce the core idea of Copy-Generation Networks, which predicts future facts based on either the historical vocabulary or the whole entity vocabulary. We evaluate our proposed method via link prediction at future times on three benchmark datasets. Through extensive experiments, we demonstrate ST-Net has superior performance on the future link prediction tasks.

Keywords: Temporal knowledge graph · Representation learning · Link prediction

1 Introduction

Knowledge graphs (KGs) is widely used in natural language processing applications due to its ability to represent structured knowledge. However, most KGs suffers from incompleteness, which limits the performance and scope of KG applications to a certain extent. Therefore, it is an important task to predict the missing facts by KG reasoning. Recently, inference task has been expanded from KGs to a more challenging field: Temporal Knowledge Graphs(TKGs). The inference task on TKGs can be simply expressed as predicting missing object entity in query (subject entity, relation, ?, timestamp). Most of their researches focus on how to effectively integrate temporal information into the model. It's suggested by some researches that the traditional KG embedding method can be extended to TKGs [1,2]. However, they only pay attention to learning the potential representation of entity in a snapshot, while ignoring modeling the dynamic evolution

© The Author(s), under exclusive license to Springer Nature Switzerland AG 2022
S. Khanna et al. (Eds.): PRICAI 2022, LNCS 13630, pp. 127–138, 2022.
https://doi.org/10.1007/978-3-031-20865-2_10

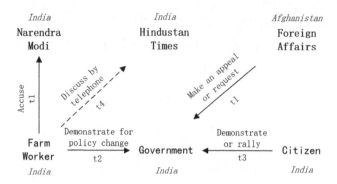

Fig. 1. Illustrates the process of ST-Net leveraging spatial information to predict future facts.

process of entity. Recently, some researchers have also conducted researches on the dynamic evolution of entity and relation [3–6], which combine historical information from previous snapshots.Another part of researchers try to enrich the potential representations of entity by incorporating multiple information [7–9], such as entity descriptions, event descriptions and uncertain information.

Inspired by this, we find that the above methods all ignore the importance of the spatial information (country, city, organization) attached to the entity. In fact, the occurrence of an event cannot be separated from spatial information, and the interaction between two entities also means the interaction between two spaces. Specifically, we found that the probability of entities in same event located in same space is 41.13% according to ICEWS18 dataset, which shows the importance of leveraging the spatial information contained in the entity to predict future facts.

To this end, we propose a innovative TKG representation learning model with both temporal and spatial perception. Mining the spatial information attached to the entity would help in fine-grained modeling of entity representation, and further strengthen the representation ability of entity embedding. At the same time, we introduce two inference modes in the copy generation network [6] to predict future facts from the historical vocabulary and the whole entity vocabulary. As shown in Fig. 1, after applying the spatial information, two nodes without interaction, *Farm Worker* and *Hindustan Times*, can be connected in the same space to pave the way for prediction.

We evaluated our proposed method on three benchmark datasets and the experimental results show that ST-Net is superior to the baseline model in link prediction task. The ablation experiment further proves that spatial information can help the model predict future facts better.

The main contributions of this work are as follows:

1. We propose a innovative TKG representation learning model ST-Net, which implements fine-grained modeling of entity representation by mining the spatial information attached to entity.

2. We introduce two inference modes in the Copy-Generation Networks [6], which predict future facts from the historical vocabulary and the whole entity vocabulary respectively.
3. We conduct extensive experiments on three public TKG datasets and demonstrate the effectiveness of ST-Net in link prediction.

2 Related Work

We discuss three relevant research directions. Since there is massive work in each direction, we can only select representative and closely related ones to elaborate.

2.1 Static Knowledge Graph Embeddings

Without considering temporal facts, researchers have made passable progress in KG embedding, which Ji et al. [10] summarizes. A classic class of models is translation model (TransE and its variants) [11–13], which leverages a distance-based scoring function to measure the reasonableness of facts. The other is the semantic matching model (such as ComplEx [14], DistMult [15], etc.), which uses a similarity-based scoring function and measure the plausibility of facts through semantic matching. Recently, some methods based on deep neural networks (such as R-GCN [16], ConvE [17], RSN [18], etc.) have emerged, which utilize CNN, RNN, and graph neural networks (GCN, R-GCN, etc.) to help models learn embedding of entity and relation. However, these methods cannot capture temporal facts.

2.2 Temporal Knowledge Graph Embeddings

TKG embedding incorporates timestamp of facts into the learning process. Some researchers attempt to extend the static KGs directly to the field of TKGs. TTransE [1] is an extension of TransE, which simply integrates time information into the scoring function; HyTE [2] replaces the unit normal vector of the hyperplane projection in TransH with a time-specific normal vector. Other researchers focus on the dynamic evolution of entity and relation. Know-Evolve [3] models the occurrence of facts as a temporal point process to learn non-linearly evolving entity representation over time; Goel et al. [4] provides the embedding of an entity at any point in time by equipping the static model with a diachronic entity embedding function. However, none of these methods correlate snapshots that have occurred in history.

To solve the problem that the model cannot capture the long-term dependency of facts, the autoregressive model is proposed. Jin et al. [5] modeled the TKGs in the way of autoregressive, that is, the snapshot at T timestamp depends on the historical snapshot before T; Han et al. [19] leverages continuous temporal embedding to encode the temporal and structure information of historical snapshots; Zhu et al. [6] utilizes the recurrence rule of facts and combines two inferring modes to predict future facts from historical vocabulary and whole entity vocabulary respectively.

2.3 Embedding with Auxiliary Information

More recent attempts have been made to combine multimodal information with structured information in KGs to promote more effective knowledge representation. SSP [8] provides more precise semantic embedding for entity and relation by projecting triples and text descriptions into semantic subspaces. Glean [7] leverages graph neural networks to fuse unstructured event descriptions and structured data from TKGs to enrich the hidden features of event participants. The uncertain KG embedding model proposed by Chen et al. [9] incorporates the confidence scores of uncertain relation facts when learning embedding. Influenced by this, we try to fuse the spatial information contained in the entity with the structured information of the TKGs. As we know, this is the first work to incorporate spatial information into TKG representation learning.

3 Spatial-Temporal Network

In this section, we start with the notations for building our model and problem definition, and then introduce the model architecture as well as its training and inference procedures in detail. Figure 2 illustrates an overview of ST-Net reasoning process. ST-Net can be decomposed into 3 sub-modules: Query Vectorization, Capture History Vocabulary, and Copy-Generation Mode.

3.1 Notations

TKGs consists of temporal facts, each of which can be simply described as subject and object entity $s \in \mathcal{E}$ and $o \in \mathcal{E}$ have a relation $r \in \mathcal{R}$ at timestamp $t \in \mathcal{T}$, denoted as quadruple (s,r,o,t), where $\mathcal{E}$, $\mathcal{R}$ represent the vocabularies corresponding to the entities and relations respectively, and $\mathcal{T}$ is the set of timestamps. The boldface $\mathbf{s,r,o,t}$ represent the corresponding embedding vectors. A TKG can be divided into a set of snapshots $\{G_1, G_2, \cdots, G_{t_k}\}$ according to the timestamps, where G_t is a snapshot of the TKG at time step t, containing all temporal facts at time step t. For each subject entity and relation pair at timestamp t_k, we define a delimited subset of $\mathcal{E}$ specific to (s, r, t_k) as $\mathbf{H}_{t_k}^{(s,r)}$, namely historical vocabulary for (s, r, t_k), which contains all object entities in temporal facts with the subject entity s and the relation r in the known snapshots $G_{(t_1, t_{k-1})} = \{G_{t_1}, G_{t_2}, \cdots, G_{t_{k-1}}\}$ before t_k, where the historical vocabulary $\mathbf{H}_{t_k}^{(s,r)}$ is an N-dimensional multi-hot indicator vector and N is the cardinality of $\mathcal{E}$, the value of entities in the historical vocabulary are masked 1 while others are 0.

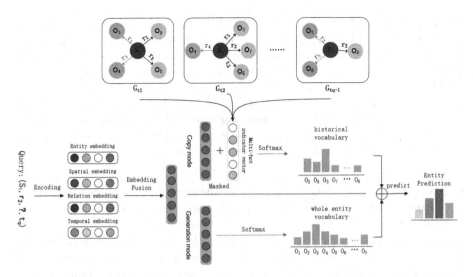

Fig. 2. Overview of ST-Net. ST-Net implement fine-grained modeling of entity representation by mining spatial information of entity, and conbines two inference modes to predict missing entity in the query. In the figure, light purple nodes are the candidate object entities in the historical vocabulary for query $(s_1, r_2, ?, t_q)$.

Prediction of a missing temporal fact aims to infer the quadruple $(s, r, ?, t_q)$ or $(?, r, o, t_q)$ from the known snapshots $G_{(t_1, t_{q-1})} = \{G_1, G_2, \cdots, G_{t_{q-1}}\}$. Without loss of generality, the task of the model is defined as predicting missing object entity.

3.2 Model Components

Query Vectorization. In encoding phase, the information contained in query needs to be converted into a continuous low-dimensional vector by the embedding layer. ST-Net first randomly initializes entity feature $\mathbf{s}_i$ and relation feature $\mathbf{r}_i$ for all $s \in \mathcal{E}$ and all $r \in \mathcal{R}$. In order for the model to be time-aware, the timestamp in temporal facts need to be encoded. Define the embedding for a unit step of time as $\mathbf{t}_u$ and $\mathbf{t}_1 = \mathbf{t}_u$, so the embedding of timestamp $\mathbf{t}_k$ is represented as follows:

$$\mathbf{t}_k = \mathbf{t}_{k-1} + \mathbf{t}_u \tag{1}$$

ST-Net expands the spatial-aware based on time-aware. Due to the complexity and uncertainty of data, the spatial information attached to entity is hard to learn by neural networks. We found that the text for most entities in TKGs already contains spatial information, like Citizen(India), Government(Pakistan). This is becasue these information have been summarized and sorted out in the process of temporal fact extraction, but they were not fully utilized. ST-Net obtains spatial information by preprocessing the text of the entity and the text in the raw data. After processing, for few of entities lacking spatial information, the entity itself can be directly used as its spatial information or use the existing mature pretraining language model to generate these message by prompt learning. After acquiring the spatial information for all entities, ST-Net randomly initializes them to get the spatial feature **sp**.

The discovered spatial information can support the model to carry out fine-grained modeling of entity representation, so that the entity has a richer and more favorable embedding to improve the effect of downstream tasks. After query Vectorization, the model needs to capture historical vocabulary of the query in advance to facilitate the next reasoning process.

Capture Historical Vocabulary. First, the training dataset can be divided into a series of snapshots $G_1, G_2, \cdots, G_{t_{train}}$ by timestamp. Then obtain the historical vocabulary for each subject entity and relation combination (s, r, t) in each snapshot, i.e. $\{\mathbf{h}_{t_1}^{(s,r)}, \mathbf{h}_{t_2}^{(s,r)}, \cdots, \mathbf{h}_{t_{train}}^{(s,r)}\}$. During training process, ST-Net is trained on each snapshot in timestamp order by incrementally maintain the historical vocabulary for all the previous snapshots. When evaluating the performance of our model on the validation set and test set, the maximum historical vocabulary from the whole training set will be used.

Specifically, for each query quadruple $(s, r, ?, t_k)$ at time t_k, during the training process, ST-Net will expand the historical vocabulary that specific to (s, r, t_k) from the snapshot before time t_k, as formalized below:

$$\mathbf{H}_{t_k}^{(s,r)} = \mathbf{h}_{t_1}^{(s,r)} + \mathbf{h}_{t_2}^{(s,r)} + \cdots + \mathbf{h}_{t_{k-1}}^{(s,r)} \tag{2}$$

where $\mathbf{H}_{t_k}^{(s,r)}$ is an N-dimensional multi-hot indicator vector where 1 is marked for all entities in the current historical vocabulary. Next two modes of reasoning will be introduced.

Copy-Generation Mode. The Copy mode aims to identify repeated facts and predict future facts by down sampling known facts of the same type in history. Given a query $(s, r, ?, t_k)$ and its corresponding historical vocabulary $\mathbf{H}_{t_k}^{(s,r)}$, the copy mode will increase the probability estimated for the object entity that are selected in the historical vocabulary. The Copy mode generates the query vector v_q with an MLP:

$$\mathbf{v}_q = tanh(\mathbf{W}_c[\mathbf{s}, \mathbf{sp}, \mathbf{r}, \mathbf{t}_k] + \mathbf{b}_c) \tag{3}$$

where $\mathbf{W}_c \in \mathbb{R}^{4d \times N}$ and $\mathbf{b}_c \in \mathbb{R}^N$ are trainable parameters. The query vector v_q is an N-dimensional vector, where N is the cardinality of the whole entity vocabulary $\mathcal{E}$.

To minimize the probability of some entities that do not form known facts with s and r in history, we first change the index value for an uninterested entity in $\mathbf{H}_{t_k}^{(s,r)}$ to a small negative number denoted $\mathbf{H}_{t_k}^{(s,r)}$. Then, the Copy mode can add the query vector and the changed multi-hot indicator vector $\mathbf{H}_{t_k}^{(s,r)}$ to limit the scope of candidate entities. After applying softmax function, the probability of the uninterested entities will be minimized.

$$\mathbf{c}_q = \mathbf{v}_q + \mathbf{H}_{t_k}^{(s,r)} \tag{4}$$

$$\mathbf{p}(c) = softmax(\mathbf{c}_q) \tag{5}$$

where $\mathbf{c}_q$ is an N-dimensional index vector. $\mathbf{p}(c)$ is an N-dimensional probability distribution vector representing the prediction probabilities on the historical vocabulary. Finally, we use the entity with the largest probability value in $\mathbf{p}(c)$ to answer the query. The advantage of the Copy mode is that it enable to predict from a more limited candidate entity space than the overall vocabulary. However, facts can also appear in upcoming snapshot, therefore a Generation mode is needed to predict such facts.

Given the same query $(s, r, ?, t_k)$ as the copy mode, the Generation mode is responsible for selecting the object entity from the whole entity vocabulary $\mathcal{E}$ to predict facts. The reasoning of Generation mode is that regards the predicted fact as a completely new fact without reference to the facts that have happened in history. The Generation mode also generates a query vector $\mathbf{g}_q$ and is further normalized using the softmax function for prediction:

$$\mathbf{g}_q = \mathbf{W}_g[\mathbf{s}, \mathbf{sp}, \mathbf{r}, \mathbf{t}_k] + \mathbf{b}_g \tag{6}$$

$$\mathbf{p}(g) = softmax(\mathbf{g}_q) \tag{7}$$

where $\mathbf{W}_g \in \mathbb{R}^{4d \times N}$ and $\mathbf{b}_g \in \mathbb{R}^N$ are trainable parameters. Similar to $\mathbf{p}(c)$ in the Copy mode, $\mathbf{p}(g)$ represents the predicted probability on the entire entity vocabulary. The maximum value in $\mathbf{p}_g$ denotes the object entity predicted by Generation mode throughout the entity vocabulary. The Generation mode is complementary to the Copy mode, with the ability to predict entirely new facts.

3.3 Parameter Learning and Inference

Given a query $(s, r, ?, t)$ to predict the object entity can be viewed as a multi-class classification task, where each class corresponds to each object entity. The learning objective is to minimize the following cross-entropy loss $\mathcal{L}$:

$$\mathcal{L} = -\sum_{t \in \mathcal{T}} \sum_{i \in \mathcal{E}} \sum_{k=1}^{K} o_{it} ln \mathbf{p}(y_{ik}|s, r, t) \tag{8}$$

where o_{it} is the i-th ground truth object entity in the snapshot G_t, $\mathbf{p}(y_{ik}|s, r, t)$ is the combined probability value of the k-th object entity in the snapshot G_t when the i-th ground truth object entity is o_i.

In order to ensure that the sum of the probability equals 1 for all entities in $\mathcal{E}$, we set a hyperparameter α to adjust the weight between the Copy mode and the Generation mode, which is defined as follows:

$$\mathbf{p}(o|s, r, t) = \alpha * \mathbf{p}(c) + (1 - \alpha) * \mathbf{p}(g) \tag{9}$$

$$o_t = argmax_{o \in \mathcal{E}} \mathbf{p}(o|s, r, t) \tag{10}$$

where $\alpha \in [0, 1]$, $\mathbf{p}(o|s, r, t)$ is the final predicted probability vector, which contains the probabilities of all entities under the current query.

4 Experiments

In this section, we evaluate our proposed method on the link prediction task on three public TKG datasets. We first introduce experimental settings in detail, including details of datasets and baselines. After that, we compare and analyze the experimental results and conduct an ablation study to evaluate the importance of spatial information.

4.1 Experimental Setup

Table 1. Statistics of the datasets.

Data	Entities	Relation	Training	Validation	Test	Granularity	Time granules
ICEWS18	23,033	256	373,018	45,995	49,545	24 h	304
ICEWS14	7,128	230	74,845	8514	7371	24 h	365
ICEWS05-15	10,488	251	368,868	46,302	46,159	24 h	4,017

Datasets and Evaluation Metrics. We evaluate ST-Net on three benchmark datasets for link prediction: ICEWS18 [20], ICEWS14 [21] and ICEWS05-15 [21]. Table 1 provides a summary of these datasets statistics. We divide each dataset into training set, validation set and testing set into 80%/10%/10% splits in the chronological order, and adopt a filited version of Mean Reciprocal Ranks(MRR) and Hits@1/3/10 to measure the performance of ST-Net.

Baselines. We compare ST-Net with multiple static knowledge graph embedding(SKGE) and temporal knowledge graph embedding(TKGE) models. The former includes TransE [11], DistMult [15], ComplEx [14], RotatE [22], and SimplE [23], while the latter includes TTransE [1], HyTE [2], TA-DistMult [21], DE-DistMult [4], DE-SimplE [4], RE-Net [5], CyGNet [6], and ATiSE [24].

Parameter Settings. The value of the hyperparameter α used to tune the weight of Copy mode and Generation mode is determined based on the MRR performance on the validation set of the current dataset. After extensive experiments, we found that the model works best when α is set to 0.8 on ICEWS14 and ICEWS18 and 0.9 on ICEWS05-15. The parameters of the model are initialized with Xavier initialization (Glorot and Bengio 2010) [25], and then optimized using an AMSGrad optimizer with a learning rate of 0.001. The batch size is set to 1024. The hidden layer embedding dimension is set to 200. The training epoch is limited to 30, which is enough for the model to converge in most cases. The baseline results are adopted from CyGNet [6] and ATiSE [24].

4.2   Results

Table 2. Results on ICEWS18, ICEWS14 and ICEWS05-15. The best results are in bold, and the second best ones are underlined.

Method	ICEWS18				ICEWS14				ICEWS05-15			
	MRR	Hits@1	Hits@3	Hits@10	MRR	Hits@1	Hits@3	Hits@10	MRR	Hits@1	Hits@3	Hits@10
TransE	17.56	2.48	26.95	43.87	28.00	9.40	–	63.70	29.40	9.00	–	66.30
DistMult	22.16	12.13	26.00	42.18	43.90	32.30	–	67.20	45.60	33.70	–	69.10
ComplEx	30.09	21.88	34.15	45.96	46.70	34.70	52.70	71.60	48.10	36.20	53.50	72.90
RotatE	23.10	14.33	27.61	38.72	41.80	29.10	47.80	69.00	30.40	16.40	35.50	59.50
SimplE	–	–	–	–	45.80	34.10	51.60	68.70	47.80	35.90	53.90	70.80
TTransE	8.36	1.94	8.71	21.93	25.50	7.40	–	60.10	27.10	8.40	–	61.60
HyTE	7.31	3.10	7.50	14.95	29.70	10.80	41.60	65.50	31.60	11.60	44.50	68.10
TA-DistMult	28.53	20.30	31.57	44.96	47.70	36.30	–	68.60	47.40	34.60	–	72.80
DE-DistMult	–	–	–	–	50.10	39.20	56.90	70.80	48.40	36.60	54.60	71.80
DE-SimplE	–	–	–	–	<u>52.60</u>	41.80	<u>59.20</u>	<u>72.50</u>	51.30	39.20	57.80	<u>74.80</u>
RE-NET	42.93	36.19	45.47	55.80	45.71	38.42	49.06	59.12	–	–	–	–
CyGNet	<u>46.69</u>	<u>40.58</u>	<u>49.82</u>	<u>57.14</u>	49.99	43.51	53.55	61.42	<u>57.22</u>	<u>50.25</u>	<u>61.77</u>	68.58
ATiSE	–	–	–	–	**55.00**	<u>43.60</u>	**62.90**	**75.00**	51.90	37.80	60.60	**79.40**
ST-Net	**47.47**	**41.07**	**50.62**	**58.52**	51.84	**44.74**	55.59	64.57	**58.34**	**51.26**	**62.85**	70.22

Table 2 report the link predition results of ST-Net and baseline methods on three TKG datasets. We observe that all SKGE methods perfrom worse than most TKGE methods, because they cannot capture temporal information in facts and cannot model dynamic interactions of entities and relations. However, their preformance generally outperform TTransE and HyTE. The reason we believe is that TTransE and HyTE only learn the representation at this timestamp for each snapshot separately, without linking entity representations at different timestamp, so it lacks the ability to capture time sequence information.

Table 2 also show that significantly outperforms other baselines on ICEWS18 and ICEWS05-15. For further analysis, we calculated the probability of repeated events in ICEWS18 to be 49.24%, which will improve the prediction effect of the Copy mode to a certain extent. And in ICEWS18, as many as 41.3% of the groups where the subject entity and the object entity are in the same space, which also explains that the reasonable use of spatial information can improve the prediction result. We argue that spatial message between entities in a fact can also help the model learn the semantic information implied by the relation, that is, the relation often occur between those spatial locations.

The experimental results indicate that ST-Net use the spatial information attached to the entity to implement fine-grained modeling of entity representation, which can effectively enrich entity information and improve the effect for link prediction.

4.3 Ablation Study

Table 3. Results (in percentage) of ablation study on the ICEWS18.

Method	ICEWS18			
	MRR	Hits@1	Hits@3	Hits@10
ST-Net-No-Spatial-Information	46.68	40.72	49.67	56.82
ST-Net-Prompt(bert-base-cased)	47.03	40.86	50.12	57.60
ST-Net	**47.47**	**41.07**	**50.62**	**58.52**

In order to explore the impact of different acquisition of spatial information on the model, we conducted an ablation study. To do this, we create variants of ST-Net by adjusting how spatial information is obtained in the model, and compare their performance gaps with ST-Net on the ICEWS18 dataset. From the results in Table 3, we can observe the importance of spatial information. After removing the spatial information, all metrics of the model have decreased, which demonstrates that the spatial information contained in entity play a vital part for predicting future facts. In addition, ST-Net-Prompt(bert-base-cased) complete the missing spatial information of entity through the Fill-Mask task in the pre-trained language model (bert-base-cased), where the template of the Fill-Mask task is set to : [Entity text]'s country is [MASK]. Its performance ranks between ST-Net and ST-Net-No-Spatial-Information, which further illustrates the importance of spatial information and reflects the shortcomings of the method we designed to complete the spatial information through the pre-trained model.

5 Conclusion

In this paper, we explore the spatial information attached to the entity and predict the future facts by combining the copy and generation reasoning mode. The experimental results show that ST-Net has promising performance in predicting the future facts in the temporal knowledge graph. In the future work, we plan to mine more accurate and effective information in entity through prompt learning, and combine them to help the model perform better. Meanwhile, further study on the utilization of spatial information is also significant.

Acknowledgements. The research is supported by The Natural Science Foundation of Guangdong Province (No.2018A030313934).

References

1. Leblay, J., Chekol, M.W.: Deriving validity time in knowledge graph. In: Companion Proceedings of the The Web Conference 2018, pp. 1771–1776 (2018)
2. Dasgupta, S.S., Ray, S.N., Talukdar, P.: HyTE: hyperplane-based temporally aware knowledge graph embedding. In: Proceedings of the 2018 Conference on Empirical Methods in Natural Language Processing, pp. 2001–2011 (2018)
3. Trivedi, R., Dai, H., Wang, Y., Song, L.: Know-evolve: deep temporal reasoning for dynamic knowledge graphs. In: International Conference on Machine Learning, pp. 3462–3471. PMLR (2017)
4. Goel, R., Kazemi, S.M., Brubaker, M., Poupart, P.: Diachronic embedding for temporal knowledge graph completion. In: Proceedings of the AAAI Conference on Artificial Intelligence, vol. 34, pp. 3988–3995 (2020)
5. Jin, W., Qu, M., Jin, X., Ren, X.: Recurrent event network: autoregressive structure inference over temporal knowledge graphs. arXiv preprint arXiv:1904.05530 (2019)
6. Zhu, C., Chen, M., Fan, C., Cheng, G., Zhan, Y.: Learning from history: modeling temporal knowledge graphs with sequential copy-generation networks. arXiv preprint arXiv:2012.08492 (2020)
7. Deng, S., Rangwala, H., Ning, Y.: Dynamic knowledge graph based multi-event forecasting. In: Proceedings of the 26th ACM SIGKDD International Conference on Knowledge Discovery & Data Mining, pp. 1585–1595 (2020)
8. Xiao, H., Huang, M., Meng, L., Zhu, X.: SSP: semantic space projection for knowledge graph embedding with text descriptions. In: Thirty-First AAAI Conference on Artificial Intelligence (2017)
9. Chen, X., Chen, M., Shi, W., Sun, Y., Zaniolo, C.: Embedding uncertain knowledge graphs. In: Proceedings of the AAAI Conference on Artificial Intelligence, vol. 33, pp. 3363–3370 (2019)
10. Ji, S., Pan, S., Cambria, E., Marttinen, P., Philip, S.Y.: A survey on knowledge graphs: representation, acquisition, and applications. IEEE Trans. Neural Netw. Learn. Syst. **33**(2), 494–514 (2021)
11. Bordes, A., Usunier, N., Garcia-Duran, A., Weston, J., Yakhnenko, O.: Translating embeddings for modeling multi-relational data. In: Advances in Neural Information Processing Systems, vol. 26 (2013)
12. Lin, Y., Liu, Z., Sun, M., Liu, Y., Zhu, X.: Learning entity and relation embeddings for knowledge graph completion. In: Twenty-ninth AAAI Conference on Artificial Intelligence (2015)
13. Wang, Z., Zhang, J., Feng, J., Chen, Z.: Knowledge graph embedding by translating on hyperplanes. In: Proceedings of the AAAI Conference on Artificial Intelligence, vol. 28 (2014)
14. Trouillon, T., Welbl, J., Riedel, S., Gaussier, É., Bouchard, G.: Complex embeddings for simple link prediction. In: International Conference on Machine Learning, pp. 2071–2080. PMLR (2016)
15. Yang, B., Yih, W.T., He, X., Gao, J., Deng, L.: Embedding entities and relations for learning and inference in knowledge bases. arXiv preprint arXiv:1412.6575 (2014)
16. Schlichtkrull, M., Kipf, T.N., Bloem, P., van den Berg, R., Titov, I., Welling, M.: Modeling relational data with graph convolutional networks. In: Gangemi, A., et al. (eds.) ESWC 2018. LNCS, vol. 10843, pp. 593–607. Springer, Cham (2018). https://doi.org/10.1007/978-3-319-93417-4_38
17. Dettmers, T., Minervini, P., Stenetorp, P., Riedel, S.: Convolutional 2d knowledge graph embeddings. In: Proceedings of the AAAI Conference on Artificial Intelligence, vol. 32 (2018)

18. Guo, L., Sun, Z., Hu, W.: Learning to exploit long-term relational dependencies in knowledge graphs. In: International Conference on Machine Learning, pp. 2505–2514. PMLR (2019)
19. Han, Z., Ding, Z., Ma, Y., Gu, Y., Tresp, V.: Learning neural ordinary equations for forecasting future links on temporal knowledge graphs. In: Proceedings of the 2021 Conference on Empirical Methods in Natural Language Processing, pp. 8352–8364 (2021)
20. Boschee, E., Lautenschlager, J., O'Brien, S., Shellman, S., Starz, J., Ward, M.: ICEWS coded event data. Harvard Dataverse, vol. 12 (2015)
21. García-Durán, A., Dumančić, S., Niepert, M.: Learning sequence encoders for temporal knowledge graph completion. arXiv preprint arXiv:1809.03202 (2018)
22. Sun, Z., Deng, Z.H., Nie, J.Y., Tang, J.: Rotate: Knowledge graph embedding by relational rotation in complex space. arXiv preprint arXiv:1902.10197 (2019)
23. Kazemi, S.M., Poole, D.: Simple embedding for link prediction in knowledge graphs. In: Advances in Neural Information Processing Systems, vol. 31 (2018)
24. Xu, C., Nayyeri, M., Alkhoury, F., Yazdi, H.S., Lehmann, J.: Temporal knowledge graph embedding model based on additive time series decomposition. arXiv preprint arXiv:1911.07893 (2019)
25. Glorot, X., Bengio, Y.: Understanding the difficulty of training deep feedforward neural networks. In: Proceedings of the Thirteenth International Conference on Artificial Intelligence and Statistics, pp. 249–256. JMLR Workshop and Conference Proceedings (2010)

Natural Language Processing

M2FNet: Multi-granularity Feature Fusion Network for Medical Visual Question Answering

He Wang, Haiwei Pan[(⊠)], Kejia Zhang, Shuning He, and Chunling Chen

College of Computer Science and Technology, Harbin Engineering University, Harbin, People's Republic of China
{whheu,panhaiwei,kejiazhang,shuning,ccl_00}@hrbeu.edu.cn

Abstract. Medical Vision Question Answer (VQA) is a combination of medical artificial intelligence and visual question answering, which is a complex multimodal task. The purpose is to obtain accurate answers based on images and questions to assist patients in understanding their personal situations as well as to provide doctors with decision-making options. Although CV and NLP have driven great progress in medical VQA, challenges still exist in medical VQA due to the characteristics of the medical domain. First, the use of a meta-learning model for image feature extraction can accelerate the convergence of medical VQA models, but it will contain different degrees of noise, which will degrade the effectiveness of feature fusion in medical VQA, thereby affecting the accuracy of the model. Second, the currently existing medical VQA methods only mine the relation between medical images and questions from a single granularity or focus on the relation within the question, which leads to an inability to comprehensively understand the relation between medical images and questions. Thus, we propose a novel multi-granularity medical VQA model. On the one hand, we apply multiple meta-learning models and a convolutional denoising autoencoder for image feature extraction, and then optimize it using an attention mechanism. On the other hand, we propose to represent the question features at three granularities of words, phrases, and sentences, while a keyword filtering module is proposed to obtain keywords from word granularity, and then the stacked attention module with different granularities is used to fuse the question features with the image features to mine the relation from multiple granularities. Experimental results on the VQA-RAD dataset demonstrate that the proposed method outperforms the currently existing meta-learning medical VQA methods, with an overall accuracy improvement of 1.8% compared to MMQ, and it has more advantages for long questions.

Keywords: Medical vision question answer · Multi-granularity · Attention mechanism · Meta-learning

© The Author(s), under exclusive license to Springer Nature Switzerland AG 2022
S. Khanna et al. (Eds.): PRICAI 2022, LNCS 13630, pp. 141–154, 2022.
https://doi.org/10.1007/978-3-031-20865-2_11

1 Introduction

Medical VQA focuses on answering questions related to the content of a given medical image by fusing the image with question information. In practice, it has a wide range of applications, such as improving patient engagement [12] and supporting clinical decision-making [7]; therefore, it has recently become a popular topic in the medical field. The Medical VQA model includes an image feature extraction module, a question feature extraction module, a feature fusion module, and an answer prediction module, each of which affects the performance of the model to varying degrees.

Image feature extraction is the basic module of the Medical VQA model, and it affects the convergence speed and accuracy of the model. Pretraining VGG [19] or ResNet [8] feature extraction networks on natural image datasets such as ImageNet [18] and then fine-tuning the medical VQA model on the medical VQA data can alleviate the training difficulties caused by the scarcity of medical data; however, the above image feature extraction approach is not effective when used in medical VQA models [1, 21] due to the content differences between medical and natural images. A mixture of enhanced visual features (MEVF) [16] combined model-agnostic meta-learning (MAML) [3] and convolutional denoising autoencoder (CDAE) [15] to extract image features. MAML can be quickly adapted to new tasks to accelerate model convergence, and CDAE is robust to noisy images. Leveraging the advantages of both, MEVF improves the accuracy of medical VQA tasks; however, the dataset used to train MAML by manual annotation may have noisy labels. Multiple meta-model quantifying (MMQ) [2] proposed a multiple meta-model quantifying method that is designed to increase meta-data by auto-annotation, deal with noisy labels, and output multiple meta-learning models that provide robust features for medical VQA. The image features extracted by different meta-learning models should have different importance, but MMQ views each image feature equivalently and applies it to the medical VQA directly. In addition, medical images such as MRI, CT, and X-ray may carry noise during acquisition and transmission, which results in image features that also contain varying degrees of noise, further affecting the accuracy of the medical VQA model.

Solving the semantic gap between images and text is the key to multimodal tasks; thus, image and question feature fusion is the core module of the medical VQA task. SAN [22] proposed a stacked attention approach to fuse image and question features. The question features are used as query vectors to find the regions in the image that are relevant to the answer, and the answer is derived by multiple reasoning. BAN [10] finds bilinear attention distributions to utilize given image and question information seamlessly. The above feature fusion methods improve the performance of general VQA tasks and are also widely used in medical VQA. However, due to the high similarity of human tissues themselves, medical images of the same part and the same body state are very similar, which makes medical image processing more difficult than natural images and thus requires stronger inference ability. Directly applying the above general VQA model to medical VQA, only a single granularity of fusing image features with question features [2,5,16] leads to a lack of inference ability and unsatisfactory performance.

To address the above problems, we propose the Multi-granularity Feature Fusion Network(M2FNet), which consists of an image feature extraction module, a multi-granularity question feature extraction module, an attention-based multi-granularity fusion module, and an answer prediction module. The image feature extraction module uses multiple meta-learning models to obtain image features understood from different perspectives and introduces the squeeze-and-excitation block (SE) [9] to assign weights to the image features extracted to suppress redundant information and emphasize important information while using CDAE to obtain the denoised high-level semantic features. The image feature extraction module obtains image features with robustness by combining the meta-learning models, CDAE and SE. The multi-granularity question feature extraction module represents question features at three granularities: word, phrase, and sentences. Further keywords are obtained from word granularity using the keyword filtering module. The attention-based multi-granularity fusion module adopts three different granularity stacked attention modules to fuse question features with image features to achieve multi-granularity mining of the relation between images and questions. The answer prediction module combines three granularities of fused features to answer questions related to medical images more accurately.

2   Related Work

2.1   Vision Question Answer

VQA is a complex multimodal task and the fusion of image and question features is the core of the VQA task. Early works applied simple concatenation, summation, or pixel-level multiplication for cross-modal feature fusion. Bilinear Fusion [6] has been proposed to apply bilinear pooling to fuse the features of two modalities to mine the high-level semantic relation between modalities. To overcome the computationally intensive problem of bilinear pooling, [4] embeds image and question features into a high-dimensional space and then performs convolution operations in Fourier space to fuse image and question information, improving performance with fewer parameters. Multimodal pooling is an important technique for fusing image features and question features, and there are some other works apply this technique, such as [11,24,25]. Since attention mechanisms are widely used in the field of CV and NLP, SAN [22] proposed a stacked attention approach to fuse image and question features; it treats the question features as query vectors to find the regions in the image that are relevant to the answer and arrive at the answer by multiple queries. Attention-based methods are also available in [5,14], and [23] further explores the application of attention in VQA by fusing features using a transformer [20]. The attention mechanism has led to the further development of VQA. However, currently existing medical VQA methods only mine the relation between medical images and questions at a single granularity [2,5,16] or focus on the relation within the question, failing to capture content in the images from multiple granularities to comprehensively understand the relation between medical images and questions.

2.2 Meta Learning

MAML [3] proposed meta-learning methods to enable rapid convergence of the model in new tasks using only small datasets. Due to data scarcity in medical VQA tasks, feature extractors pretrained with natural images are usually required to optimize the training process; however, the content differences between medical and natural images lead to unsatisfactory results of such methods. Therefore, MEVF [16] proposed a combination of MAML and CDAE; CDAE is an encoder-decoder architecture trained with unlabeled data, which improves the robustness of the model by adding noise to the image data, allowing the encoder to extract valid information from the noisy image for downstream tasks. It takes advantage of meta-learning and CDAE techniques to achieve better performance on small datasets for medical VQA, proving that meta-learning and CDAE are effective in medical VQA. MMQ [2] proposed a multiple meta-model quantifying method that is designed to increase meta-data by auto-annotation, deal with noisy labels, and output multiple meta-learning models that provide robust features for medical VQA. Although the MMQ meta-learning approach can alleviate the training difficulties associated with data scarcity in medical VQA, it views equally the image features extracted by multiple meta-learning models, and the extracted features may carry varying degrees of noise.

3 Method

3.1 Overview

In this paper, we propose the M2FNet model for medical VQA tasks, which takes images as the core and mines the relation between images and questions at multiple granularities. Figure 1 illustrates an overview of our framework.

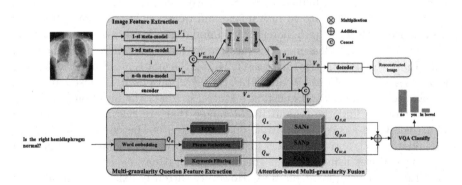

Fig. 1. The framework of our proposed M2FNet.

The M2FNet processes images and questions through two branches: image feature extraction and multi-granularity question feature extraction, and then the output of the branches is fused by the attention-based multi-granularity fusion module to obtain fused features for answer prediction.Image feature extraction consists of CDAE's encoder, n meta-learning models, and the SE module. The images are passed through n meta-learning models to obtain n feature maps $V_1 \sim V_n$ with robustness, which are input to the SE module to learn the importance of each channel after concatenation and then combine the importance weights with the feature maps to obtain the meta-learning feature map V_{meta}, while the CDAE's encoder extracts high-level semantic features V_a. The final image features V are obtained by concatenating V_{meta} and V_a. To extract question features from multiple granularities, we take the word embedding vector Q_a as the input of LSTM, Phrase Embedding, and Keywords Filtering for encoding questions to obtain sentence-granularity, phrase-granularity, and word-granularity features Q_s, Q_p, and Q_w, respectively. The question features Q_s, Q_p, and Q_w are input with the image features V to the attention-based multi-granularity fusion module consisting of SANs, SANp, and SANw to obtain the fused features $Q_{s,a}$, $Q_{p,a}$, $Q_{w,a}$, achieving multiple granularities understanding of the relation between images and questions. Finally, the three fusion features are summed at the pixel level to jointly make answer predictions. The modules are described in detail as follows.

3.2   Image Feature Extraction

We propose combining multiple meta-learning models and CDAE to extract image features and introduce a SE module to optimize the feature extraction. The meta-learning model can be quickly applied to other tasks, achieving fast convergence even on small datasets of medical VQA. CDAE is robust to noisy images and still extracts high-level semantic features from medical images such as MRI, CT, and X-ray that may carry noise. The SE module learns the importance weights of the input features for each channel, emphasizing important information and suppressing redundant information, we apply it to assign weights to the image features obtained from different meta-learning models to maximize the effect of each image feature. There are n meta-learning models in Fig. 1, and each meta-learning model consists of four 3*3 convolutional layers and a mean pooling layer. N image features V_i with robustness are obtained by feeding images to n meta-learning models,$i \in (1,n)$, and then are concatenated at the channel level to obtain V_{meta}^c. The pink part represents the SE module, including a pooling layer and two fully connected layers. V_{meta}^c is input to the SE module, the global feature representation of each channel is obtained by the pooling layer, and then the importance weight of each channel is learned by the fully connected layer, which is used to adjust the feature map to obtain V_{meta}. CDAE includes an encoder and a decoder. The encoder extracts the high-level semantic features of the image, which consists of three 3*3 convolutional layers, each of which is followed by a max-pooling layer. The decoder consisting of two

3*3 deconvolutions and two 3*3 convolutions reconstructs the image using the high-level semantic features.

We extract the image features V_a using the encoder of the pretrained CDAE and then concatenate V_{meta} and V_a to obtain the final image feature V. The above process is expressed as the following equation.

$$V_{meta}^c = [V_1, \ldots, V_n] \tag{1}$$

$$V_{meta} = SE\left(V_{meta}^c\right) \tag{2}$$

$$V = [V_{meta}, V_a] \tag{3}$$

3.3 Multi-granularity Question Feature Extraction

When people understand complex statements, they often read multiple times to understand the semantics precisely. Based on human thinking patterns, this paper argues that semantic information should also be obtained at multiple granularities in complex medical VQA tasks and therefore proposes a multi-granularity question feature extraction module to represent question features at three granularities of words, phrases, and sentences. The input question is first unified to a 12-word sentence, which is zero-padded if the length of the question is less than 12. Then, each word in the question is transformed into a vector using 600-D GloVe [17], which results in a vector $Q_a \in R^{n \times d_w}$, where $n = 12$ denotes the number of words and $d_w = 600$ denotes the word dimension. Furthermore, we pass the vector Q_a through keyword filtering (KF) to obtain keywords pointing to the pathological regions and properties, which results in word-granularity question features $Q_w \in R^{n \times d_w}$. The filter is the intersection of two lists, one of which contains words in the question of the medical VQA dataset, and the other is a stop-words list based on NLTK [13]. Input Q_a into the phrase feature extraction module to obtain the phrase-granularity question feature vector $Q_p \in R^{d_p}$, with $d_p = 1024$ denoting the dimension of the question feature. The phrase feature extraction module is shown in Fig. 2, which consists of three 1-D convolutions with different kernel sizes to output feature

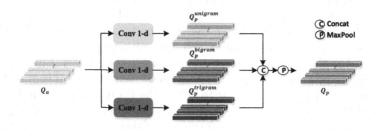

Fig. 2. Phrase feature extraction module.

vectors $Q_p^{unigram}$, Q_p^{bigram},and $Q_p^{trigram}$, and then the phrase-granularity question feature vector Q_p is obtained after concatenation and max-pooling. The above process is expressed as the following formulas.

$$Q_p^{unigram} = \tanh\left(W_1 Q_a\right) \tag{4}$$

$$Q_p^{bigram} = \tanh\left(W_2 Q_a\right) \tag{5}$$

$$Q_p^{trigram} = \tanh\left(W_3 Q_a\right) \tag{6}$$

$$Q_p = \max\left(\left[Q_p^{unigram}, Q_p^{bigram}, Q_p^{trigram}\right]\right) \tag{7}$$

We apply the 1024-D LSTM on the Q_a vector to obtain the sentence-granularity question features $Q_S \in R^{d_s}$, $d_s = 1024$. Through the above process, the multi-granularity question feature extraction module outputs three question feature vectors of sentence-granularity, phrase-granularity and word-granularity.

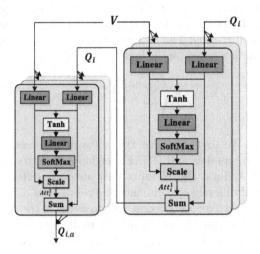

Fig. 3. Attention-Based multi-granularity fusion module: The left and right sides represent two executions of query and fusion operations, and the three layers of depth represent SANi of different granularities

3.4 Attention-Based Multi-granularity Fusion Module

In a complex task such as medical VQA, capturing key regions in an image based on semantic information at different granularities to obtain fused features that jointly participate in answer prediction helps improve model performance. In this paper, we propose an attention-based multi-granularity fusion module that fuses question features with image features at different granularities using three SANi modules, where $i \in (w, p, s)$, V and Q_i are the inputs to SANi, and the question feature vector Q_i queries image feature vector V to obtain attention vector Att_i^1. The result is combined with Q_i to obtain $Q_{\tilde{i}}$ as a new question feature vector querying the image feature V again, resulting in a high-level attention Att_i^2. High-level attention will give a more accurate attention distribution to focus on the region related to the answer, fuse it with the current question feature $Q_{\tilde{i}}$,and finally output the fusion feature $Q_{i,a}$. The three granularity fused features predict the answer together. Figure 3 shows the architecture of the fusion module. The attention-based multi-granularity fusion module enables a comprehensive understanding of the relation between images and questions to achieve deep inference and improve model performance.

3.5   Answer Prediction and Model Training

Answer Prediction. In this paper, we treat the medical VQA task as a classification task based on answer sets. We use a 2-layer MLP as a classifier to predict the category scores and obtain the final answers. The fused features $Q_{w,a}$, $Q_{p,a}$, and $Q_{s,a}$ at the word, phrase, and sentence granularity output by the fusion module are first summed at the pixel level and then fed into the classifier, resulting in category score prediction $\hat{y}$, The classifier is trained using a cross-entropy loss function. The prediction scores are calculated as follows.

$$\hat{y} = MLP \left(\sum_i q_{i,a} \right), i \in (w, p, s) \tag{8}$$

Model Training. We first initialize the network parameters using the pre-trained meta-learning models and CDAE weights and then optimize the model on the medical VQA data, the training data used by different meta-learning models are cross and different. To enhance the robustness of the model, we also introduce a CDAE image reconstruction task to assist in the optimization of the medical VQA task and train the model using a multi-task loss function. The loss function L consists of two terms. L_{vqa} is the cross-entropy loss for the medical VQA task, and L_a is the loss of the reconstruction task using MSE loss, with the following equations.

$$L = L_{vqa} + \alpha L_a \tag{9}$$

$$L_{vqa} = BCE(\hat{y}, y) \tag{10}$$

$$L_a = MSE(\hat{x}, x_o) \tag{11}$$

where α is a hyperparameter for balancing the two loss terms, $\hat{y}$ and y denote the predicted score and ground truth of the answer, $\hat{x}$ denotes the reconstructed image and x_o is the original image.

4   Experiments

4.1   Datasets and Metrics

Datasets. We evaluate the proposed M2FNet on the VQA-RAD dataset, which is a manually constructed radiology dataset, and the image set contains three parts: head, chest and abdomen, MRI and CT for head, X-ray for chest and CT for abdomen, with 315 images in total. There are 3515 question-answer pairs, and each image corresponds to 10 questions on average, of which 3064 are used as the training set and 315 as the test set. The question-answer pairs can be divided into open questions and closed questions according to the responses, where open questions are those where the responses are 'Yes/No' or give options, and closed questions are those where the responses are free-form questions. The question-answer pairs can be categorized into 11 types, such as modal, organ, and abnormal, according to the type of question. There are 458 answer types in the dataset, and our model treats medical VQA as a classification task based on the answer set. Although this dataset is small compared to other automatically constructed datasets, it is more representative of how one should answer questions as an AI radiologist due to its manual construction.

Metrics. The M2FNet is a classification-based medical VQA model, so the accuracy is used as a metric to evaluate the model on the VQA-RAD dataset. The accuracy rate is the percentage of the number of correctly predicted samples to the total number of samples, and the formula is as follows.

$$P_A = \frac{N_C}{N} * 100\% \tag{12}$$

4.2   Experimental Setup

Our model is implemented with PyTorch, and we conduct experiments on a GTX 1080ti GPU. The model is trained with a batch size of 32 and a learning rate of 0.001 using the Adamax optimizer for 40 epochs. The hyperparameter α in the loss function is set to 0.001.

4.3   Model Comparisons

The M2FNet proposed in this paper is compared with four existing meta-learning methods MAML, MEVF, MMQ and MMQ+MEVF. MAML uses a meta-learning model to initialize the weights of the image feature extraction network for fast adaptation to medical VQA tasks, which enables medical VQA models to achieve better performance even with small datasets. MEVF combines meta-learning models with CDAE to extract image features and achieves further performance improvements. MMQ proposes to mine the metadata of the dataset itself, using the metadata to train the meta-learning model, and continuously updating the training data. It iterates this process to output multiple

Table 1. Evaluation results by our proposed method and compared methods on the VQA dataset.

Method	Open-ended	Close-ended	Overall
MAML	40.1	72.4	59.6
MEVF	43.9	75.1	62.7
MMQ	53.7	75.8	67
MMQ+MEVF	56.9	75.7	68.2
M2FNet(ours)	**56.9**	**76.8**	**68.8**

meta-learning models that provide robust features for medical VQA. To achieve better performance, MMQ is combined with MEVF.

As shown in Table 1, M2FNet achieves the highest accuracy on the dataset VQA-RAD compared to the meta-learning methods in the table. Compared with the advanced meta-learning method MMQ+MEVF, the overall accuracy and close-ended accuracy improve by 0.6% and 1.1%, respectively.

4.4   Ablation Study

Effectiveness of SE and KF. We evaluate the effectiveness of SE and KF in our proposed M2FNet by performing an ablation study. In Table 2, 'baseline' represents the base model proposed in this paper, 'baseline+SE' indicates the model after introducing the SE module, and 'baseline+SE+KF' indicates the introduction of the SE and KF modules, which is the M2FNet model proposed in this paper.

Table 2. Evaluation results of the effectiveness of the SE and KF modules.

	Open-ended	Close-ended	Overall
Ours baseline	50.4	76.8	66.2
Ours baseline +SE	51.2	77.3	66.9(+0.7)
Ours baseline +SE+KF	56.9	76.8	**68.8**(+2.6)

As seen from Table 2, the overall accuracy improves by 0.7% with close-ended and open-ended accuracy increasing by 0.5% and 0.8% after the introduction of the SE module, and further, the overall accuracy achieves a large improvement of 2.6% after the introduction of the KF module. The results illustrate the effectiveness of SE and KF in our model.

Scheme of Using the SE Module. In this paper, we propose to optimize feature extraction with the SE module. To maximize the effect of the SE module, we compare the effect of the SE module acting on m meta-learning models and n meta-learning models. In Table 3, 'n' refers to the MMQ+MEVF method directly using n meta-learning models for image feature extraction, 'm+SE' means that the image features are extracted using the unfiltered m meta-learning models and the SE module acts on the m feature maps, while 'n+SE' utilizes the filtered n meta-learning models.

Table 3. Evaluation results of different SE module usage strategies.

	Open-ended	Close-ended	Overall
n	56.9	75.7	68.2
m +SE	56.1	76.8	68.5
n +SE	**56.9**	**76.8**	**68.8**

Table 3 shows that the accuracy of 'n+SE' is 0.3% higher than that of 'm+SE', which indicates that the best performance is obtained by adding the SE module to the n meta-learning model; therefore, it is the design approach ultimately adopted for our model. At the same time, the accuracy of 'n+SE' is 0.6% higher than that of 'n', which again shows the effectiveness of the SE module.

4.5   Qualitative Evaluation

The visualization experiment in Table 4 compares the effect of our proposed M2FNet and MMQ+MEVF based on the prediction confidence scores of the Top 5 answers. The table covers three types of medical images with different modalities and different organs, and the red and blue bars represent the confidence scores of correct and incorrect answers, respectively. The first three data show that the M2FNet model is more accurate in predicting answers compared to MMQ+MEVF. The fourth data shows that the M2FNet model has more advantages in dealing with long questions. This indicates that the proposed multi-granularity question feature extraction module can effectively obtain the semantic information of complex questions, thus enhancing the effect of the fusion module, which effectively improves the accuracy of the answer prediction of the medical VQA model.

Table 4. Visualization of the predicted confidence scores of M2FNet and MMQ+MEVF.

Question	Image	MMQ+MEVF	M2FNet
Question: Which side of the lungs are hyperinflated? **Ground-truth Answer**: Bilateral lungs		left 0.9999; both sides 0.0000; right side 0.0000; left axis and rt-ca 0.0000; right 0.0000	Bilateral lungs 0.9999; yes 0.0000; bilateral 0.0000; medial rectus 0.0000; left 0.0000
Question: Where are the acute infarcts? **Ground-truth Answer**: R frontal lobe		bilateral 0.9980; R frontal lobe 0.0019; bilateral lungs 0.0000; diffuse 0.0000; right cerebellum 0.0000	R frontal lobe 0.9720; bilateral 0.0279; left lung 0.0000; diffuse 0.0000; right lung 0.0000
Question: What is the mass most likely? **Ground-truth Answer**: kidney cyst		exophytic cyst 0.8898; 5mm 0.0741; kidney cyst 0.0246; well circumscribed 0.0044; infiltrative 0.0036	kidney cyst 0.9986; well circumscribed 0.0012; exophytic cyst 0.0000; extraluminal air and small fluid collection 0.0000; ischemia 0.0000
Question: Which sign do you see in the aortopulmonary window in this image? **Ground-truth Answer**: middle mogul		it is shifted to right 0.2074; lateral film as well as pa 0.1448; sinusitis 0.0815; right lung base 0.0626; both sides 0.0944	middle mogul 0.999; rounded well defined pulmonary nodules varying in size ... 0.0000; 3.4 cm 0.0000; right vertebral artery sign 0.0002; large bowel 0.0000

5   Conclusion

In this paper, we propose a novel neural network model with multiple granularities to mine the relation between images and questions for the medical VQA task. In addition, we introduce the SE module to optimize the image feature extraction process. To capture the key regions related to the answer in the image, a KF module is proposed to further fine-grain the question features of word granularity. The above enables multi-granularity inference and thus improves the model performance. Extensive experimental results on the VQA-RAD dataset show that the M2FNet model proposed in this paper outperforms the currently existing meta-learning medical VQA model. The visualization results of qualitative analyses intuitively reflect the performance of M2FNet while indicating that M2FNet is more advantageous in dealing with long questions.

Acknowledgements. This work is supported by the National Natural Science Foundation of China under (Grant No.62072135), Innovative Research Foundation of Ship General Performance (26622211), Ningxia Natural Science Foundation Project (2022AAC03346), Fundamental Research project (No. JCKY2020210B019), Fundamental Research Funds for the Central Universities (3072022TS0604).

References

1. Allaouzi, I., Ahmed, M.B., Benamrou, B.: An encoder-decoder model for visual question answering in the medical domain. In: CLEF (Working Notes) (2019)
2. Do, T., Nguyen, B.X., Tjiputra, E., Tran, M., Tran, Q.D., Nguyen, A.: Multiple meta-model quantifying for medical visual question answering. In: de Bruijne, M., et al. (eds.) MICCAI 2021. LNCS, vol. 12905, pp. 64–74. Springer, Cham (2021). https://doi.org/10.1007/978-3-030-87240-3_7
3. Finn, C., Abbeel, P., Levine, S.: Model-agnostic meta-learning for fast adaptation of deep networks. In: International Conference on Machine Learning, pp. 1126–1135. PMLR (2017)
4. Fukui, A., Park, D.H., Yang, D., Rohrbach, A., Darrell, T., Rohrbach, M.: Multimodal compact bilinear pooling for visual question answering and visual grounding. arXiv preprint arXiv:1606.01847 (2016)
5. Gao, P., et al.: Dynamic fusion with intra-and inter-modality attention flow for visual question answering. In: Proceedings of the IEEE/CVF Conference on Computer Vision and Pattern Recognition, pp. 6639–6648 (2019)
6. Gao, Y., Beijbom, O., Zhang, N., Darrell, T.: Compact bilinear pooling. In: Proceedings of the IEEE Conference on Computer Vision and Pattern Recognition, pp. 317–326 (2016)
7. Hasan, S.A., Ling, Y., Farri, O., Liu, J., Müller, H., Lungren, M.: Overview of imageclef 2018 medical domain visual question answering task. Technical Report 10–14 September 2018 (2018)
8. He, K., Zhang, X., Ren, S., Sun, J.: Deep residual learning for image recognition. In: Proceedings of the IEEE Conference on Computer Vision and Pattern Recognition, pp. 770–778 (2016)
9. Hu, J., Shen, L., Sun, G.: Squeeze-and-excitation networks. In: Proceedings of the IEEE Conference on Computer Vision and Pattern Recognition, pp. 7132–7141 (2018)
10. Kim, J.H., Jun, J., Zhang, B.T.: Bilinear attention networks. In: Advances in Neural Information Processing Systems, vol. 31 (2018)
11. Kim, J.H., et al.: Hadamard product for low-rank bilinear pooling. arXiv preprint arXiv:1610.04325 (2016)
12. Kovaleva, O., et al.: Towards visual dialog for radiology. In: Proceedings of the 19th SIGBioMed Workshop on Biomedical Language Processing.,pp. 60–69 (2020)
13. Loper, E., Bird, S.: Nltk: The natural language toolkit. arXiv preprint cs/0205028 (2002)
14. Lu, J., Yang, J., Batra, D., Parikh, D.: Hierarchical question-image co-attention for visual question answering. In: Advances in Neural Information Processing Systems, vol. 29 (2016)
15. Masci, J., Meier, U., Cireşan, D., Schmidhuber, J.: Stacked convolutional autoencoders for hierarchical feature extraction. In: International conference on artificial neural networks. pp. 52–59. Springer, (2011)

16. Nguyen, B.D., Do, T.-T., Nguyen, B.X., Do, T., Tjiputra, E., Tran, Q.D.: Overcoming data limitation in medical visual question answering. In: Shen, D., Shen, D., et al. (eds.) MICCAI 2019. LNCS, vol. 11767, pp. 522–530. Springer, Cham (2019). https://doi.org/10.1007/978-3-030-32251-9_57
17. Pennington, J., Socher, R., Manning, C.D.: Glove: global vectors for word representation. In: Proceedings of the 2014 Conference on Empirical Methods in Natural Language Processing (EMNLP), pp. 1532–1543 (2014)
18. Russakovsky, O., et al.: ImageNet large scale visual recognition challenge. Int. J. Comput. Vis. **115**(3), 211–252 (2015)
19. Simonyan, K., Zisserman, A.: Very deep convolutional networks for large-scale image recognition. arXiv preprint arXiv:1409.1556 (2014)
20. Vaswani, A., et al.: Attention is all you need. In: Advances in Neural Information Processing Systems, vol. 30 (2017)
21. Yan, X., Li, L., Xie, C., Xiao, J., Gu, L.: Zhejiang university at ImageCLEF 2019 visual question answering in the medical domain. In: CLEF (Working Notes), vol. 85 (2019)
22. Yang, Z., He, X., Gao, J., Deng, L., Smola, A.: Stacked attention networks for image question answering. In: Proceedings of the IEEE Conference on Computer Vision and Pattern Recognition, pp. 21–29 (2016)
23. Yu, Z., Yu, J., Cui, Y., Tao, D., Tian, Q.: Deep modular co-attention networks for visual question answering. In: Proceedings of the IEEE/CVF Conference on Computer Vision and Pattern Recognition, pp. 6281–6290 (2019)
24. Yu, Z., Yu, J., Fan, J., Tao, D.: Multi-modal factorized bilinear pooling with co-attention learning for visual question answering. In: Proceedings of the IEEE International Conference on Computer Vision, pp. 1821–1830 (2017)
25. Yu, Z., Yu, J., Xiang, C., Fan, J., Tao, D.: Beyond bilinear: generalized multimodal factorized high-order pooling for visual question answering. IEEE Trans. Neural Netw. Learn. Syst. **29**(12), 5947–5959 (2018)

Noise-Robust Semi-supervised Multi-modal Machine Translation

Lin Li[1](✉) [ID], Kaixi Hu[1] [ID], Turghun Tayir[1], Jianquan Liu[2], and Kong Aik Lee[3]

[1] School of Computer Science and Artificial Intelligence,
Wuhan University of Technology, Wuhan, China
{cathylilin,issac_hkx,hotpes}@whut.edu.cn
[2] Visual Intelligence Research Laboratories, NEC Corporation, Tokyo, Japan
jqliu@nec.com
[3] Institute for Infocomm Research, A*STAR, Singapore, Singapore
lee_kong_aik@i2r.a-star.edu.sg

Abstract. Recent unsupervised multi-modal machine translation methods have shown promising performance for capturing semantic relationships in unannotated monolingual corpora by large-scale pretraining. Empirical studies show that small accessible parallel corpora can achieve comparable performance gains of large pretraining corpora in unsupervised setting. Inspired by the observation, we think semi-supervised learning can largely reduce the demand of pretraining corpora without performance degradation in low-cost scenario. However, images of parallel corpora typically contain much irrelevant information, i.e., visual noises. Such noises have a negative impact on the semantic alignment between source and target languages in semi-supervised learning, thus weakening the contribution of parallel corpora. To effectively utilize the valuable and expensive parallel corpora, we propose a Noise-robust <u>Semi</u>-supervised <u>Multi</u>-modal <u>Machine</u> <u>T</u>ranslation method (Semi-MMT). In particular, a visual cross-attention sublayer is introduced into source and target language decoders, respectively. And, the representations of texts are used as a guideline to filter visual noises. Based on the visual cross-attention, we further devise a hybrid training strategy by employing four unsupervised and two supervised tasks to reduce the mismatch between the semantic representation spaces of source and target languages. Extensive experiments conducted on the Multi30k dataset show that our method outperforms the state-of-the-art unsupervised methods with large-scale extra corpora for pretraining in terms of METEOR metric, yet only requires 7% parallel corpora.

Keywords: Multimodal data · Neural machine translation · Semi-supervised learning · Noise

1 Introduction

Machine translation breaks the language barrier between people from different countries, which is of great value to modern human communication. Among

© The Author(s), under exclusive license to Springer Nature Switzerland AG 2022
S. Khanna et al. (Eds.): PRICAI 2022, LNCS 13630, pp. 155–168, 2022.
https://doi.org/10.1007/978-3-031-20865-2_12

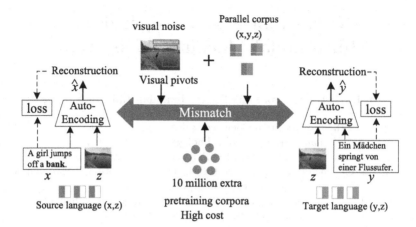

Fig. 1. An illustration of visual noises and parallel corpora in the mismatch between source and target languages in UMMT. The phrase "bank" in the source sentence has multiple meanings and the image can help the MMT model to capture the "river bank" instead of the "financial bank".

machine translation methods, multi-modal machine translation (MMT) [1,16,21] makes use of multimedia contents (e.g., texts and images) where images are treats as visual pivots [4,12] to reduce the semantic mismatch between source and target languages. As shown in Fig. 1, images and texts co-occur and they together provide a comprehensive semantics of the phrase "bank". With the enhancement of visual information, translators can understand it towards the "river bank" instead of the "financial bank". The goal of MMT is to model consistent semantic representation relationship between source and target languages via combining the visual information and derive accurate translation results.

Recently, neural machine translation methods have shown promising translation performance by modeling the relationships between different modal representations. To reduce the mismatch between different representation spaces, supervised multi-modal machine translation (SMMT) [8,10,11,26] and unsupervised multi-modal machine translation (UMMT) [4,12,16,21] are commonly training paradigms. Specifically, parallel corpora consist of two monolingual corpora and they are the translations of each other, which inherently contains the mapping relationship of two languages. SMMT is a straightforward approach to learn the semantic patterns from parallel corpora. However, the acquisition of large manually annotated parallel corpora is typically expensive. UMMT aims to achieve decent performance without using any parallel corpora. And, to align the semantic spaces from different language, UMMT typically needs large-scale extra corpora for pretraining and the cost of computation is heavy.

On the premise that small parallel corpora is relatively accessible than large monolingual pretraining corpora which incurs more resources, semi-supervised learning is a compromise strategy to reduce the mismatch of semantic spaces of different languages. And, a line of unimodal machine translation works are within this area [5, 24, 25]. It is intuitive to apply the semi-supervised setting for MMT. However, as shown in Fig. 1, images generally contain much irrelevant information and may introduce visual noises, such as sky, forest and river. It is not informed to consider texts and images equally, since the interference caused by visual noises may degrade performance and require more parallel corpora to compensate. As such, MMT is more challenging than the unimodal translation in semi-supervised learning, which motivates us to explore a noise-robust approach to effectively make use of small parallel corpora.

Inspired by recent multi-modal work [18], texts provide more effective information than images. This paper proposes a noise-robust semi-supervised multi-modal machine translation method (Semi-MMT). The visual cross-attention is introduced to balance visual and textual information in unsupervised and supervised learning, respectively. For the unsupervised learning, denoising auto-encoders [23] are employed to reconstruct source and target languages from monolingual multi-modal corpora. Then, for the supervised learning, a small set of parallel corpora is utilized to refine their representations and reduce the mismatch between source and target caused by unsupervised training. Our semi-supervised learning can achieve a trade-off between translation quality and corpora quantity, which effectively reduces the dependence on parallel corpora and monolingual pretraining corpora.

Overall, the contributions of this work are three fold:

- To our knowledge, it is the first work that focuses on the accessibility of small parallel corpora for semi-supervised MMT.
- We develop a noise-robust semi-supervised multi-modal machine translation method to balance translation quality and corpora quantity.
- Extensive experiments are conducted on the reorganized Multi30k dataset and the results show the superiority of our Semi-MMT over state-of-the-art unsupervised methods in terms of METEOR metric, yet only requires 2,014 parallel samples (30K in total), while the unsupervised methods require 10 million extra corpora for pretraining.

The remainder of this paper is organized as follows. Section 2 introduces the related work. Section 3 introduces the definition of MMT and describes the details of our proposed methodology. Section 4 introduces the experimental setup and analysis. And, Sect. 5 is the conclusion the future work.

2   Related Work

2.1   Multi-modal Machine Translation

Supervised multi-modal machine translation has achieved success in recent years [8–11, 19, 26]. These methods directly learn the paired source-target language mapping relationship from parallel corpora. However, the acquisition of sufficient parallel corpora is typically expensive, which relies on human annotation.

To reduce the reliance of parallel corpora, unsupervised multi-modal machine translation [4,12,16,21] only utilizes monolingual corpora for training. However, due to the absence of mapping relationship in monolingual data, the mismatch between the semantic spaces of source and target languages becomes a vital factor that affects translation quality. Su et al. propose a cycle-consistency loss that employs back translation to switch the two decoders of source and target languages [21]. Chen et al. propose a visual pivot based method to learn word-level and sentence-level translation progressively [4]. Huang et al. utilize visual information as an auxiliary hint for alignment [12]. Besides the visual information, the alignment between different representation spaces can also benefit from extra large-scale monolingual pretraining corpora [12,16,21]. The limitation lies that large-scale pretraining incurs more computation resource.

In this work, we argue that the accessibility of small parallel corpora enables semi-supervised training, which may not require additional monolingual corpora for high-cost pretraining and still keep good translation performance.

2.2   Semi-supervised Machine Translation

A lot of semi-supervised learning methods is proposed in unimodal machine translation [5,24,25]. Cheng et al. first propose to exploit monolingual corpora in the limitation of parallel corpora, and they reconstruct the monolingual corpora by autoencoders [5]. Inspired by the law of total probability, Wang et al. explicitly exploit the connection between the probability of target-side sentences and the conditional probability of translated sentences to improve the training of monolingual corpora [24]. Xu et al. introduce a dual reconstruction objective to incorporate monolingual training data in a unified way [25].

Despite the success of semi-supervised learning in unimodal machine translation, multi-modal corpora contains complex visual information. It is still a challenging work to study the effect of visual noises on semi-supervised learning. This paper is the first work to investigate semi-supervised multi-modal machine translation.

2.3   Noise-Robust Alignment

The early multi-modal fusion work directly treats visual and textual features equally, which ignores the irrelevant contents in images [2,3,13]. Subsequently, a line of literatures has discussed the visual noises in images, and aims to align visual information with textual information in multi-modal scenario [11,18,26]. Li et al. propose a bridge connection module that enables texts freely selecting the relevant images via relevance distance [18]. Helcl et al. [11] and Yao et al. [26] employs multi-modal self-attention to incorporate visual information in a graph perspective of Transformer.

The above works study the effect of visual noises on supervised learning. In this paper, we introduce the multi-modal self-attention to enhance our semi-supervised learning, which achieves noise-robust alignment in source and target language semantic representation spaces.

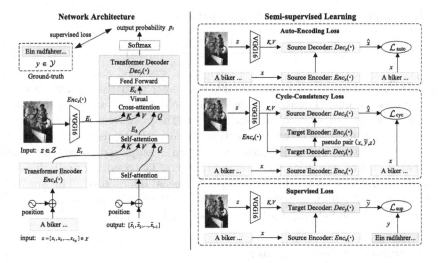

Fig. 2. The framework of our Semi-MMT. We devise forward and back translation models, i.e., $(x, z) \rightarrow y$ and $(y, z) \rightarrow x$. Each model contains a encoder and a decoder, and these encoders and decoders are designed into six combinations to compute loss functions. In terms of forward translation model, its encoder and decoder are at the left side, and its combinations are at the right side and defined in Eqs. (3), (6) and (9). For back translation model, its combinations are similar and symmetry to the forward, and defined in Eqs. (4), (8) and (9).

3   Methodology

In this section, we first formulate the definition of MMT, and introduce the overall architecture of our proposed Noise-robust Semi-supervised Multi-modal Machine Translation method (Semi-MMT). We then delve into the details of the semi-supervised learning including four unsupervised and two supervised losses.

As shown in Fig. 2, for a sample $(x, y, z) \in (\mathcal{X}, \mathcal{Y}, \mathcal{Z})$, given an image z annotated with its source sentence $x = [x_1, ..., x_{L_x}]$, we aim to train a MMT model that can translate x into target language $y = [y_1, ..., y_{L_y}]$ in low resource (i.e., the size of training corpora and computational cost), and vice versa. Here, L_x and L_y are the length of x and y.

3.1   Noise-Robust Semantic Alignment

Inspired by the work [18], the information from textual modalities is purer than that from visual modalities. We utilize texts as a guideline to filter irrelevant visual information. As shown in the left of Fig. 2, a visual cross-attention [11] sublayer is introduced into the decoder of vanilla Transformer [22] where the relevance between texts and images is measured. Formally, the image representation is a matrix E_i generated by the self-replicating output vector of a VGG16 [6] encoder, and the alignment is defined as follows:

$$E_c = softmax(\frac{(E_h W^Q)(E_i W^K)^T}{\sqrt{d}})(E_i W^V), \tag{1}$$

where W^Q, W^K and W^V are the trainable parameter matrices of query, key and value, E_h is the output matrix of the second self-attention sublayer in vanilla decoder, d is the dimension of hidden layer, i is the position of the next word.

Noting that in the visual cross-attention sublayer, the representations of texts are used as queries, and a dot-product function is employed to compare each query with a set of keys from image representations. The resulting similarities are normalized and used as weights to incorporate visual information. This sublayer is introduced into both supervised and unsupervised training to enhance the contribution of parallel corpora in semi-supervised learning.

3.2   Semi-supervised Learning.

In this paper, we highlight the contribution of small accessible parallel corpora and introduce supervised learning on the basis of unsupervised learning. In particular, to balance the corpora quantity and resource cost, we devise a hybrid training strategy by employing four unsupervised [21] and two supervised losses. During training, we randomly select several of them to learn the final mapping relationship $\mathcal{X} \times \mathcal{Z} \rightarrow \mathcal{Y}$ and $\mathcal{Y} \times \mathcal{Z} \rightarrow \mathcal{X}$. The cross-entropy is adopted to calculate the distance between the ground-truth g and the output probability distribution p of decoder. Formally, the objective function is defined as follows:

$$\mathcal{L}(p, g) = -\sum_{i=1}^{|g|}\sum_{j=1}^{|p|} g_{ij} log(p_{ij}), \tag{2}$$

where g_{ij} and p_{ij} refer to the jth value of the ith word representation of the ground-truth and probability distribution.

Unsupervised Auto-Encoding Loss. To learn a more informative encoding representation, a denoising auto-encoder [23] is used to reconstruct the source and target representations, respectively. As shown in the top right region of Fig. 2, the auto-encoding pipline and loss functions [21] are defined as follows:

$$\widehat{x} = Dec_x(Enc_x(x), Enc_z(z)),$$
$$\mathcal{L}_{auto}^x = \mathcal{L}(\widehat{x}, x), \tag{3}$$

where $\widehat{x}$ represents the reconstructed representation of x, and $Enc_x(\cdot)$ and $Dec_x(\cdot)$ refer to the encoder and decoder of source language x, respectively. Note that $Enc_z(\cdot)$ is the VGG16 [6] model. Similarly, the auto-encoding of the target language is defined as follows:

$$\widehat{y} = Dec_y(Enc_y(\mathbf{y}), Enc_z(z)),$$
$$\mathcal{L}_{auto}^y = \mathcal{L}(\widehat{y}, y). \tag{4}$$

Cycle-Consistency Loss. The auto-encoding loss learns two mapping relationships, namely $\mathcal{X} \times \mathcal{Z} \to \mathcal{X}$ and $\mathcal{Y} \times \mathcal{Z} \to \mathcal{Y}$. However, there still exists a mismatch with our final task ($\mathcal{X} \times \mathcal{Z} \to \mathcal{Y}$). To address this, two cycle-consistency loss functions are utilized to compensate such mismatch. As shown in the middle right panel of Fig. 2, for source language x, the cycle-consistency loss [14,21] first translate x into $\widetilde{y}$ as follows:

$$\widetilde{y} = Dec_y(Enc_x(x), Enc_z(z)). \tag{5}$$

However, in monolingual corpora, the ground truth y with respect to the input x and z is unknown. Therefore, we further conduct a back translation by employing a pseudo pair $(x, \widetilde{y}, z)$. In this manner, we achieve a cycle-consistency interaction between encoder and decoder from different language. Formally, for source language x, the cycle-consistency loss is defined as:

$$\mathcal{L}_{cyc}^x = \mathcal{L}(\widehat{x}, x), \tag{6}$$

given the back-translated task:

$$\widehat{x} = Dec_x(Enc_y(\widetilde{y}), Enc_z(z)). \tag{7}$$

Similarly, to model the mapping relationship $\mathcal{Y} \times \mathcal{Z} \to \mathcal{X}$, the cycle-consistency loss [21] of target language y is defined as follows:

$$\mathcal{L}_{cyc}^y = \mathcal{L}(\widehat{y}, y), \tag{8}$$

where $\widehat{y}$ represents the back-translated representation of y.

Supervised Loss. The cycle-consistency loss has limited ability to revise the mismatch, since human language is diverse and the pseudo pairs may not be precisely semantic matched. We notice that a small high-quality parallel corpora is relatively easy to collect. Therefore, a supervised loss is further utilized to refine the mapping relationship $\mathcal{X} \times \mathcal{Z} \to \mathcal{Y}$ and $\mathcal{Y} \times \mathcal{Z} \to \mathcal{X}$. Note that only a small set of high-quality parallel corpora is employed to calibrate the mismatch caused by unsupervised learning. This effectively reduce the dependency on a large-scale pretraining corpora. Formally, the supervised loss functions of the forward and back translation are defined as follows:

$$\begin{aligned} \mathcal{L}_{sup}^x &= \mathcal{L}(\widetilde{y}, y), \\ \mathcal{L}_{sup}^y &= \mathcal{L}(\widetilde{x}, x), \end{aligned} \tag{9}$$

where

$$\widetilde{x} = Dec_x(Enc_y(y), Enc_z(z)) \quad \text{and}$$
$$\widetilde{y} = Dec_y(Enc_x(x), Enc_z(z))$$

are the representation of translation results.

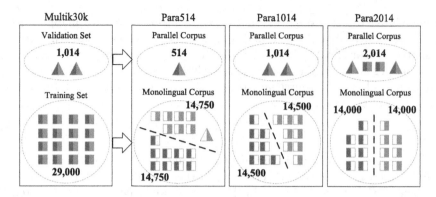

Fig. 3. Explanation of reorganized Multi30k. White boxes denote the removal of the paired language to form monolingual corpora in the source and target languages, respectively.

4   Experiment

In this section, we conduct experiments on the reorganized Multik30k dataset to reveal the effectiveness of Semi-MMT. In summary, we aim to analyze Semi-MMT from the following perspectives:

- **RQ1** How does Semi-MMT perform compared with the state-of-the-arts unsupervised methods with or without pretraining?
- **RQ2** What is the effect of different components of Semi-MMT, such as noise-robust semantic alignment, supervised learning and the size of parallel corpora?
- **RQ3** How about the translation quality of Semi-MMT in a specific case?

4.1   Experimental Setup

Experiments were conducted on the Multik30k dataset [7]. The dataset contains 29,000 training samples, 1,014 validation samples, and respective 1,000 testing samples for Test2016 and Test2017. For each sample, its image is annotated with one English sentence and its German translation.

As shown in Fig. 3, we reorganized the Multi30k dataset for semi-supervised experiment. In particular, we used the validation samples to form a parallel corpora and training samples as non-parallel corpora in Para1014. Some adjustments were conducted to generate Para514 and Para2014. To avoid paired sentences information leakage, we randomly split half of the non-parallel corpora to generate monolingual corpora.

We implemented the Semi-MMT on a machine equipped with a 12GB TITAN Xp GPU. Following [16], 10% words are randomly masked and their displacement within 2. We set the number of layers for the encoder and decoder as 4, the number of heads in attention as 8, the hidden dimension as 2048. Moreover, we

Table 1. Comparison with baselines on Test2016. "Image" means multi-modal model. "Pretrain" refers to the model pretrained in extra large-scale corpora. The best results are in **bold** and the suboptimal results are underlined

Model	BLEU[4]	METEOR	Image	Pretrain
S-txt [21]	6.27	11.6		
S-txt-img [21]	8.85	13.8	✓	
Progressive [4]	18.30	–	✓	
3rd-Iteration [16]	22.74	–	✓	✓
P-txt-img [21]	23.52	26.1	✓	✓
Base+Back_Translation [12]	**26.70**	–	✓	✓
Semi-MMT(Para2014)	<u>25.35</u>	**48.1**	✓	

train the Semi-MMT with Adam optimizer [15]. The experiments have lasted for 5 h, and the results are evaluated by BLEU[4] [20] and METEOR [17]. Note that METEOR is a more comprehensive metric that considers precision and recall. Following existing work [22], we use the average of checkpoints as the final result.

4.2 Baselines

As shown in Table 1, we trained the proposed Semi-MMT from scratch and compare it with four unsupervised models.

– S-txt,S-txt-img and P-txt-img [21] are the unimodal model, multi-modal model without pretraining and multi-modal model with pretraining, respectively. Here, the prefix "S" means monolingual corpora and "P" means the model is pretrained. These prefixes are as defined in [21].
– Progressive [4] only employs monolingual corpora in Multik30k without pretraining.
– 3rd-Iteration [16] is a MMT model that iteratively improves the model based on a reconstruction loss without any alignment.
– Base+Back_Translation [12] is a MMT model that utilizes visual information as image pivot in Transformer-based system.

Note that 3rd-Iteration [16], P-txt-img [21] and Base+Back_Translation [12] employs extra 10 millions textual corpora for pretraining, and then monolingual corpora of Multik30k for fine-tuning. All baselines results are as reported in their original papers.

4.3 Overall Comparison (RQ1)

To investigate the relationship between model performance and the demand of pretraining monolingual corpora, our proposed Semi-MMT is compared with the

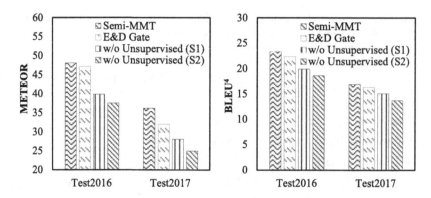

Fig. 4. The results of different alignments and supervised part.

state-of-the-art unsupervised methods with or without pretraining. The observations are below:

Semi-MMT Consistently Outperforms the Baselines Without Pretraining. As shown in Table 1, Semi-MMT achieves superior performance than S-txt-img and Progressive. It indicates that Semi-MMT improves translation quality by only employing about 2,000 parallel samples, yet the total number of samples is the same as other methods.

Semi-MMT Achieves Competitive Performance Compared with the Pretrained Baselines. Although it is unfair for us to directly compare with the UMMT methods pretrained with extra large-scale corpora, it is undeniable that Semi-MMT can still obtain comparable performance, and even outperforms some of them. In particular, Semi-MMT achieves the best in the more comprehensive metric METEOR. Compared with the heavy computation with 10 million pretraining corpora, our proposed Semi-MMT is relatively light and low cost in terms of computing resource.

The above results show that the proposed Semi-MMT can effectively utilize small parallel corpora for semi-supervised learning and achieve comparable or even better performance than unsupervised learning, which reduces the demand of large-scale monolingual pretraining corpora.

4.4   Ablation Study (RQ2)

The Effect of Noise-Robust Semantic Alignment. To investigate the effect of noises on semi-supervised learning, E&D Gate based semi-supervised method is adapted from existing supervised task [9]. In this work, we adopt the visual cross-attention layer [11] to filter noises in images. As shown in the left side of Fig. 4, we observe that when inputting identical parallel corpora, the visual cross-attention alignment [11] achieves relatively 0.9% and 4.2% absolute improvement than E&D Gate [9] in terms of METEOR in Test2016 and Test2017 datasets, respectively. In the right side of Fig. 4, the difference of performance in BLEU[4] is smaller than that in METEOR, which indicates that compared with variants, Semi-MMT not only obtains high precision, but also keep good recall. The above observations reveal that the visual cross-attention alignment in our proposed Semi-MMT can effectively reduce the effect of irrelevant information from images and enhance the contribution of parallel corpora in semi-supervised learning.

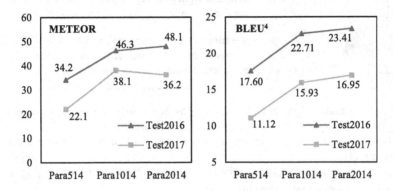

Fig. 5. The effect of gradual increment of parallel data.

The Effect of Supervised Part. Since the semi-supervised learning is a middle ground between the unsupervised and supervised learning, it will be well to compare with supervised baselines and see how much supervised MEREOR the semi-supervised model can cover with only 7% (2K/30K) parallel corpora. To this end, we further remove the unsupervised part and only keep the network architecture and supervised part. In particular, we repeatedly and randomly sample 2014 parallel corpora (S1 and S2) to conduct supervised experiments. The experimental results are shown in Fig. 4. Compared with the proposed method Semi-MMT, we observe that the performance of the best supervised baseline (S1) degrades 8.8% and 8.1% absolute METEOR values in Test2016 and Test2017, respectively. It shows that most performance gains come from the supervised part in Semi-MMT.

The Effect of the Size of Parallel Corpora. To investigate the effect of parallel corpora, we adjust the proportion of parallel corpora on the premise of constant total samples in Fig. 3. As shown in Fig. 5, we observe that the translation quality of Semi-MMT improves with the increment of the parallel corpora size and the rising trend decreases gradually. For example, compared with Para514, Semi-MMT in Para1014 achieves 12.1% absolute improvement in term of METEOR. And the improvement reduces significantly when comparing with Para2014. This shows that Semi-MMT can achieve a decent trade-off between small high-quality parallel corpora and large-scale pretraining corpora, which denotes the cost of manpower is reduced. For Test2017 dataset, the score of METEOR in Para2014 decreases by 1.9% while the score of BLEU^4 increases by 1.02%. This is because METEOR is a comprehensive metric. If the increment of parallel corpora in Test2017 is unbalanced, it will lead to higher precision while lower recall.

Source: two <u>males</u> seem to be conversing while standing <u>in front of a truck</u> across back and behind a metal item while four people stand around them

Reference: zwei <u>männer</u> stehen <u>vor dem heck lasters</u> und unterhalten sich anscheinend während vier weitere personen um sie herum stehen

- -

Baseline (Gate alignment [9]): zwei <u>menschen</u> warten auf einen <u>lastwagen</u> <u>während in der nähe</u> eines autos und einem grill unterhalten
(Translation: two people are waiting for a truck while conversing near a car and a grill)
Ours: zwei <u>männliche personen</u> die sich zu unterhalten während sie <u>vor einem lastwagen</u> stehen und hinter ihnen steht
(Translation: two male persons conversing while standing in front of a truck and standing behind them)

Fig. 6. Translation case. Red underlined words represent some of the improvements. The blue sentences are the corresponding results in English translated from Google. (Color figure online)

4.5   Case Study (RQ3)

Figure 6 depicts a translation cases in the test set. We can observe that the indoor environment contains much irrelevant information and the important information lies in the middle of the image. Compared with the Gate based semi-supervised alignment adapted from supervised work [9], our proposed Semi-MMT can effectively filter noises and capture some key information, that is two males converse in front of a truck. The Gate alignment do not capture the gender and the position relative to the truck. It indicates the effectiveness of Semi-MMT that can reduce the interference of visual noises in semi-supervised learning.

5   Conclusion and Future Work

Semi-supervised MMT is low-cost for parallel or extra pretraining corpora. In this paper, we devise a noise-robust semi-supervised learning method to reduce the mismatch between source and target semantic space. Particularly, visual cross-attention is adopted to enhance the tradeoff between translation quality and corpora quantity. The experimental results show that our method outperforms the state-of-the-art unsupervised methods with a small number of parallel corpora in terms of METEOR metric.

In future work, we would like to evaluate the balance between small parallel corpora and pretraining corpora, and explore more approaches to enhance the contribution of small parallel corpora, such as noise-robust network architectures and better training manners. Moreover, we will extent our semi-supervised training strategy to a wide range of multi-modal tasks in other applications.

Acknowledgements. This work is supported in part by the National Natural Science Foundation of China (62276196), the Key Research and Development Program of Hubei Province (No. 2021BAA030) and the China Scholarship Council (LiuJinMei [2020] 1509, 202106950041).

References

1. Calixto, I., Chowdhury, K.D., Liu, Q.: DCU system report on the WMT 2017 multi-modal machine translation task. In: Proceedings of the Second Conference on Machine Translation (WMT), pp. 440–444 (2017)
2. Calixto, I., Liu, Q.: Incorporating global visual features into attention-based neural machine translation. In: EMNLP, pp. 992–1003. Association for Computational Linguistics (2017)
3. Calixto, I., Rios, M., Aziz, W.: Latent variable model for multi-modal translation. In: ACL (1), pp. 6392–6405. Association for Computational Linguistics (2019)
4. Chen, S., Jin, Q., Fu, J.: From words to sentences: A progressive learning approach for zero-resource machine translation with visual pivots. In: Proceedings of the 28th International Joint Conference on Artificial Intelligence (IJCAI), pp. 4932–4938 (2019)
5. Cheng, Y., et al.: Semi-supervised learning for neural machine translation. In: Proceedings of the 54th Annual Meeting of the Association for Computational Linguistics (ACL) (2016)
6. Deng, J., Dong, W., Socher, R., Li, L., Li, K., Fei-Fei, L.: Imagenet: A large-scale hierarchical image database. In: Proceedings of the 2009 IEEE Conference on Computer Vision and Pattern Recognition (CVPR), pp. 248–255 (2009)
7. Elliott, D., Frank, S., Sima'an, K., Specia, L.: Multi30k: Multilingual english-german image descriptions. In: Proceedings of the 5th Workshop on Vision and Language, hosted by the 54th Annual Meeting of the Association for Computational Linguistics (VL@ACL), pp. 627–633 (2016)
8. Gehring, J., Auli, M., Grangier, D., and D.Y.: Convolutional sequence to sequence learning. In: Proceedings of the 34th International Conference on Machine Learning (ICML), pp. 1243–1252 (2017)
9. Grönroos, S., et al.: The memad submission to the WMT18 multimodal translation task. In: Proceedings of the Third Conference on Machine Translation: Shared Task Papers (WMT), pp. 603–611 (2018)
10. Han, Y., Li, L., Zhang, J.: A coordinated representation learning enhanced multi-modal machine translation approach with multi-attention. In: Proceedings of the 2020 on International Conference on Multimedia Retrieval (ICMR), pp. 571–577 (2020)
11. Helcl, J., Libovický, J., Varis, D.: CUNI system for the WMT18 multimodal translation task. In: Proceedings of the Third Conference on Machine Translation (WMT), pp. 616–623 (2018)

12. Huang, P., Sun, S., Yang, H.: Image-assisted transformer in zero-resource multi-modal translation. In: Proceedings of the 2021IEEE International Conference on Acoustics, Speech and Signal Processing (ICASSP), pp. 7548–7552 (2021)
13. Ive, J., Madhyastha, P., Specia, L.: Distilling translations with visual awareness. In: ACL, pp. 6525–6538. Association for Computational Linguistics (2019)
14. Karita, S., Watanabe, S., Iwata, T., Delcroix, M., Ogawa, A., Nakatani, T.: Semi-supervised end-to-end speech recognition using text-to-speech and autoencoders. In: Proceedings of the IEEE International Conference on Acoustics, Speech and Signal Processing (ICASSP), pp. 6166–6170 (2019)
15. Kingma, D.P., Ba, J.: Adam: A method for stochastic optimization. In: Proceedings of the Third International Conference on Learning Representations (ICLR) (2015)
16. Lample, G., Conneau, A., Denoyer, L., Ranzato, M.: Unsupervised machine translation using monolingual corpora only. In: Proceedings of the 6th International Conference on Learning Representations (ICLR) (2018)
17. Lavie, A., Agarwal, A.: METEOR: an automatic metric for MT evaluation with high levels of correlation with human judgments. In: Proceedings of the Second Workshop on Statistical Machine Translation (WMT@ACL), pp. 228–231 (2007)
18. Li, L., Hu, K., Zheng, Y., Liu, J., Lee, K.A.: Coopnet: Multi-modal cooperative gender prediction in social media user profiling. In: ICASSP, pp. 4310–4314. IEEE (2021)
19. Li, L., Tayir, T., Hu, K., Zhou, D.: Multi-modal and multi-perspective machine translation by collecting diverse alignments. In: Pham, D.N., Theeramunkong, T., Governatori, G., Liu, F. (eds.) PRICAI 2021. LNCS (LNAI), vol. 13032, pp. 311–322. Springer, Cham (2021). https://doi.org/10.1007/978-3-030-89363-7_24
20. Papineni, K., Roukos, S., Ward, T., Zhu, W.: Bleu: a method for automatic evaluation of machine translation. In: Proceedings of the 40th Annual Meeting of the Association for Computational Linguistics (ACL), pp. 311–318 (2002)
21. Su, Y., Fan, K., Bach, N., Kuo, C.J., Huang, F.: Unsupervised multi-modal neural machine translation. In: Proceedings of the 2019 IEEE Conference on Computer Vision and Pattern Recognition (CVPR), pp. 10482–10491 (2019)
22. Vaswani, A., et al.: Attention is all you need. In: Proceedings of the 31th Conference on Neural Information Processing Systems (NIPS), pp. 5998–6008 (2017)
23. Vincent, P., Larochelle, H., Bengio, Y., Manzagol, P.: Extracting and composing robust features with denoising autoencoders. In: Proceedings of the 25th International Conference on Machine Learning (ICML), pp. 1096–1103 (2008)
24. Wang, Y., et al.: Semi-supervised neural machine translation via marginal distribution estimation. IEEE ACM Trans. Audio Speech Lang. Process. 27(10), 1564–1576 (2019)
25. Xu, W., Niu, X., Carpuat, M.: Dual reconstruction: a unifying objective for semi-supervised neural machine translation. In: Findings of the Association for Computational Linguistics: EMNLP, pp. 2006–2020 (2020)
26. Yao, S., Wan, X.: Multimodal transformer for multimodal machine translation. In: Proceedings of the 58th Annual Meeting of the Association for Computational Linguistics (ACL), pp. 4346–4350 (2020)

SETFF: A Semantic Enhanced Table Filling Framework for Joint Entity and Relation Extraction

Hao Li[1], Md Tauhidul Islam[1], Kehan Huangliang[1], Zugang Chen[1],
Kaiyang Zhao[2], and Haixian Zhang[1(✉)]

[1] Machine Intelligence Laboratory, College of Computer Science, Sichuan University,
Chengdu, China
zhanghaixian@scu.edu.cn
[2] Department of Neurosurgery, West China Hospital of Sichuan University,
Chengdu, China

Abstract. In the study of text understanding and knowledge graph construction, the process of extracting entities and relations from unstructured text is crucial. Lately, joint extraction has achieved more significance in this context. Among them, table filling based method has attracted a lot of research in solving the problem of overlapping relation in complex scenarios. However, most existing table filling works need to deal with many invalid and redundant filling processes. At the same time, some semantic information is not fully considered. For instance, a token should have differentiated semantic representation when decoding triples under different relations. Moreover, the global association information between different relations is not fully utilized. In this paper, we propose a joint extraction framework: SETFF, based on table filling. Firstly, the proposed method filters out the possible relations in sentences through a relation filtering module. Then following the attention mechanism, the pre-trained relation embeddings are used to enhance the differential representation of token semantics under specified relations and obtain the mutual prompting information between different relations. In addition to these, extensive experimental results show that SETFF can effectively deal with the overlapping triples problem and achieve significant performance on two public datasets.

Keywords: Joint extraction of entities and relations · Table filling · Differentiated semantic representation · Global association information · Attention mechanism

1 Introduction

Triples are composed of two entities and the semantic relation between them, in the form of (*subject, relation, object*). Joint entity and relation extraction is to extract relation triples from unstructured text, which is very important for

© The Author(s), under exclusive license to Springer Nature Switzerland AG 2022
S. Khanna et al. (Eds.): PRICAI 2022, LNCS 13630, pp. 169–182, 2022.
https://doi.org/10.1007/978-3-031-20865-2_13

downstream tasks such as text retrieval and knowledge graph construction. The traditional method [1,12,20] uses the pipeline manner to extract entities and relations separately, which ignores the interactivity between entity recognition and relation extraction task, and causes some error propagation. To alleviate the above issues, some works based on joint extraction have achieved remarkable results [9,14,18], which integrate the associations of two tasks by sharing parameters or decoding process. Besides, some works based on table filling are suitable for relation extraction task [7,10,16,23], which usually construct a table to mark entities and relations. Each item in the table represents a token pair in the sequence. In these methods, the table is updated by simultaneously learning the token features, and the relational triples are obtained by decoding the filled table.

However, in some complex scenarios, there exist cases where different relations share a single entity or entity pairs, as shown in Fig. 1. Considering the SingleEntityOverlap (SEO) and EntityPairOverlap (EPO) overlapping patterns, some previous studies handled overlapping triples via a two-phase relation-weighted graph convolutional networks (GCNs) [5] or introduced a fresh perspective to treat relation extraction into a mapping function from subjects to objects [17].

Nevertheless, some points are still not considered in the previous methods: (1) Redundant relation processing. The previous table filling methods often need to fill a table for each relation, and a dataset might contain multiple defined relation types. In fact, there are only a few reasonable relations in a sentence, and the decoding of most other relations is redundant. (2) Differentiated semantic representation of token. The previous works often use the same token features rather than the customized token semantic features to decode the triples under the specified relation. In general, even if the same token is in the sentence, however, when used to decode different relational triples, its features should also gets changed accordingly. For instance, consider the sentence, "*Associ-azione California Chievoverona is managed by Rolando Maran, who was born in Italy and is in the Carrarese California club*". In the sentence, each token for "*Rolando Maran*" should have different semantics when referring to a person born in Italy and when defined as an administrator of a club because the same token plays different roles in different relations. (3) Global associations between relations. The semantics of different relations may be similar or contradictory, so the decoding result of any one of the two relations has a certain degree of prompting effect on the decoding of the other relation. For instance: "*Quebec, Canada's second most popular Province, after Ontario, has not decided to go that far*". Here, triple (*Ontario, /location/administrative_ division/country, Canada*) can lead us to another triple (*Canada, /location/location/contains, Ontario*), and vice versa. This is because */location/location/contains* and */location/administrative_division/country* has very close semantics. However, most existing methods did not consider the mutual prompt information between these diverse relations.

In order to solve all above issues, we propose a new table filling based framework: SETFF. Firstly, SETFF uses a *Relation Filtering Module* to identify the valid relations in a sentence. Then a *Relation-specific Semantic Enhancement Module* is designed to decode the triples under a variety of relations. The relation embedding combined with the original representation of token is used to perform additional self-attention calculations within the sentence to obtain the differentiated token features under the specific relation. At the same time, a cross-attention calculation is undertaken between the same token pairs in different table features to obtain prompt information from other tables. Therefore, the customized features can be used when filling in each table and integrate knowledge from other triples simultaneously. Moreover, a *Relation Embeddings Pre-train Module* is proposed to obtain the vector representation of the relation by designing a position prediction task.

The main contributions of this work are as follows:

- We propose a novel framework, SETFF, based on table filling for joint entity relation extraction, which effectively deals with the overlapping triple problem.
- We design a novel semantic enhancement module based on attention mechanism which can obtain the differentiated token features adjusted with the relations and integrate the global associations between the triples.
- To the best of our knowledge, we are the first to apply relation filtering to table filling methods. In addition to this, we designed a position prediction task to obtain the pre-trained relation embeddings.
- Experimental results show that SETFF achieves promising performance than the baseline models on both NYT [11] and WebNLG [6] datasets.

	Sentence	Triples
Normal	[The United States] President [Obama] has a meet with [Macron], the president of [France].	(The United States, president, Obama) (France, president, Macron)
SEO	[A Loyal Character Dancer] is written in [English] and published by [Soho Press].	(A Loyal Character Dancer, language, English) (A Loyal Character Dancer, publisher, Soho Press)
EPO	[Bill Gates], the chairman of [Microsoft], will be a keynote speaker.	(Microsoft, founders, Bill Gates) (Bill Gates, company, Microsoft)

Fig. 1. Examples of different overlapping patterns: Normal, SingleEntityOverlap(SEO) and EntityPairOverlap(EPO).

2 Related Work

In relation extraction task, due to the lack of interaction between entities and relations in the traditional pipeline manner, the method based on joint extraction has attracted more attention [4,5,22]. Among them, two main representative methods are based on sequence tagging or table filling.

Sequence tagging based methods usually use linear or binary tagging to identify the position of entities in sentences. [24] proposes a new tagging scheme, which include both entity and relation information in a unified label definition. To solve the problem of overlapping triples, [22] propose an end2end model based on sequence-to-sequence learning through a copy mechanism. [17] apply binary tagging for each relation to distinguish the start and end position of entities, which creatively treat relation classification as a mapping function from subject to object. [18] decompose the task into multiple subtasks, and use span-based tagging scheme to annotate entity boundaries and relation types. Besides, some methods based on table filling allocate the token pairs in the sentence to an table item, and decode the filled table to obtain all relation triples. For instance, the diagonal of the table is filled with the BILOU label of the token itself, and the off-diagnostic items are assigned the corresponding relation type of the token pair [10]. Unlike previous works, [7] propose a novel table filling multi-task recurrent neural network model to capture the interdependencies in entity and relation extraction tasks. A novel method of table construction is presented to integrate syntactic information to facilitate global learning [23] and a single-stage method is proposed to eliminate the exposure bias between the training and inference stages [16].

However, they ignore the differential semantic expression of tokens under different relations. [19] uses attention mechanism for assigning higher weights to the relation-related tokens in the sentence, which obtains the fine-grained sentence representation to identify triples. Yet, it does not consider the global associations between different relations, and redundant relations are not filtered out in advance.

3   The Framework

This section mainly introduces our joint entity relation extraction framework SETFF. The overall structure is shown in Fig. 2. At first, the definition of table items in our table filling strategy is introduced and then the modules a, b and c (a. Relation Embeddings Pre-train module, b. Relation Filter Module, c. Relation-specific Semantic Enhancement Module) in our framework is described. Finally, we describe the process of generating triples according to the filled table.

3.1   Table Item Definition

In order to identify a certain relation in the input sequence $S = [w_1, w_2 \ldots w_n]$, where w_i represents a token in the sentence, we first need to expand the sequence into a table according to the tokens. The position (i, j) in the table corresponds to the token pairs composed of w_i and w_j. And the table item label indicates whether the token pairs at this position are involved in the composition of a triple. The label set is defined as $L = \{N, BB, EE, BS, ES, SB, SE, SS\}$ where each label (except N) is composed of two characters. The first character indicates whether the token w_i belongs to a subject, 'B' means the head token of the

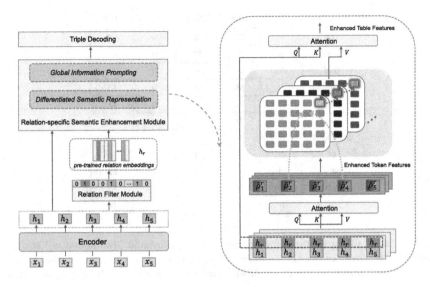

Fig. 2. The overall structure of SETFF. We use different colours to represent different relations, where blue dotted lines represent filling the corresponding table item with the features of token pairs, purple dotted lines represent mining global prompt information from different relations, and h_r represents the pre-trained relation embeddings.

subject, 'E' means the tail token of the subject, and 'S' means that the subject is composed of a single token. The second character is used to indicate the object in the triple. 'N' means none of the above. An example of the filling strategy is shown in Fig. 3, where each of the label definition contains the location and composition information of entities in triples. Therefore, it is more efficient when decoding the triples because fewer table items are filled in each table.

3.2 Methodology

Encoder. The pre-trained language model based on large-scale corpus has shown strong feature extraction ability and achieved substantial improvement in many downstream NLP tasks. The Bert [3] with multi-layer transformer [15] structure is used as the basic encoder. For the input sentence $S = [w_1, w_2 \ldots w_n]$, we can obtain the encoded representation $H = [h_1, h_2 \ldots h_n | h_i \in \mathbb{R}^{d \times 1}]$, where n is the length of the sentence, and d is the embedding size.

Relation Embeddings Pre-train Module. This module aims to obtain the vector representation of relations in low dimensional space. For a triple (subject, relation, object), the relation describes the associations between two entities. Thus, the subject or object can be predicted by combining one of them with the associate relation.

Therefore, an entity location prediction task is designed to train effective relation embeddings. It combines the representation of the subject with relation

	......	New	York	,	USA
The	N	BB	N	N	BS
Bronx	N	N	EE	N	ES
and	N	N	N	N	N
Manhattan	N	SB	SE	N	SS
are	N	N	N	N	N
tow	N	N	N	N	N
boroughs	N	N	N	N	N
of	N	N	N	N	N
New	N	N	N	N	BS
York	N	N	N	N	ES
......	N	N	N	N	N

Fig. 3. A table filling example for sentence "The Bronx and Manhattan are two boroughs of New York" under the *contains* relation. Here, N is the initialization value of the table item, and the red label indicates the recognized entity. (Color figure online)

embedding to predict the position of the object in the sentence. Through continuous iterations, the relation embeddings are gradually optimized. It is worth noting that the representation of [CLS] token is added to better integrate the context of the whole sentence. This process is described as follows:

$$
\begin{aligned}
h_{sub}^r &= h_{[CLS]} \oplus Maxpool\left(h_{w_i}, h_{w_j}, \ldots, h_{w_{i+k}}\right) \oplus h_r \\
P_{obj}^r &= Sigmoid\left(W_p h_{sub}^r + b_p\right) \in \mathbb{R}^{n \times 1}
\end{aligned}
\tag{1}
$$

where $\oplus$ indicates concatenate operation, k represents the span width of the subject, h_r represents the embedding of relation r, which is initialized randomly. W_p is a parameter matrix and b_p is a bias vector, h_{sub}^r means the representation of the subject, and P_{obj}^r indicates the score that the token at each position in the sentence belongs to the object. And those tokens belonging to the objects are expected to get higher scores.

The loss function in this module is designed as follows:

$$
Loss_{pre} = -\frac{1}{n}\sum_{i=1}^{n}\left[y_{obj}^r\left(i\right)\log p_{obj}^r\left(i\right) + \left(1 - y_{obj}^r\left(i\right)\right)\log\left(1 - p_{obj}^r\left(i\right)\right)\right]
\tag{2}
$$

where $y_{obj}^r\left(i\right)$ represents the truth label of the predicted object position for index i.

Relation Filter Module. A dataset contains the relation set $R = \{r_i\}_{i=1}^{u}$, where u indicates the number of relation categories. In order to solve the overlapping triples problem, the previous table filling methods often need to fill a table for each relation category. However, there are only several valid relations in a sentence, and so most of the filled tables are redundant. It will introduce unnecessary noise when the items in tables are very sparse.

In this module, a hyper-parameter m is set to identify a relation subset $\hat{R} = \{\hat{r}_i\}_{i=1}^m$ for each sentence. It should be set to exceed the typical number of possible relations in a sentence. Thus, only the tables of these m kinds of relations are maintained. And a binary tagging strategy is used to identify possible relations in a sentence, as shown in Eq. 3:

$$h_s = h_{[CLS]} \oplus Avg\left(h_1, \ldots, h_n\right)$$
$$P_r = Sigmoid\left(W_r h_s + b_r\right) \in \mathbb{R}^{u \times 1} \tag{3}$$
$$\{\hat{R}_i\}_{i=1}^m = f_{m,t}(P_r)$$

We use an average pool of the embeddings of n tokens in the sentence, where h_s means the representation of the whole sentence, and P_r represents the activation value predicted for different implicit relation categories. The function $f_{m,t}(\cdot)$ takes out the top m relations whose activation value is greater than the threshold value $t = 0.5$. If not enough relations are activated, we will pad $\hat{R}$ with relation "None". W_r and b_r are trainable parameters.

Relation-Specific Semantic Enhancement Module. This module enhances the semantic features of tokens and token pairs in sentences.

Differentiated Semantic Representation. Even for the same token in a sentence, it plays different roles when used to decode the triples of different relations. That is why we filled tables with differentiated token features instead of fixed token features. Therefore, it is necessary to obtain the corresponding semantic representation of tokens under the specific relation.

We concatenate the embedding of the certain relation with the original feature of the token, which means that additional condition information is attached to the token. However, its interaction within the context still needs to be considered. Therefore, we establish a self-attention operation between the fused representations of all tokens in the sentence.

$$\rho_i^r = W_\rho \left(h_i \oplus h_r\right) + b_\rho$$
$$\hat{\rho}_i^r = SelfAtten(\rho_i^r) \tag{4}$$

where $\hat{\rho}_i^r$ represents the enhancement feature of w_i under relation r. Then we build table features for different relations, and the element at (i, j) position can be obtained by the following equation:

$$t_{i,j}^r = \sigma \left[W_t \left(\hat{\rho}_i^r \circ \hat{\rho}_j^r\right) + b_t\right] \tag{5}$$

where $\circ$ represents dot product operation, and σ represents ELU activation function [2]. W_t and b_t are trainable parameters.

Global Information Prompting. Different relations of triples in the same sentence can prompt each other. Moreover, previous studies [15] show that an attention function can be described as mapping a query and a set of key-value pairs to an output. Hence, we calculate the cross attention between elements at the same position of different table features to mine the global associations. The semantic relevance of any two relation categories is reflected by the matching degrees of their embeddings in the low dimensional vector spaces.

Thus, the query vector is set as the relation embedding of the current table and the key vector is set as the relation embedding of other tables. As a result, the strength of semantic prompting from other relation triples can be determined by the attention weight. The enhanced table feature at position (i, j) is:

$$\hat{t}_{i,j}^r = Atten\left(h_r, h_r, t_{i,j}^r\right), r \in \hat{R} \tag{6}$$

The loss of training is defined as Eq. 7:

$$Loss = \sum_{r}^{\hat{R}} \sum_{i=1}^{n} \sum_{j=1}^{n} -\log P_{i,j}^r \left(y_{i,j}^r = \hat{y}_{i,j}^r\right) \tag{7}$$

here $y_{i,j}^r$ represents the truth label of token pair at position (i, j).

Triple Decoding. After obtaining the enhanced table feature, each token pairs is assigned with a corresponding label in the table, as shown in Eq. 8:

$$P_{i,j}^r = Softmax\left(W_o \hat{t}_{i,j}^r + b_o\right)$$
$$y_{i,j}^r = \underset{l \in L}{argmax}\left(P_{i,j}^r \rightarrow l\right) \tag{8}$$

where $y_{i,j}^r$ is the labeled result for the token pair w_i and w_j in the table of relation r. Then all the triples in the sentence can be decoded according to Algorithm 1.

Table 1. Statistics of the data sets used in the experiment. The *Details* table column shows the information of the test set. Note that a sentence may belong to the overlapping pattern of SEO and EPO at the same time. N represents the number of triples in a sentence, and 171* indicates that the number of relation categories in WebNLG* is 171.

Dataset	Sentences			Details					
	Train	Valid	Test	Normal	SEO	EPO	N=1	N>1	Relations
NYT	56195	5000	5000	3266	1297	978	3244	1756	24
WebNLG	5019	500	703	246	457	26	266	437	216/171*

Algorithm 1. Triple Decoding

Input:

    The relation set $\hat{R}$;

    The label set $\hat{L}$ without N;

    The sequence $S = [w_1, w_2, \ldots, w_n]$;

    The filled table Y^r of relation $r \in \hat{R}$;

Output:

    The triple result set $T \leftarrow \varnothing$;

1: **for** $r \in \hat{R}$ **do**

2:     Define empty sets $TP_{BB}, TP_{EE}, TP_{BS}, TP_{ES}, TP_{SB}, TP_{SE}, TP_{SS}$ which contain the index (i, j) of token pairs whose table item are corresponding label.

3:     **for** $y^r_{i,j} \in Y^r$ **do**

4:       **if** $y^r_{i,j} \in \hat{L}$ **then**

5:         add (i, j) to TP_l // l equals $y^r_{i,j}$

6:       **end if**

7:     **end for**

8:     **for** $(i, j) \in TP_{BB}$ **do**

9:       find an element (p, q) from TP_{EE},   // here $i < p$ and $j < q$ add $(w_{i \ldots p}, r, w_{j \ldots q})$ to T

10:     **end for**

11:     **for** $(i, j) \in TP_{BS}$ **do**

12:       find an element (p, q) from TP_{ES},   // here $i < p$ and $j = q$ add $(w_{i \ldots p}, r, w_j)$ to T

13:     **end for**

14:     **for** $(i, j) \in TP_{SB}$ **do**

15:       find an element (p, q) from TP_{SE},   // here $i = p$ and $j < q$ add $(w_i, r, w_{j \ldots q})$ to T

16:     **end for**

17:     **for** $(i, j) \in TP_{SS}$ **do**

18:       add (w_i, r, w_j) to T

19:     **end for**

20: **end for**

21: **return** T

4 Experiments

4.1 Experimental Settings

We evaluate our method on two public datasets, NYT [11] and WebNLG [6]. Both datasets have two versions with different annotation standards. The first version only annotates the last token of the entites named NYT* and WebNLG*. The second version annotates the whole entity span and is referred to as NYT and WebNLG. From this point of view, actually, we have four experimental datasets. All of them contain multiple relation categories and sentences with different overlapping patterns. Some statistics of these datasets are shown in Table 1.

    An extracted triple is considered correct only when all entities and relation are correct. In order to make a fair comparison with previous work, we use

Partial Match on NYT* and WebNLG*, and **Exact Match** on NYT and WebNLG. Consequently, either the head token or all tokens of the entity need to be predicted accurately.

We use Bert-base-cased [3] as our encoder and Adam [8] as optimizer. And the learning rate of Bert is set to 5×10^{-5} and 1×10^{-4} for other parts of the framework where the maximum length of sentences is set to 100. For relation filtering, the hyper-parameter m is set to 5, 5, 7 and 7 on NYT*, NYT, WebNLG*, and WebNLG, respectively. The size of relation embedding is set to 152/300 for NYT/WebNLG. The batch size is set to 6 with 50 training epochs in the training process.

We use standard micro Precision (Prec.), Recall (Rec.) and F1-score as evaluation metrics. Our proposed SETFF is compared with several strong baseline models, which are NovelTagging [24], CopyRE [22], GraphRel [5], OrderCopyRE [21], ETL-Span [18], RSAN [19], RIN [13], CasRel [17], PMEI [14].

Table 2. Main experimental results. Mark † indicates that the results are directly quoted from [22], and all other experimental results of the baseline models are directly quoted from the original papers. The highest experimental scores are marked in bold for reference.

Method	NYT*			NYT			WebNLG*			WebNLG		
	Prec.	Rec.	F1	Prec.	Rec.	F1	Prec.	Rec.	F1	Prec.	Rec.	F1
NovelTagging†	–	–	–	32.8	30.6	31.7	–	–	–	52.5	19.3	28.3
CopyRE	61.0	56.6	58.7	–	–	–	37.7	36.4	37.1	–	–	–
GraphRel	63.9	60.0	61.9	–	–	–	44.7	41.1	42.9	–	–	–
OrderCopyRE	77.9	67.2	72.1	–	–	–	63.3	59.9	61.6	–	–	–
ETL-Span	–	–	–	85.5	71.7	78.0	–	–	–	84.3	82.0	83.1
RSAN	–	–	–	85.7	83.6	84.6	–	–	–	80.5	83.8	82.1
RIN	87.2	87.3	87.3	83.9	85.5	84.7	87.6	87.0	87.3	77.3	76.8	77.0
CasRel	89.7	89.5	89.6	–	–	–	**93.4**	90.1	91.8	–	–	–
PMEI	90.5	89.8	90.1	88.4	88.9	88.7	91.0	**92.9**	92.0	80.8	82.8	81.8
SETFF	**91.7**	**90.8**	**91.2**	**91.6**	**90.4**	**91.0**	92.9	91.9	**92.4**	**90.9**	**88.6**	**89.7**

4.2 Main Results

It is showed that SETFF exceeds the prior baseline models in almost all evaluation metrics in Table 2. Moreover, the F1-socre on four data sets NYT*, NYT, WebNLG*, and WebNLG improved 1.1%, 2.3%, 0.4%, and 7.9% respectively, which proved the effectiveness of our semantic enhancement framework. In addition, SETFE performs better than RSAN[19] in the semantics tuning of sentences under specified relations. This shows that our semantic enhancement is more fine-grained and comprehensive. We also observed that SETFF improved more significantly on the dataset with fully labeled entity span. There are two reasons that might explain this. Firstly, for the location prediction task in relation embedding pre-training, the fully labeled entity can provide more complete information about entity span, so it can obtain more stronger relation embeddings. Secondly, the label of table items contain the character B representing the beginning and the character E representing the end. This strategy is more suitable for identifying multi-token entities. It is also observed that SETFF improved the most in WebNLG dataset. The WebNLG contains up to 216 relation categories, and the relation filtering module in this method can eliminate most irrelevant relations in a sentence.

Table 3. The report of ablation study.

Method	NYT*			WebNLG*		
	Prec	Rec	F1	Prec	Rec	F1
SETFF	**91.7**	**90.8**	**91.2**	**92.9**	**91.9**	**92.4**
-Relation Embeddings Pre-train	90.2	90.0	90.1	90.8	91.3	91.1
-Relation Filter	89.2	90.3	89.8	88.6	89.8	89.2
-Relation-specific Semantic Enhancement	86.7	89.7	88.2	87.5	90.2	88.8

4.3   Ablation Study

In this section, the ablation experiments are conducted to verify the effectiveness of each module in SETFF. Table 3 shows the experimental results of SETFF on NYT* and WebNLG* after removing different modules. When we use the relation embeddings of random initialization instead of pre-trained, the precision on both datasets is declined. It implies that our position prediction task is very suitable for this problem and can introduce some prior knowledge. And when the *Relation Filter Module* is removed, it shows a more prominent impact on WebNLG*, caused by different data distribution of the two data sets. It should be noted that there are relatively more redundant relations on WebNLG*, so it is more sensitive to the removal of this module. Finally, when *Relation-specific Semantic Enhancement Module* is removed and simply concatenate token featrues and relation embeddings, the performance of SETFF on both datasets decreases significantly, which proves that our semantic enhancement is very effective for fine-grained extraction of triples under specified relations.

4.4   Analysis on Hyper Parameter m

The associations of F1-score and parameter m are evaluated where m represents the size of the relation filtering subset. We try to search the optimal parameters in $\{2, 4, 5, 7, 9\}$. As shown in Fig. 4, the optimal m values on NYT* and WebNLG* are 5 and 7 respectively. The setting of this parameter is a trade-off result since the size of m affects both the precision and recall, wherein, on the one hand, too small m value will reduce the recall rate, and on the other hand, too large m will affect the precision. In the mean time, We observed that a smaller value of m is more harmful to the performance than a larger one. This is because the

Relation Filter Module will add "None" relation when it believes that there are not enough activated relation categories to select, and the latter modules can be trained to avoid extracting triples of this relation.

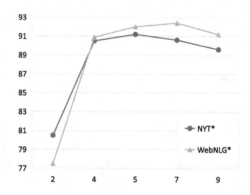

Fig. 4. F1-score under different hyper-parameter m.

4.5   Analysis on Different Sentence Types

A further evaluation of SETFF is observed on complex sentence patterns. Table 4 shows F1-score on sentences with different overlapping patterns and different numbers of triples on the NYT* dataset. We can see that in different scenarios, SETFF has made a lot of improvement compared with the baseline models and is even more obvious in harder sentences. All these improvement demonstrates the advantages of our framework. The possible game-changer is the coordination of different modules in SETFF, especially the attention-based semantic enhancement that can capture deep information to extract triples under certain relation.

Table 4. F1-score on sentences with different overlapping patterns and different numbers of triples.

Method	NYT*							
	Normal	SEO	EPO	N = 1	N = 2	N = 3	N = 4	N ≥ 5
CopyRE	66.0	48.6	55.0	67.1	58.6	52.0	53.6	30.0
GraphRel	69.6	51.2	58.2	71.0	61.5	57.4	55.1	41.1
OrderCopyRE	71.2	69.4	72.8	71.7	72.6	72.5	77.9	45.9
CasRel	87.3	91.4	92.0	88.2	90.3	91.9	94.2	83.7
SETFF	**89.1**	**93.2**	**93.3**	**89.0**	**91.6**	**92.8**	**95.6**	**91.2**

5 Conclusion

This paper propose a semantic enhanced table filling framework to solve the joint entity and relation extraction task. The proposed framework first completes the pre-training of relation embeddings. Then, filtering out the redundant relations of each sentence, the attention mechanism is used to achieve semantic enhancement, which includes obtaining the differentiated semantic expression of token under the specified relation and mining the global prompt information between different relations. The comprehensive experimental results on two benchmarks reveal the significant improvement of the proposed method, proving the ability to solve overlapping triple problem and the effectiveness in each module of SETFF.

Acknowledgements. This work was supported in part by the Science and Technology Department of Sichuan Province under Grant No.2021YFS0399 and in part by the Grid Planning and Research Center of Guangdong Power Grid Co under Grant 037700KK52220042(GDKJXM20220906).

References

1. Chan, Y.S., Roth, D.: Exploiting syntactico-semantic structures for relation extraction. In: Proceedings of the 49th Annual Meeting of the Association for Computational Linguistics: Human Language Technologies, pp. 551–560 (2011)
2. Clevert, D.A., Unterthiner, T., Hochreiter, S.: Fast and accurate deep network learning by exponential linear units (elus). arXiv preprint arXiv:1511.07289 (2015)
3. Devlin, J., Chang, M.W., Lee, K., Toutanova, K.: Bert: Pre-training of deep bidirectional transformers for language understanding. In: NAACL (2019)
4. Eberts, M., Ulges, A.: Span-based joint entity and relation extraction with transformer pre-training. arXiv preprint arXiv:1909.07755 (2019)
5. Fu, T.J., Li, P.H., Ma, W.Y.: Graphrel: Modeling text as relational graphs for joint entity and relation extraction. In: Proceedings of the 57th Annual Meeting of the Association for Computational Linguistics, pp. 1409–1418 (2019)
6. Gardent, C., Shimorina, A., Narayan, S., Perez-Beltrachini, L.: Creating training corpora for nlg micro-planning. In: 55th annual meeting of the Association for Computational Linguistics (ACL) (2017)
7. Gupta, P., Schütze, H., Andrassy, B.: Table filling multi-task recurrent neural network for joint entity and relation extraction. In: Proceedings of COLING 2016, the 26th International Conference on Computational Linguistics: Technical Papers, pp. 2537–2547 (2016)
8. Kingma, D.P., Ba, J.: Adam: A method for stochastic optimization. arXiv preprint arXiv:1412.6980 (2014)
9. Miwa, M., Bansal, M.: End-to-end relation extraction using lstms on sequences and tree structures. arXiv preprint arXiv:1601.00770 (2016)
10. Miwa, M., Sasaki, Y.: Modeling joint entity and relation extraction with table representation. In: Proceedings of the 2014 Conference on Empirical Methods in Natural Language Processing (EMNLP), pp. 1858–1869 (2014)

11. Riedel, Sebastian, Yao, Limin, McCallum, Andrew: Modeling relations and their mentions without labeled text. In: Balcázar, José Luis., Bonchi, Francesco, Gionis, Aristides, Sebag, Michèle (eds.) ECML PKDD 2010. LNCS (LNAI), vol. 6323, pp. 148–163. Springer, Heidelberg (2010). https://doi.org/10.1007/978-3-642-15939-8_10

12. Rink, B., Harabagiu, S.: Utd: Classifying semantic relations by combining lexical and semantic resources. In: Proceedings of the 5th International Workshop on Semantic Evaluation, pp. 256–259 (2010)

13. Sun, K., Zhang, R., Mensah, S., Mao, Y., Liu, X.: Recurrent interaction network for jointly extracting entities and classifying relations. arXiv preprint arXiv:2005.00162 (2020)

14. Sun, K., Zhang, R., Mensah, S., Mao, Y., Liu, X.: Progressive multitask learning with controlled information flow for joint entity and relation extraction. In: Association for the Advancement of Artificial Intelligence (AAAI) (2021)

15. Vaswani, A., et al.: Attention is all you need. In: Advances in Neural Information Processing Systems, vol. 30 (2017)

16. Wang, Y., Yu, B., Zhang, Y., Liu, T., Zhu, H., Sun, L.: Tplinker: Single-stage joint extraction of entities and relations through token pair linking. arXiv preprint arXiv:2010.13415 (2020)

17. Wei, Z., Su, J., Wang, Y., Tian, Y., Chang, Y.: A novel cascade binary tagging framework for relational triple extraction. In: ACL (2020)

18. Yu, B., et al.: Joint extraction of entities and relations based on a novel decomposition strategy. arXiv preprint arXiv:1909.04273 (2019)

19. Yuan, Y., Zhou, X., Pan, S., Zhu, Q., Song, Z., Guo, L.: A relation-specific attention network for joint entity and relation extraction. In: IJCAI, vol. 2020, pp. 4054–4060 (2020)

20. Zeng, D., Liu, K., Lai, S., Zhou, G., Zhao, J.: Relation classification via convolutional deep neural network. In: Proceedings of COLING 2014, the 25th International Conference on Computational Linguistics: Technical Papers, pp. 2335–2344 (2014)

21. Zeng, X., He, S., Zeng, D., Liu, K., Liu, S., Zhao, J.: Learning the extraction order of multiple relational facts in a sentence with reinforcement learning. In: Proceedings of the 2019 Conference on Empirical Methods in Natural Language Processing and the 9th International Joint Conference on Natural Language Processing (EMNLP-IJCNLP), pp. 367–377 (2019)

22. Zeng, X., Zeng, D., He, S., Liu, K., Zhao, J.: Extracting relational facts by an end-to-end neural model with copy mechanism. In: Proceedings of the 56th Annual Meeting of the Association for Computational Linguistics (Volume 1: Long Papers), pp. 506–514 (2018)

23. Zhang, M., Zhang, Y., Fu, G.: End-to-end neural relation extraction with global optimization. In: Proceedings of the 2017 Conference on Empirical Methods in Natural Language Processing, pp. 1730–1740 (2017)

24. Zheng, S., Wang, F., Bao, H., Hao, Y., Zhou, P., Xu, B.: Joint extraction of entities and relations based on a novel tagging scheme. arXiv preprint arXiv:1706.05075 (2017)

PEKIN: Prompt-Based External Knowledge Integration Network for Rumor Detection on Social Media

Ziang Hu[1,2], Huan Liu[1,2], Kun Li[1,2], Yuhang Wang[1,2], Zongzhen Liu[1,2], and Xiaodan Zhang[1(✉)]

[1] Institute of Information Engineering, Chinese Academy of Sciences, Beijing, China
413111617@qq.com
[2] School of Cyber Security, University of Chinese Academy of Sciences, Beijing, China

Abstract. Pretrained language models(PLMs) and additional features have been used in rumor detection with excellent performance. However, on the one hand, some recent studies find one of its critical challenges is the significant gap of objective forms in pretraining and finetuning, which restricts taking full advantage of knowledge in PLMs. On the other hand, text contents are condensed and full of knowledge entities, but existing methods usually focus on the textual contents and social contexts, and ignore external knowledge of text entities. In this paper, to address these limitations, we propose a Prompt-based External Knowledge Integration Network(PEKIN) for rumor detection, which incorporates both prior knowledges of rumor detection tasks and external knowledge of text entities. For one thing, unlike the conventional "pre-train, finetune" paradigm, we propose a prompt-based method, which brings prior knowledge to help PLMs understand the rumor detection task and better stimulate the rich knowledge distributed in PLMs. For another, we identify entities mentioned in the text and then get these entities' annotations from a knowledge base. After that, we use these annotations contexts as external knowledge to provide complementary information. Experiments on three datasets showed that PEKIN outperformed all compared models, significantly beating the old state-of-the-art on Weibo dataset.

Keywords: Rumor detection · Prompt-based · External knowledge

1 Introduction

Social psychology literature defines a rumor as a story or a statement whose truth value is unverified or deliberately false [1]. False rumors are damaging as they cause public panic and social unrest. With the rapid growth of large-scale social media platforms such as Twitter and Sina Weibo, rumors on social media have become a significant concern. Rumors can propagate very fast and affect

© The Author(s), under exclusive license to Springer Nature Switzerland AG 2022
S. Khanna et al. (Eds.): PRICAI 2022, LNCS 13630, pp. 183–196, 2022.
https://doi.org/10.1007/978-3-031-20865-2_14

people's choices because of the popularity of social media. However, it is complicated for ordinary people to identify rumors from massive online information due to limited professional knowledge, time, or space. Therefore, it is necessary to develop automatic approaches to detect rumors.

For text classification tasks, including rumor detection, transformer-based models like Bidirectional Encoder Representations from Transformers (BERT) [2], which achieved impressive results, have a significant performance variation when fine-tuned on small datasets [3]. Thus researchers proposed ensembles of multiple BERT models to provide more robust predictions. However, some recent studies find one of its critical challenges is the significant gap of objective forms in pretraining and fine-tuning, which restricts taking full advantage of knowledge in PLMs [4].

Although the existing deep learning methods have succeeded in detecting rumors based on the high-level feature representations of text contents, they ignore the external knowledge by which people usually judge the authenticity of the rumor. Rumor contents are highly condensed and comprised of a large number of entities mentioned. Generally, named entities could have rich annotated meanings, but these messages are not fed into the model.For example, as shown in (Fig. 1),a piece of rumor contains the following entity mentions:"interview", "bounty","child", "millionaire","murder","family",and "money". People usually know the annotations of these entities before reading, like we know "interview" means "a meeting (often a public one) at which a journalist asks somebody questions to...", "bounty" means "money that is offered as a reward for doing something, especially...", "murder" means "the unlawful killing of another human without justification or valid excuse, especially ...", and so on. If we take these annotations of entities as external knowledge, it can help evaluate the rumor's credibility. However, these contents cannot be provided directly based on the text contents of rumors and comments. Thus, the introduction of external knowledge is very important for rumor detection.

Content: ABC reportedly gave darren wilson 6-figures for an **interview**. if true, they essentially paid the **bounty** for killing a black **child**. #ferguson
Comment: (1)Add that to the gofundme donations, and the 133 days of paid vacay. He's well over a **millionaire** for **murder**.(2)absolutely despicable. Ugh. How much has the **family** gotten? Ugh.(3)ABC also made big **money**. Disgust!...

Fig. 1. A piece of rumor on Twitter

To alleviate these issues, in this paper, we propose a Prompt-based External Knowledge Integration Network(PEKIN) for rumor detection, which uses BERT to incorporate both prior knowledges of rumor detection tasks and external knowledge of text entities. For one thing, we propose a prompt-based method, which can further stimulate the rich knowledge distributed in PLMs to serve downstream tasks better. Previous studies suggest that prompt-tuning has remarkable superiority in the low-data scenario over the generic fine-tuning methods with extra classifiers [5–7]. The prompt is designed with prior knowledge of the rumor detection task, which brings prior knowledge to help PLMs understand the rumor detection task. For another, we identify entities mentioned in the text and then get these entities' annotations from a knowledge base. After that, we use these annotations contexts as external knowledge to provide complementary information. Thus, our proposed model can incorporate both prior knowledges of rumor detection tasks and external knowledge to detect rumors. To the best of our knowledge, PEKIN is the first to adopt prompt-based learning for rumor detection and use annotations of entities as external knowledge for this task. The main contributions of this work include:

(1) We propose a prompt-based rumor detection method, which brings prior knowledge to the rumor detection task by the hand-crafted rapid method.
(2) We propose incorporating entities and their entity annotations distilled from the knowledge base for rumor detection.
(3) We propose a Prompt-based External Knowledge Integration Network(PEKIN)for rumor detection; this network integrates knowledge into rumor content more reasonably and effectively.

Experimental results on three datasets show that PEKIN outperforms existing methods.PEKIN accuracy on Ma-Weibo [8] is higher than the old SOTA, Ma-RvNN [9]. Furthermore, PEKIN is the best of all compared methods on Twitter15 and Twitter16.

2   Related Works

In this section, we briefly revisit the following related topics: rumor detection, prompt-tuning, and external knowledge integration.

2.1   Rumor Detection

A rumor is a statement whose authenticity is certified to be false or unverified [10]. Considering the tremendous number of Twitter and Weibo users, even a little promotion of the rumor detecting accuracy is precious. Rumor detection, framed as text detection tasks, can be cracked by either traditional machine learning approaches [11] or deep neural networks [12], and comments or replies, as additional features, are widely used.

Recent deep-learning-based studies include: Wang [13] embedded source posts and comments with sentimental features and then inputted them into a two-layer Gated Recurrent Unit (GRU) network; Kumar [14] applied a tree LSTM to predict rumors with tree-structured replies; Bian [15] fed posts and replies into a Graph Convolution Network (GCN) to take advantage of propagation features, and later extended GCN to be Bi-directional GCN (viz. Bi-GCN) to explore the structures of wide dispersion on rumor detection; Zhang [16] encoded replies in a temporal order through an LSTM component; Riedel [17] profited from the cosine similarity of news content and comments while setting a threshold of similarity to filter those irrelevant comments; Lu [18] put user profiles into GCNs to extract propagation features.

2.2 Prompt-Tuning

Prompt-tuning is a new paradigm of fine-tuning inspired by GPT-3 [19], especially for language models in few-shot or zero-shot settings. It means prepending instructions and demonstrations to the input and output predictions. Recent prompt-tuning work focuses on the semi-supervised setting with many unlabeled examples. Gao [20] explore their prompt tuning methods with demonstrations of language models for some benchmark tasks, including Sentiment Classification.Prompt-tuning can induce better performances for PLMs on widespread of NLP tasks including text classification [20], relation extraction [4], NER [21], and so on. To construct better prompt for downstream tasks, several approaches [22] leverage knowledge injection to templates and fertilizer construction. Besides, there exist lots of works on prompting for mining knowledge from PLMs [23, 24].

2.3 External Knowledge Integration

Recently, there have been notable contributions toward integrating linguistic knowledge into DNNs for various NLP tasks. For sentiment analysis, Teng [25] integrates lexicon features to an RNN-based model with a custom weighted sum calculation of word features. Shin [26] proposes three convolutional neural network-specific methods of lexicon integration achieving state-of-the-art performance on two datasets. Kumar [27] concatenate features from a knowledge base to word representations in an attentive bidirectional LSTM architecture, also reporting state-of-the-art results. For sarcasm detection, Yang [28] incorporate psycholinguistic, stylistic, structural, and readability features by concatenating them to paragraph and document level representations.

3 Method

We briefly overview the proposed Prompt-based External Knowledge Integration Network (PEKIN). The framework of PEKIN is depicted in (Fig. 2). We select relatively valuable comments according to a sentimental intensity ranking. Training data1 consists of source post, comment text, and prompt text, The details of prompt learning are presented in the 3.1 subsection. Training data1 utilizes an external knowledge integration module to obtain entities in the text and then obtain annotations of the entities; those entities and associated annotations consist of training data2; the details of external knowledge extraction are described in the 3.2 subsection. In training, we use *BERT* model as the base learner. Firstly, Input training data1 into $BERT$ model, Since we want to predict whether the word in the $[MASK]$ position is yes or no, and the first token$[CLS]$ summarizes the information from input tokens using a global attention mechanism, we extract the embedding representation of $[MASK]$ position(viz. a 768-dimensional vector)and $[CLS]$ position(viz. a 768-dimensional vector) of training data1. Then, input training data2 into the BERT model, we extract the embedding representation of $[CLS]$ position(viz. a 768-dimensional vector) of training data2 as external knowledge. Finally, concatenate the three embedding representations above. The prediction layer is a dense network with softmax activation that maps the concatenated vector to two outputs to predict whether the $[MASK]$ position word is yes or no.

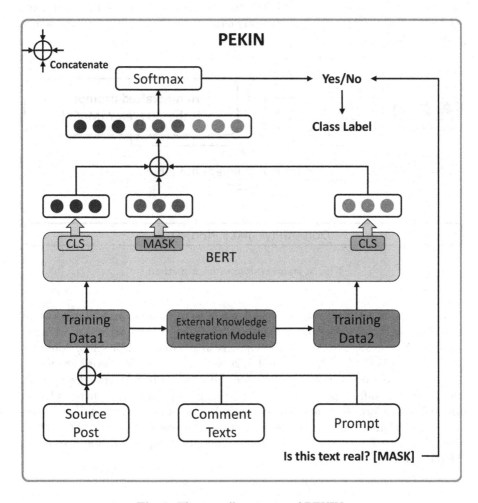

Fig. 2. The overall structure of PEKIN

3.1   Prompt Learning

Our work is based on the hand-crafted prompt learning method (HPL). We should design templates by our prior knowledge of the rumor task, so we designed 4 Chinese templates for Weibo data and 4 English templates for Twitter data, respectively, according to Social psychology's definition of rumor [1], As shown in Table 4.

The HPL model includes an input layer, hand-crafted prompt, pre-trained language model, and output layer. The pre-trained model M is used to calculate the probability values of $[MASK]$ to select the best word in the verbalizer with the maximum probability. For example, hand-crafted prompt "Is this text real? $[MASK]$ ", verbalizer"yes", "no", and then the prompt model will construct the template "source posts" and "related comments" and "Is this text real? $[MASK]$".Finally, M will return the predictive value, "no" indicating the source post is a rumor. As shown in (Fig. 3).

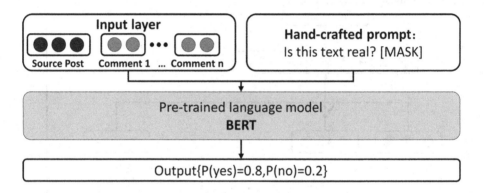

Fig. 3. Hand-crafted prompt method

In this work,let $S = \{s_1, s_2, ..., s_n\}$ be a set of source posts.Each $s_i \in S$ is a short text composed of a word (in English) or character (in Chinese) sequence $X =< X_1^i, X_2^i, ...X_l^i >$, Each s_i is associated with a set of comment texts (viz. replies) $C_i = \{c_1^i, c_2^i, ...c_n^i\}$ Like s_i,each $c_j^i \in C_i$ is a word or character sequence.We use a pre-trained model bert, verbalizer W:verbalizer{"yes", "no"},a hand-crafted prompt $P = \{p_1, p_2, ..., p_n, [MASK]\}$,where value of $[MASK]$ comes form W.The sequence input X and related comment C,and manual prompt P are separated by $[SEP]$ form a template $T = \{t_1, t_2, ..., t_n\}$.Then, input template T into model $BERT$,the template T representation learned by $BERT$ is $P = \{p_1, p_2, ..., p_n\}$

$$P_i = BERT(templateT) \tag{1}$$

Then, we extract the first element and $[MASK]$ position element of P_i respectively, which is the embedding of $[CLS]$ and $[MASK]$ in the last layer. We get the prompt learning represented PM_i derived by:

$$PM_i = concate(P_i[0], P_i[MASK]) \tag{2}$$

3.2 External Knowledge Extraction

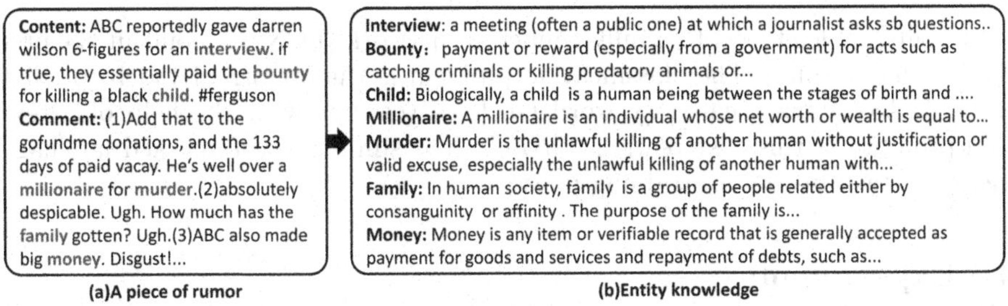

| Content: ABC reportedly gave darren wilson wilson 6-figures for an interview. if true, they essentially paid the bounty for killing a black child. #ferguson **Comment:** (1)Add that to the gofundme donations, and the 133 days of paid vacay. He's well over a millionaire for murder.(2)absolutely despicable. Ugh. How much has the family gotten? Ugh.(3)ABC also made big money. Disgust!... | **Interview:** a meeting (often a public one) at which a journalist asks sb questions.. **Bounty:** payment or reward (especially from a government) for acts such as catching criminals or killing predatory animals or... **Child:** Biologically, a child is a human being between the stages of birth and .... **Millionaire:** A millionaire is an individual whose net worth or wealth is equal to... **Murder:** Murder is the unlawful killing of another human without justification or valid excuse, especially the unlawful killing of another human with... **Family:** In human society, family is a group of people related either by consanguinity or affinity . The purpose of the family is... **Money:** Money is any item or verifiable record that is generally accepted as payment for goods and services and repayment of debts, such as... |
| (a)A piece of rumor | (b)Entity knowledge |

Fig. 4. The process of knowledge extraction

The goal of this module is to identify entities mentions in texts contents and then get these entities annotations in knowledge base. The process of knowledge extraction is shown in (Fig. 4), which includes the following steps:(1)After the 3.1 procedures, we get template $T = \{t_1, t_2, ..., t_n\}$, Through Named Entity Recognition tool, we can acquire entities sequence $E = \{e_1, e_2, ..., e_n\}$ from template t_i. (2)we can get annotations $A = \{a_1, a_2, ..., a_n\}$ for those entities in the knowledge base. For example, as shown in Fig. 1,a piece of news contains the following entity mentions: "interview", "bounty", "child", "millionaire", "murder", "family", "money". People usually know the annotations of these entities before reading the content of the text, like we know an "interview" means "a meeting (often a public one) at which a journalist asks sb questions to...", "bounty" means "money that is offered as a reward for doing something, especially..", "murder" means "the unlawful killing of another human without justification or valid excuse, especially ..", and so on.

After that, we use the $BERT$ model to get external knowledge represented.input entity annotations A into model $BERT$,the entity annotations A representation learned by $BERT$ is $K_i = \{k_1, k_2, ..., k_n\}$

$$K_i = BERT(Entity Annotations A) \tag{3}$$

Then, we extract the first element of K_i, which is the embedding of $[CLS]$ in the last layer. We get the external knowledge represented KE_i derived by:

$$KE_i = K_i[0] \tag{4}$$

3.3   Rumor Classification

After the above procedures, we get the prompt learning representation PM_i and the external knowledge representation KE_i. Both representations are important for rumor detection. Thus they are concatenated as final features for classification. The final representation PK_i is derived by:

$$PK_i = concate(PM_i, KE_i) \qquad (5)$$

Finally, we feed PK_i to a fully-connected network (FCN) and output the prediction via softmax. The classification problem is thus reformulated to predict the "$[MASK]$" as a category word (such as yes, no) with the help of a textual prompt "Is this text real? $[MASK]$". It is similar to the masked language modeling task in the pre-training phase.

4   Experiments

4.1   Datasets

The experiments were conducted on three datasets(Ma-Weibo, Twitter15, and Twitter16). These three datasets are widely used in the research line of rumor detection. Table 1 displays the basic statistics.Considering the average length of items, we allow at most 128 tokens for the post area,359 tokens for the comment area,25 tokens for the prompt area, and 330 tokens for the external knowledge area on Weibo datasets. 64 tokens for the post area, and 312 tokens for the comment area, and 25 tokens for the prompt area, and 330 tokens for the external knowledge area on two Twitter datasets.

Table 1. Statistic of datasets

Statistic	# of post	# of true	# of false	# users	# posts
Ma-weibo	4664	2351	2313	2,746,818	3,805,656
Twitter15	742	370	372	276,663	331,612
Twitter16	412	205	207	173,487	204,820

Ma-Weibo [8].*Maetal*. Collected 4664 Chinese posts published on sinaWeibo before 2016, accompanied by user-profiles and comments.

Twitter15 and Twitter16 [29]. We also experimented on two Twitter datasets. We choose only"true" and "fake" labels as the ground truth. Since the original data does not contain comments, we obtained user information and comments via Twitter API.

4.2   Experimental Setting and Data Preprocessing

We implemented PEKIN based on the pre-trained BERT base. The machine learning platform employed in the experiments is TensorFlow 1.14 with Python 3.6.9. Exerting a Xeon E5-2682 v4 CPU and a Tesla V100-32GB GPU, PEKIN ran fast on Ubuntu 16.04.6 LTS. The learning rate was set to 5e-5 on all datasets. We ran 20 epochs on Weibo datasets and 30 epochs on Twitter datasets.

Same as the original papers [8] [29], we randomly select 10% instances as the development data set and split the rest for the training and testing set with a ratio of 3:1 in all three data sets.

For Twitter datasets, we use $NLTK^1$ tool to identify the name entity.And for the Weibo data set,we use LAC^2 tool to identify the name entity. For all datasets,we use $Wikipedia^3$ knowledge base to get related entities annotations.

4.3   Compared Methods

We compared PEKIN with ten competitive methods on three datasets. We adopt the same evaluation metrics used in the prior work for a fair comparison. Thus, the accuracy, precision, recall, and F1 score are adopted for evaluation. We ran the source code of all compared methods. We used the same setting presented in the original papers for a fair comparison.

SVM-TS [30]. An SVM-based method.

Ma-RvNN [9]. They proposed a tree-structured model based on a Recursive Neural Network (RvNN). This paper declared the recent SOTA on Ma-Weibo.

CNN [31]. A CNN-based model with joint text and propagation structure learning.

Bi-GCN [15]. The Bi-Directional Graph Convolution Network (Bi-GCN) is a new technique that beats five compared models, including SVM, CNN, and RvNN.

BERT [2]. BERT is a multilayer bidirectional Transformer encoder. We experimented on BERT-base (L = 12, H = 768, A = 12,Total Parameters = 110M).

RoBERTa [32]. Liu tested important BERT design choices and training strategies to present a more robust variant of BERT.

Longformer [33]. Beltagy presented a combination of local windowed attention and task-motivated global attention, making it easy to process long sequences.

PLAN [34]. A post-level attention model which learns long-distance interactions between posts by Transformer.

Wu-Stacking [35]. Wu combined a stacking ensemble fused with feature engineering.

Geng-Ensemble [36]. An ensemble network comprises three RNN-based learners, aggregating results by majority voting.

---

[1] https://github.com/nltk/nltk.
[2] https://github.com/baidu/lac.
[3] https://github.com/goldsmith/Wikipedia.

4.4   Primary Results

Table 2 and Table 3 show primary experimental results of all compared methods on three datasets. Preliminary conclusions are:

PEKIN achieved the highest classification accuracy and F1 score on three datasets among all tested methods.

Both BERT and RoBERTa are SOTA on general text classification tasks. However, compared with BERT, PEKIN gained an up to 0.92% accuracy improvement on Weibo datasets and more than 2% accuracy improvement on Twitter datasets.

Table 2. Rumor detection results on the Twitter dataset

Method	Twitter15				Twitter16			
	F1	Rec	Prc	Acc	F1	Rec	Prc	Acc
SVM-TS	0.7372	0.7387	0.7437	0.7385	0.7589	0.7638	0.7901	0.7646
Ma-RvNN	0.9412	0.9730	0.9114	0.9392	0.9302	0.9756	0.8889	0.9268
CNN	0.8756	0.9103	0.8559	0.8721	0.9233	0.9408	0.9142	0.9214
Bi-GCN	0.9596	0.9595	**0.9599**	0.9596	0.9514	0.9514	**0.9519**	0.9515
BERT	0.9343	0.9397	0.9364	0.9367	0.9291	0.9274	0.9304	0.932
RoBERTa	0.9352	0.9354	0.9368	0.9353	0.9367	0.9371	0.94	0.9369
Longformer	0.9056	0.9056	0.9069	0.9057	0.9075	0.9076	0.911	0.9078
PLAN	0.9278	0.9133	0.951	0.9213	0.9431	0.9508	0.9336	0.9423
Wu-Stacking	0.9285	0.9285	0.9297	0.9286	0.9247	0.9246	0.9261	0.9248
Geng-Ensemble	0.9506	0.9528	0.9503	0.9512	0.9523	0.9537	0.9512	0.9518
PEKIN (best)	**0.9651**	**0.9880**	0.9431	**0.9642**	**0.9574**	**0.9782**	0.9375	**0.9569**

Table 3. Rumor detection results on the Weibo dataset

Method	Ma-Weibo			
	F1	Rec	Prc	Acc
SVM-TS	0.8827	0.8858	0.9150	0.8846
Ma-RvNN	0.9481	0.9484	0.9495	0.9481
CNN	0.9515	0.9520	0.9515	0.9510
Bi-GCN	0.9612	0.9613	0.9616	0.9612
BERT	0.9603	0.9598	0.9634	0.9603
RoBERTa	0.9603	0.9605	0.9603	0.9603
Longformer	0.8998	0.8999	0.9108	0.9084
PLAN	0.9208	0.9271	0.9159	0.9226
Wu-Stacking	0.9347	0.9352	0.9391	0.9348
Geng-Ensemble	0.9565	0.9567	0.956	0.956
PEKIN(best)	**0.9694**	**0.9750**	**0.9639**	**0.9695**

Both PLAN and Longformer are good at processing long sequences. However, PEKIN performed better than any of them, which indicates that using all comments is not the best option.

Graph-structured models include Ma-RvNN, CNN, and Bi-GCN. Ma-RvNN, the recent SOTA on Ma-Weibo, uses tree structures for propagation paths. CNN jointly learns text and propagation structure representation. Bi-GCN trains graph convolution networks. Bi-GCN performed best among these four models; however, PEKIN was superior to all of them.

We compared PEKIN with related ensemble models proposed in the recent two years. PEKIN performed better than Wu-Stacking and Geng-Ensemble, indicating the advantage of integrating BERT models and taking PEKIN.

4.5 Prompt Strategy Analysis

In this experiment, we designed 4 Chinese templates and 4 English templates, respectively, according to Social psychology's definition of rumor [1], and then we tested the effect of these templates. The experiment result is shown in Table 4. All templates are obtained from experiments on the validation set. Finally, we selected the best template for the final experiment. It can be seen that different prompts enhance the uncertainty of accuracy, but it does improve accuracy.

Table 4. Hand-prompts results

Chinese prompt	Ma-Weibo	English prompt	Twitter15	Twitter16
这段文本是否为虚假信息？（是/否）	0.9695	Is this text real? (Yes/No)	0.9583	0.9355
虚假谣言是已经被官方所辟谣的信息。这段文本是否为虚假谣言？（是/否）	0.9628	A false rumor is information that has been officially declared false. Is this text a false rumor? (Yes/No)	0.9643	0.9462
虚假谣言是已被确证的不实信息。这段文本是否为虚假谣言？（是/否）	0.9580	A false rumor is false information that has been confirmed. Is this text a false rumor? (Yes/No)	0.9404	0.9462
虚假谣言是歪曲事实并造成一定社会影响的信息。这段文本是否为虚假谣言？（是/否）	0.9571	False rumors are information that twist facts and has a certain social impact. Is this text a false rumor? (Yes/No)	0.9642	0.9569

4.6 Ablation Study

A series of ablation experiments were conducted to illustrate the influence of each module in the proposed method on the rumor detection task. We reported the average accuracy of each dataset. The experimental results are shown in Table 5. PEKIN denotes a complete model that uses all modules. The ablation experiments are organized as follows:

(1) PEKIN w/o prompt: In this experiment, the prompt module was removed, and only the source text and its corresponding comments and entity knowledge of the source text were considered.
(2) PEKIN w/o knowledge: In this experiment, the entity knowledge module was removed, and only the source text and its corresponding comments and prompt module were considered.
(3) PEKIN w/o comments: In this experiment, its corresponding comments were removed, and the source text and the entity knowledge module, and the prompt module were considered.

Table 5 shows the ablation experiment results on three datasets. There were three findings. First, the overall performance degraded most when running "PEKIN w/o knowledge," revealing the importance of entity knowledge as auxiliary data. Take the Ma-Weibo dataset as an example. Given only source posts and corresponding comments, this method only achieved an accuracy of 0.9628. However, added by entity knowledge, this model got a much higher accuracy of 0.9695 s s, the performance of "PEKIN w/o prompt" was second to last, which indicated the prompt strategy contribution to PEKIN Third, "PEKIN w/o comments " degraded, which indicated that adopting corresponding comments is effective.

Table 5. The ablation study results on the Weibo, Twitter15, and Twitter16 dataset

Model	Ma-Weibo	Twitter15	Twitter16
PEKIN	0.9695	0.9643	0.9569
PEKIN w/o knowleges	0.9628	0.9583	0.9462
PEKIN w/o prompt	0.9619	0.9619	0.9529
PEKIN w/o comments	0.9358	0.9439	0.9355

5   Conclusion and Future Works

Our work attempts to incorporate prior knowledge of rumor classification tasks and external knowledge of text entities for rumor detection. We propose a Prompt-based External Knowledge Integration Network that effectively integrates the two kinds of knowledge with Prompt-based learning. We have demonstrated the effectiveness of our proposed approach by conducting experiments on three real-world datasets. We will search for a better representation form of knowledge for future work to incorporate it into neural networks as explicit features to boost rumor detection performance further.

Acknowledgements. This work is partially supported by the Strategic Priority Research Program of the Chinese Academy of Sciences,Grant No. XDC02060400

References

1. Allport, G.W., Postman, L.: The psychology of rumor. Russel & Russell (1965)
2. Devlin, J., et al.: Bert: Pre-training of deep bidirectional transformers for language understanding. arXiv preprint arXiv:1810.04805 (2018)
3. Risch, J., Krestel, R.: Bagging BERT models for robust aggression identification. In: Proceedings of the Second Workshop on Trolling, Aggression and Cyberbullying (2020)
4. Han, X., et al.: Ptr: Prompt tuning with rules for text classification. arXiv preprint arXiv:2105.11259 (2021)
5. Zhong, R, et al.: Adapting language models for zero-shot learning by meta-tuning on dataset and prompt collections. arXiv preprint arXiv:2104.04670 (2021)
6. Schick, T., Schütze, H.: Few-shot text generation with natural language instructions. In: Proceedings of the 2021 Conference on Empirical Methods in Natural Language Processing (2021)
7. Schick, T., Schütze, H.: Exploiting cloze questions for few shot text classification and natural language inference. arXiv preprint arXiv:2001.07676 (2020)
8. Ma, J., et al.: Detecting rumors from microblogs with recurrent neural networks, vol. 3818 (2016)
9. Ma, J., et al.: An attention-based rumor detection model with tree-structured recursive neural networks. ACM Trans. Intell. Syst. Technol. (TIST) **11**(4), 1–28 (2020)
10. DiFonzo, N.: Am. Psychol. Assoc. Prashant Bordia. Social and organizational approaches, Rumor psychology (2007)
11. Del Vicario, M., et al.: Polarization and fake news: Early warning of potential misinformation targets. ACM Trans. Web (TWEB) **13**(2), 1–22 (2019)
12. Meel, P., Vishwakarma, D.S.: Fake news, rumor, information pollution in social media and web: A contemporary survey of state-of-the-arts, challenges and opportunities. Expert Syst. Appli. **153**, 112986 (2020)
13. Wang, Z., Guo, Y.: Rumor events detection enhanced by encoding sentimental information into time series division and word representations. Neurocomputing **397**, 224–243 (2020)
14. Kumar, S., Carley, K.M.: Tree lstms with convolution units to predict stance and rumor veracity in social media conversations. In: Proceedings of the 57th Annual Meeting of the Association for Computational Linguistics (2019)
15. Bian, T., et al.: Rumor detection on social media with bi-directional graph convolutional networks. In: Proceedings of the AAAI Conference on Artificial Intelligence, vol. 34(01) (2020)
16. Zhang, Q., et al.: Reply-aided detection of misinformation via bayesian deep learning. In: The World Wide Web Conference (2019)
17. Riedel, B., et al.: A simple but tough-to-beat baseline for the Fake News Challenge stance detection task. arXiv preprint arXiv:1707.03264 (2017)
18. Lu, Y-J., Li, C-T.: GCAN: Graph-aware co-attention networks for explainable fake news detection on social media. arXiv preprint arXiv:2004.11648 (2020)
19. Brown, T., et al.: Language models are few-shot learners. In: Advances in neural Information Processing Systems, vol. 33, pp, 1877–1901 (2020)

20. Gao, T., Fisch, A., Chen, D.: Making pre-trained language models better few-shot learners. arXiv preprint arXiv:2012.15723 (2020)
21. Chen, X., et al.: Lightner: A lightweight generative framework with prompt-guided attention for low-resource ner. arXiv preprint arXiv:2109.00720 (2021)
22. Hu, S., et al.: Knowledgeable prompt-tuning: Incorporating knowledge into prompt verbalizer for text classification. arXiv preprint arXiv:2108.02035 (2021)
23. Inui, K., et al.: Proceedings of the 2019 conference on empirical methods in natural language processing and the 9th international joint conference on natural language processing (EMNLP-IJCNLP). In: Proceedings of the 2019 Conference on Empirical Methods in Natural Language Processing and the 9th International Joint Conference on Natural Language Processing (EMNLP-IJCNLP) (2019)
24. Talmor, A., et al.: oLMpics-on what language model pre-training captures. Trans. Assoc. Comput Ling. 8, 743–758 (2020)
25. Teng, Z., Vo,D-T., Zhang, Y.: Context-sensitive lexicon features for neural sentiment analysis. In: Proceedings of the 2016 Conference on Empirical Methods in Natural Language Processing (2016)
26. Shin, B., Lee, T., Choi, J.D.: Lexicon integrated CNN models with attention for sentiment analysis. arXiv preprint arXiv:1610.06272 (2016)
27. Kumar, A., Kawahara, D., Kurohashi, S.: Knowledge-enriched two-layered attention network for sentiment analysis. arXiv preprint arXiv:1805.07819 (2018)
28. Yang, F., Mukherjee, A., Dragut, E.: Satirical news detection and analysis using attention mechanism and linguistic features. arXiv preprint arXiv:1709.01189 (2017)
29. Ma, J., Gao, W., Wong, K-F.: Detect rumors in microblog posts using propagation structure via kernel learning. In: Association for Computational Linguistics (2017)
30. Ma, J., et al.: Detect rumors using time series of social context information on microblogging websites. In: Proceedings of the 24th ACM International on Conference on Information and Knowledge Management (2015)
31. Tu, K., et al.: Rumor2vec: A rumor detection framework with joint text and propagation structure representation learning. Inf. Sci. 560, 137–151 (2021)
32. Liu, Y., et al.: 2019. Roberta: A robustly optimized bert pretraining approach. arXiv preprint arXiv:1907.11692 5 (2019)
33. Beltagy, I., Peters, M.E., Cohan, A.: Longformer: The long-document transformer. arXiv preprint arXiv:2004.05150 (2020)
34. Khoo, L.M.S., et al.: Interpretable rumor detection in microblogs by attending to user interactions. In: Proceedings of the AAAI Conference on Artificial Intelligence, vol. 34(05) (2020)
35. Wu, Y. et al.: Weibo rumor recognition based on communication and stacking ensemble learning. In: Discrete Dynamics in Nature and Society 2020 (2020)
36. Geng, Y., Lin, Z., Fu, P., Wang, W.: Rumor detection on social media: A multi-view model using self-attention mechanism. In: Rodrigue, J.M.F., et al. (eds.) ICCS 2019. LNCS, vol. 11536, pp. 339–352. Springer, Cham (2019). https://doi.org/10.1007/978-3-030-22734-0_25

Entity-Aware Social Media Reading Comprehension

Hao Liu[1], Yu Hong[1(✉)], and Qiao-ming Zhu[1,2]

[1] School of Computer Science and Technology, Soochow University, Suzhou, China
tianxianer@gmail.com, qmzhu@suda.edu.cn
[2] BigData Intelligence Engineering Lab of Jiangsu Province, Soochow University,
Suzhou, China

Abstract. Social media reading comprehension (SMRC) aims to answer
specific questions conditioned on short social media messages, such as
tweets. Sophisticated neural networks and pretrained language models
have been successfully leveraged in SMRC, accompanying with a series
of deliberately-designed data cleaning strategies. However, the existing SMRC techniques still suffer from unawareness of various entity
mentions, i.e., the successive tokens (words, sub-words or characters)
that fully or briefly describe named entities, such as abbreviated person
names. This unavoidably brings negative effects into question answering towards the questions of "who", "where", "which organization", etc.
To address the issue, we propose to enhance the capacity of a SMRC
model in recognizing entity mentions and, more importantly, construct
an entity-aware encoder to incorporate latent information of entities
into the understanding of questions and tweets. In order to obtain a
self-contained entity-aware encoder, we build a two-channel encoder-
shareable neural network for multitask learning. The encoder is driven to
produce distributed representations that not only facilitate decoding of
entity mentions but prediction of answers. In our experiments, we employ
12-layer transformer encoders for multi-task learning. Experiments on
the benchmark dataset TweetQA show that our method achieves significant improvements. It is also proven that our method outperforms the
state-of-the-art model NUT-RC, yielding improvements of 2.5% BLEU-
1, 3% Meteor and 2.2% Rouge-L, respectively.

Keywords: Social media reading comprehension · Named entity
recognition · Multi-task learning

1 Introduction

Machine Reading Comprehension (MRC) is a task of question answering conditioned on the semantic understanding of question and paragraph-level context.
A variety of MRC datasets have been constructed to support related research in
this field, including SQuAD [1], CoQA [2], NarrativeQA [3]), etc.

© The Author(s), under exclusive license to Springer Nature Switzerland AG 2022
S. Khanna et al. (Eds.): PRICAI 2022, LNCS 13630, pp. 197–210, 2022.
https://doi.org/10.1007/978-3-031-20865-2_15

Table 1. An example of unrecognized named entities in social media domain.

Tweet: *This forecast is deflated as much as New England Patriots footballs! I apologize.* **W NJ** has the most to lose. Dave Curren(@DaveCurren)January 27,2015
Question: *Who has the most to lose?*
Gold Answer: *W NJ*
Predict Answer: *New England Patriots*

Recently, TweetQA[1] [4] is released for the evaluation of MRC techniques, which limits the available contexts to tweets. It raises an intensive interest in exploring effective MRC solutions towards short and informal texts. The task defined on this dataset is referred to Social Media Reading Comprehension (abbr., SMRC). Table 1 illustrates an example, where a specific SMRC model is required to predict the answer *"W NJ"* given the question *"Who has the most to lose?"*. The clues that support the prediction can be merely mined from the single tweet.

Neural networks have been utilized for SMRC, which produced substantial improvements so far (Sect. 2). In particular, large pretrained language models were used to strengthen encoders of current SMRC models, such as BERT [5], UniLM [6] and T5 [7]. Due to extensive learning over large-scale data for semantic representation, the pretrained models significantly improve the understanding of questions and tweets, and therefore, boost SMRC performance. It is noteworthy that such pretrained models need to be fine-tuned over TweetQA in the mode of transfer learning, and necessarily accompanied with proper data cleaning strategies [8]. Transfer learning is applied for enhancing adaptation to domain-specific characteristics of tweets, such as that for the idiom where the stop words *"Down Under"* actually serve as the alternative name of *"Australia"*. Data cleaning is used to recover or filter grammatical errors, such as the removal of redundant spaces *"did n't"* into *"didn't"*.

Briefly, the existing neural SMRC models achieve promising performance when transferring pretrained models to tweets and coupling them with data cleaning. However, our empirical findings show that entity-oriented SMRC fails to perform perfectly, where the state-of-the-art model such as NUT-RC [8] obtains an error rate of 40.94%[2]. Though, the most noticeable fact regarding data distribution is that the proportion of entity-type answers is up to 29.13%[3] in all SMRC instances in TweetQA dataset.

---

[1] https://tweetqa.github.io/.

[2] We reproduce NUT-RC [8] and evaluate it on the development set. On the basis, we verify the error rate for entity-oriented SMRC.

[3] We employ an off-the-shelf Named Entity Recognition (NER) toolkit Twitter-Stanza to automatically determine whether gold SMRC answers are the ones containing named entities. The toolkit has been well-trained on the TweeTbank-NER dataset (https://github.com/social-machines/TweebankNLP).

Entity-oriented SMRC instances refer to the ones whose ground-truth answers are entity mentions, such as names of person (PER), organization (ORG) and location-type (LOC) entities. The reason why SMRC models fall into the misjudgement for some of them is because of the unawareness of entity knowledge [9]. For example, the clue for reasoning in the case in Table 1 is evident (i.e., the text *"W NJ has the most to lose"* which is even consistent with the question in morphology and pragmatics), though SMRC models fail to identify the entity *"W NJ"* (i.e., the abbreviated mention of *"West New Jersey"*) in it as the answer. It reveals the possibility that, to the end, SMRC models are unaware of what the mention *"W NJ"* is, or even regard it as a sequence of meaningless characters instead of the closely related entity to the *"Who"*-type question.

To address the issue, we propose to enhance the awareness of entity mentions during encoding questions and tweet contexts. The two-channel multi-task learning is utilized, where SMRC and NER tasks are considered. The shareable encoder across the two learning channels is trained to perceive interaction between question and tweet context, as well as the latent information of various entity mentions. This contributes to the construction of a self-contained entity-aware SMRC model. We experiment on the benchmark dataset TweetQA [4]. Experimental results show that our method yields substantial improvements, and it outperforms the published state-of-the-art model NUT-RC [8].

2 Related Work

A variety of innovative approaches have been proposed for SMRC. Huang et al. (2020) [8] design heuristic rules to standardize informal texts in tweets. More importantly, Huang et al. (2020) bridge generative and extractive SMRC by answer selection mechanisms. Tian et al. (2021) [10] enhance the representation learning of questions and tweets using concepts. Hashtags are used as concepts. They are extracted from the closely-related tweets, the ones retrieved and highly-ranked in terms of topic-level relevance. BERT-based pointer network is utilized for extracting concepts. Xue et al. (2022) [11] demonstrate the effectiveness of character-level models in dealing with noisy and informal datasets, such as TweetQA [4]. Instead of using the limited vocabulary to tokenize words, they directly take the UTF-8 bytes as the input. On the basis, a character-level pre-trained model is developed based on T5 [7] architecture.

Our approach is different from aforementioned approaches. We capture the exclusive characteristics that some of entity mentions play an important role for reasoning answers in tweets, or even serve as answers themselves. Accordingly, we intend to enhance the awareness of entity knowledge when encoding questions and tweets. To pursue the goal, we utilize the entity recognition as an auxiliary task, so as to drive the encoder to perceive and represent entity mentions.

3   Approach

In this section, we present the components of our SMRC model step by step, including preprocessing over tweets, entity-aware encoding by multi-task learning, as well as answer prediction.

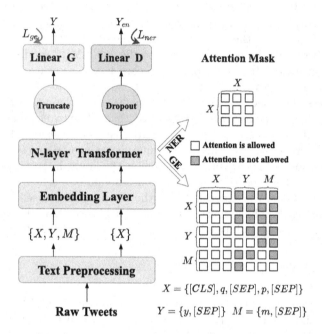

Fig. 1. Architecture of our multi-task learning model, which is used to enhance the awareness of entity information during encoding.

3.1   Text Preprocessing

We employ Huang et al. (2020)'s heuristic rules [8] to separate the mixed-tokens in tweets. Specifically, we split both Hashtags and User-Ids into formal texts (e.g., "#WhiteHouse" → "# White House"), so as to avoid the misunderstanding or omission of entity mentions.

3.2   Entity-Aware Encoding Grounded on Multi-task Learning

We conduct two-channel multi-task learning, where shareable multi-layer transformer encoders are used. One learning channel aims to train the encoder for generative SMRC (primary task), while the other performs for NER (auxiliary task). Different attention masks are utilized in the two learning channels. The neural network we used is constructed with embedding layer and transformer encoders, as well as two separate decoding layers coupled with truncation and dropout operations. Figure 1 shows the architecture of our learning model.

Embedding Layer: Given an SMRC instance in the training set, we construct two kinds of input sequences for SMRC and NER tasks respectively. For NER, we concatenate the token sequence of question q and that of tweet p, where the special tokens "*[CLS]*" and "*[SEP]*" are used (see the concatenation mode in Fig. 1). The resultant input sequence is denoted as X. For generative SMRC, we concatenate X with two additional sequences Y and M. Y comprises tokens of the ground-truth answer y and "*[SEP]*". M serves as the shuffled version of Y. Specifically, the tokens in M are duplicated from Y, though at the initialization stage, they are randomly masked by special character "*[MASK]*" or replaced with other words in the vocabulary [12]. M is primarily used for pseudo-masked fine-tuning, which contributes to the alleviation of exposure bias.

Following Devlin et al. (2019)'s practice [5], we obtain the input embeddings by conducting element-wise aggregation over token, segment and position embeddings. It is noteworthy that the embedding layer is trainable.

Encoder Layers: We apply N-layer Transformer encoders of UniLM v2.0 to convert the input embeddings to contextual semantic representations, no matter whether the input is {X,Y,M} or {X} ("{*}" denotes concatenation operation).

$$H^l = Transformer(H^{l-1}) \tag{1}$$

where, $l \in [1, N]$ signals the l-th transformer layer which produces the hidden states H^l. H^l contains the token-level hidden states of all tokens and special characters in the input sequence. We use H^N as the final hidden states, i.e., the distributed representations output by the last (N-th) transformer layer. For generative SMRC, the final hidden states act as $H^N = \{h_1^N, h_2^N, ..., h_{s+t+t}^N\}$, where, s and t constrain the maximum length of H^N which are numbers of tokens in X and Y. For NER, the final hidden states act as $\check{H}^N = \{\check{h}_1^N, \check{h}_2^N, ..., \check{h}_s^N\}$.

Selective masking mechanism is required to perform during training due to the different prediction modes (decoding modes) of generative SMRC and NER. Specifically, generative SMRC serves as a generation model, and therefore needs to possess the capacity of predicting the current token in terms of preceding predictions (and tweet context). In fact, this recursive prediction mode conforms to the fundamental limitation that ground-truth answer Y is invisible in the test process. In order to simulate the recursive prediction mode, we need to impose masks on the hidden states of subsequent tokens in H^N during training. By contrast, NER serves as a sequence labeling task, which performs B/I/O tag classification for each token separately and independently. Therefore, it is unnecessary to impose masks over the hidden states $\check{H}^N$. To facilitate the representation learning of shareable encoders between the two tasks, we establish a selective masking mechanism, where Bao et al. (2020)'s pseudo-masked attention learning [13] is used. The attention score $ATTN_l$ of the transformer l is computed as follows:

$$ATTN_l = (\frac{Q_l K_l^T}{\sqrt{d_k}} + MASK)v_l \tag{2}$$

Table 2. An example of named entities for questions and tweets

Question+Tweet: *[CLS] Who have the cavs released? [SEP] The Cavs have released Edy Tavares . No surprise . He was on a non - guaranteed contract . Roster stands at 19 . - Jason Lloyd (@ Jason Lloyd NBA) [SEP]*
Named Entities: *[CLS] O O O S-ORG O [SEP] O S-ORG O O B-PER I-PER O O O O O O O O O O O O O S-ORG O O O O O B-PER I-PER O O O O O O [SEP]*

$$MASK_{ij} = \begin{cases} 0, & \text{Attention is allowed} \\ -\infty, & \text{Attention is not allowed} \end{cases} \tag{3}$$

where, Q_l, K_l, V_l respectively denote the **Q**uery, **K**ey and **V**alue vectors that are obtained by linearly converting H^N or $\breve{H}^N$. $MASK$ denotes the attention mask. Figure 1 shows the diagrams of masked hidden states at a certain encoding step.

Decoding of SMRC and Loss Estimation: Given the pseudo-masked final hidden states H^N, we take the hidden states H_M^N of M out of H^N by truncation, which contain latent information for predicting answers. We feed H_M^N into the linear layer G with Softmax to compute the probability distribution that every token in the vocabulary serves as an answer or part of it:

$$\begin{cases} H_M^N = [h_{s+t+1}^N, h_{s+t+2}^N, ..., h_{s+t+t}^N] \\ Y_{ge} = softmax(Linear_G(H_M^N)) \end{cases} \tag{4}$$

During training, the loss of answer prediction is estimated with the probability distribution Y_{ge}. It is the reliance for back propagation. Cross entropy f_{CE} is used to estimate the loss $\mathcal{L}_{ge}$ (where Y denotes the ground-truth answer):

$$\mathcal{L}_{ge} = f_{CE}(Y_{ge}, Y) \tag{5}$$

Decoding of NER and Loss Estimation: Given the final hidden states $\breve{H}^N$, we feed them into a dropout layer for purifying their latent information. This helps to avoid overfitting. On the basis, we deliver the purified hidden states $\breve{H}^N$ to the linear layer D with Softmax, so as to predict the probability distributions Y_{en} over B/I/O tags for each token. Similarly, we utilize cross entropy f_{CE} to estimate the loss $\mathcal{L}_{ne}$. All computations of NER for decoding are as follows (where Y_{en} denotes the ground-truth B/I/O tags of NER):

$$\begin{cases} \breve{H}^{N'} = dropout(\breve{H}^N) \\ \breve{Y}_{en} = softmax(Linear_D(\breve{H}^{N'})) \\ \mathcal{L}_{ne} = f_{CE}(\breve{Y}_{en}, Y_{en}) \end{cases} \tag{6}$$

The learning in the channel of NER, frankly, requires the ground-truth B/I/O tags of entity mentions for supervision. However, TweetQA dataset doesn't possess annotation results of named entities. Therefore, we use the existing NER toolkit Twitter-Stanza [14] to automatically annotate named entities of both questions and tweets. Table 2 shows the example regarding B/I/O tags of entities towards a SMRC case in TweetQA.

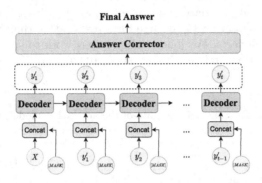

Fig. 2. The data flow produced step by step during the decoding process.

Multi-task Learning: During training, we conduct supervised learning for generative SMRC and NER tasks alternatively and iteratively in each epoch. Both the losses produced in SMRC and NER are jointly used to optimize the parameters in embedding layer, transformer encoders and predictors (i.e., generator G for SMRC while discriminator D for NER). We compute the joint loss $\mathcal{L}_{all}$ as follows (where λ denotes a trade-off coefficient):

$$\mathcal{L}_{final} = \mathcal{L}_{ge} + \lambda \mathcal{L}_{ner} \tag{7}$$

3.3 Generating Answers

Instead of extracting answers from tweets (by pointer networks), we generate answers, i.e., search the most possible tokens in the vocabulary to sequentially constitute an answer, where the greedy algorithm is used.

Specifically, conditioned on the i-th hidden state h_i^N in H_M^N (see Eq. 4), we predict the i-th token y_i' of the possible answer at the i-th time step. In order to speed up decoding, we hold up emebeddings of $\{X, y_1', ..., y_i'\}$ for each time step at run time, and concatenate them with emebedding of $\{y_i', [MASK]\}$. The resultant representation will be fed into the encoder to produce $(i+1)$-th hidden sate h_{i+1}^N in H_M^N (See Fig. 2). In this way, we iteratively predict tokens in the answer and produce the next hidden state until "$[SEP]$" is predicted.

In addition, we design an answer corrector to post-process the generated answer. It is capable of dealing with the following informal text spans. The major heuristic rules including 1) **Word Recovery** (e.g., "did n't"→"didn't") and 2) **Removing Redundant Characters** (e.g., removing "@" or "#").

4   Experimentation

4.1   Data, Evaluation and Hyperparameter Settings

- **Dataset:** We experiment on TweetQA [4]. Compared to other MRC datasets, TweetQA [4] contain a large number of unusual entities. More importantly, the answers in TweetQA [4] are free-form texts rather than the ones toughly extracted from tweets. We follow the previous work to split TweetQA. The training, validation and test sets contain 10,692, 1,086 and 1,979 instance, respecitvely.

Table 3. Performance of the state-of-the-art SMRC models and ours.

Model	BLEU-1		Meteor		Rouge-L	
	Dev	Test	Dev	Test	Dev	Test
BIDAF (Seo et al., 2016) [19]	48.3	48.7	31.6	31.4	38.9	38.6
Seq2Seq (Song et al., 2017) [18]	53.4	36.1	32.1	31.8	39.5	39.0
BERT-EX (Devlin et al., 2018) [5]	61.0	58.4	64.2	63.2	60.9	65.8
NUT-RC (Huang et al., 2020) [8]	78.2	76.1	73.3	72.1	79.6	77.9
TKR (Tian et al., 2021) [10]	68.7	69.0	64.7	65.6	70.6	71.2
EA-SMRC (Original)	**79.1**	**78.5**	**74.5**	**74.7**	**80.6**	**80.0**
EA-SMRC (Variant)	78.7	77.8	**74.5**	74.2	80.1	79.4

- **Evaluation Metrics:** For comparison, we follow the common practice to use BLEU-1 [15], Meteor [16] and Rouge-L [17] to evaluate SMRC models. The test set is not publicly available. Therefore, we submit the predicted answers to the official website of TweetQA [1] for obtaining the test performance.
- **Hyperparameter Settings:** Our source code is based on s2s-ft [12]. We use the Adam optimizer to train the MRC model. The learning rate for training is 2e-5. We set the maximum length of X to 128 and the maximum length of Y to 24. We initialize our model using the parameters of UniLM v1.2 [12], and fine-tune our model on TweetQA in 10 epochs. The batch size for training is 12. The opimal λ is set to 1. The dropout rate used for the NER task is set to 0.1.

4.2   State-of-the-art SMRC Models for Comparison

We develop two versions of SMRC models, including the aforementioned entity-aware SMRC grounded on multi-task learning (denoted as original **EA-SMRC**), as well as its variant. The variant adopts the same learning architecture, though the auxiliary task NER is implemented by Masked Language Modeling (MLM), where MLM of BERT is transferred to the learning process.

We compare our models to the state-of-the-art models including 1) **BIDAF** [4] which is an extractive MRC model based on Recurrent Neural Network

(RNN), where bi-directional attention flow is used; 2) **Seq2Seq** [18] which acts as a generative model within the RNN-based encoder-decoder framework, where copy and coverage mechanisms are leveraged; 3) **BERT-EX** [5] which is obtained by transferring the pretrained language model BERT to TweetQA and acts as an extractive MRC model; 4) **TKR** [10] which incorporates concept knowledge into the encoding process, so as to enhance the perception and representation of unusual linguistic units, where external data is applied for retrieving concept knowledge; and 5) **NUT-RC** [8] which possesses a two-channel multi-task learning architecture, where generative and extractive MRC are conducted in the two channels, and answer selection is used.

Table 4. Ablation study on TweetQA

Model	BLEU-1		Meteor		Rouge-L	
	Dev	Test	Dev	Test	Dev	Test
EA-SMRC (Original)	**79.1**	**78.5**	**74.5**	**74.7**	**80.6**	**80.0**
-NER	77.7	77.3	73.2	73.6	79.2	78.9
-NER&-CORR	75.6	76.6	71.4	72.6	77.5	78.2
-NER&-CORR&-SPLIT	74.0	75.5	69.8	71.4	75.9	77.3

4.3   Main Results

Table 3 shows the test results of our models (EA-SMRC) and the state of the art. It can be observed that both original and variant EA-SMRC models produce substantial performance gains, compared to previous work. Considering that both the models utilize entity-aware multi-task learning framework, we suggest that the proposed method is robust and capable of yielding steady improvements to some extent. Experimental results reveal the fact that original EA-SMRC achieves higher performance (BLEU-1, Meteor and Rouge-L scores) on TweetQA [4]. It is because the original version accurately introduces entity knowledge into the SMRC, while the variant one still requires to understand the semantics of context to infer the entity types, which potentially brings a certain noise due to the inadequate semantic understanding.

We concentrate on the previous work of NUT-RC [8] for advantage analysis, which used to stand on the top of leader board for a long period of time and, more importantly, it holds the same learning framework with our models (i.e., multi-task learning). From the perspective of effectiveness, our EA-SMRC models obtain better performance due to the incorporation of entity knowledge into learning. From the perspective of efficiency, frankly, EA-SMRC is relatively vest-pocket and less time-consuming because the kernel is constituted with a group of transformer encoders and two independent linear layer. By contrast, NUT-RC possesses two groups of large transformer blocks in the learning channels, which are initialized by UniLM v1.0 [6] and BERT-Large [5].

4.4 Ablation Study

We carry out ablation experiments to verify the effects of different components in EA-SMRC. The components are progressively ablated, which include 1) "-NER" denoting the ablation of the auxiliary task NER, which boils multi-task learning down to entity-unaware single-task learning, 2) "-CORR" referring to the condition that answer correction is disable, and 3) "-SPLIT" that refers to the ablation of heuristic rules for text preprocessing.

Table 4 show the experimental results. It can be found that performance constantly degrades when the components are progressively ablated. During test, the largest performance reduction results from the ablation of NER. It proves the dominant positive effect of entity-aware multi-task learning.

Table 5. Performance obtained when different pretrained models are used

Model	Framework	BLEU-1	Meteor	Rouge-L
UniLM v1.0 [6]	FT	72.5	67.5	74.5
	MTL	**73.6**	**68.4**	**75.1**
UniLM v2.0 [13]	FT	71.0	65.7	73.1
	MTL	**72.2**	**66.9**	**74.0**
BERT [5]	FT	69.7	65.4	71.5
	MTL	**70.3**	**65.6**	**72.0**

Table 6. Performance of EA-SMRC (Variant) on TweetQA using different NER tools

NER tool	BLEU-1	Meteor	Rouge-L
CoreNLP [21]	77.6	63.7	79.5
Stanza [22]	78.2	74.0	79.6
Twitter-Stanza [14]	**79.1**	**74.5**	**80.6**

4.5 Effects of Different Pretrained Models for Transfer

We verified the performance of EA-SMRC on the validation set when different pretrained models are used for initialization. Initialization is conducted by substituting off-the-shelf parameters and embeddings of pretrained models into EA-SMRC. This enables transfer learning on TweetQA within multi-task learning framework. We consider three pretrained models, including UniLM v1.0, UniLM v2.0 and BERT. The variant EA-SMRC is used due to its better performance on the validation set. Besides, two learning frameworks are considered, including our entity-aware multi-task learning (denoted as MTL) and entity-unaware single-task learning. The latter is equivalent to the case that pretrained models are directly transferred to TweetQA and fine-tuned there (denoted as FT).

Table 5 shows the performance of aforementioned pretrained models. It can be observed that utilizing different pretrained models will result in significantly performance. Nevertheless, all the models can achieve better performance when the MTL framework is used, compared to the FT framework. It illustrates that our entity-aware learning strategy generalizes well. Besides, it can be found that both UniLM v1.0 and UniLM v2.0 fail to produce competitive performance, compared to UniLM v1.2 in our EA-SMRC (see Table 3). It is because that UniLM1.2 doesn't apply relative position bias [20], and thus it is adaptive to the stationary position embeddings in our input layer.

4.6 Utility of NER Toolkits

We verify the utility of different NER toolkits in our method. Note that NER toolkits are used for obtain entity mentions in the training data, which support the learning of a self-contained encoder for perceiving entities. We consider three NER toolkits, including CoreNLP [21], Stanza [22] and Twitter-Stanza [14]. The former two provide a larger number of entity types (23 in CoreNLP and 18 in Stanza) and instances, compared to Twitter-Stanza. Nevertheless, the training data of Twitter-Stanza derives from the same domain with TweetQA.

Table 6 shows the experimental results. It can be observed that Twitter-Stanza yields relatively-substantial performance gains. It proves that domain relevance is more important than both data size and versatility of entity types for the adoption and utilization of NER toolkits.

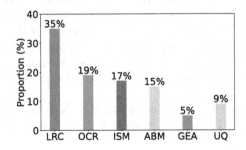

Fig. 3. The proportion of different error types.

Table 7. Examples of prediction errors produced by our SMRC models.

Type	Example
LRC	**Question:** *Who are they replying to?* **Tweet:** *This looks like blank space taken to a NEW.LEVEL. (@dunderswiftlin).* **Gold Answer:** *Gma and Taylor Swift* (**Reasons behind errors**: Be unaware of exact names of "*dunderswiftlin*" and their relationship to "*NEW.LEVEL*)
OCR	**Question:** *Who wouldn't give a long-term deal?* **Tweet:** *The Red Wings didn't believe they would get Mike Green because they wouldn't give a long-term deal.* **Gold Answer:** *The Red Wings.* (**Reasons behind errors**: Fail to correspond the co-reference "*they*" to the entity "*Red Wings*")

4.7   Error Analysis

We conduct error analysis on the predictions of our models over the validation set. The errors are caused by six classes of drawbacks, including Lack of Related Commonsense (**LRC** for short), Omission of Co-reference Resolution (**OCR**), Incorrect Segmentation of Mixed-tokens (**ISM**), Answer Boundary Misjudgement (**ABM**), Grammar Errors of the generated Answers (**GEA**), as well as Unanswerable Questions (**UQ**) caused by inexact or improper annotations. Figure 3 shows the proportions of aforementioned error types in all the misjudged answers. Table 7 gives two examples of prediction errors.

5   Conclusion

We propose an entity-aware encoding method to strengthen the current SMRC models. Multi-task learning is leveraged to enable the perception and fusion of latent information of entity mentions. Experiments on the benchmark dataset TweetQA demonstrate the effectiveness of our method. Besides of superior performance (higher BLEU-1, Meteor and Rouge-L scores), our SMRC model is vest-pocket and less time-consuming. In the future, we will enhance the entity-aware encoder from two aspects, including 1) introducing external knowledge of entities into the representation learning process, where group-based neural models will be used, and 2) conducting co-reference resolution.

Acknowledgements. This project is supported by National Key R&D Program of China (No. 2020YFB1313601) and National Natural Science Foundation of China (No.62076174 and No. 61836007).

References

1. Rajpurkar, P., Zhang, J., Lopyrev, K., Liang, P.: SQuAD: 100,000+ questions for machine comprehension of text. In: Proceedings of the 2016 Conference on Empirical Methods in Natural Language Processing, pp. 2383–2392 (2016)

2. Reddy, S., Chen, D., Manning, C.D.: CoQA: a conversational question answering challenge. Trans. Assoc. Comput. Linguist. **7**, 249–266 (2019)
3. Kočiský, T., et al.: The narrativeqa reading comprehension challenge. Trans. Assoc. Comput. Linguist. **6**, 317–328 (2018)
4. Xiong, W., et al.: TWEETQA: a social media focused question answering dataset. In: Proceedings of the 57th Annual Meeting of the Association for Computational Linguistics. pp. 5020–5031. Association for Computational Linguistics, Florence, Italy (2019). https://doi.org/10.18653/v1/P19-1496
5. Devlin, J., Chang, M.W., Lee, K., Toutanova, K.: BERT: pre-training of deep bidirectional transformers for language understanding. In: Proceedings of the 2019 Conference of the North American Chapter of the Association for Computational Linguistics: Human Language Technologies, Volume 1 (Long and Short Papers). pp. 4171–4186. Association for Computational Linguistics, Minneapolis, Minnesota (2019). https://doi.org/10.18653/v1/N19-1423
6. Dong, L., et al.: Unified language model pre-training for natural language understanding and generation. In: Advances in Neural Information Processing Systems, vol. 32 (2019)
7. Raffel, C., et al.: Exploring the limits of transfer learning with a unified text-to-text transformer. J. Mach. Learn. Res.**21**(140), 1–67 (2020). http://jmlr.org/papers/v21/20-074.html
8. Huang, R., Zou, B., Hong, Y., Zhang, W., Aw, A., Zhou, G.: NUT-Rc: noisy user-generated text-oriented reading comprehension. In: Proceedings of the 28th International Conference on Computational Linguistics, pp. 2687–2698 (2020)
9. Shao, Y., Bhutani, N., Rahman, S., Hruschka, E.: Low-resource entity set expansion: a comprehensive study on user-generated text. In: Findings of the Association for Computational Linguistics: NAACL 2022. pp. 1343–1353. Association for Computational Linguistics, Seattle, United States (2022). https://aclanthology.org/2022.findings-naacl.100
10. Tian, Z., Zhang, Y., Liu, K., Zhao, J.: Topic knowledge acquisition and utilization for machine reading comprehension in social media domain. In: Proceedings of the 20th Chinese National Conference on Computational Linguistics. pp. 988–999. Chinese Information Processing Society of China, Huhhot, China (2021). https://aclanthology.org/2021.ccl-1.88
11. Xue, L., et al.: ByT5: towards a token-free future with pre-trained byte-to-byte models. Trans. Assoc. Comput. Linguist. **10**, 291–306 (2022)
12. Bao, H., Dong, L., Wang, W., Yang, N., Wei, F.: s2s-ft: fine-tuning pre-trained transformer encoders for sequence-to-sequence learning. arXiv preprint arXiv:2110.13640 (2021)
13. Bao, H., et al.: UniLMv2: pseudo-masked language models for unified language model pre-training. In: International Conference on Machine Learning, PMLR. pp. 642–652 (2020)
14. Jiang, H., Hua, Y., Beeferman, D., Roy, D.: Annotating the tweebank corpus on named entity recognition and building NLP models for social media analysis. arXiv preprint arXiv:2201.07281 (2022)
15. Papineni, K., Roukos, S., Ward, T., Zhu, W.J.: Bleu: a method for automatic evaluation of machine translation. In: Proceedings of the 40th Annual Meeting of the Association for Computational Linguistics. Association for Computational Linguistics, Philadelphia, Pennsylvania, USA. pp. 311–318(2002). https://doi.org/10.3115/1073083.1073135

16. Denkowski, M., Lavie, A.: Meteor 1.3: Automatic metric for reliable optimization and evaluation of machine translation systems. In: Proceedings of the Sixth Workshop on Statistical Machine Translation. Association for Computational Linguistics, Edinburgh, Scotland, pp. 85–91 (2011), https://aclanthology.org/W11-2107

17. Lin, C.Y.: ROUGE: A package for automatic evaluation of summaries. In: Text Summarization Branches Out. Association for Computational Linguistics, Barcelona, Spain. pp. 74–81 (2004). https://aclanthology.org/W04-1013

18. Song, L., Wang, Z., Hamza, W.: A unified query-based generative model for question generation and question answering. arXiv preprint arXiv:1709.01058 (2017)

19. Seo, M., Kembhavi, A., Farhadi, A., Hajishirzi, H.: Bidirectional attention flow for machine comprehension. arXiv preprint arXiv:1611.01603 (2016)

20. Raffel, C., et al.: Exploring the limits of transfer learning with a unified text-to-text transformer. arXiv preprint arXiv:1910.10683 (2019)

21. Manning, C.D., Surdeanu, M., Bauer, J., Finkel, J.R., Bethard, S., McClosky, D.: The stanford corenlp natural language processing toolkit. In: Proceedings of 52nd annual meeting of the association for computational linguistics: system demonstrations, pp. 55–60 (2014)

22. Qi, P., Zhang, Y., Zhang, Y., Bolton, J., Manning, C.D.: Stanza: A python natural language processing toolkit for many human languages. In: Proceedings of the 58th Annual Meeting of the Association for Computational Linguistics: System Demonstrations. Association for Computational Linguistics, pp. 101–108.(2020). https://doi.org/10.18653/v1/2020.acl-demos.14

Aspect-Based Sentiment Analysis via Virtual Node Augmented Graph Convolutional Networks

Runzhong Xu[✉]

University of Nottingham, Nottingham NG7 2RD, UK
xrunzhong@gmail.com

Abstract. Aspect-based sentiment analysis (ABSA) refers to a fine-grained sentiment analysis task aimed at detecting sentiment polarity towards a given aspect. Recently, graph convolutional networks (GCN) integrated with dependency trees have achieved related appealing results in ABSA. Nevertheless, most existing models fail to preserve the information of the whole graph although global information can often significantly improve their performance. To address this problem, a novel virtual node augmented graph convolutional network (ViGCN) is proposed to further enhance the performance of GCNs in the ABSA task by adding a virtual node to the graph. The virtual node can connect to all the nodes in the graph to aggregate global information from the entire graph and then propagate it to each node. In particular, we construct edges between the virtual node and other nodes based on affective commonsense knowledge from SenticNet and the semantic-relative distances between contextual words and the aspect, effectively enhancing the collected global information towards the given aspect. Extensive experiments on three benchmark datasets illustrate that the ViGCN model can beat state-of-the-art models, proving its effectiveness.

Keywords: Sentiment analysis · Opinion mining · Aspect-based sentiment analysis · Graph neural network

1 Introduction

For the past few years, aspect-based sentiment analysis (ABSA) has become a popular research field in natural language processing [5, 25]. Different from sentence-level sentiment analysis, ABSA is a fine-grained task that aims at inferring the sentiment polarity (e.g., positive, negative, neural) of one specific aspect despite possible multiple aspects in a sentence. For example, in Fig. 1, the corresponding sentiment polarities of the two aspects "works" and "apple OS" are both positive.

It is a key challenge for ABSA to learn the critical sentiment information concerning the given aspect from the sentence [11, 21, 25]. In early works, attention mechanism-based deep learning models are a promising paradigm due to their

© The Author(s), under exclusive license to Springer Nature Switzerland AG 2022
S. Khanna et al. (Eds.): PRICAI 2022, LNCS 13630, pp. 211–223, 2022.
https://doi.org/10.1007/978-3-031-20865-2_16

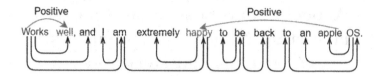

Fig. 1. An example sentence. The words in blue and red are aspects and opinions, respectively. The arrows above manifest the correspondence between aspects and opinions. The arrows below suggest dependencies between words. (Color figure online)

ability to pay attention to important parts of a sentence regarding a specific aspect [5,21]. However, these models lack a mechanism to account for sentiment dependencies between long-range words and may focus on irrelevant sentiment information to predict aspect sentiment. Recent research focuses on developing graph convolutional networks (GCN) over syntactic dependency trees [5,19,25]. Dependency trees can clarify the connections between contextual words and aspect words in a sentence. For example, in Fig. 1, there is a syntactic dependency relationship between the aspect word "Works" and its corresponding opinion word "well" as well as the other two words "am" and "and" in the sentence.

How to leverage the global structure of the graph to improve the model performance is a widely studied problem in the field of graph neural networks [1,3,12–14,23]. Most GCNs for the ABSA task, however, lack a mechanism to effectively capture the global information of the graph. To our knowledge, the GCN models in ABSA can only afford 2–3 layers [4,11,19,22,25], meaning that each node in these models can only collect local information from neighborhood nodes 2–3 hops away from it based on the message-passing scheme [14]. If a GCN model goes deeper so that each node can have a larger receptive field of the graph and learn more global information, the vanishing gradient problem will make the model unstable [11]. The nodes in the GCNs often fail to capture the critical sentiment clues due to the limitation of the receptive field. For example, in Fig. 1, the nodes representing the aspect "apple OS" are 4–5 hops away from the nodes representing the corresponding opinion word "happy". Although the opinion nodes contain significant sentiment information for determining the sentiment polarity of the aspect, this information cannot be transmitted to the aspect nodes.

To tackle the challenges mentioned above, a novel model, the virtual node augmented graph convolutional network (ViGCN), is proposed in this paper, whose architecture is shown in Fig. 2. In ViGCN, an artificial virtual node is added to the graph over the dependency tree and connected to all the real nodes to give them a global receptive field. Real nodes refer to all the nodes in the graph before adding the virtual node. The virtual node was originally proposed to represent the entire graph [9]. Recent research finds that it can be used for graph augmentation [23], because it can aggregate global information from the whole graph and propagate aggregated information to each real node. Considering that the graphs in ABSA are generated from sentences [25], the global information gathered from these graphs contains the sentiment expression of the sentences, which is crucial for the model to predict the sentiment polarities of aspects. Moreover, under the inspiration of SenticNet [2] and previously successful LCF-BERT model [24], weighted edges between the virtual node and real nodes are established based on affective commonsense knowledge and the semantic-relative distances between contextual words and the given aspect. With this approach, the virtual node can focus more on the context containing critical sentiment information in a sentence, making the preserved global information better reflect the emotional expression of the sentence towards the given aspect.

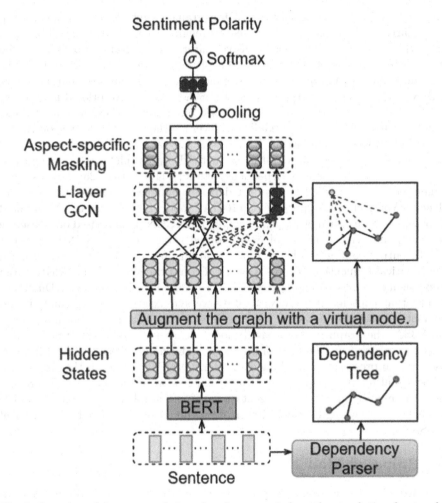

Fig. 2. Overview of the proposed virtual node augmented graph convolutional network.

This paper mainly makes the following contributions: (1) The GCN models applied to the ABSA task are reconsidered so as to exploit the global information regarding the given aspect. (2) A novel ViGCN model for the ABSA task is proposed in this paper, which can effectively preserve global information via a virtual node. Specifically, the proposed ViGCN model leverages affective commensense knowledge and semantic-relative distance to augment the preserved global information. (3) Extensive experiments on the SemEval 2014 and Twitter datasets demonstrate the superiority of the proposed ViGCN model in ABSA. The code of ViGCN is available at: https://github.com/code4scie/ViGCN.

2   Related Work

Aspect-based sentiment analysis is a fine-grained subtask for sentiment analysis. Early works in this field are feature engineering-based models like SVM [10], which are time- and labor-intensive. Later, deep neural networks have been widely used because of their ability to capture features automatically from the sentences. In general, representative works are based on recursive neural network (RNN) [7,16], long short-term memory (LSTM) [21], convolutional neural network (CNN) [8] and deep memory network [5]. However, these neural networks are generally lacking in a mechanism to leverage the syntax information that is of crucial importance for ABSA [25].

Most of the current state-of-the-art methods are graph network-based models combined with syntactic dependency trees [4,11,19,20,22,25]. For instance, Zhang et al. [25] applied GCNs over dependency trees to exploit word dependencies. Wang et al. [20] proposed an R-GAT model based on an aspect-oriented dependency tree. Chen et al. [4] developed a dotGCN model based on a discrete latent opinion tree. Tang et al. [19] adopted a bidirectional GCN to consider BERT outputs and graph-based representations jointly. Xiao et al. [22] utilized grammatical sequential features from BERT and the syntactic knowledge from dependency graphs to augment GCNs. Li et al. [11] put forward a DualGCN model that contains two GCNs to preserve syntax structure information and semantic correlation message, respectively. Despite exhibiting appealing power in ABSA, the graph network-based models learn node representations mainly based on aggregating features from the neighborhood of each node [14], overlooking the preservation of the global information of the graph that is capable of representing aspect-specific sentiment expression of the sentence. Therefore, how to enhance the node representations of the graph network-based models via effectively leveraging global information should be considered in the task of ABSA.

3   Proposed Model

The overall architecture of the proposed virtual node augmented graph convolutional network (ViGCN) is plotted in Fig. 2. In this section, the details of the ViGCN are presented. In particular, the aspect-based sentiment analysis task is first defined, and then how to initialize the node embeddings of a sentence is illustrated. After that, an introduction is made on how to build a virtual node augmented graph and feed the initial node embeddings and graph to ViGCN. Finally, how to obtain the sentiment polarity and train the model is detailed.

3.1   Task Definition

Given an n-word sentence $S = \{s_1, ..., s_{a_1}, ..., s_{a_k}, ..., s_n\}$ with a k-word aspect $A = \{s_{a_1}, ..., s_{a_k}\}$ included, ABSA is aimed at predicting the sentiment polarity p of the aspect A, where $p \in \{Negative, Neutral, Positive\}$. It is worth noting that the aspect may contain a or several words and $1 \le k < n$.

3.2   Node Embeddings Initialization

Bidirectional encoder representations from transformers (BERT) [6] is utilized as the aspect-based encoder to learn the hidden contextual representations of sentences. To be specific, under the inspiration of the model LCF-BERT [24], the sentence-aspect pair $G = [CLS] + S + [SEP] + A + [SEP]$ is first constructed as input, so that BERT can capture the semantic relationship between the sentence S and the aspect A through its next-sentence-prediction mechanism [6]. $[CLS]$ and $[SEP]$ are the special tokens of BERT. BERT first tokenizes each word in G into subwords, and the sentence sequence S is tokenized into an m-subword sequence $S_t = \{t_1, ..., t_{a_1}, ..., t_{a_j}, ..., t_m\}$. Then BERT transforms each subword in G into a hidden state vector, and S_t becomes $S_h = \{h_1, ..., h_{a_1}, ..., h_{a_j}, ..., h_m\}$, where $h_i \in \mathbb{R}^{d_h}$ is the hidden state vector of the i-th subword t_i. We use S_h as the initial real node set. Besides, the virtual node is initialized with a zero vector $0 \in \mathbb{R}^{d_h}$. The initial node embeddings are $V^0 = \{h_1, ..., h_{a_1}, ..., h_{a_j}, ..., h_m, 0\}$.

3.3   Construction of the Virtual Node Augmented Graph

For each sentence, a virtual node augmented graph $G = (V, E)$ is constructed to represent the syntactic relationship among subwords, and $A \in \mathbb{R}^{(m+1) \times (m+1)}$ is the adjacency matrix of the graph G. $V = \{x_1, ..., x_{a_1}, ..., x_{a_j}, ..., x_m, x_{m+1}\}$ is the set of nodes. The first part $\{x_1, ..., x_{a_1}, ..., x_{a_j}, ..., x_m\}$ represents the real nodes, and the latter part x_{m+1} indicates the added virtual node. E is the set of edges.

To build the edges between real nodes, a syntactic dependency tree is first constructed for each input sentence using the dependency parsing model LAL-Parser [15]. To match the subword sequence generated by BERT, the syntactic dependency of a word is expanded into all its subwords. Then, an edge is established between two subwords if a dependency is contained in them. Specifically, for $i, j \in [1, m]$:

$$A_{i,j} = \begin{cases} p_e & \text{if } t_i, t_j \text{ may contain dependency,} \\ 0 & \text{otherwise.} \end{cases} \tag{1}$$

As suggested by [11], $p_e \in (0, 1]$ here is the probability of a dependency between two subwords from a dependency parser. Its purpose is to reduce the adverse impact of parsing errors on model performance.

Inspired by [23], a virtual node is then added to the graph to preserve global information. Firstly, "naive connections" are constructed between the virtual node and real nodes. To be specific, following previous work [23], an undirectional edge is established between the virtual node and each real node in the graph. Therefore, for $i \in [1, m]$:

$$A_{i,m+1} = A_{m+1,i} = 1. \tag{2}$$

Like previous work [23], a self-loop is not added to the virtual node, thereby leading to $A_{m+1,m+1} = 0$.

To learn more global information from the words with stronger sentiment, the representation of the adjacency matrix is enhanced by utilizing affective commonsense knowledge from SenticNet. In particular, we use SenticNet 6, which is a public commonsense knowledge base that provides a set of polarity scores associated with 200,000 concepts [2]. Therefore, for $i \in [1, m]$:

$$A_{i,m+1} = A_{m+1,i} = |Sentics(t_i)| + 1, \tag{3}$$

where $Sentics(t_i) \in [-1, 1]$ represents the polarity score of the subword t_i. The value of the polarity score floats between -1 and $+1$. The polarity score of a word is closer to $+1$ when it is more positive. Conversely, the polarity score of a word is closer to -1 when it is more negative. The polarity score of each word in SenticNet 6 is obtained first and then used as the polarity score of its subwords. For those words excluded from SenticNet 6, their polarity scores are set to be 0. Consideration is only given to the strengthening of the connections between the virtual node and real nodes generated from words with an intense sentiment, regardless of whether the sentiment is positive or negative. Therefore, the absolute polarity value is taken.

In LCF-BERT [24], the semantic-relative distance (SRD) is proposed to focus on the subword tokens generated by the local context, given that the local context close to the aspect usually contains significant sentiment information. Under the inspiration of the work of [24], the connections between the virtual node and nodes representing the local context are further enhanced based on SRD:

$$A_{i,m+1} = A_{m+1,i} = \begin{cases} |Sentics(t_i)| + 2 & \text{if } SRD_i < \varphi, \\ |Sentics(t_i)| + 1 & \text{otherwise .} \end{cases} \tag{4}$$

Here, $i \in [1, m]$ and $SRD_i = |P_i - P_a| - \lfloor \frac{k}{2} \rfloor$ represents the SRD between the i-th token and targeted aspect; P_a is the central position of the aspect and P_i is the position of the context word generating the i-th token, respectively; k refers to the length of the aspect sequence; φ stands for the SRD threshold.

3.4   Virtual Node Augmented Graph Convolutional Network

GCN is a special convolutional neural network working directly on graphs and taking advantage of the graph-structured information. After the initialization of node embeddings and the construction of the graph, they are fed into an L-layer GCN to learn local and global information for the given aspect. In an L-layer GCN, $V^l = \left\{ x_1^l, ..., x_{a_1}^l, ..., x_{a_j}^l, ..., x_m^l, x_{m+1}^l \right\}$ ($l \in [1, 2, ..., L]$) is denoted as the node representations of the l-th layer, where $\left\{x_1^l, ..., x_{a_1}^l, ..., x_{a_j}^l, ..., x_m^l\right\}$ represents real nodes, and x_{m+1}^l is the virtual node. The output of the i-th node in the l-th layer can be calculated as follows:

$$x_i^l = \sigma\left(\left(\sum_{j=1}^{m+1} A_{ij} W^l x_j^{l-1}\right) / (d_i + 1) + b^l\right), \qquad (5)$$

where W^l is a trainable weight matrix and b^l is a bias vector; d_i is the outdegree of the i-th node; σ refers to an activation function and $ReLU$ is used here. The initial node set is V^0 obtained in Subsect. 3.2.

3.5 Model Training

The final output of the L-layer GCN is $V^L = \left\{x_1^L, ..., x_{a_1}^L, ..., x_{a_j}^L, ..., x_m^L, x_{m+1}^L\right\}$. Then, the final feature r is obtained through applying average pooling $f_a(\cdot)$ over aspect nodes:

$$r = f_a\left(x_{a_1}^L, ..., x_{a_j}^L\right). \qquad (6)$$

Next, the final feature r is fed into a fully connected layer, followed by a softmax layer to learn a sentiment polarity probability distribution p:

$$p = softmax(W_c r + b_c), \qquad (7)$$

where W_c and b_c are the trainable weight and bias, respectively.

The model is trained to minimize the objective function composed of a cross-entropy loss function ℓ and an L_2 regularization:

$$\mathfrak{L} = \ell + \lambda\|\Theta\|, \qquad (8)$$

where Θ represents all the trainable parameters, and λ is the coefficient of L_2 regularization. In this paper, ℓ is defined as follows:

$$\ell = -\sum_{i=1}^{D}\sum_{j=1}^{C} \hat{p}_i^j \log p_i^j, \qquad (9)$$

where D is the number of training samples, and C is the number of different sentiment polarities. $\hat{p}$ is the ground-truth sentiment polarity distribution.

4 Experiments

4.1 Datasets and Experiment Settings

We evaluate ViGCN on three public datasets. Restaurant and Laptop datasets are from the SemEval-2014 Task4 [17]. Following [5], all the data samples with the "conflict" label are removed. The Twitter dataset is provided by [7]. All three datasets contain three sentiment polarities: positive, neural and negative. Table 1 shows the statistics of the datasets.

In this experiment, we use pre-trained BERT-base-uncased model [6] to initialize word embeddings. The dimension of word embeddings and hidden states d_h is 768. The depth of ViGCN layers L is set to be 2, and the dropout rate of ViGCN is set to be 0.1 to avoid overfitting. The SRD threshold φ is set to be 3 on Restaurant and Twitter datasets, and 6 on the Laptop dataset. The Adam optimizer with a learning rate of 0.001 is utilized to optimize the model attributes. The coefficient λ of the L_2 regularization is 10^{-4}. The model is trained in 15 epochs and the batch size is set to be 16. The experimental results are obtained by averaging 10 runs with random initialization, where accuracy and macro F1 score are the evaluation metrics adopted to evaluate the model performance.

Table 1. Statistics of the experimental datasets.

Dataset	Positive		Neural		Negative	
	Train	Test	Train	Test	Train	Test
Restaurant	2164	727	637	196	807	196
Laptop	976	337	455	167	851	128
Twitter	1507	172	3016	336	1528	169

4.2   Comparison Baselines

We compare ViGCN with the following baselines: (1)**ATAE-LSTM** [21] is an attention-based LSTM model for ABSA; (2)**AEN** [18] is an attentional encoder network based on BERT; (3) **RAM** [5] uses a recurrent attention network on memory to learn the sentence representation; (4) **ASGCN** [25] is an aspect-specific GCN model over the dependency tree; (5) **BERT4GCN** [22] is a GCN augmented with intermediate layers of BERT and positional information between words for ABSA task; (6) **R-GAT+BERT** [20] proposes a relational graph attention network based on an aspect-oriented dependency tree; (7) **DualGCN + BERT** [11] integrates syntactic knowledge and semantic information simultaneously with dual GCNs, namely, SynGCN and SemGCN; (8) **DGEDT+BERT** [19] is a dual-transformer model which jointly considers graph-based representations and flat-representations; (9) **dotGCN+BERT** [4] is a graph convolutional network based on a discrete opinion tree.

4.3   Comparison Results

The main experimental results can be seen in Table 2. On all the three experimental datasets, the ViGCN model outperforms almost all compared attention-based and graph neural network-based models with respect to both accuracy and macro F1 score. Compared to the remarkable DualGCN+BERT model, it performs quite competitively as well. To be specific, ViGCN outperforms Dual-GCN+BERT on Restaurant and Twitter datasets, although its accuracy score on the Laptop dataset is slightly lower than DualGCN+BERT by 0.31. This proves that the ability to effectively preserve global information enables ViGCN to achieve significant gains in ABSA.

Compared with attention-based models such as ATAE-LSTM, AEN and RAM, ViGCN exploits a syntactic dependency tree to explicitly model the connections between the aspect and the context, which thus can avoid the noise introduced by the attention mechanism. In comparison with previous state-of-the-art graph neural network-based models like ASGCN, BERT4GCN and R-GAT+BERT, the enhancement is mainly contributed by two factors. One is that a virtual node is added to the graph because of being able to enhance node representations through leveraging the global information of the whole graph. The other is that effective weights are set for edges between the virtual node and real nodes based on affective commonsense knowledge and semantic-relative distance, which refines the process of the virtual node aggregating and propagating global information.

Table 2. Comparisons of ViGCN with baselines. Accuracy (ACC.) and macro F1 score (F1) are used for metrics. Best results are in bold and second best results are underlined.

Models	Restaurant		Laptop		Twitter	
	Acc.	F1	Acc.	F1	Acc.	F1
ATAE-LSTM	77.20	–	68.70	–	–	–
AEN	84.29	77.22	76.96	73.67	75.14	74.15
RAM	80.23	70.80	74.49	71.35	69.36	67.30
ASGCN	80.77	72.02	75.55	71.05	72.15	70.40
BERT4GCN	84.75	77.11	77.49	73.01	74.73	73.76
R-GAT+BERT	86.60	<u>81.35</u>	78.21	74.07	76.15	74.88
DualGCN+BERT	<u>87.13</u>	81.16	**81.80**	<u>78.10</u>	77.40	76.02
DGEDT+BERT	86.30	80.00	79.80	75.60	77.90	75.40
dotGCN+BERT	86.16	80.49	81.03	<u>78.10</u>	<u>78.11</u>	<u>77.00</u>
ViGCN	**87.31**	**82.27**	<u>81.49</u>	**78.29**	**78.14**	**77.04**

4.4   Ablation Analysis

To further clarify the impact of each component of constructing virtual node augmented graphs for the proposed ViGCN, ablation studies are conducted. The results are demonstrated in Table 3. First, it can be observed that the model without a virtual node performs poorly on all datasets (ViGCN w/o N+S+D) compared with the other models in Table 3. This indicates virtual node can improve the performance of GCNs in ABSA. When we only construct "naive connections" between the virtual node and real nodes (ViGCN w/o S+D), the performance of the model, although improved, is still far below the best performance. Comparatively, ViGCN w/o D and ViGCN w/o S evidently perform better. This proves the effectiveness of the SenticNet-based and SRD-based optimization methods for "naive connection". Also, the "naive connections" are indispensable to the model, given that the removal of "naive connections" leads to poorer performance (ViGCN w/o N). It is worth noting that ViGCN w/o D does not outperform ViGCN w/o S on the Twitter dataset as on the Restaurant and Laptop datasets, which may be because the data on the Twitter dataset is biased towards colloquial expressions, less sensitive to sentiment information [7]. Finally, ViGCN outperforms all its ablation models, revealing that each component of ViGCN is indispensable.

Table 3. Results of ablation analysis. "S" represents SenticNet, "D" represents SRD, "N" represents "naive connections".

Models	Restaurant		Laptop		Twitter	
	Acc.	F1	Acc.	F1	Acc.	F1
ViGCN w/o S+D+N	85.08	78.41	78.80	74.31	75.63	74.83
ViGCN w/o D+N	85.43	78.64	79.91	75.56	75.92	74.95
ViGCN w/o S+N	85.61	78.62	80.06	75.95	76.07	75.47
ViGCN w/o S+D	85.52	78.15	80.22	76.28	76.37	75.50
ViGCN w/o N	85.70	79.06	80.54	76.62	76.81	75.40
ViGCN w/o S	86.06	80.18	80.85	77.10	77.40	76.03
ViGCN w/o D	86.95	80.94	81.01	77.73	77.10	75.77
ViGCN	**87.31**	**82.27**	**81.49**	**78.29**	**78.14**	**77.04**

4.5 Parameter Sensitivity

Figure 3 illustrates the performance of ViGCN at different SRD thresholds φ from 1 to 10. It can be seen that ViGCN performs best with an SRD threshold of 3 on the Restaurant and Twitter datasets, and with an SRD threshold of 6 on the laptop dataset. As the SRD threshold φ increases, the performance of the model gradually improves until it reaches the best performance, and then the performance of the model shows a drop trend. A possible reason is that when φ is too small, the model cannot capture enough information from the local context. On the opposite, while it is too large, noise may be introduced into the global information preserved by the model.

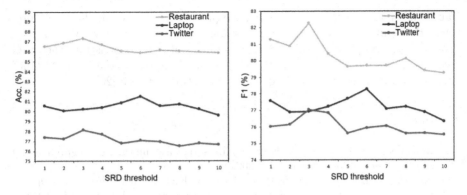

Fig. 3. Effect of the SRD threshold φ.

4.6   Case Study

ViGCN, RAM and ASGCN are compared on several sample cases. The results are demonstrated in Table 4. For the first sample, the words "apple" and "OS" in the aspect"apple OS" are five and four hops away, respectively, from the opinion word "happy" on the graph over the dependency tree. For a 2-layer ASGCN, the information contains in the opinion word cannot be passed to the aspect. In contrast, in ViGCN, information can be passed from the opinion word to the aspect in 2 hops via the virtual node. Given this, ViGCN succeeds while ASGCN fails. For the second sample, the attention-based model RAM wrongly predicts the sentiment polarity of the aspect "Saketini", which may attend to the noise word "Disappointingly". For the third sample, impacted by the noise word "wonderful", ASGCN and RAM mispredict the sentiment polarity of the aspect "burger". Nonetheless, ViGCN predicts it correctly because the model combines global information preserved from the entire sentence to make predictions, thereby significantly mitigating the interference of those noise words.

Table 4. Case study. The words in red denote the aspects. The symbols P, N and O represent positive, negative and neural sentiment, respectively.

Sentence	ViGCN	RAM	ASGCN
1. Works well, and I am extremely happy to be back to an apple OS.	P✓, P✓	P✓, P✓	P✓, O✗
2. Disappointingly, their wonderful Saketinihas been taken off the bar menu.	P✓	N✗	P✓
3. My friend had a burger and I had these wonderful blueberry pancakes.	O✓, P✓	P✗, P✓	P✗, P✓

5   Conclusion

In this paper, the task of aspect-based sentiment analysis is investigated and a virtual node augmented graph convolutional network called ViGCN is proposed.

Taking advantage of the virtual node, the proposed ViGCN can effectively preserve global information to precisely predict the sentiment polarity towards a given aspect. Empirical results on three public datasets demonstrate the effectiveness of our model. Future work includes applying the virtual node to other graph-based models in ABSA, e.g., graph attention network [20].

References

1. Buffelli, D., Vandin, F.: The impact of global structural information in graph neural networks applications. Data p. 10 (2022)
2. Cambria, E., Li, Y., Xing, F.Z., Poria, S., Kwok, K.: Senticnet 6: Ensemble application of symbolic and subsymbolic ai for sentiment analysis. In: Proceedings of the 29th ACM International Conference on Information and Knowledge Management, pp. 105–114 (2020)
3. Cao, S., Lu, W., Xu, Q.: Grarep: Learning graph representations with global structural information. In: Proceedings of the 24th ACM International on Conference on Information and Knowledge Management, pp. 891–900 (2015)
4. Chen, C., Teng, Z., Wang, Z., Zhang, Y.: Discrete opinion tree induction for aspect-based sentiment analysis. In: Proceedings of the 60th Annual Meeting of the Association for Computational Linguistics, pp. 2051–2064 (2022)
5. Chen, P., Sun, Z., Bing, L., Yang, W.: Recurrent attention network on memory for aspect sentiment analysis. In: Proceedings of the 2017 Conference on Empirical Methods in Natural Language Processing, pp. 452–461 (2017)
6. Devlin, J., Chang, M.W., Lee, K., Toutanova, K.: BERT: Pre-training of deep bidirectional transformers for language understanding. In: Proceedings of the 2019 Conference of the North American Chapter of the Association for Computational Linguistics: Human Language Technologies, pp. 4171–4186 (2019)
7. Dong, L., Wei, F., Tan, C., Tang, D., Zhou, M., Xu, K.: Adaptive recursive neural network for target-dependent twitter sentiment classification. In: Proceedings of the 52nd Annual Meeting of the Association for Computational Linguistics, pp. 49–54 (2014)
8. Fan, C., Gao, Q., Du, J., Gui, L., Xu, R., Wong, K.F.: Convolution-based memory network for aspect-based sentiment analysis. In: The 41st International ACM SIGIR Conference on Research and Development in Information Retrieval, pp. 1161–1164 (2018)
9. Gilmer, J., Schoenholz, S.S., Riley, P.F., Vinyals, O., Dahl, G.E.: Neural message passing for quantum chemistry. In: International Conference on Machine Learning, pp. 1263–1272 (2017)
10. Jiang, L., Yu, M., Zhou, M., Liu, X., Zhao, T.: Target-dependent twitter sentiment classification. In: Proceedings of the 49th Annual Meeting of the Association for Computational Linguistics: Human Language Technologies, pp. 151–160 (2011)
11. Li, R., Chen, H., Feng, F., Ma, Z., Wang, X., Hovy, E.: Dual graph convolutional networks for aspect-based sentiment analysis. In: Proceedings of the 59th Annual Meeting of the Association for Computational Linguistics and the 11th International Joint Conference on Natural Language Processing, pp. 6319–6329 (2021)
12. Liu, M., Liu, Y.: Inductive representation learning in temporal networks via mining neighborhood and community influences. In: Proceedings of the 44th International ACM SIGIR Conference on Research and Development in Information Retrieval, pp. 2202–2206 (2021)

13. Liu, M., Quan, Z.W., Wu, J.M., Liu, Y., Han, M.: Embedding temporal networks inductively via mining neighborhood and community influences. Appl. Intell. 1–20 (2022)
14. Liu, M., Wu, J.M., Liu, Y.: Embedding global and local influences for dynamic graphs. In: CIKM (2022)
15. Mrini, K., Dernoncourt, F., Tran, Q.H., Bui, T., Chang, W., Nakashole, N.: Rethinking self-attention: Towards interpretability in neural parsing. In: Findings of the Association for Computational Linguistics: EMNLP 2020, pp. 731–742 (2020)
16. Nguyen, T.H., Shirai, K.: Phrasernn: Phrase recursive neural network for aspect-based sentiment analysis. In: Proceedings of the 2015 Conference on Empirical Methods in Natural Language Processing, pp, 2509–2514 (2015)
17. Pontiki, M., Galanis, D., Pavlopoulos, J., Papageorgiou, H., Androutsopoulos, I., Manandhar, S.: Semeval-2014 task 4: Aspect based sentiment analysis. In: COLING 2014 (2014)
18. Song, Y., Wang, J., Jiang, T., Liu, Z., Rao, Y.: Attentional encoder network for targeted sentiment classification. arXiv preprint arXiv:1902.09314 (2019)
19. Tang, H., Ji, D., Li, C., Zhou, Q.: Dependency graph enhanced dual-transformer structure for aspect-based sentiment classification. In: Proceedings of the 58th Annual Meeting of the Association for Computational Linguistics, pp. 6578–6588 (2020)
20. Wang, K., Shen, W., Yang, Y., Quan, X., Wang, R.: Relational graph attention network for aspect-based sentiment analysis. In: Proceedings of the 58th Annual Meeting of the Association for Computational Linguistics, pp. 3229–3238 (2020)
21. Wang, Y., Huang, M., Zhu, X., Zhao, L.: Attention-based lstm for aspect-level sentiment classification. In: Proceedings of the 2016 Conference on Empirical Methods in Natural Language Processing, pp. 606–615 (2016)
22. Xiao, Z., Wu, J., Chen, Q., Deng, C.: BERT4GCN: Using BERT intermediate layers to augment GCN for aspect-based sentiment classification. In: Proceedings of the 2021 Conference on Empirical Methods in Natural Language Processing, pp. 9193–9200 (2021)
23. Ying, C., et al.: Do transformers really perform badly for graph representation? In: Advances in Neural Information Processing Systems, vol. 34 (2021)
24. Zeng, B., Yang, H., Xu, R., Zhou, W., Han, X.: Lcf: A local context focus mechanism for aspect-based sentiment classification. Appl. Sci. 9(16), 3389 (2019)
25. Zhang, C., Li, Q., Song, D.: Aspect-based sentiment classification with aspect-specific graph convolutional networks. In: Proceedings of the 2019 Conference on Empirical Methods in Natural Language Processing and the 9th International Joint Conference on Natural Language Processing, pp. 4568–4578 (2019)

Bidirectional Macro-level Discourse Parser Based on Oracle Selection

Longwang He, Feng Jiang, Xiaoyi Bao, Yaxin Fan, Weihao Liu, Peifeng Li, and Xiaomin Chu[✉]

School of Computer Science and Technology, Soochow University, Suzhou, China
{lwhe,fjiang,xybao,yxfan}@stu.suda.edu.cn, {pfli,xmchu}@suda.edu.cn

Abstract. Most existing studies construct a discourse structure tree following two popular methods: top-down or bottom-up strategy. However, they often suffered from cascading errors because they can not switch the strategy of building a structure tree to avoid mistakes caused by uncertain decision-making. Moreover, due to the different basis of top-down and bottom-up methods in building discourse trees, thoroughly combining the advantages of the two methods is challenging. To alleviate these issues, we propose a Bidirectional macro-level dIscourse Parser based on OracLe selEction (BIPOLE), which combines the top-down and bottom-up strategies by selecting the suitable decision-making strategy. BIPOLE consists of a basic parsing module composed of top-down and bottom-up sub-parsers and a decision-maker for selecting a prediction strategy by considering each sub-parser state. Moreover, we propose a label-based data-enhanced oracle training strategy to generate the training data of the decision-maker. Experimental results on MCDTB and RST-DT show that our model can effectively alleviate cascading errors and outperforms the SOTA baselines significantly.

Keywords: Macro discourse parsing · Label embedding · Bidirectional selection

1 Introduction

Discourse structure analysis aims to comprehend the structure and semantics of an article, which provides powerful support for the downstream task such as question answering [1], machine translation [2], automatic digesting [3], and information extraction [4]. Generally, discourse structure analysis is mainly divided into two levels: micro-level and macro-level. Micro-level discourse analysis focuses on the organizational structure and semantic relationships between sentences, whereas macro-level focuses on those between paragraphs, which reveals the main idea and content of the document from a higher level and facilitates a deeper understanding of the article. It is more challenging because it contains more complex semantic information, such as the paragraph-level elementary discourse unit (PDU) is a paragraph rather than a sentence. Figure 1 shows an example of a macro discourse tree.

© The Author(s), under exclusive license to Springer Nature Switzerland AG 2022
S. Khanna et al. (Eds.): PRICAI 2022, LNCS 13630, pp. 224–239, 2022.
https://doi.org/10.1007/978-3-031-20865-2_17

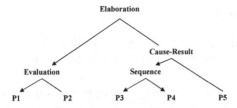

Fig. 1. A macro discourse tree with five paragraphs (leaf nodes).

Existing studies on discourse structure parsing are following two strategies: top-down parsing [6–9] and bottom-up parsing [10–14]. The top-down parsing usually splits a discourse unit (DU) into two smaller ones according to the semantic relation between two DUs. The bottom-up parsing combines two adjacent DUs into a larger one to build a discourse tree.

However, whatever the top-down or bottom-up method, these single-direction discourse parsers have cascading errors in predicting the combination or split action at each step. For example, in the top-down parser proposed by Fan et al. [6], cascading errors cause a performance loss of up to 18.72% (see Sect. 4.5 for specific evaluation methods). In the different contexts, the difficulty of predicting combination and split is different. The top-down model sometimes makes the wrong decision by choosing an uncertain split action, while a combination action is easier to predict.

On the other hand, top-down and bottom-up methods have different biases. The former focuses more on the global semantic information, while the latter focuses more on the local semantic connection between adjacent DUs. Therefore, how to combine these two unidirectional methods and gain each other's advantages becomes another challenge [22].

To address the above issues, we propose a Bidirectional dIscourse Parser based on OracLe selEction (BIPOLE), which combines the top-down and bottom-up strategies by selecting the suitable decision-making strategy. Firstly, following previous work, we design two sub-parser (split-parser and combine-parser) by pointer network as the basic parser module to construct the discourse structure tree bidirectional. Split-parser can split a DU into two new DUs, building a discourse tree from top to down, while combine-parser can combine two adjacent DUs into one new DU from bottom to up. Secondly, we propose a structured label embedding model as the decision-maker to select the current action from two sub-parsers. It not only considers the hidden state of the two sub-parsers but also obtains the basis of the switching parsing strategy from action labels and structure labels. Finally, we propose a label-based data-enhanced oracle training strategy to generate the training data of the decision-maker. We generate training data for selecting actions through the oracle strategy to enhance the error correction capability of the Decision Maker. Experimental results on the MCDTB [5] and RST-DT [18] show that our model BIPOLE is effective.

2   Related Work

Since there are no attempts at bidirectional parsing methods in known work, we have tried to divide influential work in the field into two categories: top-down and bottom-up.

The bottom-up models on discourse structure parsing mainly used various transition-based approaches to construct discourse structure trees. Mabona et al. [19] proposed a generative model based on a beam search algorithm that can track both structure and word-generating actions while avoiding the left-branching bias [20] produced by earlier RNNGs beam search methods. The beam search algorithm tries to improve the global confidence, but it does not mitigate the error propagation problem, resulting in confidence levels in the leaning back parsing steps that may not be true and reliable, and it also introduces extremely high time complexity. Zhou et al. [10] applied the shift-reduce method to build the discourse tree by extracting macro-level discourse semantic information and presenting a word-pair similarity strategy to acquire interaction information between PDUs, which enhances model performance by improving the semantic representation of PDUs. Jiang et al. [11] used the shift-reduce method leveraging the Chinese discourse structure's left-branching bias and propose a global and local reverse reading strategy to build a discourse structure tree. This work explores a new construction approach for the first time and demonstrates its effectiveness. Jiang et al. [12] introduced topic segmentation into the shift-reduce method where the lengthy text is divided into multiple small texts. Then each short text's discourse parsing efficiently reduces error propagation among the short texts, improving long text recognition. But the structure of the topics he used for training was not really labeled but transformed with rules.

As for the top-down models, Lin et al. [8] first used a pointer network with incorporating the sibling and parent node information in the decoding process. The pointer network framework is very effective in capturing global information, but the connection between neighboring PDUs is correspondingly weakened. Then, Fan et al. [6] further proposed a pointer network integrating the global and local information to strengthen the semantic interaction. Koto et al. [9] applied sequence labeling to eliminate decoders and reduce the search space for segmentation points, but ignore the possible "combine points". Zhang et al. [22] effectively improved the efficiency of the segmentation point sorting task by encoding the segmentation points in the pointer network. Zhang et al. [23] trained an adversarial robot to constraint the top-down parsing by exploiting global information from the graph to convert the predicted tree and the gold tree.

Furthermore, Kobayashi et al. [24] utilize two unsupervised parsing approaches (top-down for split parsing and bottom-up for combination parsing) based on dynamic planning and then compared and analyses them. However, they did not propose a method to combine these two parsers.

The strength of the related work mentioned above is that they have explored a lot in terms of semantic representations, semantic interactions, and parsing processes, while their weakness is that no one has tried to parse in both direc-

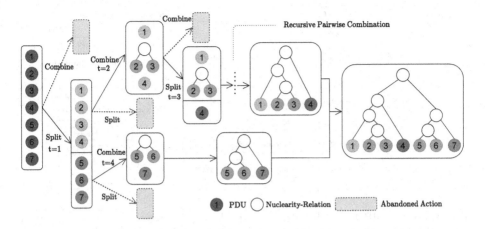

Fig. 2. Structure-building process for an article containing seven paragraphs.

tions, but only to propose conjectures. Whereas our work combines their ideas (top-down and bottom-up).

3   Bidirectional Discourse Parser on Oracle Selection

BIPOLE contains a bi-directional parsing process and a selection method. First, we introduce our bi-directional parsing process. We keep a stack to store the state of parsing, where the initial state of the stack is a DU containing the entire document. The top-of-stack unit is popped out at each decoding step and considered as Span To be Parsed (STP). The length of an STP is the number of subtrees it contains internally. Unlike the typical pointer network approach, we may not only "split" STP at each parsing step, but also "combine" two subtrees within STP, After each step of parsing, the new spans with a length greater than 2 will be pushed into the stack. Figure 2 shows our special tree-building procedure, in which spans of length 2 are combined directly without decoding and selection. The gray parts pointed by the dotted lines are the decisions that we discard, whereas the solid lines point to our chosen decision.

Each decoding step consists of two stages: 1) Basic Parser is used to obtain two candidates, and the candidate prediction results include split or combine operations and corresponding parsing positions; 2) Decision Maker selects one of them for parsing. Figure 3 shows an overview of the architecture for each decoding step.

3.1   Basic Parser

Basic Parser contains two components: split-parser and combine-parser, which both consist of a Hierarchical Encoder and an Attention-based Decoder.

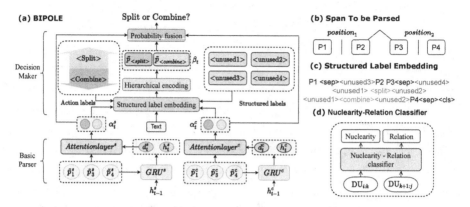

Fig. 3. (a) Our BIPOLE architecture and the decoding process at $t = 3$ in Fig. 2, with Text as the full-text document. (b) STP at $t = 3$. Since P2 and P3 have been combined in the previous steps, we use the representation of the last PDU (P3) in the subtree to represent the whole subtree (P2-3) (c) Structured Label Embedding as described in Sect. 3.2. (d) The two DUs after splitting or before combining will be fed into the Nuclearity-Relation Classifiers.

Hierarchical Encoder: Given a document $T = \{t_1, t_2, \ldots, t_n\}$ containing n tokens, which contains the $\langle sep \rangle$ after each paragraph and the $\langle cls \rangle$ at the end of the document. We first convert them all to semantic embeddings $R = \{r_1, r_2, \ldots, r_n\}$ by the popular pre-trained model XLNet [25]. To capture the global information, the embedding R with an initialized zero vector h_0 is fed into the multilayer Bi-GRU, a full-text encoding with context-awareness $P = \{p_1, p_2, \ldots, p_n\}$ and the last hidden state h_{final} of the Bi-GRU are obtained. h_{final} is considered as a document-level representation of the full text. Finally, the representation of the $\langle sep \rangle$ position spliced after each PDU is used as the compressed representation $\widetilde{P} = \{\tilde{p}_1, \tilde{p}_2, \ldots, \tilde{p}_m\}$ of that PDU, where m is the number of PDUs. It is worth noting that split-parser and combine-parser do not share an encoder, and they have their own encoder to generate $\widetilde{P}$ and h_{final} for their decoders separately, providing different parsing views.

Attention-Based Decoder: In each decoding step, we transport vector representations of all PDUs in the STP to the two sub parsers. The positions of splitting and combining operations and the corresponding probabilities are obtained respectively.

In the decoding step t, we first take the last PDU representation $\tilde{p}_{\text{tail}}$ in STP as the overall representation of STP. The hidden layer state output h_{t-1} from the previous step of the decoder and the $\tilde{p}_{\text{tail}}$ are transported to the GRU to obtain the decoder state d_t and the hidden layer state h_t of the current STP, where the initial hidden layer state h_0 in the decoder is the document-level representation h_{final} of the full text of the hierarchically encoded output. h_t contains not only the document-level representation of the full text, but also all the decoding information in the previous decoding step, and is continuously updated and passed. We use the representation of the n-th DU as the representation of the position between the n-th DU and the $(n+1)$-th DU. To obtain the probability distribution α_t, we calculate the attention score according to all the representations of the position and the attention mechanism, as shown in Eq. 1.

$$\alpha_t = softmax(\sigma(d_t, \tilde{P}_{position})) \tag{1}$$

where $\tilde{P}_{position}$ is the set of all position representations in STP, and σ is the dot product operation. α_t represents the semantic connection closeness scores between adjacent DUs in STP, and its meaning is different between the split-parser and combine-parser. In the split-parser, the higher the probability, the loosely the semantic connection between DUs beside the split position is. On the contrary, in the combine-parser, the higher the probability, the tighter the connection. As a result, based on the probability distributions α_t^s and α_t^c of the output of the split-parser and combine-parser in step t, we can obtain the split and combination positions P_t^s and P_t^c from the Basic Parser in step t.

Training Loss: We use a joint learning training method for the split-parser, the combine-parser, and the Nuclearity-Relation Classifier. Specifically, we use the negative log-likelihood function for the two sub-parsers and the cross-entropy for the Nuclearity-Relation Classifier. The total loss calculation is shown in Eq. 2, where θ^s and θ^c are the parameters of the split-parser and the combine-parser.

$$L_{total}(\theta_{total}) = L_s(\theta_s) + L_c(\theta_c) + L_{nr}(\theta_{nr}) + \frac{\gamma}{2} \|\theta_{total}\|_2^2 \tag{2}$$

In the training phase, for a document with n PDUs, split-parser keeps a stack that splits the document top-down according to the depth-first principle, while combine-parser keeps a sequence of PDUs and the sequence length is subtracted by 1 after each combination. The nodes at the same layer take a left-to-right combining order for learning. We apply L2 regularization to all parameters, where γ is the regularization strength, and θ_{total} denotes the set of all parameters in the process of joint learning.

3.2 Decision Maker

In each decoding step, Decision Maker picks between the candidates parsed by Basic Parser. Decision Maker first reorganizes the flat STP text into structured text by structured label embedding, then transports it to an additional Hierarchical Encoder for binary classification, and finally performs Probability Fusion of the binary classification results with the output from Basic Parser.

Structured Label Embedding: Label embedding can help the model identify discourse-level interactions between the text beside the labels [16], it also had a good performance in generative-based discourse parsers [27]. To fuse the parsing information of the previous step and candidate information of the current step, Decision Maker embeds two types of action labels $\langle split \rangle$ and $\langle combine \rangle$, and four types of structured labels $\langle unused1 \rangle$, $\langle unused2 \rangle$, $\langle unused3 \rangle$, and $\langle unused4 \rangle$ in the text of STP.

As an example, in Fig. 3(b)(c), STP is P1-4, and there are three DUs with two parsing positions($position_1$ and $position_2$). Assuming that the Basic Parser selects to split and combine at $position_2$ at the same time. The steps are as follows:1) Decision Maker splices the DU text in STP that was combined in the previous decoding step. 2) Adding the $\langle sep \rangle$ labels after each DU, $\langle cls \rangle$ label at the end of STP. And then nesting the $\langle unused3 \rangle$ and $\langle unused4 \rangle$ outside the combined DU to bring in the structure parsing information obtained from the previous steps. Note that in a more complex STP, $\langle unused3 \rangle$ and $\langle unused4 \rangle$ may contain multiple layers of nesting. 3) Embedding $\langle split \rangle$ and $\langle combine \rangle$ in the P_t^s and P_t^c positions respectively, and nesting the action labels with $\langle unused1 \rangle$ and $\langle unused2 \rangle$.

Finally, the restructured text is put into the Hierarchical Encoder, and the representations of the two action label positions ($\widetilde{p}_{<split>}$ and $\widetilde{p}_{<combine>}$) are spliced for classification to create the structured label embedding model's decision score distribution β_t. Unlike the commonly used label embedding approach [17], we not only naturally prevent the model from confusing label semantic information with position information, but also allow the model to learn the meaning of two abstract actions.

Probability Fusion: The final parsing strategy for the n-th step would be chosen based on a Probability Fusion, which combines the output of the Basic Parser and the Structured Label Embedding model as follows.

$$s_t^s = \lambda \beta_t^s + (1 - \lambda)max(\alpha_t^s) \tag{3}$$

$$s_t^c = \lambda \beta_t^c + (1 - \lambda)max(\alpha_t^c) \tag{4}$$

$$A_t, Position_t = \begin{cases} \text{Split}, Position_t^s & s_t^s > s_t^c \\ \text{Combine}, Position_t^c & s_t^s < s_t^c \end{cases} \tag{5}$$

where β_t^s and β_t^c are the scores of $\langle split \rangle$ label position and $\langle combine \rangle$ label position in β_t, respectively. λ is a hyperparameter to control the influence of the Basic Parser and the Structured Label Embedding model. α_t^s and α_t^c are the output of Basic Parser, s_t^s and s_t^c are the split and combine action scores of the BIPOLE at step t, respectively. And $Position_t$ is the position of the final execution decision at step t.

Finally, according to the decision, the DUs after splitting or before combining is input into the Nuclearity-Relation Classifier. Our Nuclearity-Relation Classifier is consistent with [8], which uses Biaffine Attention for classification. The DU is fed into an additional Hierarchical Encoder, and the output is subsequently max-pooling as the representation of the DU. The Nuclearity-Relation Classifier will output the binary group $\{Nuclearity, Relation\}$, and then go to step $t + 1$.

Training Loss: In the Structured Label Embedding model, we use $L_{label}(\theta_{label})$ loss for training, which consists of cross-entropy loss $L_{ce}(\theta_{label})$ and supervised contrast loss $L_{sc}(\theta_{label})$ [30], as shown in Eq. 6. θ_{label} is the parameters of the Structured Label Embedding model . We L2-regularize the two losses to get the final loss.

$$L_{label}(\theta_{label}) = \delta * L_{ce}(\theta_{label}) + (1 - \delta) * L_{sc}(\theta_{label}) + \frac{\gamma}{2} \|\theta_{label}\|_2^2 \quad (6)$$

3.3 Oracle Selection

We propose an Oracle Selection mode to generate the training data for Decision Maker. Since there are no split and combined labels in the corpus, there is no golden bidirectional tree-building process. To solve this problem, we use the Basic Parser trained in Sect. 3.1 to construct the bidirectional building process. In addition, we propose a new data augmentation method to avoid the weak variation that prevents the model from generalizing to similar contexts. In summary, our Oracle Selection mode consists of two components: 1) the bi-directional tree building principle, which determines our tree building process. 2) data enhancement, in each step of the bi-directional tree building, we use data enhancement methods to extract data for the training of decision makers.

Silver Standard Bi-direction Tree-Building Method. Hung et al. [15] propose a teacher-student mode that allows a small number of errors to be generated during training to improve the model's ability to correct error states. Inspired by this, we use the trained Basic Parser to generate separate split and combine decisions at each step. And then we compare the subtrees produced by these two decisions to the golden tree. If only one of the two decisions can generate the golden structure, that decision will be chosen for parsing and go to the next step. If both decisions can produce the correct structure or neither can, the larger one will be chosen based on the softmax probability.

Data Enhancement. At each decoding step of the Oracle Selection, we insert the ⟨*split*⟩ and ⟨*combine*⟩ labels by permutation and combination at all positions to generate more scenes samples. Then we pick out the parsing cases where only one decision in the split and combination is correct. Finally, we reorganize the text of STP using the Structured Label Embedding method described in Sect. 3.2 to generate train data for Decision Maker. Unlike common NLP data enhancement methods, our approach does not change the context and semantics. The data are chosen to focus on the critical decisions that the model can make while ignoring cases in which both are correct or incorrect. Data enhancement also eliminates the impact of data cropping due to the ignoring of non-critical decisions.

4   Experimentation

4.1   Dataset and Experimental Settings

In the past, MCDTB 1.0 was often criticized because the data set was too small. To expand the size of the corpus, 480 additional articles are annotated based on MCDTB 1.0, which constitutes MCDTB 2.0 with a total of 1200 articles (the annotation process is highly consistent with MCDTB 1.0). MCDTB 2.0 has a larger number of samples to test the generalization ability of the model. The percentage of long documents with more than 6 paragraphs in MCDTB 1.0 is 24.3%, while it is 27.1% in MCDTB 2.0, which shows that the percentage of long documents in MCDTB 2.0 is much larger and the discourse structure parsing task is more difficult. In this paper, we partitioned MCDTB 2.0 using the paragraph distribution dataset partitioning method followed by Jiang et al. [12], with 80% of the training set (960 documents) and 20% of the test set (240 documents), and 10% of the training set was randomly selected as the validation set (96 documents).

Table 1. Performance comparison of discourse tree construction (Micro-F1). $\uparrow$ and $\downarrow$ represent the bottom-up method and top-down method, respectively. BIPOLE was significantly superior to AdverParser with a p-value < 0.05 (t-test).

	Span	Nuclearity	Relation
UnifiedParser$^{\downarrow}$	52.64	36.92	31.85
TDParser$^{\downarrow}$	55.99	48.68	34.51
PNGL$^{\downarrow}$	54.23	–	–
GBLRR$^{\uparrow}$	61.87	54.25	28.35
MDParser-TS$^{\uparrow}$	59.68	45.76	27.95
DGCNParser$^{\uparrow}$	61.98	49.95	28.97
AdverParser$^{\downarrow}$	64.64	**57.96**	**40.26**
Combine-parser$^{\uparrow}_{ours}$	62.05	–	–
Split-parser$^{\downarrow}_{ours}$	63.62	–	–
BIPOLE$^{\uparrow}_{ours}$	**67.19**	56.21	39.34

We report the micro-averaged F1 score for predicting span attachments in discourse tree construction (Span), span attachments with nuclearity (Nuclearity), and span attachments with relation labels (Relation). Specifically, we use three categories to assess nuclearity recognition and fifteen categories to assess relational classification which is defined in [29].

The model parameters of split-parser and combine-parser used in this paper are set the same. In Chinese, we use the XLNet-mid[1] as our pretrained model,

---

[1]   https://github.com/ymcui/Chinese-XLNet.

while in English, we use XLNet-base[2]. And we did not fine-tune XLNet during the training process. The hidden layer dimension of all Bi-GRU and GRU used by Hierarchical Encoder and Attention-based Decoder are set to 64, and the dropout rate of both coding and decoding layers are set to 0.2, λ set to 0.4, δ set to 0.3, and τ set to 0.5. The Adam optimizer with a batch size of 2 is used, the learning rate is 1e-4, and γ is 0.0005. Basic Parser and Decision Maker were trained for 50 and 20 epochs respectively.

4.2   Experimental Results

We select two kinds of existing parsers, i.e., top-down parser and bottom-up parser, as the baselines for comparison, where the first three baselines do not use pre-trained models.

Top-Down parser. 1) **UnifiedParser** [8]: a parser incorporating information from parent and sibling nodes; 2) **TDParser** [22]: a parser encoding segmentation points; 3) **PNGL** [6]: a parser that fuses global information with local information. 4) **AdverParser** [23]: a SOTA model on micro-level, which converted predicted trees and gold trees into graphs and trains an adversarial bot to exploit global information.

Bottom-Up Parser. 5) **GBLRR** [11]: a parser that inverts the order of parsing to achieve reverse reading; 6) **MDParser-TS** [12]: a parser that uses the topic segmentation method; 7) **DGCNParser** [28]: a SOTA model on macro-level, which used topic graphs a to model the semantic relationships within and between DUs;

In our approach, **combine-parser** denotes the parsing method that does only take the combining decision into account, and **split-parser** denotes the split-only parsing method. These two ablation experiments serve as a baseline for unidirectional parsing methods that use XLNet as a pre-trained model.

In addition to comparing with the known macro discourse analysis work, we tried to migrate some of the best models at the micro level (such as Unified-Parser, TDParser, and DGCNParser) to the macro corpus. We found that these models trained for micro discourse parsing also work well at the macro level, so we included these models in the scope of assessment. Table 1 shows the performance comparison between our models and the baselines. Among all baselines, the micro-level SOTA model AdverParser also works well on the macro-level and achieves the best performance. Our model only focuses on the discourse structure parsing task and does not optimize the other nuclearity and relation recognition tasks, while AdverParser incorporated NR channels in the graph-building process for nuclearity and relation recognition. Hence, our BIPOLE outperforms AdverParser in the task of discourse structure parsing (Span) and performs comparable performance in terms of nuclearity (Nuc) and relation (Rel)

---

[2]   https://huggingface.co/xlnet-base-cased.

recognition. This result indicates the effectiveness of the bi-directional parsing strategy on the discourse structure parsing task.

Compared with our unidirectional models combine-parser and split-parser which use unidirectional parsing strategies, BIPOLE improves the F1 score of discourse structure parsing by 5.14% and 3.57%, respectively. This result also verifies the effectiveness of our bi-directional parsing strategy.

We observed the tree-building process in the testing phase, which contains 67.3% of the split decisions and 32.7% of the combination decisions. This result indicates that our bi-directional parser prefers the split decision. Among those split decisions, 69.3% can split into the correct positions, and 74.8% of the correct split decisions to avoid incorrect combinations. Similarly, among those combination decisions, 64.3% can combine the correct nodes and 63.0% of correct combination decisions effectively avoid incorrect split decisions. This demonstrates the importance of selecting a reasonable parsing method and the advantage of the bi-directional parser.

4.3   Analysis on Different Document Lengths

According to [12], existing methods perform better on short articles and worse on long articles. So improving the parsing ability on long articles should be the focus of discourse parsing research. We compared BIPOLE with the best models on macro and micro, as well as our unidirectional model. Figure 4 shows the Micro-F1 scores of all models in different length articles. In short articles of 2–4 paragraphs, our method does not pull away from other models. However, it achieves significant improvement on long articles larger than four paragraphs. The lower overall performance for long articles is due to longer parsing steps and more severe error propagation, and the results show that our model can effectively mitigate this issue.

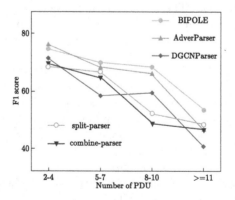

Fig. 4. Micro-F1 scores on different PDU numbers (Span).

4.4   Results on English RST-DT

English RST-DT [18] is one of the popular discourse corpora that annotate the discourse structure, nuclearity, and relationship for the whole document.

We also tested the generalization of our proposed model on English RST-DT, using the same data partitioning as [12], and transforming the non-binary trees in the original data into right binary trees. Table 2 compares the tree building performance on RST-DT. DGCNParser is the SOTA model at the macro level on RST-DT. And the first three rows of the results we obtained from [11] and [28]. Articles in Chinese MCDTB have an average length of 5.67 paragraphs, while articles in English RST-DT have an average length of 11.69 paragraphs. Our BIPOLE's great parsing capacity for large articles contributed to its strong English performance.

4.5   Error Analysis

We proposed two self-designed test modes in the testing phase: Simulation Gold mode (SG) and Oracle Selection mode (OS). Where the SG mode does not contain any error propagation, the OS mode does not contain any error selection. Therefore, we can quantify the impact of error propagation by comparing the performance results of the SG mode with the Standard Test mode (ST). Also, we can analyze the performance results of OS and ST modes to classify the performance loss into generating candidates stage loss and selection phase loss.

Specifically, in SG mode, whatever parse the model made of the STP in the previous step, we automatically perform a correct parse into the current step, eliminating the effect of error propagation (the results predicted by the model are involved in the performance evaluation, but do not affect the next step). The OS mode, uses the performance derived from the silver standard bi-directional tree building method described in Sect. 3.3. It is no different from the ST mode when both base parser choices are correct or both are incorrect, while a relatively correct choice is made when one of them is correct. This mode guarantees the absolute correctness of the choice.

We evaluated the models using our error analysis method, as shown in Table 3. The performance difference between SG (without error propagation) and ST (with error propagation) represents the extent to which the model is affected by error propagation. The larger difference represents more serious error propagation problems in the parsing process. In the three models, these differences are 16.42, 16.01, and 13.92, respectively, which shows that BIPOLE can effectively mitigate the error propagation problem. It is worth mentioning that our SG method is able to evaluate all models that contain error propagation. Since the OS mode does not contain wrong choices, then all the performance losses it incurs are generated by the generate candidates stage. So the performance loss caused by the generation candidate phase (basic parser parsing phase) is 20.17 (100%-79.83%). And the performance difference between OS (without incorrect choices) and ST (with incorrect choices) represents the performance loss incurred by BIPOLE in the selection phase, which is 12.64 (79.83%-67.19%). Meanwhile, the ST results for split-parser and combine-parser correspond to the performance without selection. The overall result proves that our method must be effective. However, as a preliminary attempt at the bi-direction parsing method, this study still has much room for improvement and deserves further exploration.

Table 2. The performance comparison on the RST-DT at the macro level.

Model	Span
GBLRR	43.70
MDParser-TS	41.56
DGCNParser	43.37
AdverParser	45.71
BIPOLE	46.79

Table 3. The results of each model in standard test mode(ST), simulated gold mode(SG), and oracle selection mode(OS) respectively.

Model	ST	SG	OS
Combine-parser	62.05	78.06	–
Split-parser	63.62	79.63	–
BIPOLE	67.19	81.11	79.83

4.6 Ablation Analysis

We compared the following simplified methods to validate the effectiveness of different components of our bi-direction selection method with the Oracle Selection training strategy and those simplified models are as follows: 1) -w/o Structured Label Embedding: only using the Basic Parser for selection; 2) -w/o Structured Labels: removing four types of structured labels in bi-direction selection; 3) -w/o Oracle Selection Strategy: using the simulated golden mode in Sect. 4.5 for training; 4) -w/o Data Enhancement: remove the data enhancement in Sect. 3.3.

Table 4. A comparison of ablation experiments.

Approach	Span
BIPOLE	**67.19**
-w/o Structured Label Embedding	−1.17
-w/o Structured Labels	−0.82
-w/o Oracle Seletion Strategy	−1.35
-w/o Data Enhancement	−1.58

Table 4 shows the results on BIPOLE and its simplified versions. Notably, when we do not use the Oracle training strategy, the performance is lower than when we do not use the entire bi-direction selection method. It implies that our training strategy and the bi-direction selection method reinforce each other.

5   Conclusion

In this paper, we propose a bidirectional macro-level discourse parser BIPOLE, which combines two mainstream parsing strategies, i.e., top-down and bottom-up, and can select one of them according to different contexts. Especially, We introduce a Basic Parser to parse out two candidates, and a Decision Maker to select one of them according to the context. Moreover, we also design an oracle selection strategy to improve the capability of the error correction for the model BIPOLE. Experimental results on MCDTB and RST-DT show that our model can effectively alleviate cascading errors and outperforms the SOTA baselines significantly. In the future, we will focus on how to improve the parsing ability of the basic parser and the selection ability of the decision maker to improve the performance of macro-level discourse parsing.

Acknowledgments. The authors would like to thank the three anonymous reviewers for their comments on this paper. This research was supported by the National Natural Science Foundation of China (Nos. 61836007, and 62006167.), and the Priority Academic Program Development of Jiangsu Higher Education Institutions (PAPD).

References

1. Liakata, M., Dobnik, S., Saha, S., Batchelor, C., Schuhmann, D.R.: A discourse-driven content model for summarising scientific articles evaluated in a complex question answering task. In: Proceedings of the 2013 Conference on Empirical Methods in Natural Language Processing, pp. 747–757 (2013)
2. Meyer, T., Popescu-Belis, A.: Using sense-labeled discourse connectives for statistical machine translation. In: Proceedings of the EACL2012 Workshop on Hybrid Approaches to Machine Translation (HyTra), no. CONF (2012)
3. Cohan, A., Goharian, N.: Scientific article summarization using citation-context and article's discourse structure, arXiv preprint arXiv:1704.06619 (2017)
4. Presutti, V., Draicchio, F., Gangemi, A.: Knowledge extraction based on discourse representation theory and linguistic frames. In: ten Teije, A., Völker, J., Handschuh, S., Stuckenschmidt, H., d'Acquin, M., Nikolov, A., Aussenac-Gilles, N., Hernandez, N. (eds.) EKAW 2012. LNCS (LNAI), vol. 7603, pp. 114–129. Springer, Heidelberg (2012). https://doi.org/10.1007/978-3-642-33876-2_12
5. Jiang, F., Xu, S., Chu, X., Li, P., Zhu, Q., Zhou, G.: Mcdtb: a macro-level chinese discourse treebank. In: Proceedings of the 27th International Conference on Computational Linguistics, pp. 3493–3504 (2018)
6. Fan, Y., Jiang, F., Chu, X., Li, P., Zhu, Q.: Combining global and local information to recognize chinese macro discourse structure. In: Proceedings of the 19th Chinese National Conference on Computational Linguistics, pp. 183–194 (2020)
7. Liu, L., Lin, X., Joty, S., Han, S., Bing, L.: Hierarchical pointer net parsing, arXiv preprint arXiv:1908.11571 (2019)
8. Lin, X., Joty, S., Jwalapuram, P., Bari, M.S.: A unified linear-time framework for sentence-level discourse parsing, arXiv preprint arXiv:1905.05682 (2019)
9. Koto, F., Lau, J.H., Baldwin, T.: Top-down discourse parsing via sequence labelling, arXiv preprint arXiv:2102.02080 (2021)

10. Zhou, Y., Chu, X., Li, P., Zhu, Q.: Constructing chinese macro discourse tree via multiple views and word pair similarity. In: Tang, J., Kan, M.-Y., Zhao, D., Li, S., Zan, H. (eds.) NLPCC 2019. LNCS (LNAI), vol. 11838, pp. 773–786. Springer, Cham (2019). https://doi.org/10.1007/978-3-030-32233-5_60

11. Jiang, F., Chu, X., Li, P., Kong, F., Zhu, Q.: Chinese paragraph-level discourse parsing with global backward and local reverse reading. In: Proceedings of the 28th International Conference on Computational Linguistics, pp. 5749–5759 (2020)

12. Jiang, F., Fan, Y., Chu, X., Li, P., Zhu, Q., Kong, F.: Hierarchical macro discourse parsing based on topic segmentation. In: Proceedings of the Conference on Artificial Intelligence (AAAI), pp. 13152–13160 (2021)

13. Feng, V.W., Hirst, G.: A linear-time bottom-up discourse parser with constraints and post-editing. In: Proceedings of the 52nd Annual Meeting of the Association for Computational Linguistics (Volume 1: Long Papers), pp. 511–521 (2014)

14. Li, Q., Li, T., Chang, B.: Discourse parsing with attention-based hierarchical neural networks. In: EMNLP, pp. 362–371 (2016)

15. Hung, S.S., Huang, H.H., Chen, H.H.: A complete shift-reduce chinese discourse parser with robust dynamic oracle. In: Proceedings of the 58th Annual Meeting of the Association for Computational Linguistics, pp. 133–138 (2020)

16. Zhou, J., Jiang, F., Chu, X., Li, P., Zhu, Q.: More Than One-Hot: Chinese Macro Discourse Relation Recognition on Joint Relation Embedding. In: Mantoro, T., Lee, M., Ayu, M.A., Wong, K.W., Hidayanto, A.N. (eds.) ICONIP 2021. CCIS, vol. 1516, pp. 73–80. Springer, Cham (2021). https://doi.org/10.1007/978-3-030-92307-5_9

17. Chen, Q., Zhang, R., Zheng, Y., Mao, .: ual contrastive learning: Text classification via label-aware data augmentation, arXiv preprint arXiv:2201.08702,(2022)

18. Carlson, L., Marcu, D., Okurowski, M.E. (2003). Building a Discourse-Tagged Corpus in the Framework of Rhetorical Structure Theory. In: van Kuppevelt, J., Smith, R.W. (eds) Current and New Directions in Discourse and Dialogue. Text, Speech and Language Technology, vol 22. Springer, Dordrecht. https://doi.org/10.1007/978-94-010-0019-2_5

19. Mabona, A., Rimell, L., Clark, S., Vlachos, A.: Neural generative rhetorical structure parsing, arXiv preprint arXiv:1909.11049 (2019)

20. Fried, D., Stern, M., Klein, D.: Improving neural parsing by disentangling model combination and reranking effects, arXiv preprint arXiv:1707.03058 (2017)

21. Zhang, L., Tan, X., Kong, F., Zhou, G.: A recursive information flow gated model for RST-style text-level discourse parsing. In: Tang, J., Kan, M.-Y., Zhao, D., Li, S., Zan, H. (eds.) NLPCC 2019. LNCS (LNAI), vol. 11839, pp. 231–241. Springer, Cham (2019). https://doi.org/10.1007/978-3-030-32236-6_20

22. Zhang, L., Xing, Y., Kong, F., Li, P., Zhou, G.: A top-down neural architecture towards text-level parsing of discourse rhetorical structure, arXiv preprint arXiv:2005.02680 2020

23. Zhang, L., Kong, F., Zhou, G.,: Adversarial learning for discourse rhetorical structure parsing. In: Proceedings of the 59th Annual Meeting of the Association for Computational Linguistics and the 11th International Joint Conference on Natural Language Processing (Volume 1: Long Papers), pp. 3946–3957 (2021)

24. Kobayashi, N., Hirao, T., Nakamura, K., Kamigaito, H., Okumura, M., Nagata, M.: Split or merge: Which is better for unsupervised rst parsing? In: Proceedings of the 2019 Conference on Empirical Methods in Natural Language Processing and the 9th International Joint Conference on Natural Language Processing (EMNLP-IJCNLP), pp. 5797–5802 (2019)

25. Yang, Z., Dai, Z., Yang, Y., Carbonell, J., Salakhutdinov, R.R., Le, Q.V.: Xlnet: Generalized autoregressive pretraining for language understanding. In: Advances in Neural Information Processing Systems, vol. 32 (2019)
26. Mann, W.C., Thompson, S.A.: Rhetorical structure theory: toward a functional theory of text organization. Text-Interdiscp. J. Study Discourse **8**(3), 243–281 (1988)
27. Zhang, Y., Kamigaito, H., Okumura, M.: A language model-based generative classifier for sentence-level discourse parsing. In: Proceedings of the 2021 Conference on Empirical Methods in Natural Language Processing, pp. 2432–2446 (2021)
28. Fan, Y., Jiang, F., Chu, X., Li, P., Zhu, Q.: Chinese macro discourse parsing on dependency graph convolutional network. In: Wang, L., Feng, Y., Hong, Yu., He, R. (eds.) NLPCC 2021. LNCS (LNAI), vol. 13028, pp. 15–26. Springer, Cham (2021). https://doi.org/10.1007/978-3-030-88480-2_2
29. Chu, X., Xi, X., Jiang, F., Xu, S., Zhu, Q., Zhou, G.: Macro discourse structure representation schema and corpus construction. J. Softw. **31**(2), 321–343 (2020)
30. Khosla, P., et al.: In: Supervised contrastive learning, In: Advances in Neural Information Processing Systems, vol. 33, pp. 18 661–18 673 (2020)

Evidence-Based Document-Level Event Factuality Identification

Heng Zhang, Zhong Qian, Peifeng Li, and Xiaoxu Zhu[✉]

School of Computer Science and Technology, Soochow University, Suzhou, China
20204227055@stu.suda.edu.cn,{qianzhong,pfli,xiaoxzhu}@suda.edu.cn

Abstract. The existing Document-Level Event Factuality Identification (DEFI) work relies on the syntactic and semantic features of event trigger and sentences. However, focusing only on the relevant features of event trigger may omit the important information for event factuality identification, while finding critical information from the whole document is still challenging. In this paper, our motivation is that DEFI can be inferred from a complete set of evidential sentences rather than the event trigger. Hence, we construct a new **E**vidence-**B**ased **D**ocument-**L**evel **E**vent **F**actuality (EB-DLEF) corpus, and introduce a new evidential sentence selection task for DEFI. Moreover, we propose a pipeline approach to solve the two-step work of evidential sentence selection and event factuality identification, which outperforms various baselines.

Keywords: Document-level event factuality identification · EB-DLEF corpus · Evidential sentence selection

1 Introduction

Event factuality describes whether an event is a fact, a possibility, or an improbable scenario. Factuality categories can be classified into the following five categories based on the degree of certainty of the event occurrence [1,2]: CerTain Positive (CT+), PoSsible Positive (PS+), CerTain Negative (CT−), PoSsible Negative (PS−), Underspecified (Uu). Furthermore, event factuality identification (EFI) can be further subdivided into sentence-level event factuality identification (SEFI) and document-level event factuality identification (DEFI), i.e., determining the factuality by a simple sentence or a complete document. EFI is an essential basic task for many other NLP applications, such as sentiment analysis [3], machine translation [4], and rumor detection [5].

EFI can be regarded as classifying the event trigger based on textual content. The left side of Fig. 1 provides an example. For SEFI, we need to focus on the negative and speculative information in the sentence, e.g., the event "reach" in S2 is affected by the speculative cue "may", so its sentence-level factuality is PS+. For DEFI, the core event of the document may occur several times, and its sentence-level factuality may have multiple values. However, from the

© The Author(s), under exclusive license to Springer Nature Switzerland AG 2022
S. Khanna et al. (Eds.): PRICAI 2022, LNCS 13630, pp. 240–254, 2022.
https://doi.org/10.1007/978-3-031-20865-2_18

Event Trigger: reach
Sentence-Level Event Factuality: CT+, CT-, PS+, CT-, PS+
Document-Level Event Factuality: CT-

[S0] According to Politico.com, it is said the United States will reach(CT+) an agreement with Mexico on the new trade deal.

[S1] Mexican Economy Minister Ildefonso Guajardo **denied** that they plan to reach(CT-) any agreement with the U.S. on the trade deal talks.

[S2] Guajardo said the two sides **may** reach(PS+) an agreement within hours.

[S3] The government has **not** been informed that any agreement will be reached(CT-) yet, said another two Mexican officials.

[S4] Some media speculate that they will **possibly** reach(PS+) an agreement.
...

Event: The bombing is linked to Bangladesh militants
Evidential Sentences: S[0], S[1], S[4]
Document-Level Event Factuality: CT-

[S0, Title]No evidence NY bomb suspect linked to Bangladesh militants: security chief.

[S1]DHAKA _ Bangladesh has found no evidence linking a Bangladeshi man charged with an attempted suicide bombing.

[S2]Ullah set off a pipe bomb in an underground pedestrian corridor between New York 's Times Square and the Port Authority Bus Terminal.

[S3]In Bangladesh we have not found any connection or have not been able to identify any of his associates who were or are involved with any terrorist groups.
...

Fig. 1. Annotation of DLEF (left) and EB-DLEF (right).

perspective of the overall semantics, its document-level event factuality can be uniquely determined, e.g., the document-level factuality of event "reach" is CT−.

Previous work on DEFI at this stage is based on the Document-Level Event Factuality (DLEF) corpus [2], an annotation example for DLEF is shown on the left side of Fig. 1, including the event trigger and sentence-level factuality values. Almost all existing studies focus on the event trigger to obtain some relevant syntactic and semantic features [2,6,7], which have the following disadvantages: (1) Since an event can be expressed in various ways, it is difficult to represent it with an event trigger. This also leads to difficulties in annotation and affects the work of DEFI, which relies heavily on the event trigger. (2) The information needed to identify the factuality is not always contained in the sentence with the event trigger. Hence, some essential information for identifying factuality may be omitted. Meanwhile, the whole document is too long and contains much noise, finding the critical information is inefficient and challenging.

To address the above issues, we construct a new evidence-based document-level event factuality corpus (EB-DLEF) with the following features: (1) A complete sentence is used instead of an event trigger as the expression of the core event. (2) The document-level event factuality is annotated with a complete set of evidential sentences containing all the information that can identify the factuality. The right side of Fig. 1 shows an example of annotation.

EB-DLEF provides a new idea for DEFI and introduces a new evidential sentence selection task, i.e., finding the complete set of evidence for an event before judging its document-level event factuality. This task is inspired by the task of evidence-based fact checking [8], which will be described in detail in Sect. 2.2. For experimentation, we propose a pipeline approach that views evidential sentence selection and event factuality identification as two independent tasks. The results show that our model outperforms all baselines.

2   Related Work

2.1   Event Factuality Identification

There are many models applied to the work on sentence-level event factuality identification (SEFI) and have achieved good performance [9–12]. Compared to SEFI, the document-level event factuality identification (DEFI) is still in its infancy and exploratory stage. Qian et al. [2] used BiLSTM to encode sentences and syntactic paths and proposed an attention mechanism to fuse semantic and syntactic information. Zhang et al. [6] introduced negation and speculation scope into DEFI work and got a significant improvement in performance. Cao et al. [7] proposed an Uncertain Local-to-Global Network, which integrated the local uncertainty as well as global structure, and achieved state-of-the-art performance.

2.2   Evidence-Based Fact Checking

Evidence-based fact checking (claim verification) aims to verify the truthfulness of a claim against evidence extracted from textual sources [13]. Usually, the task can be defined as a three-step pipeline [8], i.e., document retrieval, sentence retrieval, and claim verification. We mainly focus on sentence retrieval since this part is relevant to our evidential sentence selection task. The most common practice in sentence retrieval is to rank sentences and select top-k sentences related to the claim as the evidence or set a threshold to further filter sentences, e.g., TF-IDF [8], Logistic Regression [14], ESIM [15,16], NSMN [17].

The methods based on pre-trained models have also been widely used, e.g., BERT [18–21], XLNet [22], RoBERTa [23], ALBERT [24], T5 [25]. Unlike these jobs that focus only on high recall, Yin et al. [26] and Ma et al. [27] have conducted effective research on the work of obtaining precise evidence. In our work, the potential evidential sentences are all in one document. Focusing only on the recall may introduce too much noise for the next factuality identification task, so we work on obtaining the precise evidential sentences.

3   Corpus Annotation

As with DLEF, we use China Daily[1] and Sina Bilingual News[2] as the sources of the English corpus and Sina News[3] as the source of the Chinese corpus. Finally, 3483 English documents and 4357 Chinese documents are selected in various fields, including military, political, cultural, etc.

---

[1] http://www.chinadaily.com.cn/.

[2] https://english.sina.com/.

[3] https://news.sina.com.cn/.

3.1 Event

We use a highly summarized sentence to represent the core event in a document rather than the event trigger. If multiple events are discussed, we select the event that is most frequently mentioned. To avoid the event being a simple copy of a sentence, we ask the annotators to summarize the event from as many sentences as possible and require that only the most critical information be retained while deleting some irrelevant modifiers. The event should also be in the form of an affirmative sentence without any words that contain a tendency of factuality, such as negative or speculative cues. Finally, to ensure the difficulty of the identification, we discard some simple structured documents.

Table 1. Factuality distribution in EB-DLEF.

Datasets	Factuality values				
	CT+	CT−	PS+	PS−	Uu
English	2674 (76.77%)	456 (13.09%)	321 (9.22%)	20 (0.57%)	12 (0.34%)
Chinese	2548 (58.48%)	1145 (26.28%)	614 (14.09%)	33 (0.76%)	17 (0.39%)

Table 2. Evidential sentences distribution in EB-DLEF.

Datasets	Evidential sentences			
	n = 1	n = 2	n = 3	n > 3
English	1949 (55.96%)	1375 (39.48%)	148 (4.25%)	11 (0.32%)
Chinese	893 (20.50%)	2396 (55.99%)	990 (22.72%)	78 (1.79%)

3.2 Document-Level Event Factuality

Consistent with [2], we use the following five factuality labels: (1) PoSsible Positive (PS+): Events are governed by speculative cues (e.g., *"may"*) (2) CerTain Negative (CT−): Events are negated by negative cues (e.g., *"not"*). (3) PoSsible Negative (PS−): Events are governed by both speculative and negative cues. (4) Underspecified (Uu): Events can appear in questions (e.g., *"Is...?"*) and in the intensional contexts with underspecified semantics (e.g., *"if..."*). (5) CerTain Positive (CT+): Events are factual and do not meet the above conditions.

3.3 Evidential Sentences

Evidential sentences are the complete set of sentences that contains enough information to identify the factuality. For example, on the right side of Fig. 1, the evidential sentences of event *"The bombing is linked to Bangladesh militants"* are

S0, S1, S3. When annotating evidential sentences, we have the following guidelines: (1) Semantic similarity between different evidential sentences is allowed, as long as each sentence is strongly related to the event, i.e., the sentence can directly affect the factuality of the labeled event. (2) Based on ensuring the integrity of the evidential sentences, we do not allow the introduction of the useless noise, i.e., the sentence only mentions the entities in the event but does not affect its factuality. Assuming that without the restriction of this rule, the whole document can be considered evidence, which would make the work meaningless.

3.4   Statistics

Table 1 shows the distribution of factuality in the corpus. We can see that the CT+ category has the largest share, followed by CT− and PS+, and the two categories of PS− and Uu have a low probability of occurrence.

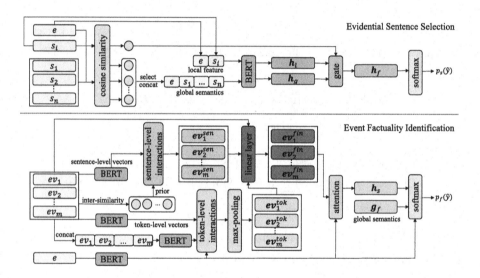

Fig. 2. The architecture of our proposed pipeline approach.

Table 2 shows the distribution of the number of evidential sentences. It can be seen that a large proportion of the events have more than one evidential sentence, which makes the selection task more difficult and practical.

The annotators are all undergraduate students familiar with both Chinese and English and have undergone our systematic training. The Kappa [28] are calculated to be 0.82 and 0.80 for the English and Chinese corpora, respectively, demonstrating the high annotation consistency of EB-DLEF.

4 Methodology

This section introduces a pipeline approach for solving the two tasks, i.e., evidential sentence selection and event factuality identification, and the overall model structure is shown in Fig. 2.

4.1 Evidential Sentence Selection

We focus on the interactions between event and candidate sentence to determine whether the candidate sentence is the evidence. Meanwhile, we design a gate mechanism that incorporates the interactions of the event with global semantics as a complement, where similarity is used for contribution assignment.

Input and Sentence Similarity. We treat evidential sentence selection as a classification task, i.e., given an event e and a candidate sentence s_i as input, the output set $\mathcal{Y}_s = \{0, 1\}$, where 1 means that s_i is the evidential sentence of e; otherwise, 0.

The event is essentially a summary or generalization of a particular sentence or several sentences. If s_i is the evidence of e, their expressions are relatively consistent. After using stanza[4] to tokenizer, we convert e and s_i into vectors e and s_i to record whether a word occurs in a sentence. The cosine similarity as follows is used to calculate the similarity of the two sequences as an important feature to determine whether s_i is evidence or not, where the subscript j means the j-th token.

$$similarity(e, s_i) = cos(\theta) = \frac{e \cdot s_i}{||e|| \cdot ||s_i||} \tag{1}$$

$$||e|| = \sqrt{\sum_{j=1}^{n}(e_j)^2}, ||s_i|| = \sqrt{\sum_{j=1}^{n}(s_{i_j})^2} \tag{2}$$

Global Semantics and Encoding. We use Eq. 1 to calculate the similarity between e and all sentences, taking the top 50% of sentences concatenated together as a sequence g_s that represents the global semantics and ensuring that the title is in g_s. When focusing only on e and s_i cannot be classified correctly, supplementing some global semantics information will have a critical effect.

We concatenate e with s_i and g_s, respectively, and put the results into BERT [29], using the final hidden state vector of the [CLS] token to get vectors $h_l, h_g \in R^d$, which denote the local and global interactions, respectively.

---

[4] https://stanfordnlp.github.io/stanza/.

Gate Mechanism. Instead of concatenating or performing an element-wise operation for h_l and h_g. We use a gate mechanism to decide how much information is needed in the two outputs and use the similarity between e and s_i for contribution assignment. To avoid sentences with low similarity ignoring local interactions, we map the similarity to a new interval as follows:

$$c^{e \leftrightarrow s_i} = a + \frac{b - a}{s_{max} - s_{min}} \cdot (s^{e \leftrightarrow s_i} - s_{min}) \tag{3}$$

where $a = 0.5$, $b = 1$, s_{max} and s_{min} are the maximum and minimum values of similarity, and $s^{e \leftrightarrow s_i}$ means the cosine similarity between e and s_i. Then the process of gating is as follows:

$$h_f = c^{e \leftrightarrow s_i} \odot h_l + (1 - c^{e \leftrightarrow s_i}) \odot h_g \tag{4}$$

where $h_f \in R^d$ is a representation that incorporates local and global interactions.

Output. Finally, we use a softmax layer to compute the probability distribution:

$$p_s(\hat{y}) = \text{softmax}(W_1 \cdot h_f + b_1) \tag{5}$$

where $W_1 \in R^{c_1 \times d}$ and $b_1 \in R^{c_1}$ are the weights and bias. Finally, the model optimize with a cross-entropy loss function:

$$\mathcal{L}_s = - \sum_{y \in \mathcal{Y}_s} \mathbb{I}\{\hat{y} = y\} log p_s(\hat{y}) \tag{6}$$

4.2   Event Factuality Identification

We design a sentence-level interactions module that uses similarity as a prior to better determine how the evidence should be integrated with other evidential sentences as a complement. Then we use dot product for token-level interactions to capture more fine-grained information while also making interactions not deviate from the event's focus. Finally, we use an attention mechanism to obtain a comprehensive representation for the final factuality classification.

Input and Encoding. Event factuality identification is treated as a 5-way classification task, the output set $\mathcal{Y}_f = \{CT+, CT-, PS+, PS-, Uu\}$. Our model defines four inputs: (1) e: core event in document. (2) $\{ev_i\}_{i=1}^n$: set of evidential sentences. (3) ev: a sequence that is the concatenation of all the evidential sentences. (4) g_f: a sequence representing the global semantics.

We use evidential sentences and their adjacent sentences, as well as sentences containing negative and speculative cues concatenated together as g_f, which proved to be useful features in previous work. The negative and speculative cues in English and Chinese come from BioScope [30] and CNeSp [31], respectively.

After unifying the inputs with length l, each sequence is encoded using BERT, and the output corresponding to each input is: $e \in R^d$; $\{ev_i\}_{i=1}^m, ev_i \in R^d$; $ev \in R^d$; $g_f \in R^d$. We also use the output of the last hidden layer of BERT as the word embedding of each token.

Sentence-Level Interactions. We adopt a multi-head self-attention [32] to capture the interactions between evidential sentences and use the computed weights to selectively decide how much information from other evidential sentences to incorporate into the current evidence representation to enhance the expressiveness. Formally, weights in the i-th head can be calculated as follows:

$$score_i = softmax(\frac{Q_i K_i^T}{\sqrt{d_k}}) \tag{7}$$

$$Q_i = QW_i^q, K_i = KW_i^k \tag{8}$$

where d_k is the size of hidden units of BERT, which equals to d. Q and K refer to the set $\{ev_i\}_{i=1}^m$, and they are multiplied by the parameters $W_i^q, W_i^k \in R^{d \times d_1}$, d_1 is d/h. h is the number of heads in the self-attention.

The importance of each evidential sentence for identifying factuality is different, with some of them being core while others being marginal. The expressions of the core evidential sentences tend to be consistent with each other. At this point, we use the similarity to predict the degree of their agreement, i.e., add a prior to the $score_i$ as follows:

$$score_i^{new} = softmax(\frac{Q_i K_i^T}{\sqrt{d_k}} + S) \tag{9}$$

where S is the similarity matrix between $\{ev_i\}_{i=1}^m$. Note that the similarity between the evidence and itself is 1, and we do not need to map the similarity to a new interval as Eq. 3.

After calculating the attention weights, the process of the multi-head self-attention can be expressed as follows:

$$head_i = score_i^{new} \cdot (VW_i^v) \tag{10}$$

$$H = [head_1; ...; head_h] \cdot W_2 \tag{11}$$

where V is the set $\{ev_i\}_{i=1}^m$, and $W_i^v \in R^{d \times d_1}$ is the parameter. The ";" denotes the concatenation operation and H is a matrix obtained by concatenating the results from h headers, the parameter $W_2 \in R^{d \times d}$. For an evidential sentence ev_i in H, we denote the result of sentence-level interactions as ev_i^{sen}.

Token-Level Interactions. For each evidential sentence ev_i, we perform token-level interactions with ev to capture more fine-grained information. Moreover, to avoid capturing information that deviates from the event's focus, we also propose to interact each token between ev_i and e. Formally, we use dot product for token-level interactions as follows:

$$c_i^j = \sum_z softmax(ev_i^j \cdot (x^z)^T) \cdot x^z \tag{12}$$

where x^z means the z-th token of e or ev. Depending on the different values of x, we can obtain the results of two token-level interactions $c1_i^j$ and $c2_i^j$, respectively.

Then the new representation of the j-th token in ev_i is as follows:

$$ev_i^j = ev_i^j \oplus c1_i^j \oplus c2_i^j \tag{13}$$

where $\oplus$ means element-wise addition. Then we use a max-pooling over $\{ev_i^j\}_{j=1}^l$ along with j, to get a representation of the whole sentence:

$$ev_i^{tok} = maxpool(\{ev_i^1, ..., ev_i^l\}) \tag{14}$$

Then we concatenate the representations of each evidential sentence and resize the dimensions with a linear layer:

$$ev_i^{fin} = W_3 \cdot [ev_i; ev_i^{sen}; ev_i^{tok}] + b_3 \tag{15}$$

where $W_3 \in R^{d \times 3d}$ and $b_3 \in R^d$ are trainable parameters, ev_i^{fin} is the final evidence representation incorporating rich interactive information.

Factuality Classification. To predict the factuality value, we use an attention mechanism to fuse the multiple evidential sentences to obtain a comprehensive representation as follows:

$$b_i = v^T \cdot tanh(W_4 \cdot ev_i^{fin} + U \cdot e) \tag{16}$$

$$s_i = \frac{exp(b_i)}{\sum_i^m exp(b_i)} \tag{17}$$

$$h_s = \sum_i^m s_i \cdot ev_i^{fin} \tag{18}$$

where $v \in R^d$, $W_4 \in R^{d \times d}$ and $U \in R^{d \times d}$ and are trainable parameters. Then we concatenate h_s with the e and g_f to get a representation, and use a softmax layer to compute the probability distribution:

$$p_f(\hat{y}) = softmax(W_5 \cdot [h_s; e; g_f] + b_5) \tag{19}$$

where $W_5 \in R^{c_2 \times d}$, $b_5 \in R^{c_2}$ are the weights and bias. The loss function is as follows:

$$\mathcal{L}_f = - \sum_{y \in \mathcal{Y}_f} \mathbb{I}\{\hat{y} = y\} log p_f(\hat{y}) \tag{20}$$

5   Experimentation

5.1   Experimental Settings

We perform 5-fold cross-validation on EB-DLEF to reflect the faithful performance of each model. Note that we mainly focus on the performance of CT+, CT− and

PS+, since the proportion of PS− and Uu categories is too small. We use bert-base-uncased and bert-base-chinese from the HuggingFace's Transformer[5] as the instances of BERT for English and Chinese, respectively.

In terms of parameter settings, the values of c_1 and c_2 in softmax layer are 2 and 5, the number of heads h is 2, and the size of hidden units d of BERT is 768. The learning rate is set to $1e-5$, and Adam algorithm is used to optimize the parameters in both tasks.

In addition to using precision, recall, and F1-Score to evaluate the performance. Inspired by [8], we add two additional metrics: (1) NoScoreEv: The accuracy of identification for all factuality categories without considering the evidence. (2) ScoreEv: In addition to the requirement of correct factuality identification, the predicted evidential sentences are an exact match to the golden.

5.2 Baselines

Previous DEFI studies [2, 6, 7] are all based on the event trigger to obtain syntactic or semantic features. However, the event trigger is not annotated in DB-DLEF, so it is not feasible to compare our model with them.

We use the following evidence-based fact checking approaches as baselines: (1) ESIM [33]: We use ESIM to infer the relationship between event and sentence, then select the top-5 sentences as evidence. (2) BERT-Rank [20]: We use BERT as a representative of the pre-trained models to select the top-5 sentences. (3) BERT [13, 16, 20]: We use a pointwise loss function and find a threshold to trade-off the recall against the precision. (4) HAN [27]: A hierarchical attention model for validating claim and selecting precise evidence. (5) TwoWingOS [26]: A joint model can identify appropriate evidence and determine whether or not the claim is supported by the evidence. (6) MLA [13]: A multi-level attention model for claim verification, which can also be used to select precise evidence.

Table 3. Experimental results of evidential sentence selection on English and Chinese corpora.

Methods	English			Chinese		
	Precision (%)	Recall (%)	F1-Score	Precision (%)	Recall (%)	F1-Score
ESIM	25.27	96.45	40.05	36.49	92.10	52.27
BERT-Rank	29.36	**97.80**	45.16	38.73	**93.46**	54.77
HAN	50.15	71.63	59.00	55.01	69.66	61.47
TwoWingOS	59.66	74.98	66.45	57.16	71.58	63.56
BERT	62.76	86.71	72.82	65.87	84.52	74.04
Ours	**67.34**	90.17	**77.10**	**70.63**	86.95	**77.95**

---

[5] https://github.com/huggingface/transformers.

Table 4. Experimental results of event factuality identification, we use F1-Score to evaluate the performance of the five categories, i.e., CT+, CT−, PS+, Macro, Micro.

Datasets	Methods	CT+	CT−	PS+	Macro	Micro	NoScoreEv	ScoreEv
English	HAN	85.97	62.55	58.63	69.26	77.73	77.15	36.22
	TwoWingOS	88.43	61.47	62.22	71.02	79.46	78.97	37.78
	MLA	91.06	72.01	**68.15**	77.32	86.24	85.82	39.73
	Ours	**92.71**	**78.72**	67.72	**80.00**	**88.52**	**87.95**	**41.46**
Chinese	HAN	80.82	69.97	65.53	72.49	74.97	74.31	30.61
	TwoWingOS	82.22	72.89	64.10	73.57	76.51	75.89	31.37
	MLA	85.80	75.11	73.76	78.35	81.04	80.39	33.26
	Ours	**87.49**	**80.34**	**74.42**	**80.83**	**83.58**	**82.91**	**35.17**

5.3 Overall Results

Table 3 shows the performance of each model on the evidential sentence selection task, and the conclusions are as follows: (1) Since all candidate sentences are in only one document, ESIM and BERT-Rank achieve a high recall. However, they achieve the lowest precision. (2) Chinese corpus has a larger proportion of events with more than one evidential sentence, so the recall in all the methods is lower than those in the English corpus. (3) The performance of the models using the pre-training method has a considerable improvement compared to those that do not use it. (4) Our method achieves a better balance between accuracy and recall. Compared with the state-of-the-art model, our method achieves 4.28 and 3.91 improvement of F1-Score on the English and Chinese corpus, respectively, which proves the effectiveness of the gate mechanism and global semantics.

Table 4 shows the performance of each model on the event factuality identification task, where we can draw the following conclusions: (1) In general, all the models perform better on the English corpus than the Chinese corpus, especially

Table 5. Ablation study results, the arrow ↓ represents the decrease, Task1 and Task2 represent the evidential sentence selection and the event factuality identification, respectively.

Methods	English corpus			Chinese corpus		
	Task1	Task2		Task1	Task2	
	F1-Score	Macro	ScoreEv	F1-Score	Macro	ScoreEv
w/o gm	↓2.21	↓1.03	↓0.31	↓1.69	↓0.79	↓0.34
w/o gs	↓4.38	↓1.45	↓0.50	↓3.16	↓1.20	↓0.44
w/o si	–	↓2.88	↓0.71	–	↓1.95	↓0.45
w/o ti	–	↓3.05	↓1.14	–	↓1.76	↓0.38
w/o am	–	↓1.93	↓0.62	–	↓1.23	↓0.40

on the NoScoreEv and ScoreEv metrics. This is due to the annotation differences between the corpora. (2) The CT+ category performs better than CT− and PS+ due to its greater number, which leads to a distance between the Macro-F1 and Micro-F1 performance as well. (3) Compared to the state-of-the-art model MLA which also uses multiple interactions between evidential sentences, our model still leads in most metrics, demonstrating that the sentence-level and token-level interactions we designed are more effective.

5.4   Ablation Study

We conduct the following ablation studies to verify the validity of our proposed components: 1) w/o gm: removing the gate mechanism and replacing it with an element-wise addition. 2) w/o gs: removing the global semantics input g_s. 3) w/o si: removing the sentence-level interactions. 4) w/o ti: removing the token-level interactions. 5) w/o am: removing the attention mechanism and replacing it with a max-pooling approach. The ablation study results are shown in Table 5.

From the results, we can observe that removing any components causes a degradation in performance, especially in the English corpus, which proves that each component has a positive effect on the experimental results.

5.5   Robustness Study

To verify whether our model can automatically filter the noise in the evidential sentences and capture the critical information for factuality identification, we add randomly sampled sentences to the evidential sentences of each sample to simulate noise. The results are shown in Fig. 3.

We can draw the following conclusions from the figure: (1) The model performs significantly better on the English corpus than on the Chinese corpus, mainly due to the higher complexity of the Chinese corpus. (2) The Macro-F1 and Micro-F1 tend to decrease as the noise increases. However, when the amount of noise reaches a threshold, more increased noise does not significantly affect the performance and even makes a slight increase within a reasonable range. (3) Two metrics gradually level off and reach a high level after decreasing, proving that the model has strong robustness and can handle the noise well.

5.6   Error Analysis

Evidential Sentence Selection. We summarize two types of errors: (1) The model incorrectly selects sentences that are not relevant to the event factuality as evidence, which directly leads to a decrease in accuracy. We also found that these sentences have some similarities to the event, which is an important reason for misclassification. (2) There are omissions in the selection of evidential sentences, which is a factor that affects the recall. Most of these omitted sentences have low similarity to the event in expression but can directly affect the event factuality. Correctly selecting this type of evidence is challenging.

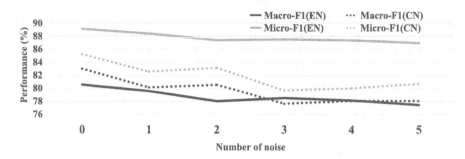

Fig. 3. Model performance with varying amounts of noise in the evidential sentences.

Event Factuality Identification. By observing instances where factuality values are misclassified, we summarize three common error cases: (1) In the evidential sentence selection task, some sentences are incorrectly classified as evidence, introducing some noise that can affect the factuality, such as negative and speculative information. (2) There are cases where some critical evidential sentences are omitted in the evidential sentence selection task, and the missing information can impact the factuality identification, especially in CT− and PS+ categories. (3) The information in evidential sentences is sometimes obscure and cannot be captured correctly by the model, resulting in misclassification.

6   Conclusion

In this paper, we construct an evidence-based document-level factuality (EB-DLEF) corpus and propose a new evidential sentence selection task, which broadens the research direction for the work of DEFI. Based on the new corpus, we propose a pipeline approach for evidential sentence selection and event factuality identification that performs better than all previous baseline models. The experimental results also demonstrate the feasibility and complexity of the task for future studies.

Acknowledgments. The authors would like to thank the three anonymous reviewers for their comments on this paper. This research was supported by the National Natural Science Foundation of China (Nos. 61836007, and 62006167), and the Priority Academic Program Development of Jiangsu Higher Education Institutions (PAPD).

References

1. Saurí, R.: A Factuality Profiler for Eventualities in Text. Brandeis University (2008)
2. Qian, Z., Li, P., Zhu, Q., Zhou, G.: Document-level event factuality identification via adversarial neural network. In: NAACL-HLT (1), pp. 2799–2809. Association for Computational Linguistics (2019)
3. Klenner, M., Clematide, S.: How factuality determines sentiment inferences. In: *SEM@ACL. The *SEM 2016 Organizing Committee (2016)

4. Born, L., Mesgar, M., Strube, M.: Using a graph-based coherence model in document-level machine translation. In: DiscoMT@EMNLP, pp. 26–35. Association for Computational Linguistics (2017)
5. Qazvinian, V., Rosengren, E., Radev, D.R., Mei, Q.: Rumor has it: identifying misinformation in microblogs. In: EMNLP, pp. 1589–1599. ACL (2011)
6. Zhang, H., Qian, Z., Zhu, X., Li, P.: Document-level event factuality identification using negation and speculation scope. In: Mantoro, T., Lee, M., Ayu, M.A., Wong, K.W., Hidayanto, A.N. (eds.) ICONIP 2021. LNCS, vol. 13108, pp. 414–425. Springer, Cham (2021). https://doi.org/10.1007/978-3-030-92185-9_34
7. Cao, P., Chen, Y., Yang, Y., Liu, K., Zhao, J.: Uncertain local-to-global networks for document-level event factuality identification. In: EMNLP (1), pp. 2636–2645. Association for Computational Linguistics (2021)
8. Thorne, J., Vlachos, A., Christodoulopoulos, C., Mittal, A.: FEVER: a large-scale dataset for fact extraction and verification. In: NAACL-HLT, pp. 809–819. Association for Computational Linguistics (2018)
9. Qian, Z., Li, P., Zhang, Y., Zhou, G., Zhu, Q.: Event factuality identification via generative adversarial networks with auxiliary classification. In: IJCAI, pp. 4293–4300. ijcai.org (2018)
10. Rudinger, R., White, A.S., Durme, B.V.: Neural models of factuality. In: NAACL-HLT, pp. 731–744. Association for Computational Linguistics (2018)
11. Huang, R., Zou, B., Wang, H., Li, P., Zhou, G.: Event factuality detection in discourse. In: Tang, J., Kan, M.-Y., Zhao, D., Li, S., Zan, H. (eds.) NLPCC 2019. LNCS (LNAI), vol. 11839, pp. 404–414. Springer, Cham (2019). https://doi.org/10.1007/978-3-030-32236-6_36
12. Veyseh, A.P.B., Nguyen, T.H., Dou, D.: Graph based neural networks for event factuality prediction using syntactic and semantic structures. In: ACL (1), pp. 4393–4399. Association for Computational Linguistics (2019)
13. Kruengkrai, C., Yamagishi, J., Wang, X.: A multi-level attention model for evidence-based fact checking. In: ACL/IJCNLP (Findings). Findings of ACL, ACL/IJCNLP 2021, pp. 2447–2460. Association for Computational Linguistics (2021)
14. Yoneda, T., Mitchell, J., Welbl, J., Stenetorp, P., Riedel, S.: UCL machine reading group: four factor framework for fact finding (HexaF). In: Proceedings of the First Workshop on Fact Extraction and VERification (FEVER), pp. 97–102 (2018)
15. Hanselowski, A., et al.: UKP-Athene: multi-sentence textual entailment for claim verification. CoRR abs/1809.01479 (2018)
16. Zhou, J., et al.: GEAR: graph-based evidence aggregating and reasoning for fact verification. In: ACL (1), pp. 892–901. Association for Computational Linguistics (2019)
17. Nie, Y., Chen, H., Bansal, M.: Combining fact extraction and verification with neural semantic matching networks. In: AAAI, pp. 6859–6866. AAAI Press (2019)
18. Nie, Y., Wang, S., Bansal, M.: Revealing the importance of semantic retrieval for machine reading at scale. In: EMNLP/IJCNLP (1), pp. 2553–2566. Association for Computational Linguistics (2019)
19. Liu, Z., Xiong, C., Sun, M., Liu, Z.: Fine-grained fact verification with kernel graph attention network. In: ACL, pp. 7342–7351. Association for Computational Linguistics (2020)
20. Soleimani, A., Monz, C., Worring, M.: BERT for evidence retrieval and claim verification. In: Jose, J.M., et al. (eds.) ECIR 2020. LNCS, vol. 12036, pp. 359–366. Springer, Cham (2020). https://doi.org/10.1007/978-3-030-45442-5_45

21. Si, J., Zhou, D., Li, T., Shi, X., He, Y.: Topic-aware evidence reasoning and stance-aware aggregation for fact verification. In: ACL/IJCNLP (1), pp. 1612–1622. Association for Computational Linguistics (2021)
22. Zhong, W., et al.: Reasoning over semantic-level graph for fact checking. In: ACL, pp. 6170–6180. Association for Computational Linguistics (2020)
23. Samarinas, C., Hsu, W., Lee, M.: Improving evidence retrieval for automated explainable fact-checking. In: NAACL-HLT (Demonstrations), pp. 84–91. Association for Computational Linguistics (2021)
24. Subramanian, S., Lee, K.: Hierarchical evidence set modeling for automated fact extraction and verification. In: EMNLP (1), pp. 7798–7809. Association for Computational Linguistics (2020)
25. Jiang, K., Pradeep, R., Lin, J.: Exploring listwise evidence reasoning with T5 for fact verification. In: ACL/IJCNLP (2), pp. 402–410. Association for Computational Linguistics (2021)
26. Yin, W., Roth, D.: TwoWingOS: a two-wing optimization strategy for evidential claim verification. In: EMNLP, pp. 105–114. Association for Computational Linguistics (2018)
27. Ma, J., Gao, W., Joty, S.R., Wong, K.: Sentence-level evidence embedding for claim verification with hierarchical attention networks. In: ACL (1), pp. 2561–2571. Association for Computational Linguistics (2019)
28. Cohen, J.: A coefficient of agreement for nominal scales. Educ. Psychol. Measur. **20**(1), 37–46 (1960)
29. Devlin, J., Chang, M., Lee, K., Toutanova, K.: BERT: pre-training of deep bidirectional transformers for language understanding. In: NAACL-HLT (1), pp. 4171–4186. Association for Computational Linguistics (2019)
30. Vincze, V., Szarvas, G., Farkas, R., Móra, G., Csirik, J.: The bioscope corpus: biomedical texts annotated for uncertainty, negation and their scopes. BMC Bioinform. **9**(S-11), 1–9 (2008)
31. Zou, B., Zhu, Q., Zhou, G.: Negation and speculation identification in Chinese language. In: ACL (1), pp. 656–665. The Association for Computer Linguistics (2015)
32. Vaswani, A., et al.: Attention is all you need. In: NIPS, pp. 5998–6008 (2017)
33. Chen, Q., Zhu, X., Ling, Z., Wei, S., Jiang, H., Inkpen, D.: Enhanced LSTM for natural language inference. In: ACL (1), pp. 1657–1668. Association for Computational Linguistics (2017)

Named Entity Recognition Model of Power Equipment Based on Multi-feature Fusion

Yun Wu, Xiangwen Ma, Jieming Yang, and Anping Wang(✉)

Northeast Electric Power University, Jilin City, Jilin, China
xiwang_xiayu@163.com

Abstract. Extracting useful information from a large number of text files in the power field is of great significance to power informatization, and the identification of power equipment entities is a key part. Aiming at the difficulties of entity recognition of power equipment in the field of Chinese electric power, such as complex entity names and difficult identification of rare entities, this paper proposes a Chinese named entity recognition model based on multi-feature fusion. From the knowledge of the electric power field (concise dictionary of electric technical terms, English dictionary of electric power terms, etc.), a large number of electric power professional terms are sorted out to construct the electric power field dictionary, and then text segmentation and part-of-speech tagging are carried out under the guidance of it. Integrate various features of characters, words and word categories into input vectors and input them into the BiLSTM-CRF model for sequence labeling. The experimental results show that the entity recognition model proposed in this paper improves the recognition effect of Chinese named entities in the field of power equipment.

Keywords: Power equipment · Chinese named entity recognition · Domain dictionary · Deep learning

1 Introduction

In recent years, the professional knowledge service platform in the field of electric power and energy [1] has been one of the key construction projects of enterprises and institutions in the domestic electric power industry such as State Grid. Chinese Power Equipment Entity Recognition (CPEER) [2] is one of the key tasks. At the same time, CPEER is also a key task for many smart grid systems [3,4], such as building a knowledge graph of the power industry [5], a knowledge recommendation system in the power field [6] and other smart grid dispatching decision-making assistance systems [7].

Supported by the science and technology research project of the Education Department of Jilin Province (Project No: JJKH20220120KJ).

© The Author(s), under exclusive license to Springer Nature Switzerland AG 2022
S. Khanna et al. (Eds.): PRICAI 2022, LNCS 13630, pp. 255–267, 2022.
https://doi.org/10.1007/978-3-031-20865-2_19

Chinese Power Equipment Entity Recognition (CPEER) aims to identify the boundaries and types of specific power equipment entities from unstructured text, that is, to identify and classify power equipment in power industry corpora. But the identification of Chinese power equipment entities is not easy. At present, Chinese power equipment entity recognition [8] still faces major challenges for the following reasons: First, as a professional field, power equipment names contain many complex and domain-specific words, and some equipment names are long and rare. For example, "电磁式电压互感器 (electromagnetic type voltage transformer)" . Second, there is a lack of public Chinese power text datasets due to the difficulty in obtaining and labeling power domain texts. Finally, Chinese is complex: on the one hand, Chinese does not have the spaces of English text as natural boundaries; on the other hand, Chinese has a complex structure with many nested and omitted sentences.

In order to improve the effect of deep learning model on power equipment entities, we introduce more feature information and perform text processing under the guidance of domain dictionaries.

The main contributions of our work can be summarized as follows:

A dataset of Chinese power equipment is constructed and the training set is augmented by the method of entity replacement of the same type to improve the entity recognition effect.

This paper proposes a Chinese power equipment entity recognition method based on character-word-word category multi-feature fusion. It gives the model more semantic information and domain information by combining multiple features of characters, words, parts of speech and word types to improve the entity recognition effect of the model.

The evaluation results show that compared with the traditional deep learning model based on character vector or word vector, this model has better performance on the power equipment data set.

2   Related Work

2.1   Named Entity Recognition in Electric Power Domain

In the early days of Chinese Named Entity Recognition (CNER), researchers used a rule-based approach, mainly applying rule templates constructed by language experts. However, this method is time-consuming and labor-intensive, and has poor portability in different fields. After this, machine learning have been applied to named entity recognition tasks, mainly using Hidden Markov Models (HMM) [9] and Conditional Random Fields (CRF) [10]. Machine learning-based methods have better adaptability and higher performance than rule-based and dictionary-based methods. But machine learning-based methods [9,10] rely on extensive feature engineering, which is too cumbersome and time-consuming.

In recent years, deep learning methods have been widely used to perform NER tasks. Deng et al. used convolutional neural network to solve the problem of event element extraction in the power field [11], to solve the problem that there is very little labeled data in the professional field, and the end-to-end learning method is difficult to achieve results. Tian et al. proposed a new entity recognition method I-BRC (integrated algorithm of BERT based BiRNN with CRF). The sequence feature information of text is extracted by iterative recurrent neural network and CRF model [12]. In 2015, Huang et al., proposed a neural network model based on bidirectional LSTM and CRF to achieve state-of-the-art performance in multiple NER tasks [13], long short-term memory network (LSTM) can automatically extract deep semantics in text sequences information, CRF considers the dependencies between tags. Yang et al., adopted the BiLSTM-CRF method to more accurately and efficiently identify power entities in power text [14]. Jia et al. used BiLSTM-CRF to improve the entity recognition accuracy of speech transcribed text in the power field, while reducing the cost of speech recognition technology in the power field [15]. Jiang et al. used the pre-training method to initialize the parameters of the general Bert to form a power Bert (PowerBert), and used Bert-BiLSTM-CRF to perform entity recognition on the power equipment troubleshooting text [16]. Although the above methods have achieved good results, they do not fully utilize the existing power knowledge and the characteristics of entity names in the power field. Deeper utilization of power domain knowledge and research on fusion methods combining multiple features have positive effects on power domain NLP tasks.

2.2   Data Augmentation

Deep learning to deal with CNER problems is based on sequence labeling methods, which require a sufficient amount of high-quality labeled corpus. However, the high cost of labeling datasets leads to the small size of named entity recognition training sets, which severely limits the final performance of named entity recognition models.

Wu et al. found that if an entity name is replaced by another entity of the same type, the new sentence is usually grammatically and semantically correct, and then proposed a method to generate pseudo-labeled data [17], which can be used as a general strategy for enhancing corpora and improving performance. In order to expand the training set size of named entity recognition without increasing labor cost, Ma et al. proposed data augmentation for named entity recognition based on EDA (Easy Data Augmentation), based on remote supervision, and based on Bootstrap (bootstrap method) technique [18] to increase the size of the training set at low cost, thereby significantly improving the performance of named entity recognition models.

3   Methods

The overall structure of the Chinese power equipment named entity recognition model constructed in this paper is shown in Fig. 1.

The model is divided into three layers, namely joint embedding layer, BiLSTM layer and CRF layer. The first layer is a joint embedding layer of character

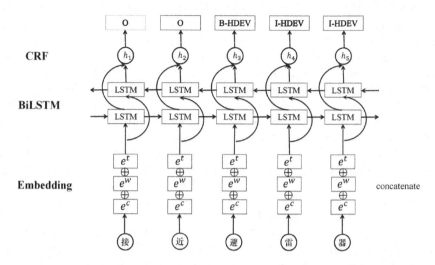

Fig. 1. Named entity recognition model of power equipment based on multi-feature fusion.

vectors, word vectors, and word category vectors. The characters and words in the dataset are replaced with pre-trained character vectors and word vectors respectively, and then the character vectors, word vectors and the initialized word category vectors are concatenated as the representation of the characters to form the final input vector. The second layer is the BiLSTM layer, which aims to automatically extract semantic and temporal features from the context. The third layer is the CRF layer, which aims to solve the dependencies between the output labels and obtain the global optimal label sequence of the text.

3.1 Data Augmentation Using Domain Dictionary

Power equipment datasets with high-quality annotations are extremely rare, so this paper draws on the research of Wu et al. and finds that the same type of entities in the domain dictionary are used to replace the original entities in the training set to form new training data to expand the dataset.

First, the words in the dictionary of electric power field are classified according to the types of power equipment entities to form several power equipment word bags. Because the electrical equipment entities in the marked corpus are divided into six categories, namely domestic electrical equipment, power generation and transmission equipment, instrumentation equipment, fire early warning equipment, electrical equipment accessories and safety protection equipment, so the domain dictionary entity nouns are classified into these six electrical equipment classes to correspond to the six types of entities marked. Then, use the jieba word segmentation tool [19] combined with the domain dictionary to segment the training set, and randomly select an entity noun from the corresponding power equipment class to replace the power equipment entity noun in a sentence after the segmentation, thereby forming a new training corpus sentence. As shown in Fig. 2 below.

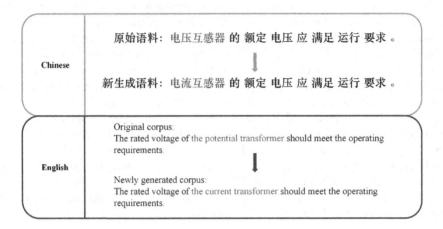

Fig. 2. Generating new corpus with synonym replacement.

Eventually a pseudo-artificially labeled training set appears. The two training sets are combined to form a data-augmented training set.

3.2 Fusion Embedding Layer

In order to improve the performance of the entity recognition model, this paper uses the vector representation of multi-feature fusion to provide more semantic information to the model. First, under the guidance of the dictionary of electric power field, the jieba word segmentation tool [19] is used to segment the corpus at the word level to improve the accuracy of the corpus segmentation. The Word2Vec model is used to train the corpus in two ways: character as the segmentation granularity and word as the segmentation granularity, to obtain a dictionary of one-to-one correspondence between characters and character vectors and a dictionary of one-to-one correspondence between words and word vectors. For the same sentence, the word segmentation methods of character and word granularity will cause different corpus lengths after word segmentation. In this paper, the word-granularity corpus length is extended to be the same as the character-granularity corpus length through word segmentation placeholders.

In order to give the segmented words more domain information and semantic information, the feature of the word category of the word in which the character is located is added to the semantic representation of the character in this paper. Class matching is performed on the words formed after word segmentation through the power equipment class word bag. For unpaired words, the jieba word segmentation tool is used to determine the part of speech, and the part of speech is used as the word category, and the parts that have a negligible impact on the sentence structure or are too few in number are merged to form other categories. Finally, a word category dictionary with 21 categories in one-to-one correspondence between words and word categories is formed.

Figure 3 shows a specific example of three vector fusions of characters, words and word categories. Through placeholder processing, the characters, words, and word categories in the corpus correspond one-to-one. In the embedding layer, the training corpus is converted into a vector through the character dictionary, the word dictionary and the word category dictionary, and the three vectors are fused as the input vector of the model by means of vector connection. This method can ensure that the same character has different vectors in different words, for example, "电缆 (electric cable)" and "电流表 (current meter)" belong to power generation and transmission equipment and instrumentation, respectively. Since the "电 (electricity)" in the two words has different semantics, after the character vector,the word vector where the character is located, and the word category vector are fused, the semantic information of the word where the character is located will not only be ignored, but will also refine the semantic information of word categories. The fused vector is expressed as.

$$e = e^c + e^w + e^t \tag{1}$$

where e^c, e^w, e^t represents the character vector, the vector of the word where the character is located, and the word category vector, respectively.

4   BiLSTM Layer

Long Short-Term Memory Network (LSTM) is a variant of Recurrent Neural Network (RNN) that has been widely used in many natural language processing (NLP) tasks such as named entity recognition, text classification, and sentiment analysis. In traditional recurrent neural network (RNN) training, the problem of vanishing or exploding gradients often occurs. To this end, LSTM introduces the cell state and utilizes input gates, forget gates, and output gates to maintain and control information to solve this problem. The mathematical expression of the LSTM model is as follows:

$$i_t = \sigma(W_i[h_{t-1}, x_t] + b_i) \tag{2}$$

$$f_t = \sigma(W_f[h_{t-1}, x_t] + b_f) \tag{3}$$

$$o_t = \sigma(W_o[h_{t+1}, x_t] + b_o) \tag{4}$$

$$\tilde{c}_t = tanh(W_c[h_{t+1}, x_t] + b_c) \tag{5}$$

$$c_t = i_t * \tilde{c}_t + f_t * c_{t-1} \tag{6}$$

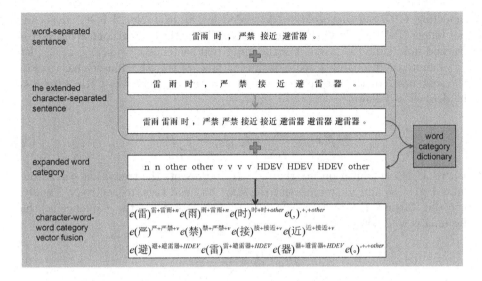

Fig. 3. Fuse character, word and word category vectors.

$$h_t = o_t * tanh(c_t) \tag{7}$$

where σ represents the sigmod activation function. tanh represents the hyperbolic tangent function. x_t represents unit input. i_t, f_t, o_t represent the output of the input gate, forget gate and output gate at the time, respectively, and W_i, W_f, W_o and b_i, b_f, b_o represent the weight and bias of the input gate, forget gate and output gate, respectively. $\tilde{c}_t$ represents the current state of the input, W_c and b_c are the weight and bias of the updated state value, respectively. c_t represents the update state at t, which can be used for the state update operation of the next LSTM cell. h_t is the output at t.

In order to use character context information at the same time, the model in this paper uses BiLSTM to obtain the context vector of each character, which is a combination of forward LSTM and reverse LSTM. For a given sentence, $x = (x_1, x_2, ..., x_n)$ denote the hidden state of the forward LSTM at t by $\overrightarrow{h_t}$, and denote the hidden state of the reverse LSTM by $\overleftarrow{h_t}$. The final context vector $h_t = [\overrightarrow{h_t}; \overleftarrow{h_t}]$ is obtained by linking the corresponding forward and reverse LSTM states.

4.1 CRF Layer

Compared with HMM, CRF does not have the strict requirements of HMM independence assumption, can effectively utilize the internal information and external observation information of the sequence, avoid the problem of labeling bias, and directly assume the possibility of labeling and execution differential modeling. CRF can capture more dependencies: for example, "I-LOC" tags cannot follow "B-PER". In CNER, the input to CRF is the contextual feature vector learned from BiLSTM layers. For the input text sentence $x = (x_1, x_2, ..., x_n)$, let $P_{i,j}$ denote the probability score of the jth label of the ith Chinese character in the sentence. For the predicted sequence $y = (y_1, y_2, ...y_n)$, the CRF score can be defined as follows:

$$f(x,y) = \sum_{n=0}^{n+1} M_{y_i,y_{i+1}} + \sum_{i=1}^{n} P_{i,y_i} \tag{8}$$

where M is the transition matrix and $M_{i,j}$ represents the transition score from label i to j. y_0 and y_{n+1} represent the start and end tags, respectively. Finally, use the softmax function to calculate the probability of the sequence y, the formula is as follows:

$$P(y \mid x) = \frac{e^{f(x,y)}}{\sum_{\tilde{y} \in Y_x} e^{f(x,y)}} \tag{9}$$

During training, maximize the log probability of the correct label sequence:

$$\log\left(P(x,y)\right) = f(x,y) - \log \sum_{\tilde{y} \in Y_x} e^{f(x,\tilde{y})} \tag{10}$$

In the decoding stage, the maximum score obtained by predicting the output sequence is as follows:

$$y^* = \underset{\tilde{y} \in Y_x}{\arg\max}\, f(x, \tilde{y}) \tag{11}$$

In the prediction stage, the optimal sequence is solved using the Viterbi dynamic programming algorithm [10].

5   Experiments and Results

5.1   Dataset

The experimental corpus of this paper is selected from the China State Grid Power Equipment Maintenance Standard Document. There are a large number of various types of power equipment entities in this standard document, which is helpful for the model to learn more information about power equipment. The original corpus selects 8000 sentences after removing useless special symbols, noise data and low-quality sentences with too short length to form a data set and ensure that all data types are covered, which can effectively reduce the risk of overfitting. The dataset covers a total of 414 power equipment entities, both primary and secondary equipment, and is labeled by Colabeler [20] by professionals with a background in electrical power. In this paper, the data set is divided into training set and test set according to the ratio of 8:2.

In this study, the BIO (begin, inside, and output) labeling method is selected to label the training and testing data, and the specific format is B-X, I-X, O. B represents the character of the starting position of the power equipment entity, I represents the character of the remaining part of the power equipment entity, and O represents the character of the non-power equipment entity. The details of the entities in the dataset are shown in Fig. 4.

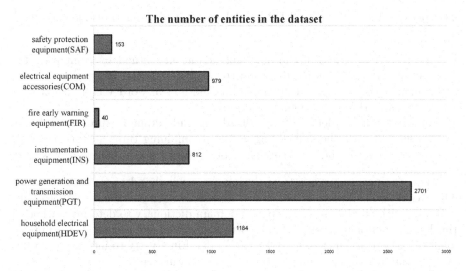

Fig. 4. The number of entities of each type in the dataset.

5.2 Evaluation Indicators

Precision, Recall, and F1-score are metrics used in named entity recognition. P (Positive) represents the positive samples among all samples. N (Negative) represents the negative sample among all samples. TP (True Positives) is the number of positive samples predicted to be positive. FN (False Negatives) is the number of positive samples predicted to be negative. FP (False Positives) is the number of negative samples predicted to be positive. TN (True Negatives) is the number of negative samples predicted to be negative. Precision is the proportion of positive samples in all predicted positive samples, defined as:

$$precision = \frac{TP}{TP + FP} \times 100\% \tag{12}$$

Recall is the proportion of positive samples predicted to be positive among all positive samples, given by:

$$recall = \frac{TP}{TP + FN} \times 100\% \tag{13}$$

F1-score is the weighted harmonic mean of precision and recall. The definition of F1-score is:

$$F1 - score = \frac{2 \times precision \times recall}{precision + recall} \tag{14}$$

5.3 Experimental Design and Parameters

The performance of the CPEER model was tested from the following three aspects:

(1) Test the effectiveness of the data augmentation method by comparing the effect of using the original data and the augmented data
(2) Comparing the effect of the embedding method of word vector fusion with and without the power domain dictionary
(3) Comparing the model effects of not adding and adding features, an ablation experiment using the embedding method combining three vector fusions of characters, words and word categories of the power domain dictionary is used.

First, the performance is tested using the original and augmented datasets. Then, compare the effect of the character-word vector fusion embedding model with and without the use of the power domain dictionary to determine whether the domain dictionary is effective for correct word segmentation and the improvement of the performance of the CPEER model. Finally, try to increase the word category information to improve the model performance.

Using the deep learning framework with Pytorch, the model runs on a single NVIDIA GeForce GTX 1660 Ti GPU. Hyperparameters are set based on trial and error. Character embedding and word embedding are pre-trained by Word2Vec, the word category is randomly initialized embedding, and the embedding size is set to 100, 80, and 20, respectively. The hidden layer size of LSTM is 100. The model is trained by the Adam optimization algorithm [21] with a learning rate of 0.005, a batch size of 64, and an epochs of 15.

5.4 Experimental Results

In order to make the experimental results have statistical significance, the experimental results in the paper are the average of 5 experiments. First, in order to judge the effectiveness of the data augmentation method used, an experimental model (BiLSTM-CRF) based on the original dataset and the augmented dataset is used for testing in this paper. The results are shown in Table 1.

Table 1. Comparison of experimental results with or without data augmentation.

Model	Augment	Precision	Recall	F1-score
BiLSTM-CRF	No	0.9216	0.8067	0.8603
BiLSTM-CRF	Yes	0.9324	0.8159	0.8703

The experimental results show that using the augmented dataset can improve the performance of CPEER, and the F1-score can be improved by about 1% on average. Subsequent experiments are based on the augmented dataset.

Then, this paper compares the effect of using the BiLSTM-CRF Model of Character-Word Vector Fusion (CWVF-BiLSTM-CRF) [22] that do not use the power domain dictionary to determine whether the domain knowledge of the domain dictionary is helpful for the improvement of the performance of the CPEER model. The results are shown in Table 2.

Table 2. Comparing the experimental results with and without domain dictionary.

Model	Domain dictionary	Precision	Recall	F1-score
CWVF-BiLSTM-CRF	No	0.9317	0.8219	0.8733
CWVF-BiLSTM-CRF	Yes	0.9458	0.8272	0.8783

It can be seen from Table 2 that the power domain dictionary is used for word segmentation, and the accuracy, recall and F1-score of the BiLSTM-CRF model based on word vector fusion have been improved to a certain extent. Therefore, combining with the power domain dictionary can improve the performance of CPEER by improving the word segmentation effect.

Finally, the word category information is added to the embedding vector, that is, the combination of the part of speech and the domain dictionary, to give the character-based vector more semantic information to improve the effect of the CPEER model. This paper selects several models (CRF, BiGRU [23], BiGRU-CRF [24], BiLSTM, CWVF-BiLSTM-CRF) commonly used in entity recognition in the Chinese power field and compares them with the model proposed in this paper. The results are shown in Table 3.

Table 3. Comparison experiment with other model.

Model	Precision	Recall	F1-score
CRF	0.9358	0.7602	0.8389
BiGRU	0.9407	0.7542	0.8309
BiGRU-CRF	0.9584	0.7721	0.8501
BiLSTM	0.9539	0.7839	0.8556
BiLSTM-CRF	0.9324	0.8159	0.8703
CWVF-BiLSTM-CRF	0.9458	0.8272	0.8783
Ours	**0.9468**	**0.8424**	**0.8884**

As can be seen from Table 3, the BiLSTM-CRF based on character-word-word category vector fusion proposed in this paper achieves the highest value in

F1-score. In contrast, several traditional models have satisfactory performance in precision, but poor performance in recall, which makes their F1-score too low. Compared with the CWVF-BiLSTM-CRF model that lacks word category information, the model in this paper has a better performance on the recall rate, which also makes the F1-score of this paper higher, with a nearly 1% improvement.

6   Conclusions

Aiming at the problems of Chinese named entity recognition in the field of power equipment, there are many complex entities and difficult to identify rare entities. This paper proposes a BiLSTM-CRF model based on character-word-word category multi-feature fusion. By making full use of the domain knowledge in the power domain to give the model more semantic information to improve the effect of the CPEER model, and using a data augmentation method to enhance the training set to solve the problem of scarce training data.

Compared with the traditional BiLSTM-CRF model that only uses character-level features, the method of adding word and word category information to the feature representation proposed in this paper can make the same Chinese character in different words have different vector representations. The experimental results show that, compared with the entity recognition model based on a single feature, the entity recognition model based on character-word-word category multi-feature fusion has superiority in the entity recognition of power equipment (CPEER).

For future work, we will try to explore the performance improvement of entity recognition tasks in the Chinese power field from two directions: (1) use more advanced and refined models, such as BERT, attention mechanism; (2) provide more domain information or features to the model.

References

1. Jinhu, L., Kun, C.: Build a power knowledge graph based on graph database. In: Second Smart Grid Conference, pp. 77–81, August 2018
2. Yuzhong, Z., Xiujie, T., Ronghui, W.: A power equipment knowledge graph application system (2020)
3. Huanan, Y., Xiaofei, B., He, W.: A fault location method for grid transmission line based on compressed sensing. J. Northeast Electr. Power Univ. 40(1), 47–55 (2020)
4. Ruosong, Y., Xiaoyue, Z., Xingfa, L.: Power enterprise material business process based on automatic data flow research on digital management system. J. Northeast Electr. Power Univ. 41(6), 100–104 (2021)
5. Xiao, T., Yongchao, L., Jing, W.: Application value of building knowledge graph system for hotline customer service in state grid corporation. Shandong Dianli Jishu 42(12), 65–67+80 (2015)
6. Yu, L., Donghai, X., Yu, B.: Optimization of combined heat and power system based on organic Rankine cycle. J. Northeast Electr. Power Univ. 42(1), 43–48 (2022)

7. Ziming, W., Liang, S., Liguo, S.: Optimization scheduling of CCHP micro-energy network based on phase change energy storage thermal resistance model. J. Northeast Electr. Power Univ. **42**(1), 96–103 (2022)
8. Kainan, J., Xin, L., Rongchen, Z.: Overview of Chinese domain named entity recognition. Comput. Eng. Appl. **57**(16), 1–15 (2021)
9. Zobaa, A., Reljin, B.: Neural network applications in electrical engineering. Neurocomputing **70**(16–18), 2613–2614 (2007)
10. Sarawagi, S., Cohen, W.W.: Semi-Markov conditional random fields for information extraction. In: Advances in Neural Information Processing Systems, vol. 17, pp. 1185–1192 (2004)
11. Junhua, D., Yunfeng, Z., Shengyu, S.: Electric event arguments extraction on convolutional neural networks. Electron. Des. Eng. **29**(3), 132–135, 140 (2021)
12. Jiapeng, T., Hui, S., Lifan, C.: Entity recognition approach of equipment failure text for knowledge graph construction. Power Syst. Technol. **46**(10), 3913–3922 (2021)
13. Huang, Z., Xu, W., Yu, K.: Bidirectional LSTM-CRF models for sequence tagging. Comput. Sci. arXiv:1508.01991 (2015)
14. Qiuyong, Y., Zewu, P., Huaquan, S.: Chinese electric power entity recognition based on BI-LSTM-CRF. XINXIJISHU **9**, 45–50 (2021)
15. Quanye, J., Qiang, Z., Bochuan, S.: A text entity recognition algorithm based on recurrent neural network for customer service voice of state grid. Distrib. Utilization **37**(6), 13–20 (2020)
16. Chen, J., Yuan, W., Junhua, H.: Power entity information recognition based on deep learning. Power Syst. Technol. **45**(6), 2141–2149 (2021)
17. Wenqiang, L., Tiehua, Z.: Research on mining and evolution methods for hot disease topics in the online health communities. Master's thesis, Northeast Electric Power University (2021)
18. Xiaoqin, M., Xiaohe, G., Yufeng, X.: Data augmentation technology for named entity recognition. J. East China Normal Univ. (Nat. Sci.) (05), 14–23 (2021)
19. Sun, J.: jieba 0.42.1 (2022). https://pypi.org/project/jieba/
20. Hangzhou Kuaiyi Technology Co., Ltd.: Collabeler 2.0.4 (2021). http://www.jinglingbiaozhu.com/
21. Graves, A., Schmidhuber, J.: Framewise phoneme classification with bidirectional LSTM and other neural network architectures. Neural Netw. **18**(5–6), 602–610 (2005)
22. Ye, N., Qin, X., Dong, L.: Chinese named entity recognition based on character-word vector fusion. Wirel. Commun. Mob. Comput. **2020**(3), 1–7 (2020)
23. Cho, K., Van Merriënboer, B., Gulcehre, C.: Learning phrase representations using RNN encoder-decoder for statistical machine translation. Comput. Sci. arXiv:1406.1078 (2014)
24. Lample, G., Ballesteros, M., Subramanian, S.: Neural architectures for named entity recognition. In: Proceedings of the 2016 Conference of the North American Chapter of the Association for Computational Linguistics: Human Language Technologies (2016)

Improving Abstractive Multi-document Summarization with Predicate-Argument Structure Extraction

Huangfei Cheng, Jiawei Wu, Tiantian Li, Bin Cao[(⊠)], and Jing Fan

Zhejiang University of Technology, Hangzhou, China
{chenghf,wujw,ttli89,bincao}@zjut.edu.cn

Abstract. Multi-Document Summarization (MDS) aims to generate a concise summary for a collection of documents on the same topic. However, the fixed input length and a large number of redundancies in source documents make the pre-trained models less effective in MDS. In this paper, we propose a two-stage abstractive MDS model based on Predicate-Argument Structure (PAS). In the first stage, we divide the redundancy of documents into intra-sentence redundancy and inter-sentence redundancy. For intra-sentence redundancy, our model utilizes Semantic Role Labeling (SRL) to covert each sentence to a PAS. Benefiting from PAS, we can filter out redundant contents while preserving the salient information. For inter-sentence redundancy, we introduce a novel similarity calculation method that incorporates semantic and syntactic knowledge to identify and remove duplicate information. The above two steps significantly shorten the input length and eliminate documents redundancies, which is crucial for MDS. In the second stage, we sort the filtered PASs to ensure important contents appear at the beginning and concatenate them into a new document. We employ a pre-trained model ProphetNet to generate an abstractive summary from the new document. Our model combines the advantages of ProphetNet and PAS on global information to generate comprehensive summaries. We conduct extensive experiments on three standard MDS datasets. All experiments demonstrate that our model outperforms the abstractive MDS baselines measured by ROUGE scores. Furthermore, the first stage of our model can improve the performance of other pre-trained models in abstractive MDS.

Keywords: Multi-document summarization · Predicate-argument structure · Semantic role labeling · Pre-trained model

1 Introduction

Multi-Document Summarization (MDS) is the task of condensing a document collection on the same topic to a short summary while retaining its most important information [12]. The task can be divided into two paradigms, extractive

© The Author(s), under exclusive license to Springer Nature Switzerland AG 2022
S. Khanna et al. (Eds.): PRICAI 2022, LNCS 13630, pp. 268–282, 2022.
https://doi.org/10.1007/978-3-031-20865-2_20

MDS and abstractive MDS. Extractive MDS assembles summaries exclusively from spans taken from the source documents, while abstractive MDS may generate novel words and phrases not featured in the source documents [30]. MDS has a wide range of real-world applications, such as Wikipedia articles generation [22], summarizing product reviews [11], and news [9].

Recent works on large-scale Pre-Trained Models (PTMs) have shown great success when fine-tuned on downstream Natural Language Processing (NLP) tasks, including text summarization [35,36]. However, the progress on abstractive MDS with pre-trained models is limited. The reasons are as follows: (1) The large input length of documents. Due to the memory limitations of current hardware, training a model that encodes all data into vectors is practically not achievable [23]. Abstractive MDS systems usually truncate the documents at the maximum input length, and the excess is discarded, which would miss lots of summary-worthy content [9,18]. (2) The duplicate content of source documents. The documents on the same topic contain semantically similar or even repetitive content [20], which leads to the summary generation to be biased towards duplicate contents and produce a verbose and repetitive summary [18].

In this paper, we propose a two-stage abstractive MDS model based on Predicate-Argument Structure (PAS). PAS is the result of syntactic analysis, using predicates and arguments to express "who did what to whom" in a sentence [13]. Our model uses PAS to filter redundant information in the original sentence and significantly shorten the sentence length. Instead of selecting certain sentences or paragraphs as the compression result [23,37], our model extracts PAS from source documents to compress documents. Using sentences or paragraphs as the extraction granularity will lose the information of the unselected parts. Our model takes semantic arguments as granularity to preserve the salient content of each sentence. Specifically, we employ a Semantic Role Labeling (SRL) [13] model to parse each sentence in a document and get Predicate-Argument Structures (PASs). There may be multiple PASs in a sentence, and reserving them all leads to redundancy within the sentence. The previous model selects the longest PAS, which makes the argument too long and contains useless content [1,15]. So we design a PAS score based on TextRank [25] to measure the importance of predicate-argument structure. For each sentence, we select the PAS whose score is the highest as the correct result of the SRL parsing. Although intra-sentence redundancy is eliminated, inter-sentence redundancy still exists. We identify semantically repeated PASs by computing similarity. Existing similarity calculation methods only consider the whole sentence semantics while ignoring syntactic information. We introduce a novel computational similarity method to measure the similarity of every two predicate-argument structures. Our model computes the similarity of PAS across multiple semantic role dimensions, combining semantic similarity and unigram overlap. The predicate-argument structure with the lower PAS score is discarded when two PASs' similarity is higher than the threshold. In the second stage, we generate a new document from the filtered PASs, then employ ProphetNet [27] to generate a fluent summary from the new document. Since PAS extraction is based on semantic arguments, the PAS document lacks more local information than the source documents. ProphetNet is a sequence-to-sequence (Seq2Seq) pre-training model with a future n-gram prediction, which can prevent the model from overfitting on strong local correlations [27]. Benefitting from the n-gram prediction mechanism, ProphetNet allows for better generation of coherent and comprehensive summary from the PAS document.

The contributions of our paper are as follows:

- We propose a two-stage abstractive MDS model, which can process much longer inputs and remove consistent information using predicate-argument structure.
- Extensive experiments demonstrate predicate-argument structure extraction is beneficial in improving other pre-trained models on abstractive MDS tasks.
- We introduce a novel similarity calculation which computes the similarity of PAS across multiple semantic role dimensions incorporating semantic and syntactic knowledge to evaluate PAS similarity in multi-document.
- Our summarization model outperforms the abstract MDS baselines by a large margin on three public datasets, including DUC-2003, DUC-2004 [26], and WCEP [12], measured by ROUGE [21] scores.

2   Preliminaries

This section introduces semantic role labeling and its advantages in document extraction.

Table 1. Common semantic roles and the corresponding semantic role labels

Semantic roles	Labels
Agent	ARG0
Patient	ARG1
Instrument, benefactive, attribute	ARG2
Locatives	ARGM-LOC
Temporal	ARGM-TMP
Adverbials	ARGM-ADV

Semantic Role Labeling. SRL systems aim to find out all the predicate-argument structures of a sentence and to determine essentially "who did what to whom," "when" and "where" [13]. SRL is a shallow semantic analysis technique that centers on the sentence's predicate. A sentence predicate typically indicates a particular action, and the predicate's syntactic arguments are associated with the participants in that action. For example, in the sentence "*Mike lost the* book", the action is a *loss* action, with *Mike* as the agent and *a lost book* as the patient. Semantic roles are defined as the relationships between syntactic arguments and the predicates [1]. As shown in Table 1, the arguments of the predicates are labeled as numbered arguments: $ARG0$, $ARG1$, $ARG2$ and so on [5], where $ARG0$ is the label of an agent, $AGR1$ is the label of a patient, $ARG2$ can be the label of instrument, benefactive, attribute. The labels prefixed with AGRM represent the modifier. For the example above, *Mike* will be labeled $AGR0$, and the book will be labeled $AGR1$. SRL is believed to be a crucial step toward natural language understanding and has been widely employed in many NLP applications such as Information Extraction [4], Question Answering [31], Machine Translation [34].

Table 2. Comparison of different extraction granularity. Words marked in red are the words that appear in the gold summary.

Original Text: newspapers reported wednesday that three top libyan officials have been tried and jailed in the Lockerbie case, but libyan dissidents said the reports appeared to be a political ploy by libya's leader, col.moammar Gadhafi. Libyan leader moammar Gadhafi said the suspects in the lockerbie bombing are "very happy" to be tried in the netherlands, and he hoped the trial would lead to a better relationship with the U.S.
Paragraph Extraction: newspapers reported wednesday that three top libyan officials have been tried and jailed in the lockerbie case, but libyan dissidents said the reports appeared to be a political ploy by libya's leader, col.moammar Gadhafi. Libyan leader moammar Gadhafi said the suspects in the lockerbie bombing are "very happy" to be tried in the netherlands, and he hoped the trial would lead to a better relationship with the U.S.
Sentence Extraction: newspapers reported wednesday that three top libyan officials have been tried and jailed in the lockerbie case, but libyan dissidents said the reports appeared to be a political ploy by libya's leader, col.moammar Gadhafi.
PAS Extraction: Three top Libyan officials jailed in the Lockerbie case. the trial would lead to a better relationship with the U.S.
Gold Summary: Three top Libyan officials reported jailed in Lockerbie case. Gadhafi sees better U.S.-Libyan relations after trial of Lockerbie suspects

SRL parses sentences to predicate-argument structures whose granularity is semantic arguments. Compared to the methods that extract sentences or paragraphs to compress documents [23,37], using semantic arguments as extraction granularity makes the compression result more concise and detailed. We select a text from DUC-2003 as an example to illustrate the advantages of PAS extraction. We can see from Table 2 that when the extraction granularity is paragraph or sentence, the extraction results contain lots of redundant contents. The result of PAS extraction is the most concise and close to the gold summary.

3   Proposed Model

Our MDS model is illustrated in Fig. 1. Details of each section are as follows.

3.1   PAS Extraction

SRL Parsing. Given the source document collection that needs to be summarized, we process each document individually. Since SRL parsing processing is based on sentences, the documents is split into sentences by periods. Different from traditional SRL model [7], we leverage pretrained model BERT [14] to achieve semantic role labeling without relying on lexical or syntactic features. We employ a BERT based SRL model [32] to parse sentences. The SRL parsing processing is two steps. The first is predicate identification. We feed the sentence into the BERT encoder to obtain the contextual representation, then use a one-hidden-layer Multilayer Perceptron (MLP) to predict the predicates. The second step is Argument identification and classification, which detects the argument spans or argument syntactic heads and assign them the correct semantic role labels. Compared with the network structure in the first step, a one-layer Bidirectional Long Short-Term Memory (BiLSTM) is added to obtain hidden states before the MLP.

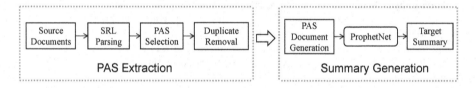

Fig. 1. Pipeline of our multi-document summarization system.

Table 3. The result of the SRL parsing for a sample sentence, the PASs containing only predicate but no other arguments are not displayed

Original Sentence: U.S. officials who toured some of the hardest-hit regions of North Korea this summer said 2 million people may have died because of famine
PAS1: [ARG0: U.S. officials] [R-ARG0: who] [V: toured] [ARG1: some of the hardest - hit regions of North Korea] [ARGM-TMP: this summer]
PAS2: [ARGM-MNR: hardest] - [V: hit] [ARG1: regions]
PAS3: [ARG0: U.S. officials who toured some of the hardest - hit regions of North Korea this summer] [V: said] [ARG1: 2 million people may have died because of famine]
PAS4: [ARG1: 2 million people] [ARGM-MOD: may] have [V: died] [ARGM-CAU: because of famine]

PAS Selection. For each sentence, one or more predicate-argument structures are produced as the result of SRL parsing. As shown in Table 3, the sample sentence gets four PASs. Since the PASs from the same sentence have lots of duplicate content, reserving them all leads to semantic duplication within the sentence. So it is necessary to choose a summary-worthy PAS for each sentence. Aksoy et al. and Khan et al. consider the predicate-argument structure that leaves the least number of terms unlabeled as the correct parse of the sentence [1, 15]. Namely, they select the PAS whose spliced length is most extended. In this case, the chosen predicate-argument structure will be the complete original sentence. This causes arguments to include redundant information, making it impractical to analyze semantic arguments between different PASs. For example, we can see from Table 3 that PAS3 is the longest PAS. PAS3 is the original sentence and contains worthless content, while PAS4 contains salient information and is more concise than PAS3. However, selecting the shortest PASs is also not reasonable, which leads to losing lots of information in the sentence, such as PAS2.

To solve this problem, we use the PAS Score based on TextRank. TextRank is essentially a way of deciding the importance of a vertex within a graph, based on global information recursively drawn from the entire graph, which helps select the summary-worthy PAS. First, for each document sentence, we perform word segmentation and part-of-speech tagging, filter out stop words and retain only words with specified parts of speech, such as nouns, verbs, and adjectives. Next, we construct an undirected graph $G = (V, E)$ with the set of vertexes V and set of edges E. The vertexes of the graph are words that pass the syntactic filter. And an edge is added between those lexical units co-occurring within a window of words [25]. The score of vertexes is set to an initial value of 1. The score of a vertex V_i is defined as follows:

$$S(V_i) = (1 - d) + d * \sum_{j \in In(V_i)} \frac{1}{|Out(V_j)|} S(V_j) \qquad (1)$$

where d is a damping factor that can be set between 0 and 1. For a given vertex V_i, let $In(V_i)$ be the set of vertices that point to it (predecessors), and $Out(V_j)$ let be the set of vertices that vertex $i \in V$ points to successors. According to formula (1), iteratively calculate the weight of each vertex on the graph until convergence. So far, we have built a dictionary D, whose key is the words corresponding to the vertexes, and the value is the score of the vertex. We add words not in the current graph to D and set their values to 0.

Next, we calculate the PAS score based on the dictionary D. Its calculation formula is as follows:

$$PAS\ score(p) = \sum_{w \in p} D(w)/N(p) \qquad (2)$$

where p is a predicate-argument structure, and $PAS\ score(p)$ is the score of p.w is the word in p, $D(w)$ is the value of w in D, and $N(p)$ is the number of words in p. To make the results less inclined to select more extended predicate-argument structures, we divide the final sum of $D(w)$ by $N(p)$. It means the PAS's importance depends on the proportion of keywords contained in the PAS, regardless of length. In each sentence, we select the PAS whose score is the highest. So far, we have converted source documents to a collection of predicate-argument structures.

Duplicate Removal. The source documents are topic-related, so multi-document has more duplicate contents than single-document. Although intra-sentence redundancy is removed by PAS selection, semantic repetition between PASs still exists, which leads to repeated texts in summary and makes the summary less concise. Also, eliminating duplicate contents can further compress the document. To identify semantically repetitive PASs, we propose the PAS similarity in multi-document conditions to measure predicate-argument structures' similarity. Our similarity calculation method incorporates syntactic and semantic information, which can compare across multiple semantic argument dimensions. The formula is defined as follows:

$$PAS\_SIM(a,b) = \sum_{i \in S}(cos\_sim(a_i, b_i) + ROUGE\text{-}1\,(a_i, b_i))/(2 * |S|) \quad (3)$$

$$cos\_sim(a_i, b_i) = cosine(BERT(a_i), BERT(b_i)) \quad (4)$$

where $PAS\_SIM(a,b)$ is the PAS similarity of two predicate-argument structures, a, and b, S is the set of semantic roles. As shown in Table 1, this set contains $ARG0$, $ARG1$, $ARG2$, $ARG-LOC$, $ARG-TMP$, and $ARG-ADV$, respectively, and i is a semantic role in set S. In addition, we added the predicate as a special semantic role to S. a_i is the semantic argument corresponding to semantic role i. $cos\_sim(a_i, b_i)$ is the cosine similarity of a_i and b_i, their representations are obtained from the BERT encoder. $ROUGE\text{-}1(a_i, b_i)$ is the ROUGE-1 F1 score of a_i and b_i. We multiply the result by $1/2$ so that the final result is between 0 and 1, which matches our intuition that similarity ranges from 0 to 1.

We use the above formulas to calculate the similarity between two PASs. If the similarity exceeds the threshold, the one with the lower PAS score will be deleted from the collection of PASs.

3.2 Summary Generation

PAS Document Generation. In this section, we generate a PAS Document with the collection of predicate-argument structures obtained in the last step. For each PAS, we splice all the semantic arguments in the order of original places in the sentence. The PASs from the same document is arranged in the original sentence order. Because source documents are disordered, we rank documents by the PAS scores to ensure the important contents appear at the beginning. If arranged in random order, more informative documents may be lost due to exceeding the input length limit. We add up the PAS scores in the same document and use this score as the document's score. Finally, we concatenate the documents in descending order of scores.

Summary Generation. ProphetNet is a sequence-to-sequence (Seq2Seq) pre-training model, which is based on Transformer encoder-decoder architecture. In addition to the traditional Seq2Seq model that optimizes one-step-ahead prediction, the ProphetNet learns n-step ahead prediction [27]. This n-gram prediction is served as extra guidance that prevents overfitting on strong local correlations such as the bigram combination. The model achieves better global coherence and long-term dependency, which is helpful for our model. The reasons are as follows. First, PAS selection is based on TextRank, a graph ranking algorithm that considers global information. Second, compared to sentences or paragraphs as the extraction granularity, our model takes semantic arguments as granularity to preserve the main content of each sentence. This means the PAS document has more comprehensive information but lacks more local related information than source documents. Therefore, in the last step, we feed the PAS Document obtained in the previous step into ProphetNet and generate an abstractive summary with the fine-tuned ProphetNet model.

4 Experiments

4.1 Datasets and Evaluation Metrics

We conduct experiments on three public datasets, as described below. DUC-2003 and DUC-2004 [26] are standard MDS datasets containing 30/50 topics, and each topic includes ten documents with four different human-generated reference summaries. We follow Fabbri et al. [9] to truncate input articles to 500 tokens in the following way. For each example with X source input documents, we take the first $500/X$ tokens from each source document. We iteratively determine the number of tokens to take from each document until the 500 token quotas are reached. WCEP [12] dataset consists of 10,200 clusters with one human-written summary and 235 articles per cluster on average. We follow [12] to use WCEP-10, which refers to a truncated version with a maximum cluster size of 10. We truncate WCEP-10 to 500 tokens, which uses the same process as DUC-2004.

We evaluated summarization quality using Recall-Oriented Understudy for Gisting Evaluation (ROUGE) F1 [21]. We report unigram and bigram overlap (ROUGE-1 and ROUGE-2) as a means of assessing informativeness and the longest common subsequence (ROUGE-L) as a means of assessing fluency.

4.2 Baselines

We compare our model against a broad spectrum of strong baselines. They are described below.

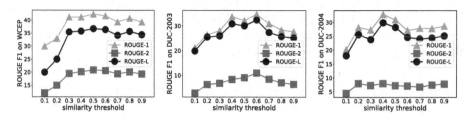

Fig. 2. Comparison of different similarity thresholds on the WCEP, DUC-2003, DUC-2004 validation set using ROUGE F1.

- **LEAD:** We concatenate the first sentence of each article in a document cluster as the system summary. For the WCEP dataset, we follow Ghalandar et al. [12] to use the lead of an individual article with the best ROUGE-1 F1 score within a document collection as the system summary.
- **TextRank:** It is an unsupervised graph-based ranking model. TextRank regards sentences in the text as nodes and uses the similarity between sentences as the weights of edges, and calculates the importance scores of sentences according to the voting mechanism.
- **BART:** BART is a pre-trained model which combines Bidirectional and Auto-Regressive Transformers. It is a denoising autoencoder built with a sequence-to-sequence model [19].
- **T5:** The basic idea underlying T5 is to treat every text processing problem as a "text-to-text" problem, taking the text as input and producing new text as output [29].
- **ProphetNet:** ProphetNet is a sequence-to-sequence pre-training model, which is based on Transformer encoder-decoder architecture. It learns to predict future n-gram at each time step to prevent overfitting on strong local correlations [27].

4.3   Experimental Setup

All models are trained on the GPU (NVIDIA 3090) for 6 epoches. Weight decay is set to 0.001. The optimizer is Adam [16] with learning rate 0.00001, $beta1 = 0.9$ and $beta2 = 0.999$. Label smoothing [33] with smoothing factor 0.1 is also used. The warmup steps are set as 2000 for WCEP, while 50 for DUC-2003 and DUC-2004. During decoding, we use beam search with beam size 5. Other model configurations are in line with the corresponding pre-trained models. We choose the base version of ProphetNet, BART, and T5 in our experiments. In the similarity calculation, we use the base version of BERT. The maximum co-occurrence window in keywords extraction is set to 6, and the damping factor d is set to 0.85.

4.4   Results

Tuning for Similarity Threshold. Figure 2 shows the broken lines of ROUGE scores at different thresholds on three datasets. The similarity threshold is taken from 0.1 to 0.9. For each threshold experiment on a dataset, we determine the final parameters based on the model's ROUGE-L score on the validation set as the evaluation criterion. Due to the different sources of documents in the three datasets, the proportion of sentences with semantic repetition is different. It can be found that the similarity threshold for our model to achieve the best performance on the three datasets is different. We set the similarity thresholds of WCEP, DUC-2003, and DUC-2004 to be 0.5, 0.4, and 0.6, respectively, in the following experiments. At smaller thresholds such as 0.1 and 0.2, the model's ROUGE scores on all datasets are significantly lower than other thresholds. This is because a too low similarity threshold removes a lot of semantically non-repetitive information contents, preventing the model from generating comprehensive summaries. As the threshold increases, the ROUGE score falls after reaching the highest, which is formally consistent with the performance of the ideal similarity calculation method.

Table 4. Evaluation results on the WCEP, DUC-2003, DUC-2004 test set.

Model	WCEP			DUC-2003			DUC-2004		
	R-1	R-2	R-L	R-1	R-2	R-L	R-1	R-2	R-L
LEAD	32.90	13.10	23.30	22.85	4.13	19.0	23.46	4.86	18.29
TextRank	34.10	13.11	25.01	24.32	3.27	18.45	25.20	4.57	19.77
T5	34.74	14.09	30.16	26.49	6.61	23.48	27.19	8.24	24.75
BART	38.30	17.83	33.93	26.32	6.70	24.30	28.74	6.68	23.04
ProphetNet	39.45	19.31	34.23	30.81	8.85	29.71	28.19	7.13	26.03
PAS+T5	35.24	15.03	30.41	27.26	6.63	23.74	29.47	5.99	29.24
PAS+BART	40.80	18.59	34.34	27.13	6.68	24.69	29.91	6.43	27.40
PAS+ProphetNet	**42.36**	**20.88**	**36.70**	**34.79**	**9.96**	**32.45**	**32.88**	**7.97**	**29.88**

Results on WCEP. Table 4 summarizes the evaluation results on WCEP, DUC-2003, and DUC-2004, respectively. Our model is named as PAS+ProphetNet where PAS is the first stage of our model. The PAS+T5 model and the PAS+BART model are named in the same way. Our model outperforms the comparative models by a large margin on all ROUGE F1 metrics, reaching 42.36, 20.88, and 36.70 on ROUGE-1, ROUGE-2, and ROUGE-L, respectively. Our model uses predicate-argument structure to reduce the lengths of documents and eliminates intra-sentence and inter-sentence redundancy. These allow our model to contain more valuable information in a much shorter document. In addition, the performances of the PAS+T5 model and PAS+BART model are also better than their origin model, which demonstrates the potential of predicate-argument structure in improving the performances of other Transformer based pre-trained models in abstractive MDS.

Results on DUC-2003 and DUC-2004. Compared with the WCEP dataset, the DUC-2003 and DUC-2004 datasets contain little training data, while the model still greatly improves ROUGE scores. This shows that our model can effectively improve abstractive MDS with a small number of training data, which benefits from both the large-scale pre-training for ProphetNet and the compression by using PAS. It can be found from Table 4 that the PAS extraction barely improves the ROUGE-2 score for PAS+T5 and PAS+BART, and even reduces it on the DUC-2004 dataset. Similar to the case of the WCEP dataset, the improvement of PAS+ProphetNet brought by PAS extraction is more significant than PAS+BART and PAS+T5. Since in addition to the traditional Seq2Seq model that optimizes one-step-ahead prediction, ProphetNet also learns n-step ahead to prevent overfitting on strong local correlations. Therefore, ProphetNet can generate better summaries from a PAS document.

Table 5. Ablation study on the WCEP, DUC-2003, DUC-2004 test set.

Model	WCEP			DUC-2003			DUC-2004		
	R-1	R-2	R-L	R-1	R-2	R-L	R-1	R-2	R-L
w/o document rank	41.89	20.26	35.93	33.87	9.24	31.91	32.05	7.21	29.66
w/o duplicate removal	39.67	19.27	34.65	33.02	9.82	30.26	31.33	7.25	29.02
w/o PAS extraction	40.28	19.21	34.87	31.33	8.25	29.02	28.19	7.13	26.03
PAS+ProphetNet	**42.36**	**20.88**	**36.70**	**34.79**	**9.96**	**32.45**	**32.88**	**7.97**	**29.88**

Ablation Study. Table 5 summarizes the results of ablation studies aiming to validate the effectiveness of individual components. The w/o document rank model doesn't rank documents in the section of PAS document generation. The w/o duplicate removal model doesn't remove duplicate contents. The w/o PAS extraction model doesn't extract PASs. The ablation study demonstrates the positive effect of removing duplicate information and ranking documents. The ablation study also shows the feasibility of our similarity calculation method in evaluating sentence similarity for MDS.

5   Related Work

Non-neural Methods. Traditional methods are mainly extractive summarization. Carbonell et al. present the Maximal Marginal Relevance (MMR) criterion to reduce redundancy, and the clear advantage is demonstrated in constructing non-redundant multi-document [6]. Radev et al. generate summaries for multi-document using cluster centroids produced by a topic detection and tracking system [28]. Erkan et al. introduce a stochastic graph-based method for computing the relative importance of textual units [8]. There are also traditional abstractive methods. Barzilay et al. present a method to automatically generate a concise summary by identifying and synthesizing similar elements across a related text from a set of multiple documents [3]. Ganesan et al. present a novel graph-based summarization framework [10]. Unlike these models, we use predicate-argument structure to compress documents and generate final summaries using a pre-trained language model.

Neural Methods. Li Wei et al. develop a neural abstractive MDS model which can leverage graph representations of documents [20]. Yang et al. propose a model that augments a previously proposed Transformer architecture with the ability to encode documents in a hierarchical manner [23]. Several two-stage summarization systems have emerged from recent work [2,35]. Lebanoff et al. and Xu et al. [17,24] follow an *extract-then-compress* architecture, which extracts some fragments of the original text first, then compresses them. Our model can be viewed as a *compress-then-rewrite* framework, which uses PAS to compress documents and employs ProphetNet to rewrite summaries.

6 Conclusion

In this paper, we explore the potential of predicate-argument structure in MDS and propose to use predicate-argument structure to improve the performance of abstractive MDS. Our model extract PAS to reduce document length and eliminate consistent information to process longer inputs. Our model preserves more global information by taking semantic argument as extraction unit, which can combine with ProphetNet's future n-gram prediction to generate comprehensive and concise summaries. We also propose an effective similarity calculation method to evaluate PAS similarity in multi-document. Experimental results show that our model outperforms several strong baselines by a wide margin and has extensive reference value for abstractive MDS based on pre-trained models.

Acknowledgements. This research was supported by Key Research Project of Zhejiang Province (2022C01145).

References

1. Aksoy, C., Bugdayci, A., Gur, T., Uysal, I., Can, F.: Semantic argument frequency-based multi-document summarization. In: 2009 24th International Symposium on Computer and Information Sciences, pp. 460–464. IEEE (2009)
2. Bae, S., Kim, T., Kim, J., Lee, S.G.: Summary level training of sentence rewriting for abstractive summarization. In: Proceedings of the 2nd Workshop on New Frontiers in Summarization, pp. 10–20 (2019)

3. Barzilay, R., McKeown, K., Elhadad, M.: Information fusion in the context of multi-document summarization. In: Proceedings of the 37th Annual Meeting of the Association for Computational Linguistics, pp. 550–557 (1999)
4. Bastianelli, E., Castellucci, G., Croce, D., Basili, R.: Textual inference and meaning representation in human robot interaction. In: Proceedings of the Joint Symposium on Semantic Processing. Textual Inference and Structures in Corpora, pp. 65–69 (2013)
5. Bonial, C., Hwang, J., Bonn, J., Conger, K., Babko-Malaya, O., Palmer, M.: English propbank annotation guidelines. Center for Computational Language and Education Research, Institute of Cognitive Science, University of Colorado at Boulder, p. 48 (2012)
6. Carbonell, J., Goldstein, J.: The use of MMR, diversity-based reranking for reordering documents and producing summaries. In: Proceedings of the 21st Annual International ACM SIGIR Conference on Research and Development in Information Retrieval, pp. 335–336 (1998)
7. Carreras, X., Màrquez, L.: Introduction to the CoNLL-2005 shared task: semantic role labeling. In: Proceedings of the Ninth Conference on Computational Natural Language Learning (CoNLL-2005), pp. 152–164 (2005)
8. Erkan, G., Radev, D.R.: LexRank: graph-based lexical centrality as salience in text summarization. J. Artif. Intell. Res. **22**, 457–479 (2004)
9. Fabbri, A.R., Li, I., She, T., Li, S., Radev, D.: Multi-news: a large-scale multi-document summarization dataset and abstractive hierarchical model. In: Proceedings of the 57th Annual Meeting of the Association for Computational Linguistics, pp. 1074–1084 (2019)
10. Ganesan, K., Zhai, C.X., Han, J.: Opinosis: a graph-based approach to abstractive summarization of highly redundant opinions. In: 23rd International Conference on Computational Linguistics, COLING 2010 (2010)
11. Gerani, S., Mehdad, Y., Carenini, G., Ng, R., Nejat, B.: Abstractive summarization of product reviews using discourse structure. In: Proceedings of the 2014 Conference on Empirical Methods in Natural Language Processing (EMNLP), pp. 1602–1613 (2014)
12. Ghalandari, D.G., Hokamp, C., Glover, J., Ifrim, G., et al.: A large-scale multi-document summarization dataset from the Wikipedia current events portal. In: Proceedings of the 58th Annual Meeting of the Association for Computational Linguistics, pp. 1302–1308 (2020)
13. He, L., Lee, K., Lewis, M., Zettlemoyer, L.: Deep semantic role labeling: what works and what's next. In: Proceedings of the 55th Annual Meeting of the Association for Computational Linguistics (Volume 1: Long Papers), pp. 473–483 (2017)
14. Kenton, J.D.M.W.C., Toutanova, L.K.: BERT: pre-training of deep bidirectional transformers for language understanding. In: Proceedings of NAACL-HLT, pp. 4171–4186 (2019)
15. Khan, A., Salim, N., Kumar, Y.J.: A framework for multi-document abstractive summarization based on semantic role labelling. Appl. Soft Comput. **30**, 737–747 (2015)
16. Kingma, D.P., Ba, J.: Adam: a method for stochastic optimization. In: ICLR (Poster) (2015)
17. Lebanoff, L., et al.: Scoring sentence singletons and pairs for abstractive summarization. In: Proceedings of the 57th Annual Meeting of the Association for Computational Linguistics, pp. 2175–2189 (2019)
18. Lebanoff, L., Song, K., Liu, F.: Adapting the neural encoder-decoder framework from single to multi-document summarization. In: EMNLP (2018)

19. Lewis, M., et al.: BART: denoising sequence-to-sequence pre-training for natural language generation, translation, and comprehension. In: Proceedings of the 58th Annual Meeting of the Association for Computational Linguistics, pp. 7871–7880 (2020)
20. Li, W., Xiao, X., Liu, J., Wu, H., Wang, H., Du, J.: Leveraging graph to improve abstractive multi-document summarization. In: Proceedings of the 58th Annual Meeting of the Association for Computational Linguistics, pp. 6232–6243 (2020)
21. Lin, C.Y.: ROUGE: a package for automatic evaluation of summaries. In: Text Summarization Branches Out, pp. 74–81 (2004)
22. Liu, P.J., et al.: Generating Wikipedia by summarizing long sequences. In: International Conference on Learning Representations (2018)
23. Liu, Y., Lapata, M.: Hierarchical transformers for multi-document summarization. In: Proceedings of the 57th Annual Meeting of the Association for Computational Linguistics, pp. 5070–5081 (2019)
24. Mendes, A., Narayan, S., Miranda, S., Marinho, Z., Martins, A.F., Cohen, S.B.: Jointly extracting and compressing documents with summary state representations. In: Proceedings of the 2019 Conference of the North American Chapter of the Association for Computational Linguistics: Human Language Technologies, Volume 1 (Long and Short Papers), pp. 3955–3966 (2019)
25. Mihalcea, R., Tarau, P.: TextRank: bringing order into text. In: Proceedings of the 2004 Conference on Empirical Methods in Natural Language Processing, pp. 404–411 (2004)
26. Over, P., Yen, J.: An introduction to DUC-2004. National Institute of Standards and Technology (2004)
27. Qi, W., et al.: ProphetNet: predicting future n-gram for sequence-to-sequencepre-training. In: Findings of the Association for Computational Linguistics: EMNLP 2020, pp. 2401–2410 (2020)
28. Radev, D.R., Jing, H., Styś, M., Tam, D.: Centroid-based summarization of multiple documents. Inf. Process. Manag. **40**(6), 919–938 (2004)
29. Raffel, C., et al.: Exploring the limits of transfer learning with a unified text-to-text transformer. J. Mach. Learn. Res. **21**, 1–67 (2020)
30. See, A., Liu, P.J., Manning, C.D.: Get to the point: summarization with pointer-generator networks. In: Proceedings of the 55th Annual Meeting of the Association for Computational Linguistics (Volume 1: Long Papers), pp. 1073–1083 (2017)
31. Shen, D., Lapata, M.: Using semantic roles to improve question answering. In: Proceedings of the 2007 Joint Conference on Empirical Methods in Natural Language Processing and Computational Natural Language Learning (EMNLP-CoNLL), pp. 12–21 (2007)
32. Shi, P., Lin, J.: Simple BERT models for relation extraction and semantic role labeling. arXiv preprint arXiv:1904.05255 (2019)
33. Szegedy, C., Vanhoucke, V., Ioffe, S., Shlens, J., Wojna, Z.: Rethinking the inception architecture for computer vision. In: Proceedings of the IEEE Conference on Computer Vision and Pattern Recognition, pp. 2818–2826 (2016)
34. Wu, D., Fung, P.: Semantic roles for SMT: a hybrid two-pass model. In: Proceedings of Human Language Technologies: The 2009 Annual Conference of the North American Chapter of the Association for Computational Linguistics, Companion Volume: Short Papers, pp. 13–16 (2009)
35. Zhang, H., Cai, J., Xu, J., Wang, J.: Pretraining-based natural language generation for text summarization. In: Proceedings of the 23rd Conference on Computational Natural Language Learning (CoNLL), pp. 789–797 (2019)

36. Zhang, J., Zhao, Y., Saleh, M., Liu, P.: PEGASUS: pre-training with extracted gap-sentences for abstractive summarization. In: International Conference on Machine Learning, pp. 11328–11339. PMLR (2020)
37. Zhong, M., Liu, P., Chen, Y., Wang, D., Qiu, X., Huang, X.: Extractive summarization as text matching. In: ACL (2020)

A Structure-Aware Method
for Cross-domain Text Classification

Yuhong Zhang[1,2], Lin Qian[1,2], Qi Zhang[1,2], Peipei Li[1,2(✉)], and Guocheng Liu[3]

[1] School of Computer and Information Engineering, HeFei University of Technology,
Hefei, China
{zhangyh,peipeili}@hfut.ed.cn, {2020171174,zhangq}@mail.hfut.edu.cn
[2] Key Laboratory of Knowledge Engineering with Big Data,
Hefei University of Technology, Ministry of Education, Hefei 230601, China
[3] Anhui Mobile Communication Co., Ltd., Hefei 230031, China
liuguocheng@ah.chinamobile.com

Abstract. Cross-domain text classification utilizes the labeled source domain to train a well-performing classifier for the unlabeled target domain. It is an important task in natural language processing. Owing to the outstanding performance for representations learning, deep learning models are introduced into cross-domain classification to learn domain invariant representations. However, existing methods assume that features in text are independent, ignoring the correlation between features. To this end, we propose a structure-aware method for cross-domain text classification, which uses both the feature semantics and the structure among features to learn the invariant representations. Firstly, a knowledge graph is introduced as an additional resource to capture the structure among features, and the text in both domains is mapped into two sub-graphs. Then, the invariant structure representations between two sub-graphs are learned based on Graph Attention Network (GAT) and correlation alignment. Lastly, the invariant structure representations and the invariant feature representations are combined together to learn higher-level invariant representations for cross-domain classification. Extensive experiments demonstrate that our method achieves better classification accuracy compared with state-of-the-art methods.

Keywords: Cross-domain · Text classification · Knowledge graph

1 Introduction

Cross-domain text classification [12] is one of the important tasks in natural language processing. It aims to train a classifier for the unlabeled target domain with the labeled source domain, where the source and target domain follow different but similar distributions. The cross-domain text classification has been widely concerned in applications.

Supported by the National Natural Science Foundation of China under grant 61976077 and the Natural Science Foundation of Anhui Province under grant 2208085MF170.

© The Author(s), under exclusive license to Springer Nature Switzerland AG 2022
S. Khanna et al. (Eds.): PRICAI 2022, LNCS 13630, pp. 283–296, 2022.
https://doi.org/10.1007/978-3-031-20865-2_21

The recent advances in cross-domain text classification reveal that deep learning models can learn more transferable representations. Existing methods can be divided into two categories. One is with feature independence assumption, and the other is with graphs. The former methods learn the invariant representations with bags-of-word (BOW) or word embedding, where the features are independent. And deep neural networks with distance metrics, such as MMD [18], COARL [16], or Generative Adversarial Network (GAN) [9] are used to learn domain-invariant representations. These methods have achieved good performance on text classification. However, these methods have some limitations, as shown in case 1 of Fig. 1. There exist semantic gaps between features for methods with BOW representations. Although word embedding can measure the semantic similarity between features, it is not easy to explicitly express the structure relations among features. The latter methods have begun to focus on the structure relations among features for cross-domain text classification, as shown in case 2 of Fig. 1. Its main idea is to construct a homogeneous graph based on word co-occurrence [22] and word similarity [21], and then some models for graph representations, such as Graph Convolutional Networks (GCN) [27], GAT [19], are used to address cross-domain classification [25]. These methods only represent the correlation among features with the homogeneous similar or co-occurrence relations. However, the correlation of features is varied in application. As shown in case 3 of Fig. 1, $Kobe$ and USA are connected by $nationality-of$, while $Kobe$ and $Lakers$ are connected by $play-for$, where $nationality-of$ and $play-for$ are two relations with different semantics. This kind of graph structure containing different types of nodes and rich relations is also called the Heterogeneous Information Network (HIN) [15]. Obviously, the heterogeneous relations included in HIN are beneficial to the learning of semantic representations of text, thereby improving the performance of cross-domain classification.

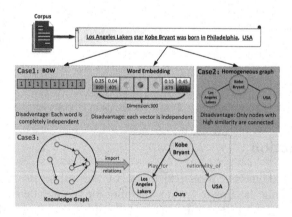

Fig. 1. The illustration for our motivation. Case 1 shows the limitation of methods with feature independence assumption, case 2 show the limitation of methods with homogeneous graph, and case 3 shows our method with heterogeneous graph.

To this end, we introduce the knowledge graph (KG) as external information to capture the heterogeneous relations and propose a structure-aware method for cross-domain text classification. Specifically, two sub-graphs of source and target are obtained from the external KG, and two embedding spaces are learned with GAT. Then, the invariant structure representations of the two sub-graphs are solved based on covariance alignment. Lastly, the invariant structure representations and the invariant feature representations are further fused to address cross-domain classification. Our contributions are summarized as follows:

- With the help of knowledge graph, two heterogeneous sub-graphs are constructed to learn the invariant structure representations. Compared with existing methods with graphs, our heterogeneous graphs contain rich semantic structure information, which benefits cross-domain text classification.
- Existing methods learn the invariant representations in view of either features or structure, while our method combines features and structure together, and both structure-invariant and feature-invariant representations are used for cross-domain classification.

2 Related Works

Domain adaptation methods based on deep models have become the mainstream, and these methods can be divided into the following two categories.

2.1 Cross-domain Text Classification with Independence Assumption

Most of the cross-domain text classification methods use BOW or word embedding as the representations of features with the independence assumption. These models are mainly divided into two sub-categories: discrepancy-based [10,11,16,18] and adversarial-based [6,17,24]. The former methods learn the invariant representations by minimizing the distance between two domains. DDC [18] uses MMD as the measure for distance to reduce the discrepancy. DAN [10] proposes MK-MMD to measure the distance. In addition, to minimize the marginal distribution difference, JAN [11] proposes the joint MMD, which combines the marginal and conditional distribution. In addition, Deep Coral [16] is proposed to align the features of two domains by using the second-order statistic covariance. And the latter methods have attracted extensive attention due to their excellent performance. The generator generates features to confuse the discriminator while the discriminator distinguishes which domain the features come from. RevGrad [6] incorporates the adversarial learning into domain adaptation for the first time, which extracts domain-invariant features in an adversarial way. DM-ADA [24] guarantees domain-invariance in a more continuous latent space and guides the domain discriminator in judging samples' difference relative to source and target domains. DADA [17] encourages a mutually inhibitory relation between category and domain predictions for any input instance.

2.2   Cross-domain Text Classification Methods with Graphs

In applications, the feature independence assumption does not usually hold, and there do exist correlations among features. Thus, some studies have begun to focus on graph-based methods. Most methods construct the graph based on the similarity between features and then use the graph neural network (GNN) to learn the representations of graph. DAGNN [22] constructs a graph for each document to be classified according to word similarity, then uses GCN to learn the representations of graph, and finally, the adversarial network is used to learn the invariant representations for cross-domain classification. CLHG [21] constructs the document graph and word graph, respectively, according to the semantic relevance, and then uses Hetero-GCN to aggregate two-hop neighbors. There are only a few studies focusing on the heterogeneous graph. Kingdom [8] enriches the semantic information of original documents by obtaining domain aggregation subgraphs containing source and target domains from the ConceptNet. However, Kingdom only aggregates the features connected by the same relation, ignoring the influence of relational representations on domain alignment.

3   Preliminary Knowledge

Many excellent GNN models, such as GCN, GAT, have been proposed to represent graphs with low-dimensional vectors, in which more similar nodes will be closer. Regarding that the neighbors and relations are similar in semantics to the central nodes, GCN and GAT represent the nodes with rich semantics by aggregating their neighbors or relations of nodes. GCN makes the node's embedding representations retain its structural information by aggregating the node's k-hop neighbors, And in the aggregation, the propagation rules from the i-th hop to the $(i+1)$-th hop are as follows:

$$\boldsymbol{X}^{(l+1)} = \text{ReLU}(\tilde{D}^{-\frac{1}{2}}\tilde{A}\tilde{D}^{-\frac{1}{2}}\boldsymbol{X}^{(l)}) \tag{1}$$

where $\tilde{A} = A + I$, A is the adjacency matrix of KG, I is an identity matrix, $\tilde{D}$ is the diagonal matrix of $\tilde{A}$, X is a vector matrix of nodes in the graph.

To reduce the influence of noise accumulated by layers, RDGCN [23] further uses a two-layer highway network to balance node and its neighbors, adjusts the weight of neighbors at the highway network layer. The final node representations are obtained through the weighted summation of nodes and neighbors.

$$T\left(X^{(l)}\right) = \sigma\left(X^{(l)}W^{(l)} + b^{(l)}\right) \tag{2}$$

$$X^{(l+1)} = T\left(X^{(l)}\right) \cdot X^{(l+1)} + \left(1 - T\left(X^{(l)}\right)\right) \cdot X^{(l)} \tag{3}$$

4   Our Method

4.1   Problem Definition

Given a labeled source domain $X^S = \left\{ \left(x_i^S, y_i^S \right) \right\}_{i=1}^{n_s}$, an unlabeled target domain $X^T = \left\{ \left(x_j^T \right) \right\}_{j=1}^{n_t}$, and an external knowledge graph $KG = (E, R)$, the feature spaces of source and target domains can be denoted as W^S and W^T, n_s and n_t are the number of features in two domains respectively, our task is to train a classifier for target domain with the labeled source domain and external KG.

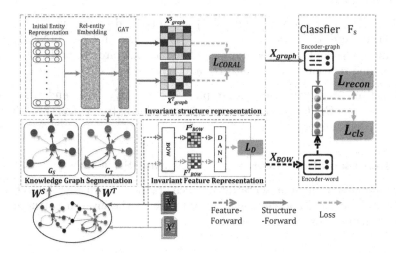

Fig. 2. The Framework of our method. The blue nodes and green nodes represent the feature nodes in source data and target data respectively. The orange lines and black lines represent the structural and semantics representations. The blue dotted line represents the loss, the solid line represents structure forward, dotted lines in other colors represent feature forward. (Color figure online)

Figure 2 shows the framework of our proposed method, which consists of four parts. (1) Representations learning for invariant features. With BOW features, the adversarial methods are used to learn inter-domain invariant feature representations X_{BOW}. In this paper, DANN [7] with the adversarial loss $\mathcal{L}_D$ is used to learn the feature invariant representations. Thus it will not be described in detail later. (2) The construction of heterogeneous graphs. According to the features in two domains, two subgraphs G_S and G_T are constructed from the external KG, where the features are treated as nodes. (3) Representations learning for invariant structure. GAT is used to learn the embedding for two graphs X_{graph}^S and X_{graph}^T, respectively, and the invariant structure representations of the two subgraphs are solved by covariance alignment. (4) Classifier training with features and structure. Both feature and structure invariant representations are used to train cross-domain classifiers.

4.2   The Construction of Heterogeneous Graphs

In this paper, ConceptNet [15] is introduced as an external resource to describe the heterogeneous correlations among textual features. With the textual features from the source domain as nodes, their 1-hop neighbors and relations are also divided from ConceptNet to construct the source heterogeneous graph. In a similar way, the target graph is constructed. As for a triple in the heterogeneous graph, $(novacor, IsA, controlled-vocabulary-types)$, $novacor$ and $controlled-vocabulary-types$ are two features from text, IsA is the corresponding relation coming from knowledge graph. The process of heterogeneous graph division is shown as follows:

(1) $G_S = \{E_S, R_S\}$ and $G_T = \{E_T, R_T\}$ are initialized to empty;
(2) Each feature $w_i^S \in W^S$ or $w_j^T \in W^T$ is searched in ConceptNet, and the found nodes and their one-hop neighbors are put into E_S or E_T, the corresponding relations are put into R_S and R_T.

Based on this, the source graph $G_S = \{E_S, R_S\}$ and the target graph $G_T = \{E_T, R_T\}$ can be obtained, in which, $(w_i^S \in E_S, r_h^S \in R_S)$ and $(w_j^T \in E_T, r_h^T \in R_T)$.

4.3   Representations Learning for Invariant Structure

In this subsection, the representations of each graph are learned with GAT firstly, and then the correlation alignment is used to learn the invariant structure representations for cross-domain classification.

The Representations for Each Graph. GCN is a popular model for graph representations. In this paper, we initialize the vectors of the graph with glove [14] and then use GCN to learn the representations, as other methods do [28]. The vectors of nodes can be represented $w^S = \{w_1^S, w_2^S, w_3^S, \dots, w_{n_s}^S \mid w_i^S \in R^{d_e}\}$, in which, d_e is the dimension of the feature vectors, w_i^S denote the embedding of feature nodes in source network.

Since there are heterogeneous relations in our graphs, we try to optimize the representations of graphs with these heterogeneous relations to enrich the semantic representations. Generally speaking, the types of relations are much smaller than that of nodes, and it is difficult to effectively improve the node representations based on GAT only aggregating the relations. Thus, we propose to enrich the representations by aggregating the triple $(w_i^S \| r_h^S \| w_k^S)$ as a unit, instead of aggregating the independent features $(w_i^S$ and $w_k^S)$ and their relation (r_h^S), in which, w_i^S is the vector of nodes in source network and w_k^S is the vector for one of the neighbors of w_i^S. Therefore, given a relation r_h^S, the attention of its corresponding triple $(w_i^S \| r_h^S \| w_k^S)$ to the feature w_i^S is calculated as follows:

$$\alpha_{ihk}^t = \frac{\exp\left(\boldsymbol{\alpha}^T \left[\, w_i^S \,\|\, r_h^S \,\|\, w_k^S \,\right]\right)}{\sum\limits_{w_{k'} \in N_i} \sum\limits_{r_{h'}^S \in R_{w_i^S w_{k'}^S}^S} \exp\left(\boldsymbol{\alpha}^T \left[w_i^S \,\|\, r_{h'}^S \,\|\, w_{k'}^S \right]\right)} \tag{4}$$

where N_i is the neighbor set of node w_i^S, $R_{w_i^S w_{k'}^S}^S$ is the set of all relationships between node w_i^S and its neighbor $w_{k'}^S$, k' is the index for set.

By aggregating the triples with attentions, the representations of the feature nodes can be expressed as following.

$$w_{i-rel}^S = \text{ReLU} \left(\sum_{w_k \in N_i} \sum_{r_h^S \in R_{w_i^S w_k^S}^S} \alpha_{ihk}^S \left[w_i^S \| r_h^S \| w_k^S \right] \right) \tag{5}$$

where $\|$ is the concatenation operation. N_i is the neighbor set of the w_i^S, $R_{w_i^S w_{k'}^S}^S$ is the set of all relationships.

In the aggregating of neighborhoods, we adopt one-layer graph attention to ensure that the dimension of the embedded representations are controllable, owing to that stacking multiple-layer relation will lead to the explosion of physical dimensions. The calculation process is as follows:

$$\alpha_{ik}^S = \frac{\exp \left(\text{LeakyRELU} \left(\alpha^T w_{i-rel}^S + \beta^T w_{k-rel}^S \right) \right)}{\sum\limits_{k'-rel \in N_i} \exp \left(\text{LeakyRELU} \left(\alpha^T w_{i-rel}^S + \beta^T w_{k'-rel}^S \right) \right)} \tag{6}$$

$$x_{\text{graph}}^S = \left[\left(w_{i-rel}^S \otimes c \right) \oplus \left(\left(\sum_{k \in N_i} \alpha_{ik}^S w_{i-rel}^S \right) \otimes (1-c) \right) \right] \tag{7}$$

where α and β are learnable parameter vectors. $\oplus$ means the addition of vectors, $\otimes$ means the multiplication of vectors, the trad-off parameter $c = 0.5$.

Finally, we get source graph feature representations X_{graph}^S after graph embedding. Similarly, we can get target graph feature representations X_{graph}^T.

The Learning for Invariant Structure Representations. To address cross-domain classification, the invariant representations need to be learned. In this paper, the correlation alignment [16] is used to match the second-order statistics represented in two graphs. The correlation loss is defined as the difference of structure feature representations between two graphs.

$$\mathcal{L}_{CORAL} = \frac{1}{4d^2} \| C_S - C_T \|_F^2 \tag{8}$$

where d is the feature dimension, $\| \cdot \|_F^2$ represents the square matrix of the Frobenius norm, C_S and C_T are the covariance matrix of source KG and target KG respectively, and they are computed as follows.

$$C_S = \frac{1}{N_S - 1} \left(\left(X_{graph}^S \right)^T X_{graph}^S - \frac{1}{N_S} \left(1^T X_{graph}^S \right)^T \left(1^T X_{graph}^S \right) \right) \tag{9}$$

$$C_T = \frac{1}{N_T - 1} \left(\left(X_{graph}^T \right)^T X_{graph}^T - \frac{1}{N_T} \left(1^T X_{graph}^T \right)^T \left(1^T X_{graph}^T \right) \right) \tag{10}$$

where N_S, N_T are the sizes of the two graphs respectively, and 1 denotes an all-one column vector.

4.4 Classifier Training with Features and Structure

Both the learned invariant structure representations X_{graph} and the feature invariant representations X_{BOW} are used together to train the classifier. Two encoders are designed to combine the invariant structure representations and feature invariant representations to obtain higher invariant representations, which are used as the input to train the classifier.

The reconstruction loss of the encoder is added to minimize the domain invariance, and it is shown as follows:

$$\mathcal{L}_{recon}\left(X_{graph}\right) = -\mathbb{E}_{X_{graph}}\left(\left\|D_{recon}\left(X_{graph}\right) - X_{graph}\right\|_2^2\right) \qquad (11)$$

And the cross entropy is used as loss function to train the classifier.

$$\mathcal{L}_{\text{cls}} = \frac{1}{n_s}\sum_{i=1}^{n_s}L\left(F_s\left[E_{word}\left(X_{BOW}^S\right)\|E_{graph}\left(X_{graph}^S\right)\right]\right) \qquad (12)$$

where L is the cross-entropy loss, F_s is the classifier, E_{graph} is the graph feature encoder, and E_{word} is the bag-of-words feature encoder.

In summary, the overall objective function and the optimization are shown respectively as following:

$$\mathcal{L}\left(\theta_{cls},\theta_{recon},\theta_{CORAL},\theta_D\right) = \mathcal{L}_{cls} + \mathcal{L}_{recon} + \mathcal{L}_{CORAL} + \mathcal{L}_D \qquad (13)$$

$$\left(\hat{\theta}_{cls},\hat{\theta}_{recon},\hat{\theta}_{CORAL},\hat{\theta}_D\right) = \underset{\theta_{cls},\theta_{recon},\theta_{CoRAL}}{\arg\min}\ \underset{\theta_D}{\max}\,\mathcal{L}\left(\theta_{cls},\theta_{recon},\theta_{CORAL},\theta_D\right) \qquad (14)$$

5 Experiment

5.1 Setup

Datasets. Two popular datasets are used in this paper to validate the effectiveness of our method. **Amazon review** [3] consists of four domains, including Books(B), DVDs(D), Electronics(E), and kitchens(K), and 12 cross-domain tasks can be constructed. Each domain contains 2k labeled training samples and 3k-6k samples for testing. With TF-IDF, the top-5000 features are selected for each domain. **SemEval Corpora** [2] is provided by the organizer of SemEval2013, which we call S13. These tweets contain positive, negative, and neutral sentiments. In order to address the cross-domain classification from Semeval to Amazon, we also remove the neutral tweets as Barnes et al. (2018) [2] did. For the comparative experiments on SemEval Corpora, we use the source code provided by the author.

Baselines. Three categories of baselines are compared in this paper. 1) Methods based on independent assumption include three adversarial-based methods and four discrepancy-based methods. The former includes DANN [7], MADAOT [5], F-domain [1], and the latter includes CMD [26], CoCMD [13], DDC [18] and Deep coral [16]. 2) Methods based on homogeneous graph include DAGNN [22] and GAC [20]. Owing to that the source codes are unavailable, we reproduce the methods proposed in the original papers. Specially, we simulate the edges of graphs with the relations from KG, ignoring the type difference of edges, and the subsequent processing is the same as the original paper. At the same time, in order to apply the single-domain method GAC to cross-domain, we put the features processed by GAC into DANN for domain adaptation. 3) Methods based on the heterogeneous graph include KINGDOM [8] and our method.

Table 1. Performance (accuracy %) on Amazon datasets. * is a semi-supervised method. c means the results are from their original paper, and r means the results are gotten by re-implemented codes.

Tasks	B->D	B->E	B->K	D->B	D->E	D->K	E->B	E->D	E->K	K->B	K->D	K-E	AVG
CMD^c [26]	80.50	78.70	81.30	79.50	79.70	83.00	74.40	76.30	86.00	75.60	77.50	85.40	79.80
CoCMD^{c*} [13]	83.10	**83.00**	**85.30**	81.80	**83.40**	**85.50**	76.90	78.30	87.30	77.20	79.60	87.20	82.40
DANN^c [7]	78.40	73.30	77.90	72.30	75.40	78.30	71.30	73.80	85.40	70.90	74.00	84.30	76.30
MADAOT^c [5]	82.40	75.00	80.40	80.90	73.50	81.50	77.20	78.10	88.10	75.60	75.90	87.10	79.60
F-DAL^c [1]	**84.00**	80.90	81.40	80.60	81.80	83.9	76.70	78.30	87.90	76.50	79.50	87.5	81.60
DAGNN^r [22]	82.05	80.95	84.22	81.16	80.80	84.05	75.55	77.86	88.36	76.90	79.39	87.10	81.54
GAC^r [20]	82.07	80.85	84.10	81.16	81.12	84.36	75.80	78.00	88.19	77.07	80.93	87.20	81.73
KINGDOM^c [8]	83.10	82.20	85.00	81.40	81.70	84.6	76.90	78.80	88.40	78.20	80.70	87.40	82.30
Ours	83.38	82.64	85.28	**81.97**	83.00	85.28	**78.03**	**80.26**	**88.71**	**78.97**	**82.00**	**87.80**	**83.10**

5.2   Results and Analysis

Table 2. Performance (accuracy %) on Semeval datasets. s means the results are from their shared codes, and r means the results are gotten by re-implemented codes.

Tasks	S13->B	S13->E	S13->D	S13->K	AVG
DDC^s [18]	50.82	50.52	50.39	50.45	50.54
Deep Coral^s [16]	50.84	50.39	51.00	50.53	50.69
DANN^s [7]	50.77	52.35	51.09	50.31	51.13
DAGNN^r [22]	53.59	52.12	50.70	50.34	51.68
GAC^r [20]	52.95	52.30	50.75	51.64	51.91
KINGDOM^s [8]	53.75	53.18	50.73	52.09	52.43
Ours	**53.91**	**54.59**	**51.31**	**54.33**	**53.53**

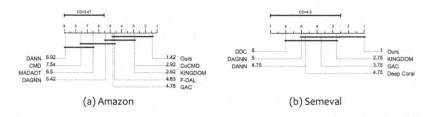

(a) Amazon   (b) Semeval

Fig. 3. Comparison of ours and baselines with the Nemenyi test

The Overall Classification Performance. We compare our model with baselines on two datasets, as shown in Tables 1 and 2. Owing to the unavailability of source codes and the difference of datasets, the baselines in Tables 1 and 2 are different. Some baselines, including CMD, CoCMD, MADAOT and F-DAL, are not compared in Table 2, and baselines including DDC, Deep Coral are not compared in Table 1. Some observations can be gotten. 1) Compared with the methods with independence assumption, the methods with graphs perform better on average. This shows that the introduction of structure representations between features can rich the semantics of features and benefit the classification. 2) Compared with homogeneous graph methods, including DAGNN and GAC, heterogeneous graph-based methods, including KINGDOM and Ours, generally outperform. It indicates that the heterogeneous relations among features can enrich the semantic representations of features and benefit the cross-domain classification. 3) As for the two methods with heterogeneous graphs, our method performs significantly better. It indicates that combining both the structure and feature representations is better than using only the invariant feature representations for cross-domain classification. 4) It is worthy to note that the performance of five tasks in Table 1 is not the best. Firstly, CoCMD is a semi-supervised method, while our method does not use the semi-supervised learning. Compared with CMD, which is the variant of CoCMD ignoring the semi-supervised learning, our method perform best in 11 tasks. In addition, the improvement of our method on some tasks (such as K-D) is more obvious than other tasks (such as B-K). It is because that there are some features that do not exist in graph, which makes the number of nodes in subgraphs for B domain and K domain small.

Statistical Test. To validate whether the improvement of our method is significant, we perform Nemenyi test [4], which is widely used to statistically compare different algorithms. The critical difference (CD) diagram of the Nemenyi test is plotted in Fig. 3 (a) and (b), where the average rank of each baseline is marked along the axis (lower ranks to the right). It can be seen from Fig. 3 that our model performs best on both datasets. We notice that ours performs significantly better than baselines on Amazon datasets.

5.3 Ablation Experiment

In this subsection, we design several variants of our method to validate the contribution of each step in our method, as shown in Tables 3 and 4. Only-BOW ignores the graph structure representations and only trains classifier with BOW features. Only-HoG ignores the BOW and replaces the heterogeneous relations in ConceptNet with the homogeneous relations. Only-HeG means ignoring BOW and only using the heterogeneous graph to train classifier. BOW+HoG means that both BOW and the homogeneous graph are considered. Bow+HeG means that only relations, not the corresponding triples, are aggregated in the representations of heterogeneous graph.

The experimental results show that the performance of each variant decreases, which shows the effectiveness of each component in our method. 1) The combination of BOW and graph representations are more effective than single representations. Compared with Only-BOW, the performances of the BOW+HoG and BOW+HeG improves by 1.0% and 1.4% on average. It indicates that the introduction of the relation among features is effective. Compared with Only-HoG and Only-HeG, BOW+HoG and Bow+HeG improve the performance by 28% and 2.3% on two datasets. It indicates that traditional BOW are also useful for cross-domain classification. 2) Heterogeneous graph is more effective than homogeneous graph. Only-HeG achieves higher performance by 1.1% than the Only-HoG. And Our performance achieves 1% higher than Bow+HoG on average. It shows that heterogeneous relations contain richer semantic information and are more conducive to cross-domain classification. 3) Aggregating the triples is better than aggregating the independent neighbors and relations in the representations of the heterogeneous graph. Compared with BOW+HeG, the performance of our method improves by 0.4% and 0.7% respectively, which shows that our aggregation of triples can learn richer semantics and benefit the classification. 4) It can be noted that BOW contributes more than the graph for cross-domain adaptation. Compared with our method, Only-BOW decreases by 3%, while Only-HeG and Only-HoG both decrease about 28% on Amazon. But it does not work on Semeval. This is mainly because some features in Amazon do not occur in the ConceptNet. It leads to that the number of nodes in the source and target graph is much smaller than the number of features. Then the heterogeneous graph is sparse, which may lead to the performance difference between the two datasets.

Table 3. Performance (accuracy %) on Amazon datasets.

Methods	B->D	B->E	B->K	D->B	D->E	D->K	E->B	E->D	E->K	K->B	K->D	K-E	AVG
Only-Bow	82.60	79.90	81.80	80.30	79.90	83.00	74.90	78.60	88.60	75.90	79.20	86.90	80.90
Only-HoG	52.09	51.84	54.57	52.34	51.06	54.03	50.87	50.81	54.55	51.04	51.73	56.82	52.64
Only-HeG	53.35	58.83	56.84	51.76	52.77	50.55	53.21	53.54	53.37	52.30	51.59	56.29	53.70
Bow+HoG	82.93	81.94	84.24	81.52	81.98	84.81	77.78	79.00	88.43	78.01	81.09	87.19	82.40
Bow+HeG	83.32	81.99	84.88	81.61	82.01	85.08	78.01	79.81	88.61	78.30	81.32	87.47	82.70
Ours (Bow+HeG-Tri)	**83.38**	**82.64**	**85.28**	**81.97**	**83.00**	**85.28**	**78.03**	**80.26**	**88.71**	**78.97**	**82.00**	**87.80**	**83.10**

Table 4. Performance (accuracy %) on Semeval datasets.

Methods	S13->B	S13->E	S13->D	S13->K	AVG
Only-Bow	53.26	52.91	50.47	50.68	51.83
Only-HoG	50.54	50.29	50.19	49.79	50.20
Only-HeG	50.97	50.29	50.5	50.31	50.51
Bow+HoG	53.30	52.83	50.73	52.62	52.37
Bow+HeG	53.82	54.22	50.67	52.65	52.84
Ours (Bow+HeG-Tri)	**53.91**	**54.59**	**51.31**	**54.33**	**53.53**

5.4 Parameter Discussion

Figure 4 shows the performance changing with different neighbor scopes including one-hop, two hops and three hops. We can see that the performance of one-hop and three-hop both drop by 1% and 1.5%. This shows that two-hops neighbors can enrich the semantic of nodes by aggregating their similar neighbors, while one-hop ignores these similar information, three-hops will cover more noise, although it may cover similar information.

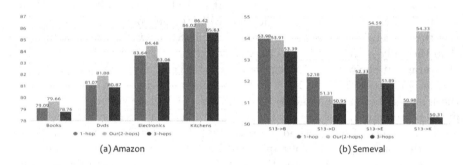

(a) Amazon   (b) Semeval

Fig. 4. the performance changing with different neighbor scopes on two datasets

6   Conclusions

In this paper, we explore the role of heterogeneous relations among features for cross-domain classification and propose a structure-aware method for cross-domain text classification. A KG is introduced to obtain the relations among features. With heterogeneous relations, the structure invariant representations are learned, which is combined with the feature representations together to train the cross-domain classifier. Extensive experiments show that the effectiveness of our method. In addition, the mis-matching between features and graphs is one of the limitations for our method, which is our focus in the near future.

Acknowledgement. This work is supported by the National Natural Science Foundation of China under grants (62076087, 61976077), and Anhui Provincial Natural Science Foundation under grants (2208085MF170).

References

1. Acuna, D., Zhang, G., Law, M.T., Fidler, S.: f-domain adversarial learning: theory and algorithms. In: Proceedings of the 38th International Conference on Machine Learning, ICML. Proceedings of Machine Learning Research, vol. 139, pp. 66–75 (2021)
2. Barnes, J., Klinger, R., im Walde, S.S.: Projecting embeddings for domain adaption: joint modeling of sentiment analysis in diverse domains. In: Proceedings of the 27th International Conference on Computational Linguistics, COLING, pp. 818–830 (2018)
3. Blitzer, J., Dredze, M., Pereira, F.: Biographies, bollywood, boom-boxes and blenders: domain adaptation for sentiment classification. In: Proceedings of the 45th Annual Meeting of the Association for Computational Linguistics. ACL (2007)
4. Demsar, J.: Statistical comparisons of classifiers over multiple data sets. J. Mach. Learn. Res. **7**, 1–30 (2006)
5. Dhouib, S., Redko, I., Lartizien, C.: Margin-aware adversarial domain adaptation with optimal transport. In: Proceedings of the 37th International Conference on Machine Learning, ICML. Proceedings of Machine Learning Research, vol. 119, pp. 2514–2524 (2020)
6. Ganin, Y., Lempitsky, V.S.: Unsupervised domain adaptation by backpropagation. In: Proceedings of the 32nd International Conference on Machine Learning, ICML. JMLR Workshop and Conference Proceedings, vol. 37, pp. 1180–1189 (2015)
7. Ganin, Y., et al.: Domain-adversarial training of neural networks. J. Mach. Learn. Res. **17**, 59:1–59:35 (2016)
8. Ghosal, D., Hazarika, D., Roy, A., Majumder, N., Mihalcea, R., Poria, S.: Kingdom: knowledge-guided domain adaptation for sentiment analysis. In: Proceedings of the 58th Annual Meeting of the Association for Computational Linguistics, pp. 3198–3210. ACL (2020)
9. Goodfellow, I., et al.: Generative adversarial nets. In: Advances in Neural Information Processing Systems, vol. 27 (2014)
10. Long, M., Cao, Y., Wang, J., Jordan, M.I.: Learning transferable features with deep adaptation networks. In: Proceedings of the 32nd International Conference on Machine Learning, ICML. JMLR Workshop and Conference Proceedings, vol. 37, pp. 97–105 (2015)
11. Long, M., Zhu, H., Wang, J., Jordan, M.I.: Deep transfer learning with joint adaptation networks. In: Proceedings of the 34th International Conference on Machine Learning, ICML. Proceedings of Machine Learning Research, vol. 70, pp. 2208–2217 (2017)
12. Pan, S.J., Yang, Q.: A survey on transfer learning. IEEE Trans. Knowl. Data Eng. **22**(10), 1345–1359 (2010)
13. Peng, M., Zhang, Q., Jiang, Y., Huang, X.: Cross-domain sentiment classification with target domain specific information. In: Proceedings of the 56th Annual Meeting of the Association for Computational Linguistics, pp. 2505–2513. ACL (2018)
14. Pennington, J., Socher, R., Manning, C.D.: GloVe: global vectors for word representation. In: Proceedings of the 2014 Conference on Empirical Methods in Natural Language Processing, EMNLP, pp. 1532–1543 (2014)
15. Speer, R., Chin, J., Havasi, C.: ConceptNet 5.5: an open multilingual graph of general knowledge. In: Proceedings of the Thirty-First AAAI Conference on Artificial Intelligence, pp. 4444–4451 (2017)

16. Sun, B., Saenko, K.: Deep CORAL: correlation alignment for deep domain adaptation. In: Hua, G., Jégou, H. (eds.) ECCV 2016. LNCS, vol. 9915, pp. 443–450. Springer, Cham (2016). https://doi.org/10.1007/978-3-319-49409-8_35
17. Tang, H., Jia, K.: Discriminative adversarial domain adaptation. In: The Thirty-Fourth AAAI Conference on Artificial Intelligence, AAAI, pp. 5940–5947 (2020)
18. Tzeng, E., Hoffman, J., Zhang, N., Saenko, K., Darrell, T.: Deep domain confusion: maximizing for domain invariance. CoRR abs/1412.3474 (2014)
19. Velickovic, P., Cucurull, G., Casanova, A., Romero, A., Lio, P., Bengio, Y.: Graph attention networks. Stat **1050**, 20 (2017)
20. Wang, L., Huang, Y., Hou, Y., Zhang, S., Shan, J.: Graph attention convolution for point cloud semantic segmentation. In: IEEE Conference on Computer Vision and Pattern Recognition, CVPR, pp. 10296–10305 (2019)
21. Wang, Z., Liu, X., Yang, P., Liu, S., Wang, Z.: Cross-lingual text classification with heterogeneous graph neural network. In: Proceedings of the 59th Annual Meeting of the Association for Computational Linguistics and the 11th International Joint Conference on Natural Language Processing, ACL/IJCNLP, pp. 612–620 (2021)
22. Wu, M., Pan, S., Zhu, X., Zhou, C., Pan, L.: Domain-adversarial graph neural networks for text classification. In: 2019 IEEE International Conference on Data Mining, ICDM, pp. 648–657 (2019)
23. Wu, Y., Liu, X., Feng, Y., Wang, Z., Yan, R., Zhao, D.: Relation-aware entity alignment for heterogeneous knowledge graphs. In: Proceedings of the Twenty-Eighth International Joint Conference on Artificial Intelligence, IJCAI, pp. 5278–5284 (2019)
24. Xu, M., et al.: Adversarial domain adaptation with domain mixup. In: The Thirty-Fourth AAAI Conference on Artificial Intelligence, AAAI. pp. 6502–6509 (2020)
25. Yao, L., Mao, C., Luo, Y.: Graph convolutional networks for text classification. In: The Thirty-Third AAAI Conference on Artificial Intelligence, AAAI, pp. 7370–7377 (2019)
26. Zellinger, W., Grubinger, T., Lughofer, E., Natschläger, T., Saminger-Platz, S.: Central moment discrepancy (CMD) for domain-invariant representation learning. In: 5th International Conference on Learning Representations, ICLR (2017)
27. Zhang, Y., Qi, P., Manning, C.D.: Graph convolution over pruned dependency trees improves relation extraction. In: Proceedings of the 2018 Conference on Empirical Methods in Natural Language Processing, pp. 2205–2215 (2018)
28. Zhu, R., Ma, M., Wang, P.: RAGA: relation-aware graph attention networks for global entity alignment. In: Karlapalem, K., et al. (eds.) PAKDD 2021. LNCS (LNAI), vol. 12712, pp. 501–513. Springer, Cham (2021). https://doi.org/10.1007/978-3-030-75762-5_40

SICM: A Supervised-Based Identification and Classification Model for Chinese Jargons Using Feature Adapter Enhanced BERT

Yifei Wang, Haochen Su, Yingao Wu, and Haizhou Wang[✉]

School of Cyber Science and Engineering, Sichuan University, Chengdu, China
{wangyife1,suhaochen,yeowu}@stu.scu.edu.cn, whzh.nc@scu.edu.cn

Abstract. In recent years, cybercriminals in darknet markets are becoming increasingly rampant and they usually converse in jargons to avoid surveillance. These jargons distort the original meaning of innocent-looking words, which makes it difficult for network regulators to understand the true meaning of dialogues content. Existing studies mainly explored jargon detection based on unsupervised methods. However, those solutions generally face significant challenges in setting appropriate jargon evaluation thresholds. To the best of our knowledge, we are the first to propose a **S**upervised-based jargon **I**dentification and **C**lassification **M**odel (SICM). Specifically, we transform jargon detection into a sequence labeling problem. In order to better represent the unique characteristics of Chinese jargon and facilitate more effective feature fusion, we innovatively propose a Chinese jargon identification and classification model based on Feature Adapter enhanced BERT, which uses attention mechanism to integrate phonetic, glyph and lexical features into the lower layers of BERT. The experimental results demonstrate that our model outperforms existing state-of-the-art jargon detection methods, with an F1-score of 91.99%. This study provides a brand-new research idea for the Chinese jargon detection in the darknet marketplace.

Keywords: Chinese jargons · BERT adapter · Supervised learning · Sequence labeling · Feature fusion

1 Introduction

Background. Due to the anonymity of the dark web, cybercriminals in darknet markets are becoming increasingly rampant [5]. They usually conduct illegal transactions in underground markets, such as spreading gambling information, leaking personal private data through hacking, selling firearms and drugs in regulated areas. These activities seriously endanger the normal order of cyberspace and real society.

© The Author(s), under exclusive license to Springer Nature Switzerland AG 2022
S. Khanna et al. (Eds.): PRICAI 2022, LNCS 13630, pp. 297–308, 2022.
https://doi.org/10.1007/978-3-031-20865-2_22

However, because of the obscurity of information in the darknet underground markets [5], it is a significant challenge for its regulation. Cybercriminals often use jargons to disguise transactions and avoid surveillance. Jargons distort the original meaning of innocent-looking words. It is not easy to discover the harmful implications of jargons, which makes cybercrime monitoring and investigation very difficult. For example, "猪肉" (pork) is a word that is common in real life, but it may refer to "冰毒" (methamphetamine) in the underground market; "道料" (rail material) actually refers to the bank card information obtained by modifying the POS (Point of Sale) machine. Due to these characteristics of jargons, it is quite difficult for network regulators to grasp what the cybercriminals are saying. The research work on automatic jargons identification and classification is of significant importance for network regulators to better understand the various types of cybercrime.

There have been several studies using unsupervised methods to detect jargons [4,12,13,15,17,20–22]. The main idea of their works is to compare the similarity of word embeddings of the same word in different corpora. Usually, for a specific word, its word embeddings are generated not only in a normal corpus, but also in a malicious corpus in which words may have hidden harmful meanings. Then, the similarity of the same word's two different embeddings will be calculated. The value of the similarity is the key indicator to determine whether the word is a jargon [4,12,13,17]. Besides, there are also some unsupervised methods that use BERT-based MLM (Masked Language Model) to predict jargons [21,22].

Challenges. All the existing research works of jargon detection use unsupervised methods, and they generally face the following significant challenges.

Firstly, in their algorithms, it is challenging to set the appropriate threshold for determining the jargons. Existing unsupervised approaches set a threshold for the result of similarity calculation [4,12,13,17] or the result predicted by the Masked Language Model [21,22] to obtain the jargon candidates. Nevertheless, the threshold value is usually set subjectively based on experience, and meanwhile the results of jargon prediction are extremely sensitive to the threshold value. If the threshold value is not set properly, it can easily cause normal words to be incorrectly recognized as jargons. Although this problem can be avoided by using the supervised approach, there is no precedent research on jargon identification based on supervised methods, to the best of our knowledge.

Secondly, for Chinese jargon detection, previous methods also have some other problems: most of them only consider the textual information and do not extract the linguistic features of Chinese jargons [4,13,15,20]. Actually, there are many Chinese jargons created based on the similarity of character pronunciation or morphology. For instance, members of gambling websites use the word "菠菜" (spinach) instead of "博彩" (Gambling), which are completely different words but very similar in their Chinese pronunciations. Another example is that people often use the word "果" (fruit) instead of "裸" (nude) when it comes to pornography. The two words are pronounced differently but have similar Chinese character roots. Therefore, we believe that using an appropriate way to introduce information about the similarity of pronunciation and morphology between different Chinese characters can be of great help in Chinese jargon detection.

Contributions. To address the above challenges, the main contributions of this paper are summarized as follows:

- We design and publish the first Chinese jargon identification and classification model based on a supervised approach (SICM[1]), to the best of our knowledge. We transform the jargon detection into a sequence labeling problem. For an input sentence, the location of the jargons in the sentence and the crime category they belong to can be identified.
- We extract brand-new features based on the unique characteristics of Chinese jargons. Considering the characteristics of pronunciation and morphology of Chinese jargons, we extract phonetic features and glyph features for each Chinese character. Meanwhile, lexical features are added to the model in order to learn the boundary information related to jargons. The experimental results show that these features can significantly improve the effect of jargon detection.

2 Related Work

Until now, jargon detection is a relatively new research area. Existing researches mainly focus on Chinese [4,13,15,20], English [17,21,22] and Japanese [12].

In 2016, Zhao et al. [20] proposed the first Chinese jargon detection method. The authors used Word2Vec model to generate word embeddings and clustered jargons in underground market QQ groups by LDA (Latent Dirichlet Allocation) model. In another study on the detection of Chinese jargons by Yang et al. [15], the authors investigated the underground business promoted through blackhat SEO (Search Engine Optimization), and then built KDES (Keyword Detection and Expansion System) to find Chinese jargons in Baidu search engine. These two methods achieve the clustering of jargons, but do not take into account the differences between words when used as jargons and when used as normal semantics.

In subsequent studies [4,12,13,17], researchers tried to introduce the cross-corpus information into the model to detect jargons. Yuan et al. [17] proposed a new technique called Cantreader, which is able to recognize and understand the English jargons in darknet marketplace. The authors modified the Word2Vec model to perform model training in dark corpora containing jargons and benign corpora in normal contexts simultaneously. Similarly, Takuro et al. [12] used Word2Vec for each of the two corpora and detected Japanese jargons in Twitter. Wang et al. [13] designed the CJI-Framework to identify Chinese jargons in Telegram by extracting seven novel features. Ke et al. [4] constructed a word-based pre-training language model called DC-BERT to generate high-quality

---

[1] https://github.com/yiyepianzhounc/SICM.

contextual word embeddings for the corpus of darknet Chinese forums, and then perform cross-corpora jargon detection by computing the cosine similarity. Zhu et al. [22] took a different idea and used the Masked Language Model to self-supervisedly analyze the context to detect English euphemism and its hidden meanings. In addition, Zhu et al. [21] used a similar method which focuses on English euphemistic phrases detection.

In conclusion, existing studies have some common limitations: (1) Most of them obtain jargon candidates by setting a threshold. However, the threshold value is usually sensitive, and if the threshold value is not set properly, it can easily cause normal words to be incorrectly identified as jargons. (2) They did not consider the pronunciation and morphology characteristics of Chinese jargons.

3   Methodology

In this section, we give a detailed introduction of the proposed SICM model, which is shown in Fig. 1.

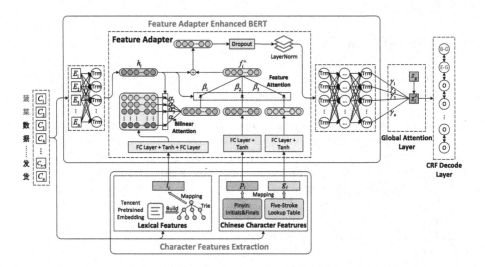

Fig. 1. Model structure of SICM

3.1   Character Feature Extraction Module

Phonetic Feature Extraction. Inspired by the 'Trans-pinyin' system proposed by Li et al. [6], we use a similar approach to extract the phonetic features of Chinese characters. The approach of 'Trans-pinyin' is to combine Chinese Pinyin with the IPA (International Phonetic Alphabet) system[2]. Specifically, for

---

[2] https://www.internationalphoneticassociation.org.

each Chinese character in the input sequence, we first use the 'pypinyin' library[3] to get its Pinyin representation. Then, we divide the Pinyin representation into two parts: the initial and the final, and map them to the representations in the IPA system respectively, according to the conversion table[4]. Therefore, each part will be represented by a one-hot encoding. There is also a one-dimensional phonetic weight for each character. If two initials are similar in pronunciation, they will be represented as the same one-hot encoding with different phonetic weights. At last, we concatenate two one-hot encodings of the character and its phonetic weight to obtain its phonetic embedding representation.

Glyph Feature Extraction. We use the Five-stroke (or Wubi) encoding[5] of Chinese characters to generate glyph features, so that characters with similar morphology have similar vector representations. The Five-stroke encoding creates mappings between different Chinese character roots and 25 English letters, with each Chinese character represented by no more than five English letters. For each character, we represent each bit of the Five-stroke encoding with a 25-dimensional one-hot encoding, and then concatenate them together to get the final glyph embedding.

Lexical Feature Extraction. Unlike English, Chinese words are not separated by spaces and lack distinct lexical boundaries, which makes Chinese sequence labeling a challenging task. There have been some works attempting to integrate lexical information into Chinese sequence labeling model to learn the boundary information related to Chinese words [2,7–9,19]. To allow our model to learn the boundary information related to Chinese jargons, we use a popular pre-trained embedding corpus from Tencent AI Lab[6], which is pre-trained on large-scale high-quality data using directional skip-gram model [10] and contains over 12 million words and phrases. More importantly, the corpus has advantages in coverage and freshness, including a large number of domain-specific words.

We use the method proposed by Liu et al. [8] to obtain lexical features. Specifically, a Trie is first constructed based on the pre-trained lexicon $\mathbf{D}$. Then, for an input sentence sequence $X = \{x_1, x_2, x_3, ..., x_n\}$, all its character subsequences are traversed and matched with the Trie, such that each character x_i is given a word list $W_i = \{w_i^1, w_i^2, w_i^3, ..., w_i^m\}$. The m indicates the maximum number of words matched by a character. If the number of words is less than m, the remaining positions will be filled with '<PAD>'. Finally, based on W_i, we get the Character lexical feature $l_i = \{v_i^1, v_i^2, v_i^3, ..., v_i^m\}$, which is a set of

---

[3] https://github.com/mozillazg/python-pinyin.

[4] https://github.com/untunt/PhonoCollection/blob/master/Standard%20Chinese.
md.

[5] https://en.wikipedia.org/wiki/Wubi_method.

[6] https://ai.tencent.com/ailab/nlp/en/embedding.html.

word embeddings. The v_i^j is the word embedding of w_i^j and is obtained by the following equation:

$$v_i^j = \mathbf{E}\left(w_i^j\right) \tag{1}$$

where $\mathbf{E}$ denotes the lookup table of the pre-trained lexicon $\mathbf{D}$. We treat the lexical feature l_i as a m-by-d_w matrix, where d_w denotes the dimension of the word embedding in $\mathbf{D}$.

3.2   Feature Adapter Enhanced BERT Module

We use the Chinese BERT pre-trained model [1] to extract text features. The traditional feature fusion is usually performed after the output of BERT model. However, such approaches do not take full advantage of the powerful representation capability of BERT. To make our feature fusion more effective, we modify the structure of BERT. Inspired by studies [8] and [14], we design the Feature Adapter to integrate Chinese character features (including phonetic features and glyph features) and lexical features into the lower layers of BERT directly. Specifically, we place the Feature Adapter between the first and second Transformer layers of BERT.

Feature Adapter accepts four inputs, which are text features, phonetic features, glyph features and lexical features of characters. For the i-th character x_i in the input sentence sequence $X = \{x_1, x_2, x_3, ..., x_n\}$, the input of Feature Adapter can be represented as (h_i, p_i, g_i, l_i), where $h_i \in \mathbb{R}^{d_h}$ denotes the character vector output by the previous Transformer layer; and $p_i \in \mathbb{R}^{d_p}$, $g_i \in \mathbb{R}^{d_g}$ denote the phonetic features and glyph features obtained by the Chinese character feature extractor, respectively; and $l_i \in \mathbb{R}^{m \times d_w}$ denotes the lexical features. To align the different feature representations, we apply the following transformations to the phonetic features and glyph features:

$$\hat{p}_i = \tanh\left(\mathbf{W}_p p_i + \mathbf{b}_p\right) \tag{2}$$

$$\hat{g}_i = \tanh\left(\mathbf{W}_g g_i + \mathbf{b}_g\right) \tag{3}$$

where $\mathbf{W}_p$ is a d_h-by-d_p matrix, $\mathbf{W}_g$ is a d_h-by-d_g matrix, $\mathbf{b}_p$ and $\mathbf{b}_g$ are bias.

The lexical feature $l_i = \left\{v_i^1, v_i^2, v_i^3, ..., v_i^m\right\}$ of each character is an m-by-d_w matrix. Here, we use the method of [8] to further process the lexical features. First, a nonlinear transformation is applied to l_i that maps the lexical features to the same dimensions as the text features:

$$l_i^{'} = \mathbf{W}_2\left(\tanh\left(\mathbf{W}_1 l_i^T + \mathbf{b}_1\right)\right) + \mathbf{b}_2 \tag{4}$$

where $\mathbf{W}_1$ is a d_h-by-d_w matrix, $\mathbf{W}_2$ is a d_h-by-d_h matrix, $\mathbf{b}_1$ and $\mathbf{b}_2$ are bias. In our approach, each character is matched to up to m words. However, not all of these words are useful. To be able to allow the model to select the most appropriate words and thus learn the correct boundary information, a bilinear attention mechanism is used here to calculate the weights of different words under the same character:

$$\alpha_i = \text{softmax}\left(h_i \mathbf{W}_{att} l_i'\right) \tag{5}$$

$$\hat{l}_i = \sum_{j=1}^{m} \alpha_i^j v_i^j \tag{6}$$

where $\mathbf{W}_{att}$ is a d_h-by-d_h matrix, which is a learnable parameter and represents the weight matrix of the bilinear attention mechanism; α_i is the attention weight distribution representing the relevance between the current character x_i and the words it matches (i.e. words in W_i). Finally, we obtain the final lexical embedding $\hat{l}_i$ by attention-weighted summation.

As mentioned above, the transformed phonetic embedding $\hat{p}_i$, glyph embedding $\hat{g}_i$ and lexical embedding $\hat{l}_i$ are all d_h-dimensional vectors. Let $f_i = \left\{\hat{p}_i, \hat{g}_i, \hat{l}_i\right\}$, representing the 3-by-$h$ feature matrix of character x_i. Different jargons have different sensitivities to various features, so we design the following attention-based feature fusion strategy:

$$h_i' = \tanh\left(\mathbf{W}_h h_i + \mathbf{b}_h\right) \tag{7}$$

$$\beta_t = \frac{\exp\left(h_i'(f_i^t)^T\right)}{\sum_{k=1}^{3} \exp\left(h_i'(f_i^k)^T\right)} \tag{8}$$

$$\hat{f}_i = \sum_{t=1}^{3} \beta_t f_i^t \tag{9}$$

where $\mathbf{W}_h$ is a d_h-by-d_h matrix and f_i^t denotes the t-th row in the feature matrix f_i. The β_t denotes the attention weights of different features. Then, we add the final character features $\hat{f}_i$ with h_i to obtain the character vector fused with the character features:

$$\hat{h}_i = h_i + \hat{f}_i \tag{10}$$

Finally, $\hat{h}_i$ is output as Feature Adapter after a dropout layer and layer normalization, and input to the next Transformer layer.

3.3 Global Attention Layer

In the Chinese jargon corpus, it is usually possible to recognize the category of crime present in the sentence by observing the contextual background of the whole sentence. Therefore, we believe that introducing global information of sentences for the model is beneficial to the identification and classification of jargons. It should be noted that words in a sentence contribute differently to the global information. Referring to [18], we designed a global attention layer to introduce weighted global contextual information for each character in the sentence sequence. We denote the output of the last Transformer layer by $Z = \{z_1, z_2, z_3, ..., z_n\}$, and then calculate the attention score using the following:

$$z_g = \text{avg}\{z_1, z_2, z_3, ..., z_n\} \tag{11}$$

$$e_i = \mathbf{V}^T \tanh(\mathbf{W}_g z_g + \mathbf{W}_z z_i) \tag{12}$$

$$\gamma_i = \frac{\exp(e_i)}{\sum\limits_{k=1}^{n} \exp(e_k)} \tag{13}$$

where z_g denotes the global representation of the whole sentence; $\mathbf{V} \in \mathbb{R}^{d_h}$, $\mathbf{W}_g \in \mathbb{R}^{d_h \times d_h}$ and $\mathbf{W}_z \in \mathbb{R}^{d_h \times d_h}$ are all trainable parameters; γ_i denotes the attention score of the i-th character in the sentence sequence, reflecting the importance of that character in the global information of the whole sentence. Then, the sentence representation is generated by weighted summation:

$$s = \sum_{i=1}^{n} \gamma_i z_i \tag{14}$$

Finally, the global attention layer combines the generated sentence representation with the output of the last Transformer layer as the input to the following CRF (Conditional Random Field) decoding layer:

$$\hat{z}_i = z_i + s \tag{15}$$

4   Experiments

4.1   Dataset Construction

First, we adopt the raw data of the darknet which has been published by Ke et al. [4]. The data comes from multiple popular Chinese darknet websites[7], covering most types of cybercrimes. Then, In order to balance the amount of data in different crime categories, we supplement data from additional Chinese darknet forums[8]. All these raw data are not annotated.

We refer to the existing classification rules of Chinese jargons [4] and fine tune it, classifying jargons into seven categories: 'Drugs', 'Gambling', 'Pornography', 'Violence', 'Fraud', 'Hacking' and 'Others', which covers most types of cybercrime in darknet markets. In the end, our dataset contains 33,668 sentences, including 19,675 sentences containing jargons and 13,993 normal sentences. A total of 45,079 jargons were labeled, including 1,796 unduplicated jargons. We randomly divide our dataset into training, validation and test sets in the ratio of 6:2:2. The specific information is shown in Table 1.

---

[7] https://github.com/KL4MVP/Chinese-Jargon-Detection/tree/master/dataset.
[8] https://github.com/yiyepianzhounc/CJC.

Table 1. Dataset statistics

Category	#Sentences	#Jargons	#Unduplicated jargons	Example of jargons
Drug	1,936	3,920	225	叶子 (leaf), 猪肉 (pork)
Gambling	1,831	3,713	239	菠菜 (spinach), 博彩 (fight color)
Pornography	4,132	10,560	362	果体 (fruit body), 狼友 (wolf friend)
Violence	1,456	3,469	203	气狗 (air dog), (bald eagle)
Fraud	4,284	10,320	381	道料 (rail material), 裸条 (bare strip)
Hacking	4,138	8,147	341	蜜 (Mellivora capensis), 炸机 (bomber)
Others	2,998	4,860	47	梯子 (ladder), 洋葱 (onion)

4.2 Sequence Labeling Baseline Model Comparison Experiment

To demonstrate the effectiveness of the proposed model SICM, we tested the performance of the model against seven baseline methods on our dataset CJC. These baselines are all sequence labeling models because no supervised jargon detection method has been proposed before. In particular, BERT-FeatureLSTM-CRF is a traditional feature fusion method, which concatenates the output of the last Transformer layer with the phonetic embedding, the glyph embedding and the weighted lexical embedding, and then uses BiLSTM as the fusion layer. This baseline can be used as a comparative experiment for feature fusion methods. In this experiment, we use *Precision, Recall* and *F1-score* as evaluation metrics. The results are shown in Table 2.

Table 2. Results for sequence labeling baseline model comparison experiment

Models	Precision	Recall	F1-score
BiLSTM-CRF [3]	87.91	87.42	87.66
IDCNN-CRF [11]	87.44	87.19	87.31
LatticeLSTM [19]	89.82	88.03	88.92
BERT-CRF	89.68	90.43	90.06
BERT-BiLSTM-CRF	90.05	90.87	90.46
LEBERT [8]	90.43	90.93	90.68
BERT-FeatureLSTM-CRF	90.28	90.99	90.64
SICM (our model)	**91.73**	**92.25**	**91.99**

Among all eight models, our model SICM shows the best results in each metric. The results of LEBERT outperformed the first five baselines, probably because it uses a more advanced lexicon feature extraction method and is able to inject it into the lower layers of BERT, thus allowing the model to better capture the boundary information between words. In addition, SICM outperforms BERT-FeatureLSTM-CRF because the use of Feature Adapter for feature fusion takes full advantage of the powerful representation capabilities of BERT.

Experimental results show that our model SICM outperforms various advanced sequence labeling models for jargon detection, and our feature fusion approach is more effective than the traditional method.

4.3   Unsupervised Methods Comparison Experiment

In this experiment, we apply four existing unsupervised jargon detection methods to our dataset CJC and compare their results with our model SICM.

Each unsupervised method generates a jargon list. Considering that these are unsupervised methods, we rank the jargon lists generated by each method and then use Precision at k ($P@k$) as the evaluation metric, which is often used in the field of information retrieval to assess the relevance of search results to a query [16]. The criterion for judging jargons here are those labeled in our dataset CJC.

Table 3. Results for unsupervised methods comparison experiment

Methods	Language	$P@10$	$P@20$	$P@30$	$P@40$	$P@50$	$P@60$	$P@80$	$P@100$
CantReader [17]	English	0.00	0.00	0.07	0.05	0.04	0.07	0.10	0.10
CJI-Framework [13]	Chinese	**0.70**	**0.40**	0.30	0.30	0.28	0.30	**0.33**	**0.33**
DC-BERT [4]	Chinese	0.50	0.35	**0.40**	**0.38**	**0.36**	**0.33**	0.29	0.27
MLM [22]	English	0.10	0.20	0.17	0.18	0.16	0.15	0.13	0.12

The results are shown in Table 3. It can be observed that CJI-Frameworks and DC-BERT, the two detection methods for Chinese jargons, can achieve relatively good results. However, even for the $P@10$ metric, CJI-Frameworks, the best performer among the unsupervised methods, can only reach 0.70, i.e., only 7 of the top 10 most likely words are jargons. In contrast, the *Precision, Recall* and *F1-score* of SICM can all reach above 0.90, which achieves better results. CantReader performs poorly on our dataset, whose conclusion is similar to the research work [22]. We infer that this is because the method requires an additional benign corpus and it is difficult for us to guarantee that the selected Chinese corpus[9] is appropriate. MLM also does not work well, the method uses a native BERT model and cannot predict multiple tokens at the same time, so it is not well suited for Chinese jargon detection.

Experiments show that our method is significantly better than existing state-of-the-art unsupervised methods and can better detect jargons in the dark web.

---

[9] https://github.com/brightmart/nlp_chinese_corpus.

5   Conclusion

In this paper, we propose the first supervised-based Chinese jargon identification and classification model, to the best of our knowledge. We transform jargon detection into a sequence labeling problem and propose our brand-new model based on Feature Adapter enhanced BERT, which uses attention mechanism to integrate phonetic, glyph and lexical features into the lower layers of BERT. Experiments show that our model outperforms existing state-of-the-art jargon detection methods.

Acknowledgements. This work is supported by the National Natural Science Foundation of China (NSFC) under grant nos. 61802271, 61802270, 81602935, and 81773548. In addition, this work is also partially supported by Joint Research Fund of China Ministry of Education and China Mobile Company (No. CM20200409), Science and Technology Plan Transfer Payment Project of Sichuan Province (No. 2021ZYSF007); The Key Research and Development Program of Science and Technology Department of Sichuan Province (No. 2020YFS0575, No. 2021YFG0159, No. 2021KJT0012-2021YFS0067). The authors thank Liang Ke, Hailin Wang, and Yiwei Hou for their helpful suggestions to improve the paper.

References

1. Cui, Y., Che, W., Liu, T., Qin, B., Yang, Z.: Pre-training with whole word masking for Chinese BERT. IEEE/ACM Trans. Audio Speech Lang. Process. **29**, 3504–3514 (2021)
2. Ding, R., Xie, P., Zhang, X., Lu, W., Li, L., Si, L.: A neural multi-digraph model for Chinese NER with gazetteers. In: Proceedings of the 57th Annual Meeting of the Association for Computational Linguistics, pp. 1462–1467 (2019)
3. Huang, Z., Xu, W., Yu, K.: Bidirectional LSTM-CRF models for sequence tagging. arXiv preprint arXiv:1508.01991 (2015)
4. Ke, L., Chen, X., Wang, H.: An unsupervised detection framework for Chinese jargons in the darknet. In: Proceedings of the 15th ACM International Conference on Web Search and Data Mining, pp. 458–466 (2022)
5. Kovalchuk, O., Masonkova, M., Banakh, S.: The dark web worldwide 2020: anonymous vs safety. In: Proceedings of the 11th International Conference on Advanced Computer Information Technologies, pp. 526–530 (2021)
6. Li, J., Meng, K.: MFE-NER: multi-feature fusion embedding for Chinese named entity recognition. arXiv preprint arXiv:2109.07877 (2021)
7. Li, X., Yan, H., Qiu, X., Huang, X.J.: Flat: Chinese NER using flat-lattice transformer. In: Proceedings of the 58th Annual Meeting of the Association for Computational Linguistics, pp. 6836–6842 (2020)
8. Liu, W., Fu, X., Zhang, Y., Xiao, W.: Lexicon enhanced Chinese sequence labeling using BERT adapter. In: Proceedings of the 59th Annual Meeting of the Association for Computational Linguistics and the 11th International Joint Conference on Natural Language Processing, pp. 5847–5858 (2021)
9. Ma, R., Peng, M., Zhang, Q., Wei, Z., Huang, X.J.: Simplify the usage of lexicon in Chinese NER. In: Proceedings of the 58th Annual Meeting of the Association for Computational Linguistics, pp. 5951–5960 (2020)

10. Song, Y., Shi, S., Li, J., Zhang, H.: Directional skip-gram: explicitly distinguishing left and right context for word embeddings. In: Proceedings of the 16th Conference of the North American Chapter of the Association for Computational Linguistics: Human Language Technologies, pp. 175–180 (2018)
11. Strubell, E., Verga, P., Belanger, D., McCallum, A.: Fast and accurate entity recognition with iterated dilated convolutions. In: Proceedings of the 22nd Conference on Empirical Methods in Natural Language Processing, pp. 2670–2680 (2017)
12. Takuro, H., Yuichi, S., Tahara, Y., Ohsuga, A.: Codewords detection in microblogs focusing on differences in word use between two corpora. In: Proceedings of the 3rd International Conference on Computing, Electronics and Communications Engineering, pp. 103–108 (2020)
13. Wang, H., Hou, Y., Wang, H.: A novel framework of identifying Chinese jargons for telegram underground markets. In: Proceedings of the 30th International Conference on Computer Communications and Networks, pp. 1–9 (2021)
14. Wang, R., et al.: K-adapter: infusing knowledge into pre-trained models with adapters. In: Proceedings of the 59th Annual Meeting of the Association for Computational Linguistics and the 11th International Joint Conference on Natural Language Processing, pp. 1405–1418 (2021)
15. Yang, H., et al.: How to learn Klingon without a dictionary: detection and measurement of black keywords used by the underground economy. In: Proceedings of the 38th IEEE Symposium on Security and Privacy, pp. 751–769 (2017)
16. Yang, P., Fang, H., Lin, J.: Anserini: enabling the use of Lucene for information retrieval research. In: Proceedings of the 40th International ACM SIGIR Conference on Research and Development in Information Retrieval, pp. 1253–1256 (2017)
17. Yuan, K., Lu, H., Liao, X., Wang, X.: Reading thieves' cant: automatically identifying and understanding dark jargons from cybercrime marketplaces. In: Proceedings of the 27th USENIX Security Symposium, pp. 1027–1041 (2018)
18. Yuan, Y., Zhou, X., Pan, S., Zhu, Q., Song, Z., Guo, L.: A relation-specific attention network for joint entity and relation extraction. In: Proceedings of the 29th International Joint Conference on Artificial Intelligence, pp. 4054–4060 (2020)
19. Zhang, Y., Yang, J.: Chinese NER using lattice LSTM. In: Proceedings of the 56th Annual Meeting of the Association for Computational Linguistics, pp. 1554–1564 (2018)
20. Zhao, K., Zhang, Y., Xing, C., Li, W., Chen, H.: Chinese underground market jargon analysis based on unsupervised learning. In: Proceedings of the 14th IEEE Conference on Intelligence and Security Informatics, pp. 97–102 (2016)
21. Zhu, W., Bhat, S.: Euphemistic phrase detection by masked language model. In: Proceedings of the 26th Conference on Empirical Methods in Natural Language Processing, pp. 163–168 (2021)
22. Zhu, W., et al.: Self-supervised euphemism detection and identification for content moderation. In: Proceedings of the 42nd IEEE Symposium on Security and Privacy, pp. 229–246 (2021)

HS²N: Heterogeneous Semantics-Syntax Fusion Network for Document-Level Event Factuality Identification

Zihao Zhang, Chengwei Liu, Zhong Qian, Xiaoxu Zhu[✉], and Peifeng Li

School of Computer Science and Technology, Soochow University, Suzhou, China
zhzhangpro@stu.suda.edu.cn, liuliuchengwei@gmail.com,
{qianzhong,xiaoxzhu,pfli}@suda.edu.cn

Abstract. Event factuality identification (EFI) aims to assess the veracity degree to which an event mentioned in a document has happened, and both semantic and syntactic features are crucial for this task. Most of the previous studies only focused on sentence-level event factuality, which may lead to conflicts among mentions of a specific event in a document. Existing studies on document-level EFI (DEFI) are still scarce and mainly focus on semantic features. To address the above issues, we propose a novel Heterogeneous Semantics-Syntax-fused Network (HS²N) for DEFI, which not only integrates both semantic and syntactic information in an efficient way using Biaffine Attention and differentiated alignment method, but also considers both inter-and-intra sentence interaction. Experimental results on the English and Chinese datasets show that our proposed HS²N outperforms the state-of-the-art model.

Keywords: Document-level event factuality identification · Feature fusion · Graph convolutional network

1 Introduction

Event factuality is defined as the level of information expressing the veracity of relevant sources towards the factual nature of events mentioned in a certain discourse [1], which is essential and crucial for many natural language understanding (NLU) applications, e.g., rumor detection [2–4]. In general, event factuality identification (EFI) is a five-class classification task that can be classified into five categories: Certain Positive (CT+), Certain Negative (CT−), Possible Positive (PS+), Possible Negative (PS−) and Underspecified (Uu).

Most existing studies on EFI have mainly focused on sentence level, where various state-of-the-art models have emerged in the last few years [1,5,7–10]. When a sentence is given, a sentence-level EFI (SEFI) task is supposed to assess the veracity of the event mentioned in it. Nevertheless, events reported in the real world is always annotated with an authenticated factuality value. Consequently, this will lead to an unavoidable scene in performing SEFI trials, where

© The Author(s), under exclusive license to Springer Nature Switzerland AG 2022
S. Khanna et al. (Eds.): PRICAI 2022, LNCS 13630, pp. 309–320, 2022.
https://doi.org/10.1007/978-3-031-20865-2_23

> **Event**: Trump and Kim Jong-un meet(PS-) 'any time soon': White House.
> **The Document-Level Event Factuality**: PS-
> [S1] China on Saturday urged(CT+) the ... system.
> [S2] The White House said on Monday US President Donald Trump's meeting(CT+) with ... .
> ...
> [S6] Earlier on Monday, Trump told Bloomberg that he would meet(CT+) Kim Jong-un under the right circumstances.
> [S7] "If it would be appropriate for me to meet(Uu) with him, I would absolutely, I would be honored to do it."

Fig. 1. An example of document-level event factuality, where event factualities vary from sentences to document.

the predicted event factuality may be contrary to the actual situation according to the whole document as Fig. 1 shows, i.e., though the event truth of sentences is mainly CT+, the document-level event factuality is PS−.

Generally, the factuality of an event should be uniquely determined by its whole passage, rather than having multiple truth values from a sentence perspective. However, document-level event factuality identification (DEFI) is nontrivial. When assessing document-level event factuality, in addition to the inconsistencies of event factuality between sentences and document, there are often conflicts between truth values of the sentences, as S6 and S7 shown in Fig. 1. Such inter-sentence conflicts can increase the complexity and difficulty of DEFI task. Qian et al. [11] proposed an adversarial neural network to embark on DEFI. Cao et al. [12] proposed a graph-based model by using graph convolutional networks [15] with Gaussian distribution (ULGN), which mainly focused on semantics, while previous work [2,7–10] has demonstrated the importance of both semantic and syntactic information when considering EFI task. Besides, the redundant fully-connected graph structure of ULGN will reduce intra-sentence interaction and lead to perturbation of inter-semantics.

According to the above analysis, document-level EFI is mainly challenged by: 1) the insufficient interaction from both inter-sentence and intra-sentence; 2) the lack of use of syntactic dependency information altogether with semantics.

To address the above issues, we propose a novel **Heterogeneous Semantics-Syntax-fused Network (HS^{2}N)** to identify document-level event factuality. Specifically, we first construct a heterogeneous graph containing rich inter-/intra-sentence information with various nodes and edges to process the complicated interaction between sentences and encode event at the document level. To further improve the graph structure, we devise a fine-grained fusion module at the lexical level to combine syntactic dependency information with semantics to initialize sentence nodes by using a differentiated alignment method and Biaffine Attention mechanism. To verify the effectiveness of our model, we conduct extensive experiments on two widely used datasets, and the results show that our model achieves state-of-the-art performances. In summary, our contributions are as follows.

1. We propose a novel **HS^{2}N** for document-level event factuality identification. To our best knowledge, this is the first method that considers both semantic and syntactic information for document-level EFI task by using a heterogeneous graph structure hierarchically.

2. We design an information fusion mechanism for better learning the interactions between a document's semantic and syntactic dependency information. By adequately utilizing the interactions, both semantics and syntactic dependency information can be mutually improved to enhance model performance.
3. Extensive experiments are conducted to verify the effectiveness of our model. The experimental results demonstrate that our model achieves state-of-the-art performances.

2 Related Work

Event factuality identification (EFI) is a very challenging task in event extraction, which is crucial and helpful for many NLU applications, e.g., rumor detection [2–4], fake news detection [16,17] and knowledge base construction [6]. Studies on EFI are mostly limited to sentence-level due to its relative simplicity.

Saurí et al. [1,5] constructed a widely-used sentence-level EFI corpus–FactBank, and proposed a rule-based model in the early phase of SEFI studying. On the basis of FactBank, Qian et al. [7,8] first proposed a two-step framework combining rule-based approaches and machine learning, and further devised a generative adversarial network with auxiliary classification for SEFI. Current deep learning models have demonstrated the importance of syntactic and semantic structures of sentences to identify important context words for EFI tasks. Based on this, Veyseh et al. [9] proposed a graph-based neural network for SEFI. Le et al. [10] devised a novel model that explicitly considers multi-hop paths with both syntax-based and semantic-based edges among words to obtain sentence structures for representation learning in SEFI.

Existing studies on document-level event factuality are still scarce. Qian et al. [11] constructed the first and only document-level event factuality dataset–DLEF with two widely used English and Chinese subcorpus, and proposed an LSTM-based adversarial neural network (Att_2+AT) for DEFI. Zhang et al. [13] used a gated convolutional network and self-attention layer to capture the feature representation of the overall information for DEFI task, which outperforms Att_2+AT. Recently, Cao et al. [12] proposed a state-of-the-art graph-based method (ULGN) by utilizing Gaussian distribution to aggregate uncertain local information into a global document structure to assess document-level event factuality.

3 Methodology

We propose a heterogeneous semantics-syntax fusion network (HS^2N) for document-level EFI. Our approach is schematically illustrated in Fig. 2, which consists of three major components: (1) Graph Construction and Initialization, which construct a heterogeneous graph and aggregate enriched information into sentence nodes; (2) Semantic and Syntactic Information Fusion, which fuse the semantic and syntactic information by a differentiated alignment we devised and

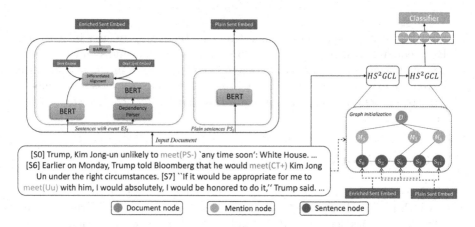

Fig. 2. The architecture of our proposed HS^{2}N network for document-level event factuality identification. Lines with an arrow indicate the flow direction of vectors, dashed lines with an arrow represent the initialization of graph/node.

Biaffine Attention mechanism; (3) Graph Inferring for Identification, which utilizes the graph structure we proposed for event factuality identification. Each component will be illustrated in detail.

3.1 Semantics-Syntax Fusion

Previous studies [2,7–10] have demonstrated the importance of both semantic and syntactic information for EFI task. As the early stage of document-level EFI study, existing DEFI studies mainly focus on utilizing semantics. To synthesize richer intra-sentence information, we devise a fusion module of both semantic and syntactic information. Specially, we categorized sentences of a document into two types: **Event-related Sentences (ES)** and **Plain Sentences (PS)**.

- **ES** is defined as sentences with the corresponding event in a document. Sentence of this kind is crucial to the DEFI task, yet existing state-of-the-art models [12] haven't taken syntactic information into consideration. To obtain richer latent text information, we use spaCy for dependency parsing of its related event's shortest dependency path. Precisely, we devise a differentiated alignment method and use Biaffine Attention for data fusion.
- **PS** refers to sentences with no event in a document, which mainly contribute to the inter-sentence interaction.

BERT [14] has been demonstrated as the state-of-the-art pre-trained model for many natural language processing applications, including EFI task. We adopt BERT to embed each sentence of a document as input of the fusion module and that is defined as follows:

$$S_i = [w_1, w_2, \ldots, w_n], i = 1, 2, \ldots, N \tag{1}$$

$$E_i = \text{BERT}([w_1, w_2, \ldots, w_n]) \tag{2}$$

$$E_{i,j}^{es} = \text{BERT}(s\_path(e_j^{S_i^{es}})) \tag{3}$$

where S_i denotes the i-th sentence of a document with a sentence type, i.e., S_i^{es} or S_i^{ps}, and N, n denote the length of document and sentence, respectively. E_i denotes the corresponding embedding of the i-th sentence, i.e., E_i^{es} or E_i^{ps}. Additionally, E_i^{ps} is directly used to initialize PS-type sentence nodes, and E_i^{es} will be put into the fusion module to integrate with syntax information. $s\_path(\cdot)$ denotes the shortest dependency path of $e_j^{S_i^{es}}$, i.e., the j-th event of S_i^{es}, obtained by spaCy dependency parser, and the related embedding is denoted as $E_{i,j}^{es}$.

Differentiated Alignment. We expect that two types of embedding learned from BERT model can represent distinct information contained within the syntactic shortest dependency paths and semantic correlations. Therefore, we adopt a differentiated alignment between the embedding of semantic and syntactic information. The differentiated alignment is defined as:

$$DA(E_i^{es}, E_{ij}^{es}) = \frac{1}{\|E_i^{es} - E_{ij}^{es}\|_{\text{F}}} \tag{4}$$

where the subscript F denotes the Frobenius norm [19].

Biaffine Attention. Inspired by studies in Dependency Parsing [20] and Named Entity Recognition [21], we introduce a biaffine module for information fusion after getting embedded from BERT and being aligned. Dozat and Manning [21] demonstrated that the biaffine mapping performs significantly better than just the concatenation of pairs. The biaffine fusion module is defined as follows:

$$f_i^{es} = \begin{bmatrix} E_i^{es} \\ 1 \end{bmatrix}^\top W_{biaffine} E_{ij}^{es} + b \tag{5}$$

where $W_{biaffine} \in \mathbb{R}^{d \times d}$ denotes the Biaffine Attention matrix, b denotes bias, f_i^{es} denotes the semantics-syntax fusion feature obtained by biaffine fusion module.

3.2 Heterogeneous Graph

Previous work [12] mainly focuses on the semantic information of document, and its fully-connected graph structure will perturb model for a better prediction. To synthesize the enriched intra-sentence information obtained by our fusion module and learn the representation of document event as global contexts, we propose a heterogeneous graph with multiple nodes and edges.

Graph Construction. An event factuality document has different properties for DEFI, i.e., document structure, sentences, and sentence-level event factuality. Thus, we devise a heterogeneous graph [22] to handle these attributes for factuality identification as shown in Fig. 2. Specifically, there are three types of nodes to encode information of different semantics:

- *document node*, which captures the global semantics of a document. We initialize this node with the output of BERT, which takes the entire document text as input.
- *sentence node*, which is initialized by f_i^{es} or E_i^{ps} according to its sentence type.
- *mention node*, which encodes the event of a sentence by BERT.

Therefore, the types of edges can be defined as follows:

- *document-mention edge*: Document node is connected with all mention nodes.
- *sentence-mention edge*: ES-type sentence node is connected with its corresponding mention node.
- *sentence-sentence edge*: A sentence node is connected with its previous and next sentence nodes if there are.

Compared with Cao et al. [12], which uses a fully-connected graph, our HS^{2}N graph structure is more rational because we only connect document node, which is the final identification node for EFI, with mention node. Such connection excludes the perturbations that come from global document node. Besides, it allows nodes of all kinds to interact with each other by using mention nodes as a hub.

Graph Inferring. We apply an l-layer GCN [15] to convolute the graph. The optimal l is set to be 2 after extensive experiments on the performance of GCN [15]. The $(l+1)$-th GCN-layer-wise inference is defined as:

$$H^{(l+1)} = \sigma(\tilde{D}^{-\frac{1}{2}}\tilde{A}\tilde{D}^{-\frac{1}{2}}H^{(l)}W^{(l)}) \tag{6}$$

where $\tilde{A} = A + I$, A and I denotes the adjacency matrix of the constructed graph and identity matrix, respectively. $\sigma(\cdot)$ denotes an activation function, such as $ReLU(\cdot) = max(0, \cdot)$. $W^{(l)}$ denotes a layer-specific trainable weight matrix.

To be precise, the i-th element of the $(l+1)$-th GCN-layer-wise inference matrix is defined as:

$$h_i^{(l+1)} = \sigma\left(\sum_{j \in ne(i)} \frac{1}{\sqrt{\tilde{D}_{i,i}\tilde{D}_{j,j}}} h_j^{(l)} W^{(l)}\right) \tag{7}$$

where $ne(i)$ denotes the neighbor nodes set of the i-th node. $\tilde{D}_{i,i} = \sum_{j \in ne(i)} \tilde{A}_{j,j}$.

Following Qian et al. [11], we use cross-entropy as the loss function below:

$$\mathcal{L}_\mathcal{D}(\theta) = -\frac{1}{M}\sum_{i=0}^{M-1} \log p(y_j^{(i)}|x^{(i)};\theta) \tag{8}$$

where M is the number of instances, $p(y_j^{(i)}|x^{(i)};\theta)$ denotes the probability of instance x_i being predicted as the golden label $y^{(i)}$. θ is a hyper-parameter.

4 Experimentation

4.1 Datasets

To verify the effectiveness of our model, we conduct experiments on two widely used English and Chinese datasets constructed by Qian et al. [11]. The statistics of these two datasets are shown in Table 1.

Table 1. Statistics of the documents in DLEF dataset. DEFC denotes document-level event factuality class, and SEFC denotes the number of sentence-level event factuality categories within a document.

Dataset	DEFC	SEFC = 1	SEFC = 2	SEFC ≥ 3
DLEF_en	CT+	1022	119	9
	CT−	162	97	20
	PS+	93	157	24
	PS−	2	6	4
	Uu	5	6	1
	Total	1284	385	58
DLEF_zh	CT+	2061	290	52
	CT−	491	612	239
	PS+	321	425	102
	PS−	9	11	16
	Uu	8	5	7
	Total	2890	1343	416

4.2 Experimental Settings

We use AdamW algorithm [18] to optimize model parameters. The optimal dropout rate and learning rate is set to 0.7 and 2e−5, respectively. The number of HS^2-graph convolution layers is set to 2. The size of hidden states of the HS^2-graph convolution layer is 768. In our implementations, our method uses the HuggingFace's Transformers library[1] to implement the BERT Base model.

The PS− and Uu documents cover only 1.39% and 1.20% in DLEF English and Chinese corpus, respectively. To be fairly compared with previous studies [11–13], we mainly focus on the performance of CT+, CT−, and PS+ and

---

[1] https://github.com/huggingface/transformers.

conduct 10-fold cross-validation on both English and Chinese dataset. F1 score is adopted to evaluate each category of event factuality, micro-/macro-averaged F1 score is also adopted for overall performance evaluation of event factuality categories.

4.3 Baselines

To verify the effectiveness of our HS^2N, we conduct the following strong baselines for comparison.

- **BERT Base** [14], which utilizes the BERT-base to encode the document, and uses the [CLS] token for prediction.
- **Att_2+LSTM** [11], which utilizes an intra-sentence attention to capture the most important information in sentences, and employs the long short-term memory network (LSTM) for DEFI.
- **Att_2+AT** [11], which leverages the intra-sentence and inter-sentence attention to learn the document representation. Adversarial training is adopted to improve the robustness.
- **MaxEntVote** [11], which uses maximum entropy model to identify sentence-level event factuality, and considers voting mechanism, i.e., choose the value committed by the most sentences as the document-level factuality value.
- **SentVote** [11], which is similar to MaxEntVote model, voting mechanism is used to identify document-level event factuality. Inter-sentence is not considered in it.
- **GCNN** [13], which uses a gated convolution network and self-attention layer to capture the feature representation of the overall information to identify the document-level event factuality.
- **ULGN** [12][2], which proposes a graph-based model [15] by using Gaussian distribution to aggregate local uncertainty into global structure to capture document feature for DEFI. The original results of ULGN somewhat are far to reach in practice, so we adopt the best implementation results via its publicly available code instead.

4.4 Result and Analysis

Experimental results on the document-level event factuality datasets are shown in Table 2, and we can observe from the experimental results that:

1. Our model performs the best and outperforms all baseline models on both English and Chinese DLEF dataset. Notably, on the English dataset, our model's micro-/macro-F1 score outperforms the current state-of-the-art model ULGN by 3.13/5.18, and outperforms the previous state-of-the-art model Att_2+AT by 7.4/12.46, which showcases the robustness and effectiveness of our proposed method for document-level event factuality identification. Though spaCy achieved the state-of-the-art performance for parsing,

---

[2] https://github.com/CPF-NLPR/ULGN4DocEFI.

Table 2. Experimental results on the document-level event factuality datasets (English and Chinese respetively). The best performance is in **bold**.

Dataset	Methods	CT+	CT−	PS+	Micro-F1	Macro-F1
DLEF_en	MaxEntVote	75.14	58.17	35.89	68.42	56.40
	Att_2+LSTM	79.18	65.25	53.65	73.23	66.03
	SentVote	83.98	70.22	57.85	78.06	70.68
	Att_2+AT	89.84	76.87	62.14	83.56	76.28
	BERT	89.38	71.82	69.09	83.53	76.76
	GCNN	91.19	80.28	70.76	86.37	80.74
	ULGN	92.25	85.53	74.01	87.83	83.26
	HS^{2}N(Ours)	**93.39**	**88.46**	**84.37**	**90.96**	**88.74**
DLEF_zh	MaxEntVote	72.22	62.44	58.29	67.72	64.32
	Att_2+LSTM	81.89	68.82	49.78	71.12	67.28
	SentVote	80.68	72.66	58.39	74.70	70.58
	Att_2+AT	87.52	83.35	74.06	84.03	81.64
	BERT	84.79	88.71	79.33	85.83	84.28
	GCNN	89.60	85.38	76.81	86.03	83.93
	ULGN	**93.16**	94.12	86.78	92.48	91.35
	HS^{2}N(Ours)	92.89	**94.42**	**88.93**	**92.95**	**92.08**

    its parsing result in Chinese is still unsatisfactory, which leads to the slight improvement of micro-/macro-F1 score of 0.47/0.73 and 8.92/10.44 compared with ULGN and ATT_2+AT on Chinese dataset, respectively.

2. According to the experimental gap between graph-based models, i.e., HS^{2}N and ULGN, and traditional deep learning models, i.e., Att_2+AT and GCNN, it can be inferred that graph structure is more suitable for processing document-level tasks. This is due to the fact that traditional models are limited by their structure, which is more linear in processing the input document text, while the graph structure can better encapsulate document and its corresponding data, and better utilizes documents for global prediction.

3. BERT has been proved to be one of the best models that can obtain deeper semantic information. Our model outperforms BERT on both English and Chinese datasets. We attribute the performance to the effectiveness of our semantics-syntax fusion method and the simplicity and efficiency of our proposed graph structure that can guarantee a deep and profound interaction from both inter-sentence and intra-sentence perspectives, which can dig deeper for enriched semantic information.

Table 3. Experimental results on ablation study. DA refers to the differentiated alignment method for information fusion. SF means syntactic information fusion module. That is, without SF means to experiment only with the heterogeneous graph. The best performance is in **bold**.

Dataset	Methods	CT+	CT−	PS+	Micro-F1	Macro-F1
DLEF_en	**HS²N(Ours)**	**93.39**	**88.46**	**84.37**	**90.96**	**88.74**
	w/o DA	93.16	88.19	77.55	90.58	86.97
	w/o SF	92.31	85.71	74.07	88.37	84.03
	ULGN	92.25	85.53	74.01	87.83	83.26
DLEF_zh	**HS²N(Ours)**	92.89	94.42	**88.93**	**92.95**	92.08
	w/o DA	**93.27**	94.27	88.21	92.82	91.84
	w/o SF	90.91	**95.08**	87.50	91.16	**92.52**
	ULGN	93.16	94.12	86.78	92.48	91.35

4.5 Ablation Study

To verify the effectiveness of our proposed model, we design an ablation test to investigate the effectiveness of these modules separately. As shown in Table 3, we can observe that:

1. After removing the differentiated alignment (DA) method from fusion module, the macro-F1 score of HS²N dropped by 1.77 on DLEF English dataset, which demonstrated the effectiveness of our pre-fusion processing.
2. After removing the syntax fusion module (SF), the macro-F1 score of HS²N dropped by 4.71 on DLEF English dataset. Such experimental results demonstrate that dependency syntax and semantic information are equally important for this task.
3. To be precise, there is only a heterogeneous graph remained after removing the SF module, only considering semantics as ULGN did. However, the macro-F1 score of HS²N still outperforms ULGN by 0.77 and 1.17 on both English and Chinese datasets, respectively. We attribute this success to the rational and straightforward structure of our HS²-graph, which considering mention nodes as a hub for interaction within a document, reducing perturbation from redundant information as in the fully-connected graph structure of ULGN.

5   Conclusion

In this paper, we propose a novel fusion graph neural network–HS²N for document-level event factuality identification, which not only integrates both semantic and syntactic information efficiently by using Biaffine Attention and a differentiated alignment method but also considers both inter and intra sentence interaction of a specific document more carefully. Extensive experiments showed that our model achieves state-of-the-art performances.

Acknowledgements. The authors would like to thank the two anonymous reviewers for their comments on this paper. This research was supported by the National Natural Science Foundation of China (No. 61836007 and 62006167.), and Project Funded by the Priority Academic Program Development of Jiangsu Higher Education Institutions (PAPD).

References

1. Saurí, R., Pustejovsky, J.: FactBank: a corpus annotated with event factuality. Lang. Resour. Eval. **43**(3), 227–268 (2009)
2. Qazvinian, V., Rosengren, E., Radev, D., Mei, Q.: Rumor has it: dentifying misinformation in microblogs. In: Proceedings of the 2011 Conference on Empirical Methods in Natural Language Processing, pp. 1589–1599. Association for Computational Linguistics, USA (2011)
3. Bian, T., Xiao, X., Xu, T., et al.: Rumor detection on social media with bidirectional graph convolutional networks. In: Proceedings of the Thirty-Fourth AAAI Conference on Artificial Intelligence, pp. 549–556. AAAI Press, USA (2020)
4. Tu, K., Chen, C., Hou, C., Yuan, J., Li, J., Yuan, X.: Rumor2Vec: a rumor detection framework with joint text and propagation structure representation learning. Inf. Sci. **560**, 137–151 (2021)
5. Saurí, R., Pustejovsky, J.: Are you sure that this happened? Assessing the factuality degree of events in text. Comput. Linguist. **38**(2), 261–299 (2012)
6. Vroe, S., Guillou, L., Stanojević, M., McKenna, N., Steedman, M.: Modality and negation in event extraction. In: Proceedings of the 4th Workshop on Challenges and Applications of Automated Extraction of Socio-political Events from Text (CASE), pp. 31–42. Association for Computational Linguistics, Online (2021)
7. Qian, Z., Li, P., Zhu, Q.: A two-step approach for event factuality identification. In: 2015 International Conference on Asian Language Processing (IALP), pp. 103–106. IEEE, China (2015)
8. Qian, Z., Li, P., Zhang, Y., Zhou, G., Zhu, Q.: Event factuality identification via generative adversarial networks with auxiliary classification. In: Proceedings of the 27th International Joint Conference on Artificial Intelligence, pp. 4293–4300. AAAI Press, Sweden (2018)
9. Veyseh, A., Nguyen, T., Dou, D.: Graph based neural networks for event factuality prediction using syntactic and semantic structures. In: Proceedings of the 57th Annual Meeting of the Association for Computational Linguistics, pp. 4393–4399. Association for Computational Linguistics, Italy (2019)
10. Le, D., Nguyen, T.: Does it happen? Multi-hop path structures for event factuality prediction with graph transformer networks. In: Proceedings of the Seventh Workshop on Noisy User-generated Text, pp. 46–55. Association for Computational Linguistics, Online (2021)
11. Qian, Z., Li, P., Zhu, Q., Zhou, G.: Document-level event factuality identification via adversarial neural network. In: Proceedings of the 2019 Conference of the North American Chapter of the Association for Computational Linguistics: Human Language Technologies, pp. 2799–2809. Association for Computational Linguistics, Minnesota (2019)
12. Cao, P., Chen, Y., Yang, Y., Liu, K., Zhao, J.: Uncertain local-to-global networks for document-level event factuality identification. In: Proceedings of the 2021 Conference on Empirical Methods in Natural Language Processing, pp. 2636–2645. Association for Computational Linguistics, Online and Dominican Republic (2021)

13. Zhang, Y., Li, P., Zhu, Q.: Document-level event factuality identification method with gated convolution networks. Comput. Sci. **47**(3), 5 (2020)
14. Devlin, J., Chang, M., Lee, K., Toutanova, K.: BERT: pre-training of Ddeep bidirectional transformers for language understanding. In: Proceedings of the 2019 Conference of the North American Chapter of the Association for Computational Linguistics: Human Language Technologies, pp. 4171–4186. Association for Computational Linguistics, Minnesota (2019)
15. Kipf, N., Welling, M.: Semi-supervised classification with graph convolutional networks. In: Proceedings of the 5th International Conference on Learning Representations, France (2017)
16. Baly, R., Karadzhov, G., Alexandrov, D., Glass, J., Nakov, P.: Predicting factuality of reporting and bias of news media sources. In: Proceedings of the 2018 Conference on Empirical Methods in Natural Language Processing, pp. 3528–3539. Association for Computational Linguistics, Belgium (2018)
17. Singhal, S., Shah, R., Chakraborty, T., Kumaraguru, P., Satoh, S.: SpotFake: a multi-modal framework for fake news detection. In: 2019 IEEE Fifth International Conference on Multimedia Big Data (BigMM), pp. 39–47. IEEE (2018)
18. Loshchilov, I., Hutter, F.: Decoupled weight decay regularization. In: Proceedings of the 7th International Conference on Learning Representations (ICLR), pp. OpenReview.net, New Orleans (2018)
19. Paatero, P., Tapper, U.: Positive matrix factorization: a non-negative factor model with optimal utilization of error estimates of data values. Environmetrics **5**(2) (1994)
20. Dozat, T., Manning, C.: Deep biaffine attention for neural dependency parsing. In: Proceedings of 5th International Conference on Learning Representations (ICLR), pp. OpenReview.net, Toulon (2017)
21. Yu, J., Bohnet, B., Poesio, M.: Named entity recognition as dependency parsing. In: Proceedings of the 58th Annual Meeting of the Association for Computational Linguistics, pp. 6470–6476. Association for Computational Linguistics, Online (2020)
22. Shi, C., Li, Y., Zhang, J., Sun, Y., Philip, S.Y.: A survey of heterogeneous information network analysis. IEEE Trans. Knowl. Data Eng. **29**(1), 17–37 (2016)

Pay Attention to the "Tails": A Novel Aspect-Fusion Model for Long-Tailed Aspect Category Detection

Wei Nie, Heng-yang Lu[(✉)], and Wei Fang[(✉)]

Jiangsu Provincial Engineering Laboratory of Pattern Recognition and Computational Intelligence, Jiangnan University, Jiangsu, China
niewei@stu.jiangnan.edu.cn, {luhengyang,fangwei}@jiangnan.edu.cn

Abstract. Aspect Category Detection (ACD), which belongs to the research of fine-grained sentiment analysis, aims to identify the aspect categories mentioned in given sentences. However, the distribution of data from the real world is imbalanced or even long-tailed. This fact poses significant challenges for ACD because it is hard to fully extract the features of tail classes. Since a sentence usually contains one or more aspect categories, we model ACD as a multi-label text classification task. Under the long-tailed setting, this paper proposes a novel Aspect-Fusion model for Long-Tailed Aspect Category Detection (AFLoT-ACD). AFLoT-ACD first extracts the fine-grained aspect features from sentence vectors by the mechanism of Interactive Attention Network with characteristics of Long-Tailed distribution (IAN-LoT). A long-tailed distribution-based attention mechanism is also incorporated, which integrates contextual aspect-level semantic information. Additionally, an Advanced Distribution-Balanced loss (A-DB) is introduced to overcome the problems of label co-occurrence and the dominance of negative classes in training a long-tailed multi-label text classifier. We conduct experiments on three datasets and compare AFLoT-ACD with eight baselines. AFLoT-ACD outperforms the SOTA with over 7% improvements in Macro F1 score for tail classes and also achieves higher detection performance in general.

Keywords: Aspect category detection · Fine-grained sentiment analysis · Long-tailed distribution · Multi-label classification

1 Introduction

Aspect-based sentiment analysis (ABSA) [1,4,23] is a fine-grained sentiment analysis task, which has a wide range of applications, such as public opinion analysis and information retrieval. As a major subtask of ABSA, Aspect Category Detection (ACD) plays a significant role in ABSA which affects sentiment classification tasks [26]. Given a set of predefined aspect categories, ACD attempts to identify all aspect categories in a sentence. Figure 1 illustrates a simple example:

© The Author(s), under exclusive license to Springer Nature Switzerland AG 2022
S. Khanna et al. (Eds.): PRICAI 2022, LNCS 13630, pp. 321–334, 2022.
https://doi.org/10.1007/978-3-031-20865-2_24

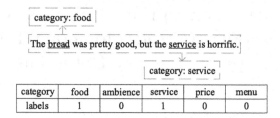

Fig. 1. An example of the ACD task. The underlined words are the aspect categories to be detected. The corresponding label is 1 if the sentence contains the aspect category.

food and *service* are two aspect categories to be identified in the given sentence. The aspect categories, which are words or phrases in the given sentence, can be expressed as explicit ones (e.g. service) or implicit ones (e.g. bread).

Since a sentence may contain one or more aspect categories, the ACD task needs to consider information of different aspect categories. Some existing works apply deep learning-based methods to address the ACD task [7]. Recently, Hu et al. [9] discovered that the datasets used for ACD show the long-tailed tendency. For example, as seen from Fig. 2, two public ACD datasets present approximately long-tailed distributions, in which the number of training instances per aspect varies significantly from thousands for *food* to as few for *price*. Long-tailed distribution has brought huge challenges for machine learning tasks [11,20], which may cause bias for classification to head classes. Therefore, a critical problem arises: **how to improve the detection of tail classes in ACD under the long-tailed distribution settings?**

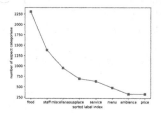 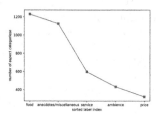

Fig. 2. The distributions of aspect categories on MAMS (left) and SemEval2014 (right).

In this paper, we model ACD as a multi-label classification task and propose a novel Aspect-Fusion model for Long-Tailed Aspect Category Detection (AFLoT-ACD). It can be effectively applied to long-tailed data. This model introduces the Interactive Attention Network with characteristics of Long-Tailed distribution, namely IAN-LoT mechanism. Besides, AFLoT-ACD incorporates an attention mechanism based on the long-tailed distribution. We also propose an Advanced Distribution-Balanced (A-DB) loss function to improve the prediction of tail classes. The main contributions include:

1. We consider the long-tail phenomenon in ACD task, which is rarely discussed previously. We propose an AFLoT-ACD model which can effectively improve the detection of tail classes, and achieve strong performance in general.
2. We adopt an A-DB loss function for ACD to address the problems of label co-occurrence and dominance of negative classes in long-tailed scenarios.
3. To extract the fine-grained aspect features and additional context-level semantics, we propose an IAN-LoT mechanism that combines the long-tailed characteristics. Additionally, we introduce a fused attention mechanism to capture the most relevant aspect category information.

2 Related Work

2.1 Aspect Category Detection

The previous works on ACD mainly include two categories: lexicon-based methods and machine learning-based methods. The lexicon-based methods primarily integrate a dictionary of opinion words and certain grammatical rules [24]. Compared with the lexicon-based methods, the most recent machine learning-based methods have better performance. Ghadery et al. [7] addressed the ACD task in multiple languages by using different fully connected layers to detect aspect categories. Huang et al. [12] fused the sentence and the aspect category attention feature representation by multi-head attention. In addition, some works had developed joint models ecuting ACD and sentiment classification tasks simultaneously [17,25,26]. Li et al. [17] proposed a multi-instance multi-label learning network for aspect-category sentiment analysis, in which attention-based ACD generates effective attention weights for different aspect categories. However, the above methods neglect the fact that aspect categories generally show the characteristics of long-tailed distribution. Recently, Hu et al. [9] formulated the ACD task in the few-shot learning scenario to solute the long-tailed challenge.

2.2 Long-Tailed Distribution in Multi-label Classification

Re-sampling is a common strategy that includes oversampling of minority classes [30] and undersampling of majority classes [3]. However, re-sampling methods are ineffective in the multi-label scenario, since re-sampling samples may not lead to a balance when majority classes co-occur with minority classes. Recently, loss function manipulation has been explored to solve long-tailed multi-label classification. For example, Lin et al. [18] presented focal loss function based on the standard cross entropy loss. It allowed the model to focus on hard samples while reducing the weight of easy samples. Wu et al. [27] provided a distribution-balanced loss function aiming at the co-occurrence of labels and the dominance of negative labels in the computer vision (CV) domain. Huang et al. [11] introduced the distribution-balanced loss function to the natural language processing (NLP) domain for multi-label text classification tasks. This paper incorporates long-tailed distribution information and aspect category information. Meanwhile, we present an A-DB loss inspired by [27]. It effectively improves the identification effect in long-tailed ACD.

3   Methodology

3.1   Problem Formulation

There are m predefined aspect categories $A = \{a_1, a_2, \ldots, a_m\}$, where a_j is a word or phrase that describes the j-th aspect. $D = \left\{ \left\{ S_l, \hat{A}_l \right\} \middle| 1 \le l \le N \right\}$ is the dataset composed of N sentences along with their aspect categories $\hat{A}_l$, where $\hat{A}_l \subseteq A$. Given a sentence $S_l = \{w_1, w_2, \ldots, w_n\}$, we can represent the aspect categories $\hat{A}_l$ as $Y_l = \{y_1^l, y_2^l, \ldots, y_m^l\}$, where $y_j^l \in \{0,1\}$, and $y_j^l = 1$ if and only if the l-th sentence contains the j-th aspect category a_j. ACD aims to detect all of the aspect categories in a sentence S_l. Therefore, it can be modeled as a multi-label classification problem. In long-tailed settings, there are around 80% of instances that appear in less than 20% of classes, called **head classes**, and the remaining classes with a low frequency called **tail classes** [29].

3.2   Proposed Model

This section describes the proposed AFLoT-ACD. Figure 3 illustrates the architecture of AFLoT-ACD, which contains six layers: input layer, embedding layer, LSTM layer, IAN-LoT layer, fused attention layer, and prediction layer.

Input Layer. The inputs of AFLoT-ACD are m predefined aspect categories $A = \{a_1, a_2, \ldots, a_m\}$, and a sentence $S_l = \{w_1, w_2, \ldots, w_n\}$ in the dataset.

Embedding Layer. For each word w_i, we can get a vector $w_e^i \in R^d$ from $E_1 \in R^{|V| \times d}$, where $|V|$ is the vocabulary size and d is the embedding dimension. Meanwhile, for each aspect a_i, we can get a vector $a_e^i \in R^d$ from $E_2 \in R^{m \times d}$. The l-th sentence S_l and the predefined aspect categories A are respectively converted to word embeddings of the sentence $\boldsymbol{S}_l = \left\{ w_e^1, w_e^2, \ldots, w_e^n \right\} \in R^{n \times d}$ and word embeddings of aspect categories $\boldsymbol{A}_l = \left\{ a_e^1, a_e^2, \ldots, a_e^m \right\} \in R^{m \times d}$, where n is the number of words, m is the number of aspect categories.

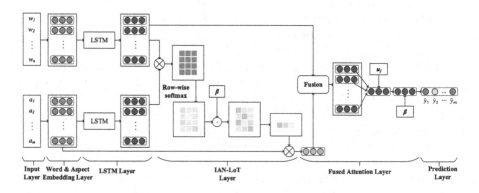

Fig. 3. The architecture of AFLoT-ACD.

LSTM Layer. To better perceive contextual semantic, word embeddings of the sentence and aspect categories are fed into a LSTM network [8], which can output hidden states $H_w = \{h_w^1, h_w^2, \ldots, h_w^n\}$ and $H_a = \{h_a^1, h_a^2, \ldots, h_a^m\}$. The hidden states of LSTM h_w^i and h_a^j are computed by Eq. 1:

$$h_w^i = LSTM\left(h_w^{i-1}, w_i\right), \quad h_a^j = LSTM\left(h_a^{j-1}, a_j\right), \tag{1}$$

where the sizes of the hidden state is set to be d.

IAN-LoT Layer. This layer applies the proposed IAN-LoT mechanism. Inspired by the use of attention-over-attention (AOA) in sentiment classification [10], we introduce a fine-grained interactive attention matrix to learn better representations of aspect categories and the sentence. The entire aspect vector that incorporates long-tailed characteristics is obtained. Specifically, we first calculate the interactive attention matrix $I \in R^{n \times m}$ with the hidden states H_w and H_a. The process is as follows:

$$I = H_w \cdot H_a^T. \tag{2}$$

Then, the softmax function is applied to each row of the attention matrix I, which is calculated by Eq. 3:

$$k_{ij} = \frac{\exp\left(I_{ij}\right)}{\sum_i \exp\left(I_{ij}\right)}, \tag{3}$$

where k_{ij} is the i-th row and j-th column of $k \in R^{n \times m}$. k represents the attention weight of the sentence to aspect categories. Given k, we introduce long-tailed characteristics as follows:

$$\hat{I} = \beta \cdot k, \tag{4}$$

where the weight parameters $\beta = \{\beta_1, \beta_2, \ldots, \beta_m\}$, which are calculated as $\beta_j = \frac{1}{N_{a_j}}$, N_{a_j} is the number of instances for aspect category a_j in the training dataset. For example, a tail class a_j can achieve more attention when training by a larger weight β_j. And $\hat{I} \in R^{n \times m}$ represents weight information for each aspect category.

The finer-grained weight information I_L of aspect categories based on the long-tailed distribution can be obtained through the max-pooling of $\hat{I}$. The weight information is then multiplied by A_l to generate the entire aspect category vector representation s, $s \in R^{1 \times d}$. The process is as follows:

$$s = I_L \times A_l. \tag{5}$$

Fused Attention Layer. This layer takes the output s of the IAN-LoT layer and $H_w = \{h_w^1, h_w^2, \ldots, h_w^n\}$ as inputs, the fused vetor $\hat{h}$ is computed by:

$$\hat{h} = W \cdot s + H_w, \tag{6}$$

where $W \in R^{n \times 1}$ is a learnable weight parameter, and $\hat{h} \in R^{n \times d}$ is a vector that fuses contextual aspect level semantic information. Fine-grained learnable weights allow for better integration of aspect information with context. $\hat{h}$ is fed into an attentional mechanism to generate attention weight for each predefined aspect category [28]. For the j-th aspect category:

$$\alpha_j = softmax \left(u_j^T \cdot \beta \cdot \tanh \left(W_j \cdot \hat{h}_j + b_j \right) \right), j = 1, 2, \ldots, m, \qquad (7)$$

where $W_j \in R^{d \times d}$, $b_j \in R^d$, $u_j \in R^d$ are learnable parameters, and $\alpha_j \in R^n$ is the attention weight vector.

Prediction Layer. We use the $\hat{h}$ as the sentence representation for prediction. For the j-th aspect category:

$$\hat{y}_j = sigmoid \left(W_j \cdot \hat{h} \cdot \alpha_j^T + b_j \right), j = 1, 2, \ldots, m, \qquad (8)$$

where $W_j \in R^{d \times 1}$, b_j is a scalar, $\hat{y}_j$ is the prediction of the j-th aspect category.

3.3   Loss Function

In this section, we introduce the A-DB loss function. Binary cross entropy (BCE) loss is commonly used for multi-label classification problems [2]. However, BCE may focus on learning features from negative samples because positive and negative classes are uniformly processed in BCE. In Fig. 4, it can be seen intuitively that the head class *food* has a high possibility of occurring simultaneously with other aspect categories. Inspired by [27], we introduce A-DB loss function aiming at the co-occurrence of labels and the dominance of negative labels in ACD. We improve the weight of the rebalance calculation method to ensure that the weights of head and tail classes are more appropriate for ACD and modify the smoothing function to further improve the performance of the model.

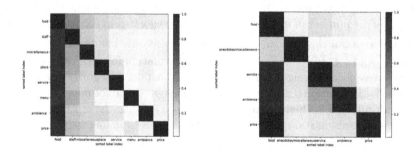

Fig. 4. The label co-occurrence on MAMS-LT (left) and SemEval2014-LT (right) (refer to Sect. 4.1). The color coding of the co-occurence matrix is based on the conditional probability $p(i|j)$ of class in the i-th column on class in the j-th row.

Specifically, $n_j = \sum_{l=1}^{|N|} y_j^l$ is the number of instances contained the j-th aspect category in the dataset. Without considering classes co-occurrence, the sampling frequency expectation is calculated by $P_j(S_l) = \frac{1}{m}\frac{1}{n_j}$ for the j-th aspect category. The instance sampling frequency is calculated based on the repeated sampling of each positive class in the instance, and the process is as follows:

$$P^I(S_l) = \frac{1}{m} \cdot \sum_{j=1}^{m} \frac{1}{n_j} \cdot y_j^l. \tag{9}$$

Rebalanced weight r_j^l is calculated by:

$$r_j^l = \left[\frac{P_j(S_l)}{P^I(S_l)} \right]^{\gamma-1}, \tag{10}$$

where γ is a hyper-parameter. The modified smoothing function is used to map r_j^l into a suitable value as follows:

$$\hat{r}_j^l = \omega + \log\left(1 + exp\left(-\varphi \times (r_j^l - \mu)\right)\right), \tag{11}$$

where ω, φ and μ are scalars. In order to avoid the advantage of negative classes, A-DB introduces a hyper-parameter λ and a specifical bias τ_j as follows:

$$\tau_j = \eta \cdot \log\left(\frac{1}{\rho_j} - 1\right), \tag{12}$$

where ρ_j is the proportion of the number of j-th aspect category to the total number of samples, and η is a hyper-parameter. The proposed A-DB loss function is as follows:

$$\begin{aligned} L = \frac{1}{m} \cdot \sum_{j=0}^{m} \hat{r}_j^l \cdot \Big[& y_j^l \cdot \log\left(1 + e^{-(z_j^l - \tau_j)}\right) \\ & + \frac{1}{\lambda} \cdot \left(1 - y_j^l\right) \cdot \log\left(1 + e^{\lambda(z_j^l - \tau_j)}\right) \Big]. \end{aligned} \tag{13}$$

4 Experiments

4.1 Datasets

We conduct experiments on three datasets, including original MAMS [13], MAMS-LT and SemEval2014-LT. First, we compare the performance of AFLoT-ACD on original MAMS, which is a widely used and public dataset for ACD tasks [16,17]. In addition, to better show the advantages of AFLoT-ACD under long-tailed distributions, we use MAMS-LT and SemEval2014-LT, which fit the standard long-tailed distribution. This kind of experiment follows the previously long-tailed practice [27]. SemEval2014-LT and MAMS-LT come from the SemEval2014 dataset [23] and MAMS dataset [13] respectively. The procedure includes: we first sort all aspect categories based on the original data and determine the head and tail classes; then, instances are added or removed based on the Pareto Distribution [19].

SemEval2014-LT training set contains 1422 sentences. We randomly cut out 12.5% to be validation set and the rest to be the training set. Experiments are evaluated on original SemEval2014 testing set. **MAMS-LT** training set contains 1502 sentences. We evaluate experiments on original MAMS testing set.

Figure 5 shows the distribution of MAMS-LT and SemEval2014-LT datasets. It can be seen that a few aspect categories occupy the majority of the samples while the majority of aspect categories have few samples on MAMS-LT and SemEval2014-LT.

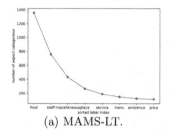 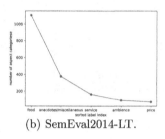

(a) MAMS-LT.   (b) SemEval2014-LT.

Fig. 5. The distributions on MAMS-LT and SemEval2014-LT.

4.2 Implementation Details

We implement AFLoT-ACD in PyTorch 1.2 [21]. The word embedding vectors are initialized using 300-dimensional word vectors pre-trained by GloVe [22], and the aspect embedding vectors are randomly initialized. The batch sizes are set to 64. AFLoT-ACD is optimized by the Adam optimizer [15]. The learning rate is set to 0.001.We set $d = 300$, $\lambda = 5$, $\eta = 0.05$, $\omega = 10$, $\varphi = 0.2$, and $\mu = 0.1$. In order to adjust the weight of the head classes and the tail classes appropriately, the experiment is used to confirm the hyperparameter γ. Figure 6 depicts the effect of γ for the head classes, tail classes and total classes respectively. Synthetically, the results reveal that $\gamma = 2$ is the optimal solution to the problem.

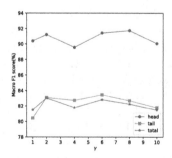

Fig. 6. The effect of γ on the Macro F1 scores of the head classes, tail classes, and total classes.

We compare AFLoT-ACD with the following six baselines: four ACD models: **TextCNN** [14], **LSTM** [8], **SVR** [6], **SCAN** [16]; two joint models that perform the ACD and ACSC simultaneously: **AS-Capsules** [26], **AC-MIMLLN** [17]. We also design the **AFLoT-ACD-BERT** model which combines BERT [5] and AFLoT-ACD. We replace the embedding layer and the LSTM in AFLoT-ACD with the uncased basic pre-trained BERT. AFLoT-ACD-BERT takes "[CLS] sentence [SEP] aspect category [SEP]" as input like ACMIMLLN-BERT [17].

4.3 Experimental Results and Analysis

Comparisons with Baseline Methods. To evaluate the performance of AFLoT-ACD, we first compare the AFLoT-ACD with baseline methods on MAMS-LT and SemEval2014-LT. The following conclusions can be taken based on the experimental results in Table 1. First, AFLoT-ACD outperforms all baseline methods on MAMS-LT and SemEval2014-LT, and AFLoT-ACD can obtain better improvement by using more powerful sentence encoders. Experimental results show that AFLoT-ACD has a greater capacity for long-tailed ACD. Second, AFLoT-ACD has a distinct advantage in Macro F1 scores on MAMS-LT, indicating that AFLoT-ACD performs better for sentences with multiple aspect categories. Third, AFLoT-ACD outperforms on MAMS-LT than on SemEval2014-LT, which could be owing to the SemEval2014-LT containing more sentences with only one aspect category. It weakens the effect of the re-balancing weight we designed for the label co-occurrence problem. But it can be seen that the effect is greatly improved on MAMS-LT.

Table 1. Macro F1 scores by baseline methods and AFLoT-ACD on MAMS-LT and SemEval2014-LT with the best results represented by boldface.

Methods	MAMS-LT	SemEval2014-LT
(1) SVR	74.13%	63.20%
(2) LSTM	77.27%	76.55%
(3) TextCNN	80.04%	77.48%
(4) SCAN	76.18%	79.55%
(5) AC-MIMLLN	76.18%	78.87%
(6) AS-Capsules	80.76%	80.18%
(7) AFLoT-ACD (ours)	**83.04%**	**82.10%**
(8) BERT	84.19%	82.11%
(9) AC-MIMLLN-BERT	83.08%	81.23%
(10) AFLoT-ACD-BERT (ours)	**86.79%**	**84.44%**

Table 2. The results of comparisons for tail classes on the Semeval2014-LT.

Methods	Anecdotes/ miscellaneous	Service	Ambience	price	Macro F1
AC-MIMLLN	73.62%	85.99%	72.16%	78.83%	78.87%
AS-Capsules	72.37%	**89.17%**	70.1%	79.72%	80.18%
AFLoT-ACD (ours)	**74.6%**	88.0%	**77.98%**	**85.71%**	**82.10%**
BERT	68.94%	88.82%	73.96%	87.58%	82.11%
AC-MIMLLN-BERT	71.09%	**89.38%**	73.68%	84.56%	81.23%
AFLoT-ACD-BERT (ours)	**75.05%**	86.23%	**79.41%**	**92.02%**	**83.44%**

Effectiveness of AFLoT-ACD on Tail Classes. We conduct experiments to show the performance of tail classes in Table 2. Comparing the best baseline AS-Capsules and recent work AC-MIMLLN on Semeval2014-LT, we can observe that AFLoT-ACD achieves 5.99% and 5.82% higher F1 scores than AS-Capsules respectively for tail classes *price* and *ambience*, and AFLoT-ACD performs slightly than AS-capsules for *service*. Besides, AFLoT-ACD-BERT surpasses all BERT-based models for most aspect categories, especially for *ambience* and *price*. We can observe that AFLoT-ACD effectively enhances the effect of tail classes.

Performance Comparisons the Original Dataset. In order to show the performance of our AFLoT-ACD on original MAMS dataset, we compare the results of AC-MIMLLN and AFLoT-ACD for each aspect category. As seen in Table 3, AFLoT-ACD outperforms AC-MIMLLN for most aspect categories. Especially for tail classes *price*, the result of AFLoT-ACD is 11.25% higher than AC-MIMLLN. Besides, we can observe that significant increases for tail classes can

Table 3. F1 scores of AC-MIMLLN and AFLoT-ACD for each aspect category on the MAMS and the best results are represented by boldface.

Classes	Aspects	Methods	
		AC-MIMLLN	AFLoT-ACD (ours)
head	food	**94.42%**	93.76%
	Staff	94.52%	**95.07%**
tail	miscellaneous	70.45%	**73.0%**
	place	**83.71%**	**83.71%**
	Ambience	85.25%	**88.89%**
	price	68.75%	**80.0%**
	menu	**95.0%**	94.34%
	Service	81.0%	**83.87%**
Macro F1 scores		84.14%	**86.58%**

compensate slight decreases for head classes, which makes up for the performance of total results. The experimental results indicate that AFLoT-ACD is also effective on the original dataset in the ACD task.

Table 4. F1 scores of AFLoT-ACD with different loss functions for long-tailed tasks.

Loss Function	MAMS-LT	SemEval2014-LT
BCE Loss	82.68%	79.92%
DB Loss	81.04%	80.10%
DB-Focal Loss	82.10%	81.60%
A-DB Loss (ours)	**83.04%**	**82.10%**

Effectiveness of the Proposed Loss Function. Table 4 compares performances of AFLoT-ACD with various long-tailed loss functions, including **BCE** [2], **DB** [27], **DB-Focal** [27] and **A-DB** (our proposed). For MAMS-LT and SemEval2014-LT dataset, we can observe that A-DB loss outperforms the previous long-tailed loss functions in the ACD task.

4.4 Ablation Study

We conduct an ablation study to better assess the effects of components of AFLoT-ACD. Table 5 shows the experimental results of Macro F1 scores of each part of AFLoT-ACD. Note that Table 5(1) is compared to Table 5(4) using standard BCE loss; for Table 5(2) and Table 5(3), we apply deletion to compare with Table 5(4). We can observe that removing any one of the three components will result in a decrease for the performance of AFLoT-ACD.

Table 5. Experimental results of Macro F1 scores of each component of AFLoT-ACD.

	IAN-LoT	A-DB loss	Fused attention	MAMS-LT	SemEval2014-LT
(1)	√		√	82.68%	79.92%
(2)	√	√		80.79%	81.22%
(3)		√	√	81.6%	81.21%
(4)	√	√	√	**83.04%**	**82.10%**

5 Conclusion

In this study, we propose an AFLoT-ACD model for ACD tasks in the long-tailed scenario. Specifically, we design an A-DB loss function to focus on the problems of label co-occurrence and dominance of negative classes. Besides, to better learn long-tailed information and aspect information, we propose the IAN-LoT mechanism and the fused attention. Experimental results on three datasets show that AFLoT-ACD outperforms eight baselines in general. Additionally, to exhibit the effectiveness of the proposed A-DB loss function, we compare the performance by using different loss functions. We also conduct the ablation study to further show the effectiveness of AFLoT-ACD.

Acknowledgements. This work was supported in part by the National Natural Science foundation of China under Grant 62073155, 62002137, and 62106088, in part by "Blue Project" in Jiangsu Universities, China, in part by Guangdong Provincial Key Laboratory under Grant 2020B121201001, in part by the China Postdoctoral Science Foundation under Grant 2022M711360.

References

1. Ahmed, M., Chen, Q., Wang, Y., Li, Z.: Hint-embedding attention-based LSTM for aspect identification sentiment analysis. In: PRICAI 2019: Trends in Artificial Intelligence: 16th Pacific Rim International Conference on Artificial Intelligence, Cuvu, Yanuca Island, Fiji, August 26–30, 2019, Proceedings, Part II (2019)
2. Bengio, Y.: Courville, aaron, vincent, pascal: representation learning: a review and new perspectives. IEEE Trans. Pattern Anal. Mach. Intell. **35**(8), 1798–1828 (2013)
3. Buda, M., Maki, A., Mazurowski, M.A.: A systematic study of the class imbalance problem in convolutional neural networks. Neural Netw. **106**, 249–259 (2018)
4. Dai, Z., Peng, C., Chen, H., Ding, Y.: A multi-task incremental learning framework with category name embedding for aspect-category sentiment analysis. In: Proceedings of the 2020 Conference on Empirical Methods in Natural Language Processing (EMNLP), pp. 6955–6965 (2020)
5. Devlin, J., Chang, M.W., Lee, K., Toutanova, K.: BERT: pre-training of deep bidirectional transformers for language understanding. In: Proceedings of the 2019 Conference of the North American Chapter of the Association for Computational Linguistics: Human Language Technologies, Volume 1 (Long and Short Papers), pp. 4171–4186. Association for Computational Linguistics, Minneapolis, Minnesota, June 2019. https://doi.org/10.18653/v1/N19-1423
6. Dilawar, N., et al.: Understanding citizen issues through reviews: a step towards data informed planning in smart cities. Appl. Sci. **8**(9), 1589 (2018)
7. Ghadery, E., Movahedi, S., Faili, H., Shakery, A.: MNCN: a multilingual ngram-based convolutional network for aspect category detection in online reviews. In: Proceedings of the AAAI Conference on Artificial Intelligence, vol. 33, pp. 6441–6448 (2019)
8. Hochreiter, S., Schmidhuber, J.: Long short-term memory. Neural Comput. **9**(8), 1735–1780 (1997)
9. Hu, M., et al.: Multi-label few-shot learning for aspect category detection. In: Proceedings of the 59th Annual Meeting of the Association for Computational Linguistics and the 11th International Joint Conference on Natural Language Processing (Volume 1: Long Papers), pp. 6330–6340 (2021)
10. Huang, B., Ou, Y., Carley, K.M.: Aspect level sentiment classification with attention-over-attention neural networks. In: International Conference on Social Computing, Behavioral-Cultural Modeling and Prediction and Behavior Representation in Modeling and Simulation (2018)

11. Huang, Y., Giledereli, B., Köksal, A., Özgür, A., Ozkirimli, E.: Balancing methods for multi-label text classification with long-tailed class distribution. CoRR abs/2109.04712 (2021)
12. Huang, Z., Zhao, H., Peng, F., Chen, Q., Zhao, G.: Aspect category sentiment analysis with self-attention fusion networks. In: Nah, Y., Cui, B., Lee, S.-W., Yu, J.X., Moon, Y.-S., Whang, S.E. (eds.) DASFAA 2020. LNCS, vol. 12114, pp. 154–168. Springer, Cham (2020). https://doi.org/10.1007/978-3-030-59419-0_10
13. Jiang, Q., Chen, L., Xu, R., Ao, X., Yang, M.: A challenge dataset and effective models for aspect-based sentiment analysis. In: Proceedings of the 2019 Conference on Empirical Methods in Natural Language Processing and the 9th International Joint Conference on Natural Language Processing (EMNLP-IJCNLP) (2019)
14. Kim.Y: Convolutional neural networks for sentence classification. arXiv preprint arXiv:1408.5882 (2014)
15. Kingma, D.P., Ba, J.: Adam: a method for stochastic optimization. arXiv preprint arXiv:1412.6980 (2014)
16. Li, Y., Yin, C., Zhong, S.: Sentence constituent-aware aspect-category sentiment analysis with graph attention networks. In: Zhu, X., Zhang, M., Hong, Yu., He, R. (eds.) NLPCC 2020. LNCS (LNAI), vol. 12430, pp. 815–827. Springer, Cham (2020). https://doi.org/10.1007/978-3-030-60450-9_64
17. Li, Y., Yin, C., Zhong, S.H., Pan, X.: Multi-instance multi-label learning networks for aspect-category sentiment analysis. In: Proceedings of the 2020 Conference on Empirical Methods in Natural Language Processing (EMNLP), pp. 3550–3560 (2020)
18. Lin, T.Y., Goyal, P., Girshick, R., He, K., Dollár, P.: Focal loss for dense object detection. IEEE Trans. Pattern Anal. Mach. Intell. $\mathbf{PP}$(99), 2999–3007 (2017)
19. Liu, Z., Miao, Z., Zhan, X., Wang, J., Gong, B., Yu, S.X.: Large-scale long-tailed recognition in an open world. In: Proceedings of the IEEE/CVF Conference on Computer Vision and Pattern Recognition, pp. 2537–2546 (2019)
20. Movahedi, S., Ghadery, E., Faili, H., Shakery, A.: Aspect category detection via topic-attention network. arXiv e-prints pp. arXiv-1901 (2019)
21. Paszke, A., et al.: Automatic differentiation in pytorch (2017)
22. Pennington, J., Socher, R., Manning, C.D.: Glove: global vectors for word representation. In: Proceedings of the 2014 Conference on Empirical Methods in Natural Language Processing (EMNLP), pp. 1532–1543 (2014)
23. Pontiki, M., Galanis, D., Pavlopoulos, J., Papageorgiou, H., Androutsopoulos, I., Manandhar, S.: Semeval-2014 task 4: aspect based sentiment analysis. In: Nakov, P., Zesch, T. (eds.) Proceedings of the 8th International Workshop on Semantic Evaluation, SemEval@COLING 2014, Dublin, Ireland, August 23–24, 2014. pp. 27–35. The Association for Computer Linguistics (2014)
24. Schouten, K., Weijde, O., Frasincar, F., Dekker, R.: Supervised and unsupervised aspect category detection for sentiment analysis with co-occurrence data. IEEE Trans. Cybern. $\mathbf{48}$(4), 1263–1275 (2018)
25. Siyu, W., Jiangtao, Q., Chuanyang, H.: A joint self-attention model for aspect category detection in e-commerce reviews. In: PACIS 2021 Proceedings (2021)
26. Wang, Y., Sun, A., Huang, M., Zhu, X.: Aspect-level sentiment analysis using as-capsules. In: The World Wide Web Conference, pp. 2033–2044 (2019)
27. Wu, T., Huang, Q., Liu, Z., Wang, Yu., Lin, D.: Distribution-balanced loss for multi-label classification in long-tailed datasets. In: Vedaldi, A., Bischof, H., Brox, T., Frahm, J.-M. (eds.) ECCV 2020. LNCS, vol. 12349, pp. 162–178. Springer, Cham (2020). https://doi.org/10.1007/978-3-030-58548-8_10

28. Yang, Z., Yang, D., Dyer, C., He, X., Smola, A., Hovy, E.: Hierarchical attention networks for document classification. In: Proceedings of the 2016 conference of the North American chapter of the association for computational linguistics: human language technologies, pp. 1480–1489 (2016)
29. Yuan, M., Xu, J., Li, Z.: Long tail multi-label learning. In: 2019 IEEE Second International Conference on Artificial Intelligence and Knowledge Engineering (AIKE), pp. 28–31. IEEE (2019)
30. Zhou, B., Cui, Q., Wei, X.S., Chen, Z.M.: BBN: bilateral-branch network with cumulative learning for long-tailed visual recognition. In: Proceedings of the IEEE/CVF Conference on Computer Vision and Pattern Recognition, pp. 9719–9728 (2020)

Choice-Driven Contextual Reasoning for Commonsense Question Answering

Wenqing Deng[1], Zhe Wang[2], Kewen Wang[2(✉)], Xiaowang Zhang[1], and Zhiyong Feng[1]

[1] College of Intelligence and Computing, Tianjin University, Tianjin, China
{2019218039,xiaowangzhang,zhiyongfeng}@tju.edu.cn
[2] School of Information and Communication Technology, Griffith University, Brisbane, Australia
{zhe.wang,k.wang}@griffith.edu.au

Abstract. The task of question answering is to find the most appropriate answer for an input question in natural language from a given custom knowledge base of information. While the performance of question answering systems has been significantly improved, they still struggle to answer questions that require commonsense reasoning. To capture common sense beyond associations, a challenging dataset CommonsenseQA for commonsense question answering is proposed. As a result, several models have been developed for tackling this challenge. But existing approaches are still limited in handling contextual representation and reasoning. In this paper, we propose a model for commonsense question answering by implementing a form of choice-driven contextual reasoning through novel encoding strategies and choice differentiation mechanisms. We have conducted experiments on major baselines for commonsense question answering and our experimental results show that the proposed model significantly outperforms strong baselines.

Keywords: Commonsense question answering · Multiple choice questions · Contextual reasoning

1 Introduction

A key component in many practical AI systems, such as chatbots, virtual assistants, and exam robots [3,5] is to answer complex questions that require specialised knowledge with a level of accuracy, but existing models for question answering are still limited in reasoning about commonsense knowledge. Thus commonsense question answering (QA) has been proposed as an initiative for answering questions in natural language by understanding the contextual information of a given question and performing commonsense reasoning to select the best answer from a set of candidate answers [2,22]. Figure 1 shows an example, where five choices (candidate answers) are provided and sometimes they are indistinguishable if certain subtle contextual information is missing. In particular, without establishing the connection between *"business restaurant"* and

© The Author(s), under exclusive license to Springer Nature Switzerland AG 2022
S. Khanna et al. (Eds.): PRICAI 2022, LNCS 13630, pp. 335–346, 2022.
https://doi.org/10.1007/978-3-031-20865-2_25

Q:Where is a business restaurant **likely to be located?**
A. town   B. at hotel   C. mall   D. business sector   **E. yellow pages**

Commonsense Knowledge

-Town is a settlement that is smaller than a city but bigger than a large village (or borough in some areas).

-Hotel is business enterprise that provides lodging in a single building paid on a short-term basis.

-Mall is a large indoor shopping center, usually anchored by department stores.

-Business sector is a subset of the economy made up by companies, excluding the economic activities of general government, private households, and nonprofit organizations serving individuals.

-Yellow pages means telephone directory of businesses by category.

....

Fig. 1. An example from the CommonsenseQA dataset.

"business sector", pre-trained language models alone, such as ALBERT [10], may not be able to select the correct answer.

As pre-trained language models for QA [6,10,14,17] do not explicitly process knowledge and commonsense reasoning, much research effort has been made in developing QA models that are both accurate and interpretable by modelling human commonsense reasoning. In particular, knowledge graphs such as ConceptNet [13] have been used as a source of external knowledge, and there are several approaches that model commonsense reasoning through the graph connectedness of concepts [11,23]. Some proposals have been reported along this line, e.g., [15,22], but it still remains a challenge to effectively model commonsense reasoning into QA systems in the purpose of obtaining interpretable and better accurate QA models.

While existing QA models are still limited in commonsense reasoning, human beings are good at building semantic connections between concepts through background knowledge and cognitive strategies. For instance, to refine the semantic connections established and to eliminate distractor choices that are semantically close to the answers, a human may compare the choices to understand their subtle differences. For example, while *"hotel"*, *"mall"* and *"business sector"* are all buildings that may have a *"business restaurant"*, a *"business sector"* stands out with the features of its business activities. Hence, a comparison among the choices can help to focus their differences and highlight those differentiable features of each choice. Some attempts have been made to simulate contextual reasoning using deep neural networks [20,24]. However, the accuracy of these models needs to be further improved. Moreover, the two different semantic representations produced from two reading strategies in [20] are aggregated in a naive way by only merging their confidence degree in the last stage. It would be interesting to directly aggregate the semantic representations. A two-way matching strategy for reading comprehension is introduced in [24] and thus the correlations between choices are used in their model. The strategy targets five reading comprehension datasets, but it doesn't illustrate its role in the commonsense question answering. Meanwhile, it is unclear whether correlations between choices can be reduced to increase differences by reducing correlations.

In this paper, we aim to model some aspects of contextual reasoning in natural language processing (NLP) and thus propose a method of commonsense reasoning for better accuracy (we call it Choice-driven Contextual Reasoning or CCR). Given a question-choice pair, by employing a pre-trained language model, such as ALBERT [10], we simulate human beings' cognitive strategies, including contextual information extraction from the question to the choice, as well as from the choices to the question, and from external knowledge bases. The proposed approach is able to compare choices w.r.t. the question and integrate contextual information using attention mechanisms. Evaluation shows that our model outperforms major models that do not use heavyweight language models (like T5 [17]), ConceptNet [13], or its source corpus OMCS [19]. This is not a restriction since the use of ConceptNet or OMCS will make the commonsense question answering much less challenging. Also, some cognitive strategies we propose can further enhance the performance of other QA models such as ALBERT [10], KCR[1] and XLNET+GR [15]. Our model through case study shows our strategies are able to help intuitively rank the choices in some tricky cases.

Codes and data for our model can be found at https://www.dropbox.com/sh/dryl2c00vh612fg/AABXg0FmU5OAB6ltByQUHgqia?dl=0.

2   Our Approach

Our approach focuses on the task of commonsense QA. Formally, given a natural language question q and m choices (or candidate answers) $a_1, a_2, \ldots, a_m$, the goal is to find the most plausible answer by employing commonsense knowledge and reasoning. In datasets like CommonsenseQA [21], some key concepts $\{c_q^{(1)}, c_q^{(2)}, \ldots, c_q^{(n)}\}$ in the question q are also annotated.

An overview of our model ALBERT+CCR for commonsense QA is shown in Fig. 2. The new model has four major modules, namely, Context Retrieval, Contextualized Encoding, Similarity-based Differentiation, and Confidence Aggregation. In what follows, we introduce the design of our model.

2.1   Context Retrieval

In this module, we aim to retrieve textual descriptions of the key concepts in the question and the choices from Wiki knowledge that can provide most relevant and concise contextual information for the QA. As discussed in the Introduction, this is essential for contextual reasoning.

For each concept in the questions or the choices, we retrieve several descriptions through the MediaWiki API. Since the descriptions returned by the MediaWiki API are sorted according to the degrees of matching, we can often adopt

---

[1] https://github.com/jessionlin/csqa/blob/master/Model_details.md.

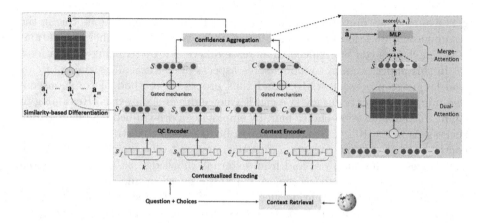

Fig. 2. A framework overview.

the first description as the description of the concept. To form the queries or the search keywords, we process the words in the concept into the following three forms: i) the original form without any change; ii) the lemma form produced by Spacy [7]; and iii) the basic word, which is the last noun by default. For instance, for the concept "raise children", its original form and its lemma form are both "raise children", whereas the basic word is "children".

For each key concept $c_q^{(i)}$ in the question and each choice a, we obtain their descriptions $d_q^{(i)}$ and d_a respectively.

2.2   Contextualized Encoding

When human beings answer a multiple choice question, one can first read the question and then the choices, and/or first read the choices and then the question. To simulate such cognition strategies in QA, we encode both forward (i.e., from questions to choices) and backward (i.e., from choices to questions) reading sequences.

For each pair of a question q and a choice a, the forward QA input s_f is obtained by concatenating the question q, the key concepts $c_q^{(i)}$'s, and the choice a, whereas the backward QA input s_b is in the reverse order, by concatenating a, q, and $c_q^{(i)}$'s. Note that we include the key concepts to establish connection with the knowledge retrieved in the Context Retrieval module. Existing models often only encode the forward reading, which cannot capture the connection building process from choices to questions, whereas our backward encoding simulate the case when the choice a is read before the question q. Note that this is different from a bidirectional encoding, where the same forward reading sequence is encoded forth and back word by word.

The language encodings for the forward and backward QA inputs can be obtained from pre-trained language model like ALBERT [10], denoted S_f and S_b, which are $k \times h$ matrices with k being the number of tokens in s_f (same for s_d)

and h being the dimension of the encoding for each token. Inspired by [1], we integrate S_f and S_b into a single embedding $S = \mathsf{fuse}(S_f, S_b)$ as follows.

$$\lambda_s = \sigma(W_s[S_f - S_b; S_f \circ S_b]) \tag{1}$$

$$\mathsf{fuse}(S_f, S_b) = \lambda_s \cdot S_f + (1 - \lambda_s) \cdot S_b \tag{2}$$

where σ is the sigmoid activation function, W_s is a parameter matrix, $X - Y$ is subtraction of two matrices X and Y, $X \circ Y$ is their element-wise multiplication, and $[X; Y]$ is matrix concatenation in the second dimension.

Similarly, we encode the retrieved contextual information in a bi-directional manner, to obtain the forward and backward context inputs t_f and t_b. We use a separate ALBERT encoder to encode the forward and backward context inputs, denoted S_f and S_b, which are $l \times h$ matrices with l being the number of tokens in t_f (same for t_d). This is different from existing methods that combine the background knowledge in the same input to the language encoder, where the encoding fuses q and a with their contexts. Separately encoding the QA inputs and contexts allow us to apply attention-based mechanisms to focus on most relevant parts of the contexts. And C_f and C_b are integrated into a single embedding $C = \mathsf{fuse}(C_f, C_b)$ with a different parameter matrix from above.

2.3 Similarity-Based Differentiation

When solving multi-choice questions, a human often compares the differences of all the choices to find some differentiable features of the correct answer. Such a strategy is particularly effective in eliminating distractor choices. In order to compare choices and highlight their subtle differences, we use an attention mechanism to obtain a refined embedding for each choice.

For each choice a, it may contain p words $x_1, x_2, \ldots, x_p$. We obtain the language encoding of each word x_i $(1 \leq i \leq p)$, denoted $\mathbf{x}_i$ from s_f. As p is often small (averagely 1.5), we assume each word x_i has the same weight. And we aggregates the encodings of all the words in the choice a to obtain an embedding $\mathbf{a} = \sum_{1 \leq i \leq p} \mathbf{x}_i$. Then, we calculate the correlation score $\gamma_{a,a'}$ between each pair of choices a and a', and the correlation vector of a with the other choices, denoted $\mathbf{a}_\Delta$. Intuitively, $\mathbf{a}_\Delta$ captures the parts in the features of a that have interaction with the other choices. Hence, we subtract $\mathbf{a}_\Delta$ from $\mathbf{a}$ to focus on the differences and obtain a refined embedding $\hat{\mathbf{a}}$ for a as follows.

$$\gamma_{a,a'} = \mathsf{softmax}(\mathbf{a}^T W_a \mathbf{a}') \tag{3}$$

$$\mathbf{a}_\Delta = \sum_{a' \in \mathcal{A}, a' \neq a} \gamma_{a,a'} \cdot \mathbf{a} \tag{4}$$

$$\hat{\mathbf{a}} = \mathbf{a} - \mathbf{a}_\Delta \tag{5}$$

where $\mathcal{A}$ consists of all the choices to the question and W_a is a parameter matrix.

2.4 Confidence Aggregation

The embedding S contains semantic information of the question and the choice, whereas C provides useful contextual information which helps to establish semantic connections between the question and the choice. Also, the embedding $\widehat{a}$ contains the differentiable features of the choice that are distinct from other choices. In this module, we aggregate the information in S, C and $\widehat{a}$ through attention mechanisms to generate a confidence score for the choice.

There is a naive method that sums the each token encoding in $S[i]$ $(0 \leq i < k)$ and $C[j]$ $(0 \leq j < l)$ respectively, and uses simple gate mechanisms to combine the two resulting vectors. However, we note that tokens in the external context information may have contribute differently to the semantic connections, and these tokens should have different weights. Therefore, our aggregation method applies dual-attention to obtain an intergrated embedding $\widehat{S}$ at the token-level, which is based on the weights from each token to selectively incorporate the contextual information C to the embedding S. Then, we use a merge-attention to give the higher weights to the more important tokens in $\widehat{S}$. Therefore, we will divide the section into two parts: dual-attention and merge-attention.

Dual-Attention. We use a dual-attention layer to capture the interaction between the QC statement and the context description. In particular, the interaction between the i-th token in S and the j-th token in C is put into the weight $\alpha_{i,j}$, and $\widehat{C}[i]$ captures the contribution of the i-th token in the context description to the establishment of contextual connections.

$$\alpha_{i,j} = \mathsf{softmax}(S[i]^T W_\alpha C[j]) \tag{6}$$

$$\widehat{C}[i] = \sum_{0 \leq j < l} \alpha_{i,j} \cdot C[j] \tag{7}$$

where W_α and W_c are parameter matrices, $0 \leq i < k$ and $0 \leq j < l$.

Unlike the dual-attention in model GENMC [8], our model not only uses the contextual information $\widehat{C}$, we also incorporate it into the QC statement embedding S to generate a new statement embedding $\widehat{S} = \mathsf{fuse}(S, \widehat{C})$ with its unique parameter matrix.

Merge-Attention. After combining the statement and context embeddings through the improved dual-attention layer, we aggregate the embeddings of tokens in $\widehat{S}$ via a merge-attention layer. Similarly, the contribution of the i-th token in $\widehat{S}$ is captured by the weight β_i, and by aggregating the weighted token-level contributions, we obtain the embedding $\mathbf{s}$ as follows:

$$\beta_i = \mathsf{softmax}(\mathbf{w}^T \widehat{S}[i]) \tag{8}$$

$$\mathbf{s} = \sum_{0 \leq i < k} \beta_i \cdot \widehat{S}[i] \tag{9}$$

where $\mathbf{w}$ is a parameter vector and $0 \leq i < k$.

Finally, the confidence score of the answer choice a w.r.t. the question q can be computed through a MLP and softmax layer as $\mathsf{score}(q, a) = \mathsf{softmax}\,(\mathsf{MLP}\,[\mathbf{s}, \hat{\mathbf{a}}])$.

3 Experiments

We evaluated our model ALBERT+CCR (Choice-driven Contextual Reasoning) on the CommonsenseQA dataset [21].

3.1 Comparison on CommonsenseQA

Our ALBERT+CCR model was compared with ten baselines, which fall into three groups: the pre-trained language models, models that can use both Wiki knowledge and ConceptNet/OMCS (but ConceptNet/OMCS is not used for a fair comparison), and models that use external knowledge but not (directly use) ConceptNet or OMCS.

Table 1. Comparison on CommonsenseQA. * indicates the Wiki-only results from the ablation studies of the corresponding papers or technical reports on the leaderboard. The Dev results are from the corresponding papers or technical reports, and the Test results are from the leaderboard.

Group	Model	Dev	Test
Pre-trained language models	ALBERT	80.5	73.5
	FREELB-ROBERTA	78.8	72.2
	ROBERTA	78.5	72.1
Support both Wiki and ConceptNet/OMCS with ConceptNet/OMCS turned off	ALBERT+MSKF*	80.6	–
	ALBERT+DESC-KCR*	80.1	–
	XLNET+GR*	73.5	–
Support external knowledge other than ConceptNet/OMCS	KEDGN	80.8	72.5
	ROBERTA+IR	78.9	72.1
	ROBERTA+KE	78.7	73.3
	DREAM	73.0	66.9
Ours	ALBERT+CCR	**81.9**	**75.3**

In our first set of evaluations, we have included major models on the CommonsenseQA leaderboard[2] that are comparable to ours, that is, we exclude those models that use ConceptNet or Open Mind Common Sense (OMCS) corpus [19]

---

[2] https://www.tau-nlp.org/csqa-leaderboard. We consider models that are ranked among top 25 by September 2021.

as their external knowledge, and those ensemble models. In particular, as the CommonsenseQA dataset is constructed from ConceptNet, it is concerned that using ConceptNet may help to eliminate human provided distractor choices. Indeed, models based on ConceptNet are no long accepted by the CommonsenseQA leaderboard. And ConceptNet originates from the Open Mind Common Sense (OMCS) project [19]. In addition, following other approaches in the literature [4], a few heavyweight models such as T5[3] and UnifiedQA [9], which is based on T5, were not included in the comparison.

As shown in Table 1, our model ALBERT+CCR outperforms the baselines in terms of the accuracy on both the Dev and Test data, and achieves state-of-the-art performance among models that do not use ConceptNet/OMCS as external knowledge and are not based on heavyweight language models. In particular, our model improves the language model ALBERT by 1.8% on Test. Compared with the strong baselines ALBERT+MSKF* and ALBERT+DESC-KCR* in Group 2, which use the same language model ALBERT and (only) Wiki knowledge, our model achieves 1.3% and 1.8% improvement on Dev. This demonstrates the advantage of our model over other comparable models.

3.2   Ablation Study

To understand the individual contributions of each component in our model, we carried out various ablation studies on the Dev data.

Table 2. Ablation study on CommonsenseQA.

Variants	Dev (%)
ALBERT+CCR	**81.9**
w/o Wiki knowledge	80.8
w/o dual-attention	81.2
w/o merge-attention	80.0
two-layered attention → GateCat	80.3
w/o forward and backward encoding strategy	80.9
w/ a single ALBERT encoder, both forward encoding	80.9
w/ a single ALBERT encoder, both backward encoding	81.4
w/ two ALBERT encoders, both forward encoding	80.5
w/ two ALBERT encoders, both backward encoding	81.6
w/o similarity-based differentiation	81.1

From Table 2, if without Wiki knowledge, the performance dropped by 1.1%, which shows the importance of external knowledge in providing necessary contextual information. Yet incorporating Wiki knowledge is not straightforward as

---

[3] It is reported that the number of parameters in T5 is about 30 times more than other models [4].

it may introduce noise, and the confidence aggregation is shown to be necessary for effective knowledge integration. In particular, if the improved dual-attention was not used to integrate more relevant contextual information, the performance would drop by 0.7%; and if without the merge-attention mechanism to help focusing on more relevant parts of information, the performance with Wiki knowledge (-1.9%) would be lower. It is a similar case when the Confidence Aggregation module is replaced with a simple gate mechanism GateCat (-1.6%), which shows the vital role of this module in incorporating contextual information. Finally, it also establishes that the modules Contextualized Encoding and Similarity-based Differentiation are effective in guiding the contextual reasoning, as without them will cause 0.8% to 1.0% decrease of accuracy. To show that the encoding strategy is not simply information enhancement, we included four variants, with a single or two separate ALBERT encoders with both forward or both backward encoding, which establishes the advantages of our bi-directional encodings.

3.3   The Effectiveness of Choice-Driven Strategy

Table 3. The performance gain of existing models with the Contextualized Encoding and Similarity-based Differentiation modules. All results are from our evaluations.

Model	ALBERT	KCR	XLNET+GR
Original	79.4	81.5	78.8
+ encoding strategy	80.6	82.2	79.4
+ similarity-based differentiation	79.7	82.2	79.8
+ both	**80.8**	**82.6**	**81.1**

We explore the benefit of our contextual reasoning strategies in ALBERT+CCR to some other existing models for CommonsenseQA. In particular, we added the Contextualized Encoding and Similarity-based Differentiation modules to the language model ALBERT, KCR[1] and XLNET+GR [15], which utilises ConceptNet as external knowledge, and we evaluated their performance gain on the official Dev data.

From Table 3, by adding Contextualized Encoding and Similarity-based Differentiation respectively to ALBERT, its performance is improved by 1.2% and 0.3%, and is improved by 1.4% when both modules are added. Note that the enhanced performance is still lower than our model ALBERT+CCR. Similarly, by adding Contextualized Encoding and Similarity-based Differentiation to KCR, we observed a 0.7% and a 0.7% performance gain respectively, and a 1.1% performance gain when both are added. In addition, when adding Contextualized Encoding and Similarity-based Differentiation modules to XLNET+GR, we obtained the improvements of 0.8% and 1.0% respectively. The highest boost(2.3%) was obtained when they were added at the same time. These results show that major reasoning strategies introduced in our ALBERT+CCR are not only effective for ALBERT+CCR itself, they are also effective for some other models for commonsense QA.

4   Related Work

CommonsenseQA Models. There are several works on commonsense question answering, which differ in the form of external knowledge they apply and how they perform commonse reasoning. Approaches using ConceptNet as the external knowledge base typically explore relationship between the questions and answer choices based on the graph structure, which often involves extracting paths connection the key concepts from the question and those from the answer choices [11,23].

Some other approaches introduce unstructured knowledge bases. Besides extracting knowledge from ConceptNet, the approach in [15] enriches the extracted graph with Wikipedia. The method in [22] uses a pre-trained language model to simultaneously encode the triples from ConceptNet and concept definitions from Wikitionary. We use only concept descriptions extracted using MediaWiki API as contextual knowledge. Different from the existing approaches, we apply a choice-driven approach and attention-based confidence aggregation to focus on most relevant parts of the retrieved Wiki knowledge and perform effective contextual reasoning.

Commonsense Reasoning Approaches. There have been an increasing interest in incorporating commonsense reasoning into reading comprehension tasks. Most models use neural networks to incorporate commonsense knowledge and perform reasoning [16,18], whereas some approaches [12] mine the reasoning rules of different knowledge types, and then use the rules for reasoning. What's more, GenMc [8] model does not rely on any external knowledge, and it generates relevant clues from questions to help reasoning.

5   Conclusions

In this work, we have developed a novel choice-driven contextual reasoning approach for commonsense question answering. The contextual information is retrieved from Wiki knowledge as plain text, and the contextual reasoning is performed by simulating human cognitive behaviour, including forward and backward reading of questions/choices and context descriptions, similarity-based differentiation among choices, and confidence aggregation. Evaluation on the CommonsenseQA dataset shows the superior accuracy of our model over comparable models on the leaderboard. Ablation studies establish the significance of each modules in our model, and case study also shows how each module contributes to the contextual reasoning on tricky cases. We also show that our strategies can be applied to existing QA models. Our base encoder is ALBERTA, and in the future we expect to experiment with other base encoder, such as DEBERTA [6].

Acknowledgements. This work was partially supported by the National Natural Science Foundation of China under grant 61976153.

References

1. Bauer, L., Wang, Y., Bansal, M.:: Commonsense for generative multi-hop question answering tasks. In: Proceedings of the 2018 Conference on Empirical Methods in Natural Language Processing (EMNLP-18), pp. 4220–4230 (2018)
2. Bian, N., Han, X., Chen, B., Sun, L.: Benchmarking knowledge-enhanced commonsense question answering via knowledge-to-text transformation. In: Proceedings of the 35th AAAI Conference on Artificial Intelligence (AAAI-21), pp. 12574–12582 (2021)
3. Cheng, G., Zhu, W., Wang, Z., Chen, J., Qu, Y.: Taking up the gaokao challenge: an information retrieval approach. In: Proceedings of the 25th International Joint Conference on Artificial Intelligence (IJCAI-16), pp. 2479–2485. IJCAI/AAAI Press (2016)
4. Feng, Y., Chen, X., Lin, B.Y., Wang, P., Yan, J., Ren, X.: Scalable multi-hop relational reasoning for knowledge-aware question answering. In: Proceedings of the 2020 Conference on Empirical Methods in Natural Language Processing, EMNLP 2020, Online, November 16–20, 2020, pp. 1295–1309. Association for Computational Linguistics (2020)
5. Fujita, A., Kameda, A., Kawazoe, A., Miyao, Y.: Overview of todai robot project and evaluation framework of its NLP-based problem solving. In: Proceedings of the 9th International Conference on Language Resources and Evaluation (LREC-14), pp. 2590–2597. European Language Resources Association (ELRA) (2014)
6. He, P., Liu, X., Gao, J., Chen, W.: Deberta: decoding-enhanced bert with disentangled attention. In 9th International Conference on Learning Representations, ICLR 2021, Virtual Event, Austria, May 3–7, 2021. OpenReview.net (2021)
7. Honnibal, M., Montani, I.: spacy 2: natural language understanding with bloom embeddings. Convolut. Neural Networks Incremental Pars. **7**(1), 411–420 (2017)
8. Huang, Z., Wu, A., Zhou, J., Gu, Y., Zhao, Y., Cheng, G.: Clues before answers: Generation-enhanced multiple-choice QA. CoRR, abs/2205.00274 (2022)
9. Khashabi, D., et al.: Unifiedqa: crossing format boundaries with a single QA system. In: Findings of the Association for Computational Linguistics (EMNLP-20), volume EMNLP 2020 of Findings of ACL, pp. 1896–1907 (2020)
10. Lan, Z., Chen, M., Goodman, S., Gimpel, K., Sharma, P., Soricut, R.: ALBERT: a lite BERT for self-supervised learning of language representations. In: Proceedings of the 8th International Conference on Learning Representations (ICLR-20) (2020)
11. Lin, B.Y., Chen, X., Chen, J., Ren, X.: Kagnet: knowledge-aware graph networks for commonsense reasoning. In: Proceedings of the 2019 Conference on Empirical Methods in Natural Language Processing and the 9th International Joint Conference on Natural Language Processing (EMNLP-IJCNLP-19), pp. 2829–2839 (2019)
12. Lin, H., Sun, L., Han, X.: Reasoning with heterogeneous knowledge for commonsense machine comprehension. In: Proceedings of the 2017 Conference on Empirical Methods in Natural Language Processing (EMNLP-17), pp. 2032–2043 (2017)
13. Liu, H., Singh, P.: Conceptnet-a practical commonsense reasoning tool-kit. BT Technol. J. **22**(4), 211–226 (2004)
14. Liu, Y., et al.: Roberta: a robustly optimized BERT pretraining approach. CoRR, abs/1907.11692, 2019

15. Lv, S., et al.: Graph-based reasoning over heterogeneous external knowledge for commonsense question answering. In: Proceedings of the 34th AAAI Conference on Artificial Intelligence (AAAI-20), pp. 8449–8456 (2020)
16. Mihaylov, T., Frank, A.: Knowledgeable reader: enhancing cloze-style reading comprehension with external commonsense knowledge. In: Proceedings of the 56th Annual Meeting of the Association for Computational Linguistics (ACL-18), pp. 821–832 (2018)
17. Raffel, C., et al.: Exploring the limits of transfer learning with a unified text-to-text transformer. J. Mach. Learn. Res. **21**, 140:1-140:67 (2020)
18. Rajani, N.F., McCann, B., Xiong, C., Socher, R.: Explain yourself! leveraging language models for commonsense reasoning. In: Proceedings of the 57th Conference of the Association for Computational Linguistics (ACL-19), pp. 4932–4942 (2019)
19. Singh, P., Lin, T., Mueller, E.T., Lim, G., Perkins, T., Li Zhu, W.: Open mind common sense: knowledge acquisition from the general public. In: Meersman, R., Tari, Z. (eds.) OTM 2002. LNCS, vol. 2519, pp. 1223–1237. Springer, Heidelberg (2002). https://doi.org/10.1007/3-540-36124-3_77
20. Sun, K., Yu, D., Yu, D., Cardie, C.: Improving machine reading comprehension with general reading strategies. In Proceedings of the 2019 Conference of the North American Chapter of the Association for Computational Linguistics: Human Language Technologies (NAACL-HLT-19), pp. 2633–2643 (2019)
21. Talmor, A., Herzig, J., Lourie, N., Berant, J.: Commonsenseqa: a question answering challenge targeting commonsense knowledge. In: Proceedings of the 2019 Conference of the North American Chapter of the Association for Computational Linguistics: Human Language Technologies (NAACL-HLT-19), pp. 4149–4158 (2019)
22. Xu, Y., Zhu, C., Xu, R., Liu, Y., Zeng, M., Huang, X.: Fusing context into knowledge graph for commonsense reasoning. CoRR, abs/2012.04808 (2020)
23. Yan, J., et al.: Learning contextualized knowledge structures for commonsense reasoning. In: Findings of the Association for Computational Linguistics (ACL/IJCNLP-21), pp. 4038–4051 (2021)
24. Zhang, S., Zhao, H., Wu, Y., Zhang, Z., Zhou, X., Zhou, X.: DCMN+: dual co-matching network for multi-choice reading comprehension. In: Proceedings of the 34th AAAI Conference on Artificial Intelligence (AAAI-20), pp. 9563–9570 (2020)

Implicit Discourse Relation Recognition Based on Multi-granularity Context Fusion Mechanism

Yuxiang Lu, Yu Hong[✉], Xiao Li, and GuoDong Zhou

School of Computer Science and Technology, Soochow University, Suzhou, China
tianxianer@gmail.com, gdzhou@suda.edu.cn

Abstract. Implicit discourse relation recognition is a NLP task that identifies the semantic relation between arguments without explicit connectives. Existing studies are mostly based on interactive attention. However, if arguments have incomplete semantics, it will be difficult for the model to deeply understand the argument, which negatively impacts the information interaction. In addition, although there is valid information in the context that can mitigate the negative effects caused by the semantic loss, the unfiltered context usually contains much distracting information. We propose a multi-granularity context fusion method for the above problems. Specifically, we first reduce contextual interference by constructing an information extraction mechanism. Then, we fuse the denoised context with the arguments for better learning the semantics. The experiment results in the Penn Discourse Treebank corpus show that, compared with the baseline, our method increases F1 score by 4.11%, 5.46%, 3.26%, and 7.03% in the scenarios of binary classification. For 4-way F1 and 4-way accuracy, we get 65.34% and 71.18% performances. Most of them surpass state-of-the-art systems.

Keywords: Discourse relation recognition · Multi-granularity context fusion · Information extraction

1 Introduction

Discourse relation recognition is an essential subtask in discourse structure analysis, which aims to judge the semantic relation between two arguments (e.g., sub-sentences, clauses, and text blocks). It is fundamental research in Natural Language Processing (NLP) and has been applied to many downstream tasks, such as machine translation [15], sentiment analysis [21], automatic summarization [24], and question answering systems [18].

Every sample of discourse relation recognition is a triple (Arg1; R; Arg2). The former argument in the sentence is Arg1, the next argument is Arg2, and R is the relation. The Penn Discourse Treebank (PDTB) [17] is currently the largest and most authoritative discourse relation recognition corpus. Its defined

© The Author(s), under exclusive license to Springer Nature Switzerland AG 2022
S. Khanna et al. (Eds.): PRICAI 2022, LNCS 13630, pp. 347–358, 2022.
https://doi.org/10.1007/978-3-031-20865-2_26

argument relation consists of three layers. The first layer includes four coarse-grained discourse relations: Comparison, Contingency, Expansion, and Temporal. The second and third layers are subdivided based on the previous layer. Consistent with the previous works, we conduct binary and 4-way classification for the first layer.

In addition, PDTB corpus divide discourse relations into explicit and implicit relation types. The connective can be directly used as a relation discrimination feature in explicit type. In contrast, the implicit discourse relation recognition is still challenging due to the lack of connectives. It has been found that profoundly understanding the semantics of the argument promotes the model to make correct relation predictions. Therefore, fully mining the semantic information of arguments is crucial in the Implicit Discourse Relation Recognition (abbr., IDRR) task. Existing interactive attention-based neural networks [14] help two arguments fully exchange identifiable information through the attention mechanism and have achieved considerable performance improvements in the task. However, we find that many samples in the PDTB corpus have the problem of missing or incomplete semantics in a single argument. These problems can be the interference items, affecting the model's determination of the real discourse relation.

We propose a method based on a multi-granularity context fusion mechanism to address the above problems. First, the method is based on a word-level interactive attention mechanism and obtains the preliminary encoding of the argument. In addition, the method introduces a context vital information extractor to denoise the context information. Ultimately, we use a sentence-level interactive attention mechanism to interact the two arguments with the denoised context and finally obtain the argument encoding. It provides compelling relation judgment clues for the relation recognition decoder model.

Overall, the main contributions of this paper include the following two aspects:

- We propose a multi-granularity context interaction attention mechanism, which uses the word-level information in the context to make up for the semantic lack of the arguments. Further, the information extraction mechanism is employed to reduce the influence of the noisy information in the context. The optimized context interacts with the argument to obtain the argument encoding with advanced contextual information.
- Compare a variety of context fusion mechanisms to extract context information and get the best method to encode context semantics more accurately.

2 Related Work

Reliable argument encoding is a crucial inference clue in IDRR. In the early years, traditional machine learning was widely used. For example, Pitler et al. [16] construct classification features with the help of elements of the sentence (e.g., word pairs, verb types). Lin et al. [10] exploit the syntactic and dependency structures to mine the semantic features.

A large number of researches have shown that fully mining the interactive semantic information between arguments can improve the relation recognition ability of the model. For instance, Chen et al. [2] adopt the gating mechanism to obtain the semantic information between the two arguments at the word and phrase levels. With the assistance of this information, the performance has made a breakthrough. In addition, methods based on attention mechanism are shown to assist the information interaction within arguments. Liu and Li [12] design a neural network based on multi-layer attention. With the help of external memory vectors, the argument representation under each layer of the attention mechanism is gradually updated. Shi and Demberg [20] migrate the BERT model proposed by Devlin et al. [4], which utilizes the NSP (Next Sentence Prediction) task in BERT to assist in IDRR. He et al. [6] use a multi-level encoder to mine the underlying geometric structure information in the discourse relation instances to assist the model in representing the semantics of arguments.

In addition, attention-based methods have made progress in the information interaction process of arguments. Guo et al. [5] mine key information from the two arguments and feed it into the attention mechanism to obtain the better semantic representation. What is more, Ruan et al. [19] combine self-attention and interactive attention to construct a propagative attention learning model. Further, due to the problem that the weight distribution of the attention learning model is too smooth, Li et al. [8] propose a penalty-based loss re-evaluation method, thereby optimizing the IDRR methods. In particular, Zhang et al. [25] extract the semantic interaction between argument pairs based on a semantic graph convolutional network. This work constructs an information graph on the arguments.

Contextual features have become a relatively reliable breakthrough point for the problems of ambiguity and lack of semantics in discourse-related corpora. Therefore, Dai and Huang [3] conduct a paragraph-level method to search the interdependence between chapter units and the continuity of chapter relationships. Liu et al. [11] use multi-view cosine similarity to match the contextual information of arguments. Further, Zhang et al. [26] capture the contextual information of the current argument by constructing a paragraph association graph.

3 Method

We propose a method based on multi-granularity context fusion to improve the performance of IDRR. The overall model framework of the method is shown in Fig. 1, which is divided into the following four parts: (1) Splice the argument pair (Arg1, Arg2) and its context sentences (context sentence1 and context sentence2) and feed them to the pre-trained model [22] (BERT or RoBERTa) for encoding. Through the multi-head self-attention in the Transformer architecture, the argument pair interacts with its contexts at the word granularity. Then, we truncate the context encoding and argument encoding ($R_{\theta 1}$ and $R_{\theta 2}$). (2) The context encoding H will be sent to the information extraction mechanism for

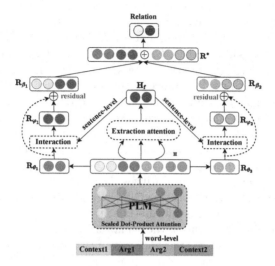

Fig. 1. Overall model frame diagram

denoising the contextual information and obtaining a more reliable contextual encoding H_f. (3) Employing the sentence-level interactive attention mechanism, the encoding of the two arguments ($R_{\theta 1}$ and $R_{\theta 2}$) interacts with H_f respectively and obtain the enhanced argument encoding ($R_{\varphi 1}$ and $R_{\varphi 2}$) with contextual information. (4) Our method conducts residual connections in the training phase. Specifically, we fuse the enhanced argument encoding ($R_{\varphi 1}$ and $R_{\varphi 2}$) with the original argument encoding ($R_{\theta 1}$ and $R_{\theta 2}$) to obtain more semantically informative argument encoding ($R_{\beta 1}$ and $R_{\beta 2}$). Finally, we concatenate the encoding and send it (R^*) to the softmax layer for classification.

3.1   Word Interaction Between Argument and Context (WIBAC)

Input Layer. In order to track the semantics information of the arguments and the context, we use BPE (Byte-Pair Encoding) to divide the input text into subword sequences. Specifically, the representations of Arg1 and Arg2 are $R_1 = (x_1^1, x_2^1, ..., x_L^1)$ and $R_2 = (x_1^2, x_2^2, ..., x_L^2)$ respectively. Besides, we describe the two critical statements with argument pairs as $C_1 = (c_1^1, c_2^1, ..., c_L^1)$ and $C_2 = (c_1^2, c_2^2, ..., c_L^2)$. The context information used here consists of C_1, R_1, R_2, and C_2. In order to truncate the encoded representation of arguments from the whole last-layer hidden state, we set the maximum sequence length of arguments to L. Therefore, the composition of the model input I is shown in Eq. (1).

$$I = \{[CLS], C_1, [SEP], R_1, [SEP], R_2, [SEP], C_2, [SEP]\} \tag{1}$$

where C_1 refers to the former n sentences adjacent to R_1, and C_2 refers to the following n sentences adjacent to R_2.

Word-Level Attention Mechanism. We use the argument pair and critical sentence splicing as the pre-trained model's input. Then, we employ the multi-head self-attention integrated into Transformer [22] to achieve word-level information. The input I is constructed as a set composed of query and key-value pair for calculation. The multi-head attention fuses the semantic information of the arguments and the context information in the word granularity to assist the model in understanding the incomplete arguments. Further, in order to capture the features in different sub-spaces, the multi-head attention performs h linear transformations on I^Q, I^K, and I^V. Then, it feeds the transformed vectors into the scaled dot product attention mechanism and obtains h attention vectors. Finally, the mechanism splices these vectors and sends them to a linear layer to obtain the fusion of word information in different sub-spaces.

Context Information Extraction Mechanism. In order to alleviate the uncertainty caused by the noise of the context, we propose to build a context information extraction mechanism (Extraction Attention). In this way, the model's attention to the interference information is reduced, and the reliability of the context representation is improved. As shown in Fig. 2, the extraction mechanism is constructed by the self-attention proposed by Lin et al. [9]. It calculates the attention weight matrix $\alpha \in R^L$ by the context-based encoding H. As shown in Eq. (2), the weight matrix assigns a higher attention value to the context keywords, and relatively, the noise information is assigned a lower value. Finally, the Extraction Attention conducts a weighted summation of the α and the H to obtain the context encoding $H^f = (e_1, e_2, \ldots, e_L)$, $e_i \in R^{(d_h)}$ as shown in Eq. (3). It is worth noting that the context covers the original semantic information of the argument pair. Therefore, the critical information extracted from this context can better assist the model in understanding the argument's deep semantics.

$$\alpha = \mathrm{softmax}\left(W_\alpha^2 \tanh\left(W_\alpha^1 H\right)\right) \qquad (2)$$

$$H^f = \alpha H \qquad (3)$$

where $W_\alpha^1 \in R^{d_\partial \times d_{\mathrm{model}}}$ and $W_\alpha^2 \in R^{d_\partial}$ are trainable weight parameters, and d_∂ is the dimension size set when performing dimension transformation on the encoded representation of the input vector.

3.2 Sentence Interaction Between Argument and Context (SIBAC)

Although the argument pair has interacted with its context at the word level, some noisy information is also introduced. Therefore, if the above method uses the information of the unfiltered context, it will be difficult for the useful information to be fused with the two arguments.

Thus, we have to fuse the denoised context with the argument for effective information. Specifically, under the action of sentence-granular interactive attention (as shown in Fig. 3), we combine the word-granular context-enhanced argument encoding ($R_{\theta 1}$ and $R_{\theta 2}$) with the key information highlighted in Sect. 3.2.

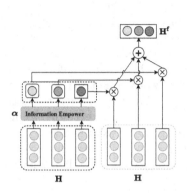

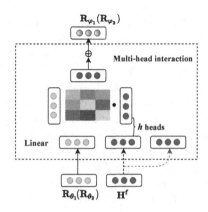

Fig. 2. Attention-based context information extraction

Fig. 3. Sentence level context information fusion

The interactive attention mechanism used in this work is the multi-head attention. The encoding of the arguments ($R_{\theta 1}$ or $R_{\theta 2}$) as query, and H^f as key and value. The sentence-level interactive attention mechanism conducts h linear transformations on $R_{\theta 1}$ ($R_{\theta 2}$), H^f, and calculates the interactive attention based on the transformation results of each $R_{\theta 1}$ (query) and H^f (key) weight matrix. We perform a weighted summation of the transformation result of H^f. On h different sub-spaces, we obtain h argument features fused with context information. In addition, we concatenate h and conduct a linear transformation to obtain the argument representation $R_{\partial 1}(R_{\partial 2})$ enhanced by the contextual key information.

3.3   Residual Network

The semantic encoding of argument pairs is a crucial inference clue in the task of IDRR. Under the multi-granularity context fusion, the model understands the deep semantic information of the argument with the help of the vital information of the context. However, this mechanism often leads the model to bias the semantic of context information, diluting the semantic of the original arguments.

Therefore, we employ the residual network during training. Specifically, we fuse the encoding of the argument after the fusion of multi-granularity information with the encoding of the original argument to reduce the loss of the original semantic information. As shown in Fig. 1, we add the argument encoding $R_{\partial}1$ ($R_{\partial}2$) and $R_{\theta 1}$ ($R_{\theta 2}$) produced by the fine-tuned pre-trained model (BERT [4] or RoBERTa [13]) to obtain the jointly encoding.

Table 1. Performance (%) comparison to state of the art. Our method based on BERT and RoBERTa is considered for comparison, respectively.

Model	COM.	CON.	EXP.	TEM.	4-way F1	4-way Acc.
Chen [2]	40.17	54.76	–	31.32	44.61	57.84
Bai and Zhao [1]	47.85	54.47	70.60	36.97	51.06	–
Guo et al. [5]	40.35	56.81	72.11	38.65	47.59	59.06
Ruan et al. [19]	46.75	**59.56**	75.83	39.35	–	–
Zhang et al. [26]	46.86	55.63	73.71	45.90	53.11	–
Ours (BERT)	**49.15**	58.03	**76.19**	40.13	**55.92**	**64.96**
Liu et al. [11]	**59.44**	60.98	77.66	**50.26**	63.39	69.06
Ours (RoBERTa)	57.67	**64.81**	**79.16**	41.93	**65.34**	**71.18**

4 Experiments

4.1 Dataset and Evaluation Metrics

In order to be consistent with predecessors, we use the PDTB [17] dataset for IDRR task. We use Section 02–20 in the PDTB corpus as the training set, Section 00–01 as the development set, and Section 21–22 as the test set. Among them, the category of all samples is one of the four relations: Comparison (COM.), Contingency (CON.), Expansion (EXP.), and Temporal (TEM.). In evaluating the binary classifier, the F1 value (F1-score) is used as the evaluation metric. The macro F1 value (Macro-F1) and the accuracy rate (Acc.) are used as evaluation metrics when evaluating the quaternary classification model.

4.2 Hyperparameter Setting

The benchmark model is BERT-base and RoBERTa-base. The maximum sequence length L of an argument is 100. The context includes the argument and two adjacent sentences in the document, and its maximum sequence length is $4L$. The weight matrix dimension d_{model} in all attention mechanisms is 128. The h of the multi-head attention in the sentence-level context fusion mechanism is set to 6, and the word-level fusion mechanism h is set to 12. Furthermore, the batch size is set to 8, the learning rate is 5e-6, and the model parameters are updated using the Adam [7] optimizer. In particular, to alleviate the problem of overfitting, the model uses dropout after each layer of modules, where the ratio of random dropout is set to 0.2.

4.3 Results

We compare our methods with the existing state-of-the-art IDRR models. Table 1 shows the comparison results.

Table 2. Ablation experiment results (%), our method based on BERT and RoBERTa is constructed by expanding the baseline step by step.

Method	COM.	CON.	EXP.	TEM.
Baseline (BERT)	43.33	56.64	73.33	35.63
+WIBAC	45.24	55.87	74.58	35.90
+WIBAC&SIBAC	45.15	57.70	75.07	38.35
+WIBAC&SIBAC&Residual	**49.15**	**58.03**	**76.19**	**40.13**
Baseline (RoBERTa)	53.56	59.34	75.90	33.42
+WIBAC	55.03	62.12	77.68	34.90
+WIBAC&SIBAC	54.27	64.36	**79.59**	38.92
+WIBAC&SIBAC&Residual	**57.67**	**64.80**	79.16	**41.93**

Bai and Zhao [1] employ different text granularities to obtain rich implications. Guo et al. [5] used bidirectional LSTM to mine the critical information in the two arguments. In contrast, Ruan et al. [19] used the self-attention mechanism to extract critical information from the argument. Zhang et al. [26] transformed the context into a paragraph association to obtain a context-fused argument encoding. Compared with Zhang et al. [26], our method based on BERT has advantages in Comparison, Contingency, and Expansion relations. However, its performance on Temporal relation is lower than Zhang et al. [26]. The analysis shows that the method of Zhang et al. [26] can regularize the context information and reduce the interference in the context. Nevertheless, it ignores the information interaction between arguments and context to some extent.

In order to examine the performance of the pr oposed method on different pre-trained models, we further compare the state-of-the-art models, which use RoBERTa [13] as the benchmark system. Specifically, Liu et al. [11] used multiview cosine similarity to match the critical information of arguments, which significantly improved performance compared with previous works. Using the same baseline model, our performance is better than Liu et al. [11] in Contingency, Expansion. Furthermore, our method gets the best performance of all in the 4-way classification. It shows the effectiveness of the method proposed in this paper and proves that it has strong generality on different pre-trained models.

4.4 Ablation Experiments

We conduct ablation experiments to examine the influence of each module in the multi-granularity context fusion mechanism on the experimental results. Analysis of Table 2 shows that the trend results under different pre-trained models is consistent. Therefore, we will focus on the experimental results under the BERT benchmark.

BERT/RoBERTa (baseline). Two arguments are concatenated as the pre-trained model's input in our method. Then, we feed the splicing results (r_1 and r_2) into the fully connected layer for relation classification. **WIBAC** We

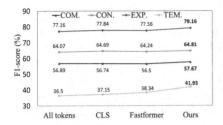
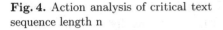

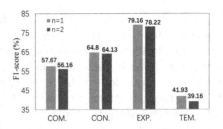

Fig. 4. Action analysis of critical text sequence length n

Fig. 5. Effect for the results with different context extraction methods

concatenate two arguments and their adjacent sentences as the input for the first time and jointly feed them into a pre-trained model for encoding. This experiments truncate the context-enhanced argument encoding from the last hidden state of the model's output and concatenate them as the input of the fully connected layer for classification. According to the experimental results, the word-level context fusion mechanism achieves better results than the baseline model. **SIBAC** The experiment uses the context information extraction mechanism in Sect. 3.1 to obtain the context encoding after noise reduction. Further, we fuse the argument encoding with the context encoding based on the sentence-level context fusion mechanism. After, we obtain the enhanced argument representation encoding. We will use it as a clue to infer the category of relations. Finally, we concatenate the enhanced argument representations and send them into the classifier. At this time, the performance of the 4-way classification has been further improved, while the results of the Comparison have slightly decreased. The reason is that the Comparison samples in PDTB can usually be inferred from a keyword pair. Too much attention to the context information will interfere with the model's judgment when we introduce the context. **Residual Network (Residual)** Besides, after employing the residual connection in the experiment, compared with before, the performance of the four relation types has been dramatically improved.

4.5 Effects and Analysis of Different Context Fusion Mechanisms

In order to extract more critical information from the context and reduce the attention of irrelevant words, various information extraction mechanisms are tried in the experiments. The experimental results are shown in Table 5 (taking RoBERTa as the benchmark system). In the experiment, RoBERTa encodes the input context and obtain the context encoding H. We adopt four information extraction mechanisms to obtain the context encoding: 1) All token: use H as the context representation; 2) CLS: use the first token in H as the context representation; 3) Fast-former [23]: Use the additive attention mechanism to extract critical information for H; 4) Extraction-attention: Use the information extraction mechanism introduced in Sect. 3.2.

According to Fig. 4, our method achieves the best experimental performance compared with the other three fusion mechanisms. We can conclude that the first two information extraction methods (All token and CLS) do not distinguish the key and non-key information in the context, resulting in a lot of disturbing semantic information in the representation of the argument. Furthermore, the third method (Fastformer) is an efficient version of Transformer, which incorporates a multi-layer attention mechanism. Therefore, if the Fastformer is stacked into the model constructed by the multi-granularity context fusion mechanism, the entire model will be too complicated. There will be problems of overfitting and network degradation. Therefore, this section finally uses the context information extraction mechanism (Extraction-attention), which assigns higher weight values to keywords in the context than non-keywords, thereby reducing the contextual representation of non-critical information.

4.6   Selection of Critical Text Sequence Length

The context information used in our method consists of input argument pairs and their critical sentences. The critical sentences of Arg1 and Arg2 are selected from their most adjacent n sentences. As shown in Fig. 5, it analyzes the changes caused by different values of n in the final classification. Expressly, we set n to 1 and 2, respectively, and analyze the impact of changes in the value of n on performance. This experiment uses RoBERTa as the benchmark system, and the evaluation metric is the F1 value. According to the experimental results in Fig. 5, when the n is increased from 1 to 2, the F1 value significantly decreases in the three categories of Comparison, Expansion, and Temporal. At the same time, in terms of Contingency relation, the increase of n also leads to a small decrease in the performance. Thus, when the length of the sequence is too long, a large amount of noise information may be introduced, which will negatively affect the context information fusion process.

5   Conclusion

In the research of implicit discourse relation recognition based on argument information interaction, this paper proposes a method based on multi-granularity context fusion to alleviate the negative impact of argument fragmentation semantic missing problem in argument semantic representation. At the same time, this paper verifies the effectiveness of the proposed method based on multiple sets of controlled experiments and employs a key information extraction mechanism when characterizing contextual semantics. This mechanism highlights the critical information in the context. It reduces the model's over-attention to unimportant or even disturbing information. Compared with the model without an information extraction mechanism, the enhanced model based on the information extraction method used in this paper has achieved noticeable performance improvement in implicit discourse relation recognition.

Acknowledgements. The research is supported by National Key R&D Program of China (2020YFB1313601) and National Science Foundation of China (62076174).

References

1. Bai, H., Zhao, H.: Deep enhanced representation for implicit discourse relation recognition. arXiv preprint arXiv:1807.05154 (2018)
2. Chen, J., Zhang, Q., Liu, P., Qiu, X., Huang, X.J.: Implicit discourse relation detection via a deep architecture with gated relevance network. In: Proceedings of the 54th Annual Meeting of the Association for Computational Linguistics (Volume 1: Long Papers), pp. 1726–1735 (2016)
3. Dai, Z., Huang, R.: Improving implicit discourse relation classification by modeling inter-dependencies of discourse units in a paragraph. arXiv preprint arXiv:1804.05918 (2018)
4. Devlin, J., Chang, M.W., Lee, K., Toutanova, K.: Bert: Pre-training of deep bidirectional transformers for language understanding. arXiv preprint arXiv:1810.04805 (2018)
5. Guo, F., He, R., Jin, D., Dang, J., Wang, L., Li, X.: Implicit discourse relation recognition using neural tensor network with interactive attention and sparse learning. In: Proceedings of the 27th International Conference on Computational Linguistics, pp. 547–558 (2018)
6. He, R., Wang, J., Guo, F., Han, Y.: Transs-driven joint learning architecture for implicit discourse relation recognition. In: Proceedings of the 58th Annual Meeting of the Association for Computational Linguistics, pp. 139–148 (2020)
7. Kingma, D.P., Ba, J.: Adam: A method for stochastic optimization. arXiv preprint arXiv:1412.6980 (2014)
8. Li, X., Hong, Y., Ruan, H., Huang, Z.: Using a penalty-based loss re-estimation method to improve implicit discourse relation classification. In: Proceedings of the 28th International Conference on Computational Linguistics, pp. 1513–1518 (2020)
9. Lin, Z., et al.: A structured self-attentive sentence embedding. arXiv preprint arXiv:1703.03130 (2017)
10. Lin, Z., Kan, M.Y., Ng, H.T.: Recognizing implicit discourse relations in the penn discourse treebank. In: Proceedings of the 2009 Conference on Empirical Methods in Natural Language Processing, pp. 343–351 (2009)
11. Liu, X., Ou, J., Song, Y., Jiang, X.: On the importance of word and sentence representation learning in implicit discourse relation classification. arXiv preprint arXiv:2004.12617 (2020)
12. Liu, Y., Li, S.: Recognizing implicit discourse relations via repeated reading: neural networks with multi-level attention. arXiv preprint arXiv:1609.06380 (2016)
13. Liu, Y., et al.: Roberta: a robustly optimized bert pretraining approach. arXiv preprint arXiv:1907.11692 (2019)
14. Ma, D., Li, S., Zhang, X., Wang, H.: Interactive attention networks for aspect-level sentiment classification. arXiv preprint arXiv:1709.00893 (2017)
15. Meyer, T., Popescu-Belis, A.: Using sense-labeled discourse connectives for statistical machine translation. In: Proceedings of the EACL2012 Workshop on Hybrid Approaches to Machine Translation (HyTra). No. CONF (2012)
16. Pitler, E., Louis, A., Nenkova, A.: Automatic sense prediction for implicit discourse relations in text (2009)

17. Prasad, R., et al.: The penn discourse treebank 2.0. In: Proceedings of the Sixth International Conference on Language Resources and Evaluation (LREC 2008) (2008)
18. Riaz, M., Girju, R.: Another look at causality: Discovering scenario-specific contingency relationships with no supervision. In: 2010 IEEE Fourth International Conference on Semantic Computing, pp. 361–368. IEEE (2010)
19. Ruan, H., Hong, Y., Xu, Y., Huang, Z., Zhou, G., Zhang, M.: Interactively-propagative attention learning for implicit discourse relation recognition. In: Proceedings of the 28th International Conference on Computational Linguistics, pp. 3168–3178 (2020)
20. Shi, W., Demberg, V.: Next sentence prediction helps implicit discourse relation classification within and across domains. In: Proceedings of the 2019 Conference on Empirical Methods in Natural Language Processing and the 9th International Joint Conference on Natural Language Processing (EMNLP-IJCNLP), pp. 5790–5796 (2019)
21. Somasundaran, S., Namata, G., Wiebe, J., Getoor, L.: Supervised and unsupervised methods in employing discourse relations for improving opinion polarity classification. In: Proceedings of the 2009 Conference on Empirical Methods in Natural Language Processing, pp. 170–179 (2009)
22. Vaswani, A., et al.: Attention is all you need. Advances in Neural Information Processing Systems 30 (2017)
23. Wu, C., Wu, F., Qi, T., Huang, Y., Xie, X.: Fastformer: additive attention can be all you need. arXiv preprint arXiv:2108.09084 (2021)
24. Yoshida, Y., Suzuki, J., Hirao, T., Nagata, M.: Dependency-based discourse parser for single-document summarization. In: Proceedings of the 2014 Conference on Empirical Methods in Natural Language Processing (EMNLP), pp. 1834–1839 (2014)
25. Zhang, Y., Jian, P., Meng, F., Geng, R., Cheng, W., Zhou, J.: Semantic graph convolutional network for implicit discourse relation classification. arXiv preprint arXiv:1910.09183 (2019)
26. Zhang, Y., Meng, F., Li, P., Jian, P., Zhou, J.: Context tracking network: Graph-based context modeling for implicit discourse relation recognition. In: Proceedings of the 2021 Conference of the North American Chapter of the Association for Computational Linguistics: Human Language Technologies, pp. 1592–1599 (2021)

Chinese Medical Named Entity Recognition Using External Knowledge

Lin Zhang, Peichao Lai, Feiyang Ye, Ruixiong Fang, Ruiqing Wang,
Jiayong Li, and Yilei Wang[✉]

School of Computer and Big Data, Fuzhou University, Fuzhou, China
yilei@fzu.edu.cn

Abstract. Chinese medical named entity recognition (NER) task usually lacks sufficient annotation data, and it contains many medical professional terms and abbreviations, making the NER task more difficult. In addition, compared with English NER, Chinese NER is more challenging because it lacks standard feature symbols to determine named entity boundaries. Therefore, Chinese NER needs to perform word segmentation. In this paper, we are inspired by lexicon-based BERT and propose a novel method for Chinese medical NER task. Besides, We design a template-based strategy to enrich the words' information and improve the model's ability to distinguish medical professional terms and abbreviations. Our method enhances the word segmentation accuracy by introducing the external medical lexicon. To verify the effectiveness of our method, we carry out experiments on three medical datasets and our method improves them by 0.92%, 1.18% and 1.55% F1-score compared to baseline.

Keywords: Chinese medical NER · External knowledge · Prompt

1 Introduction

Nowadays, medical information systems have accumulated many medical data, including electronic medical records, physical examination reports, and medical reports. The widespread use of information technology in the medical field has contributed to a dramatic increase in medical data. With the continuous accumulation of data, using natural language processing (NLP) technology and deep learning methods to mine valuable data has become hot research in medicine and artificial intelligence.

NER is a fundamental task in information extraction for the NLP task. It is a fine-grained sequence labeling task where entity boundaries and class labels are jointly predicted. Chinese NER is divided into character-based and lexicon-based methods. The lack of lexicon, grammar, domain knowledge, and other types of information in character-based NER makes it difficult for the model to understand the correct meaning, significantly affecting its performance. Lexicon-based methods suffer from the inaccuracy of word segmentation. However, we

© The Author(s), under exclusive license to Springer Nature Switzerland AG 2022
S. Khanna et al. (Eds.): PRICAI 2022, LNCS 13630, pp. 359–371, 2022.
https://doi.org/10.1007/978-3-031-20865-2_27

can improve model's ability to understand the lexicon by introducing external knowledge, so as to improve the accuracy of word segmentation.

With the explosion of Chinese medical data, using Chinese medical NER to extract medical entities from electronic medical records and physical examination reports can help decrease the time spent in manually annotating medical entities. Chinese medical NER has become increasingly important in recent years. However, existing Chinese medical datasets have the following problems. First, the high cost of manual labeling makes the existing medical datasets have less labeled data, making large-scale model training impossible. Secondly, it contains many medical professional terms and abbreviations rarely used daily. And the Chinese NER boundary problem is always the main problem in the NER task. Because of the complexity of Chinese grammar, word segmentation becomes difficult. Therefore, Chinese medical NER is a challenging task.

In this paper, we propose a novel Chinese medical NER method based on lexicon enhancement. Besides, We design a template-based strategy that uses a pre-trained language model (PLM) to stimulate the model's ability to recognize Chinese medical entities. The experimental results based on the CCKS and CDD datasets prove the validity of introducing external medical knowledge and demonstrate the performance of the proposed method. We also perform experimental validation on the FN medical examination dataset. To sum up, our contributions are as follows:

- We propose a structure by using external knowledge to improve the accuracy of Chinese word segmentation.
- We design a template-based strategy to enrich the words' information and improve the model's sensitivity to medical professional terms and abbreviations.
- Experimental results show that the proposed method achieves good state-of-the-art performance on three datasets.

2   Related Work

In recent years, the research on NER has developed continuously. In the early stage, the primary methods are based on rules [7,24] and dictionaries [19,21,25]. Later, researchers have proposed many handcrafted feature-based NER models, such as hidden markov model (HMM) [1], decision tree [20], support vector machine (SVM) [23] and conditional random field (CRF) [18].

With the development of deep learning, many deep learning models have been applied to NER task and achieved excellent results. For example, convolutional neural networks (CNN), long short term memory (LSTM) and bidirectional long short term memory (BiLSTM) have proven effective. It also brings breakthroughs for medical NER. Kuru [12] describes a character-level tagger employing a deep bidirectional LSTM architecture. He and Sun [11] propose a semi-supervised learning model based on a BiLSTM neural network to take advantage of traditional methods in NER such as CRF and combine transition probability with deep learning. After the pre-trained models like BERT [5] were proposed, the accuracy of the NER task was significantly improved. However, in the Chinese NER task, BERT cannot effectively utilize the lexicon information.

To solve the impact caused by the lack of clear separators in Chinese NER. More and more lexicon-based methods are proposed. Zhang and Yang [27] introduced a lattice LSTM to encode both characters and words for Chinese NER. Gui and Ma [9] introduced a Lexicon-Based CNNs (LR-CNN) model that fusion lexical information using an attention mechanism and used CNN to encode potential words at different window sizes. Lexicon-based Graph Networks [10] and Collaborative Graph Networks [22] convert lattices into graphs and use Graph Neural Networks (GNN) to its encoding them. Lattice LSTM and LR-CNN have the problem of not capturing long-distance dependencies, and Li and Yan [13] proposed using Transformer to solve this problem. Liu proposed LEBERT [14] to integrate lexicon knowledge into BERT layers and achieved state-of-the-art performance in multiple Chinese NER datasets. However, the above Chinese NER models cannot fully exert their performance in special domains including medical domain.

With the emergence of GPT-3, prompt tuning has become more and more popular. By choosing an appropriate template and manipulating the model's input during pre-training, PLM can be used to predict the desired output. Cui and Wu [3] investigated template-based few-shot NER using BART as the backbone model. When there are new entity categories, they can be fine-tuned directly for the target domain. Chen and Zhang [2] propose a novel generative framework with prompt-guided attention (LightNER), which can recognize unseen entities using a few examples. By constructing semantic-aware answer space of entity types for prompt- tuning, LightNER can maintain consistent pre-trained and fine-tuning procedures.

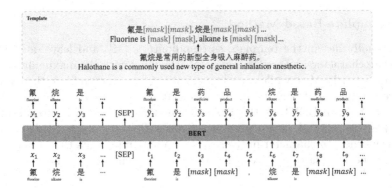

Fig. 1. Training of template-based method.

3   Methods

In this paper, we propose a template-based method. We use a PLM and train the model by designing a template, as shown in Fig. 1.

And we propose a lexicon-based Chinese medical NER model. The overall architecture of our model is shown in Fig. 2. Specifically, our model is comprised of a multi-feature layer, transformer layers and a BiLSTM-CRF layer.

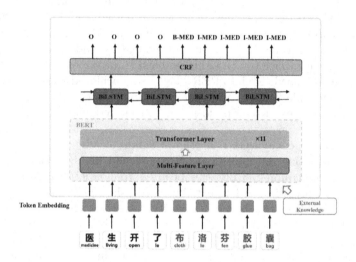

Fig. 2. The overall architecture of our model.

3.1   Template-Based Method

We manually design the template as (candidate is [M]) and leave one slot for candidate characters, where [M] represents the label with the maximum amount of Chinese words. Meanwhile, we use non-entity characters to fill in the template for pre-training, and each template is concatenated with a comma, as shown in Fig. 1. We use BERT as the PLM. Then we converte each input sentence $X = \{x_1,\ x_2,\ ...,x_n\}$ into a prompt sequence $T = \{t_1,\ t_2,\ ...,t_m\}$, where x_i represents the i-th character in the sentence, and t_i represents the i-th character filled in the template, and combine the original sentence X and the prompt sequence T.

$$X_{prompt} = [CLS]X[SEP]T \tag{1}$$

[CLS] and [SEP] are the special token of BERT. Then we feed the new sequence X_{prompt} into the PLM for pre-training and compute the loss as follow:

$$\mathcal{L} = -\sum_i \widetilde{y}_i log\left(P\left(\widetilde{y}_i|X\right)\right) \tag{2}$$

where $\widetilde{y}$ represented the predicted label. In pre-training, the model can learn the information contained in words.

We set maximum input sentence length for pre-training is 512. When the length of X_{prompt} is greater than the maximum length, we will discard the prompt sequence that is greater than maximum length. And when the length of X_{prompt} is less than the length we set, we use [PAD] to pad to the maximum length, [PAD] is a special token of BERT. We set a threshold and stop pre-training when the loss falls below 10^{-3}. Then we use the pre-trained BERT model for our proposed Chinese medical NER model.

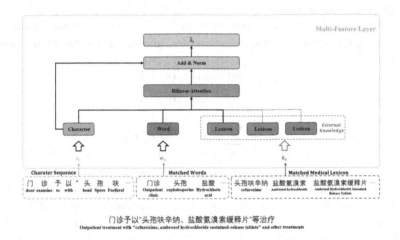

Fig. 3. The architecture of the multi-feature layer.

3.2 Multi-feature Layer

The architecture of the multi-feature layer is shown in Fig. 3; it receives character features, word features, and external knowledge features. A Chinese medical sentence with n characters $s_c = \{c_1, c_2, ..., c_n\}$, a Chinese Lexicon $\mathbf{D}_1$ for matching words, and a Chinese Medical Lexicon $\mathbf{D}_2$ are given to provide external knowledge features. Then, find all the words that the characters in the sentence can form by matching the sequence of characters against $\mathbf{D}_1$ and $\mathbf{D}_2$. We construct the lexicon tree on the $\mathbf{D}_1$ and $\mathbf{D}_2$, then iterate over the subsentence containing the current character and match the lexicon tree to get all potential words. In this way, we get word features and external knowledge features. After that, we combine the embedding of character, word, and external lexicon into a character-word pair and a character-lexicon pair, respectively. We construct $s_{cw} = \{(c_1, w_{s1}), (c_2, w_{s2}), ..., (c_n, w_{sn})\}$ character-word pair and $s_{ck} = \{(c_1, k_{s1}), (c_2, k_{s2}), ..., (c_n, k_{sn})\}$ character-lexicon pair, where w_{si} and k_{si} represent matched words assigned to c_i.

We send the sequence of character, character-word pair and character-lexicon pair to the model. In this way, the model can directly fuse medical lexicon information into the multi-feature layer. And denote the input as (h_i^c, x_i^w, k_i^w), where h_i^c is a character vector, x_i^w is a set of word embeddings, and k_i^w is a set of medical lexicon embeddings. The j-th word in x_i^w and k_i^w is represented as follows:

$$x_{ij}^w = e^w(w_{ij}^x) \tag{3}$$

$$k_{ij}^w = e^w(w_{ij}^k) \tag{4}$$

where e^w is a pre-trained word embedding lookup table and w_{ij}^x is the j-th of w_{si}, w_{ij}^k is the j-th of k_{si}.

We use a non-linear transformer to transform the word vectors into v_{ij}^x and v_{ij}^k, align word feature with character feature, and calculate the attention score as follows:

$$a_i^x = softmax(h_i^c W_{attn}^x V_{xi}^T) \tag{5}$$

$$a_i^k = softmax(h_i^c W_{attn}^k V_{ki}^T) \tag{6}$$

$$Z_i^w = \sum_{j=1}^u a_{ij}^x v_{ij}^x + \sum_{j=1}^l a_{ij}^k v_{ij}^k \tag{7}$$

where $V_{xi}^T = \{v_{i1}^x, v_{i2}^x, \ldots, v_{im}^x\}$ represents the vectors of i-th character in word vectors and the same to the $V_{ki}^T = \{v_{i1}^k, v_{i2}^k, \ldots, v_{il}^k\}$ about medical lexicon vectors, W_{attn}^x and W_{attn}^k is the attention weight matrix, u is the total number of words, and l is the total number of medical lexicon. Then, we use a bilinear attention layer to combine the three inputs separately to get Z_i^w and then combine h_i^c and the feature vector to send to the transform layer.

$$\widetilde{h}_i = Z_i^w + h_i^c \tag{8}$$

3.3 Label Prediction

This part contains BiLSTM layer and CRF layer. BiLSTM has a strong non-linear fitting ability and can more accurately capture long-distance dependencies. The outputs of BiLSTM are independent, and each step outputs the label with the maximum probability value, which may lead to unreasonable label connections. To avoid this problem, we add a CRF layer after BiLSTM.

To train the CRF layer [26], we minimize a negative log-likelihood function consisting of real path score and total score of all possible paths where a path means a candidate label sequence of the input sentences. The real path is the gold label sequence and we denote P_{real} as the real path score. Suppose there are M kinds of labels and n characters in the sentence. There will be M^n paths. We denote $P_{total} = P_1 + P_2 + \ldots + P_{M^n}$ as the total path score. The loss function of the CRF layer is defined as follows:

$$LossFunction = -\log \frac{P_{real}}{P_{total}} \tag{9}$$

P_t is the path score of path t, and we define P_t as $exp(S_t)$. S_t is defined as follows:

$$S_t = \sum_{i=1}^{n} E_{i,label_i} + \sum_{i=2}^{n} T_{label_{i-1},label_i} \tag{10}$$

where $label_i$ denotes the i-th label of path t. E is the emission score, the score represents the fact that j is the label of i. T is the transition score, the score represents the fact that label i transitions to label j. The emission score comes from the BiLSTM layer. It is a matrix of size n by M, and $E_{i,j}, 1 \leq i \leq n, 1 \leq j \leq M$. The transition score is a square matrix T of size M by M, and $T_{i,j}, 1 \leq i, j \leq M$. The transition score is trainable parameter of the CRF layer.

In order to find the best label sequence for an input sentence, we used the Viterbi algorithm [6], one of dynamic programming algorithms.

4 Experiments

In this section, we conduct a series of experiments on three Chinese medical NER datasets to prove the effectiveness of our method.

4.1 Dataset

There are three datasets, all of which are Chinses medical NER datasets. The statistical details of the three datasets are shown in Table 1.

The first dataset is the CCKS2019, all samples of which are clinical text. This dataset contains six categories. The second dataset, named CDD, is from the China Disease Resource Database's laboratory examination text and other auxiliary examination text. Zhang et al. [8] constructed this dataset. It contains only one category. The third dataset, named FN, is from the hospital examination text; 500 samples are annotated according to the Medical Named Entity Recognition labeling standard. It contains only one category.

4.2 Setting

The lexicon $\mathbf{D}_1$ is from Tencent AI Lab[1] and the lexicon $\mathbf{D}_2$ consists of Chinese medical thesaurus words organized by THUOCL[2] (THU Open Chinese Lexicon), and medical examination summary words obtained from hospitals.

Character Embedding: In our experiments, our model is constructed based on $BERT_{wwm\_ext}$ [4], with 12 layers of transformers.

---

[1] https://ai.tencent.com/ailab/nlp/en/embedding.html.
[2] https://github.com/thunlp/THUOCL.

Table 1. The statistical details of the datasets.

Dataset	Type	Train	Dev	Test
CCKS	Sentence	1.0k		0.4k
	Char	418.4k		132.7k
CDD	Sentence	5.6k	0.9k	0.9k
	Char	527.7k	83.0k	90.3k
FN	Sentence	0.4k		0.1k
	Char	400.4k		100.5k

Hyper-parameter Setting: the Multi-feature Layer and the Transformer Layer are trained for 30 epochs with the learning rate of 2e–5 using the AdamW [16] optimizer and the BiLSTM-CRF Layer with the learning rate of 1e–2. The number of hidden units is 300. The batch size is 8 in all datasets. The max length of the sequence of FN is set to 512, CCKS and CDD is set to 150. And for each experiment, we record the best result of 5 runs.

4.3 Evaluation

We use F1-score to evaluate all methods and report precision (PRE) and recall (REC) to ensure fairness in model comparisons.

4.4 Results

Lexicon Enhancement Methods: To illustrate the effectiveness of our method, we compare it with others in Table 2. We set the BERT+BiLSTM+CRF and LEBERT methods as our baselines, and we also compare them with six other lexicon-based methods, as can be seen from the table. Our method obtains good performance, with the F1-score of 83.24% for the CCKS, 62.22% for the CDD and 69.55% for the FN. And our method with a template-based pre-trained model achieves 83.84%, 62.35% and 70.23%, respectively.

Compared with LEBERT, our method with a template-based pre-trained model improves by 0.92%, 1.18% and 1.55%, respectively. And the effects of other models do not achieve good results. We believe that this reflects the particularity of the Chinese medical NER dataset: a small amount of data and a large number of professional terms and abbreviations. Therefore, these NER models cannot achieve the expected results. Our model improves the model's word segmentation accuracy for medical named entities by fusing medical lexicon information to address the impact of professional terms and abbreviations.

Table 2. The main results of Chinese medical NER.

Methods	CCKS			CDD			FN		
	Pre	Rec	F1	Pre	Rec	F1	Pre	Rec	F1
Lattice LSTM [27]	67.19	60.14	63.47	**73.71**	48.68	58.64	64.21	57.39	60.61
LR-CNN [9]	59.38	53.15	56.09	68.04	52.56	59.31	65.94	63.13	64.50
CCW [15]	82.66	81.91	82.28	72.19	50.78	59.62	62.89	58.97	60.87
LGN [10]	79.77	81.54	80.65	58.06	43.13	49.49	63.2	56.41	59.61
Sample-Lattice [17]	54.88	35.16	42.86	71.82	51.37	59.90	–	–	–
FLAT [13]	77.56	74.24	75.87	70.30	53.79	60.95	47.63	45.13	46.34
BERT+BiLSTM+CRF	83.36	81.95	82.65	59.98	**63.91**	61.88	67.41	70.04	68.70
+ prompt	84.34	82.19	83.25	68.73	56.30	61.90	**73.06**	66.61	69.69
LEBERT [14]	82.70	83.14	82.92	**71.86**	53.24	61.17	69.23	68.14	68.68
+ prompt	83.50	83.35	83.43	70.94	54.24	61.48	71.58	66.68	69.04
Our method	**84.66**	81.87	83.24	65.41	59.32	62.22	67.89	**71.30**	69.55
+ prompt	83.66	**84.03**	**83.84**	66.55	58.65	**62.35**	72.14	68.43	**70.23**

Low-Resource: To prove that our method can still maintain good performance in the case of low resources, similar to the experiments above, we evaluate 0.5k sentences randomly sampled from the CCKS dataset and 0.5k, 1k and 2k sentences randomly sampled from the CDD dataset. We report the F1 of CCKS and CDD in Tables 3 and 4. As can be seen from Tables 3 and 4, our method maintains good results in low-resource scenarios. When there are only 500 training data, the effect of BERT+BiLSTM+CRF exceeds our method, and as the training data increases, our method surpasses it.

Table 3. The effectiveness of Low-Resource on the CCKS.

Method	0.5k			1k (All)		
	Pre	Rec	F1	Pre	Rec	F1
Lattice LSTM [27]	56.00	48.95	52.24	67.19	60.14	63.47
LR-CNN [9]	43.65	38.46	40.89	59.38	53.15	56.09
CCW [15]	82.39	79.30	80.82	82.66	81.91	82.28
LGN [10]	77.62	77.37	77.50	79.77	81.54	80.65
FLAT [13]	65.08	67.36	66.20	77.56	74.24	75.87
BERT+BiLSTM+CRF	82.30	81.49	81.90	83.36	81.95	82.65
+ prompt	81.92	82.20	82.06	84.34	82.19	83.25
LEBERT [14]	79.86	81.15	80.5	82.70	83.14	82.92
+ prompt	81.48	**83.37**	82.41	83.50	83.35	83.43
Our method	80.53	81.91	81.21	**84.66**	81.87	83.24
+ prompt	**82.35**	83.12	**82.73**	83.66	**84.03**	**83.84**

Table 4. The effectiveness of Low-Resource on the CDD.

Method	0.5k			1k			2k		
	Pre	Rec	F1	Pre	Rec	F1	Pre	Rec	$F1$
Lattice LSTM [27]	58.25	38.81	46.59	58.19	47.49	52.30	**68.19**	45.61	54.66
LR-CNN [9]	–	–	–	–	–	–	21.42	0.16	0.32
CCW [15]	61.38	37.98	46.92	63.68	48.01	54.74	66.67	49.64	47.69
LGN [10]	44.24	31.05	36.49	53.46	38.71	44.90	55.73	41.67	47.69
FLAT [13]	14.78	6.59	9.11	40.80	26.42	32.07	50.03	39.57	44.19
BERT+BiLSTM+CRF	58.97	54.40	56.59	60.17	**59.13**	59.65	64.81	55.75	59.94
+ prompt	56.79	56.78	56.79	62.90	57.42	60.03	64.73	56.31	60.23
LEBERT [14]	57.92	52.53	55.09	60.05	58.86	59.45	60.81	**57.88**	59.31
+ prompt	57.43	53.03	55.15	65.13	55.17	59.73	62.79	57.04	59.78
Our method	**64.13**	49.88	56.11	**65.32**	55.97	60.28	66.86	54.57	60.09
+ prompt	56.19	**57.42**	**56.80**	63.82	57.13	**60.29**	66.94	55.21	**60.52**

Word Segmentation: Figure 4 shows the results predicted by LEBERT and our model. As can be seen from the figure, the introduction of external medical knowledge improves the model's ability to recognize medical professional terms, and our model can effectively predict professional terms in external knowledge. When these professional terms contain nouns for body parts, LEBERT can only predict body parts as entities, and other characters as non-entities.

Fig. 4. The effect of word segmentation.

4.5   Ablation Study

We designed an ablation experiment to verify whether various modules of our model would affect the performance. The added modules are checked by removing BiLSTM and the external medical knowledge feature. Therefore, we conduct three experiments: (1) Remove external medical knowledge feature: we use the Lexicon Adapter layer of LEBERT and connect the Transformer and BiLSTM-CRF layers. In this case, the external medical knowledge feature is removed from the entire model. (2) Remove BiLSTM: the model cannot capture bidirectional semantic information after the removal of BiLSTM. Add the CRF layer directly after the Transformer layer. (3) Proposed model: Models (1) and (2) are compared with our proposed model. The experimental results are shown in Table 5. We can see from the results that removing any one of these two modules will affect the overall effect of the model.

Table 5. Ablation experiment on the dataset.

Dataset	Method	Pre	Rec	F1
CCKS	– External medical knowledge	83.40	82.33	82.86
	– BiLSTM	82.34	**82.80**	82.57
	Our method	**84.66**	81.87	**83.24**
CDD	– External medical knowledge	**67.39**	56.98	61.75
	– BiLSTM	66.83	57.75	61.96
	Our method	65.41	**59.32**	**62.22**
FN	– External medical knowledge	**71.70**	67.43	69.50
	– BiLSTM	68.84	68.38	68.61
	Our method	69.34	**72.40**	**70.84**

5 Conclusion

We propose a novel Chinese medical NER model. The core of our model is the lexicon-based method, which integrates the external medical lexicon information into the model, and improves the ability of word segmentation. We also design a template-based strategy to enrich the words' information and improve the model's sensitivity to medical professional terms and abbreviations. The performance of the proposed method is validated on three Chinese medical datasets. Experimental results show that our model is feasible and outperforms other lexicon-based NER models in performance and efficiency. And our method maintains good performance in the case of low resources. In addition, we conduct ablation experiments to verify the effect of each module.

Acknowledgments. The research was supported by Natural Science Foundation of Fujian Province, PR China (2022J01120).

References

1. Bikel, D.M., Miller, S., Schwartz, R., Weischedel, R.: Nymble: a high-performance learning name-finder. arXiv preprint arXiv:cmp-lg/9803003 (1998)

2. Chen, X., et al.: Lightner: a lightweight generative framework with prompt-guided attention for low-resource NER. arXiv preprint arXiv:2109.00720 (2021)
3. Cui, L., Wu, Y., Liu, J., Yang, S., Zhang, Y.: Template-based named entity recognition using bart. arXiv preprint arXiv:2106.01760 (2021)
4. Cui, Y., Che, W., Liu, T., Qin, B., Yang, Z.: Pre-training with whole word masking for chinese bert. IEEE/ACM Trans. Audio Speech Lang. Process. **29**, 3504–3514 (2021)
5. Devlin, J., Chang, M.W., Lee, K., Toutanova, K.: Bert: pre-training of deep bidirectional transformers for language understanding. arXiv preprint arXiv:1810.04805 (2018)
6. Forney, G.D.: The viterbi algorithm. Proc. IEEE **61**(3), 268–278 (1973)
7. Fukuda, K.J., Tsunoda, T., Tamura, A., Takagi, T., et al.: Toward information extraction: identifying protein names from biological papers. In: Pacific Symposium on Biocomputing, vol. 707, pp. 707–718. Citeseer (1998)
8. Gan, Z., et al.: Incorporate lexicon into self-training: a distantly supervised chinese medical NER. In: Wang, L., Feng, Y., Hong, Yu., He, R. (eds.) NLPCC 2021. LNCS (LNAI), vol. 13028, pp. 338–349. Springer, Cham (2021). https://doi.org/10.1007/978-3-030-88480-2_27
9. Gui, T., Ma, R., Zhang, Q., Zhao, L., Jiang, Y.G., Huang, X.: CNN-based chinese NER with lexicon rethinking. In: IJCAI, pp. 4982–4988 (2019)
10. Gui, T., et al.: A lexicon-based graph neural network for Chinese NER. In: Proceedings of the 2019 Conference on Empirical Methods in Natural Language Processing and the 9th International Joint Conference on Natural Language Processing (EMNLP-IJCNLP), pp. 1040–1050 (2019)
11. He, H., Sun, X.: F-score driven max margin neural network for named entity recognition in chinese social media. arXiv preprint arXiv:1611.04234 (2016)
12. Kuru, O., Can, O.A., Yuret, D.: Charner: character-level named entity recognition. In: Proceedings of COLING 2016, the 26th International Conference on Computational Linguistics: Technical Papers, pp. 911–921 (2016)
13. Li, X., Yan, H., Qiu, X., Huang, X.: FLAT: Chinese NER using flat-lattice transformer. In: Proceedings of the 58th Annual Meeting of the Association for Computational Linguistics, pp. 6836–6842. Association for Computational Linguistics, Online (2020). https://doi.org/10.18653/v1/2020.acl-main.611, https://aclanthology.org/2020.acl-main.611
14. Liu, W., Fu, X., Zhang, Y., Xiao, W.: Lexicon enhanced Chinese sequence labeling using BERT adapter. In: Proceedings of the 59th Annual Meeting of the Association for Computational Linguistics and the 11th International Joint Conference on Natural Language Processing (Volume 1: Long Papers), pp. 5847–5858. Association for Computational Linguistics, Online 2021). https://doi.org/10.18653/v1/2021.acl-long.454, https://aclanthology.org/2021.acl-long.454
15. Liu, W., Xu, T., Xu, Q., Song, J., Zu, Y.: An encoding strategy based word-character LSTM for chinese NER. In: Proceedings of the 2019 Conference of the North American Chapter of the Association for Computational Linguistics: Human Language Technologies, Volume 1 (Long and Short Papers), pp. 2379–2389 (2019)
16. Loshchilov, I., Hutter, F.: Decoupled weight decay regularization. arXiv preprint arXiv:1711.05101 (2017)
17. Ma, R., Peng, M., Zhang, Q., Huang, X.: Simplify the usage of lexicon in chinese NER. arXiv preprint arXiv:1908.05969 (2019)
18. Mccallum, A., Li, W.: Early results for named entity recognition with conditional random fields, feature induction and web-enhanced lexicons. Assoc. Comput. Linguist. **4**, 188–191 (2003)

19. Rindflesch, T.C., Tanabe, L., Weinstein, J.N., Hunter, L.: Edgar: extraction of drugs, genes and relations from the biomedical literature. In: Biocomputing 2000, pp. 517–528. World Scientific (1999)
20. Sekine, S.: Description of the japanese NE system used for met-2. In: Seventh Message Understanding Conference (MUC-7): Proceedings of a Conference Held in Fairfax, Virginia, April 29-May 1, 1998 (1998)
21. Song, M., Yu, H., Han, W.S.: Developing a hybrid dictionary-based bio-entity recognition technique. BMC Med. Inform. Decis. Mak. **15**(1), 1–8 (2015)
22. Sui, D., Chen, Y., Liu, K., Zhao, J., Liu, S.: Leverage lexical knowledge for chinese named entity recognition via collaborative graph network. In: Proceedings of the 2019 Conference on Empirical Methods in Natural Language Processing and the 9th International Joint Conference on Natural Language Processing (EMNLP-IJCNLP), pp. 3830–3840 (2019)
23. Takeuchi, K., Collier, N.: Use of support vector machines in extended named entity recognition. In: COLING-02: The 6th Conference on Natural Language Learning 2002 (CoNLL-2002) (2002), https://aclanthology.org/W02-2029
24. Tsai, R.T.H., Sung, C.L., Dai, H.J., Hung, H.C., Sung, T.Y., Hsu, W.L.: Nerbio: using selected word conjunctions, term normalization, and global patterns to improve biomedical named entity recognition. In: BMC bioinformatics, vol. 7, pp. 1–14. BioMed Central (2006)
25. Tsuruoka, Y., Tsujii, J.: Improving the performance of dictionary-based approaches in protein name recognition. J. Biomed. Inform. **37**(6), 461–470 (2004)
26. Wu, Y., Fang, X., Li, J., Zhang, L., Chen, Z., Wang, Y.: A deep learning approach with conditional random field for automatic sleep stage scoring. In: Proceedings of the 2021 5th International Conference on Electronic Information Technology and Computer Engineering, pp. 901–906 (2021)
27. Zhang, Y., Yang, J.: Chinese NER using lattice LSTM. In: Proceedings of the 56th Annual Meeting of the Association for Computational Linguistics (Volume 1: Long Papers), pp. 1554–1564. Association for Computational Linguistics, Melbourne, Australia (2018). https://doi.org/10.18653/v1/P18-1144, https://aclanthology.org/P18-1144

Neural Networks and Deep Learning

Trajectory Prediction with Heterogeneous Graph Neural Network

Guanlue Li[1,2], Guiyang Luo[1], Quan Yuan[1], and Jinglin Li[1(✉)]

[1] Beijing University of Posts and Telecommunications, Beijing, China
{liguanlue,luoguiyang,yuanquan,jlli}@bupt.edu.cn
[2] Science and Technology on Communication Networks Laboratory, Shijiazhuang, China

Abstract. Trajectory prediction with dense traffic is a challenging task. The heterogeneity caused by multi-type of road agents complicates the mutual and dynamic relationship between agents. Besides, scene context will affect the trajectory of agents. To address the aforementioned challenges, we present a novel model named HTFNet. Specifically, we use a heterogeneous graph network to model multi-type of agents in traffic. In order to handle varying influence between nodes, interactions between nodes are modelled by a heterogeneous transformer neural network, which uses mate-relation-dependent parameters to distinguish heterogeneous attention over each edge. In addition, scene contexts are considered in multi-model destinations prediction. Through extensive experiments on Stanford Drone Dataset, the results show that our model achieves superior performance on the heterogeneous traffic dataset and produces more reasonable trajectories for different types of road agents.

Keywords: Trajectory prediction · Heterogeneous graph transformer · Multi-type agents

1 Introduction

Predicting trajectory is an essential component for many applications. For example, autonomous driving needs accurate trajectory prediction to avoid collisions and ensure safety. When robots deliver goods in a complex environment, trajectory forecasting can help them take appropriate strategies to improve efficiency.

In a traffic scenario, there are multi-type road agents, such as cars, buses, pedestrians and bicycles. Different types of road agents increase the uncertainty of interaction effects between them. Most existing trajectory prediction works focus on one type of road agents such as pedestrians [1,3,6,26] or vehicles [10,25]. However, these methods ignore the difference in social interaction and dynamic patterns between multi-type road agents. For example, people will pay more attention to motor vehicles with greater speed and inertia than pedestrians.

© The Author(s), under exclusive license to Springer Nature Switzerland AG 2022
S. Khanna et al. (Eds.): PRICAI 2022, LNCS 13630, pp. 375–387, 2022.
https://doi.org/10.1007/978-3-031-20865-2_28

Hence, learning different interaction patterns is required to predict trajectories in dense traffic.

Many models divide the prediction into two steps [2,8,28], which predict destinations firstly, then predict the final trajectory based on a generated destination. Generative Adversarial Networks (GANs) and Variational Autoencoders are used to predict the destination distribution [9,21]. Static scene feature need to be added in destination prediction, which prevents unrealistic predictions.

This work aims to develop a trajectory prediction model suitable for dense traffic with multi-type road agents. We follow the target-driven trajectory prediction framework and use conditional variational autoencoders (CVAEs) to predict the destination distribution. With the success of graph neural networks in processing graph-structured data, road agents can be modelled as a graph with rich relation information. We propose HTFNet, which uses a heterogeneous graph transformer network to model interactions between road agents. Meta-relation-based parameters are used to get adaptive scaling attention. We add scene information in the process of destinations and trajectories prediction, which increases the accuracy and reality of trajectories. We empirically validate our model on Stanford Drone Datasets. Experimental results show that our model significantly improves trajectory prediction tasks compared to baselines.

The contributions of this paper are summarized as follows:

- We model multi-type of agents as a dynamic heterogeneous graph and propose HFTNet to learn heterogeneous message transmission between nodes.
- In the destination and trajectory prediction process, we consider scene information and the dynamic pattern of the agents.
- Our model is evaluated in the short-term and long-term trajectory prediction tasks. The result shows that our model can produce more reasonable and accurate trajectories in complex traffic.

2   Related Work

There are considerable works on trajectory prediction for moving agents. Many approaches rely on recurrent neural networks (LSTMs or GRUs) to exploit temporal dependencies of time series. Many models take into account the interaction between road agents. Alahi et al. [1] introduces social pooling to pool nearby pedestrians' hidden features. Deo et al. [10] use convolutional social pooling to improve the pooling process. Another relevant work is STGAT by Huang et al. [15]. STGAT treats each agent as a graph node and exploits the graph attention network to share information across different pedestrians. Some algorithms consider heterogeneous data: Trajectron++ by Salzmann et al. [24] accounts for multiple interacting agents from heterogeneous input data and produces dynamically-feasible trajectory forecasts. TraPHic by Chandra et al. [7] uses a hybrid network LSTM-CNN to predict trajectories and take into account heterogeneous interactions. The dynamics of a bus-pedestrian interaction differ significantly from a pedestrian-pedestrian or a car-pedestrian. In order to process dense, heterogeneous traffic scenarios in-depth, we model the interactions among different types of agents by using a dynamic heterogeneous graph. Some methods also use reinforcement learning to model the interaction and communication between agents [17,20].

Graph Neural Networks (GNNs) are aimed to process graph structured data and use message passing between the nodes to capture information from its neighbourhood with arbitrary depth. GNN has been used in many fields such as biology [12], traffic forecasting [19] and mobile networks [18]. The graph convolutional neural network can be divided into two categories: spectral domain and non-spectral domain. Spectral approaches represent the graph as spectral embedding based on adjacency matrices, while non-spectral approaches use convolutions directly on the graph based on groups of spatial neighbours. A heterogeneous graph is defined as a graph have several kinds of nodes and edges. The heterogeneous graph embedding mainly focuses on meta-relation, which utilizes the nodes' paths to model the context of a node. Meta-relation can group the neighbours according to their node types and distances. HAN by Wang et al. [27] proposed the heterogeneous graph attention network, which utilizes meta-relation to model node level and semantic attention and learns the weights of different neighbours. HGT by Hu et al. [14] uses transformer-like self-attention architecture for learning node representation.

3   Model Design

In this section, we introduce our HTFNet for trajectory prediction with multiple types of agents. Our approach is visualized in Fig. 1. There are three key components 1) Feature Encoder, 2) Destination Generator, and 3) Interaction and Prediction Module. We begin the section by describing the problem definition. Then we present details on how the proposed components are adapted to the task.

3.1   Problem Formulation

Problem Setup. Multi-agent trajectory prediction is a task of forecasting the future states of agents. The inputs of model are the historical state of N agents $X = [x^{-t_h}, ..., x^{-1}, x^0]$ and scene context S in the time period $[-t_h, 0]$, where $x^t = (x_1^t, x_2^t, ...x_N^t)$ is the joint state of N agents at time t. The goal of model is predicting the position of N agents $Y = (Y^1, Y^2, ...Y^{t_p})$ in the future time period $[1, t_p]$.

This paper is focused on a complex traffic scenario involving multi-type road agents, such as cars, pedestrians and bicycles. The scenario can be modeled by dynamic heterogeneous graph denoted as a series of snapshots $\{G\}_{-t_h}^{t_p}$, where nodes represent road agents and edges represent their interactions. The graph G at each time t represented as $G_t = (\mathcal{V}_t, \mathcal{E}_t, \mathcal{A}, \mathcal{R})$, where the nodes $\mathcal{V}_t$ and edges $\mathcal{E}_t$ change when the dynamic graph evolving. $\mathcal{A}$ and $\mathcal{R}$ are node and edge type sets respectively. Each node $v \in \mathcal{V}_t$ and each edge $e \in \mathcal{E}_t$ are associated with their type by mapping functions $\gamma(v) : \mathcal{V}_t \to \mathcal{A}$ and $\lambda(e) : \mathcal{E}_t \to \mathcal{R}$.

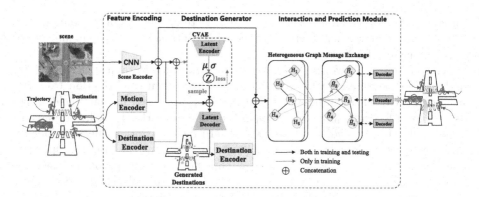

Fig. 1. Overview of the model architecture. Our model consists of three components: 1) Feature Encoder, 2) Destination Generator, and 3) Interaction and Prediction Module. The Destination Generator Module combines the motion feature of the historical trajectories and scene context to infer the destination distribution. The Interaction and Prediction Module uses the HGT network to exchange features between nodes.

3.2   Feature Extraction Module

The input of the model includes 2D location series of agents. We use a fully connected layer (FCL) with Relu activation as the motion encoder to extract temporal information of history state F_x:

$$F_x = \mathrm{MLP}_x(\{x_k\}^0_{-t_h}), \tag{1}$$

where $\{x_k\}^0_{-t_h}$ is the 2D location series of agent k. We follow target-driven framework that predicts the destination distribution firstly. Therefore we need to extract the trajectory endpoint for destination generative module. We also use a FCL and Relu activation as the destination encoder:

$$F_d = \mathrm{MLP}_d(D_k). \tag{2}$$

where $D_k = x_k^{t_p}$ is the ground-truth destination of agent k. Trajectories are significantly oriented by scene context. The objective of the scene encoder is to detect the scene edge information (e.g., sidewalk, boundaries and buildings). We use the hand-designed convolutional neural network (CNN) to extract visual features F_s:

$$F_s = \mathrm{CNN}(S_t). \tag{3}$$

where S_t is the image of traffic environment at time t.

3.3   Scene Context Aware Destinations Prediction

In this model, CAVE is used to learn the destination distribution. The goal of destination generator module is to model the destination distribution $p_\theta(D|X, S)$

conditioned on history motion X and contextual information S. To consider the stochasticity of destination in complex traffic scenarios, latent variables Z are introduced. The future destination distribution of agents can be represented as:

$$p(D_k|X_k, S_k) = \int p_\theta(D_k|Z_k, X_k, S_k)p_\nu(Z_k|X_k, S)dZ_k \tag{4}$$

where D_k is the ground-truth destination of agent k. Z_k, X_k is the latent intent and historical trajectory of agent k, respectively. S_k is the scene context in this period of time. Deep neural network are used to approximate prior network $p_\nu(Z_k|X_k, S)$ and decoder network $p_\theta(D_k|Z_k, X_k, S_k)$, where ν and θ denote the parameters of corresponding networks. The generative process of D_k is:

1. Sample a latent variable z from the prior network $p_\nu(Z_k|X_k, S_k)$.
2. Generate destinations $\widehat{D}_k$ through the response decoder $p_\theta(D_k|Z_k, X_k, S_k)$.

The goal of CVAE is maximizing the conditional log likelihood $\log p(D_k|X_k, S_k)$, which can be trained by maximizing the variational lower bound of the conditional log likelihood. Finally, the loss function of the destination generator can be represented as:

$$L_d(\theta, \nu; D, X, S) = \text{KL}\left(q_\nu(Z|D, X, S) \| p_\theta(S|X, S)\right)$$
$$- E_{q_\nu(Z|D,X,S)}[\log p_\theta(D|Z, X, S)]. \tag{5}$$

3.4 Heterogeneous Graph Message Exchange

In a dense and complex traffic scene, different types of road agents have various types of interactions. In order to transmit information between them, we consider each road agent as a node of the graph and use a heterogeneous graph transformer network (HGTNet) to exchange messages. Our HGTNet is based on Heterogeneour Graph Transformer architecture [14]. HGTNet allows for aggregating information from neighbours by assigning different attention to different types of nodes. It also puts different attention within the same type. For example, vehicles and bicycles extract different information from the road agent in front and sides of them to avoid collisions.

There are two stages in the HGTNet. Firstly, the heterogeneous multi-head attention mechanism is used to calculate attention and messages. Then we use the heterogeneous message passing framework to exchange information between nodes. HGTNet is constructed by stacking HGT layers. The structure of a single HGT layer is shown in Fig. 2. We concatenate motion feature F_x, scene feature F_s and generated destination feature F_{gd} as the input of the Heterogeneous Message Exchange Module:

$$H = \oplus(F_x, F_{gd}, F_s), \tag{6}$$

We map trajectory hidden feature of target node k and source node s into Query vector and Key vector, respectively. Then calculate their dot product as attention. For a meta relation $< \gamma(s), \lambda(e), \gamma(k) >$, the influence from source node s to the target node k are calculated by a meta-relation-based attention network:

$$K^i(s) = K^i_{\gamma(s)}(H^{l-1}[s]), \tag{7}$$

$$Q^i(k) = Q^i_{\gamma(k)}(H^{l-1}[k]), \tag{8}$$

$$Att^{h_i}(s, e, k) = K^i(s)Q^i(k)^T \varphi^{att}_{<\gamma(s),\lambda(e),\gamma(k)>}, \tag{9}$$

where $Att^{h_i}(s, e, k)$ means one of multi-head attention. H^l means the output of l-th HGT layer, which is also the input of the $(l+1)$-th layer. In order to distinguish different meta relation between attention, a matrix $\varphi^{att}_{<\gamma(s),\lambda(e),\gamma(k)>}$ for meta relation is used to donate the difference. Then we concatenate different representations of attention and make them through the softmax procedure:

$$ATT_{HGT}(s, e, k) = \underset{\forall s \in N(k)}{Softmax}(\underset{i \in [1,h]}{\|} Att^{h_i}(s, e, k)). \tag{10}$$

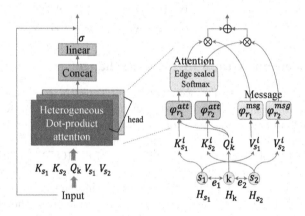

Fig. 2. Overview of architecture of heterogeneous graph transformer

After we get the multi-head attention, the message passing process can be computed in a similar way. We use a matrix $\varphi^{msg}_{<\gamma(s),\lambda(e),\gamma(k)>}$ to distinguish different mate relation. Then all heads of message are aggregated:

$$Msg^{h_i}(s, e, k) = M^i_{\gamma(s)}(H^{l-1}[s])\varphi^{msg}_{<\gamma(s),\lambda(e),\gamma(k)>}, \tag{11}$$

$$MSG_{HGT}(s, e, k) = \underset{i \in [1,h]}{\|} Msg^{h_i}(s, e, k). \tag{12}$$

As show in Fig. 2, φ_r^{att} and φ_r^{msg} denote the meta-relation-based attention and message. After getting heterogeneous multi-head attention and message, we need to aggregate them to get the final target node feature representation:

$$\widetilde{H}^l[k] = \sum_{\forall s \in N(k)} (ATT_{HGT}(s, e, k) \cdot MSG_{HGT}(s, e, k)), \tag{13}$$

following the residual connection, the output of the l-th layer is

$$H_{[k]}^{l+1} = \sigma(A_{\gamma(k)}\widetilde{H}_{[k]}^l) + H_{[k]}^l, \tag{14}$$

$A_{\gamma(k)}$ is a linear function mapping target note's vector back to its node type-specific distribution.

3.5   Trajectory Prediction

The final trajectory feature H of each node is passed through the prediction decoder to get the future trajectory. We use a FCL as the trajectory generator:

$$\{Y_k\}_1^{t_f} = MLP_y(H_k). \tag{15}$$

To train the full model HTFNet, we use the following losses:

$$L = L_d(\theta, \nu; D, X, S) + \|\widehat{Y} - Y\|^2, \tag{16}$$

where $L_d(\theta, \nu; D, X, S)$ measures destination error and $\|\widehat{Y} - Y\|^2$ measures how far the generated trajectories from the ground truth.

4   Experiments

4.1   Dataset

We conduct experiments on Stanford Drone Datasets (SDD) [22]. SDD is a heterogeneous dataset which consists of the following road agents categories: pedestrians, skateboarders, bikers, cars, carts and buses. To make the category more general, we combine car, cart and bus into one type and denote as the vehicle. In total, there are eight unique top view scenes recorded by drone, 60 videos and 10300 unique trajectories. We follow the dataset split defined in TrajNet benchmark [4] which used in prior work [5,23].

4.2   Experimental Settings

We use the Average Displacement Error (ADE) and Final Displacement Error (FDE) as performance metrics. The error is measured in the pixel space. We conduct the trajectory prediction task in three different time steps. In detail, We sample the data at 25 fps. The length of input sequence is $t_p = 8$ (3.2 s) while the length of output sequence is $t_f = 12, 24, 36$ (4.8, 9.6, 14.4 s). For the adjacent matrix, we build a binary adjacency matrix, which based on spatial and temporal correlation. $\mathcal{E}_{i,j} = 1$ if the spatial and temporal correlations are satisfied between agent i and agent j:

$$\sqrt{(x_i - x_j)^2} \leq \delta_d,$$
$$\min(\min |t^i_{begin} - t^j_k|, \min |t^i_{end} - t^j_k|) \leq \delta_t, \quad (17)$$

where δ_t and δ_d is the spatial and temporal threshold values, respectively.

The scene images are downsampled and resized to the same size. The entire network are trained end to end by ADAM optimizer and we use 2 layers HGT network to handle interaction between road agents.

4.3 Baselines

We compare the performance of our proposed model with the following baselines.
Social GAN [13]: In this approach SeqtoSeq model are used to encode motion histories and predict future trajectories. The outputs of LSTM are the generator of GAN. The diverse predictions are evaluated against with ground truth by the discriminator.
DESIRE [16]: This model use CAVE to generate diverse set of hypothetical future trajectories. Then use a scoring-regression module rank every prediction. A feedback mechanism further increases the prediction accuracy.
SoPhie [23]: This model predicts future trajectories based on GAN and consider two sources of information, which are history trajectories and scene context information. This model proposes physical attention and social attention to model interaction between agents.
CF-VAE [5]: This model use Conditional Flow Variational Autoencoder(CF-VAE) to learning multi-modal trajectories distributions. And it also proposed posterior regularization and condition regularization to stabilize training.
P2TIRL [11]: This model use MaxEnt IRL to infer goals and paths by learning rewards and it also defined coarse 2-D grid over the scene to predict trajectories.
PECNET [21]: This model first use CVAE to predict multi-modality destination of road agents. Then predict trajectories based on these destinations.

4.4 Quantitative Evaluation

We conduct trajectory prediction with different future time steps form 12 to 36. Table 1 shows the ADE and FDE values of our proposed method against the baselines on SDD. Our proposed HTFNet shows consistent lowest errors for different future time periods compared to the prior approaches. HTFNet outperforms PECNet by 1.2%, 3.4% and 3.8% on ADE in three time steps, respectively. This can be reasonably expected, since we add heterogeneous interaction between different types of road agents and static scene context, which help to find the reasonable destination.

Table 1. Different time steps comparison of recent methods on SDD. We report two metrics: minADE and minFDE of the trajectory with least error among K = 20 predicted trajectories. The units of ADE/FDE are pixels.

Methods	12-step		24-step		36-step	
	min ADE	min FDE	min ADE	min FDE	min ADE	min FDE
Social-GAN(k = 20)	27.25	41.44	56.28	123.39	114.87	267.40
DESIRE(k =5)	19.25	34.05	49.25	111.78	99.82	233.45
SoPhie(k = 20)	16.27	29.38	36.05	81.14	79.09	172.47
CF-VAE(k = 20)	12.60	26.30	33.89	68.66	73.09	138.47
P2TIRL(k = 20)	12.58	22.07	24.07	42.40	53.47	93.05
PECNET(k = 20)	9.96	15.88	24.88	43.51	53.71	94.71
HTFNet(ours)(k = 20)	**9.84**	**15.76**	**24.01**	**42.46**	**52.80**	**89.46**

We show the results of different types of agents in Table 2. Our method outperforms Social-GAN in all types of agents. Furthermore, our model has better performance in pedestrian, bicycle and vehicle categories compared to PECNet. This is because these categories have more complex interaction with scene context and other road agents. Our model can predict more reasonable trajectories through the heterogeneous transformer network.

Table 2. Performance of different types of road agents. minADE and minFDE are the least error among K = 20 predicted trajectories.

Metric	Type	Social-GAN	PECNet	HTFNet (ours)
minADE	Pedestrian	24.66	9.57	**9.03**
	Bicycle	312.33	311.34	**303**
	Vehicle	204.26	177.72	**160.89**
	Skater	69.75	**39.25**	51.34
	Average	27.25	9.96	**9.84**
minFDE	Pedestrian	36.69	15.02	**14.72**
	Bicycle	589.77	578.82	**569.53**
	Vehicle	254.51	264.36	**167.67**
	Skater	92.55	**70.04**	83
	Average	41.44	15.88	**15.76**

4.5 Ablation Study

We further conduct ablation studies to investigate the contribution of key technical components in our method. The ablation results are summarized in Table 3. We investigate the role of (1) heterogeneous interaction, (2) scene context and (3) destination prediction, and we denote the corresponding variants as "w/o

HI", "w/o SC" and "w/o DP". We can see that three variants lead to worse performance compared to our proposed method. After removing this heterogeneous interaction learning, the performance of the model has dropped since the different interactions between road agents are not considered. After removing the scene context feature in destination and trajectories prediction, the model achieves 14.72 on ADE metric and 25.22 on FDE metric. This shows that extracting scene context has a certain effect on the accuracy of the model. The multi-model destination prediction also improves the performance of ADE and FDE metrics.

Table 3. Ablation study on effectiveness of heterogeneous interaction (HI), scene context (SC) and destination prediction (DP).

	w/o HT	w/o SC	w/o DP	Ours (HTFNet)
ADE	16.22	14.72	13.04	9.84
FDE	30.90	25.22	26.84	15.76

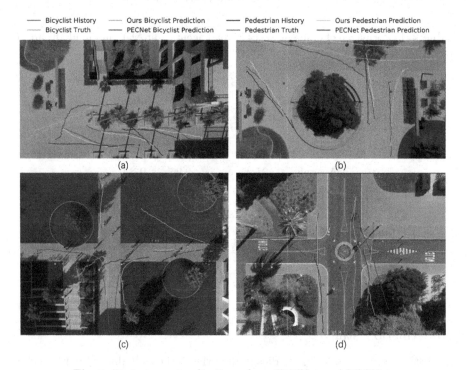

(a)   (b)

(c)   (d)

Fig. 3. Trajectory visualization of our HTFNet and PECNet

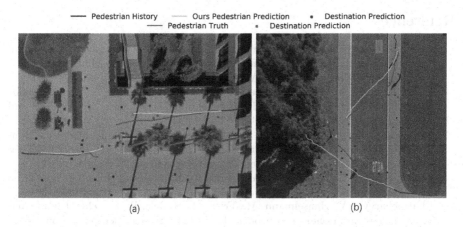

Fig. 4. Destination visualization of HTFNet

4.6   Qualitative Evaluation

Trajectory Visualization. In Fig. 3, we visualize predicted trajectories of our method and PECNet. We can see that our model provides significant improvement especially in long-range trajectory prediction. In Fig. 3(a, b), The distribution of trajectories and destination points of our model will avoid obstacles and buildings. In Fig. 3 (c, d), our model can extract the contour of the scene, and then follow the interaction with the scene and other road agents.

Destination Visualization. Figure 4 show the predicted destination results obtained by our model. We use blue and red points to denote the sampled destination by CVAE. We can see that our model captures the multi-modality of the trajectory by destination distribution. In Fig. 4a, we can see that the distribution of destination depends on the scene context and history trajectory. In Fig. 4b, the prediction shows the pedestrians choose to cross the road.

5   Conclusion

In this work, we propose a model for motion prediction. This model first generates possible future destinations and then predicts trajectories based on multi-model destinations. We add scene information and dynamic pattern in the forecasting process. In order to model different interactions between different types of road agents, we use HGT to model their interactions with each other. We evaluate our model on a heterogeneous traffic dataset and prove that our model can predict a reasonable and accurate future trajectory.

Acknowledgments. This work was supported in part by the Natural Science Foundation of China under Grant 61876023 and in part by the Foundation of Science and Technology on Communication Networks Laboratory.

References

1. Alahi, A., Goel, K., Ramanathan, V., Robicquet, A., Fei-Fei, L., Savarese, S.: Social lSTM: Human trajectory prediction in crowded spaces. In: Proceedings of the IEEE Conference On Computer Vision And Pattern Recognition, pp. 961–971 (2016)
2. Albrecht, S.V., et al.: Interpretable goal-based prediction and planning for autonomous driving. In: 2021 IEEE International Conference on Robotics and Automation (ICRA), pp. 1043–1049. IEEE (2021)
3. Amirian, J., Hayet, J.-B., Pettré, J.: Social ways: learning multi-modal distributions of pedestrian trajectories with GANS. In: Proceedings of the IEEE/CVF Conference on Computer Vision and Pattern Recognition Workshops (2019)
4. Becker, S., Hug, R., Hübner, W., Arens, M.: An evaluation of trajectory prediction approaches and notes on the trajnet benchmark. CoRR, abs/1805.07663 (2018)
5. Bhattacharyya, A., Hanselmann, M., Fritz, M., Schiele, B., Straehle, C.-N.: Conditional flow variational autoencoders for structured sequence prediction. arXiv preprint arXiv:1908.09008 (2019)
6. Brito, B., Zhu, H., Pan, W., Alonso-Mora, J.: Social-VRNN: one-shot multi-modal trajectory prediction for interacting pedestrians. arXiv preprint arXiv:2010.09056 (2020)
7. Chandra, R., Bhattacharya, U., Bera, A., Manocha, D.: Traphic: trajectory prediction in dense and heterogeneous traffic using weighted interactions. In: Proceedings of the IEEE/CVF Conference on Computer Vision and Pattern Recognition, pp. 8483–8492 (2019)
8. Chiara, L.F., Coscia, P., Das, S., Calderara, S., Cucchiara, R., Ballan, L.: Goal-driven self-attentive recurrent networks for trajectory prediction. In: Proceedings of the IEEE/CVF Conference on Computer Vision and Pattern Recognition, pp. 2518–2527 (2022)
9. Dendorfer, P., Osep, A., Leal-Taixé, L.: Goal-gan: Multimodal trajectory prediction based on goal position estimation. In: Proceedings of the Asian Conference on Computer Vision (2020)
10. Deo, N., Trivedi, M.M.: Convolutional social pooling for vehicle trajectory prediction. In: Proceedings of the IEEE Conference on Computer Vision and Pattern Recognition Workshops, pp. 1468–1476 (2018)
11. Deo, N., Trivedi, M.M.: Trajectory forecasts in unknown environments conditioned on grid-based plans. arXiv preprint arXiv:2001.00735 (2020)
12. Ganea, O.-E., et al.: Independent se(3)-equivariant models for end-to-end rigid protein docking. In: The Tenth International Conference on Learning Representations, ICLR 2022, Virtual Event, 25–29 April 2022. OpenReview.net (2022)
13. Gupta, A., Johnson, J., Fei-Fei, L., Savarese, S., Alahi, A.: Social GAN: Socially acceptable trajectories with generative adversarial networks. In: Proceedings of the IEEE Conference on Computer Vision and Pattern Recognition, pp. 2255–2264 (2018)
14. Ziniu, H., Dong, Y., Wang, K., Sun, Y.: Heterogeneous graph transformer. In: Proceedings of The Web Conference, pp. 2704–2710 (2020)
15. Huang, Y., Bi, H., Li, Z., Mao, T., Wang, Z.: Stgat: modeling spatial-temporal interactions for human trajectory prediction. In: Proceedings of the IEEE/CVF International Conference on Computer Vision, pp. 6272–6281 (2019)
16. Lee, N., Choi, W., Vernaza, P., Choy, C.B., Torr, P.H.S., Chandraker, M.: Desire: distant future prediction in dynamic scenes with interacting agents. In: Proceedings of the IEEE Conference on Computer Vision and Pattern Recognition, pp. 336–345 (2017)

17. Luo, G., Zhang, H., He, H., Li, J., Wang, F.Y.: Multiagent adversarial collaborative learning via mean-field theory. IEEE Trans. Cybern. 1–14 (2020)
18. Luo, G., Yuan, Q., Li, J., Wang, S., Yang, F.: Artificial intelligence powered mobile networks: From cognition to decision. IEEE Network, pp. 1–8 (2021)
19. Luo, G., Zhang, H., Yuan, Q., Li, J., Wang, F.-Y.: Estnet: embedded spatial-temporal network for modeling traffic flow dynamics. IEEE Trans. Intell. Transp. Syst. 1–12 (2022)
20. Luo, G., et al.: Software-defined cooperative data sharing in edge computing assisted 5g-vanet. IEEE Trans. Mob. Comput. **20**(3), 1212–1229 (2021)
21. Karttikeya, M., et al.: It is not the journey but the destination: endpoint conditioned trajectory prediction. In: Andrea, V., Horst, B., Thomas, B., Jan-Michael, F. (eds.) ECCV 2020. LNCS, vol. 12347, pp. 759–776. Springer, Cham (2020). https://doi.org/10.1007/978-3-030-58536-5_45
22. Alexandre, R., Amir, S., Alexandre, A., Silvio, S.: Learning social etiquette: human trajectory understanding in crowded scenes. In: Bastian, L., Jiri, M., Nicu, S., Max, W. (eds.) ECCV 2016. LNCS, vol. 9912, pp. 549–565. Springer, Cham (2016). https://doi.org/10.1007/978-3-319-46484-8_33
23. Sadeghian, A., Kosaraju, V., Sadeghian, A., Hirose, N., Rezatofighi, H., Sophie, S.S.: An attentive GAN for predicting paths compliant to social and physical constraints. In: Proceedings of the IEEE/CVF Conference on Computer Vision and Pattern Recognition, pp. 1349–1358 (2019)
24. Salzmann, T., Ivanovic, B., Chakravarty, P., Pavone, M.: Trajectron++: dynamically-feasible trajectory forecasting with heterogeneous data. arXiv preprint arXiv:2001.03093 (2020)
25. Sheng, Z., Xu, Y., Xue, S., Li, D.: Graph-based spatial-temporal convolutional network for vehicle trajectory prediction in autonomous driving. IEEE Trans. Intell. Transp. Syst. **23** (2022)
26. Shi, L., et al.: SGCN: Sparse graph convolution network for pedestrian trajectory prediction. In: Proceedings of the IEEE/CVF Conference on Computer Vision and Pattern Recognition, pp. 8994–9003 (2021)
27. Wang, X., et al.: Heterogeneous graph attention network. In: The World Wide Web Conference, pp. 2022–2032 (2019)
28. Zhao, H., et al.: TNT: Target-driven trajectory prediction. arXiv preprint arXiv:2008.08294 (2020)

EEF1-NN: Efficient and EF1 Allocations Through Neural Networks

Shaily Mishra$^{(\boxtimes)}$, Manisha Padala, and Sujit Gujar

Machine Learning Lab, International Institute of Information Technology,
Hyderabad, India
{shaily.mishra,manisha.padala}@research.iiit.ac.in,
sujit.gujar@iiit.ac.in

Abstract. Our goal is to allocate items to maximize efficiency while ensuring fairness. Since Envy-freeness may not always exist, we consider the relaxed notion, Envy-freeness up to one item (EF1) that is guaranteed to exist. We add the further constraint of maximizing efficiency, utilitarian social welfare (USW) among fair allocations. In general, finding USW allocations among EF1, i.e., EEF1, is an NP-Hard problem even for additive valuations. Neural networks (NNs) have shown state-of-the-art performance in designing optimal auctions as well as in learning algorithms. We design a NN inspired by U-Net for learning EEE1 allocations which we refer to as EEF1-NN. EEF1-NN is generic and scales to any number of agents and items once trained. We empirically demonstrate that EEF1-NN finds allocation with higher USW and ensures EF1 with a high probability for different distributions over input valuations.

Keywords: Resource allocation · Neural networks · EEF1

1 Introduction

Consider a situation where a social planner needs to allocate a set of indivisible items (goods or/and chores) among interested agents. Agents have valuations for the items, i.e., an item might be a *good* – positive valuation for one while it might be a *chore* – negative valuation for the other. The agents reveal their valuations upfront to the *social planner*. The social planner is responsible for the fair and efficient allocation of these items among the agents. For example, a Government needs to distribute resources and delegate tasks amongst its subdivisions. The subdivisions should not feel mistreated in the system. While ensuring this, the Government would like to optimally allocate items for the system's growth.

Fair division is well-explored in literature [10,30,34]. Economists have proposed various fairness and efficiency notions applicable in real-world settings, such as division of investments and inheritance, vaccines, tasks, etc. There are web-based applications such as Spliddit, The Fair Proposals System, Coursematch, Divide Your Rent Fairly, etc., used for credit assignment, land allocation, division of property, course allocation, and even task allotment. All these applications assure certain fairness and efficiency guarantees.

© The Author(s), under exclusive license to Springer Nature Switzerland AG 2022
S. Khanna et al. (Eds.): PRICAI 2022, LNCS 13630, pp. 388–401, 2022.
https://doi.org/10.1007/978-3-031-20865-2_29

One of the most popular fairness criteria is envy-freeness (EF) [17]. An allocation is envy-free if each agent values its share at least as much as they value any other agent's share. EF is also trivially satisfied by allocating empty bundles to every agent. Hence we must also have efficiency guarantees. When we consider a complete allocation of indivisible items, EF may not exist (two agents, one good). Finding whether EF exists or not is known to be Δ_2^pcomplete [9], let alone finding an efficient allocation among EF. To overcome this limitation, we consider a prominent relaxation of EF - EF1 (Envy-freeness up to one item) [12]. Unlike EF, EF1 always exists and can be computed in polynomial time [25].

In this work, we focus on *utilitarian* social welfare (USW), i.e., the sum of utilities of individual agents. When valuations are additive, finding allocation that maximize USW (MUW) is polynomial-time solvable. While finding EF1 or MUW allocations are polynomial-time solvable, maximizing USW within EF1 allocations, i.e., *EEF1*; efficient and envy-free up to one item, is an NP-hard problem, even when valuations are additive for two agents [4,6]. There is no known approximation algorithm for EEF1. With these theoretical limitations, we propose a data-driven learning approach, i.e., given the agents' valuations, we aim to learn EEF1. It is widely known that neural networks (NNs) outperform existing approaches in finding an optimal mapping between the given input and output data. NNs can learn algorithms [22], mechanisms [16] or solve Mixed Integer Programs [31]. Motivated by the success of NNs, we aim to learn algorithm for EEF1 using NN. We list our major challenges as follows,

Challenges. (i) In the existing integration of NNs and mechanism design, payments are at their disposal. In our work, there are no payments, and we learn discrete allocations, i.e., our solution space is binary. Whereas the output of NNs is real numbers, it can easily learn optimal fractional allocations. If we convert fractional solutions to integral, fairness guarantees no longer hold. (ii) Further, we aim to design a generalized network for any number of agents or items, even for configurations not seen during training. Most of the existing NN based approaches in EconCS train the models separately for each configuration [16,27]. We overcome the above challenges as described below.

Contributions. To the best of our knowledge, this is the first study that integrates deep learning and fair resource allocation. In particular,

- We propose a neural network EEF1-NN inspired by U-Net to learn EEF1.
- We transform our valuations and augment them with additional channels to enhance the network's performance.
- We use a series of convolutional and up-convolutional layers to learn EEF1; EEF1-NN is generalized for any number of agents and items.
- We sample valuations from various distributions and report the expected fairness and efficiency achieved. Even for large instances, our network performs well. Moreover,[1] the network quickly computes the output; hence we can improvise this approach to be adept in practical real-time applications.
- We show that, for our setting, bagging of networks improves performance.

---

[1] We evaluated IP solver to solve maximizing USW w.r.t. EF1 constraints, and for 10×100, it was taking several minutes.

2   Related Work

Fair resource allocation is well studied in the literature across various fairness and efficient notions [10,30,34]. When a definition of fairness is too strong or may not exist, we always look for its relaxation/approximation. There is existing work that provides approximate efficiency and fairness guarantees in [1,7,11,24]. In this paper, we majorly focus on EEF1. Authors in [11] presents a framework to compute ϵ-Efficient and $\mathcal{F}$-Fair allocation, using parametric integer linear programming, which is double exponential in terms of n and m. They explored group Pareto Efficiency, which is equivalent to USW. Authors in [4] provides a pseudopolynomial-time algorithm to find MUW within EF1, which is exponential in n and polynomial in m and V, where V bounds the valuation per item.

EF1 allocations always exist and can be found in polynomial time even for general valuations [2,14,25]. Finding MUW allocations is also polynomial-time solvable for additive valuations, i.e., we iterate over items assign the item to the agent who values it the most. However, finding MUW allocation amongst EF1 allocations is NP-hard even for two agents with additive valuations. Also finding a truthful way for allocating EF1 is also challenging [33].

There is always a trade-off between fairness and efficiency, corresponding to the study of the price of fairness [5,8]. Researchers have also studied how likely a fairness notion will not exist [15,28,29]. When agents' valuations are additive and drawn randomly from a uniform distribution, EF exists with a high probability when m is at least $\Omega(n \log n)$ and can be obtained by MUW allocations proved by [15]. However, the hidden constants might be high[2], and it leaves scope to explore. [29] show that RR is envy-free when $m \geq \Omega(n \log n/ \log \log n)$.

Recently the EconCS community has been interested in learning mechanisms/algorithms using NN, especially in a setting of theoretical limitations [16, 21,22,27,37–39]. Researchers have studied mechanism design widely [18,19]. [16] and [21] learns optimal auctions and multi-facility mechanism using NN. [40] uses NN in the combinatorial auction for preference elicitation. [26,27,38] learns optimal redistribution mechanisms and MAB through NN. [39] uses NN to maximize the expected number of consumers and the expected social welfare for public projects. Additionally, [31] solves MIP on large-scale real-world application datasets and MIPLIB using a neural network that performs significantly better than the MIP solver. [32] proposed a neural network-based solution to achieve fairness in classification. Given enough data, hyper-parameter tuning, and proper training, the networks are adept at learning effective transformations. Another line of work is Reinforcement Mechanism Design, such as learning dynamic price in sponsored search auctions [13,36].

3   Preliminaries

We consider the problem of allocating $M = [m]$ indivisible items among $N = [n]$ interested agents, where $m, n \in \mathbb{N}$. We only allow complete allocation and no

---

[2] Our experiments show that in the case of uniform distribution, even for 10 agents, 150 items, the probability of MUW allocation being EF1 is less than 0.5.

two agents can receive the same item. That is, $A = (A_1, \ldots, A_n)$, $A \in \Pi_n(M)$ s.t., $\forall i, j \in N$, $i \neq j; A_i \cap A_j = \emptyset$ and $\bigcup_i A_i = M$. Each agent $i \in N$ has a valuation function $v_i : 2^M \rightarrow \mathbb{R}$ and $v_i(S)$ is its valuation for a $S \subseteq M$ s.t. $v_i(\emptyset) = 0$. We represent valuation profile $v = (v_1, v_2, \ldots, v_n)$. We only consider additive valuations. The valuation of an agent $i \in N$ for bundle A_i is $v_i(A_i) = \sum_{j \in A_i} v_i(\{j\})$. For an agent i, an item $j \in M$ is a *good* if, $v_i(\{j\}) \geq 0$, and a *chore* if, $v_i(\{j\}) < 0$. We consider three settings - pure goods, pure chores, and a combination of goods and chores. With this notation, we now define fairness and efficiency properties as follows.

Definition 1 (Envy-free (EF) and relaxations). *An allocation A that satisfies $\forall i, j \in N$,*

$$v_i(A_i) \geq v_i(A_j) \text{ is EF}$$
$$v_i(A_i \backslash \{k\}) \geq v_i(A_j \backslash \{k\}); \exists k \in \{A_i \cup A_j\} \text{ is EF1}$$

Definition 2 (Maximum Utilitarian Welfare (MUW)). *An allocation A^* is said to be efficient or MUW if it maximizes the USW, $sw(A, v) = \sum_{i \in N} v_i(A_i)$*

$$A^* \in \underset{A \in \Pi_n(M)}{\arg\max}\ sw(A, v)$$

Definition 3 (EEF1 Allocation). *We say an allocation is EEF1 if it satisfies EF1 fairness and maximizes USW amongst EF1 allocations.*

Given agents' valuation profile $v = (v_1, v_2, \ldots, v_n)$, we learn EEF1 allocations using a data-driven approach. We randomly draw $v_i \sim \mathcal{F}_i$ and assume $\mathcal{F} = \mathcal{F}_1 \times \mathcal{F}_2, \ldots, \times \mathcal{F}_n$ to be a known prior distribution over agents' valuations. We use the notation $n \otimes m$ to represent a setting with n agents and m items.

4 Our Approach: EEF1-NN

We construct the optimization problem for EEF1 Sect. 4.1; we then formulate the Lagrangian loss function Sect. 4.2 and provide the detail of EEF1-NN Sects. 4.3 and 4.4.

4.1 Optimization Problem

We are given a set of valuation profile $v = (v_1, v_2, \ldots, v_n)$, where v_i is drawn randomly from a distribution $\mathcal{F}_i$. Among all possible allocations, we need to find an optimal A^* that maximizes USW $sw(A, v)$ and satisfies a fairness constraint. We formulate two (generalized) fairness constraints - EF and EF1 as follows.

$$ef_i(A, v) = \sum_{k \in N} \max\left\{0, (v_i(A_k) - v_i(A_i))\right\} \tag{1}$$

$$ef1_i(A, v) = \sum_{k \in N} \max \left\{ 0, (v_i(A_k) - v_i(A_i)) + \min \left\{ -\max_{j \in A_k} v_i(\{j\}), \min_{j \in A_i} v_i(\{j\}) \right\} \right\}$$

$$(2)$$

Our goal is to maximize the expected welfare w.r.t. to the expected fairness.

$$\text{minimize } -\mathbb{E}_v \left[sw(A, v) \right] = \mathbb{E}_v [\sum_{i \in N} v_i(A_i)]$$

$$\text{subject to } \mathbb{E}_v \left[\sum_{i \in N} ef_i(A, v) \right] = 0 \text{ or, } \mathbb{E}_v \left[\sum_{i \in N} ef1_i(A, v) \right] = 0$$

$$(3)$$

In the above optimization problem, we have 'OR' among fairness constraints, which we elaborate more on this in the Ablation Study in Sect. 5.1.

4.2 EEF1-NN: Lagrangian Loss Function

EEF1-NN represents a mapping from valuation to allocation space, i.e., $\mathcal{A}^w : \mathbb{R}^{\{n \times m\}} \to \{0, 1\}^{n \times m}$, where w represents the network's parameters. To learn w, we formulate our problem to optimize welfare w.r.t. to fairness constraints in Eq. 3 and formulate Lagrangian loss function ($\lambda \in \mathbb{R}_{\geq 0}$). Given $\mathcal{L}$ samples of valuation profiles $(v^1, \ldots, v^{\mathcal{L}})$ drawn from $\mathcal{F}$, the loss per sample (I_v^l) is,

$$Loss(I_v^l, w, \lambda) = \left[-sw(\mathcal{A}^w(I_v^l), v^l) + \lambda \frac{\sum_{i \in N} envy_i(\mathcal{A}^w(I_v^l), v^l)}{n} \right]$$

$$(4)$$

We minimize the following loss w.r.t w, $\mathbf{L}_{EEF1}(I_v^l, w, \lambda) = \frac{1}{\mathcal{L}} \sum_l Loss(v^l, w)$.

4.3 Network Details

We describe EEF1-NNś various components, including the input, architecture, and other training details in this section. EEF1-NN is a fully convolutional network (FCN) and processes input of varied sizes (i.e., height × width).

EEF1-NN: Input. We transform our valuations and augment with additional channels to enhance performance. We construct an input tensor of size $n \times m \times 6$, i.e., $I_v \in \mathbb{R}^{n \times m \times 6}$. The first channel is an $n \times m$ matrix of given valuations, i.e., $\forall i, j; I_v[i, j, 1] = v_i(\{j\})$. We take a matrix X of size $n \times m$ that contains valuation for items only corresponding to the agent who values it the most, and the rest are zero. We break ties arbitrarily and expand X into five channels.

$$\forall j \in M; \; X[i.j, 1] = \begin{cases} v_i(\{j\}) & \text{if } i \in argmax_i v_i(\{j\}) \\ 0 & \text{otherwise} \end{cases}$$

The next channel contains information about items indexed as $0, 5, \ldots, \lfloor m/5 \rfloor$,

$$I[i.j, 2] = \begin{cases} X[i, j, 1] & \text{if } j \in \{0, 5, 10, \ldots, \lfloor m/5 \rfloor\} \\ 0 & \text{otherwise} \end{cases}$$

The next channel contains data from the previous channel along with items indexed as $1, 6, \ldots, 1 + \lfloor m/5 \rfloor$. And so on. The last channel $I_v[i, j, 6]$ is X. We observe that single channeled input performs sub-optimal. We study the effect of input complexity on the performance in Sect. 5.1.

EEF1-NN: Architecture. Our architecture is inspired by U-Net architecture [35]. U-Net is a fully convolutional network built to segment bio-medical images; it also requires assigning labels to image patches and not just classifying the image as a whole. While we are working on valuation profiles rather than images, one of the primary motivations to use U-Net is to process arbitrary size images. If we use a feed-forward fully functional neural network to learn fair and efficient allocations, we need a different network for each $n \otimes m$. Moreover, just using a feed-forward functional network (multi-layer perceptron) learns EEF1 allocations for smaller values of n, but cannot learn as n increases.

EEF1-NN contains series of convolution and up-convolution layers, as given by Fig. 1. EEF1-NN has three series of Conv-UpConv layers. The convolutional layers consist of 4 repeated 3×3 convolution, each followed by a non-linear activation function, tanh. The up-convolution layers consist of 4 repeated 3×3 up-convolution, each followed by a tanh activation. Note that we are not using maxpool or skip connections as we found that they degraded the performance. We apply softmax activation function across all agents for every item to ensure each item is allocated exactly once, i.e., $\forall j \in M \sum_{i \in N} \mathcal{A}_i^w(\{j\}) = 1$. The final output represents the probability with which agent i receives item j. Using an FCN, we have a generalized network for $n \otimes m$; however, learning EEF1 is not easy. We need to learn integral variables, while NNs are known for learning continuous output. We describe these challenges next.

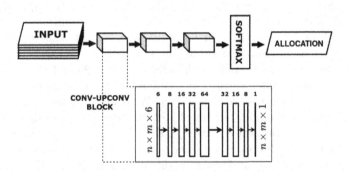

Fig. 1. EEF1-NN Architecture

4.4 Training Details

Integral Allocations. The global optima of the optimization problem in Eq. 3 might lie in a continuous allocation setting, i.e., similar to allocating divisible items. If a network learns to distribute an item equally among all agents, then the gradient vanishes. Assigning an equal partition of each item is indeed an optimum. Converting these non-integral allocation to integral is non-trivial. Hence we set a *temperature* parameter T in the softmax layer of the network to prevent getting stuck at such optima. Let $o_j = \{o_{j_1}, \ldots, o_{j_n}\}$ denote the output of our network before the final layer. The final allocation for agent i is given by, $\mathcal{A}_i^w(\{j\}) = \text{softmax}(o_{j_i}) = \frac{e^{o_{j_i}/T}}{\sum_{k=1}^{n} e^{o_{j_k}/T}}$ which represents the probability of assigning item j to all the agents. It is common to start with a large T for initial exploration and gradually reduce T to reach the global optima. While training, when we set T to 1, we get fractional allocations. As we decrease the value of T, the network outputs allocation close to discrete. The approach we want is while training, allocation output is almost discrete, but not exactly discrete. When we keep the value too low, the output is exact discrete allocations, and there is no learning because of the vanishing gradients. We appropriately choose T based on our experiments. Once the network learns, we set the parameter low enough to ensure discrete allocations.

Inefficient Local Optima. Due to the low T value, the training of EEF1-NN is highly unstable and often gets stuck at inefficient local optima. To overcome this, we use the technique of *Bootstrap Aggregation* or Bagging. It combines the predictions from multiple classifiers to produce a single classifier. We train multiple weak networks with varied hyper-parameters on the same data set, capturing different sets of local optima. While testing, the final allocation is aggregated from these networks. We pass a test sample through all networks and select the allocation that is EF1 with maximum USW. In total, we bag seven networks with varied $\lambda \in [0.1, 2]$ for increased performance. We further analyze how Bagging affects our results in the ablation study.

We implement EEF1-NN using PyTorch. We initialize the network weights using Xavier Initialization [20]. To train, we use Adam Optimizer [23] with learning rate 0.001 for 1000 epochs with $T = 0.01$. We use a batch size of 256 samples. We sample valuations from $U[0, 1]$ (goods), $U[-1, 0]$ (chores) and $U[-1, 1]$ (combination). We sample $150k$ training data for both $10 \otimes 20$ and $13 \otimes 26$ for goods, chores, and combinations, so in total, we have $300k$ training samples, and we sample $10k$ testing samples for each setting. We train seven networks with varied $\lambda \in [0.1, 2]$ and bag them for enhanced performance. The training process takes 5–6 h to train a single network using GPU. We are training the network for $10 \otimes 20$ and $13 \otimes 26$. however, we show our test results for various $n \otimes m$. We test for network performance for $n \in [7, 15]$. We also train an individual network over different distributions such as Gaussian, Log-normal, and Exponential. We validate EEF1-NN efficacy in the next section.

5   Experiments and Results

In this section, we conduct an ablation study to set appropriate hyper-parameters and 3 types of experiments showcasing performances across different item types, distributions, and scalability. To report the network performance, we define the following two metrics: the measure of fairness (probability of an allocation to be EF1) and the other of efficiency (how close our social welfare is to optimal).

Evaluation Metrics

1. α_{EF1}^{ALG} - It measures the probability with which an algorithm ALG outputs EF1 allocation. α_{EF1} is the ratio of the number of samples that are EF1 to the total number of samples.
2. β_{SW}^{ALG} - It measures the ratio of expected USW of an algorithm ALG by expected USW of MUW allocation. $\beta_{SW}^{ALG} = \mathbb{E}(sw^{ALG})/\mathbb{E}(sw^{MUW})$.

Note that $\beta_{SW}^{ALG} \in [0,1]$ for goods, $\beta_{SW}^{ALG} \geq 1$ for chores, and will depend on the overall social welfare (positive/negative) for a combination of goods and chores. We will use that notation $(\alpha_{EF1}, \beta_{sw})$ to report performance.

5.1 Ablation Study

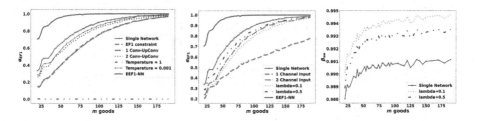

Fig. 2. Ablation Study over varied hyper-parameters (Color figure online)

We illustrate the effect of specific hyper-parameters in the performance of EEF1-NN in Fig. 2. We set $n = 10$ goods for all the experiments. In the plots, the red line with the label EEF1-NN denotes the α_{EF1} for optimal parameters. Corresponding to EEF1-NN, a single network from this bagged network is labeled as *Single Network*. This *Single Network* trained with six-channeled input, $\lambda = 1$, and $T = 0.01$ is the baseline to compare across this ablation study. Only one parameter is changed w.r.t. the *Single Network* for the study.

(i) Effect of Temperature T. In Fig. 2(left), when $T = 1$, it converges to fractional allocation represented by the blue line at the bottom of the plot. When $T = 0.001$ (violet line), it is too low, and performs sub-optimally compared to single network. We also noticed that the performance for $T = 0.01$ and $T = 0.1$ are close to each other. We set $T = 0.01$ for all the bagged networks in EEF1-NN.

(ii) Effect of Series of Conv-UpConv layers. We select three series of Conv-UpConv for EEF1-NN as illustrated in Fig. 2(left). As seen from Fig. 2(left), a performance increase between 1-series (green dashed line) and 2-series (red dotted line) is significant compared to 2-series and 3-series (single network). The complexity of the network having 4-series is far more than the performance improvement.

(iii) Effect of Loss Function We empirically analyze how different envy definitions (Eq. 3) affects the training of EEF1-NN. As shown in Fig. 2(left), when we train our network using EF, i.e., Eq. 1 (*Single Network*, the network performs significantly better than when trained using EF1, i.e., Eq. 2 (orange dashed line). For example, for $10 \otimes 20$, the performance of *Single Network* is (0.3358,17.9611), whereas the performance of the EF1 trained network is (0.1530,17.8708).

iv) Number of Input Channels. To enhance our network performance, we experimented with different channel inputs. For 2-channeled input, we set the first channel of input tensor as the valuation and the second to X. Like 6-channeled input, we expand X to 11 channels. As shown in Fig. 2(right), the performance of a 1-channeled network is (0.2113, 17.8976), 2-channeled network is (0.2365, 17.8991), *Single Network* is (0.3358, 17.9611), and 11-channeled network is (0.3925, 17.9395). The network cannot be generalized for 11-channeled.

v) Effect of Bagging. We bag different combination of networks, each trained for varied λ in Fig. 2(right). More the λ, more penalty is given to envy. When λ is too small, the network learns a more efficient but less fair allocation. As we increase λ up to a certain value, the network learns less efficient but more fair allocations. We observed that varying λ results in converging to the different optimum. We bagged seven networks trained with $\lambda \in [0.1, 2]$. Bagging (EEF1-NN) outperforms the performance of a single network.

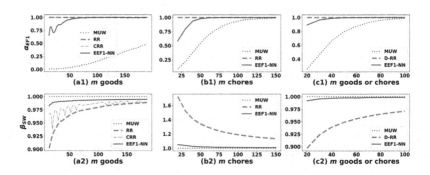

Fig. 3. Exp1 ($n = 10$, Uniform Distribution)

5.2   Experiment Details and Observations

We conduct three types of experiments, Exp1: Different kinds of resources, Exp2: Input distributions, and Exp3: Scalability. Since approaches in [4,11] are exponential, we cannot report results on our experimentation configuration. We compare EEF1-NN with the following existing methods,

– MUW- We compare our results with MUW since we don't have EEF1. Note that EEF1-NN welfare is close to MUW; we can say it is also close to EEF1.

- ROUND ROBIN (RR)- [14] finds EF1 for goods or chores. *Double Round Robin* (D-RR) [2] finds EF1 for the combination of goods and chores.
- CONSTRAINED ROUND ROBIN (CRR)- We implement CRR [3] to find RB sequences to increase efficiency. An RB sequence for goods.

EXP1: Performance Across Differed Resources for Uniform Distribution. For $n = 10$, we compare α_{EF1} in Fig. 3 (a1, b1, c1) and β_{SW} in Fig. 3 (a2, b2, c2). As m increases, all the approaches move closer to EEF1. We observe that MUW (blue dotted line) converges towards EEF1 much faster for chores or combinations than goods. While RR converges to EEF1 much faster in goods compared to chores or combinations. We discuss this convergence in detail in Table 1. We observe that EEF1-NN consistently has better α_{EF1} than MUW and β_{sw} than RR/CRR. We observe that $\alpha_{EF1}^{EEF1-NN}$ is close to 1 after a certain m. At the same time, EEF1-NN is far more efficient than *RR*. (Fig 3 (a2, b2, c2)). Note that the CRR is only for goods. We observe that compared to CRR, EEF1-NN obtains marginally better β_{SW}, in Fig. 3(a2).

EXP2: Performance Across Different Distributions. We provide the performance of EEF1-NN when the valuations are sampled from different distributions such as Gaussian ($\mu = 0.5$, $\sigma = 1$) in Fig. 4(a1, a2), Log-normal ($\mu = 0.5$, $\sigma = 1$) in Fig. 4(b1, b2), and Exponential ($\lambda = 1$) in Fig. 4(c1, c2). We observe that in all three $\alpha_{EF1}^{EEF1-NN} > 0.99$ and $\beta_{SW}^{EEF1-NN} > 0.99$ for $m \geq 40$ in Fig. 4.

EXP3: Scalability to Larger Number of Agents. EEF1-NN is trained only for $10 \otimes 20$ and $13 \otimes 26$. As we have seen in the previous results and in Fig. 5, the performance scales across varying m and n seamlessly. We provide the performance of EEF1-NN when $n = 7, 12, 14$ in Fig. 5[3].

Analysis of Convergence to EEF1 Allocations (Uniform Distribution)

Definition 4 $(m^\star(n))$. *For a given n, we say an algorithm converges to EEF1 allocation at $m^\star(n)$ if $\forall m > m^\star(n)$,*

(i) For goods: $\alpha_{EF1}^{ALG} \geq 0.99$ *and* $\beta_{sw}^{ALG} \geq 0.99$.
(ii) For chores: $\alpha_{EF1}^{ALG} \geq 0.99$, *and* $\beta_{sw}^{ALG} \leq 1.02$.

We empirically study $m^\star(n)$ value after which EEF1-NN, RR, and MUW start converging towards EEF1 for uniform distribution in Table 1. We don't report CRR in this; as we see fluctuations in β_{sw}, it doesn't increase smoothly in Fig. [35]; For goods, EEF1-NN reaches close to EEF1 faster than MUW and RR, and RR reaches close to EEF1 faster than MUW. EEF1-NN converges first, then MUW, and finally RR for chores in Table 1. For chores, we report the value of $m^\star$ for RR when $\beta_{sw} \leq 1.064$ since m is significantly higher than MUW and RR, concluding that RR converges after a considerably larger m. As m increases, $\alpha_{EF1}, \alpha_{EFX}$, and α_{EF} of MUW gets closer. Note that we do not experiment with all possible m; the actual value of $m^\star(n)$ may be slightly different from Table 1. We aim to observe a pattern among approaches to achieve EEF1.

---

[3] To report performance for $n \in [7, 9]$, we reduce a Conv-UpConv layer and train accordingly with $7 \otimes 14$ and $10 \otimes 20$ valuation profiles.

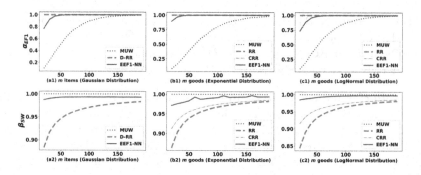

Fig. 4. Exp2 ($n = 10$, different distributions)

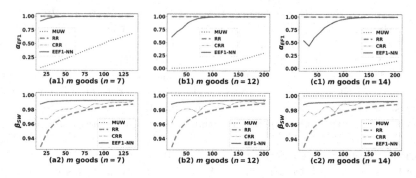

Fig. 5. Exp3 ($n = 7, 12, 14$ goods, Uniform Distribution)

Table 1. Value of $m^*(n)$ as different approaches converge to EEF1 allocations

n	(m) Goods			(m) Chores		
	EEF1-NN	R	MUW	EEF1-NN	R	MUW
7	38	159	380	44	195	112
8	46	172	450	44	240	120
9	57	186	530	53	295	130
10	70	196	610	60	340	148
11	82	206	660	68	400	160
12	94	214	740	75	455	167
13	110	220	840	83	505	180
14	134	228	940	87	565	190

Discussion. $\alpha_{EF1}^{EEF1-NN}$ reaches 1 much faster than α_{EF1}^{MUW}, and $\beta_{sw}^{EEF1-NN}$ reaches close to β_{sw}^{MUW} much faster than RR, D-RR, CRR. EEF1-NN shows a better trade-off between EF1 and efficiency than the existing approaches for different input distributions. We trained our network with fixed $n \otimes m$ for goods or/and chores, it is interesting that the performance scales for any m and a large

n. We conclude that EEF1-NN effectively learns and provides a better trade-off when m is not too large or small compared to n but is in a specific range.

6 Conclusion

In this paper, we proposed a neural network EEF1-NN to find EEF1, an NP-hard problem. We designed architecture and input representation combined with other training heuristics to learn approximate EEF1 on average. We studied the effect of each proposed constituent on performance. Our experiments demonstrated the efficacy of EEF1-NN for different input distributions across various n and m over existing approaches. With theoretical limitations and the success of neural networks, we believe that the path of amalgamating deep learning and resource allocation is worth exploring further with more complex objective functions.

References

1. Amanatidis, G., Markakis, E., Nikzad, A., Saberi, A.: Approximation algorithms for computing maximin share allocations. ACM Trans. Algorithms **13**(4), 1–28 (2017)
2. Aziz, H., Caragiannis, I., Igarashi, A.: Fair allocation of combinations of indivisible goods and chores (2018). http://arxiv.org/abs/1807.10684
3. Aziz, H., Huang, X., Mattei, N., Segal-Halevi, E.: The constrained round robin algorithm for fair and efficient allocation (2019)
4. Aziz, H., Huang, X., Mattei, N., Segal-Halevi, E.: Computing fair utilitarian allocations of indivisible goods (2020). https://arxiv.org/abs/2012.03979
5. Barman, S., Bhaskar, U., Shah, N.: Optimal bounds on the price of fairness for indivisible goods. In: Chen, X., Gravin, N., Hoefer, M., Mehta, R. (eds.) WINE 2020. LNCS, vol. 12495, pp. 356–369. Springer, Cham (2020). https://doi.org/10.1007/978-3-030-64946-3_25
6. Barman, S., Ghalme, G., Jain, S., Kulkarni, P., Narang, S.: Fair division of indivisible goods among strategic agents. pp. 1811–1813. AAMAS 2019 (2019)
7. Barman, S., Krishnamurthy, S.K., Vaish, R.: Finding Fair and Efficient Allocations, pp. 557–574. EC 2018, Association for Computing Machinery, New York, NY, USA (2018)
8. Bei, X., Lu, X., Manurangsi, P., Suksompong, W.: The price of fairness for indivisible goods. In: Proceedings of the 28th International Joint Conference on Artificial Intelligence, pp. 81–87. IJCAI 2019, AAAI Press (2019)
9. Bouveret, S.: Efficiency and envy-freeness in fair division of indivisible goods: logical representation and complexity. J. Artif. Intell. Res. **32** (2008)
10. Bouveret, S., Chevaleyre, Y., Maudet, N., Moulin, H.: Fair Allocation of Indivisible Goods, pp. 284–310. Cambridge University Press (2016)
11. Bredereck, R., Kaczmarczyk, A., Knop, D., Niedermeier, R.: High-multiplicity fair allocation: lenstra empowered by n-fold integer programming. In: Proceedings of the 2019 ACM Conference on Economics and Computation. pp. 505–523. EC 2019 (2019)
12. Budish, E.: The combinatorial assignment problem: approximate competitive equilibrium from equal incomes. J. Polit. Econ. **119**(6), 1061–1103 (2011)

13. Cai, Q., Filos-Ratsikas, A., Tang, P., Zhang, Y.: Reinforcement mechanism design for e-commerce. In: Proceedings of the 2018 World Wide Web Conference, pp. 1339–1348. WWW 2018 (2018)
14. Caragiannis, I., Kurokawa, D., Moulin, H., Procaccia, A.D., Shah, N., Wang, J.: The unreasonable fairness of maximum nash welfare. In: Proceedings of the 2016 ACM Conference on Economics and Computation, pp. 305–322. EC 2016, Association for Computing Machinery, New York, NY, USA (2016)
15. Dickerson, J.P., Goldman, J., Karp, J., Procaccia, A.D., Sandholm, T.: The computational rise and fall of fairness. In: Proceedings of the Twenty-Eighth AAAI Conference on Artificial Intelligence, pp. 1405–1411. AAAI 2014, AAAI Press (2014)
16. Duetting, P., Feng, Z., Narasimhan, H., Parkes, D., Ravindranath, S.S.: Optimal auctions through deep learning. In: Chaudhuri, K., Salakhutdinov, R. (eds.) Proceedings of the 36th International Conference on Machine Learning. Proceedings of Machine Learning Research, vol. 97, pp. 1706–1715. PMLR (2019)
17. Foley, D.K.: Resource allocation and the public sector (1967)
18. Garg, D., Narahari, Y., Gujar, S.: Foundations of mechanism design: a tutorial part 2-advanced concepts and results. Sadhana **33**(2), 131–174 (2008)
19. Garg, D., Narahari, Y., Gujar, S.: Foundations of mechanism design: a tutorial part 1-key concepts and classical results. Sadhana **33**(2), 83–130 (2008)
20. Glorot, X., Bengio, Y.: Understanding the difficulty of training deep feedforward neural networks. In: Teh, Y.W., Titterington, M. (eds.) Proceedings of the Thirteenth International Conference on Artificial Intelligence and Statistics. Proceedings of Machine Learning Research, vol. 9, pp. 249–256. JMLR Workshop and Conference Proceedings, Chia Laguna Resort, Sardinia, Italy (2010). http://proceedings.mlr.press/v9/glorot10a.html
21. Golowich, N., Narasimhan, H., Parkes, D.C.: Deep learning for multi-facility location mechanism design. In: Proceedings of the 27th International Joint Conference on Artificial Intelligence, pp. 261–267. IJCAI 2018, AAAI Press (2018)
22. Kim, H., Jiang, Y., Rana, R.B., Kannan, S., Oh, S., Viswanath, P.: Communication algorithms via deep learning. In: International Conference on Learning Representations (2018). https://openreview.net/forum?id=ryazCMbR-
23. Kingma, D., Ba, J.: Adam: a method for stochastic optimization. International Conference on Learning Representations (2014)
24. Kurokawa, D., Procaccia, A.D., Wang, J.: Fair enough: guaranteeing approximate maximin shares. J. ACM **65**(2) (2018)
25. Lipton, R.J., Markakis, E., Mossel, E., Saberi, A.: On approximately fair allocations of indivisible goods. In: Proceedings of the 5th ACM Conference on Electronic Commerce, pp. 125–131. EC 2004 (2004)
26. Manisha, P., Gujar, S.: Thompson sampling based multi-armed-bandit mechanism using neural networks. In: Proceedings of the 18th International Conference on Autonomous Agents and MultiAgent Systems, pp. 2111–2113. AAMAS 2019 (2019)
27. Manisha, P., Jawahar, C.V., Gujar, S.: Learning optimal redistribution mechanisms through neural networks. In: Proceedings of the 17th International Conference on Autonomous Agents and MultiAgent Systems, pp. 345–353. AAMAS 2018 (2018)
28. Manurangsi, P., Suksompong, W.: When do envy-free allocations exist? SIAM J. Discrete Math. **34**, 1505–1521 (2020)
29. Manurangsi, P., Suksompong, W.: Closing gaps in asymptotic fair division. SIAM J. Discret Math. **35** (2021)
30. Markakis, E.: Approximation algorithms and hardness results for fair division with indivisible goods. In: Endriss, U. (ed.) Trends in Computational Social Choice, chap. 12, pp. 231–247. AI Access (2017)

31. Nair, V., et al.: Solving mixed integer programs using neural networks. ArXiv abs/2012.13349 (2020)
32. Padala, M., Gujar, S.: FNNC: achieving fairness through neural networks. In: Proceedings of the Twenty-Ninth International Joint Conference on Artificial Intelligence,{IJCAI-20}, International Joint Conferences on Artificial Intelligence Organization (2020)
33. Padala, M., Gujar, S.: Mechanism design without money for fair allocations. In: IEEE/WIC/ACM International Conference on Web Intelligence and Intelligent Agent Technology, pp. 382–389 (2021)
34. Procaccia, A.D., Moulin, H.: Cake Cutting Algorithms, pp. 311–330. Cambridge University Press (2016)
35. Ronneberger, O., Fischer, P., Brox, T.: U-net: convolutional networks for biomedical image segmentation. vol. 9351, pp. 234–241 (2015)
36. Shen, W., et al.: Reinforcement mechanism design, with applications to dynamic pricing in sponsored search auctions (2017). http://arxiv.org/abs/1711.10279
37. Shen, W., Tang, P., Zuo, S.: Automated mechanism design via neural networks. In: Proceedings of the 18th International Conference on Autonomous Agents and Multiagent Systems, pp. 215–223 (2019)
38. Tacchetti, A., Strouse, D., Garnelo, M., Graepel, T., Bachrach, Y.: A neural architecture for designing truthful and efficient auctions (2019). http://arxiv.org/abs/1907.05181
39. Wang, G., Guo, R., Sakurai, Y., Ali Babar, M., Guo, M.: Mechanism design for public projects via neural networks. In: Proceedings of the 20th International Conference on Autonomous Agents and MultiAgent Systems, pp. 1380–1388. AAMAS 2021, International Foundation for Autonomous Agents and Multiagent Systems, Richland, SC (2021)
40. Weissteiner, J., Seuken, S.: Deep learning–powered iterative combinatorial auctions. Proceedings of the AAAI Conference on Artificial Intelligence, vol. 34, issue(02), pp. 2284–2293 (2020). https://doi.org/10.1609/aaai.v34i02.5606

Weighted Adaptive Perturbations Adversarial Training for Improving Robustness

Yan Wang, Dongmei Zhang, and Haiyang Zhang[(✉)]

Beijing University of Posts and Telecommunications, Beijing, China
{usebywang,zhangdm,zhhy}@bupt.edu.cn

Abstract. Adversarial Training (AT) is one of the most effective defense methods against adversarial examples, in which a model is trained on both clean and adversarial examples. Although AT improves the robustness by smoothing the small neighborhood, it reduces accuracy on clean examples. We propose Weighted Adaptive Perturbation Adversarial Training (WAPAT) to reduce the loss of clean accuracy and improve robustness, which is motivated by the adaptive learning rate of the model optimizer. In the adversarial examples generation stage of adversarial training, We introduce weights based on feature changes to adaptively adjust the perturbation step size for different features. In iterative attacks, if a feature is frequently attacked, we increase the attack strength of this area, otherwise, we weaken the attack strength of this area. WAPAT is a data augmentation method that shortens the distance of adversarial examples to the classification boundary. The generated adversarial examples maintain good adversarial effects while retaining more clean examples information. Therefore, such adversarial examples can help us to obtain a more robust model while reducing the loss of recognition accuracy for clean examples. To demonstrate our method, we implement WAPAT in three adversarial training frameworks. Experimental results on CIFAR-10 and MNIST show that WAPAT significantly improves adversarial robustness with less sacrifice of accuracy.

Keywords: Adversarial examples · Adversarial training · Weighted perturbations

1 Introduction

In recent years deep learning has enjoyed tremendous success in solving a variety of machine learning tasks such as computer vision [6], speech recognition [19] and natural language processing [22], even achieving or surpassing human-level performance in certain cases [8,17]. However, deep neural networks (DNNs) could be vulnerable to adversarial perturbations: carefully computed small perturbations added to clean examples to get adversarial examples can cause misclassification on machine learning models [2,5,16,21]. This vulnerability of DNNs raises serious concerns in security-critical applications [3,4,12]. Recent research focuses

© The Author(s), under exclusive license to Springer Nature Switzerland AG 2022
S. Khanna et al. (Eds.): PRICAI 2022, LNCS 13630, pp. 402–415, 2022.
https://doi.org/10.1007/978-3-031-20865-2_30

on improving their robustness mainly by two defense approaches, i.e., certified defense and empirical defense. Certified defense tries to learn provably robust DNNs against adversarial perturbations. Empirical defense incorporates adversarial examples into the training process. For instance, adversarial training (AT) [5,13,24] is an empirical defense, which is recognized as the current best defense method to adversarial attack [1,11].

Adversarial training is formulated as a minimax optimization problem [13,25]. To conduct this minimax optimization, project gradient descent (PGD) is a common method to generate the most adversarial data that maximizes the loss, updating the current model. The adversarial training seeks to train an adversarial robust deep network whose predictions are locally invariant to a small neighborhood of its inputs. Although adversarial training can improve the robustness against adversarial examples by smoothing the small neighborhood, it sometimes hurts accuracy on clean examples [15,18,24]. And it is impossible to introduce all unknown attack examples into the adversarial training. Among substantial works of adversarial training, there still is a big robust generalization gap between the training data and the testing data. Adversarial perturbations in practice are typically defined to be imperceptible to humans (e.g. small perturbations in vision). Hence by definition, the human is a classifier that is both robust and accurate with no trade-off in the clean data and adversarial data [23]. Furthermore, deep neural networks are expressive enough to fit not only adversarial but also clean data perfectly. Unfortunately, the model obtained through adversarial training does not reach the capabilities of human being. Model robustness is obtained at the cost of accuracy. Is this phenomenon caused by the unreasonable generation of adversarial examples? Motivated by the above, the core problem we raise and address in this paper is:

For adversarial training, how to generate adversarial examples closer to human vision, which can make the model have better robustness and less sacrifice in accuracy?

We propose a novel Weighted Adaptive Perturbations Adversarial Training (WAPAT) framework that tries to solve the problem. WAPAT is established on top of adversarial training, yet augmenting adversarial data with a new approach. It changes the adversarial attack module with a fixed step length in adversarial training and further refines the perturbation step size of different features during the attack process. We call this method as Weighted Adaptive Perturbations Attack (WAP-Attack). WAP-attack divide perturbation into the perturbation step size and perturbation direction. WAP-Attack implements perturbation weighting when iteratively adding adversarial perturbations on clean data, which is used to control the perturb granularity of different features in an iteration. The improvement of this method is mainly inspired by the adaptive learning rate of the model training optimizer. The adversarial examples generated by this method not only retain the features of the weak attack areas but also enhance the attack strength in the strong attack areas. WAP-Attack will make the perturbations at different features better discriminated, but this method will reduce the attack strength. To solve this problem, we give a basic attack when weighting the perturbation of the example. On this basis, different features will have different perturbations. The WAP-Attack gives the adversarial attack process feature-level adaptability using weighted adversarial perturbations. Figure 1 shows clean examples from the MNIST dataset, as well as adversarial examples from PGD and WAP attacks. Compared with figure (b), the shaded part of figure (c) is more fragmented and retains more clean examples' information. The WAP-Attack examples have fewer perturbation areas, but Table 1 shows that the same level of attack effect is achieved with shorter perturbation distances.

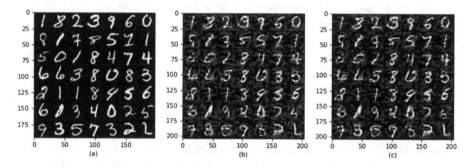

Fig. 1. On the MNIST dataset, (a) are clean examples, (b) are adversarial examples generated using PGD, and (c) are adversarial examples generated using WAP-Attack

Our contributions can be briefly summarized as below:

- We propose a novel method to get more powerful adversarial examples, which is called Weighted Adaptive Perturbations Attack (WAP-Attack). This method adjusts the examples' perturbation step size based on the change value of different features to generate adversarial examples for training.
- We propose a variant of adversarial training called WAPAT, which uses adversarial examples generated by WAP-Attack for adversarial training. The WAPAT framework improves the robustness of the model while less impairing clean accuracy.
- Experimental results show that compared with other adversarial training results, WAPAT trades more robustness gains with less accuracy reduction. Our thoughts are more effective in the defense of iterative attacks. We provide the process of evaluating experimental results.

2   Related Work

2.1   Adversarial Attacks

Let $F(x)$ be a probabilistic classifier based on a neural network with the logits function $f(x)$ and the probability distribution $P(x)$. Let $L(F(x),y)$ be the cross entropy loss for image classfication. The goal of Adversarial attacks is to get an example $x^{adv} \in \mathcal{B}_\epsilon(x) = \{x^{adv} :=\| x^{adv} - x \|_p \leq \epsilon\}$ in the ℓ_p norm bounded perturbations, where ϵ denotes the perturbation budget. In the paper, we use $p = \infty$ to align with previous work. Adversarial attacks can be divided into single-step attacks and iterative attacks according to the number of attacks. Fast Gradient Sign Method (FGSM) [5] is the most commonly used single-step attack method. Projected Gradient Descent (PGD) [13] is a stronger iterative variant of FGSM, which iteratively solves the optimization problem $\max_{x^{adv} \in B_\epsilon(x)} L(F(x^{adv}), y)$ with a step size α:

$$x^{t+1} = \Pi_{x^{adv} \in \mathcal{B}_\epsilon(x)}(x^t - \alpha \cdot sign(\nabla_x L(F(x^t), y))) \tag{1}$$

where $\Pi_{x^{adv} \in \mathcal{B}_\epsilon(x)}$ indicates the projection of set $\mathcal{B}_\epsilon(x)$. Carlini-Wagner attack (CW) [2] is a sophisticated method to directly solve for the adversarial example x^{adv} by using an auxiliary variable w:

$$x^{adv} = \frac{1}{2} \cdot (\tanh(w) + 1) \tag{2}$$

The objective function to optimize the auxiliary variable w is defined as:

$$\min_w \| x^{adv} - x \| + c \cdot F(x^{adv}) \tag{3}$$

where $F(x^{adv}) = max(f_y(x^{adv}) - max\{f_i(x^{adv}) : i \neq y\}, -k)$. The constant k controls the confidence gap between the adversarial class and the true class.

2.2   Standard Adversarial Training

Despite a wide range of defense methods, adversarial training is considered the most effective way to defend against adversarial examples. The idea of adversarial training is to solve the min-max optimization problem, as show in Eq. (4):

$$\min_{F(\bullet)} \frac{1}{n} \sum_{i=1}^n \{ \max_{x_i^{adv} \in \mathcal{B}(x_i)} L(F(x_i^{adv}), y_i)\} \tag{4}$$

where x_i^{adv} is the adversarial example within the ϵ-ball centered at x_i, $F(\bullet) : X \to \mathbb{R}^c$ is a classifier, and the loss function $L : \mathbb{R}^c \times y \to \mathbb{R}$ is a composition of a base loss $l_B : \Delta^{c-1} \times y \to \mathbb{R}$ (e.g. the cross-entropy loss) and an inverse link function $l_L : \mathbb{R}^c \to \Delta^{c-1}$ (e.g. the soft-max activation), in which Δ^{c-1} is the corresponding probability simplex-in other words, $L(F(x), y) = l_B(l_L(F(x), y))$.

Here we introduce two adversarial training frameworks.

PGDAT. PGD Adversarial Training (PGDAT) [13] leverages the PGD attack to generate adversarial examples, and trains only with the adversarial examples. The objective function is formalized as follows:

$$L(F(x), y) = L(F(x^{adv}), y) \tag{5}$$

where x^{adv} obtained by the PGD attack in Eq. (1).

GAIRAT. Geometry-Aware Instance-Reweighted Adversarial Training (GAIRAT) [26] considered the unequal importance of adversarial data. A natural data point closer to/farther from the class boundary is less/more robust, and the corresponding adversarial data point should be assigned with larger/smaller weight. The objective function is shown in Eq. (6):

$$L(F(x), y) = w(x, y) \cdot L(F(x^{adv}), y) \tag{6}$$

where $w(x, y)$ is the weight of the current example, which can indicate how important the current example is to robustness. $w(x, y) = f(t)$, is a function of the minimum number of steps t used to generate adversarial examples, t is used to measure the distance from the classification boundary.

After adversarial training, the network learns a new decision boundary to incorporate both clean and adversarial examples.

3 Weighted Adaptive Perturbation Adversarial Training

3.1 Motivations of WAPAT

In the standard training, the model has more than enough model capacity, which can easily fit the natural training data entirely [23,26]. However, according to the existing research, it is difficult for the model to fit both clean examples and adversarial examples. Why is there such a problem? We think that the generation process of adversarial examples needs improvement. Our motivation comes from the optimizer in the model training process. We can simplify the process of image classification by the model to a feature map. As shown in Eq. 7, we call this feature map a scoring function.

$$F(x) = Wx + b \tag{7}$$

When we fix x, the training process is realized by adjusting the model parameters W and b through the loss function. The optimization of parameters mainly depends on optimization direction and optimization step size. The optimization direction is determined by the gradient of the loss function to the model parameters. The optimization step size is called the learning rate, which is an important hyperparameter used to control the parameter update process. Adam [7] is a representative of adaptive learning rate optimizer. It adaptively selects the learning rate according to the different parameters in the training process. If we fix the parameters of the model and update the examples in the opposite direction of the gradient, adversarial examples will be generated. Existing research on the iterative generation methods of adversarial examples, such as PGD, BIM [9], *etc.*, ignores the adaptability of the perturbation step size. We believe that the different features in examples and parameters in the model have the same properties. When performing an iterative adversarial attack, the perturbation step size should be adaptively selected considering the difference of examples' features.

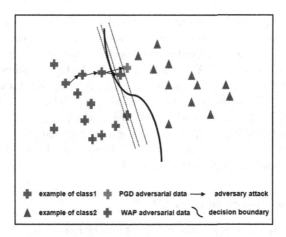

Fig. 2. WAP-Attack uses a more refined iteration adversarial perturbations to push clean examples across the decision boundary. The generation process of these adversarial examples takes into account the difference based on the feature position

Table 1. On the MNIST dataset and CIFAR-10 dataset, we present the distances of adversarial examples generated with PGD and WAP from clean examples and the attack success rates of the two methods. We use the test data of the two datasets separately for experiments, and the distances are averaged

Dataset	Method	Distance(l_2)	Accuracy
MNIST	PGD	5.8703	0.01%
MNIST	WAP	5.4097	0.09%
CIFAR-10	PGD	1.1842	0.01%
CIFAR-10	WAP	0.9856	0.02%

WAPAT achieves adaptability using a feature-based weighting of the perturbation step size. If the feature of a certain area changes greatly from the original feature, it means that the feature contributes greatly to the generation of adversarial examples; otherwise, the contribution is small. Therefore, different features should be treated differently when weighting and the attack strength should be increased if the contribution is large, and the attack strength should be weakened if the contribution is small. This method is different from other methods in the following two points:

1. In other iterative attacks, there are only two changes to the examples' features in each iteration, $+\alpha$ or $-\alpha$, where α is the perturbation step size of the iterative attacks. WAP-Attack makes the change of each features more diverse. Through the iterative attack, the algorithm adaptively selects the perturbation step size according to the contribution of features to adversarial examples.

2. From the perspective of examples distribution, the process of moving from clean examples to adversarial examples (see Fig. 2) is refined. Compared with early stopping [25] with a fixed feature perturbation step size, the adversarial examples generated by WAP-attack are closer to the classification boundary and have better adversarial properties. We present the data of two attack methods on the classification models of the two datasets in Table 1. We fix the perturbation direction and attack clean examples. WAP-Attack achieves the same level of attack success rate using a shorter distance from the original example. Because the attack direction is the same, the shorter the distance from the original example, the shorter the distance classification boundary.

3.2 Learning Objective of WAPAT

WAPAT's objective function implies the optimization of adversarial robust networks, with one step generating adversarial examples and one step minimizing loss on the generated adversarial data w.r.t the model parameter θ. The outer optimization for the minimization problem still follows Eq. (4). The inner optimization for generating x^{adv} is

$$x_i^{adv} = \underset{x^{adv} \in \mathcal{B}(x_i)}{\arg max} \; L(F(x^{adv}), y) \tag{8}$$

x^{adv} is obtained through the iterative attack. We refer to the idea of attention mechanism and increase the weight when the adversarial perturbation is added. As shown in Fig. 3, WEI is the perturbation weight assignment function when generating the adversarial example x^{adv}.

$$x^{t+1} = x^t + w(s(t), b) \cdot \alpha \cdot sign(\nabla_{x^t} L(F_\theta(x^t), y)), t \in n \tag{9}$$

where $w(s(t), b)$ is the core of weighted perturbations module (WEI). $s(t)$ is the sum of gradient sign multiple iterative attacks, which is used to represent the size of the example change. b is the basic adversarial perturbation. $w(s(t), b)$ shows the feature changes on examples' different areas. If the change value of the features increases with the number of iterations, it means that these features are located in the strong attack areas, and the attack strength should be increased; otherwise, they are located in the weak attack area, and the attack strength should be reduced. We introduce the hyperparameter b to control the size of basic perturbations.

3.3 Realization of WAPAT

When generating adversarial examples, as shown in Fig. 3, we divide the adversarial perturbation into a perturbation direction and a perturbation size. The perturbation direction provides the change direction of features to generate adversarial examples. The perturbation size is the core improvement part of the WAPAT framework, which gives an adaptive weight to distinguish strong and weak attack areas. According to the number of iterations and the sum of

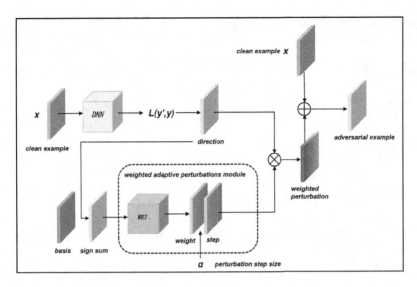

Fig. 3. The illustration of weighted adaptive perturbations adversarial attack framework. The weighted perturbations module (WEI) is the improvement on the generation of adversarial examples. The weight matrix and the perturbation step size α are used to generate the weighted adversarial perturbations, and it is combined with the gradient direction to obtain the final adversarial perturbations

gradient signs, the WEI module helps examples get the perturbation weight based on different features. We introduce a hyperparameter b as the basis of the perturbation, which is the minimum change value of the perturbation at the feature level. On this basis, the perturbations step size when generating adversarial examples is different for the different features. As the core of the weighted adaptive perturbations module, WEI is very simple to implement (Algorithm 1). It is based on an iterative process. In the completed iteration, if the accumulated attack is large, this feature is important for adversarial examples. This means that we should increase the perturbation step size for this feature. If the cumulative attack of a feature is small, which indicates that the feature has a limited impact on adversarial examples, we should reduce the perturbation step size. Extending to the entire examples, a weighted adaptive perturbation size is calculated. This is like the dynamic adaptation of learning rate in model training, which adds the attention mechanism to adversarial perturbation according to features.

We combine these two parts to generate adversarial perturbations.We call this iterative attack method which distinguishes different characteristics as weighted adaptive perturbation attack. It is summarized in Algorithm 1. Model training through these adversarial examples is the process of WAPAT.

Algorithm 1. WAP-Attack Algorithm

Input: data $x \in X$, label $y \in Y$, loss function L, weight w, attack step K, perturbation bound ϵ, perturbation step size α, base perturbation b.
Output: x^{adv}

1: Let $x^{adv} \leftarrow x + 0.001 \cdot \mathcal{N}(0, I); i, t \leftarrow 0; s_0, w_0 \leftarrow 0$.
2: **for** t=1,...,K **do**
3:     $s_t \leftarrow s_{t-1} + sign(\nabla_{x^{adv}} L(F(x^{adv}), y))$.
4:     $w_t \leftarrow abs(s_t)/K$
5:     $base \leftarrow b/K$
6:     **if** The value of w_t is 0 in a area **then**
7:         In this area: $w_t = base$
8:     **else**
9:         In this area: $w_t = w_t + base$
10:     **end if**
11:     $x_t^{adv} \leftarrow x_{t-1}^{adv} + w_t \cdot \alpha \cdot sign(\nabla_{x_t^{adv}} L(F(x_t^{adv}), y))$
12: **end for**
13: **return** x^{adv}

---

4   Experiments

In this section, we conduct a set of experiments to verify the effectiveness of WAPAT and then evaluate its robustness on benchmark datasets.

4.1   Experimental Setup

Baselines. Standard Training;AT(use PGD attack) [13]; TRADES [24]; MART [20]. We compare with adversarial training variants, since they are recognized as the most effective defense.

Architecture and Datasets. We used two benchmark datasets (CIFAR-10 [6] and MNIST [10]), which are commomly used in the adversarial robustness literature. The CIFAR-10 dataset consists of 60000 color images each of size 32 × 32, split between 50K training and 10K test images. The MNIST dataset consists of 70000 handwritten digits each of size 28 × 28, split between 60K training and 10K test images. For CIFAR-10, we use the same neural network architecture as [6] i.e., the ResNet18. We set perturbation $\epsilon = 0.031$, perturbation step size $\alpha = 0.007$, number of iterations $K = 10$, learning rate $lr = 0.1$, batch size $m = 128$, and run 80 epochs on the training dataset. For MNIST, We use the Small_CNN architecture with four convolutional layers, followed by three fully-connected layers. We set perturbation $\epsilon = 0.3$, perturbation step size $\alpha = 0.075$, number of iterations $K = 10$, learning rate $lr = 0.01$, batch size $m = 128$, and run 50 epochs on the training dataset. For TRADES, we set $\lambda = 6.0$. For MART, we set $\lambda = 5.0$. Hyperparameters of the baselines are configured as per their original papers. Hyperparameter of WAPAT is set $b = 3.0$.

Table 2. On the MNIST and CIFAR-10 datasets, we attack the standard trained models with PGD and WAP-PGD. We explore the role of hyperparameter b using the distance between adversarial and clean examples and recognize accuracy as evaluation criteria

Attack	DataSet	CIFAR-10		MNIST	
	Eval	Distance(l_2)	Accuracy	Distance(l_2)	Accuracy
PGD	Unweighted	1.1845	0.02%	5.0984	1.10%
WAP+PGD	b = 0	0.7209	0.20%	2.6075	43.91%
	b = 1	0.8297	0.08%	3.1058	21.27%
	b = 2	0.9090	0.03%	3.6056	9.26%
	b = 3	0.9855	0.01%	4.4037	4.25%
	b = 4	1.0449	0.01%	4.6040	2.13%
	b = 5	1.0900	0.02%	4.9163	1.43%
	b = 6	1.1288	0.01%	5.0528	1.23%
	b = 7	1.1652	0.01%	5.1762	1.05%
	b = 8	1.1945	0.01%	5.2864	1.01%
	b = 9	1.2092	0.01%	5.3569	0.87%
	b = 10	1.2201	0.01%	5.4290	0.77%

4.2 Effectiveness of WAP-Attack

We evaluated the effectiveness of adversarial examples obtained using WAP-Attack. We train the standard classification model on CIFAR-10 and MNIST, and then tested the PGD attack and WAP+PGD attack on standard classification models. The experimental results are shown in Table 2, where $Distance = \| x^{adv} - x \|$. We use the l_2 distance to measure the distance between adversarial examples and clean examples. On the premise that the perturbation direction remains unchanged, this distance can indirectly represent the distance of the adversarial example from the classification boundary. The specific value of this distance is the average of all the data in the test set. For the CIFAR-10 dataset, the l_2 distance of the adversarial examples obtained by the PGD attack from the clean examples is 1.1845, and the accuracy is 0.02%. WAP+PGD uses a perturbation distance of 0.9090 to achieve almost the same attack effect. For the MNIST dataset, the l_2 distance of the adversarial examples obtained by the PGD attack from the clean examples is 5.0984, and the accuracy is 1.10%. While WAP+PGD uses a perturbation distance of 4.9163 to achieve a similar attack effect. At the same time, we found that the basic attack b affects the distance. When b = 5, a balance can be achieved, which is the perturbation distance is smaller and the attack effect is similar. At this point, we can say that the adversarial examples generated by WAP-Attack are more powerful. Therefore, a more robust classification model can also be obtained through adversarial training.

Table 3. Experimental results on the CIFAR10 dataset

Defense methods	No-attack	FGSM	PGD(7)	PGD(10)	PGD(20)	DeepFool
Standard training	**93.49%**	16.59%	0.00%	0.00%	0.00%	5.29%
AT(PGD)	83.66%	55.19%	49.92%	46.88%	44.97%	61.32%
WAPAT	83.40%	56.11%	51.25%	48.10%	46.29%	62.42%
TRADES	81.65%	57.32%	54.08%	51.49%	50.60%	63.51%
WAP+TRADES	83.68%	59.35%	55.51%	53.21%	52.08%	**64.50%**
MART	80.08%	57.37%	53.37%	53.76%	51.68%	61.58%
WAP+MART	80.13%	**59.58%**	**56.89%**	54.86%	**53.87%**	63.73%

Table 4. Experimental results on the MNIST dataset

Defense methods	No-attack	FGSM	PGD(7)	PGD(10)	PGD(20)	DeepFool
Standard training	**99.43%**	48.13%	22.84%	10.80%	1.88%	2.55%
AT(PGD)	99.00%	96.72%	97.22%	96.39%	94.59%	96.90%
WAPAT	99.32%	97.48%	98.00%	97.40%	96.17%	97.52%
TRADES	99.26%	97.15%	97.58%	96.82%	95.30%	96.92%
WAP+TRADES	99.16%	97.90%	97.85%	97.47%	96.67%	97.92%
MART	99.13%	98.07%	97.71%	97.06%	96.34%	97.51%
WAP+MART	99.33%	**98.26%**	**98.25%**	97.86%	**97.07%**	**98.06%**

4.3 Evaluation Results for WAPAT

The above three methods(AT, TRADES, MART) are chosen as the baselines because they all generate adversarial examples iteratively, and none of their improvements involve the process of generating adversarial examples. This allows us to easily add the WAP-Attack module to these methods. We evaluate the robustness and clean accuracy of three methods against three types of attacks for both MNIST and CIFAR-10: FGSM, PGD, DeepFool [14]. We used three kinds of PGD attacks with the different numbers of iterations. For the CIFAR-10 dataset, we applied the WAP-Attack module to AT(PGD), TRADES and MART. For the setting of the adversarial attack method of the test model, we have made the following settings. For FGSM, we set perturbation $\epsilon = 0.031$. For a series of PGD adversarial attacks, we set perturbation $\epsilon = 0.031$, perturbation step size $\alpha = 0.007$, number of iterations includes 7, 10, and 20 steps. For DeepFool attack, we set perturbation $\epsilon = 0.031$. The perturbations of the above three methods are all limited to the infinity norm l_∞. The experiment results of CIFAR-10 and MNIST are reported in Table 3 and Table 4, where "No-Attack" denotes the accuracy on clean test images. The results show that the accuracy of the clean examples of the three methods has been improved. Compared with the accuracy of standard training, the downward trend has been alleviated to a certain extent. While ensuring the accuracy of clean examples, the model's robustness to adversarial examples has also been improved. Before and after adding the WAP-Attack module, the accuracy and robustness changes of the three adversarial training methods are shown in Table 5 and Table 6. Taking PGD (20) as an example, the accuracy of adversarial examples in the AT(PGD) method has increased by 1.32%, from 44.97% to 46.29%; the accuracy of adversarial examples in the TRADES method has increased by 1.48%, from 50.60% to 52.08%; The accuracy of adversarial examples in the MART method is increased by 2.19%, from 51.68% to 53.87%.

Table 5. The robustness change value of the three methods before and after adding the WAP module on the CIFAR-10 dataset.

Defense	AT	TRADES	MART
No-attack	−0.26%	+2.03%	+0.05%
FGSM	+0.92%	+2.03%	+2.21%
PGD(20)	+1.32%	+1.48%	+2.19%
DeepFool	+1.10%	+1.01%	+2.15%

Table 6. The robustness change value of the three methods before and after adding the WAP module on the MNIST dataset.

Defense	AT	TRADES	MART
No-attack	+0.32%	−0.10%	+0.20%
FGSM	+0.76%	+0.75%	+0.19%
PGD(20)	+1.58%	+1.37%	+0.73%
DeepFool	+0.62%	+1.00%	+0.55%

For the MNIST dataset, we also do the same change to the three methods. However, the setting of the adversarial attack methods is different from the CIFAR-10 dataset. For FGSM, we set perturbation $\epsilon = 0.3$. For a series of PGD adversarial attacks, we set perturbation $\epsilon = 0.3$, perturbation step size $\alpha = 0.03$, the number of iterations includes 7, 10, and 20 steps. For the DeepFool attack, we set perturbation $\epsilon = 0.3$. The MNIST dataset and CIFAR-10 dataset do not perform well in the accuracy of clean examples. This may be the examples in the MNIST dataset are relatively simple. But after introducing the WAP-Attack module and adversarial training, the robustness of the model is improved. We still take PGD (20) as an example. The robustness of the models trained by the three methods is improved by 1.58%, 1.37%, and 0.73% respectively.

5   Conclusion and Future Work

In this paper, we are motivated by the model optimizer's adaptive learning rate to investigate the impact of adaptive adversarial perturbations on adversarial training defense. Based on this idea, we designed a method for weighting adversarial perturbations in the process of attacking and used the adversarial examples generated by this method to complete adversarial training, which is called *Weighted Adaptive Perturbations Adversarial Training* (WAPAT). Experimental results show that compared with standard training, WAPAT reduces the accuracy loss of clean examples to a certain extent, and also improves the model's robustness to different adversarial attacks.

In the future, we plan to investigate the influence of different weighted adaptive perturbation methods such as attention mechanism on the process of generating adversarial examples and study the influence on the defense effect of adversarial training using this kind of adversarial examples.

References

1. Athalye, A., Carlini, N., Wagner, D.: Obfuscated gradients give a false sense of security: circumventing defenses to adversarial examples. In: ICML, pp. 274–283. PMLR (2018)
2. Carlini, N., Wagner, D.: Towards evaluating the robustness of neural networks. In: 2017 IEEE Symposium on Security and Privacy (sp), pp. 39–57. IEEE (2017)
3. Chen, C., Seff, A., Kornhauser, A., Xiao, J.: Deepdriving: learning affordance for direct perception in autonomous driving. In: ICCV, pp. 2722–2730 (2015)
4. Finlayson, S.G., Bowers, J.D., Ito, J., Zittrain, J.L., Beam, A.L., Kohane, I.S.: Adversarial attacks on medical machine learning. Science **363**(6433), 1287–1289 (2019)
5. Goodfellow, J.I., Shlens, J., Szegedy, C.: Explaining and harnessing adversarial examples. In: International Conference on Learning Representations (2015)
6. He, K., Zhang, X., Ren, S., Sun, J.: Deep residual learning for image recognition. In: CVPR, pp. 770–778 (2016)
7. Kingma, D.P., Ba, J.: Adam: a method for stochastic optimization. arXiv preprint arXiv:1412.6980 (2014)
8. Krizhevsky, A., Sutskever, I., Hinton, G.E.: Imagenet classification with deep convolutional neural networks. Commun. ACM **60**(6), 84–90 (2017)
9. Kurakin, A., Goodfellow, I.J., Bengio, S.: Adversarial examples in the physical world. In: Artificial Intelligence Safety and Security, pp. 99–112. Chapman and Hall/CRC (2018)
10. LeCun, Y., Bottou, L., Bengio, Y., Haffner, P.: Gradient-based learning applied to document recognition. Proc. IEEE **86**(11), 2278–2324 (1998)
11. Li, Y., Li, L., Wang, L., Zhang, T., Gong, B.: Nattack: learning the distributions of adversarial examples for an improved black-box attack on deep neural networks. In: ICML, pp. 3866–3876. PMLR (2019)
12. Ma, X., et al.: Understanding adversarial attacks on deep learning based medical image analysis systems. Pattern Recogn. **110**, 107332 (2021)
13. Madry, A., Makelov, A., Schmidt, L., Tsipras, D., Vladu, A.: Towards deep learning models resistant to adversarial attacks. arXiv preprint arXiv:1706.06083 (2017)

14. Moosavi-Dezfooli, S.M., Fawzi, A., Frossard, P.: Deepfool: a simple and accurate method to fool deep neural networks. In: Proceedings of the IEEE Conference on Computer Vision and Pattern Recognition, pp. 2574–2582 (2016)
15. Raghunathan, A., Xie, S.M., Yang, F., Duchi, J.C., Liang, P.: Adversarial training can hurt generalization. arXiv preprint arXiv:1906.06032 (2019)
16. Szegedy, C., et al.: Intriguing properties of neural networks. In: International Conference on Learning Representations (2014)
17. Tian, J., Zhou, J., Li, Y., Duan, J.: Detecting adversarial examples from sensitivity inconsistency of spatial-transform domain. arXiv preprint arXiv:2103.04302 (2021)
18. Uesato, J., Alayrac, J.B., Huang, P.S., Stanforth, R., Fawzi, A., Kohli, P.: Are labels required for improving adversarial robustness? arXiv preprint arXiv:1905.13725 (2019)
19. Wang, Y., Deng, X., Pu, S., Huang, Z.: Residual convolutional ctc networks for automatic speech recognition. arXiv preprint arXiv:1702.07793 (2017)
20. Wang, Y., Zou, D., Yi, J., Bailey, J., Ma, X., Gu, Q.: Improving adversarial robustness requires revisiting misclassified examples. In: ICLR (2019)
21. Wu, D., Wang, Y., Xia, S.T., Bailey, J., Ma, X.: Skip connections matter: on the transferability of adversarial examples generated with resnets. arXiv preprint arXiv:2002.05990 (2020)
22. Zeng, M., Wang, Y., Luo, Y.: Dirichlet latent variable hierarchical recurrent encoder-decoder in dialogue generation. In: EMNLP-IJCNLP, pp. 1267–1272 (2019)
23. Zhang, C., Bengio, S., Hardt, M., Recht, B., Vinyals, O.: Understanding deep learning requires rethinking generalization. ICLR (2017)
24. Zhang, H., Yu, Y., Jiao, J., Xing, E., El Ghaoui, L., Jordan, M.: Theoretically principled trade-off between robustness and accuracy. In: ICML, pp. 7472–7482. PMLR (2019)
25. Zhang, J., et al.: Attacks which do not kill training make adversarial learning stronger. In: ICML, pp. 11278–11287. PMLR (2020)
26. Zhang, J., Zhu, J., Niu, G., Han, B., Sugiyama, M., Kankanhalli, M.: Geometry-aware instance-reweighted adversarial training. ICLR (2021)

Improved Network Pruning via Similarity-Based Regularization

Shaopu Wang[1,2] (ID), Xiaoying Li[1,2], Jiaxin Zhang[3], Xiaojun Chen[2](✉),
and Jinqiao Shi[4]

[1] School of Cyber Security, University of Chinese Academy of Sciences,
Beijing, China
[2] Institute of Information Engineering, Chinese Academy of Sciences, Beijing, China
{wangshaopu,lixiaoying,chenxiaojun}@iie.ac.cn
[3] DUT-RU International School of Information Science and Engineering at DUT,
Dalian, China
[4] Beijing University of Posts and Telecommunication, Beijing, China
shijinqiao@bupt.edu.cn

Abstract. Network pruning has been shown as an effective technique
for compressing neural networks by removing weights directly. Although
the pruned network consumes less training and inference costs, it tends
to suffer from accuracy loss. Some recent works have proposed several
norm-based regularization terms to improve the generalization ability
of pruned networks. However, their penalty weights are usually set to
a small value since improper regularization hurts performance, which
limits their efficacy. In this work, we design a similarity-based regularization term named *focus coefficient*. Differing from previous regularization methods of directly pushing network weights towards zero,
the focus coefficient encourages them to be statistically similar to zero.
The loss produced by our method does not increase with the number of
network parameters, which allows it easy to tune and compatible with
large penalty weights. We empirically investigate the effectiveness of our
proposed method with experiments on CIFAR-10/100, Tiny-ImageNet,
and ImageNet. Results indicate that focus coefficient can improve model
generalization performance and significantly reduce the accuracy loss
encountered by ultra sparse networks.

Keywords: Regularization · Network pruning · Deep learning

1 Introduction

Neural networks with an enormous number of parameters have achieved remarkable practical success. In recent years, the capacity of networks has increased
substantially, from 100 million parameters [23], to 340 million parameters [4],

Supported by The National Key Research and Development Program of China No.
2020YFE0200500.

© The Author(s), under exclusive license to Springer Nature Switzerland AG 2022
S. Khanna et al. (Eds.): PRICAI 2022, LNCS 13630, pp. 416–429, 2022.
https://doi.org/10.1007/978-3-031-20865-2_31

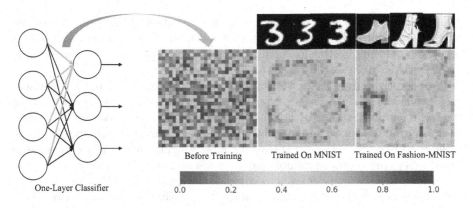

Fig. 1. The heatmap of a neuron's weights. We reshape values into 28×28 for a more intuitive demonstration, and attach some training samples above. Normalization scales the range in $[0, 1]$. Blue means that the input pixel is positively correlated with the neuron's assigned label, while red means the opposite. Consequently, one can see a fuzzy green '3' from the weights trained on MNIST, and an ankle boot on Fashion-MNIST. (Color figure online)

and finally 530 billion parameters [25]. An arms race of training large networks has begun.

Although these over-parameterized models usually exhibit remarkable generalization performance, they come at a hefty cost in terms of computing and storage. Therefore, some model compression methods [1,11,14] have been proposed to trim neural networks. Network pruning [8] is one of these methods that is known for achieving improved compression by directly removing unimportant weights. It typically has a minor impact on test performance, but can vastly enhance computational and memory efficiency. In particular, ultra sparse networks [16,30] could potentially enable real-time inference on edge devices with single-core CPUs.

When it comes to identifying unimportant weights, there are two types of algorithms: importance-based and regularization-based. The former is constituted of importance criteria, such as norm [8], gradient [15], etc. The algorithm, given a sparsity, removes all weights with low scores in the dense network at once to produce a sparse network. While the latter generally imposes an additional regularization term to identify unimportant weights or channels by pushing parameters towards zero [18,19,28]. However, existing studies are limited to small penalty weight regime to avoid downgrading the model. Therefore, the effect of regularization-based approaches is restricted. To demonstrate the principle of pruning, we train a single-layer network, apply Min-Max normalization to the weights, and then display the weights of one of the neurons in Fig. 1.

One can see that the optimization has tuned these random values into a certain distribution, which enables a model to determine whether the neuron should be activated. For inputs (elements of a sample) that substantially correlate with the neuron's delegated class, the weights are boosted to large values, resulting in a high activation value. However, most weights are tuned near 0 (that is 0.5 after normalization), making their inputs slightly affect the activation value. Intuitively, the neuron ignores most inputs and infers using only a few pixels. This interesting mechanism allows us to observe some training sample characteristics from weights.

Apparently, only some dimensions in the sample contribute to the classification, while the rest can be safely pruned. It is a widely held view that focusing on certain inputs is key to the success of ReLU [7] and attention [27]. Thus, network pruning can be improved by adding a regularization term to drive more weights to zero. Nevertheless, is lowering most weights numerically close to zero a necessary condition to produce sparse representations? Intuitively, raising the remaining weights away from zero could achieve the same effect of making a few inputs dominate the activation values. Obviously, the order relation within weights plays a more crucial role in generalization and pruning.

In this work, we propose a similarity-based regularization term named *focus coefficient* (FC). Differing from previous norm-based regularization components, our term measures the statistical similarity of the neural network weights to zero, which theoretically indicates the importance that weights attach to inputs. Therefore, FC motivates the neural network to focus on fewer inputs when serving as a proximal term. Furthermore, FC is easily tunable since it regularizes layer-wise and independent of the number of weights.

We first empirically evaluate the effect of regularization on generalization. Results show that FC manages to regularize the network and therefore slightly improve generalization behavior as expected. Most notably, it does not significantly reduce accuracy even trained with large penalty weights.

Then we investigate its improvement on network pruning. It has commonly been assumed that model compression can benefit from incorporating proper regularization [20]. However, our experiments show that even the dense network performance has increased, data augmentation **downgrades** the generalization of sparse networks. The output-based regularizers (confidence penalty [22] and label smoothing [26]) have a minor impact on network pruning. FC, in contrast, can improve the performance of ultra sparse networks dramatically. More experiments on ViT [6] show that our approach is also applicable to the Transformer architecture [27].

Contributions: our contributions in this paper are as follows.

- We discuss the relationship between regularization and pruning, and argue that the traditional wisdom of letting the weights be close to zero numerically is unnecessary.
- We propose a similarity-based regularization term called focus coefficient, which encourages the neural network to focus on fewer inputs. Our approach can introduce strong regularization to improve network pruning.
- The experiments in Sect. 4 verify that our method could regularize the network and slightly improves the generalization. Besides, it is compatible with large penalty weights without seriously hurting accuracy. More experiments in Sect. 5 demonstrate that FC can be used to obtain well-behaved ultra sparse networks.

2   Related Work

A typical pruning involves three stages: (1) pre-training a dense network (2) pruning unimportant weights to obtain a sparse network (3) fine-tuning the sparse network to recover accuracy.

Regularization. Regularization-based pruning mainly aimed to push the weight values towards zero by introducing norm regularization in the pre-training process. Among them, the most applied ones were L_0 and L_1 [18,19], which could implement pruning in training. Regularization methods could also be used to estimate sparsity [8]. The majority of the early work focused on unstructured pruning. Although higher sparsity could be achieved, it had limited effectiveness for acceleration. Therefore, some regularization-based structured pruning methods had been presented [29]. The penalty weights of these approaches could typically only be set to a moderate value because unduly strong regularization interfered with training. In order to introduce strong regularization, some works [5] proposed to apply different penalty weights to various weights. While other studies [28] suggested gradually increasing the strength of regularization.

Our suggested similarity-based regularization, unlike other techniques, is inherently compatible with large penalty weights and does not require additional settings to strongly regularize the neural network.

Importance. Some importance-based methods were proposed for application in the pruning stage. Specifically, these methods designed algorithms that could identify and removed unimportant weights from the trained network. The initial group of works [9,14] was to use the Hessian matrix, but it involved huge computational effort. As a result, the most applied are simple magnitude-based schemes. Both the L1 [18] and L2 norm [8] of the weights could be used for unstructured or structured pruning.

3   Method

3.1   Notations

We consider an n-layer neural network using fixed nonlinearity ρ. For the i-th layer with input dimension d_i and output dimension c_i, its weight tensor is denoted as $\boldsymbol{w}_i$, so $i \in \{1, \ldots, n\}$ and $\boldsymbol{w}_i \in \mathbb{R}^{c_i \times d_i}$. While the output of the neural network is as follows[1]:

$$f(\boldsymbol{x}; \boldsymbol{w}) := \rho(\boldsymbol{w}_n \rho(\boldsymbol{w}_{n-1} \cdots \rho(\boldsymbol{w}_1 \boldsymbol{x}) \cdots))$$

For $\boldsymbol{w}_i$, let $\boldsymbol{w}_i^{min}$ and $\boldsymbol{w}_i^{max}$ correspond to tensors filled with minimum w_i^{min} and maximum w_i^{max} respectively. Both tensors have the same shape as $\boldsymbol{w}_i$. When $\boldsymbol{w}_i$ is full of 0.5, it is denoted as $\boldsymbol{w}_i^{0.5}$. The l_1 norm $| \cdot |$ and l_2 norm $\| \cdot \|$ are always computed entry-wise. Thus, the l_2 norm corresponds to the Frobenius norm $\| \cdot \|_F$ for a matrix.

---

[1] Since weights account for most of the neural network parameters, we do not consider other parameters, such as bias.

3.2   Focus Coefficient

We use cosine similarity to derive *focus coefficient*. First, we bring the weights onto the same range $[0, 1]$ to obtain the dimensionless version. For $\boldsymbol{w}_i$, we apply Min-Max normalization for simplicity as follows:

$$\boldsymbol{w}_i^N = \frac{\boldsymbol{w}_i - \boldsymbol{w}_i^{min}}{w_i^{max} - w_i^{min}} \tag{1}$$

As mentioned in Sect. 1, 0 in the weights can be roughly considered as 0.5 after normalization. Therefore, we compute the cosine of $\boldsymbol{w}_i^N$ and $\boldsymbol{w}^{0.5}$ to obtain the statistical similarity of $\boldsymbol{w}_i$ to $\mathbf{0}$.

$$
\begin{aligned}
\gamma(\boldsymbol{w}_i) &= 1 - \cos(\boldsymbol{w}_i^N, \boldsymbol{w}^{0.5}) = 1 - \frac{\boldsymbol{w}_i^N \cdot \boldsymbol{w}^{0.5}}{\|\boldsymbol{w}_i^N\| \times \|\boldsymbol{w}^{0.5}\|} \\
&= 1 - \frac{1}{\sqrt{c_i \times d_i}} \cdot \frac{|\boldsymbol{w}_i - \boldsymbol{w}_i^{min}|}{\|\boldsymbol{w}_i - \boldsymbol{w}_i^{min}\|}
\end{aligned}
\tag{2}
$$

The above derivation is just plain algebra. After obtaining $\gamma(\boldsymbol{w}_i)$ of each layer, we further define the FC of a neural network $\Gamma(\boldsymbol{w})$ as follows:

$$\Gamma(\boldsymbol{w}) = \frac{1}{n} \cdot \sum_{i=1}^{n} \gamma(\boldsymbol{w}_i) \tag{3}$$

A linear layer with a smaller $\gamma(\boldsymbol{w}_i)$ tends to allow fewer inputs to affect its output. Correspondingly, the simpler the model becomes. Therefore, we next work on reducing $\Gamma(\boldsymbol{w})$ to regularize the neural network.

3.3   Regularization

For a given dataset, consisting of m i.i.d tuples $\{(\boldsymbol{x}_1, y_1), \ldots, (\boldsymbol{x}_m, y_m)\}$, we let $\boldsymbol{x}_i \in \mathbb{R}^{d \times 1}$ denotes the input data and y_i denotes the corresponding class label. We regularize the neural network f trained on it by applying the following loss function:

$$\ell(f(\boldsymbol{x}; \boldsymbol{w})) = \frac{1}{m} \sum_{i=1}^{m} CE(f_w(\boldsymbol{x}_i), y) + \lambda \cdot \Gamma(\boldsymbol{w}) \tag{4}$$

where $CE(\cdot)$ indicates the cross-entropy loss and λ denotes the focus penalty.

For a neural network trained using gradient descent scheme, the j-th weight of its i-th layer iterates the following equation at time t:

$$\boldsymbol{w}_i^{(t+1)}[j] = \boldsymbol{w}_i^{(t)}[j] - \alpha \cdot \left. \frac{\partial \ell(f(\boldsymbol{x}; \boldsymbol{w}))}{\partial \boldsymbol{w}_i[j]} \right|_{\boldsymbol{w}_i[j] = \boldsymbol{w}_i^{(t)}[j]} \tag{5}$$

where α is the learning rate. Next we obtain the gradient of $\ell(f(\boldsymbol{x}; \boldsymbol{w}))$ on $\boldsymbol{w}_i[j]$:

$$\frac{\partial \ell(f(\boldsymbol{x}; \boldsymbol{w}))}{\partial \boldsymbol{w}_i[j]} = \frac{\partial \mathcal{L}}{\partial \boldsymbol{w}_i[j]} - \frac{\lambda}{\sqrt{c_i \times d_i}} \cdot \frac{\partial \frac{|\boldsymbol{w}_i - \boldsymbol{w}_i^{min}|}{\|\boldsymbol{w}_i - \boldsymbol{w}_i^{min}\|}}{\partial \boldsymbol{w}_i[j]} \tag{6}$$

where $\mathcal{L} = \dfrac{\partial \frac{1}{m} \sum_{i=1}^{m} CE(f_w(\boldsymbol{x}_i), y)}{\partial \boldsymbol{w}_i[j]}$.

Since FC is computed layer-wise, we only consider the current i-th layer when computing the gradient. Specifically, we have:

$$\frac{\partial \frac{|\boldsymbol{w}_i - \boldsymbol{w}_i^{min}|}{\|\boldsymbol{w}_i - \boldsymbol{w}_i^{min}\|}}{\partial \boldsymbol{w}_i[j]} = \frac{1}{\|\boldsymbol{w}_i - \boldsymbol{w}_i^{min}\|} - \frac{|\boldsymbol{w}_i - \boldsymbol{w}_i^{min}|}{\|\boldsymbol{w}_i - \boldsymbol{w}_i^{min}\|^3}(\boldsymbol{w}_i[j] - w_i^{min}) \tag{7}$$

Next, we substitute Eq. (6) and (7) into Eq. (5) to obtain the following formula:

$$\boldsymbol{w}_i^{(t+1)}[j] = (\underbrace{1 - \frac{\alpha \cdot \lambda}{\sqrt{c_i \times d_i}} \cdot \frac{|\boldsymbol{w}_i - \boldsymbol{w}_i^{min}|}{\|\boldsymbol{w}_i - \boldsymbol{w}_i^{min}\|^3}}_{A1})\boldsymbol{w}_i[j]$$

$$+ \underbrace{\frac{\alpha \cdot \lambda}{\sqrt{c_i \times d_i}} \cdot (\frac{1}{\|\boldsymbol{w}_i - \boldsymbol{w}_i^{min}\|} + \frac{|\boldsymbol{w}_i - \boldsymbol{w}_i^{min}|}{\|\boldsymbol{w}_i - \boldsymbol{w}_i^{min}\|^3} \cdot w_i^{min})}_{A2} - \alpha \cdot \frac{\partial \mathcal{L}}{\partial \boldsymbol{w}_i[j]}$$

$$\tag{8}$$

We see that FC, when serving as a regular term, imposes the following two transforms on the weights: (1) Shrinking to $A1$ times; (2) Adding $A2$. Note that the weights in the same layer share the same $A1$ and $A2$ values. In this way, our method makes each input to be labeled with similar weights. Therefore, FC can be considered as an adaptive version of weight decay.

4 Improvements to Dense Networks

In this section, we investigate the impact of FC on dense network generalization. Specifically, we first perform vanilla training on models as baselines. Then we apply Eq. (4) as the optimization objective and gradually increased λ from 0. Note that λ is raised to an unreasonably high value, such as 50 for AlexNet. Figure 2 presents the test accuracy of these networks. We also report the value of $\Gamma(\boldsymbol{w})$ to demonstrate the effect of λ on regularization.

The FC curve (orange) indicates that our method manages to regularize the network as expected. At first, the network generalization improves with FC integration. The suitable value of λ is affected by the task difficulty and the number of parameters. In our setting, focus coefficient can improve large networks (AlexNet and VGG-16) when λ equals 0.01. For a small network (ResNet-20) or challenging task (ImageNet), a smaller value such as 5e-4 could be a better

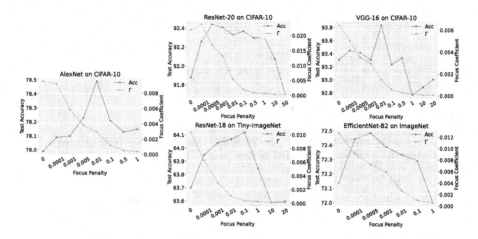

Fig. 2. Accuracy (%) and FC of the network with various regularizers.

choice. On the other hand, we note that there is only a slight performance loss from continuing to boost λ rather than making learning fail like L_1 and L_2 [21]. We next demonstrate that this compatibility with large weight penalties leads to stronger regularization, resulting in higher sparsity.

5   Improvements to Sparse Networks

Regularization is generally considered to enable neural networks to achieve low-complexity solutions, which require less network capacity. In this section, we explore the impact of FC on sparse networks and compare it with other regularization techniques. We employ the two-step process proposed by [17] to construct sparse networks. An additional regularizer is enabled when first pre-training the dense network. After pruning the low-magnitude weights, we perform normal training to fine-tune the sparse network for fairness.

Table 1. Test accuracy (%) of sparse network with various data augmentation strategies on CIFAR-10.

Sparsity (%)	AlexNet			ResNet-20		
	None	Mixup	Rand augment	None	Mixup	Rand augment
0	78.18	78.51	**79.57**	92.04	92.46	**93.29**
50	**77.76**	76.67	76.75	92.12	92.50	**93.22**
90	**79.84**	77.97	78.65	89.72	90.38	**90.52**
99	**74.22**	73.47	73.04	**72.39**	70.46	72.07
99.5	**59.45**	59.09	55.89	**64.77**	61.04	63.44

Table 2. Test accuracy (%) of sparse network with various data augmentation strategies on CIFAR-100.

Sparsity (%)	AlexNet			ResNet-20		
	None	Mixup	Rand augment	None	Mixup	Rand augment
0	46.21	48.65	**50.82**	67.63	68.71	**68.80**
50	47.42	47.44	**48.62**	67.98	68.12	**68.58**
90	49.15	**49.77**	46.28	62.67	62.50	**62.90**
99	**46.48**	42.14	40.11	**40.69**	40.02	39.42
99.5	**40.56**	39.24	38.33	**31.28**	30.24	28.84

5.1 Data Augmentation Hurts Network Pruning

We begin by adding more data augmentation methods to the pre-training process. In practice, mixup [31] and RandAugmentation [2] are considered to introduce large data perturbation and thus regularize the network. The former introduces linear behavior by synthesizing a new sample by randomly overlaying another one on each image in the dataset. While the latter is an automated augmentation strategy. While both are thought to help dense networks by incorporating strong regularization, can sparse networks also benefit from it?

We train AlexNet [13] and ResNet-20 [10] on CIFAR-10 [12] and CIFAR-100, respectively. The test accuracy is shown in Table 1 and Table 2. Results show that dense neural networks trained with data augmentation perform better as claimed by the authors. The following pruning, on the other hand, would not gain improvement. Surprisingly, providing additional data augmentation to the pre-training process actually degrades the performance of the ultra sparse network. RandAugment, for example, improves AlexNet by 4.6% on CIFAR-100, yet at a sparsity of 99%, it leads to a 6.4% accuracy loss instead. Our results show that data augmentation during the pre-training period can impede network pruning. Furthermore, the relationship between data augmentation and regularization is called into question.

5.2 Explicit Regularizers

Next we turn to compare the following explicit regularizers with our proposed FC for network pruning.

- L_1 **Regularization** is also known as LASSO. It is often used to improve network pruning due to its sparsity-inducing property.
- **Confidence Penalty** [22] is a penalty term based on the maximum entropy principle. It prevents peaked distributions by regularizing the output distribution of the network.
- **Label Smoothing** [26] is a widely-used regularization term based on output restrictions. It penalizes overfitting by replacing hard labels in the dataset with soft ones. Its regularization strength is controlled by the smoothing factor.

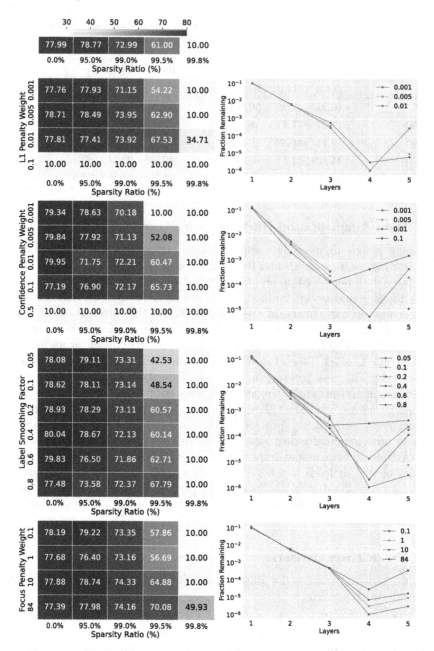

Fig. 3. Left: Accuracy (%) of sparse AlexNet with explicit regularizers. **Right**: Parameter remaining ratio per layer of AlexNet with extreme sparsity (99.8%). Points not drawn in the dashed line indicate that a layer collapse has occurred.

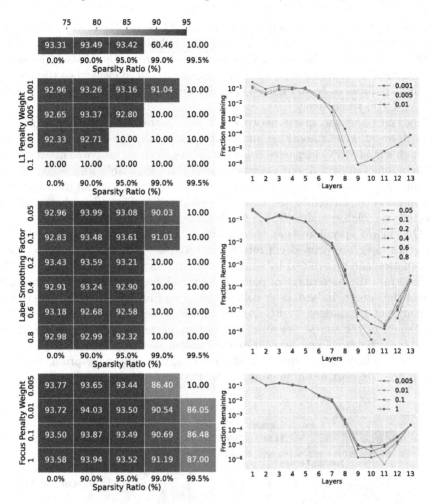

Fig. 4. Left: Accuracy (%) of sparse VGG-16 with explicit regularizers. **Right**: Parameter remaining ratio per layer of VGG-16 with extreme sparsity (99.5%). Points not drawn in the dashed line indicate that a layer collapse has occurred.

Table 3. Test accuracy (%) of networks with various sparsity. (a): ResNet-18 on Tiny-ImageNet. (b):EfficientNet-B2 on ImageNet.

(a)					(b)				
λ	95%	99%	99.9%	99.95%	λ	90%	95%	99%	99.95%
0	60.03	52.14	30.44	18.85	0	71.03	66.95	25.82	18.85
0.1	60.54	53.02	30.43	25.69	0.001	72.03	66.81	27.05	25.69
0.5	61.02	55.19	36.90	30.96	0.01	70.86	66.99	28.19	30.96

PlainNets. We start by training AlexNet and VGG-16 [24] on CIFAR-10. The hyperparameter of the regularization are gradually increased until the accuracy of the dense network drop to random guessing. Interestingly, VGG-16 is incompatible with the confidence penalty and cannot be trained even when the penalty weight is reduced to 1e–8. Figure 3 and Fig. 4 report the performance of AlexNet and VGG-16, respectively.

By and large, the sparse network performs better with stronger regularization. However, label smoothing and confidence penalty are ineffective in achieving high sparsity. FC surpasses conventional regularizers in sparse networks. As we mentioned in Sect. 4, our proposed method is compatible with large penalty weights, which allows it to provide stronger regularization without disturbing the neural network. Therefore, the network regularized by FC still predicts properly even at very high sparsity (99.8% for AlexNet and 99.5% for VGG-16).

One might speculate that this is due to the fact that the parameters of a certain layer are pruned entirely (layer-collapse), and that serious accuracy degradation can be avoided by simply restricting the sparsity of each layer. We demonstrate the percentage of parameters remaining at each layer on the right side of the figures. Indeed, layer collapse happens from time to time in networks that are not regularized by FC. Although this conjecture can partially explain the failure of the sparse network, there exists networks without layer collapse (solid line) that are no more accurate the random guessing. Therefore, we believe that layer collapse is a sufficient and unnecessary condition for pruning failure, and proper regularization remains an effective way to improve pruning.

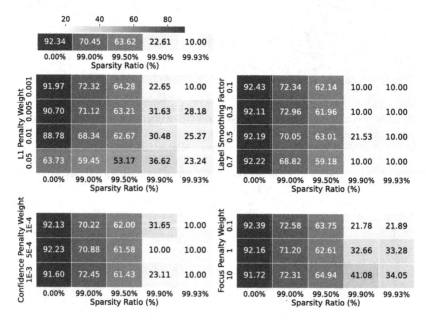

Fig. 5. Accuracy (%) of ResNet-20 on CIFAR-10 with various regularizers.

Modern Networks with Shortcut Connections. We next validate our method on ResNet. Differing from PlainNets above, the collapsed layer in the ResNet can be bypassed by shortcuts, resulting in higher sparsity. However, the accuracy still decreases because of the network shortening caused by the disappearance of some convolutional layers. As shown in Fig. 5, the accuracy of the sparse network improves with the increase of the regularization strength, while FC presents better results. Table 3 then shows that our method is still applicable on the more challenging Tiny-ImageNet and ImageNet [3].

5.3   Transformer Architecture

We extend our discussion from CNN to Vision Transformer (ViT) [6]. We train ViT on CIFAR-10 and prune its linear layers in multi-head self-attention [32].

As shown in Fig. 6, ViT can clearly gain performance from pruning. We speculate that this is due to the high redundancy of the linear layer used by the original self-attention module. As a result, the regularization brought by FC slightly improves the effectiveness of ViT. As the sparsity and penalty weights increase, the performance improvement becomes larger.

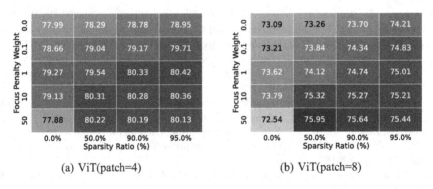

(a) ViT(patch=4)   (b) ViT(patch=8)

Fig. 6. Test accuracy (%) of Vision Transformer with FC.

6   Conclusion

In this work, we proposed the *focus coefficient*, a regularization term that drives the weights to be statistically equal to zero. Our proposed regularizer improved the pruning process by focusing the network on fewer inputs via layer-wise regularization. FC was compatible with large penalty weights, which allows us to bring stronger regularization to the neural network. Preliminary evaluations revealed that FC could simplify the model and enhance accuracy slightly. We also compare FC with existing regularizers in sparse convolutional neural networks and ViT. The results show that network pruning tends to benefit from strong regularization, and FC usually produces better results.

References

1. Cheng, J., Wang, P., Li, G., Hu, Q., Lu, H.: Recent advances in efficient computation of deep convolutional neural networks. Front. Inf. Technol. Electron. Eng. **19**(1), 64–77 (2018). https://doi.org/10.1631/FITEE.1700789
2. Cubuk, E.D., Zoph, B., Shlens, J., Le, Q.V.: Randaugment: practical automated data augmentation with a reduced search space. In: Proceedings of the IEEE/CVF Conference on Computer Vision and Pattern Recognition Workshops, pp. 702–703 (2020)
3. Deng, J., Dong, W., Socher, R., Li, L.J., Li, K., Fei-Fei, L.: Imagenet: a large-scale hierarchical image database. In: 2009 IEEE Conference on Computer Vision and Pattern Recognition, pp. 248–255 (2009)
4. Devlin, J., Chang, M.W., Lee, K., Toutanova, K.: Bert: pre-training of deep bidirectional transformers for language understanding. arXiv preprint arXiv:1810.04805 (2018)
5. Ding, X., Ding, G., Han, J., Tang, S.: Auto-balanced filter pruning for efficient convolutional neural networks. In: Proceedings of the AAAI Conference on Artificial Intelligence, vol. 32 (2018)
6. Dosovitskiy, A., et al.: An image is worth 16x16 words: transformers for image recognition at scale. In: International Conference on Learning Representations (2020)
7. Glorot, X., Bordes, A., Bengio, Y.: Deep sparse rectifier neural networks. In: Proceedings of the Fourteenth International Conference on Artificial Intelligence and Statistics, pp. 315–323. JMLR Workshop and Conference Proceedings (2011)
8. Han, S., Pool, J., Tran, J., Dally, W.: Learning both weights and connections for efficient neural network. In: Advances in Neural Information Processing Systems, vol. 28. Curran Associates, Inc. (2015)
9. Hassibi, B., Stork, D.: Second order derivatives for network pruning: optimal brain surgeon. Adv. Neural Inf. Process. Syst. **5** (1992)
10. He, K., Zhang, X., Ren, S., Sun, J.: Deep residual learning for image recognition. In: Proceedings of the IEEE Conference on Computer Vision and Pattern Recognition, pp. 770–778 (2016)
11. Hinton, G., Vinyals, O., Dean, J.: Distilling the Knowledge in a Neural Network. arXiv:1503.02531 [cs, stat] (2015)
12. Krizhevsky, A., Hinton, G., et al.: Learning multiple layers of features from tiny images (2009)
13. Krizhevsky, A., Sutskever, I., Hinton, G.E.: ImageNet classification with deep convolutional neural networks. In: Advances in Neural Information Processing Systems, vol. 25. Curran Associates, Inc. (2012)
14. LeCun, Y., Denker, J., Solla, S.: Optimal brain damage. In: Advances in Neural Information Processing Systems, vol. 2. Morgan-Kaufmann (1989)
15. Lee, N., Ajanthan, T., Torr, P.: SNIP: single-shot network pruning based on connection sensitivity. In: International Conference on Learning Representations (2018)
16. Liu, N., Ma, X., Xu, Z., Wang, Y., Tang, J., Ye, J.: AutoCompress: an automatic DNN structured pruning framework for ultra-high compression rates. Proc. AAAI Conf. Artif. Intell. **34**(04), 4876–4883 (2020). https://doi.org/10.1609/aaai.v34i04.5924
17. Liu, N., et al.: Lottery ticket preserves weight correlation: is it desirable or not? In: Proceedings of the 38th International Conference on Machine Learning, pp. 7011–7020. PMLR (2021)

18. Liu, Z., Li, J., Shen, Z., Huang, G., Yan, S., Zhang, C.: Learning efficient convolutional networks through network slimming. In: Proceedings of the IEEE International Conference on Computer Vision, pp. 2736–2744 (2017)
19. Louizos, C., Welling, M., Kingma, D.P.: Learning sparse neural networks through L_0 regularization. In: International Conference on Learning Representations (2018)
20. Mirzadeh, S.I., Farajtabar, M., Li, A., Levine, N., Matsukawa, A., Ghasemzadeh, H.: Improved knowledge distillation via teacher assistant. Proc. AAAI Conf. Artif. Intell. **34**(04), 5191–5198 (2020). https://doi.org/10.1609/aaai.v34i04.5963
21. Park, D.H., Ho, C.M., Chang, Y.: Achieving Strong Regularization for Deep Neural Networks (2018)
22. Pereyra, G., Tucker, G., Chorowski, J., Kaiser, L., Hinton, G.: Regularizing Neural Networks by Penalizing Confident Output Distributions (2017)
23. Radford, A., Narasimhan, K., Salimans, T., Sutskever, I.: Improving language understanding by generative pre-training (2018)
24. 1. Simonyan, K., Zisserman, A.: Very Deep Convolutional Networks for Large-Scale Image Recognition. arXiv:1409.1556 [cs] (2015)
25. Smith, S., et al.: Using DeepSpeed and Megatron to Train Megatron-Turing NLG 530B, A Large-Scale Generative Language Model. Technical Report arXiv:2201.11990, arXiv (2022)
26. Szegedy, C., Vanhoucke, V., Ioffe, S., Shlens, J., Wojna, Z.: Rethinking the inception architecture for computer vision. In: Proceedings of the IEEE Conference on Computer Vision and Pattern Recognition, pp. 2818–2826 (2016)
27. Vaswani, A., et al.: Attention is all you need. In: Advances in Neural Information Processing Systems, vol. 30. Curran Associates, Inc. (2017)
28. Wang, H., Qin, C., Zhang, Y., Fu, Y.: Neural pruning via growing regularization. In: International Conference on Learning Representations (2020)
29. Wen, W., Wu, C., Wang, Y., Chen, Y., Li, H.: Learning structured sparsity in deep neural networks. In: Advances in Neural Information Processing Systems, vol. 29. Curran Associates, Inc. (2016)
30. Ye, S., et al.: Progressive DNN compression: a key to achieve ultra-high weight pruning and quantization rates using ADMM. arXiv preprint arXiv:1903.09769 (2019)
31. Zhang, H., Cisse, M., Dauphin, Y.N., Lopez-Paz, D.: Mixup: beyond empirical risk minimization. In: International Conference on Learning Representations (2018)
32. Zhu, M., Tang, Y., Han, K.: Vision transformer pruning. arXiv preprint arXiv:2104.08500 (2021)

Dynamic-GTN: Learning an Node Efficient Embedding in Dynamic Graph with Transformer

Thi-Linh Hoang and Viet-Cuong Ta[(✉)]

HMI Laboratory, University of Engineering and Technology,
VNU Hanoi, Hanoi, Vietnam
{hoanglinh,cuongtv}@vnu.edu.vn

Abstract. Graph Transformer Networks (GTN) use an attention mechanism to learn the node representation in a static graph and achieves state-of-the-art results on several graph learning tasks. However, due to the computation complexity of the attention operation, GTNs are not applicable to dynamic graphs. In this paper, we propose the Dynamic-GTN model which is designed to learn the node embedding in a continous-time dynamic graph. The Dynamic-GTN extends the attention mechanism in a standard GTN to include temporal information of recent node interactions. Based on temporal patterns interaction between nodes, the Dynamic-GTN employs an node sampling step to reduce the number of attention operations in the dynamic graph. We evaluate our model on three benchmark datasets for learning node embedding in dynamic graphs. The results show that the Dynamic-GTN has better accuracy than the state-of-the-art of Graph Neural Networks on both transductive and inductive graph learning tasks.

Keywords: Graph Transformer Network · Dynamic graph · Node sampling

1 Introduction

In recent years, Graph Neural Networks (GNN) have gained a lot of attention for learning in graph-based data such as social networks [1,2], author-papers in citation networks [3,4], user-item interactions in e-commerce [2,5,6] and protein-protein interactions [7,8]. The main idea of GNN is to find a mapping of the nodes in the graph to a latent space, which preserves several key properties of the graphs. Given that every single node has a certain influence on its neighbors, node embedding is created by GNN based on a message passing mechanism to aggregate information from the neighborhood nodes, which can be used for downstream tasks such as node classification, edge prediction, or graph classification.

The embedding learned by traditional GNN methods can describe the local and global structures on a static graph with the constraint that the graph's nodes

© The Author(s), under exclusive license to Springer Nature Switzerland AG 2022
S. Khanna et al. (Eds.): PRICAI 2022, LNCS 13630, pp. 430–443, 2022.
https://doi.org/10.1007/978-3-031-20865-2_32

and edges do not change over time. For online systems such as social networks or e-commerce, this assumption usually does not hold. In order to deal with dynamic graphs, one could employ a snapshot-based approach. More specifically, a GNN model such as Graph Convolution Network (GCN) [3], Graph Attention Network (GAT) [4], or Graph Transformer [9] is trained to learn the graph representation at a specific timestamp. The drawback of this approach is that the learned representation at each snapshot ignores the temporal interactions because each models is trained separately. The trained embedding model in this case can only capture the graph specific structures at the end of a time interval. In addition to that, the snapshot-based approach is a time-consuming one because it has to retrain the model from scratch.

Dynamic-based graph learning methods overcome these issues by learning both temporal and structural properties of the dynamic graph. Recent works can be classified into discrete-time approaches and continuous-time approaches. Discrete-time methods improve the snapshot-based approach by adding the temporal relations to the node representation. Several architectures are proposed such as DynGEM [10] with regularized weights or DySAT [11] with structural attention layers. Discrete-time methods have issues in learning the fine-grained temporal structure of the dynamic graph. Continuous-time methods avoid the issues by seeing the dynamic graph as a sequence of nodes' interaction with a timestamp. Then, a sequence learning network is employed to extract the temporal pattern of interactions. For example, RNN [12] is used in DeepCoevolve [6] and LSTM [13] is used in Temporal Dependency Interaction Graph [14].

Although continuous-time approaches are more natural in learning temporal information in dynamic graphs than the discrete ones, they still have significant drawbacks. The usage of RNN-like architectures to aggregate information from temporal neighbors are unable to capture long-term dependencies. When the temporal information spreads over a long period of time, the learnt dynamic representations usually degrade. Secondly, these approaches usually compute dynamic embeddings of the two target interactions nodes independently without taking into account the semantic relatedness between their temporal regions (i.e. historical behaviors), which could be a causal element for the target interactions.

To address the above limitations, in this work, we extend the Graph Transformer network to capture the long-term dependencies of temporal interactions between nodes in the dynamic graphs. We introduce a Time Projection layer which is added after the standard transformer layer. Firstly, the multi-head attention layer is used to aggregate both time-based node interactions and local structures of the graph. Then, the projection layer uses node embedding with temporal interactions to predict the future node representation of the graph. In order to reduce the computing complexity of the multi-head attention layer, a node sampling component is added based on the dynamic embedding of the projection layer. The attention operation only includes similar nodes which are defined by a clustering process on the node embedding. We evaluate our model on three time-dynamic graph datasets: Wikipedia, Reddit, and MOOC [15]. The experiments show that our proposed Dynamic-GTN could improve the overall accuracy of downstream tasks, and also reduce the computational time of the model.

2   Related Works

The existing modeling approaches are roughly divided into two categories based on how the dynamic graph is constructed: discrete-time methods and continuous-time methods.

Discrete-Time Methods: This category of methods deals with a sequence of discretized graph snapshots that coarsely approximate a time-evolving graph. DynGEM [10] is an auto-encoding method that minimizes reconstruction loss and learns incremental node embeddings from previous time steps. DySAT [11] computes dynamic embeddings by employing structural attention layers on each snapshot, followed by temporal attention layers to capture temporal variations among snapshots, as inspired by the self-attention mechanism. EvolveGCN [16] recently leverages RNNs to regulate the GCN model (i.e., network parameters) at each time step in order to capture the dynamism in the evolving network parameters. Regardless of progress, snapshot-based methods will always fail to capture fine-grained temporal and structural information due to the coarse approximation of continuous-time graphs. It is also difficult to specify an appropriate aggregation granularity.

Continuous-Time Methods: Methods in this category operate directly on time-evolving graphs without time discretization and focus on designing various temporal aggregators to extract information. The dynamic graphs are represented as a series of chronological interactions with precise timestamps. DyRep [17] is based on a temporal point process to capture immediate information and long-term information at the same time by consider both association events and communication events. DeepCoevolve [6] and it's variant JODIE [15] see two coupled RNNs to update dynamic node embeddings based on each interaction. They provide an implicit way to construct the dynamic graph in which only the historical interaction information of the two involved nodes of the interactions at time t is used. TDIG-MPNN [14] provides a graph creation approach called Temporal Dependency Interaction Graph (TDIG), which generalizes the above implicit construction and is formed from a sequence of cascaded interactions to explicitly leverage the topology structure of the temporal graph. To acquire the dynamic embeddings, they use a graph-informed Long Short Term Memory (LSTM) [13] based on the topology of TDIG.

Recent work such as TGAT [18] and TGNs [19] use a different graph creation technique, namely a time-recorded multi-graph, which allows for more than one interaction (edge) between two nodes. A single TGAT layer is used to collect one-hop neighborhoods, similar to the encoding process in static models (e.g.. GraphSAGE [20]). By stacking numerous layers, the TGAT model can capture high-order topological information. TGNs generalize TGAT's aggregation and use a node-wise memory to keep track of long-term dependencies.

Node Sampling: Node sampling or graph pooling in GNN is often used to reduce the computing complexity in the aggregate. The idea to connect between graph learning and local node structures is not new. In [21], they arrange the nodes into a binary tree to fast pool adjacent nodes. The GraphSAGE [20] framework defines a neighborhood set with a fixed number of nodes to reduce the computational footprint. By exploiting the graph clustering structure, the authors propose a novel GCN training algorithm, namely Cluster-GCN [22]. The Cluster-GCN restricts the neighborhood search into a sub-graph in each learning batch. The sub-graphs are split from the original graph by a graph clustering algorithm. Our work is motivated by the work of Cluster-GCN. Instead of defining the learning batches for updating the graph cluster, we utilize the time step in a time-dynamic graph to define a learning batch.

3   Continuous-Time Dynamic Graph

We define a dynamic continuous graph as $\mathcal{G}_t = (\mathcal{V}_t, \mathcal{E}_t)$ consists of a node set $\mathcal{V}_t$ and an set of edges $\mathcal{E}_t$ ordered by time $t \in \mathbb{R}^+$ and described chronological interactions up to time t. An interaction appearing at time t is denoted as $e_{u,v,t}$, where nodes $u, v \in \mathcal{V}_t$ are two nodes involved in this interaction, $e_{u,v,t}$ has features extract from the interaction between two nodes. One node can have multiple interactions at different time points, we let $u(t)$ represent the node u at time t.

Since t can also indicate the order of interactions between two nodes, by recording the time or order of each edge, a dynamic graph can capture the evolution of the relationship between nodes. Given the topology of a graph $\mathcal{G}_t$, dynamic graph embedding aims to learn mapping function at time t:

$$f_t : \mathcal{V}_t \rightarrow \mathbb{R}^d, \tag{1}$$

where d is the number of node embedding dimensions. As long as the correctness of node representation in latent space, the downstream tasks such as node classification, and link prediction will more benefit from it. With interaction nodes $u(t)$ and $v(t)$, i.e., $h_{u(t)}$, $h_{v(t)}$ are node embedding of u, v at time t.

For example, Fig. 1 shows a graph evolve with time, which describes interactions between users and items. Given an ordered sequence of temporal node interactions at time $0 < t_1 < t_2 < t_3 < t$, the target is learning embedding of node u at time t: $u(t)$ (square symbol). And uses the previous observed state $u(t)$ and the elapsed time Δt to predict the future embedding of the node at $t + \Delta t$. For each node, its dynamic associated nodes and their neighbor from a graph structure, which includes more time/order information than conventional static graphs. It is not trivial to encode the preference of each user from this dynamic graph.

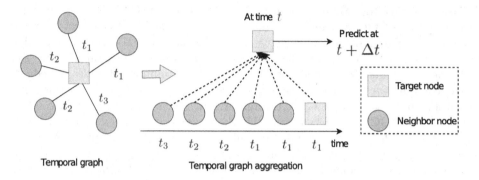

Fig. 1. Illustration of the temporal graph aggregation and label prediction with continuous time event

4   Graph Transformer Network for Continuous-time Dynamic Graph

Our proposed model, Dynamic-GTN, works on the chronological interactions between two nodes in the continuous-time dynamic graph. It includes three major components as illustrated in Fig. 2:

- *Node sampling*: A sampled subgraph of an original graph G should obtain a good sample quality. The goal of this component is to find a better way to evaluate the entire sample clustering process which integrates node sampling with clustering. Node sampling base on cluster can remove the edges with high similarity centrality and then optimize the calculation of multi-head attention steps in Graph Transformer.
- *Graph Transformer Network and Time Projection layer*: the Graph Transformer Network (GTN) layer based on GT [9] is used to aggregate both continuous-time embedding and structural information of the graph. Output embedding from the GTN layer is used to project the self-node to the future embedding by the Time Projection layer. The resulting embedding are used to improve the node sampling and representing as dynamic embedding for the Prediction Layer.
- *Output layer*: it utilizes output embedding from the Time Projection layer to calculate the target values. In Fig. 2, the link prediction task is computed by concatenating the output of two related nodes. In the node classification task, we could omit the Concatenation layer and feed the embedding into the feed-forward layer directly.

4.1   Node Sampling

At the first block, we employ a node sampling method based on cluster with dynamic information to extract relevant nodes based on the latent space of the

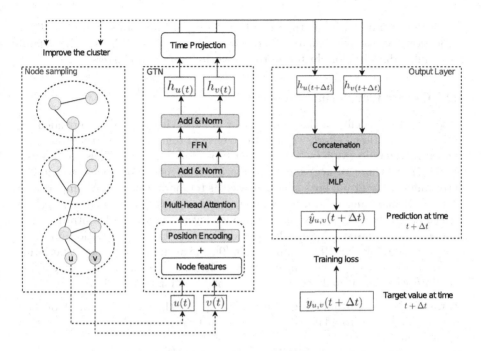

Fig. 2. Illustration of the architecture of the proposed model

graph. This component allows the Graph Transformer to learn different graph attention kernels for different regions based on a gradient-based self-clustering assignment such that different regions are treated differently in spatial dependency modeling.

First, a vertex-level soft-assignment to M clusters is learnt from the temporal pattern of each vertex. To partition the graph, we employ graph clustering methods. Node sampling component try to build partitions over the vertices in the graph such that within-cluster ties are significantly more than between-cluster links in order to better represent the graph's clustering and community structure. This is precisely what we require because: As previously stated, the embedding usage for each batch is equal to within-cluster linkages. Intuitively, each node and its neighbors are usually in the same cluster, hence neighborhood nodes with a high chance of being in the same cluster after a few hops are still in the same cluster.

$$C = \sigma_s \left(\sigma_r \left(h_{i(t)} \mathbf{W}_f \right)_t \mathbf{W}_t \right), \tag{2}$$

where C is the cluster assignment score for each vertex to M clusters. $\mathbf{h}_{i(t)}$ represent embedding of node i at time t and $\mathbf{W}_t$ is parameters for linear layers on the feature mode and temporal mode, respectively, and σ_r and σ_s represent the relu and softmax activation functions. The feature dimension of input tensor $h_{i(t)}$ is first squeezed to 1 using $\mathbf{W}_f$, in order to provide a summarized temporal pattern at each vertex. The $\mathbf{W}_t$ is further applied to the temporal pattern to calculate a M-dimensional cluster assignment score.

At the beginning, i.e at time $t = 0$, the output embedding from the Time Projection layer is not available. Therefore, the Dynamic-GTN uses the default node embedding PE for clustering the nodes as the initial clusters.

4.2   Graph Transformer Network

Observing the benefits of the Transformer in capturing long-term dependencies and in computational effort, we propose to extract temporal and structural information of dynamic graph by Transformer type of architecture. Thus, We use the Graph Transformer to aggregate information from neighbor nodes, and it will derive information from both spatial as well as temporal features. An importance of using Transformer in graph is that we need to have position encoding (PE) to feed as an input in Transformer Encoder layer. Several works introduce PE to Transformer-based GNNs to help model capture the node position information. We use Laplacian PE is employed in [9], the authors prove that it performs better than other PE. To enhance node's positional information, we also employ time intervals that usually convey important behavior information.

Dynamic Node Embedding: Firstly, we update the hidden feature h of the i th node in a graph from layer l to layer $l + 1$ at time t when there is a interaction of node i as follows:

$$h_i^{\ell+1}(t) = \sum_{j \in \mathcal{N}(i)} w_{ij} \left(V^\ell h_j^\ell \right) \tag{3}$$

where

$$w_{ij} = \text{softmax}_j \left(\frac{Q^\ell h_i^\ell \cdot K^\ell h_j^\ell}{\sqrt{d}} \right) \tag{4}$$

and $j \in \mathcal{N}(i)$ denotes the set of neighbor nodes of node i in graph and Q^ℓ, K^ℓ, V^ℓ are learnable linear weights (denoting the Query, Key and Value for the attention computation, respectively). $\mathcal{N}(i)$ is neighborhood of node i evolve by time and after node or edge event such as create a new node, delete/edit edge $\mathcal{N}(i)$ can be change, also have many version of interactions, thus we formulate neighbor of node i at time t as $\mathcal{N}_t(i)$, which describes in Fig 2. The method uses for sampling neighborhoods is cluster-based sampling as we introduced in the previous section. The attention mechanism is performed parallelly for each node in the neighbor nodes to obtain their updated features in one shot-another plus point for Transformers over RNNs, which update features node-by-node.

Multi-head Attention: Getting this straightforward dot-product attention mechanism to work proves to be tricky. Bad random initializations of the learnable weights can destabilize the training process. We can overcome this by parallelly performing multiple 'heads' of attention and concatenating the result (with each head now having separate learnable weights):

$$\hat{h}_i^{\ell+1}(t) = O_h^\ell \|_{k=1}^H \left(\sum_{j \in \mathcal{N}_i} w_{ij}^{k,\ell} V^{k,\ell} h_j^\ell \right), \tag{5}$$

where,

$$w_{ij}^{k,\ell} = \text{softmax}_j \left(\frac{Q^{k,\ell}h_i^\ell \cdot K^{k,\ell}h_j^\ell}{\sqrt{d_k}} \right), \tag{6}$$

and $Q^{k,\ell}, K^{k,\ell}, V^{k,\ell}$ are the learnable weights of the kth attention head and O^ℓ is a down-projection to match the dimensions of $h_i^{\ell+1}$ and h_i^ℓ across layers. The attention outputs $\hat{h}_i^{\ell+1}(t)$ are then passed to a Feed Forward Network (FFN) preceded and succeeded by residual connections and normalization layers, as:

$$z_i^{\ell+1}(t) = \text{Norm} \left(h_i^\ell(t) + \hat{h}_i^{\ell+1}(t) \right), \tag{7}$$

$$\hat{z}_i^{\ell+1}(t) = W_2^\ell \, \text{ReLU} \left(W_1^\ell z_i^{\ell+1}(t) \right), \tag{8}$$

$$h_i^{\ell+1}(t) = \text{Norm} \left(z_i^{\ell+1}(t) + \hat{z}_i^{\ell+1}(t) \right), \tag{9}$$

where $W_1^\ell, W_2^\ell, z_i^{\ell+1}(t), \hat{z}_i^{\ell+1}(t)$ denote intermediate representations, and Norm can either be LayerNorm or BatchNorm.

Time Projection: Our proposed model projects the embedding to capture temporal information, and predicts the future embedding at a time. After a short duration Δ_t the node i's projected embedding is update to as follow:

$$h_{i(t+\Delta t)} = (1 + w) * h_{i(t)} \tag{10}$$

where w is time-context vector is converted from Δt by using a linear layer: $w = W_p \Delta t$. The vector $(1 + w)$ works as a temporal attention vector to scale the past node embedding.

4.3   Output Layer

In the link prediction task, The interaction of two nodes u and v at time $t + \Delta t$ for link prediction task represent by:

$$\hat{y}_{u,v}(t + \Delta t) = W * \left(h_{u(t+\Delta t)} \, \| \, h_{v(t+\Delta t)} \right) + b \tag{11}$$

To learn model parameters, we optimize the cross entropy loss. The objective function $\mathcal{L}$ is defined follows:

$$\mathcal{L} = - \sum_{\mathcal{S}} \mathbf{y}_{u,v} \log (\hat{\mathbf{y}}_{u,v}) + (1 - \mathbf{y}_{u,v}) \log (1 - \hat{\mathbf{y}}_{u,v}) + \lambda \|\Theta\|_2 \tag{12}$$

where $\mathcal{S}$ denotes the training samples, $\mathbf{y}_{u,v}$ is input interaction of node u and node v and $\hat{\mathbf{y}}_{u,v}$ is the predicted interaction of node u and node v from the classification layer of the model.

   In the node classification task, we could directly use the embedding in Eq. 10 without the concatenation layer for predicting the label of a specific node at time $t + \Delta t$.

5   Experiments

5.1   Datasets

For testing our proposed Dynamic-GTN model, we use three popular time-continous dynamic graph datasets: Wikipedia, Reddit, and MOOC, these datasets public in [15]. These datasets consist of one month of interaction between user and item (i.e., MOOC: MOOC online course, Reddit: post, Wekipedia: page). The detail statistics of each dataset is described in Table 1. We evaluate the efficiency of our model output embedding on both transductive and inductive settings. Our experiments follow the setting in [19] in continuous-time graph learning.

More specifically, we split the data by time for training, validating and testing. We use the first 70% interaction to train, next 15% to evaluate, and the final 15% to test. For example, on Reddit dataset consist of four weeks of posts created by users on subreddits, in a week the models take the first 5 days data of week to train, the next day to evaluate, and the last day to test. The fixed evaluation period is selected at one week duration. Because our proposed model can learn continuously, the duration could be changed freely.

Table 1. Statistics of the datasets used in our experiments

Information	MOOC	Reddit	Wikipedia
#Nodes	7,144	10,984	9,227
#Edges	411,749	672,447	157,474
#Dynamic Nodes	4,066	366	217
Nodes' Label Type	Course dropout	Posting ban	Editing ban

5.2   Baseline

In the transductive edge prediction and inductive node classification, we use the state-of-the-art algorithms for representation learning on temporal graphs as baselines: Discrete-Time Methods: EvolveGCN [16] and DySAT [11]; Continuous-Time Methods: JODIE [15] , TGAT [18], DyRep [17], and TGN [19] for comparison.

Evaluation Metric: With future link prediction task, given an interaction $e_{u,v,t}$ each method outputs calculate the node u's preference score over node v at time t in test set. This score is used to classify if there is a connection between two nodes at time t. To evaluate the performance of the proposed method and baseline we use average precision for future edge prediction task in transductive setting. In the node classification task, we aim to represent a node u at time t as $u(t)$, and base on this representation these model prediction status of node u at time t. Accuracy is used to measure the achievement of methods.

5.3   Performance

We implement our method in PyTorch. For the other methods, we use all the original papers' code from their github pages. For all the methods we use the Adam optimizer with learning rate as 0.01, dropout rate as 20%, weight decay as zero. The mean aggregator proposed by TGN is adopted and the number of hidden units is the same for all methods. All the results were averaged over 10 runs. For Dynamic-GTN, the number of partitions and clusters per batch for each dataset are listed in Table 5 and we show that graph clustering only takes a small portion of preprocessing time. Note that clustering is seen as a preprocessing step and its running time is not taken into account in training.

Table 2 and Table 3 shows the performance results on dynamic node classification task and future link prediction task, respectively. In general, the continuous-time methods perform better than the discrete-time methods. This can be explained by the fact that continuous-time methods can access to a more fine-gained temporal and structural information. Built on continuous-time approach, our model Dynamic-GTN outperforms all the competitors on all the datasets. The improvements are stable across the two down stream tasks. The nearest competitor to our model is the TGN architecture. By combining the time-based embedding with the self-attention operation, our model likely captures more interaction information than the compared baselines without the need to retrain the models.

Table 2. The performance of our model and base line on node classification task

Method	Model	MOOC	Wikipedia	Reddit
Discrete-time	EvolveGCN	70.26 ± 0.5	63.41 ± 0.3	81.77 ± 1.2
	DySAT	72.11 ± 0.5	61.79 ± 0.3	74.82 ± 1.2
Continuous-time	Jodie	73.39 ± 2.1	61.23 ± 2.5	84.35 ± 1.2
	TGAT	74.23 ± 1.2	65.43 ± 0.7	83.12 ± 0.7
	DyRep	75.12 ± 0.7	62.79 ± 2.3	84.82 ± 2.2
	TGN	77.47 ± 0.8	67.11 ± 0.9	87.41 ± 0.3
	Dynamic-GTN (ours)	$\mathbf{78.13 \pm 0.9}$	$\mathbf{69.74 \pm 1.3}$	$\mathbf{89.03 \pm 0.3}$

5.4   Discussion

We perform further experiments to highlight different components of our propose Dynamic-GTN for learning an efficient node representation in dynamic graphs.

Impact of Dynamic-GTN in Long Period: We test the accuracy of our proposed model by varying the time projecting window Δt. The node classification task results on Reddit dataset of our model and other baselines are shown in Table 4. In general, it is more difficult to predict for a long period updating time Δt than the short one. While all of the tested models drop accuracy, our model still achieve the best accuracies. At the longest $\Delta t = 7$, the proposed

Table 3. The performance of our model and base line on link prediction task

Method	Model	MOOC	Wikipedia	Reddit
Discrete-time	EvolveGCN	78.33 ± 0.3	89.71 ± 0.5	80.79 ± 0.4
	DySAT	74.05 ± 0.4	88.13 ± 0.5	87.23 ± 0.4
Continuous-time	Jodie	76.34 ± 0.5	90.74 ± 0.3	79.11 ± 0.4
	TGAT	75.36 ± 0.5	92.87 ± 0.3	87.42 ± 0.2
	DyRep	73.45 ± 0.4	92.21 ± 0.3	86.89 ± 0.4
	TGN	81.20 ± 0.6	92.37 ± 0.2	88.17 ± 0.2
	Dynamic-GTN (ours)	**84.42 ± 0.5**	**93.71 ± 0.3**	**89.69 ± 0.2**

Dynamic-GTN achieves around 85.36% accuracy. The second highest accuracy is the TGN with 82.53% accuracy. This demonstrates that our architectures is more stable on learning node representation in dynamic graphs.

Table 4. The accuracy of node classification task on Reddit dataset by varying the time projection $\Delta t(days)$ of different models

Model	$\Delta t = 1$	$\Delta t = 3$	$\Delta t = 5$	$\Delta t = 7$
EvolveGCN	81.77 ± 1.2	70.39 ± 0.7	71.22 ± 0.5	74.07 ± 0.5
DySAT	82.32 ± 0.7	75.13 ± 0.5	74.05 ± 0.4	71.39 ± 0.5
Jodie	84.35 ± 1.2	81.71 ± 0.8	81.13 ± 0.5	79.38 ± 0.7
TGAT	83.12 ± 0.7	84.46 ± 0.5	83.18 ± 0.7	78.59 ± 1.2
DyRep	84.82 ± 2.2	80.33 ± 0.5	81.05 ± 0.5	79.77 ± 1.1
TGN	87.41 ± 0.3	87.58 ± 0.5	86.11 ± 0.3	82.53 ± 0.5
Dynamic-GTN (ours)	**89.03 ± 0.3**	**88.11 ± 0.2**	**86.43 ± 0.5**	**85.36 ± 0.7**

Impact of Node Sampling: To evaluate the effects of node sampling step with temporal information, we iterate the number of clustering components and compare the accuracy and run time performance against the baseline architecture. Table 5 compares three different node partitioning and model without clustering. The usage of clustering could improve both accuracy and training time. From our experimental results, the optimal number of clusters depend heavily on the temporal and local structures of the graph. More investigation should be done in future works to have a more accurate estimation of the number.

Impact of the Number of Attention Head Number: As the number of attention head plays an important role in projecting between consecutive latent spaces, we perform further experiments to test how it affects the performance on down stream tasks. We plot the test accuracy on MOOC dataset with different number of heads in Fig 3. The model's performance improves when the head number increases from 1–5, reaching highest accuracy at 5 attention heads, which demonstrates the effectiveness of multi-head attention in learning node

Table 5. The training time and the Accuracy (%) of node sampling component in Dynamic-GTN, testing on node classification task with Reddit dataset. The average time is reported per epoch with lower is better.

Model	Avg. time (s)	Accuracy
Dynamic-GTN (10 cluster)	**50.23**	90.67
Dynamic-GTN (15 clusters)	52.37	**90.81**
Dynamic-GTN (20 clusters)	52.58	90.08
Dynamic-GTN (w/o node sampling)	75.83	89.72

relationship in dynamic graph. Our results relate to the works in [23] that the best performance can be achieved with 3 layers and 2 heads (6 effective heads).

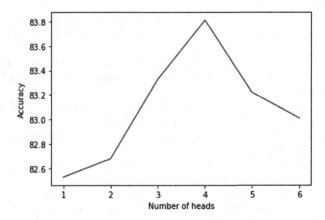

Fig. 3. The comparison of number head attention in Dynamic-GTN on MOOC's node classification

6   Conclusion

In this paper, we propose a continuous-time dynamic graph representation learning method, called Dynamic-GTN. Dynamic-GTN generalizes the Graph Transformer Network (GTN) to extract temporal-based local structure information on dynamic graphs via node embedding projection. Due to the cost computation in sampling graph in the temporal network, we utilize a cluster-based sampling to help model to train faster both in inductive and transductive learning. Several experiments are made to evaluate the characteristics of our proposed architecture. The overall results on three benchmark datasets show that our model achieves better performance than previous state-of-the-art GNN models on continuous-time graphs.

References

1. He, X., Deng, K., Wang, X., Li, Y., Zhang, Y., Wang, M.: Lightgcn: simplifying and powering graph convolution network for recommendation. In: Proceedings of the 43rd International ACM SIGIR conference on research and development in Information Retrieval, pp. 639–648 (2020)
2. Fan, W., et al.: Graph neural networks for social recommendation. In: The World Wide Web Conference, pp. 417–426 (2019)
3. Hamilton,W., Ying, Z., Leskovec, J.: Inductive representation learning on large graphs. In: Proceedings of the 31st International Conference on Neural Information Processing Systems, pp. 1025–1035 (2017)
4. Veličković, P., Cucurull, G., Casanova, A., Romero, A., Lio, P., Bengio, Y.: Graph attention networks. arXiv preprint arXiv:1710.10903 (2017)
5. Qiu, R., Li, J., Huang, Z., Yin, H.: Rethinking the item order in session-based recommendation with graph neural networks. In: Proceedings of the 28th ACM International Conference on Information and Knowledge Management, pp. 579–588 (2019)
6. Dai, H., Wang, Y., Trivedi, R., Song, L.: Deep coevolutionary network: Embedding user and item features for recommendation. arXiv preprint arXiv:1609.03675 (2016)
7. You, J., Liu, B., Ying, Z., Pande, V., Leskovec, J.: Graph convolutional policy network for goal-directed molecular graph generation. Adv. Neural Inf. Process. syst. **31** (2018)
8. Jiang, M., et al.: Drug-target affinity prediction using graph neural network and contact maps. RSC Adv. **10**(35), 20701–20712 (2020)
9. Dwivedi, V.P., Bresson, X.: A generalization of transformer networks to graphs. arXiv preprint arXiv:2012.09699 (2020)
10. Goyal, P., Kamra, N., He, X., Liu, Y.: Dyngem: Deep embedding method for dynamic graphs. arXiv preprint arXiv:1805.11273 (2018)
11. Sankar, A., Wu, Y., Gou, L., Zhang, W., Yang, H.: Dysat: deep neural representation learning on dynamic graphs via self-attention networks. In: Proceedings of the 13th International Conference on Web Search and Data Mining, pp. 519–527 (2020)
12. Medsker, L.R., Jain, L.C.: Recurrent neural networks. Des. Appl. **5**, 64–67 (2001)
13. Hochreiter, S., Schmidhuber, J.: Long short-term memory. Neural Comput. **9**(8), 1735–1780 (1997)
14. Chang, X., et al.: Continuous-time dynamic graph learning via neural interaction processes. In: Proceedings of the 29th ACM International Conference on Information & Knowledge Management, pp. 145–154 (2020)
15. Kumar, S., Zhang, X., Leskovec, J.: Predicting dynamic embedding trajectory in temporal interaction networks. In: Proceedings of the 25th ACM SIGKDD International Conference on Knowledge Discovery & Data Mining, pp. 1269–1278 (2019)
16. Pareja, A., et al.: Evolvegcn: evolving graph convolutional networks for dynamic graphs. In: Proceedings of the AAAI Conference on Artificial Intelligence, vol. 34, no. 04, pp. 5363–5370 (2020)
17. Trivedi, R., Farajtabar, M., Biswal, P., Zha, H.: Dyrep: learning representations over dynamic graphs. In: International Conference on Learning Representations (2019)
18. Xu, D., Ruan, C., Korpeoglu, E., Kumar, S., Achan, K.: Inductive representation learning on temporal graphs. arXiv preprint arXiv:2002.07962 (2020)

19. Rossi, E., Chamberlain, B., Frasca, F., Eynard, D., Monti, F., Bronstein, M.: Temporal graph networks for deep learning on dynamic graphs. arXiv preprint arXiv:2006.10637 (2020)
20. Hamilton, W., Ying, Z., Leskovec, J.: Inductive representation learning on large graphs. Adv. Neural Inf. Process. Syst. **30** (2017)
21. Defferrard, M., Bresson, X., Vandergheynst, P.: Convolutional neural networks on graphs with fast localized spectral filtering. Adv. Neural Inf. Process. Syst. **29** (2016)
22. Chiang, W.L., Liu, X., Si, S., Li, Y., Bengio, S., Hsieh, C.J.: Cluster-GCN: an efficient algorithm for training deep and large graph convolutional networks. In: Proceedings of the 25th ACM SIGKDD International Conference on Knowledge Discovery & Data Mining, pp. 257–266 (2019)
23. Ma, X., Pino, J., Cross, J., Puzon, L., Gu, J.: Monotonic multihead attention. arXiv preprint arXiv:1909.12406 (2019)

ICDT: Incremental Context Guided Deliberation Transformer for Image Captioning

Xinyi Lai, Yufeng Lyu, Jiang Zhong$^{(\boxtimes)}$, Chen Wang, Qizhu Dai, and Gang Li

Chongqing University, Shapingba, Chongqing, China
{laixinyi,lvyufeng,zhongjiang,chenwang,daiqizhu}@cqu.edu.cn

Abstract. Image Captioning is a task to generate descriptions for given images. Most encoder-decoder methods suffer from lacking the ability to correct the mistakes in predicted word. Though current deliberation motivated models can refine the generated text, they use single level image features throughout two stages. Due to the insufficient image information provided for the second-pass, deliberation action is ineffective in some cases. In this paper, we propose Incremental Context Guided Deliberation Transformer, namely **ICDT**, which consists of three modules, including: 1) Incremental Context Encoder, 2) Raw Caption Decoder and 3) Deliberation Decoder. Motivated by human writing habits in daily life, we treat the process of generating a caption as a deliberation procedure. The Raw Caption Decoder in first-pass constructs a draft sentence and then the Deliberation Decoder in second-pass polishes it to a better high-quality caption. In particular, for image encoding process, we design an Incremental Context Encoder that can provide cumulative encoded context based on different levels of image features for the deliberation procedure. Our encoder makes image features at different levels play specific roles in each decoding pass, instead of being simply fused and fed into the model for training. To validate the performance of the ICDT model, we evaluate it on the MSCOCO dataset. Compared with both Transformer-based models and deliberation-motivated models, our ICDT improves the state-of-the-art results and reaches 81.7% BLEU-1, 40.6% BLEU-4, 29.6% METEOR, 59.7% ROUGE and 134.6% CIDEr.

Keywords: Image captioning · Deliberation networks · Transformer

© The Author(s), under exclusive license to Springer Nature Switzerland AG 2022
S. Khanna et al. (Eds.): PRICAI 2022, LNCS 13630, pp. 444–458, 2022.
https://doi.org/10.1007/978-3-031-20865-2_33

1   Introduction

Image captioning task aims to generate a descriptive sentence for a given image, and its challenges lie not only in comprehensive image understanding but also in generating a sentence that matches the visual semantics of the image. The majority of proposed image captioning models following the encoder-decoder framework [2, 4, 10, 13, 25, 31, 32] has achieved promising progress on public datasets.

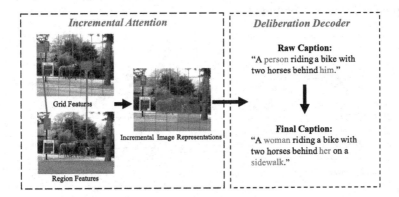

Fig. 1. An illustration of incremental context guided deliberation process. The left part shows how attention works to obtain incremental representation, and the right part summarizes the deliberation results. The blue arrow indicates attention operation and the blue mask denotes the attended area in original image (Color figure online).

Despite the great success, such single-pass decoding process suffer from lacking the ability to correct the mistakes in predicted words. To overcome this limitation, deliberation motivated models are introduced to image captioning [6–8, 14, 28, 30] for better decoding. Motivated by human writing behaviours, deliberation models should firstly generate a rough caption of the image from a global perspective, and then use the details to modify the rough caption. However, most of deliberated-based models are especially focus on text refinement, but use single level image features throughout two stages. These methods suffer from a drawback: the visual features from the first stage is insufficient for fixing the wrong words in the deliberation process. To utilize more diverse image features, Some works are proposed to fusion or interact of grid and region features to complement each other's advantages by using attention modules [5, 10, 18, 19, 27]. However, the direct use of two sources of features is prone to produce semantic noise. e.g. A grid containing a horse's leg may interact with the incorrect region containing a branch just because they have similar appearances. Therefore, merits of the two features should be leveraged separately with different functions instead of being used equally, and that can be well applied through two processes of deliberation.

To tackle the above problems and effectively combine two different stages, we try to design a method to utilize grid and region features in an incremental way to guide the deliberation procedure. As shown in Fig. 1, the grid level features attend to semantically related regions to get the incremental image representation. With the condition of grid attentive regions, the missing details of objects in the image can be captured, which guides the deliberation decoder to modify the word *person* to the correct detailed word *women*. Besides, unpredicted words in the raw caption like *sidewalk* can also be decoded by the incremental context. To this end, the introduction of the deliberation decoder and the rational use of the two features are organically combined, which inspires us to design a comprehensive end-to-end model.

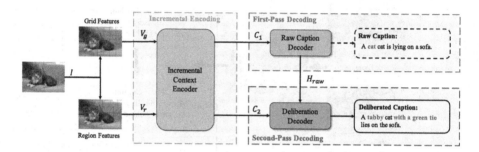

Fig. 2. Overview of our incremental context guide deliberation transformer model.

In this paper, we propose Incremental Context Guided Deliberation Transformer, namely ICDT. As shown in Fig 2, ICDT is a two-pass decoding model, consisting of three modules:1) Incremental Context Encoder: encode grid level features as global first-pass context while adding local region level features to it as incremental second-pass context, 2) Raw Caption Decoder: a non-autoregressive Transformer decoder use the global information provided by first-pass context to generate a raw caption, 3) Deliberation Decoder: polish the raw caption to a fine caption under the guidance of incremental second-pass context.

The major contributions of our paper can be summarized as follows:

- We propose a novel two-pass decoding model ICDT to achieve polishing generated sentence guided by two different level image features in an incremental way.
- We design an Incremental Context Encoder to obtain both global image features and incremental image features. With the Incremental Context Encoder, the second decoder of ICDT can be guided correctly to modify and detail the raw caption in the deliberation procedure.
- Experiments on MS-COCO dataset demonstrate that our model achieve new state-of-art performance for image captioning, *i.e.*, 134.6% CIDEr scores on *Karpathy* [12] test set.

2   Related Work

2.1   Image Encoding Over Different Features

With the advantage of covering the information of the entire image without over-compressing the information, grid features were used in many image captioning models [17,21,29]. Compared with grid features, region features can provide object-level information of the image. By introduing region features [2,5,9,10], the quantitative performance of image captioning was significantly improved. Nevertheless, the above works predicted sentences by using only one kind of features and lack full utilization of image information.

In order to integrate the advantages of both grid and region features, Wang et al. [26] proposed a hierarchical attention network to combine text, grid, and region features and explore the intrinsic relationship between different features. Luo et al. [18] proposed a cross-attention module with a graph to exploit complementary advantages of region and grid features.

2.2   Deliberation-Motivated Methods

Motivated by human behaviour in the process of describing an image, deliberation aims to polish the existing caption results for further improvement. Wang et al. [30] proposed Review Net as a rudiment of the deliberation network for image captioning, which outputs a thought vector after each review step to capture the global properties in a compact vector representation. Sammani et al. [22] introduced a Modification Network to modify existing captions from a given framework by modeling the residual information. Latterly, [23] proposed a caption-editing model to perform iterative adaptive refinement of an existing caption. Related to ruminant decoder [8,14] introduced a two-pass decoding framework, where a Cross Modification Attention is used to enhance the semantic expression of the image features and filter out error information from the draft caption to get better image captions. Although the above methods involve the deliberation process, they still focus only on the relationship between original image features and the draft caption, ignoring the effect of using different granularity image features throughout the process of generation.

3   Methodology

3.1   Problem Statement

In order to obtain a precise caption, we define the image captioning task as generating a refined sentence based on a raw caption. Formally, give an image I, we first need to generate a sequence $Y^{*'} = \{y_1^{*'}, y_2^{*'}, ..., y_T^{*'}\}$, where $y_T^{*'} \in \mathcal{D}$ is the predicted word in the raw caption, $\mathcal{D}$ is the dictionary, and T denotes the sequence length. In the deliberation procedure, we polish the raw caption guided by the extra image information, and finally get a fine caption $Y^* = \{y_1^*, y_2^*, ..., y_T^*\}, y_T^* \in \mathcal{D}$.

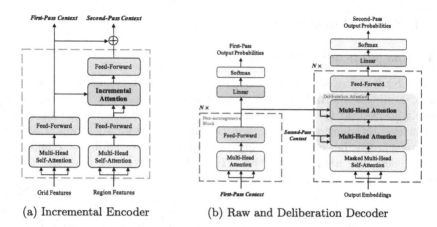

Fig. 3. The architecture of Encoder and Decoder modules.

3.2   Incremental Context Encoder

Efficient encoding of visual features of images is a prerequisite for generating high-quality captions. The deliberation-motivated methods usually encode single features like grids or regions, and then use the same encoded context when generating raw captions and final captions. This makes the deliberation process can not acquire additional information to modify the generated text and only focus on optimizing the language model. In this paper, we try to design an Incremental Context Encoder (ICE) that can provide incremental context for the two-pass decoder, so that it can provide extra information to guide the generation of final captions when deliberating raw captions. As shown in Fig. 3a, the grid features are encoded as first-pass context while integrating the region features through incremental attention as the second-pass context.

Basic Encoding. The ICE employs a vanilla Transformer encoder module for basic encoding. Since Grid features can cover the full content of a given image to describe the global scenes, we utilize it as input for basic encoding to obtain a first-pass context for generating a raw caption. The input grid features are directly extracted from the RCNN model. Considering the positional information of grids, we introduce a learnable embedding layer and combine them:

$$V_g = E_g + E_{pos} \tag{1}$$

where E_{pos} indicates the positional embedding and E_g stands for the extracted encoding grid features.

After that, we feed the combined feature V_g to the Transformer encoder module. Each encoder layer contains two sub-layers, including a multi-head self-attention (MHA) layer and a feed-forward network (FFN) layer:

$$H_g^{'(l)} = MHA(H_g^{(l)}, H_g^{(l)}, H_g^{(l)}) \tag{2}$$

$$H_g^{(l+1)} = FFN(H_g^{'(l)}) \tag{3}$$

where $H_g^{(0)} = V_g$ and l is the number of encoder layer. The hidden states of grids $H_g^{(l)}$ are fed into the $(l+1)$-th MHA layer. Specifically, the FFN is a position-wise fully connected layer consisting two linear projections with a ReLU activation in between:

$$FFN(x) = max(0, xW_1 + b_1)W_2 + b_2 \tag{4}$$

Through the Transformer encoder, we get the encoded hidden state from N-th layer H_g^N as the first-pass context C_1.

Incremental Attention Encoding. Once the first-pass context was obtained through basic encoding, we need to add extra information to it to guide the deliberation pass. Although grids can provide information covering the entire image, it still lacks attention to the salient objects. So we take region features as object-level information to improve the capability of understanding the objects. In order to achieve the purpose of integrating region features on the basis of the grid, we design an Incremental Attention Encoding mechanism.

Same as basic encoding, we first feed the extracted region features to the MHA and FFN component to get the middle encoded context $C_r^{(l)}$:

$$H_r^{'(l)} = MHA(H_r^{(l)}, H_r^{(l)}, H_r^{(l)}) \tag{5}$$

$$C_r^{(l)} = FFN(H_r^{'(l)}) \tag{6}$$

where $H_r^{(0)} = V_r$, which denotes region feature vector extracted from object detection model.

Then we use the encoded first-pass context C_1 as the query matrix and $C_r^{(l)}$ as the key and value matrix. The scale-dot product between grids and regions stands for attentive relationships, which can be leveraged as a weight matrix applying to region features. For each grid, the weighted context contains region information at the corresponding location. The incremental attention can be stated recursively as follows:

$$H_{inc}^{'(l)} = \text{softmax}\left(\frac{(C_1)\left(C_r^{(l)}\right)^T}{\sqrt{d_{C_r^{(l)}}}}\right) C_r^{(l)} \tag{7}$$

After incremental attention, an FFN layer is also applied to $H_{inc}^{'}$:

$$H_{inc}^{(l)} = FFN(H_{inc}^{'(l)}) \tag{8}$$

Notice that the incremental attention encoding and basic encoding are computed in the same layer. Finally, we directly add N-th incremental encoded context H_{inc}^N to C_1 and get the second-pass context C_2:

$$C_2 = C_1 + H_{inc}^N \tag{9}$$

With the first-pass context C_1, the Raw Caption Decoder (RCD) generates a sequence of raw caption $Y^{*} = \{y_1^{*'}, y_2^{*'}, ..., y_T^{*'}\}$, where T is the length of the raw caption. Different from other deliberation-motivated models, we use a non-autoregressive decoder as RCD. The non-autoregressive decoder enables parallel prediction during inference decoding. As shown in Fig 3b, the RCD removes the softmax layer during prediction, and directly use the vector output by the linear layer as the raw caption embedding feeding to the deliberation decoder.

Therefore, we remove the Masked Multi-head Self-attention layer of the vanilla Transformer decoder, and use the first-pass context from ICE directly to the MHA layer:

$$H_{raw}^{'(l)} = MHA(H_1^{(l)}, H_1^{(l)}, H_1^{(l)}) \tag{10}$$

where $H_1^{(0)} = C_1$. After that, A Feed-forward layer also is introduced:

$$H_{raw}^{(l)} = FFN(H_{raw}^{'(l)}) \tag{11}$$

And then we add a projection linear layer and a softmax layer for the training stage.

$$Y^{*'} = \text{softmax}(\text{proj}(H_{raw}^N)) \tag{12}$$

Due to the non-autoregressive design, the RCD executes in parallel for both training and inference stages. However, this makes RCD unable to directly generate coherent sentences.

3.3 Deliberation Decoder

The deliberation decoder (DD) aims to polish the preliminary caption guided by the second-pass context. To achieve the deliberation procedure, we design a Transformer-like autoregressive decoder. Fig 3b illustrates the detailed structure of DD. As the same as vanilla Transformer, the output embedding of target sentence E_s is fed into a Masked Multi-head self-attention (MMHA) layer during the training state:

$$H_s^{'(l)} = MMHA(H_s^{(l)}, H_s^{(l)}, H_s^{(l)}) \tag{13}$$

where $H_s^{(0)} = E_s$. After that, DD incorporates the second-pass context which contains the attentive region features by grids. Since the ICE can leverage the extra region features to enhance the detailed information of objects, we use the Multi-head attention layer to stress the relationship between caption and attentive regions:

$$H_{deli}^{'(l)} = \text{softmax}\left(\frac{\left(H_s^{'(l)}\right)(C_2)^T}{\sqrt{d_{C_2}}}\right)C_2 \tag{14}$$

Then we add an additional multi-head attention layer and take the embedding of the raw caption as input:

$$H_{deli}^{(l)} = \text{softmax}\left(\frac{\left(H_{deli}^{'(l)}\right)(H_{raw})^T}{\sqrt{d_{H_{raw}}}}\right)H_{raw} \tag{15}$$

where $H_{deli}^{(l)}$ and H_{raw} are treated as query and key matrix respectively, which contributes to learning a weight for refining the raw caption. Notice that the projection layer of RCD and output embedding layer of DD shares the same parameter weights which are used to embed the vocabulary of the caption. And H_{raw} is extracted from the projection layer of RCD to avoid the extra embedding layer breaking the end-to-end structure of ICDT.

Finally, the DD also uses a FNN layer before the projection linear layer:

$$Y^* = \text{softmax}\left(FFN(H_{deli}^N)\right) \tag{16}$$

3.4 Training Details

Following standard practice of image captioning, we first calculate the cross-entropy loss for each decoder:

$$L_{XE}^i(\theta) = -\sum_{t=0}^{T-1} \log\left(p_\theta\left(Y_t^* \mid Y_{0:t-1}^*, I\right)\right) \tag{17}$$

where Y_t^* is the ground-truth word, and θ is the parameter of i-th decoder. We obtain the overall learning objective by adding the losses of Raw Caption Decoder and Deliberation Decoder:

$$L_{XE} = L_{XE}^{raw} + L_{XE}^{delib} \tag{18}$$

Following Cornia et al. [5], we also introduce reinforcement learning for further finetune to make up the difference between cross-entropy loss and evaluation metrics between cross-entropy loss and evaluation metrics. When training with reinforcement learning, we use the CIDEr-D score as a reward through Self-Critical Sequence Training (SCST) [21]. At prediction time, we simplify the Raw Caption Decoder as an inner decoder layer instead of generating sentences. After that, the Deliberation Decoder can generate the final caption directly through beam search, and the highest scored sequence has been kept as the best caption.

4 Experiments

4.1 Experimental Settings

Dataset and Evaluation Metrics. Microsoft COCO 2014 dataset [16] is the widely used benchmark for image captioning. Each image is annotated with 5 caption sentences. We follow the setting of Karpathy and Fei-Fei [12] for the offline evaluation, where 113,287 images are used for training, 5,000 images for validation and 5,000 images for testing. To evaluate the quality of generated captions, we use COCO caption evaluation tool[1] to calculate the standard evaluation metrics, including BLEU-1/4 [20], METEOR [3], ROUGE [15], CIDEr [24] and SPICE [1]. All metrics can reflect the quality of the generated caption text from different aspects.

Implementation Details. Since our ICDT model needs to use both grid and region features, we adopt the same data preprocessing method as Luo et al. [18]. The pre-trained Faster R-CNN provided by Jiang et al. [11] was used to extract features from both levels simultaneously. For extracting features, it removes the delation and uses a normal C5 layer to extract grid features. For grid features, an additional average-pool was applied to get 7×7 grid size vectors. Meanwhile, the 2048-d output vector from the first FC-layer of the detection head was used as region features.

In our implementation, we set the dimension of each layer in encoder and decoders to 512, the number of heads to 8. The number of layers for both encoder and decoder is set to 4. We set the dimension d_f of FFN to 2048. We employ dropout with keep probability 0.9 after each attention and feed-forward layer. In the XE pre-training stage, we warm up our model for 4 epochs with the learning rate linearly increased to $1e^{-4}$, and then decays by rate 0.8 every 3 epochs. When training with SCST, the learning rate starts from $5e^{-5}$ and decays by rate 0.1 every 50 epochs. We train all models using the Adam optimizer with momentum of 0.9 and 0.999, a batch size of 128. We use beam search with a beam size of 5 to generate captions when validating and testing.

4.2 Quantitative Analysis

Compared with Transformer-based Methods. As shown in Table 1, we compare ICDT with other Transformer-based model for image captioning. Since ICDT considers both image grid and region granularity features, the models selected for comparison are divided into three groups, including:

- Grid Only: The model only takes the grid features to generate the image caption, where RSTNet [33] is the original model, and AoA, M^2 and X-Transformer are the experimental models used to compare with region features in the original paper.
- Region Only: Models that only use region features, Because R-CNN model is the mainstream way of the region feature extraction in image captioning, all the baselines in this group take the official results of the original model.
- Grid and Region: Models that utilize both grid and region features at the same time,

---

[1] https://github.com/tylin/coco-caption.

Table 1. Comparison results on Transformer-based models. For fair comparison, all 'Grid Only' models takes the result based on features extracted from ResNext-101 backbone, and all 'Region Only' models use ResNet-101 backbone.

Feature	Model	BLEU-1	BLEU-4	METOR	ROUGE	CIDEr	SPICE
Grid only	AoA	80.7	39.0	28.9	58.7	129.5	22.6
	M^2	80.8	38.9	29.1	58.5	131.7	22.6
	X-Transformer	81.0	39.7	29.4	58.9	132.5	23.1
	RSTNet	81.1	39.3	29.4	58.8	133.3	23.0
Region only	ETA	81.5	39.9	28.9	59.0	127.6	22.6
	ORT	80.5	38.6	28.7	58.4	128.3	22.6
	CPTR	**81.7**	40.0	29.1	59.4	129.4	–
	AoA	80.2	38.9	29.2	58.8	129.8	22.4
	M^2 Transformer	80.8	39.1	29.2	58.6	131.2	22.6
	X-Transformer	80.9	39.7	29.5	59.1	132.8	**23.4**
	DRT	**81.7**	40.4	29.5	59.3	133.2	23.3
Grid and Region	I^2RT	80.9	39.2	29.3	58.9	130.9	22.9
	DLCT	81.4	39.8	29.5	59.1	133.8	23.0
	ICDT(Our model)	**81.7**	**40.6**	**29.6**	**59.7**	**134.6**	23.2

From the results of the model on different evaluation metrics, our method fully surpasses the previous Transformer-based methods in terms of BLEU-1, BLEU-4, METOR, ROUGE and CIDEr. The CIDEr score of our DLCT reaches 134.6%, wich advances DLCT 0.8%. The boost of performance demonstrate the advantages of our ICDT which use incremental context encoder instead of cross fusion of region and grid features. In addition, according to the evaluation results, the model using two features achieves higher scores on CIDEr and SPICE metrics than the model using only single feature. In particular, compared with the Transformer-based SOTA model DLCT, our method achieves better performance in all indicators, reflecting the advantages of introducing a deliberation decoder. Next we will compare ICDT with all deliberation-motivated models.

Table 2. Comparison results on deliberation-motivated models

Model	BLEU-1	BLEU-4	METOR	ROUGE	CIDEr	SPICE
Review net	–	29.0	23.7	–	88.6	–
Skeleton key	74.2	33.6	26.8	55.2	107.3	19.6
Stack-Captioning	78.6	36.1	27.4	56.9	120.4	20.9
Deliberate attention	79.9	37.5	28.5	58.2	125.6	22.3
Ruminant decoding	80.5	38.6	28.7	58.7	128.3	22.3
ETN	80.6	39.2	–	58.9	128.9	22.6
CMA-DM	80.6	39.2	29.0	58.9	129.0	22.6
ICDT(Our model)	**81.7**	**40.6**	**29.6**	**59.7**	**134.6**	**23.2**

Compared with Deliberation-motivated Methods. Table 2 summaries all models designed with deliberation actions. As shown in Table 2, our ICDT model consistently exhibits better performance than the others. Since all of the deliberation-motivated models use LSTM instead of Transformer, their feature encoding and sequence generation capabilities are not as good as our proposed Transformer-based Model. However, the deliberation idea still shows its capability on image captioning task and deserves to be generalized more widely.

4.3   Ablation Study

In order to verify the effectiveness of each module in ICDT, we design ablation experiments based on the vanilla Transformer. As shown in Table 3, we separately use different visual features to validate the impact of Incremental Context Encoder. Further, all models are extended to two-pass decoders that we can evaluate the influence of Deliberation Decoder.

Table 3. Performance comparison of Incremental Context Encoder (ICE) and Raw Caption Decoder & Deliberation Decoder (R&D) for grids (G) and regions (R). E+D denotes traditional encoder-decoder framework which is based on vanilla Transformer.

Feature	BLEU-1	BLEU-4	METOR	ROUGE	CIDEr	SPICE
E+D(G)	81.2	39.0	29.0	58.6	131.2	22.4
E+D(R)	80.1	39.0	28.9	58.6	130.1	22.4
E+D(G + R)	80.9	38.9	29.2	58.6	131.6	22.7
ICE+D(G + R)	81.1	39.3	29.5	58.9	132.8	22.9
E+R&D(G)	81.2	39.2	29.0	59.0	131.5	22.4
E+R&D(R)	80.8	39.1	29.1	58.9	130.1	22.3
E+R&D(G + R)	81.3	39.4	**29.8**	58.9	132.4	22.8
ICE+R&D(G + R)	**81.7**	**40.6**	29.6	**59.7**	**134.6**	**23.2**

Impact of Incremental Context Encoder. To better understand the effect of our Incremental Context Encoder, we conduct four experiments on different features. The ICE+D model surpasses both single feature and fusion feature encoded models, which illustrates the effectiveness of Incremental Context Encoder. By integrating the attentive region feature and adding it to grid feature, the captioning model can better understand the corresponding region information and enrich the final encoded context. In sum, ICE+D outperforms E+D in most of the metrics and performs slightly worse in BLUE-1. We believe this is due to the fact that the Grid feature tends to highlight individual words rather than object entities in the raw image after self-attention.

Impact of Deliberation Decoder. As shown in the lower part of Table 3, we also conduct several experiments to demonstrate the effectiveness of our Deliberation Decoder. After adding the deliberation decoder, the performance of experimental models can be further improved whether using the ordinary Transformer encoder or our proposed ICE. Specifically, the BLEU-4, ROUGE and CIDEr scores have the most significant improvements. The results also show that after the introduction of Deliberation Decoder, the fluency and correctness of the final generated caption can be significantly improved through the polishing.

In addition, we analyzed the experimental results of E+R&D(G+R) and ICE+R&D(G+R). ICE+R&D surpassed E+R&D by nearly 2% on the CIDEr metric. Owing to the ICE we designed can guide two decoding passes, although ordinary E+R&D can perform second-pass polishing, same encoded context from single encoder leads the difficulty to perform effective refinement on the raw caption generated in the first-pass. However, ICE+R&D adds incremental image representations to deliberation decoder, which allows to obtain additional information to correct and polish the raw caption.

Fig. 4. Examples of image captioning results by vanilla Transformer and our ICDT with ground truth sentences.

4.4   Qualitative Analysis

We show several example image captions generated by vanilla Transformer and ICDT in Fig. 4. In genegral, our ICDT can generate more detailed and correct captions. For two examples in the first column, both Transformer and ICDT can provide accurate descriptions. For examples in the middle column, we can see that our ICDT is able to capture more contextual information from the image to generate richer and more correct descriptions in some cases. The third column shows that both Transformer and ICDT fail to provide a high-quality caption which contains some specific information in the ground truth sentences. One possible reason is that human can get the information such as *"conference room"* and *"brave"* based on their background knowledge or associations about this scene, while Transformer and ICDT do not currently have such capabilities. This can propose a valuable direction for future research in image captioning.

5   Conclusion

In this paper, we propose a novel comprehensive two-pass decoding based model, Incremental Context Guided Deliberation Transformer (ICDT) for image captioning. In the first-pass a Raw Caption Decoder uses grid features alone to obtain a raw description for the image, and in the second-pass a Deliberation Decoder guided by rich image feature representations to polish the raw description to a high-quality caption . In order to cooperate with deliberation decoding procedure, we propose an Incremental Context Encoder to encode more accurate and detailed image information incrementally. As far as we know, ICDT is the only model that comprehensively considers different level features to guide the deliberation process. Results show that our approach outperforms the state-of-the-art methods.

Acknowledgements. This work is supported by the National Natural Science Foundation of China (Grant No: 62176029).

References

1. Anderson, P., Fernando, B., Johnson, M., Gould, S.: SPICE: semantic propositional image caption evaluation. In: Leibe, B., Matas, J., Sebe, N., Welling, M. (eds.) Computer Vision – ECCV 2016, pp. 382–398. Springer International Publishing, Cham (2016)
2. Anderson, P., et al.: Bottom-up and top-down attention for image captioning and visual question answering. In: 2018 IEEE/CVF Conference on Computer Vision and Pattern Recognition, pp. 6077–6086. IEEE, Salt Lake City, UT (2018)
3. Banerjee, S., Lavie, A.: METEOR: an automatic metric for MT evaluation with improved correlation with human judgments. In: Proceedings of the ACL Workshop on Intrinsic and Extrinsic Evaluation Measures for Machine Translation and/or Summarization, pp. 65–72. Association for Computational Linguistics, Ann Arbor, Michigan (2005)
4. Cho, K., Courville, A., Bengio, Y.: Describing multimedia content using attention-based encoder-decoder networks. IEEE Trans. Multimedia **17**(11), 1875–1886 (2015)
5. Cornia, M., Stefanini, M., Baraldi, L., Cucchiara, R.: Meshed-memory transformer for image captioning. In: Proceedings of the IEEE/CVF Conference on Computer Vision and Pattern Recognitionpp. 10578–10587 (2020)
6. Gao, L., Fan, K., Song, J., Liu, X., Xu, X., Shen, H.T.: Deliberate attention networks for image captioning. In: Proceedings of the AAAI Conference on Artificial Intelligence, vol. 33, no. 01, pp. 8320–8327 (2019)
7. Gu, J., Cai, J., Wang, G., Chen, T.: Stack-captioning: coarse-to-fine learning for image captioning. In: Proceedings of the AAAI Conference on Artificial Intelligence, vol. 32, no. 1 (2018)
8. Guo, L., Liu, J., Lu, S., Lu, H.: Show, Tell, and polish: ruminant decoding for image Captioning. IEEE Trans. Multimedia **22**(8), 2149–2162 (2020)
9. Herdade, S., Kappeler, A., Boakye, K., Soares, J.: Image captioning: transforming objects into words. Adv. Neural Inf. Process. Syst. **32**. Curran Associates, Inc. (2019)

10. Huang, L., Wang, W., Chen, J., Wei, X.Y.: Attention on attention for image captioning. In: 2019 IEEE/CVF International Conference on Computer Vision (ICCV), pp. 4633–4642. IEEE, Seoul, Korea (South) (2019)
11. Jiang, H., Misra, I., Rohrbach, M., Learned-Miller, E., Chen, X.:. In defense of grid features for visual question answering. In: Proceedings of the IEEE/CVF Conference on Computer Vision and Pattern Recognition, pp. 10267–10276 (2020)
12. Karpathy, A., Fei-Fei, L.: Deep visual-semantic alignments for generating image descriptions. In: Proceedings of the IEEE Conference on Computer Vision and Pattern Recognition, pp. 3128–3137 (2015)
13. Li, L., Tang, S., Zhang, Y., Deng, L., Tian, Q.: GLA: global-local attention for image description. IEEE Trans. Multimedia 20(3), 726–737 (2018)
14. Lian, Z., Zhang, Y., Li, H., Wang, R., Hu, X.: Cross Modification Attention Based Deliberation Model for Image Captioning. arXiv:2109.08411 [cs] (2021)
15. Lin, C.Y.: ROUGE: a package for automatic evaluation of summaries. In: Text Summarization Branches Out: Proceedings of the ACL-04 Workshop, pp. 74–81. Association for Computational Linguistics, Barcelona, Spain (2004)
16. Lin, T.Y., et al.: Microsoft COCO: common objects in context. In: Fleet, D., Pajdla, T., Schiele, B., Tuytelaars, T. (eds.) Computer Vision – ECCV 2014, pp. 740–755. Springer International Publishing, Cham (2014)
17. Lu, J., Xiong, C., Parikh, D., Socher, R.: Knowing when to look: adaptive attention via a visual sentinel for image captioning. In: 2017 IEEE Conference on Computer Vision and Pattern Recognition (CVPR), pp. 3242–3250. IEEE, Honolulu, HI (2017)
18. Luo, Y., et al.: Dual-level collaborative transformer for image captioning. Proceedings of the AAAI Conference on Artificial Intelligence, vol. 35, no. 3, pp. 2286–2293 (2021)
19. Pan, Y., Yao, T., Li, Y., Mei, T.: X-Linear attention networks for image captioning. In: Proceedings of the IEEE/CVF Conference on Computer Vision and Pattern Recognition, pp. 10971–10980 (2020)
20. Papineni, K., Roukos, S., Ward, T., Zhu, W.J.: Bleu: a method for automatic evaluation of machine translation. In: Proceedings of the 40th Annual Meeting of the Association for Computational Linguistics, pp. 311–318. Association for Computational Linguistics, Philadelphia, Pennsylvania, USA (2002)
21. Rennie, S.J., Marcheret, E., Mroueh, Y., Ross, J., Goel, V.: Self-critical sequence training for image captioning. In: Proceedings of the IEEE Conference on Computer Vision and Pattern Recognition, pp. 7008–7024 (2017)
22. Sammani, F., Elsayed, M.: Look and Modify: Modification Networks for Image Captioning. arXiv:1909.03169 [cs] (2020)
23. Sammani, F., Melas-Kyriazi, L.: Show, edit and tell: a framework for editing image captions In: Proceedings of the IEEE/CVF Conference on Computer Vision and Pattern Recognition, pp. 4808–4816 (2020)
24. Vedantam, R., Lawrence Zitnick, C., Parikh, D.: Cider: consensus-based image description evaluation. In: Proceedings of the IEEE Conference on Computer Vision and Pattern Recognition, pp. 4566–4575 (2015)
25. Vinyals, O., Toshev, A., Bengio, S., Erhan, D.: Show and tell: a neural image caption generator. In: 2015 IEEE Conference on Computer Vision and Pattern Recognition (CVPR), pp. 3156–3164. IEEE, Boston, MA, USA (2015)
26. Wang, W., Chen, Z., Hu, H.: Hierarchical attention network for image captioning. Proceedings of the AAAI Conference on Artificial Intelligence, vol. 33, no. 01, pp. 8957–8964 (2019)

27. Wang, Y., Zhang, W., Liu, Q., Zhang, Z., Gao, X., Sun, X.: Improving intra- and inter-modality visual relation for image captioning. In: Proceedings of the 28th ACM International Conference on Multimedia, pp. 4190–4198. Association for Computing Machinery, New York, NY, USA (2020)
28. Wang, Y., Lin, Z., Shen, X., Cohen, S., Cottrell, G.W.: Skeleton key: Image captioning by skeleton-attribute decomposition. In: Proceedings of the IEEE Conference on Computer Vision and Pattern Recognition, pp. 7272–7281 (2017)
29. Xu, K., et al.: Show, attend and tell: neural image caption generation with visual attention. In: Proceedings of the 32nd International Conference on Machine Learning, pp. 2048–2057. PMLR (2015), iSSN: 1938–7228
30. Yang, Z., Yuan, Y., Wu, Y., Cohen, W.W., Salakhutdinov, R.R.: Review networks for caption generation. Adv. Neural Inf. Process. Syst. **29**. Curran Associates, Inc. (2016)
31. Yao, T., Pan, Y., Li, Y., Mei, T.: Exploring visual relationship for image captioning. In: Proceedings of the European Conference on Computer Vision (ECCV), pp. 684–699 (2018)
32. Yao, T., Pan, Y., Li, Y., Qiu, Z., Mei, T.: Boosting image captioning with attributes. In: Proceedings of the IEEE International Conference on Computer Vision, pp. 4894–4902 (2017)
33. Zhang, X., et al.: RSTNet: captioning with adaptive attention on visual and non-visual words. In: Proceedings of the IEEE/CVF Conference on Computer Vision and Pattern Recognition, pp. 15465–15474 (2021)

Semantic-Adversarial Graph Convolutional Network for Zero-Shot Cross-Modal Retrieval

Chuang Li[1], Lunke Fei[1], Peipei Kang[1(✉)], Jiahao Liang[2], Xiaozhao Fang[2], and Shaohua Teng[1]

[1] School of Computer Science and Technology, Guangdong University of Technology, Guangzhou, China
ppkanggdut@126.com,shteng@gdut.edu.cn,mllandlcc@gmail.com,flksxm@126.com
[2] School of Automation, Guangdong University of Technology, Guangzhou, China
ljh2365532081@163.com,xzhfang168@126.com

Abstract. Traditional cross-modal retrieval (CMR) methods assume that training data holds all the categories appearing in retrieval stage. However, when some multimodal data of new categories come, the learned model may achieve disappointing performance. Based on the theory of zero-shot learning, zero-shot cross-modal retrieval (ZS-CMR) emerges to solve this problem and becomes a new research topic. Existing ZS-CMR methods have the following limitations. (1) The semantic association between seen and unseen categories is important but ignored. Therefore, the semantic knowledge cannot be fully transferred from seen classes to unseen classes. (2) The cross-modal representations are not semantically aligned. Thus, samples of new categories cannot obtain semantic representations, further leading to unsatisfactory retrieval results. To tackle the above problems, this paper proposed the semantic-adversarial graph convolutional network (SAGCN) for ZS-CMR. Specifically, graph convolutional network is introduced to mine the potential relationship between categories. Besides, the techniques of adversarial learning and semantic similarity reconstruction are utilized to learn a common space, where multimodal embedding and class embedding are semantically fused. Finally, a shared classifier is adopted to enhance the discriminant ability of the common space. Experiments on three data sets illustrated the effectiveness of SAGCN on both traditional CMR and ZS-CMR tasks.

Keywords: Cross-modal retrieval · Zero-shot learning · Graph convolutional network · Adversarial learning

1 Introduction

In recent decades, the rapid development of information technology, especially the development of social media, makes people obtain information more timely and diversified. With this development, single-modal retrieval, such as text

© The Author(s), under exclusive license to Springer Nature Switzerland AG 2022
S. Khanna et al. (Eds.): PRICAI 2022, LNCS 13630, pp. 459–472, 2022.
https://doi.org/10.1007/978-3-031-20865-2_34

retrieval, can no longer meet people's needs. Cross mode retrieval (CMR), which utilizes one modality as the query to retrieve other semantically related modalities, has attracted more and more attention [16], such as image-text retrieval [7].

However, CMR faces a serious challenge of "heterogeneous gap". It comes from the distribution difference among multimodal data, which makes it difficult to measure cross-modal similarity. In order to eliminate the "heterogeneous gap", various methods have been proposed [6]. There are also some hasing-based methods [29] and attention-based methods [8]. The key of these work is to construct a common space, where cross-modal representations can be aligned.

Although the CMR methods have made remarkable success in eliminating the "heterogeneous gap", they are still limited in practical application. Traditional CMR assumes that training data embodies all the categories that may appear during retrieval stage. However, in practical scenarios, people often face the problem that the information they are looking for comes from a new emerging category. In other words, the model has some unseen categories during training, thus it cannot appropriately deal with the data of unseen categories. For example, a robot is trained with multimodal data of "cutting potatoes" and "cutting tomatoes". When it is required to cut beans, the performance is disappointing.

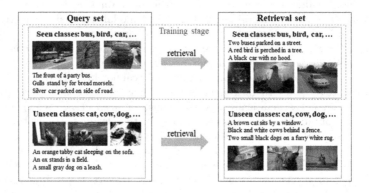

Fig. 1. The scenario of ZS-CMR. Only seen class data are used during training.

Zero-shot learning [11,24] transfers knowledge from known categories to unknown categories. Based on this theory, zero-shot cross-modal retrieval (ZS-CMR) emerges, which makes it possible to deal with multimodal samples of new categories. Figure 1 shows the scenario of ZS-CMR. Recently, scholars consider that a pretrained natural language processing (NLP) model contains human knowledge, because it was trained on a large amount of text information. Therefore, some methods are put forward by utilizing the pretrained model to extract semantic embedding for categories [3]. Some researches [26] further introduce the generative adversarial network (GAN) [10] to construct a common semantic space for multimodal data. Differently, Xu et al [25] adopted GAN to enhance training data, so as to expand the knowledge storage. Consequently, the model can learn more knowledge from synthetic samples.

In spite of the achievements, existing ZS-CMR methods still have the following limitations. (1) The semantic embedding of categories is often simply used to align multimodal embedding. However, the important semantic association between seen and unseen categories is ignored. Therefore, the semantic knowledge cannot be fully transferred from seen classes to unseen classes. (2) Multimodal embedding and category embedding lack semantic interaction, which makes cross-modal representations unable to be semantically aligned. Thus, samples of new categories cannot obtain semantic representations, further leading to unsatisfactory retrieval results.

In this paper, we proposed the semantic-adversarial graph convolutional network (SAGCN) for ZS-CMR. Firstly, to acquire semantic embedding of categories, SAGCN integrates pretrained NLP model with GCN, and mines the potential relationship between seen and unseen categories. Besides, to obtain the semantic-aligned space, SAGCN introduces the adversarial learning and semantic similarity reconstruction, which brings in the semantic interaction between multimodal embedding and category embedding. In addition, a shared classifier is adopted to enhance the discriminant ability of the space. The contributions of this paper are as follows:

- A novel ZS-CMR approach, named SAGCN, is proposed in this paper. To the best of our knowledge, it firstly utilizes GCN to mine the semantic association between seen and unseen categories.
- SAGCN introduces the techniques of adversarial learning and semantic similarity reconstruction, so as to realize the semantic interaction between multimodal embedding and category embedding.
- Extensive experiments and analyses on three data sets illustrate the effectiveness of SAGCN on both traditional CMR and ZS-CMR tasks.

2 Related Work

The main problem in CMR is how to eliminate the "semantic gap" and the "heterogeneous gap" among multimodal data. The widely adopted manner is to utilize the correlation between cross-modal data and learn their common presentations. For example, canonical correlation analysis (CCA) [20] introduces linear transformation matrices to correlate cross-modal data. Cross-modal factor analysis (CFA) [15] minimizes the Frobenius norm of the correlated cross-modal data. Beyond that, joint representation learning (JRL) [31] learns the common representation by taking advantage of the semantic information, and extends the CMR on five kinds of modalities. Along with the development of deep neural networks (DNN), the DNN-based methods become popular. Deep canonical correlation analysis (DCCA) [28] improves the linear CCA by utilizing neural networks. Adversarial cross-modal retrieval (ACMR) [22] uses generative adversarial networks to fuse heterogeneous cross-modal data.

Although these methods can eliminate the "heterogeneous gap" to some extent, they still have some limitations in practical applications. To be specific, when multimodal data of new categories come, the approaches cannot learn appropriate representations for them. That is to say, these methods is not applicable to unseen categories. To tackle this problem, some zero-shot CMR techniques were proposed. Felix et al [9] utilized the attribute information as additional knowledge for zero-shot single-modal and cross-modal retrieval, which can transfer semantic knowledge from seen categories to unseen categories. Then, dual adversarial networks for zero-shot cross-media retrieval (DANZCR) [3] and dual adversarial distribution network (DADN) [4] were proposed. They adopted the category attribute to generate class embedding that was used to learn common semantic space. Xu et al [27] proposed the generative adversarial network (AAEGAN) to construct class embedding. Furthermore, Chakraborty et al [2] applied the attention mechanism to multimodal fusion, thereby solving the ZS-CMR problem. Differently, prototype-based adaptive network (PAN) [30] takes the advantages of prototype learning and adaptive network for this problem. Deep multimodal transfer learning (DMTL) [32] employs a joint learning paradigm to transfer knowledge by assigning a pseudo label to each target sample.

However, they all ignore the semantic associations between seen and unseen categories. Therefore, the semantic knowledge cannot be fully transferred from seen classes to unseen classes. Besides, the semantic interaction between multimodal embedding and category embedding is insufficient, which leads to unsatisfactory representation learning for new-category samples. In this work, we introduce the graph convolution network, adversarial learning, and semantic similarity reconstruction to solve these problems.

3   Proposed Method

3.1   Problem Definition

The goal of ZS-CMR is to learn a semantic space from the multimodal data of seen classes, and appropriately express multimodal data of unseen classes. Without loss of generality, this paper focuses on two modalities, i.e., image and text. Suppose we have the multimodal dataset O with N samples, i.e., $O = \{o_i\}_{i=1}^{N}$. $o_i = \{v_i, t_i, l_i, y_i\}$ is the i-th object in O, where v_i, t_i, l_i and y_i denote its image feature, text feature, class feature and the class label (category), respectively. It should be noted that the feature vectors are obtained by using the pre-trained CNN model and NLP model. In addition, $y_i \in \mathbb{R}^K$ is the one-hot encoding of category, where K represents the number of categories.

For the traditional CMR task, we divide the whole dataset O into a retrieval set O_r and a query set O_q, i.e., $O = \{O_r, O_q\}$. In addition, for the ZS-CMR task, we further divide the categories into seen categories and unseen categories. Assume the category set is $\mathcal{Y} = \{\mathcal{Y}_s, \mathcal{Y}_u\}$, where $\mathcal{Y}_s$ is the seen-class set, $\mathcal{Y}_u$ is the unseen-class set, and $\mathcal{Y}_s \cap \mathcal{Y}_u = \varnothing$. Accordingly, the data partition for ZS-CMR is as follows: $O = \{O_r^s, O_r^u, O_q^s, O_q^u\}$, which respectively represent the seen-class retrieval set, unseen-class retrieval set, seen-class query set and unseen-class query set. O_r^s and O_q^s only contain the categories in $\mathcal{Y}_s$, while O_r^u and O_q^u only contain the categories in $\mathcal{Y}_u$.

One step further, all image features in O_r^s are represented as $V_r^s = [v_j]_{j=1}^{n_r^s}$, where n_r^s is the number of samples in O_r^s. Similarly, all text features are represented as $T_r^s = [t_j]_{j=1}^{n_r^s}$, all label features are represented as $L_r^s = [l_j]_{j=1}^{n_r^s}$, and all classes are represented as $Y_r^s = [y_j]_{j=1}^{n_r^s}$. It should be noted that we only use O_r^s for training. For the traditional CMR task in the test phase, we view O_q^s as queries to retrieve semantically relevant cross-modal instances in O_r^s, symbolized as $O_q^s \rightarrow O_r^s$. While for the ZS-CMR task, we view O_q^u as queries to retrieve O_r^u, symbolized as $O_q^u \rightarrow O_r^u$.

3.2 SAGCN

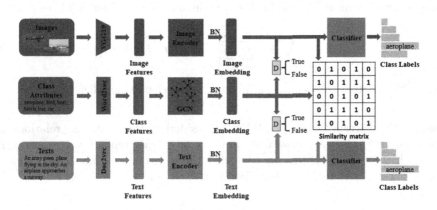

Fig. 2. The framework of SAGCN. For the upper and the lower branches, image and text have their encoders respectively, and the shared classifier ensures the discriminability of multimodal embedding. For the middle branch, GCN is utilized to extract semantic embedding of the classes. Discriminator D determines whether the embedding is the semantic class embedding. Semantic similarity reconstruction further fuses the multimodal embedding with the semantic class embedding.

Model Architecture. The whole framework of SAGCN is illustrated in Fig. 2. As shown, we introduce the class attributes that help the model learn semantic representations. Specifically, there are three branches respectively for images, texts, and class attributes. Pre-trained models are utilized to extract their features. Then after that, two encoders are designed to transform image and text features into the common semantic space. To enhance the discriminant ability of the space, a shared classifier C is designed. For the class features, GCN is brought in to mine category relationships and learn semantic class embedding. Besides, a shared discriminator is adversarial to the encoders. Finally, it makes the model difficult to distinguish the multimodal embedding and the class embedding. Furthermore, enhanced by the semantic similarity reconstruction among three branches, SAGCN can acquire aligned semantic representations. Next, we will describe each module in detail.

Discriminant Regularization. Cross-modal data have different feature representation and distribution. We design two encoders, Enc_v and Enc_t, to transform images V and texts T into the shared space, respectively. Then after the batch normalization operation (BN), we can obtain the corresponding image embedding F_v and the text embedding F_t. The process is formulated as:

$$\begin{cases} F_v = BN(Enc_v(V, \theta_v)); \\ F_t = BN(Enc_t(T, \theta_t)), \end{cases} \tag{1}$$

where θ_v and θ_t represent the parameters of the image encoder and the text encoder respectively. To enhance the discriminant ability of the space, we introduce a shared classifier C that classifies F_v and F_t to correct categories. The cross-entropy term is utilized in this module, and the loss function is as follows:

$$L_{ce} = -\frac{1}{n_r^s} \sum_m^{\{v,t\}} \sum_{i=1}^{n_r^s} \sum_{k=1}^{K} y_{ik} \log\left((C(F_m, \theta_c))_{ik}\right), \tag{2}$$

where θ_c denotes the network parameters of the shared classifier C.

Semantic Extraction by GCN. Considering the semantic relationship between categories, we construct the GCN to extract semantic representation for each category. In detail, we construct the adjacency matrix A for all categories according to their attribute features $Z^{(0)} = [(L_r^s)^T, (L_q^s)^T, (L_r^u)^T, (L_q^u)^T]^T$, i.e.,

$$A_{ij} = \frac{z_i^{(0)} \cdot z_j^{(0)}}{|z_i^{(0)}||z_j^{(0)}|}, \tag{3}$$

where $z_i^{(0)}$ is the i-th row of $Z^{(0)}$. A_{ij} represents the cosine similarity between the i-th class feature and the j-th class feature. After this, the semantic representations of the categories can be calculated by:

$$Z^{(h+1)} = \sigma(\widetilde{D}^{-\frac{1}{2}} \widetilde{A} \widetilde{D}^{-\frac{1}{2}} Z^{(h)} W^{(h)}), \tag{4}$$

where $\widetilde{A} = A + I$, and I is the identity matrix. $\widetilde{D}$ is the degree matrix of A, that is, $\widetilde{D}_{ii} = \sum_j \widetilde{A}_{ij}$. $Z^{(h)}$ is the input class feature matrix of the h-th layer in GCN, and it is initialized as $Z^{(0)}$. $W^{(h)}$ and $Z^{(h+1)}$ are the parameter matrix and the output matrix respectively of the h-th layer. σ is the nonlinear activation function like $Relu(\cdot) = max(0, \cdot)$. By taking the first n_r^s rows of $Z^{(h+1)}$, we obtain the corresponding semantic embedding of categories, denoted as F_l:

$$F_l = Z^{(h+1)}[0 : n_r^s, :]. \tag{5}$$

Adversarial Learning. To fuse heterogeneous multimodal data in the common space, we add a discriminator D, which can be combined with Enc_v and Enc_t to form adversarial relationship. Specifically, image embedding F_v, text embedding

F_t and semantic class embedding F_l are taken as the input of the discriminator D, and it determines whether they are class embedding. During the adversarial learning, discriminator D is trained to distinguish the embedding as much as possible, while the encoders Enc_v and Enc_t are trained to confuse D as much as possible. Therefore, multimodal data can learn semantic embedding that is similar to the class embedding. The adversarial loss function is defined as follows:

$$L_{adv}(\theta_v, \theta_t, \theta_l, \theta_D) = E_{p \sim P_{F_l(p,\theta_l)}}[\log D(p, \theta_D)]$$

$$+ \sum_m^{\{v,t\}} E_{q \sim P_{F_m(q,\theta_m)}}[\log(1 - D(q, \theta_D))], \qquad (6)$$

where θ_v, θ_t, and θ_l are the parameters of Enc_v, Enc_t, and the GCN, respectively. To optimize θ_D, we fix other parameters, and maximize L_{adv} (i.e., minimizing $-L_{adv}$), which enables D to distinguish semantic class embedding from image and text embedding. To optimize θ_v, θ_t, and θ_l, θ_D is fixed, and L_{adv} is minimized to make the encoders deceive the discriminator as much as possible. Finally, the discriminator can hardly distinguish the embedding. Therefore, the multimodal embedding is fused with the semantic class embedding in the common space.

Semantic Similarity Reconstruction. To further fuse the multimodal data in the common space, and preserve the semantic similarity relationship between samples, we propose the cross-modal semantic similarity reconstruction. According to the samples' categories, we construct their similarity matrix S by the following formula.

$$S_{ij} = \begin{cases} 1, & \text{if } l_i = l_j; \\ 0, & \text{otherwise}, \end{cases} \qquad (7)$$

where $l_i = l_j$ means that the i-th object and j-th object have the same category. The similarity matrix is used as supervisory information. It guides the similarity relationship learning among different modalities, i.e., image-text, image-class and text-class. Given the embedding matrices F_{m_1} and F_{m_2} of two modalities, where $m_1, m_2 \in \{v, t, l\}$, and $m_1 \neq m_2$, we would like the cross-modal embedding to reconstruct the similarity matrix. Since Cosine similarity can well describe the similarity of high dimensional vectors, we calculate the similarities between F_{m_1} and F_{m_2} as $cos(F_{m_1}, F_{m_2})$:

$$(\cos(F_{m_1}, F_{m_2}))_{ij} = \frac{F_{m_1 i} \cdot F_{m_2 j}}{|F_{m_1 i}||F_{m_2 j}|}, \qquad (8)$$

where $F_{m_1 i}$ means the i-th sample embedding of F_{m_1}, and $F_{m_2 j}$ means the j-th sample embedding of F_{m_2}. The loss function of this part is formulated as follows:

$$L_{rec} = \sum_{m_1, m_2, m_1 \neq m_2}^{v,t,l} \|\cos(F_{m_1}, F_{m_2}) - S\|_F, \qquad (9)$$

where $\|\cdot\|_F$ is the Frobenius norm.

Overall Objective. After defining the loss function of each module, we get the overall objective function as follows:

$$L_{obj} = L_{ce} \pm \alpha L_{adv} + \beta L_{rec}, \tag{10}$$

where "$\pm$" becomes "$-$" when optimizing the discriminator, and becomes "$+$" when optimizing other network parameters. α and β are the trade-off parameters. The training procedure of SAGCN is summarized in Algorithm 1.

Algorithm 1: SAGCN

Input: Seen-class images, seen-class texts, all classes and the corresponding attributes, batch size n, the number of epochs T.

1 Initialize the network parameters $\theta_v, \theta_t, \theta_l, \theta_c$, and θ_D;
2 Extract features by pre-trained models, and get V_r^s, T_r^s, L, and Y;
3 **for** $epoch = 1$ to T **do**
4 | **for** $i = 1$ to N/n **do**
5 | | Forward-propagate to calculate the overall loss through equation (10);
6 | | Back-propagate to update parameters $\theta_v, \theta_t, \theta_c, \theta_l$, and θ_D;
7 | **end**
8 **end**

Output: The acquired $\theta_v, \theta_t, \theta_c, \theta_l$, and θ_D in SAGCN.

---

4 Experiment

4.1 Experimental Setting

Dataset. To validate the effectiveness of our proposed method, we do experiments on three public datasets, including Wikipedia [20], Pascal Sentences [19] and NUS-WIDE [5]). For fair comparison, the way of data preprocessing and data partition follows the reference [3]. Specifically, we extract the $4,096$-d image features that are the output from the 7th layer of VGG19 [21]. Besides, the Doc2Vec [14] model is utilized to extract the 300-d text features, and the pretrained Word2Vec [17] model is utilized to extract class attribute features.

Implemental Details. For our network architecture, the image encoder and the text encoder contain three fully-connected layers with dimensions [4096, 4096, K_*], where K_* is the dimension of the common space. Each fully connected layer is activated by Relu. Batch normalization (BN) and dropout are adopted after Relu except the last layer. The GCN module is a three-layer graph convolutional network with dimensions [1024, 1024, K_*]. Similar to the encoders, each layer is activated by Relu, followed by BN and dropout except the last layer. The discriminator includes three fully-connected layers with dimensions [4096, 2048, 1], and all layers are activated by Relu. The fc1 and fc2 in discriminator are followed by BN and dropout. As for the classifier, we built it with three fully-connected layers with dimensions [4096, 4096, K_m], where K_m is the number of seen categories. Note that only fc1 and fc2 are activated by Relu followed by BN, while fc3 is activated by the softmax function. The Adam optimizer is applied to each module for back-propagation. The initial learning rate is set to 0.0001, and "MultiStepLR" is selected as the learning rate decay strategy. The batch size is set to 64, and the model is implemented on Pytorch [18].

Evaluation Details. In this paper, we evaluate SAGCN on two kinds of tasks, i.e., traditional CMR and ZS-CMR. Traditional CMR includes two subtasks of image-to-text retrieval (I2T) on seen classes and text-to-image retrieval (T2I) on seen classes. Similarly, ZS-CMR also includes two subtasks of image-to-text retrieval on unseen classes and text-to-image retrieval on unseen classes, as mentioned in Sect. 3.1.

We select twelve methods as baselines, and among the comparison methods, DANZCR [3], DADN [4], and DMTL [32] were proposed for ZS-CMR, and others were proposed for traditional CMR. Besides, CCA [20], JRL [31], CFA [15], KCCA [1] and LGCFL [12] are shallow methods, while others are deep methods.

As for the evaluation metric, we adopt the mean average precision (MAP), because it takes into account not only the precision, but also the ranking information. Concretely, the average precision (AP) scores of all queries w.r.t. all returned results are firstly calculated. Then, MAP is the mean of the APs.

4.2   Overall Results

Zero-Shot CMR. Table 1 shows the ZS-CMR results of the proposed SAGCN and other methods. From the table, we have the following observations.

- Compared with shallow methods, deep ones usually obtain better results, showing that deep models have stronger learning ability than shallow ones.
- Different from the traditional methods, DANZCR, DADN, DMTL, and SAGCN are particularly designed for ZS-CMR with obviously higher results.
- SAGCN acquires the best MAP scores on the two small data sets. Specifically, it increases the second best results by 18.8% and 3.7% on the Pascal Sentence dataset and the Wikipedia dataset respectively. The advantage comes from its full use of the semantic information, i.e., mining the semantic relationship by GCN, adversarial learning, and cross-modal semantic similarity reconstruction. It enables knowledge to be transfered from known categories to unknown categories.
- SAGCN does not obtain the best retrieval performance on the NUS-WIDE dataset. Because NUS-WIDE is a huge multi-label dataset, the large amount of categories and the multi-label property make SAGCN excessively construct the semantic relationship.

Table 1. The MAP results of SAGCN and other methods for zero-shot cross-modal retrieval. Best results are highlighted in bold.

Methods	Pascal sentences			Wikipedia			NUS-WIDE		
	I2T	T2I	Avg.	I2T	T2I	Avg.	I2T	T2I	Avg.
CCA [20]	0.207	0.183	0.195	0.238	0.236	0.237	0.400	0.397	0.399
CFA [15]	0.270	0.294	0.282	0.275	0.285	0.280	0.410	0.355	0.383
KCCA [1]	0.310	0.321	0.316	0.279	0.288	0.284	0.402	0.413	0.408
DCCA [28]	0.297	0.264	0.281	0.282	0.266	0.274	0.406	0.407	0.407
JRL [31]	0.298	0.283	0.291	0.264	0.266	0.265	0.401	0.449	0.425
LGCFL [12]	0.273	0.258	0.266	0.261	0.258	0.260	0.396	0.422	0.409
SAE [13]	0.302	0.220	0.261	0.301	0.234	0.268	0.400	0.464	0.432
ACMR [22]	0.306	0.291	0.299	0.276	0.262	0.269	0.407	0.425	0.416
Deep-SM [23]	0.276	0.251	0.264	0.265	0.258	0.262	0.401	0.414	0.408
DANZCR [3]	0.334	0.338	0.336	0.297	0.287	0.292	0.416	0.469	0.443
DADN [4]	0.359	0.353	0.356	0.305	0.291	0.298	0.423	0.472	0.448
DMTL [32]	0.359	0.363	0.361	0.306	0.297	0.301	**0.572**	**0.576**	**0.574**
SAGCN	**0.421**	**0.436**	**0.429**	**0.322**	**0.302**	**0.312**	0.423	0.447	0.435

Table 2. The MAP results of SAGCN and other methods for traditional cross-modal retrieval. Best results are highlighted in bold.

Methods	Pascal sentences			Wikipedia			NUS-WIDE		
	I2T	T2I	Avg.	I2T	T2I	Avg.	I2T	T2I	Avg.
CCA [20]	0.214	0.183	0.199	0.261	0.267	0.264	0.432	0.438	0.435
CFA [15]	0.594	0.590	0.592	0.464	0.457	0.461	0.466	0.475	0.471
KCCA [1]	0.493	0.497	0.495	0.421	0.520	0.471	0.423	0.482	0.453
DCCA [28]	0.511	0.507	0.509	0.448	0.446	0.447	0.428	0.430	0.429
JRL [31]	0.636	0.677	0.657	0.522	0.604	0.563	0.480	0.616	0.548
LGCFL [12]	0.592	0.638	0.615	0.510	0.586	0.548	0.459	0.529	0.494
SAE [13]	0.670	0.827	0.749	0.574	0.841	0.708	0.483	0.600	0.542
ACMR [22]	0.726	0.756	0.741	0.674	0.863	0.769	0.604	0.702	0.653
Deep-SM [23]	0.728	0.841	0.785	0.674	0.872	0.773	0.680	0.667	0.674
DANZCR [3]	0.737	0.868	0.803	0.672	0.887	0.780	0.727	0.709	0.718
DADN [4]	0.748	0.878	0.813	0.677	0.892	0.785	0.732	0.712	0.722
DMTL [32]	–	–	–	–	–	–	–	–	–
SAGCN	**0.840**	**0.880**	**0.860**	**0.687**	**0.895**	**0.791**	**0.846**	**0.833**	**0.840**

Table 3. Ablation study of SAGCN on the Pascal Sentences and Wikipedia data sets.

Methods	Pascal sentences			Wikipedia		
	I2T	T2I	Ave.	I2T	T2I	Ave.
SAGCN (without L_{ce})	**0.427**	0.399	0.413	**0.324**	0.293	0.309
SAGCN (without L_{rec})	0.327	0.305	0.316	0.267	0.266	0.267
SAGCN (without L_{adv})	0.422	0.418	0.415	0.323	0.298	0.311
SAGCN	0.421	**0.436**	**0.429**	0.322	**0.302**	**0.312**

Traditional CMR. To more comprehensively evaluate the performance of our proposed model, we also tested the model on traditional CMR tasks, and the comparison results are shown in Table 2. From the results shown in the table, we have the following findings.

- Compared with the ZS-CMR tasks, traditional CMR tasks obtain significantly higher retrieval results. This indicates the difficulty of ZS-CMR.
- On traditional CMR tasks, the ZS-CMR methods still achieve higher MAP scores than the traditional CMR methods, which is beyond our expectation. The reason may be that ZS-CMR methods further consider the semantic information based on the traditional ones.
- SAGCN gets the best results on all data sets. Specifically, it exceeds the second best method (DADN) by 5.8%, 0.8%, and 16.3% respectively on the Pascal Sentence dataset, Wikipedia dataset, and the NUS-WIDE dataset.

4.3 Further Analysis

Ablation Study. To study the effect of each module in SAGCN, we designed three variants of the model by discarding each module separately, and compared SAGCN with its variations. The comparison results on the Pascal Sentences and Wikipedia data sets are shown in Table 3. According to Table 3, we can see that:

- When the semantic similarity reconstruction module is discarded (i.e., SAGCN without L_{rec}), the performance significantly decreases. This module is used for cross-modal semantic similarity reconstruction, which not only enables embedding to preserve semantic information, but also fuses multimodal data in the common space. Therefore, this part plays a necessary role.
- Giving up the discriminator or the adversarial learning (i.e., SAGCN without L_{adv}), the performance is also negatively affected because of the loss of multimodal fusion. However, the effect is not remarkable since the L_{rec} term also tries to achieve this goal, and they have some overlap.
- Abandoning the discrimination regularization (i.e., SAGCN without L_{ce}) causes a slight decline of the performance. It indicates that the discrimination regularization module also plays an important role, since it is responsible to enhance the discriminant ability of the embedding.

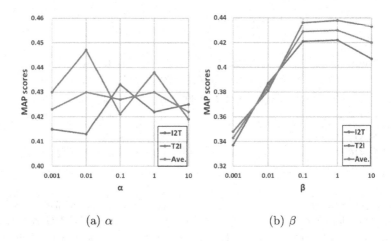

(a) α (b) β

Fig. 3. MAP scores versus the parameters on the Pascal Sentence dataset.

Parameter Sensitivity. There are two trade-off parameters in the final objective of SAGCN, i.e., α and β. In this part, we discuss the sensitivity to these parameters. Figure 3 shows the MAP variation along with the parameters on the Pascal Sentence dataset. The range of the two parameters are set to $[0.001, 10]$. To be fair, when discussing one, the other one is fixed. From the figure, we find that the MAP score does not vary a lot with the change of α, which means SAGCN is not sensitive to α. Comparatively, the change of β brings in obvious difference of the MAP score. On one hand, this phenomenon illustrates that SAGCN is sensitive to β. On the other hand, β controls the semantic similarity reconstruction term. When β varys from a small value to a high value, the MAP score rises, which shows the significance of this term.

5 Conclusion

In this paper, we proposed a novel ZS-CMR method, named SAGCN. It is composed of an image encoder, a text encoder, a GCN, a discriminator, and a classifier. The GCN mines the potential relationship between seen and unseen categories, thus learning more appropriate class embedding. Besides, we consider the image encoder, text encoder, and the GCN as a whole encoder. Based on adversarial learning, we semantically fused the multimodal embedding and the class embedding. Additionally, the proposed semantic similarity reconstruction term can further fuse these embedding. Finally, the shared classifier enhanced the discriminant ability of the embedding space. Extensive experiments illustrated the effectiveness of SAGCN on both traditional CMR and ZS-CMR tasks.

Acknowledgements. This work is supported in part by the Key-Area Research and Development Program of Guangdong Province under Grant 2020B010166006, in part by the National Natural Science Foundation of China under Grant 62176065, 62176066,

62202107, and 61972102, and in part by the Natural Science Foundation of Guangdong Province under Grant 2019A1515011811 and 2021A1515012017.

References

1. Ballan, L., Uricchio, T., Seidenari, L., Del Bimbo, A.: A cross-media model for automatic image annotation. In: Proceedings of International Conference on Multimedia Retrieval, pp. 73–80 (2014)
2. Chakraborty, B., Wang, P., Wang, L.: Inter-modality fusion based attention for zero-shot cross-modal retrieval. In: 2021 IEEE International Conference on Image Processing (ICIP), pp. 2648–2652. IEEE (2021)
3. Chi, J., Peng, Y.: Dual adversarial networks for zero-shot cross-media retrieval. In: Proceedings of the International Joint Conference on Artificial Intelligence, pp. 663–669 (2018)
4. Chi, J., Peng, Y.: Zero-shot cross-media embedding learning with dual adversarial distribution network. IEEE Trans. Circ. Syst. Video Technol. **30**(4), 1173–1187 (2019)
5. Chua, T.S., Tang, J., Hong, R., Li, H., Luo, Z., Zheng, Y.: Nus-wide: a real-world web image database from national university of singapore. In: Proceedings of the ACM International Conference on Image and Video Retrieval, pp. 1–9 (2009)
6. Chun, S., Oh, S.J., De Rezende, R.S., Kalantidis, Y., Larlus, D.: Probabilistic embeddings for cross-modal retrieval. In: Proceedings of the IEEE/CVF Conference on Computer Vision and Pattern Recognition, pp. 8415–8424 (2021)
7. Diao, H., Zhang, Y., Ma, L., Lu, H.: Similarity reasoning and filtration for image-text matching. arXiv preprint arXiv:2101.01368 (2021)
8. Dong, X., Zhang, H., Dong, X., Lu, X.: Iterative graph attention memory network for cross-modal retrieval. Knowl.-Based Syst. **226**, 107138 (2021)
9. Felix, R., Vijay Kumar, B.G., Reid, I., Carneiro, G.: Multi-modal cycle-consistent generalized zero-shot learning. In: Ferrari, V., Hebert, M., Sminchisescu, C., Weiss, Y. (eds.) ECCV 2018. LNCS, vol. 11210, pp. 21–37. Springer, Cham (2018). https://doi.org/10.1007/978-3-030-01231-1_2
10. Goodfellow, I., et al.: Generative adversarial nets. Adv. Neural Inf. Process. Syst. **27** (2014)
11. Han, Z., Fu, Z., Chen, S., Yang, J.: Contrastive embedding for generalized zero-shot learning. In: Proceedings of the IEEE/CVF Conference on Computer Vision and Pattern Recognition, pp. 2371–2381 (2021)
12. Kang, C., Xiang, S., Liao, S., Xu, C., Pan, C.: Learning consistent feature representation for cross-modal multimedia retrieval. IEEE Trans. Multimedia **17**(3), 370–381 (2015)
13. Kodirov, E., Xiang, T., Gong, S.: Semantic autoencoder for zero-shot learning. In: Proceedings of the IEEE/CVF Conference on Computer Vision and Pattern Recognition, pp. 3174–3183 (2017)
14. Le, Q., Mikolov, T.: Distributed representations of sentences and documents. In: International Conference on Machine Learning, pp. 1188–1196. PMLR (2014)
15. Li, D., Dimitrova, N., Li, M., Sethi, I.K.: Multimedia content processing through cross-modal association. In: Proceedings of the Eleventh ACM International Conference on Multimedia, pp. 604–611 (2003)
16. Liu, S., Fan, H., Qian, S., Chen, Y., Ding, W., Wang, Z.: Hit: hierarchical transformer with momentum contrast for video-text retrieval. In: Proceedings of the IEEE/CVF International Conference on Computer Vision, pp. 11915–11925 (2021)

17. Mikolov, T., Chen, K., Corrado, G., Dean, J.: Efficient estimation of word representations in vector space. arXiv preprint arXiv:1301.3781 (2013)
18. Paszke, A., et al.: Pytorch: an imperative style, high-performance deep learning library. Adv. Neural Inf. Process. Syst. **32** (2019)
19. Rashtchian, C., Young, P., Hodosh, M., Hockenmaier, J.: Collecting image annotations using amazon's mechanical turk. In: Proceedings of the NAACL HLT 2010 workshop on creating speech and language data with Amazon's Mechanical Turk, pp. 139–147 (2010)
20. Rasiwasia, N., et al.: A new approach to cross-modal multimedia retrieval. In: Proceedings of the 18th ACM International Conference on Multimedia, pp. 251–260 (2010)
21. Simonyan, K., Zisserman, A.: Very deep convolutional networks for large-scale image recognition. arXiv preprint arXiv:1409.1556 (2014)
22. Wang, B., Yang, Y., Xu, X., Hanjalic, A., Shen, H.T.: Adversarial cross-modal retrieval. In: Proceedings of the ACM International Conference on Multimedia, pp. 154–162 (2017)
23. Wei, Y., et al.: Cross-modal retrieval with cnn visual features: a new baseline. IEEE Trans. Cybern. **47**(2), 449–460 (2016)
24. Xu, W., Xian, Y., Wang, J., Schiele, B., Akata, Z.: Attribute prototype network for zero-shot learning. Adv. Neural Inf. Process. Syst. **33**, 21969–21980 (2020)
25. Xu, X., Lin, K., Lu, H., Gao, L., Shen, H.T.: Correlated features synthesis and alignment for zero-shot cross-modal retrieval. In: Proceedings of the International ACM SIGIR Conference on Research and Development in Information Retrieval, pp. 1419–1428 (2020)
26. Xu, X., Song, J., Lu, H., Yang, Y., Shen, F., Huang, Z.: Modal-adversarial semantic learning network for extendable cross-modal retrieval. In: Proceedings of the ACM International Conference on Multimedia Retrieval, pp. 46–54 (2018)
27. Xu, X., Tian, J., Lin, K., Lu, H., Shao, J., Shen, H.T.: Zero-shot cross-modal retrieval by assembling autoencoder and generative adversarial network. ACM Trans. Multimedia Comput. Commun. Appl. (TOMM) **17**(1s), 1–17 (2021)
28. Yan, F., Mikolajczyk, K.: Deep correlation for matching images and text. In: Proceedings of the IEEE Conference on Computer Vision and Pattern Recognition, pp. 3441–3450 (2015)
29. Yang, Z., et al.: Nsdh: a nonlinear supervised discrete hashing framework for large-scale cross-modal retrieval. Knowl.-Based Syst. **217**, 106818 (2021)
30. Zeng, Z., Wang, S., Xu, N., Mao, W.: Pan: prototype-based adaptive network for robust cross-modal retrieval. In: Proceedings of the 44th International ACM SIGIR Conference on Research and Development in Information Retrieval, pp. 1125–1134 (2021)
31. Zhai, X., Peng, Y., Xiao, J.: Learning cross-media joint representation with sparse and semisupervised regularization. IEEE Trans. Circ. Syst. Video Technol. **24**(6), 965–978 (2013)
32. Zhen, L., Hu, P., Peng, X., Goh, R.S.M., Zhou, J.T.: Deep multimodal transfer learning for cross-modal retrieval. IEEE Trans. Neural Netw. Learn. Syst. **33**(2) (2022)

DAST: Depth-Aware Assessment and Synthesis Transformer for RGB-D Salient Object Detection

Chenxing Xia[1], Songsong Duan[1(✉)], Xianjin Fang[1], Bin Ge[1], Xiuju Gao[1], and Jianhua Cui[2]

[1] Anhui University of Science and Technology, Huainan, Anhui, China
cxxia@aust.edu.cn, 1440377954@qq.com
[2] Anyang Cigarette Factory, China Tobacco Henan Industrial Co., Ltd., Anyang, Henan, China

Abstract. The introduction and popularity of depth maps have brought new vitality and growth into salient object detection (SOD), and plentiful RGB-D SOD methods have been proposed, which mainly focus on how to utilize and integrate the depth map. Although existing methods have achieved promising performance, the negative effects of low-quality depth maps have not been effectively addressed. In this paper, we solve the problem with a strategy of judging low-quality depth maps and assigning low factors to low-quality depth maps. To this end, we proposed a novel Transformer-based SOD framework, namely Depth-aware Assessment and Synthesis Transformer (DAST), to further improve the performance of RGB-D SOD. The proposed DAST involves two primary designs: 1) a Swin Transformer-based encoder is employed instead of a convolutional neural network for more effective feature extraction and long-range dependencies capture; 2) a Depth Assessment and Synthesis (DAS) module is proposed to judge the quality of depth maps and fuse the multi-modality salient features by computing the difference of saliency maps from RGB and depth streams in a coarse-to-fine manner. Extensive experiments on five benchmark datasets demonstrate that the proposed DAST achieves favorable performance as compared with other state-of-the-art (SOTA) methods.

Keywords: Salient object detection · Swin transformer · Low-quality · Depth map · Assessment and synthesis

1 Introduction

Salient object detection (SOD) is a fundamental and important task in computer vision. The purpose of SOD is to highlight and segment the most distinctive objects or regions in a given scene. It has been applied to many other computer vision tasks, such as image retrieval [6] and visual tracking [32].

© The Author(s), under exclusive license to Springer Nature Switzerland AG 2022
S. Khanna et al. (Eds.): PRICAI 2022, LNCS 13630, pp. 473–487, 2022.
https://doi.org/10.1007/978-3-031-20865-2_35

In the past, most SOD methods only focus on RGB images. Although RGB-based SOD methods have achieved significant results due to the advance of Convolutional Neural Network (CNN), challenges still remain in dealing with complex scenes, for instance, low-contrast, confused background, transparent objects, and multi-object scenes. With the popularity of depth sensors, such as smartphones and digital cameras, the acquisition and collection of depth maps have become growing convenient. In this situation, depth maps are introduced into the field of SOD, known as RGB-D SOD. Different from RGB images, depth maps can offer additional cues to obtain the spatial structure and 3D layout. The participation of depth maps for the SOD task is hopeful of salving some thorny issues. As shown in Fig. 1, RGB-D methods achieve better performance than RGB methods in terms of a complex scene, where the salient objects and their surroundings are low-contrasts.

Unfortunately, low-quality depth maps are usually mixed with noise and redundancy information, which may lead to negative interference for detecting salient objects. It is a pity that most early algorithms ignore the quality of depth maps, leading to suboptimal performance.

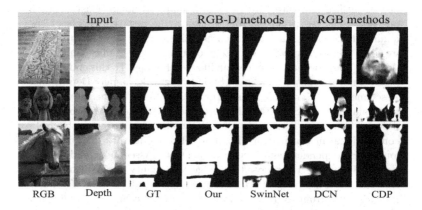

Fig. 1. Visual comparison of RGB-D methods and RGB methods for SOD, which can reflect the role of depth cues. The compared methods are SwinNet [19] and our method for RGB-D methods while DCN [30] and CPD [29] for RGB methods.

Recently, some works [13,27,31] have started paying attention to the qualities of the input for saliency detection, especially the quality of depth maps. These methods mainly adopt two strategies to tackle low-quality depth issues: 1) depth estimation techniques are employed to generate pseudo depth maps; 2) adaptive or dynamic mechanisms are adopted to selectively fuse multi-modality features. However, the two strategies have several problems. On the one hand, the depth estimation process is time-consuming and may not produce a high-quality depth map, which may be inferior to the original depth map. Meanwhile, the adaptive or dynamic fusion mechanisms mainly focus on the complementarity among different modalities, resulting in the inability to effectively confirm the quality of depth maps.

To address the aforementioned issues, we proposed a novel and concise RGB-D SOD method, namely depth-aware assessment and synthesis transformer (DAST). The core of our method contains two key units: 1) pure Swin Transformer-based backbone for extracting multi-modality features; 2) depth-aware assessment and synthesis (DAS) module for fusing RGB and depth features through computing weights of depth maps. Unlike most existing RGB-D SOD methods that used CNN (e.g., VGG16, ResNet, and Inception) to capture RGB and depth features, we leverage the Swin Transformer as the encoder to extract the multi-modality features from RGB and depth images. There are two reasons to use the Swin Transformer: (1) Swin Transformer is able to capture long-range dependencies for better saliency reasoning; (2) Swin Transformer is specially designed Transformer architecture for image processing field, which can be well migrated to the SOD task. To assess the role of the depth maps, we instinctively intend to compute a weighting factor, which is used to measure the degree of importance for depth maps. To this end, we compute the difference of the two-modality features in multiple scales to generate the weighting factor, then generate an attention mask by the weighting factor to tell which regions to pay attention to. Finally, to integrate multi-scale features, we design a feature aggregation (FA) module to fuse two-scale features by an up-sample operation.

Overall, the main contributions of our work include:

- We propose a novel depth-aware assessment and synthesis transformer (DAST), which adopts two Swin Transformers as backbones to extract multi-modality features due to the capture ability of long-range dependencies.
- We present a depth-aware assessment and synthesis (DAS) module to assess the quality of depth maps by formulating a weighting factor and an attention mask. The former measures whether the quality of the depth map is good while the latter tells the model which regions to pay attention to in features.
- We conduct comprehensive experiments on five RGB-D SOD datasets, including quantitative analysis and visual comparison, proving that the proposed DAST outperforms other state-of-the-art RGB-D SOD methods.

2   Related Work

Our method designs a Depth-aware Assessment and Synthesis Network based on Transformer for RGB-D SOD, which mainly contains three aspects of works: RGB-D SOD, Depth-aware RGB-D SOD, and Transformer. Next, we introduce the related work from the three aspects.

RGB-D Salient Object Detection: Early RGB-D SOD methods mainly focused on the fusion of multi-modality features, and a massive of algorithms and models [3,10,15,16,37] were designed to implement the fusion. Chen et al. [3] proposed a disentangled cross-modal fusion network to explore structural and content representations of both modalities by cross-modal reconstruction. Li *et al.* [15] designed an information conversion mechanism to capture the complex correlation between the RGB and depth images via a siamese network structure with shared weights. Huang *et al.* [10] exploited the cross-modal features from the RGB-D images and the unimodal features from the input RGB and depth images for saliency detection. Zhao *et al.* [37] proposed a Bilateral attention network (BiANet) for RGB-D SOD via exploring salient information from the background and foreground. In recent years, thanks to advances in deep learning, a crowd of significant technologies, like attention mechanism [16], neural architecture search [24], and 3D convolutional neural networks [4] have been applied to saliency detection and achieved remarkable performance.

Depth-Aware RGB-D Salient Object Detection: Since depth quality usually affects the performance of the RGB-D SOD model, some researchers have considered the depth quality issue in RGB-D SOD, devoting to alleviating the negative impact of low-quality depth. As an attempt, some works proposed to conduct depth estimation from RGB images and obtain a pseudo depth map. Xiao *et al.* [31] firstly adopted the depth estimation method to generate a pseudo depth map, which was used to take place the original depth maps. Jin *et al.* [13] adaptively fused the original depth maps and estimation depth maps obtained by depth estimation technology to generate depth features. In recent years, some researchers adopted an adoptive or dynamic manner to selectively fusion RGB and depth modalities. Wen *et al.* [27] designed a dynamic selective module (DSM) to dynamically mine the cross-modal complementary information between RGB images and depth maps. Different from the above existing two strategies, our method adopts a depth quality assessment manner to solve the low-quality issue by measuring multi-modality differences, which is more efficient and suitable to reduce the effect of low-quality depth maps.

Transformer: Due to the emergence and advance of the self-attention mechanism [25], Transformer can effectively capture the long-range dependencies and extract global context information. In recent years, Transformer has shown powerful advantages over the convolutional neural network (CNN) in various computer vision downstream tasks, like image classification, object detection, image segmentation, and visual tracking. For instance, DETR [2] employed Transformer to the field of object detection and achieved SOTA performance. ViT [7] first use the patch embedding technology to achieve efficient classification results on computer vision. SETR [39] adopted a pure Transformer as the encoder, combined with a simple decoder, to achieve a powerful semantic segmentation model. To effective feature extraction, Swin Transformer [18] proposed a shifted window-based multi-head attention to reduce the computational complexity, and obtained marvelous performance for dense prediction tasks. Due to its significant superiority, Swin Transformer is used as the backbone network of our method.

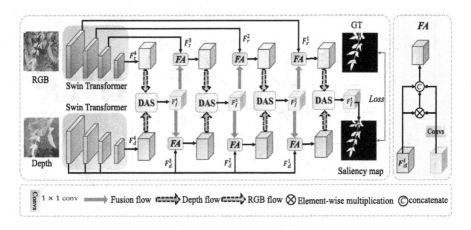

Fig. 2. Overview architecture of the proposed method.

3 Methodology

3.1 Overview

The overview architecture of the proposed DAST is illustrated in Fig. 2, which consists of a two-stream Swin Transformer encoder, depth-aware assessment and synthesis (DAS), and decoder with feature aggregation (FA). Overall, the proposed DAST adopts an end-to-end structure for saliency reasoning. On the encoder stage, we adopt Swin Transformer [18] to extract the RGB features $\{F_r^i\}_{i=1}^4$ and depth features $\{F_d^i\}_{i=1}^4$, where r and d present the RGB and depth branches, and i indicates the ith level on the encoder. On the decoder stage, DAS fuses the multi-modality features ($\{F_r^i\}_{i=1}^4$ and $\{F_d^i\}_{i=1}^4$) through the calculated weighting factor and attention mask to achieve the fused feature $\{F_f^i\}_{i=1}^4$. Next, the fused features $\{F_f^i\}_{i=1}^4$ are embedded into the FA module to integrate multi-scale features. The details can be seen in the following sections.

3.2 Two-Stream Swin Transformer Encoder

We adopt the Swin Transformer [18] to generate multi-scale features with hierarchical scales at four stages, starting with small-sized image patches and gradually merging neighboring patches in deeper layers. In the first stage, the shape of the input is $H \times W \times 3$, which is partitioned into non-overlapping patches of size 4×4. A linear embedding layer is then employed to project this raw-valued feature into an arbitrary dimension (denoted as C), respectively. Then, forming features in a shape of $(H/4 \times W/4 \times C)$, where H and W indicate the height and width of the input. Similar to the first stage, a sequence of Swin Transformer blocks is applied to the merged patches at each following stage, while keeping the number of tokens unchanged. As a result, the following three features are produced by Swin Transformer with the hierarchical shapes $(H/8 \times W/8 \times 2C)$, $(H/16 \times W/16 \times 4C)$, and $(H/32 \times W/32 \times 8C)$.

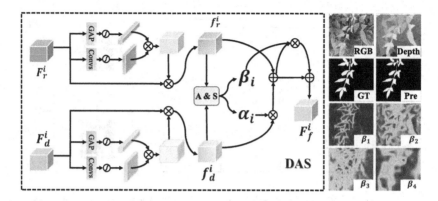

Fig. 3. The structure of the DAS. GAP means global average pooling operation; $\otimes$ and $\oplus$ are element-wise addition and element-wise multiplication, respectively. The right is the visualization of attention masks $\{\beta_i\}_{i=1}^{4}$ in our method.

3.3 Depth-Aware Assessment and Synthesis (DAS)

As shown in Fig. 3, the core of the DAS is to evaluate the quality of depth map and synthesis of the attention mask to further improve the performance of the SOD model. The former tells whether the depth quality is good or not while the latter highlights which regions to pay attention to. Concretely, the DAS contains three key stages, including channel-spatial attention feature enhancement, depth-aware assessment and synthesis, and quality-aware multi-modality fusion.

Channel-Spatial Attention Feature Enhancement: Considering the difference in information representation between RGB and depth features, we elaborate on the enhancement process for RGB and depth features by leveraging channel-spatial attention [28]. As we all know, RGB image shows more appearance, color, and texture cues while depth map usually exhibits spatial information and 3D layout. The existing difference between the two modalities demands the SOD model to distinguish the importance of channels and emphasize their respective salient content. Therefore, spatial attention and channel attention are jointly adopted to implement this purpose.

Specifically, given the RGB feature F_r^i and depth feature F_d^i at i^{th} level, we compute the spatial and channel attention maps, which can be defined as follows:

$$CA_t^i = Sigmoid(GAP(F_t^i)), \tag{1}$$

$$SA_t^i = Sigmoid(Conv_s(F_t^i)), \tag{2}$$

where $t \in \{r, d\}$, $i \in \{1, 2, 3, 4\}$, CA_t^i and SA_t^i present the channel and spatial attention maps at i^{th} level. GAP means global average pooling operation and $Conv_s$ indicates a 1×1 convolution operation.

Different from previous works [19,28], our method adopts a parallel manner to integrate the outputs of the two attention modules instead of a serial way.

The rationale behind this is that the parallel channel-spatial attention can focus on channel and spatial significant cues at the same time, which bring new performance gains for SOD. Next, we combine the original features and attention maps to obtain the enhanced features, which can be described as follows:

$$f_t^i = F_t^i \times (CA_t^i \times SA_t^i), \tag{3}$$

where $t \in \{r, d\}$, f_t^i is the feature enhanced by channel-spatial attention.

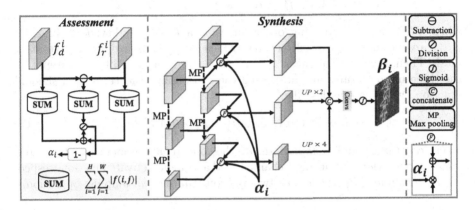

Fig. 4. The architecture of the Assessment and Synthesis. "1−" means 1 subtract the input of the equation.

Depth-Aware Assessment and Synthesis: As shown in Fig. 4, we design an Assessment and Synthesis (A&S) mechanism to compute a weighting factor and an attention mask, which is used to judge whether the depth quality is positive or negative and decide which regions to pay attention to, respectively.

Firstly, we introduce an assessment process. To effectively compute the weighting factor, we adopt a simple subtraction operation to calculate the difference between enhanced RGB and depth features. The motivation of this operation is that high-quality RGB images and depth maps should be consistent and possess similar salient features [12,16,36]. Hence, we use a simple subtraction operation to generate the absolute discrepancy of the two-modality features at the pixel level. Then, the weighting factor α_i can be achieved by dividing the obtained discrepancy by the absolute sum of pixel values from the multi-modality features, which can be formulated as:

$$S_{rd}^i = Conv_t(f_r^i) - Conv_t(f_d^i), \tag{4}$$

$$\alpha_i = 1 - \frac{SUM(S_{rd}^i)}{SUM(f_r^i) + SUM(f_d^i)}, \tag{5}$$

where $SUM(f) = \sum_{i=1}^{W} \sum_{j=1}^{H} (|f(i,j)|)$, $|\cdot|$ means the absolute value operation, H and W are the height and width of feature f, respectively. $Conv_t$ indicates the 3×3 convolution operation. The α_i means the generated weighting factor in i^{th} level.

Secondly, we leverage the α_i to generate the attention mask. In the processing of synthesis, we use the max-pooling operation to capture the salient information, which can be defined as:

$$\begin{cases} Att_k^i = f_r^i + \alpha_i \times f_d^i, & k = 1 \\ Att_k^i = MP_k(f_r^i) + \alpha_i \times MP_k(f_d^i), & k \in \{2,4\} \end{cases} \tag{6}$$

where MP_k is a max-pooling operation with a $k \times k$ window; $k \in \{1,2,4\}$; Att_k^i presents obtained fused features, which is used to generate an attention mask. Then, the attention mask β_i at i^{th} level can be achieved by concatenating the three fused features and activating the concatenated features by a sigmoid function, which can be described as:

$$\beta_i = Sigmoid(Conv1(cat(Att_1^i, UP_2(Att_2^i), UP_4(Att_4^i)))), \tag{7}$$

where cat, $Conv1$, and $Sigmoid$ indicate the concatenation operation, 1×1 convolution operation with a single channel, and a sigmoid activate function, respectively; UP_2 and UP_4 present the two and four times of upsampling operation.

Quality-Aware Multi-Modality Fusion: Next, we fuse RGB and depth features in a quality-aware manner through the weighting factor α_i and the attention mask β_i. A residual connection is adopted to integrate the original features. The fusion can be formulated as:

$$f_i = f_r^i + \alpha_i \times f_d^i, \tag{8}$$

$$F_f^i = f_i + \beta_i \times f_i, \tag{9}$$

where α_i and β_i mean the weighting factor and attention mask, respectively. F_f^i is the fused feature in a quality-aware manner. As shown in the right part of Fig. 3, we display some visualization graphic of the attention mask β_i, which can observably highlight the salient objects of the scene from visual view.

3.4   Decoder with Feature Aggregation (FA)

In the decoder section, we employ a top-down progressive aggregation way to integrate the multi-scale features for saliency prediction. First, the fused feature F_f^4 from the top-level is embedded into the next level. Note that the fused features with multi-modality information flow to RGB and depth branches, respectively. Then, a feature aggregation (FA) module is designed to integrate the two-scale features, which can be described as:

$$\begin{cases} D_t^i = F_t^i, & i = 4 \\ D_t^i = cat(F_t^i, UP(Conv_s(F_f^i)), F_t^i \times UP(Conv_s(F_f^i))), i \in \{1,2,3\} \end{cases} \tag{10}$$

where $t \in \{r, d\}$, UP is the up-sample operation, D_r^i and D_d^i are encoder features from RGB and depth branches, respectively. At the top-level, the RGB F_r^4 and depth feature F_d^4 are directly deemed as decoder feature D_r^4 and D_d^4 without multi-scale feature integration. In the remaining layers, the multi-modality fused features are integrated in a top-down progressive manner. Finally, we activate the F_f^1 by a sigmoid function to generate the saliency prediction P.

3.5 Loss Function

Similar to works [33, 36], we adopt the binary cross-entropy (BCE) to train our network, which is a universal loss function in the SOD tasks, defined as:

$$L_{bce} = \frac{1}{H \times W} \sum_h^H \sum_w^W [g \log p + (1 - g) \log (1 - p)], \tag{11}$$

where $P = \{p | 0 < p < 1\} \in R^{1 \times H \times W}$ and $G = \{g | 0, 1\} \in R^{1 \times H \times W}$ represent the predicted value and the corresponding ground truth, respectively. H and W represent the height and width of the input, respectively. L_{bce} calculates the error between the ground truth G and the predicted P for each pixel.

Table 1. Quantitative comparisons of the proposed method against the other 19 state-of-the-art RGB-D SOD methods. ↑/↓ indicates that a larger/smaller is better. The top three results are highlighted in red, **blue**, and green, respectively.

Dataset	Metric	SSF	UCNet	CoNet	DANet	D3Net	SMEG	BiANet	CCAF	DSNet	DCFNet	DSA2F	CDINet	DFMNet	RD3D	SwinNet	VST	DAST
		2020	2020	2020	2020	2020	2021	2021	2021	2021	2021	2021	2021	2021	2021	2022	2021	Ours
		CVPR	CVPR	ECCV	ECCV	TNNLS	NP	TIP	TMM	TMM	CVPR	CVPR	MM	MM	AAAI	TCSVT	ICCV	
		CNN-based														Transformer-based		Swin
NLPR	E_ξ^{adp}↑	0.951	0.955	0.934	0.944	0.945	0.953	0.939	0.954	0.957	0.956	0.952	0.955	0.954	0.969	0.969	0.956	0.973
	F_β^{adp}↑	0.875	0.089	0.848	0.865	0.861	0.878	0.849	0.882	0.886	0.893	0.896	0.883	0.880	0.892	0.908	0.886	0.928
	WF↑	0.874	0.878	0.849	0.849	0.848	0.873	0.833	0.885	0.881	0.892	0.889	0.882	0.877	0.889	0.908	0.887	0.921
	MAE↓	0.026	0.025	0.031	0.031	0.029	0.025	0.032	0.026	0.024	0.023	0.024	0.024	0.024	0.022	0.018	0.023	0.016
NJU2K	E_ξ^{adp}↑	0.935	0.934	0.924	0.926	0.926	0.933	0.907	0.942	0.947	0.941	0.937	0.945	0.937	0.942	0.954	0.943	0.957
	F_β^{adp}↑	0.886	0.889	0.872	0.876	0.865	0.893	0.848	0.898	0.907	0.898	0.901	0.907	0.894	0.901	0.922	0.900	0.928
	WF↑	0.871	0.867	0.856	0.852	0.854	0.875	0.811	0.885	0.892	0.884	0.889	0.892	0.879	0.886	0.913	0.888	0.917
	MAE↓	0.044	0.043	0.046	0.046	0.046	0.040	0.056	0.040	0.044	0.039	0.035	0.034	0.039	0.035	0.033	0.034	0.029
SSD	E_ξ^{adp}↑	0.873	0.909	0.898	0.909	0.904	–	0.888	–	0.923	0.906	0.912	0.906	–	–	0.924	0.922	0.925
	F_β^{adp}↑	0.761	0.847	0.806	0.831	0.813	–	0.772	–	0.858	0.829	0.852	0.827	–	–	0.863	0.842	0.871
	WF↑	0.692	0.814	0.791	0.797	0.776	–	0.725	–	0.829	0.800	0.815	0.795	–	–	0.844	0.829	0.849
	MAE↓	0.084	0.049	0.059	0.049	0.058	–	0.071	–	0.045	0.053	0.047	0.056	–	–	0.040	0.041	0.038
STERE	E_ξ^{adp}↑	0.935	0.941	0.941	0.926	0.926	0.934	0.934	0.925	0.947	0.945	0.942	0.942	0.939	0.944	0.950	0.942	0.955
	F_β^{adp}↑	0.880	0.884	0.885	0.858	0.859	0.866	0.869	0.870	0.894	0.897	**0.898**	0.890	0.875	0.886	0.893	0.878	0.915
	WF↑	0.862	0.866	0.871	0.829	0.837	0.852	0.833	0.855	0.876	0.887	**0.887**	0.866	0.860	0.871	0.882	0.866	0.903
	MAE↓	0.044	0.039	0.040	0.047	0.046	0.043	0.043	0.046	0.040	0.036	0.039	0.041	0.044	0.041	0.033	0.038	0.026
RGBD135	E_ξ^{adp}↑	0.948	0.974	0.945	0.960	0.951	0.959	0.925	0.976	0.970	0.960	0.957	0.972	0.972	0.975	0.980	**0.979**	0.976
	F_β^{adp}↑	0.876	0.917	0.861	0.891	0.870	0.895	0.830	0.916	0.910	0.910	0.898	0.913	0.907	0.917	0.926	0.917	0.935
	WF↑	0.860	0.908	0.856	0.848	0.828	0.884	0.774	**0.915**	0.893	0.884	0.890	0.901	0.902	0.904	0.919	0.913	0.919
	MAE↓	0.025	0.019	0.027	0.028	0.031	0.022	0.038	0.018	0.021	0.022	0.021	0.020	0.019	0.019	0.016	**0.017**	0.016

4 Experiments

4.1 Experimental Setting

Datasets: To verify the effectiveness of the proposed DAST, we conduct a comprehensive comparison on five RGB-D benchmark datasets, including RGBD135 [5], NLPR [23], NJU2K [14], SSD [41], and STERE [22]. RGBD135 [5] is a small-scale dataset captured by the Kinect camera, which includes 135 pairs of indoor images. SSD [41] contains 80 images picked up from three stereo movies. NLPR [23] contains 1000 RGB images and corresponding depth maps. Moreover, there is a mass of multi-objective scenarios in this dataset. NJU2K [14] contains 1985 pairs of RGB images and depth maps, where the depth maps are estimated from stereo images. STERE [22] is the first proposed dataset containing 1000 pairs totally with low-quality depth maps.

Evalution Metrics: To quantitatively evaluate the results of our network and other comparison methods, we adopt widely used evaluation metrics to analyze the performance of different methods, including F-measure [1], E-measure [8], and Mean Absolute Error (MAE) [26]. F-measure is proposed to balance the precision and recall scores. Weighted F-measure (WF) [21], a weighted precision, is designed to improve F-measure. E-measure is utilized to compute the similarity of characterizes both image-level statistics and local pixel matching. We employ adaptive E-measure (E_ξ^{adp}) to evaluation. MAE computes the pixel-level mean absolute errors between the predicted saliency map S and ground truth G.

Implementation Details: Following [35,40], we randomly select 650 samples from NLPR, 1400 samples from NJU2K, and 800 samples from DUT as the training set, the remaining samples are classified as testing set. We implement the proposed network with PyTorch framework on a PC with an NVIDIA GTX 2080Ti GPU. All training and testing samples are resized to 384×384. We deploy the Adam optimizer to train our model. Parameters of the backbone network are initialized with a pre-trained Swin-B network [18]. Besides, the batch size and initial learning rate are set to 4 and $5e^{-5}$, and the learning rate will be divided by 10 every 50 epochs. The proposed DAST converges within 120 epochs.

4.2 Comparison with SOTA Methods

To evaluate the performance of the proposed DAST, we compare our network with other 16 SOTA RGB-D SOD methods, including SSF [35], UC-Net [34], CoNet [12], DANet [38], D3Net [9], ICNet [15], SMEG [20], BiANet [37], CCAF [40], DSNet [27], DCFNet [11], DSA2F [24], CDINet [33], DFMNet [36], RD3D [4], SwinNet [19], and VST [17]. Saliency maps of these methods are generated by the original code under default parameters, or provided by the authors.

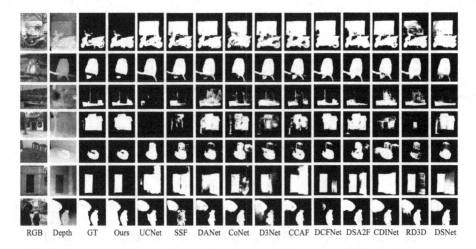

RGB Depth GT Ours UCNet SSF DANet CoNet D3Net CCAF DCFNet DSA2F CDINet RD3D DSNet

Fig. 5. Visual comparisons of our method and other SOTA RGB-D SOD methods.

Quantitative Comparisons: Table 1 lists the comparison results in metrics of E_ξ^{adp}, F_β^{adp}, WF, and MAE on all the five benchmarks datasets. As can be seen, our method consistently outperforms all the SOTA methods in terms of all evaluation metrics, which indicates the superior overall performance of the proposed method. Take the challenging STERE for example, our method can obtain a percentage gain of 0.5%, 2.5%, 2.4%, and 12.1% in metrics of E_ξ^{adp}, F_β^{adp}, WF, and MAE over the second best method SwinNet. Compared with the model using Swin Transformer (like, SwinNet [19]), our algorithm still achieves superior performance.

Visual Comparisons: To qualitative comparison results of the proposed DAST, various challenging scenarios are visualized in Fig. 5, including complex background, foreground similar to background, low contrast, obscured objects, and multiple objects. It can be observed that the proposed DAST are closer to the ground truth, which validates the strong potential of the proposed method in handling various challenging scenarios.

4.3   Ablation Studies

The Importance of Each Component in the DAST: We intend to investigate the contribution of each component of the proposed DAST. To this end, we conduct several ablation studies. Specifically, the whole DAS module is removed from the DAST to prove its effectiveness, denoted as w/o DAS; Further, we omit the assessment and synthesis (A & S) of DAS, denoted as w/o AS; Deleting the assessment procedure from DAS, denoted as w/o A; similar with w/o A, removing the synthesis procedure from DAS, denoted as w/o S.

Table 2. Results of ablation studies. The best results are highlighted in red.

Nomber	Variants	SIP				NJU2K				SSD				STERE			
		E_ε^{adp} ↑	F_β^{adp} ↑	WF ↑	MAE ↓	E_ε^{adp} ↑	F_β^{adp} ↑	WF ↑	MAE ↓	E_ε^{adp} ↑	F_s^{adp} ↑	WF ↑	MAE ↓	E_ε^{adp} ↑	F_β^{adp} ↑	WF ↑	MAE ↓
No.1	w/o A	0.930	0.883	0.852	0.042	0.946	0.909	0.894	0.029	0.923	0.841	0.829	0.042	0.951	0.904	0.887	0.033
No.2	w/o S	0.921	0.863	0.830	0.050	0.939	0.893	0.883	0.0344	0.917	0.835	0.816	0.042	0.941	0.884	0.864	0.042
No.3	w/o AS	0.931	0.884	0.853	0.047	0.944	0.905	0.893	0.033	0.916	0.833	0.808	0.049	0.948	0.900	0.882	0.035
No.4	w/o DAS	0.929	0.878	0.845	0.051	0.939	0.896	0.883	0.035	0.907	0.826	0.803	0.050	0.947	0.897	0.878	0.037
No.5	w/o MP-0	0.928	0.875	0.844	0.048	0.941	0.901	0.888	0.035	0.912	0.829	0.801	0.053	0.946	0.896	0.879	0.036
No.6	w/o MP-1	0.935	0.891	0.859	0.045	0.943	0.906	0.890	0.031	0.919	0.842	0.816	0.048	0.953	0.908	0.889	0.034
No.7	w/o MP-3	0.926	0.885	0.848	0.050	0.950	0.914	0.900	0.032	0.921	0.842	0.820	0.045	0.952	0.907	0.889	0.033
No.8	VGG16	0.922	0.875	0.843	0.049	0.942	0.908	0.890	0.037	0.909	0.842	0.806	0.048	0.940	0.889	0.865	0.040
No.9	VGG19	0.934	0.871	0.862	0.046	0.943	0.903	0.890	0.037	0.917	0.848	0.827	0.043	0.942	0.889	0.867	0.040
No.10	ResNet50	0.933	0.887	0.860	0.043	0.938	0.896	0.876	0.035	0.922	0.853	0.830	0.042	0.946	0.894	0.871	0.037
No.11	Ours(MP-2)	0.940	0.910	0.885	0.038	0.957	0.928	0.917	0.026	0.925	0.871	0.849	0.038	0.955	0.915	0.903	0.029

The results of the four variants are presented in Table 2, the performance of w/o DAS has a significant decline (*e.g.*,MAE: 0.051→0.038 on SIP, 0.035→0.026 on NJU2K, 0.049→0.038 on SSD, and 0.037→0.029 on STERE) compared with the proposed DAST, which confirms that the DAS module is extremely beneficial to SOD tasks. Besides, the results of ablation studies of the used inner mechanisms (assessment and synthesis) in DAS indicate the rationality and effectiveness of the assessment and synthesis.

The Effectiveness of Attention Mask from Feature Synthesis: In DAS, we adopt two max-pooling operations to capture the significant information of features. To confirm the rationality of our design, we design four variants, denoted as MP-0, MP-1, MP-2, and MP-3, which indicate the times of max-pooling operation are 0, 1, 2, and 3, respectively. As reported in Table 2, compared with MP-0, MP-1 can significantly improve the performance of saliency detection, which proves the positive role of adopted max-pooling operation. Furthermore, compared with MP-1, we can observer that MP-2 (Ours) can further improve the accuracy of SOD task while MP-3 with three max-pooling operations cannot keep up the performance growth, which confirms our method with two max-pooling operations is reasonable.

The Effectiveness of the Swin Transformer: we adopted the Swin Transformer as our encoder to extract multi-modality features due to its good ability to capture long-range dependencies. To certify the advance of the Swin Transformer, we replace the Swin Transformer with VGG and ResNet, denoted as VGG16, VGG19, and ResNet50, respectively. From Table 2, we can find that the use of the Swin Transformer significantly improves the detection performance. This may result from the integration of the locality merit of CNN and the global-aware ability of transformer.

5   Conclusion

In this article, we propose a pure Transformer-based RGB-D SOD model, namely DAST. To handle the issue of low-quality depth maps, we propose a depth-aware assessment and synthesis (DAS) module to judge the quality of depth maps and fuse the multi-modality salient features by computing the difference between RGB and depth modalities in a coarse-to-fine manner. In DAS, a weighted factor and an attention mask can be generated to tell whether the depth quality is good or not, resulting in deciding which regions in features need attention. Furthermore, a feature aggregation (FA) module is proposed to integrate the multi-scale features for better saliency reasoning. Comprehensive experiments prove that the proposed DAST achieves SOTA performance on five benchmark datasets.

Acknowledgements. This work was supported by National Science Foundation of China (62102003), Anhui Natural Science Foundation (2108085QF258), Natural Science Research Project of Colleges and Universities in Anhui Province (KJ2020A0299), and University Synergy Innovation Program of Anhui Province (GXXT-2021-006).

References

1. Achanta, R., Hemami, S., Estrada, F., Susstrunk, S.: Frequency-tuned salient region detection. In: CVPR, pp. 1597–1604 (2009)
2. Carion, N., Massa, F., Synnaeve, G., Usunier, N., Kirillov, A., Zagoruyko, S.: End-to-end object detection with transformers. In: Vedaldi, A., Bischof, H., Brox, T., Frahm, J.-M. (eds.) ECCV 2020. LNCS, vol. 12346, pp. 213–229. Springer, Cham (2020). https://doi.org/10.1007/978-3-030-58452-8_13
3. Chen, H., Deng, Y., Li, Y., Hung, T.Y., Lin, G.: Rgbd salient object detection via disentangled cross-modal fusion. IEEE TIP **29**, 8407–8416 (2020)
4. Chen, Q., Liu, Z., Zhang, Y., Fu, K., Zhao, Q., Du, H.: RGB-D salient object detection via 3D convolutional neural networks. In: AAAI, pp. 1063–1071 (2021)
5. Cheng, Y., Fu, H., Wei, X., Xiao, J., Cao, X.: Depth enhanced saliency detection method. In: ICIMCS, pp. 23–27 (2014)
6. Dey, S., Dutta, A., Ghosh, S.K., Valveny, E., Lladós, J., Pal, U.: Aligning salient objects to queries: a multi-modal and multi-object image retrieval framework. In: ACCV, pp. 241–255 (2018)
7. Dosovitskiy, A., Beyer, L., Kolesnikov, A., Weissenborn, D., Zhai, X., Unterthiner, T.: An image is worth 16×16 words: transformers for image recognition at scale. In: ICLR. pp. 1 (2020)
8. Fan, D.P., Gong, C., Cao, Y., Ren, B., Cheng, M.M., Borji, A.: Enhanced-alignment measure for binary foreground map evaluation. arXiv preprint arXiv:1805.10421 (2018)
9. Fan, D.P., Lin, Z., Zhang, Z., Zhu, M., Cheng, M.M.: Rethinking rgb-d salient object detection: models, data sets, and large-scale benchmarks. IEEE TNNLS **32**(5), 2075–2089 (2020)
10. Huang, N., Liu, Y., Zhang, Q., Han, J.: Joint cross-modal and unimodal features for rgb-d salient object detection. IEEE TMM **23**, 2428–2441 (2020)

11. Ji, W., et al.: Calibrated rgb-d salient object detection. In: CVPR, pp. 9471–9481 (2021)
12. Ji, W., Li, J., Zhang, M., Piao, Y., Lu, H.: Accurate RGB-D salient object detection via collaborative learning. In: Vedaldi, A., Bischof, H., Brox, T., Frahm, J.-M. (eds.) ECCV 2020. LNCS, vol. 12363, pp. 52–69. Springer, Cham (2020). https://doi.org/10.1007/978-3-030-58523-5_4
13. Jin, W.D., Xu, J., Han, Q., Zhang, Y., Cheng, M.M.: Cdnet: complementary depth network for rgb-d salient object detection. IEEE TIP **30**, 3376–3390 (2021)
14. Ju, R., Ge, L., Geng, W., Ren, T., Wu, G.: Depth saliency based on anisotropic center-surround difference. In: ICIP, pp. 1115–1119 (2014)
15. Li, G., Liu, Z., Ling, H.: Icnet: information conversion network for rgb-d based salient object detection. IEEE TIP **29**, 4873–4884 (2020)
16. Liu, N., Zhang, N., Han, J.: Learning selective self-mutual attention for rgb-d saliency detection. In: CVPR, pp. 13756–13765 (2020)
17. Liu, N., Zhang, N., Wan, K., Shao, L., Han, J.: Visual saliency transformer. In: ICCV, pp. 4722–4732 (2021)
18. Liu, Z., et al.: Swin transformer: hierarchical vision transformer using shifted windows. In: ICCV, pp. 10012–10022 (2021)
19. Liu, Z., Tan, Y., He, Q., Xiao, Y.: Swinnet: swin transformer drives edge-aware rgb-d and rgb-t salient object detection. IEEE TCSVT **32**, 4486–4497 (2021)
20. Liu, Z., Wang, K., Dong, H., Wang, Y.: A cross-modal edge-guided salient object detection for rgb-d image. Neurocomputing **454**, 168–177 (2021)
21. Margolin, R., Zelnik-Manor, L., Tal, A.: How to evaluate foreground maps? In: CVPR, pp. 248–255 (2014)
22. Niu, Y., Geng, Y., Li, X., Liu, F.: Leveraging stereopsis for saliency analysis. In: CVPR, pp. 454–461 (2012)
23. Peng, H., Li, B., Xiong, W., Hu, W., Ji, R.: RGBD salient object detection: a benchmark and algorithms. In: Fleet, D., Pajdla, T., Schiele, B., Tuytelaars, T. (eds.) ECCV 2014. LNCS, vol. 8691, pp. 92–109. Springer, Cham (2014). https://doi.org/10.1007/978-3-319-10578-9_7
24. Sun, P., Zhang, W., Wang, H., Li, S., Li, X.: Deep rgb-d saliency detection with depth-sensitive attention and automatic multi-modal fusion. In: CVPR, pp. 1407–1417 (2021)
25. Vaswani, A., et al.: Attention is all you need. In: NeurIPS, vol. 30 (2017)
26. Wang, W., Lai, Q., Fu, H., Shen, J., Ling, H., Yang, R.: Salient object detection in the deep learning era: an in-depth survey. IEEE TPAMI **44**(6), 3239–3259 (2021)
27. Wen, H., et al.: Dynamic selective network for rgb-d salient object detection. IEEE TIP **30**, 9179–9192 (2021)
28. Woo, S., Park, J., Lee, J.-Y., Kweon, I.S.: CBAM: convolutional block attention module. In: Ferrari, V., Hebert, M., Sminchisescu, C., Weiss, Y. (eds.) ECCV 2018. LNCS, vol. 11211, pp. 3–19. Springer, Cham (2018). https://doi.org/10.1007/978-3-030-01234-2_1
29. Wu, Z., Su, L., Huang, Q.: Cascaded partial decoder for fast and accurate salient object detection. In: CVPR, pp. 3907–3916 (2019)
30. Wu, Z., Su, L., Huang, Q.: Decomposition and completion network for salient object detection. IEEE TIP **30**, 6226–6239 (2021)
31. Xiao, X., Zhou, Y., Gong, Y.J.: Rgb-'d'saliency detection with pseudo depth. IEEE TIP **28**(5), 2126–2139 (2018)
32. Zhan, J., Zhao, H., Zheng, P., Wu, H., Wang, L.: Salient superpixel visual tracking with graph model and iterative segmentation. Cogn. Comput. **13**(4), 821–832 (2021)

33. Zhang, C., et al.: Cross-modality discrepant interaction network for rgb-d salient object detection. In: ACM MM, pp. 2094–2102 (2021)

34. Zhang, J., et al.: Uc-net: uncertainty inspired rgb-d saliency detection via conditional variational autoencoders. In: CVPR, pp. 8582–8591 (2020)

35. Zhang, M., Ren, W., Piao, Y., Rong, Z., Lu, H.: Select, supplement and focus for rgb-d saliency detection. In: CVPR, pp. 3472–3481 (2020)

36. Zhang, W., Ji, G.P., Wang, Z., Fu, K., Zhao, Q.: Depth quality-inspired feature manipulation for efficient rgb-d salient object detection. In: ACM MM, pp. 731–740 (2021)

37. Zhang, Z., Lin, Z., Xu, J., Jin, W.D., Lu, S.P., Fan, D.P.: Bilateral attention network for rgb-d salient object detection. IEEE TIP **30**, 1949–1961 (2021)

38. Zhao, X., Zhang, L., Pang, Y., Lu, H., Zhang, L.: A single stream network for robust and real-time RGB-D salient object detection. In: Vedaldi, A., Bischof, H., Brox, T., Frahm, J.-M. (eds.) ECCV 2020. LNCS, vol. 12367, pp. 646–662. Springer, Cham (2020). https://doi.org/10.1007/978-3-030-58542-6_39

39. Zheng, S., et al.: Rethinking semantic segmentation from a sequence-to-sequence perspective with transformers. In: CVPR, pp. 6881–6890 (2021)

40. Zhou, W., Zhu, Y., Lei, J., Wan, J., Yu, L.: CCAFNET: crossflow and cross-scale adaptive fusion network for detecting salient objects in rgb-d images. IEEE TMM **24**, 2192–2204 (2021)

41. Zhu, C., Li, G.: A three-pathway psychobiological framework of salient object detection using stereoscopic technology. In: ICCV, pp. 3008–3014 (2017)

A Vehicle Re-ID Algorithm Based on Channel Correlation Self-attention and Lstm Local Information Loss

Tiantian Qi[1] , Song Qiu[1(✉)], Li Sun[1], Zhuang Liu[1], Mingsong Chen[2], and Yue Lyu[1]

[1] Shanghai Key Laboratory of Multidimensional Information Processing, East China Normal University, Shanghai 200241, China
sqiu@ee.ecnu.edu.cn
[2] Software Engineering Institute, East China Normal University, Shanghai 200241, China

Abstract. Recently, the rapid development of vehicle re-identification (ReID) technology has facilitated the construction of intelligent transport systems. Mainstream ReID methods rely on the fusion of global and local features. In the global feature extraction, the channel attention modules are usually exploited in the network, most of which only focus on the channels' importance and ignore the interactions among channels. In the local feature extraction, the additional annotation-based local feature extraction methods can focus on local information and improve the model's performance but increase the workload of the data annotation and reduce the generalizability of the model. In this article, we put forward a new ReID Algorithm called CCSAM-LL. Firstly, a plug-and-play module based on channel correlation self-attention called CCSAM is introduced, which focuses on channel relevance and improves the characterization of global features. Secondly, we propose an Lstm-based loss, named LstmLocal loss, which takes into account local features without additional annotation. LstmLocal loss is trained with Triplet Hard loss and ID loss to improve the model's ability to capture detailed features and accuracy in the retrieval task. Experimental results demonstrate that our approach outperforms the state-of-the-art methods on the challenging dataset VeRi776. Specifically, our approach achieves 83.18% mAP, 98.79% Rank5, and 48.83% mINP. The model is available at https://gitee.com/qitiantian128/ccsam-ll.

Keywords: Vehicle re-identification · Deep learning · Channel attention · Lstm · Local information

This work was supported by National Key Research and Development Program of China 2018YFB2101300 and the Dean's Fund of Engineering Research Center of Software/Hardware Co-design Technology and Application, Ministry of Education, East China Normal University.

© The Author(s), under exclusive license to Springer Nature Switzerland AG 2022
S. Khanna et al. (Eds.): PRICAI 2022, LNCS 13630, pp. 488–500, 2022.
https://doi.org/10.1007/978-3-031-20865-2_36

1 Introduction

Vehicle ReID is an image retrieval technology aiming to identify specific vehicles from images or video sequences across shots using computer vision technology. Currently, vehicle re-identification technology based on license plate recognition is the most reliable method. However license plate information is not always valid due to factors such as lighting, camera angle, masking, and smudging. Therefore, the research of vehicle re-identification algorithms for unlicensed vehicles is essential.

In the article, we concentrate on deep learning-based approaches in the research on vehicle re-identification technology based on unlicensed vehicles. These re-recognition algorithms face a significant challenge in practical applications. Different camera positions can produce light variations, viewpoint variations, and resolution differences, resulting in small differences between classes and large differences within classes, as shown in Fig. 1. The addition of attention mechanisms is one way to address this problem by enhancing the importance of critical features and suppressing useless features. Moreover, the success of many recent re-recognition tasks has shown that it is also important to combine other mechanisms to mine local information from images, such as view segmentation [17], key point detection [12], and viewpoint estimation [12,30]. These methods use local information such as critical points and vehicle orientation to provide supplementary information for global features. Some methods require additional annotation of the dataset, such as crucial point marking, which limits the generalisability of these methods.

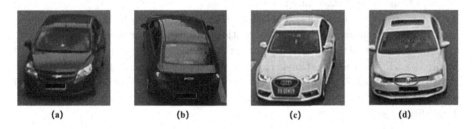

Fig. 1. (a) and (b) are the front and rear views of the same ID vehicle, (c) and (d) are front views of a different vehicle.

Therefore, designing efficient attention mechanisms and mining local and detailed information are the keys to improving the re-recognition accuracy. Based on this, we propose a vehicle re-recognition algorithm based on channel correlation self-attention and lstm local information loss, which named CCSAM-LL. Two main contributions are included in the proposed algorithm. One is a channel correlation self-attention module called CCSAM for capturing the correlation between channels, with higher correlation channels being given greater weight, thus enhancing the global representation of features. The other is an lstm-based loss, named LstmLocal loss, which takes into account local features without additional annotation. It has the advantage that image regions can be processed sequentially, thus making full use of contextual information to enhance the model's ability to differentiate between individuals. Through extensive experiments, the combined performance of the newly proposed structure on the challenging dataset VeRi776 exceeds the state-of-the-art.

2 Related Work

Deep learning-based vehicle re-identification methods have become a hot research topic recently. In this section, we briefly review the recent work related to vehicle ReID in the direction of deep learning. Liu et al. [15] designed a Couple Cluster Loss to improve triplet loss, which is the first metric-based learning method for vehicle ReID. Hermans A et al. [9] proposed Triplet Hard loss to improve the robust representation of appearance. At the same time, the idea of multi-task learning is applied. Classification loss and triplet loss are used to jointly train the network, making the different loss functions constrain each other. To solve the problem of intra-class differences and inter-class similarities caused by perspective changes, Bai et al. [28] proposed a Group-Sensitive-Triplet Embedding method and considered inter-group differences as well as differences between vehicles in the loss function. Varior et al. [24] proposed an LSTM-based network to model the spatial contextual information. Khorramshahi et al. [12] and Guo et al. [5] used an attention mechanism to extract features with discriminative power through vehicle essential part localization and critical point detection. Chen et al. [3] proposed a new 3D segmentation strategy to extract more local features from each image dimension.

However, the correlation between channel information is not effectively exploited in the above-mentioned attention-based mechanism network. And in numerous local feature extraction-based methods, feature representations are required additional annotations. Hence this article puts forward a vehicle ReID algorithm based on channel correlation self-attention and lstm local information loss, facilitating the model to learn more global significant features and local detail features.

3 Proposed Method

We first present the baseline model and the general architecture of our proposed methods (CCSAM-LL). Next, more details about the channel correlation self-attention module (CCSAM) are discussed in Sect. 3.2. In Sect. 3.3, we focus on the LstmLocal loss.

3.1 Architecture of Our Proposed Method

Baseline. Taking inspiration from the literature [7], we choose ResNet50 for global feature extraction. We insert the IBN [18] structure into ResNet50 to learn more discriminative structures. Then we change the stride of the last stage to 1, remove the fully connected layers(FC) and add the pooling layer and the batch normalization layer(BN). The network is trained using Triplet Hard loss (TriHard loss) [9] and label smooth-based Cross-Entropy loss (ID loss). In the testing phase, the 2048-dimensional vector of all images is obtained and then the cosine similarity is calculated as a basis for ranking.

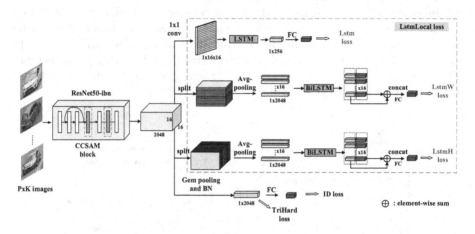

Fig. 2. Overview of our framework. ResNet50-ibn is our backbone, CCSAM block is our proposed channel correlation self-attention module, and LstmLocal loss is our added loss module. In the figure, Avgpoolng denotes average pooling, BN denotes batch normalization, FC denotes fully connected layer, concat denotes concatenation, Gem pooling denotes Generalized Mean Pooling.

Our Proposed Method (CCSAM-LL). Our approach is based on the baseline, firstly inserting the proposed channel correlation self-attention module (CCSAM) into the stage of ResNet50-ibn. We use the idea of self-attention [25] to extract correlation features between channels, enhancing the feature representation capability of important channels and improving the global feature representation ability. Secondly, based on TriHard loss and ID loss, LstmLocal loss is proposed to enhance the model's discriminative capability of local feature representation. The idea of multi-task and joint learning is used to reduce network overfitting and enhance the model's generalization ability. The framework of our proposed method is shown in Fig. 2.

3.2   CCSAM

Attention allows the model to learn to pay attention autonomously, suppressing irrelevant information and focusing on critical information. SEnet [10] is the more popular plug-and-play channel attention, which reduces the redundancy of channel information by giving channel weights through the Squeeze-Excitation operation. It plays an active role in many downstream tasks in computer vision. Meanwhile, with the popularity of self-attention, attention based on this idea, such as nonlocal [27], has also been proposed to optimize the feature extraction ability of the network from the perspective of contextual relevance, primarily used in the direction of NLP.

Based on this, we innovatively propose a channel correlation self-attention module named CCSAM. It makes the weight coefficient of each channel is related to its correlation with the rest of the channels and each position of the feature map combines the relevant information for all channels. The SEnet is used to obtain the weights of the channels directly through global average pooling and FC layers. It is not related to the mutuality among channels, which is different from CCSAM. The structure of the CCSAM is shown in Fig. 3.

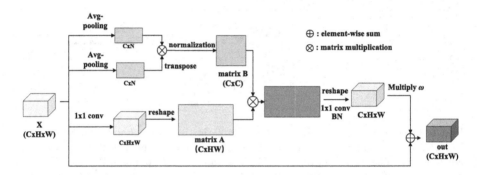

Fig. 3. Channel correlation self-attention module(CCSAM block). In the figure, N equals H multiplied by W divided by 16 Avgpoolng denotes average pooling, BN denotes batch normalization, HW equals H by W, Multiply denotes each element of the matrix multiplied by the learnable variable w.

First, features are extracted from the feature map X using a 1×1 convolutional layer (Conv), and then the length and width dimensions are stitched together to obtain the channel matrix A. At the same time, the feature map X is average-pooled to produce the channel feature vectors. The channel feature vectors are multiplied with their transposed results to obtain a matrix of size CXC. Each element of the matrix represents the correlation among the different channels. Normalized this matrix to obtain the channel weight matrix B. The normalization method can be softmax. Our module divides the number of channels directly to normalize. Multiply B with the channel matrix A to obtain the interaction among all channels at each position in the feature map. Reshape the result to the original feature map size, and use 1×1 Conv and batch normalization to get the new feature map. Finally, we multiply the new feature map with the learnable variable w and add it to feature map X. The presence of w allows the model to continuously learn the proportional relationship between the original feature map and the new feature map, facilitating network optimization.

The above-mentioned channel correlation self-attention module can also be summarised by the following equation:

$$out = X + wx' \tag{1}$$

$$x' = \frac{1}{N_c} \sum_j f(x_i, x_j)g(x_j) \tag{2}$$

where X denotes the input feature map, w denotes the learnable weight, and the add operation indicates a residual connection structure that can be plugged into the backbone easily. N_c denotes normalization factor, $f(x_i, x_j)$ denotes the interaction relationship between any two channels and $g(x_j)$ denotes the value of the features of the input feature map at position j.

3.3   LstmLocal Loss

Many methods have shown that methods based on local features [3,5] are beneficial for vehicle identification. However, these methods increase the complexity and training difficulty of the network and some methods require additional annotation of the dataset, such as crucial point marking, which limits the generalisability of these methods. To overcome these problems, our method proposes the LstmLocal loss. The vehicle can be thought of as a sequence from top to bottom, including structures such as roof, windows, doors, wheels, etc. We use lstm to model the serialization of local features and capture the correlation between local features. Benefiting from the gate unit within lstm, lstm can selectively retain the more relevant information and filter the less relevant information. The serialized feature vectors output by lstm are stitched together and computed the classification loss, prompting the network to focus on locally important detail information. During re-identification task, attention to important detail information can contribute to retrieval accuracy.

$$Loss = TriHard\ loss + ID\ loss + LstmLocal\ loss \tag{3}$$

$$LstmLocal\ loss = Lstm\ loss + 0.25 * (LstmH\ loss + LstmW\ loss) \tag{4}$$

As shown in Fig. 2, we input the feature map from ResNet50-ibn to the lstm branches(the red dashed box in Fig. 2) to calculate the LstmLocal loss. The first branch is to downscale the feature map by 1×1 Conv to obtain a $1 \times 16 \times 16$ feature map. Each row vector of the feature map is considered as a representation of the local feature and input to the LSTM in top-to-bottom order. The last feature vector of the output sequence of the LSTM is calculated as the Cross-Entropy loss, named Lstm loss. The second branch is to make the feature map average pooled by row or column to obtain 16 row or column vectors of 2048 dimension. They are treated as representations of local features and input to the BiLSTM to extract serialized features in the horizontal or vertical direction, respectively. The first half of the serialized features is added to the second half. Then the result is concatenated and, after FC layer, to calculate the

Cross-Entropy loss, called LstmH loss and LstmW loss. The last branch in Fig. 2 applies the Generalized Mean Pooling and BN of the feature map to obtain the 2048-dimensional feature vector, which is used for the calculation of the TriHard loss; the 2048-dimensional feature vector after FC layer is used to calculate the Cross-Entropy loss, also known as the ID loss. The loss of the model can be expressed by Eq. 3 and 4.

4   Experiments

4.1   Datasets

We trained and tested our method on the challenging dataset VeRi776 [16]. The VeRi776 dataset is one of the more commonly used vehicle re-identification datasets, where each vehicle is captured by at least two and at most 18 cameras. The vehicle images have different viewing angles, lighting, resolutions, and occlusions, constituting a highly reproducible dataset in realistic scenarios. The VeRi776 dataset contains 49,360 images of 776 vehicles.

4.2   Implementation Details

We randomly cropped, flipped, and padded the input images, uniformly resized them to a size of 256×256, and finally normalized them by the mean and variance of the dataset. The pre-training weights were chosen from the ResNet50-ibn model pre-trained at imagenet dataset. The Batch size was set to 160, including 40 classes with four samples per class. The optimizer used SGD with a learning rate starting at 0.01, utilizing a warm-up strategy and a CosineAnnealingLR strategy. The total training numbers were set to 60 epochs. The w in CCSAM was initialized to 1. The LSTM was set to two layers, and the hidden nodes were 256. The BiLSTM was set to one layer, and the hidden nodes were 256.

4.3   Evaluation

We follow the standard evaluation protocol. Rank1, Rank5, mAP, and mINP are standard evaluation metrics used in Reid tasks. Rank-k indicates the percentage of correct matches for the first k graphs; The mAP indicates the accuracy rate of all search results; The mINP [29] is used to evaluate the ability of the model to search for the most difficult-to-find samples. The experimental results of the method in this paper are all the average of five experiments.

4.4   Comparison with Related Methods

We compare the proposed method with state-of-the-art methods, and as shown in Table 1, the proposed method achieves compelling results on the VeRi776 dataset.

Specifically, we compare the metrics of state-of-the-art methods on mAP, Rank1, Rank5 and mINP. As seen from the table, our method has the highest

Table 1. Comparison with state-of-the-art results(%) on VeRi776.The 1st best result is bolded. CCSAM-LL is the name of our model.

Method	Publication	mAP	Rank1	Rank5	mINP
AAVER [12]	ICCV19	61.18	88.97	94.70	–
DMML [2]	ICCV19	70.1	91.2	96.3	–
PART [6]	CVPR19	74.3	94.3	98.7	–
GLAMOR [23]	–	80.3	96.5	98.6	–
PGAN [31]	IEEE TITS20	79.3	96.5	98.3	–
CFVMNet [22]	ACM MM'20	77.1	95.3	–	–
SAN [19]	MST20	72.5	93.3	97.1	–
UMTS [11]	AAAI20	75.9	95.8	–	–
SPAN [4]	ECCV20	68.9	94.0	97.6	–
PVEN [17]	CVPR20	79.5	95.6	98.4	–
DFLNet [1]	IJCAI20	73.2	93.2	97.5	–
SAVER [13]	ECCV20	79.6	96.4	98.6	–
GB+AB+SB [14]	ICCV21	81.0	96.7	98.6	–
TBE-Net [21]	IEEE TITS21	79.5	96	98.5	–
Transreid [8]	ICCV21	81.7	**97.1**	98.7	–
Fastreid [7]	–	81.9	97.0	98.51	44.79
Baseline		81.93	96.50	98.35	47.24
Ours(CCSAM-LL)		**83.18**	96.80	**98.79**	**48.83**

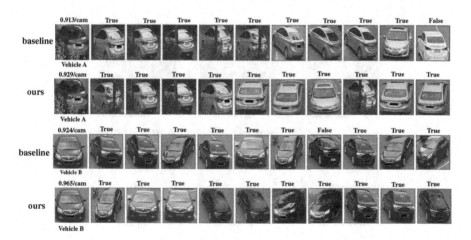

Fig. 4. Comparison of the results of our proposed method with the baseline model. The left-most column shows the test image and the right-hand side shows the top ten matches images in terms of similarity to the test image. The red box indicates a correct match and the blue box indicates an incorrect match. The indicators at the top of the Vehicle A and Vehicle B represent the mAP and cam ID respectively. (Color figure online)

metrics on mAP, Rank5, and mINP, achieving improvements of 1.25, 0.44, and 1.59, respectively. This demonstrates that our proposed method can enhance the ability of the model to match complex samples and strengthen the robustness of the model. We visualize the matching results for vehicle A and vehicle B in the test set. In Fig. 4, the left column shows the test image(vehicle A and vehicle B), and the right column shows the top ten matches images. It is evident that the mAP of our proposed method is higher than the mAP of the baseline model, with an improvement of 1.6 for sample A's mAP and 4.11 for sample B'mAP. The Baseline model makes an error of judgment on the 7th matched image of sample B, but our model is correct. Although the Rank1 metric does not outperform existing methods, in a real-world vehicle image retrieval application, not only one image will be matched, but in most cases, multiple images with high similarity rankings will be retrieved.

To demonstrate the effectiveness of our proposed method more directly, we use Gradcam [20] for heat map visualization. Figure 5(b) and (e) clearly show that the baseline can already focus on the preliminary information about the vehicle, but the presence of the background distracts the model's attention. It is not easy to find important feature information in the view. Hence, our proposed model uses the relevance of the channels to learn the essential features in the view, reducing the distraction of the background and focusing the vast majority of attention on the vehicle itself, which is relevant to the task, as in Fig. 5(c). Meanwhile, Fig. 5(f) show that the presence of LstmLocal loss improves model's attention to detailed information such as vehicle logos, reflectors and light outlines.

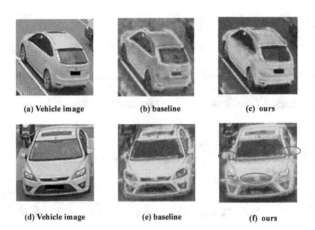

(a) Vehicle image   (b) baseline   (c) ours

(d) Vehicle image   (e) baseline   (f) ours

Fig. 5. (b)(e) show the visualisation of the baseline model using Gradcam; (c)(f) show the visualisation of our method using Gradcam. The red circles in the diagram indicate the detailed features that the model focuses on. (Color figure online)

4.5   Ablation Study

To further evaluate the effectiveness and robustness of the CCSAM module and LstmLocal loss proposed in this paper, we conduct ablation experiments on the VeRi776 dataset.

Effectiveness of CCSAM. CCSAM is a plug-and-play channel correlation self-attention module that can be easily inserted at any position in the backbone. we compare CCSAM with the popular plug-and-play components in recent years, such as SEnet [10] and ECAnet [26]. Compared to them, CCSAM removes the dimensionality reduction operation to reduce information loss and enhances the interaction between channels using a channel weight matrix. As shown in Table 2, the mAP of our method improves by 1.09 and 0.49 over SEnet and ECAnet, which has certain advantages. In terms of number of parameters, CCSAM has 139.7MB parameters, which is higher than the other two. This is mainly because using all channels for convolution operations increases model accuracy at the cost of computational effort.

Table 2. Performance comparison(%) of CCSAM added at different locations in ResNet50-ibn on VeRi776. The 1st best result is bolded.

Method	mAP	Rank1	Rank5	mINP
Baseline	81.93	96.50	98.35	47.24
+SEnet	81.63	96.77	**98.70**	46.98
+ECAnet	82.23	96.61	98.69	46.97
+CCSAM(stage2,3,4)	82.59	96.96	98.69	48.17
+CCSAM(stage3,4)	82.61	96.78	98.67	48.15
+CCSAM(stage2,3)	**82.72**	**96.98**	98.62	**48.43**

Furthermore, we conduct experimental comparisons by inserting attention into different positions of ResNet50-ibn. Attention is not inserted at stage1 because the feature map size of stage1 is 64×64, which would introduce more extensive parameters when computing channel attention. Table 2 compares the performance of CCSAM added to ResNet50-ibn at different locations. It can be seen that mAP, Rank1, and mINP are highest when CCSAM is inserted at stage2 and stage3. The model with CCSAM inserted at stage2, stage3, and stage4 not only has an increased number of parameters and a lower mAP. Therefore, the CCSAM in this paper is inserted in stage2 and stage3.

Effectiveness of LstmLocal Loss. The addition of LstmLocal loss is another important innovation in our approach. We put LstmLocal loss on the baseline and combine TriHard loss and ID loss. LstmLocal loss consists of Lstm loss, LstmH loss, and LstmW loss. Lstm loss is calculated by taking each row of the feature map as a local feature, thus learning the association information between contexts. LstmH loss and LstmW loss are calculated by 16×2048 dimensional vectors, which are obtained via average pooling by row or column of the feature map. We conduct separation and weight scaling experiments for these two kinds of loss. As shown in Table 3, the different coefficients can affect the experimental results and thus reduce the validity of the method. However, our method is still more accurate than the baseline method. The most significant improvement is achieved when the coefficient of Lstm loss is one, and the coefficient of LstmH loss and LstmW loss is 0.25. MAP improved by 1.0 to 82.93, and Rank1, Rank5, and mINP improved by 0.44, 0.35, and 1.12, respectively. It indicates that contextual association information can further constrain the classification loss of the model, thus improving the model's ability to extract detailed feature and the discriminate detailed information.

Table 3. Performance comparison(%) with different weighting factors of LstmH loss and LstmW loss on VeRi776. The 1st best result is bolded.

Method	mAP	Rank1	Rank5	mINP
Baseline	81.93	96.50	98.35	47.24
+Lstm loss	82.25	96.73	98.64	47.65
+0.25*(LstmH loss+LstmW loss)	82.55	96.83	98.72	48.11
+Lstm loss+1*(LstmH loss+LstmW loss)	82.33	96.73	98.58	47.96
+Lstm loss+0.5*(LstmH loss+LstmW loss)	82.59	96.71	98.59	**48.45**
+Lstm loss+0.25*(LstmH loss+LstmW loss)	**82.93**	**96.94**	**98.73**	48.36

5 Conclusion

In this paper, we first propose the channel correlation self-attention module (CCSAM), where each position of the feature map combines the relevant information for all channels. Secondly, LstmLocal loss is proposed to be trained in collaboration with TriHard loss and ID loss. Based on these losses, the network is able to capture local detailed features and improve the model's accuracy without additional annotation. But the coefficients among these loss functions need to be chosen carefully, as it affects the final effect of the method. Through extensive experiments, it has been shown that our proposed algorithm named CCSAM-LL improves the re-identification accuracy of the VeRi776 dataset, ranking top among the latest methods in recent years, with 83.18% mAP, 98.79% Rank5, and 48.83% mINP. In the future, we plan to optimize the structure of CCSAM to reduce the amount of computation and explore in depth the scaling relationship between various loss functions to achieve improved network accuracy.

References

1. Bai, Y., et al.: Disentangled feature learning network for vehicle re-identification. In: IJCAI, pp. 474–480 (2020)
2. Chen, G., Zhang, T., Lu, J., Zhou, J.: Deep meta metric learning. In: Proceedings of the IEEE/CVF International Conference on Computer Vision, pp. 9547–9556 (2019)
3. Chen, H., Lagadec, B., Bremond, F.: Partition and reunion: a two-branch neural network for vehicle re-identification. In: CVPR Workshops, pp. 184–192 (2019)
4. Chen, T.-S., Liu, C.-T., Wu, C.-W., Chien, S.-Y.: Orientation-aware vehicle re-identification with semantics-guided part attention network. In: Vedaldi, A., Bischof, H., Brox, T., Frahm, J.-M. (eds.) ECCV 2020. LNCS, vol. 12347, pp. 330–346. Springer, Cham (2020). https://doi.org/10.1007/978-3-030-58536-5_20
5. Guo, H., Zhu, K., Tang, M., Wang, J.: Two-level attention network with multi-grain ranking loss for vehicle re-identification. IEEE Trans. Image Process. **28**, 4328–4338 (2019)
6. He, B., Li, J., Zhao, Y., Tian, Y.: Part-regularized near-duplicate vehicle re-identification. In: 2019 IEEE/CVF Conference on Computer Vision and Pattern Recognition (CVPR) (2019)
7. He, L., Liao, X., Liu, W., Liu, X., Cheng, P., Mei, T.: Fastreid: a pytorch toolbox for real-world person re-identification, vol. 1, no. 6. arXiv preprint arXiv:2006.02631 (2020)
8. He, S., Luo, H., Wang, P., Wang, F., Li, H., Jiang, W.: Transreid: transformer-based object re-identification. In: Proceedings of the IEEE/CVF International Conference on Computer Vision, pp. 15013–15022 (2021)
9. Hermans, A., Beyer, L., Leibe, B.: In defense of the triplet loss for person re-identification. arXiv preprint arXiv:1703.07737 (2017)
10. Hu, J., Shen, L., Sun, G.: Squeeze-and-excitation networks. In: Proceedings of the IEEE Conference on Computer Vision and Pattern Recognition, pp. 7132–7141 (2018)
11. Jin, X., Lan, C., Zeng, W., Chen, Z.: Uncertainty-aware multi-shot knowledge distillation for image-based object re-identification. In: Proceedings of the AAAI Conference on Artificial Intelligence, pp. 11165–11172 (2020)
12. Khorramshahi, P., Kumar, A., Peri, N., Rambhatla, S.S., Chen, J.C., Chellappa, R.: A dual-path model with adaptive attention for vehicle re-identification. In: Proceedings of the IEEE/CVF International Conference on Computer Vision, pp. 6132–6141 (2019)
13. Khorramshahi, P., Peri, N., Chen, J., Chellappa, R.: The devil is in the details: self-supervised attention for vehicle re-identification. In: Vedaldi, A., Bischof, H., Brox, T., Frahm, J.-M. (eds.) ECCV 2020. LNCS, vol. 12359, pp. 369–386. Springer, Cham (2020). https://doi.org/10.1007/978-3-030-58568-6_22
14. Li, M., Huang, X., Zhang, Z.: Self-supervised geometric features discovery via interpretable attention for vehicle re-identification and beyond. In: International Conference on Computer Vision (2021)
15. Liu, H., Tian, Y., Wang, Y., Lu, P., Huang, T.: Deep relative distance learning: tell the difference between similar vehicles. In: 2016 IEEE Conference on Computer Vision and Pattern Recognition (CVPR) (2016)
16. Liu, X., Liu, W., Mei, T., Ma, H.: A deep learning-based approach to progressive vehicle re-identification for urban surveillance. In: Leibe, B., Matas, J., Sebe, N., Welling, M. (eds.) ECCV 2016. LNCS, vol. 9906, pp. 869–884. Springer, Cham (2016). https://doi.org/10.1007/978-3-319-46475-6_53

17. Meng, D., et al.: Parsing-based view-aware embedding network for vehicle re-identification. In: Proceedings of the IEEE/CVF Conference on Computer Vision and Pattern Recognition, pp. 7103–7112 (2020)
18. Pan, X., Luo, P., Shi, J., Tang, X.: Two at once: enhancing learning and generalization capacities via ibn-net. In: Proceedings of the European Conference on Computer Vision (ECCV), pp. 464–479 (2018)
19. Qian, J., Jiang, W., Luo, H., Yu, H.: Stripe-based and attribute-aware network: a two-branch deep model for vehicle re-identification. Measure. Sci. Technol. **31**(9), 095401 (2020)
20. Selvaraju, R.R., Cogswell, M., Das, A., Vedantam, R., Parikh, D., Batra, D.: Gradcam: Visual explanations from deep networks via gradient-based localization. In: Proceedings of the IEEE International Conference on Computer Vision, pp. 618–626 (2017)
21. Sun, W., Dai, G., Zhang, X., He, X., Chen, X.: Tbe-net: a three-branch embedding network with part-aware ability and feature complementary learning for vehicle re-identification. IEEE Trans. Intell. Transp. Syst. (2021)
22. Sun, Z., Nie, X., Xi, X., Yin, Y.: Cfvmnet: a multi-branch network for vehicle re-identification based on common field of view. In: Proceedings of the 28th ACM International Conference on Multimedia, pp. 3523–3531 (2020)
23. Suprem, A., Pu, C.: Looking glamorous: vehicle re-id in heterogeneous cameras networks with global and local attention. arXiv preprint arXiv:2002.02256 (2020)
24. Varior, R.R., Shuai, B., Lu, J., Xu, D., Wang, G.: A siamese long short-term memory architecture for human re-identification. In: Leibe, B., Matas, J., Sebe, N., Welling, M. (eds.) ECCV 2016. LNCS, vol. 9911, pp. 135–153. Springer, Cham (2016). https://doi.org/10.1007/978-3-319-46478-7_9
25. Vaswani, A., et al.: Attention is all you need. Adv. Neural Inf. Process. Syst. **30** (2017)
26. Wang, Q., Wu, B., Zhu, P., Li, P., Hu, Q.: Eca-net: efficient channel attention for deep convolutional neural networks. In: 2020 IEEE/CVF Conference on Computer Vision and Pattern Recognition (CVPR) (2020)
27. Wang, X., Girshick, R., Gupta, A., He, K.: Non-local neural networks. In: Proceedings of the IEEE Conference on Computer Vision and Pattern Recognition, pp. 7794–7803 (2018)
28. Bai, Y., Lou, Y., Gao, F., Wang, S., Wu, Y., Duan, L.Y.: Group-sensitive triplet embedding for vehicle reidentification. IEEE Trans. Multimedia **20**(9), 2385–2399 (2018)
29. Ye, M., Shen, J., Lin, G., Xiang, T., Shao, L., Hoi, S.C.: Deep learning for person re-identification: a survey and outlook. IEEE Trans. Pattern Anal. Mach. Intelligence **44**(6), 2872–2893 (2021)
30. Yi, Z., Ling, S.: Viewpoint-aware attentive multi-view inference for vehicle re-identification. In: IEEE/CVF Conference on Computer Vision and Pattern Recognition (2018)
31. Zhang, X., Zhang, R., Cao, J., Gong, D., You, M., Shen, C.: Part-guided attention learning for vehicle instance retrieval. IEEE Trans. Intell. Transp. Syst. **23**, 3048–3060 (2020)

A Self-supervised Graph Autoencoder with Barlow Twins

Jingci Li, Guangquan Lu$^{(\boxtimes)}$, and Jiecheng Li

Guangxi Key Lab of Multi-Source Information Mining and Security,
Guangxi Normal University, Guilin 541004, China
lugq@mailbox.gxnu.edu.cn, lijiecheng@stu.gxnu.edu.cn

Abstract. Self-supervised graph learning has attracted significant interest, especially graph contrastive learning. However, graph contrastive learning heavily relies on the choices of negative samples and the elaborate designs of architectures. Motivated by Barlow Twins, a method in computer vision, we propose a novel graph autoencoder named Core Barlow Graph Auto-Encoder(CBGAE) which does not rely on any special techniques, like predictor networks or momentum encoders. Meanwhile, we set a core view to make maximize agreement between the learned feature information. In contrast to the most existing graph contrastive learning models, it is negative-sample-free.

Keywords: Graph autoencoder · Graph representation learning · Self-supervised learning · Barlow Twins

1 Introduction

In recent years, graph representation learning has become increasingly popular in deep learning, especially in social networks, knowledge graphs, chemistry protein molecular domains, and so on. In these domains, original data is graph-structured data rather than Euclidean data. Therefore, convolutional neural networks(CNNs) [3] and recurrent neural networks (RNNs) [30] can not tackle well with graph-structured data. Graph representation learning can map graph-structured data into low-dimensional space and preserve graph topology and node feature information as much as possible. Previous works studying graph representation learning always need many well-annotated manual labels, namely, they are based on supervised learning or semi-supervised learning. Although previous works have achieved great success in many tasks of representation learning, there are several shortcomings. Firstly, collecting and annotating labels cost too much time during the experimental period. Secondly, however, labels are usually sparse in real-world scenarios and extracted from complex interaction systems so it is difficult to collect. Thirdly, relying on labels can cause an over-fitting problem, which runs in the opposite direction of our research goals.

To tackle the above shortcomings, a series of graph representation learning methods based on self-supervised learning have been proposed. They have no

© The Author(s), under exclusive license to Springer Nature Switzerland AG 2022
S. Khanna et al. (Eds.): PRICAI 2022, LNCS 13630, pp. 501–512, 2022.
https://doi.org/10.1007/978-3-031-20865-2_37

reliance on manual labels and solve several auxiliary tasks with signals acquired from the data itself [18]. In self-supervised graph representation learning, contrastive learning has become a mainstream method, especially for node and graph classification tasks. The keys to graph contrastive learning are generating data augmentations and then using the additional mutual information(MI) [20] estimator to score positive and negative pairs. For example, DGI [29] and MVGRL [9] utilize an estimator to score local-global representations and representations from augmentation views, taking about 10%-30% of the training time [19]. However, graph contrastive learning still suffers some limitations. Firstly, the MI estimator occupies expensive memory during the training process and the proposed model is sensitive to the choice of the MI estimator [28]. Secondly, the proposed method is also sensitive to the choice of negative pairs. The negative pairs can be generated by node-level, graph-level, edge-level, or feature-level. Thirdly, the proposed method usually relies on data augmentations in order to generate both input contents and their related contents [19].

Not the same as graph contrastive learning became a dominant approach, what is easy to be ignored in self-supervised graph learning is graph autoencoder which is an end-to-end approach, with no label required. Most existing models based on graph autoencoder or graph variational autoencoder just focus on link prediction and graph clustering based on single-view and have not explored deeply contrastive learning. Besides, major graph models based on contrastive learning focus on node classification and graph classification rather than link prediction or graph clustering. So, how do apply contrastive learning to graph autoencoder for link prediction or graph clustering? And how do we avoid the above shortcomings of contrastive learning?

To address the above issues, we propose a novel self-supervised graph autoencoder. Inspired by Barlow Twins [31], a self-supervised approach for computer vision by constructing two data augmentation views and trying to maximize the agreement between two learned representations from the above views. Therefore, feature information between two learned representations can resemble deeply to each other and minimize the feature redundancy. Notice that this is a negative-sample-free contrastive method, which just we need. Not just apply simply Barlow Twins to graph autoencoder, we propose Core Barlow Graph Auto-Encoder(CBGAE) which utilizes three views to learn the graph representation with comprehensive network topology and node feature information. Specifically, there will be three graph representations learned from the original input data, data augmentation based on global topology information, and data augmentation based on feature information. The original input data as the core view to maximize the feature agreement with the global topology view and feature similarity view, respectively. And the final graph representation is obtained by the attention mechanism.

The main contributions of this paper are summarized as follows:

- We propose a novel graph autoencoder optimized by Barlow Twins. We set the original data as the core view to promise the learned embeddings that can contain the most critical information.

- Not only do we obtain data augmentation on the graph structure, but also we get feature data augmentation simultaneously. Through the above process, the proposed method can aggregate comprehensive information and does not rely on any special techniques, like predictor networks or momentum encoders.
- The experimental results on four graph datasets demonstrate that the proposed model obtains solid competitive performance on link prediction tasks.

2   Related Work

2.1   Graph Autoencoder Models

Normally, a graph autoencoder contains two parts: an encoder that maps the graph-structured data into low-dimensional space and a decoder that reconstructs the adjacency matrix or node feature matrix through the hidden emddedings obtained from the encoder. Kipf et al. [14] first proposed graph autoencoder(GAE) and graph variational autoencoder(GVAE) stacked by two GCN [15] layers as the encoder and an inner product decoder to reconstruct the adjacency matrix.

Following GAE and GVAE, an increasing number of models based on them have been proposed. ARGA [22] combined generative adversarial network(GAN) [6] with GAE and improved GAE with adversarial regularization. ARVGA [22] is the variant of ARGA, like GVAE. TVGA [25] used a triad decoder to replace the inner product decoder, which can predict the three edges involved in a local triad. DGVAE [16] replaced normal distribution with the Dirichlet distributions as priors on the latent variables. GNAE and VGNAE [2] utilized L2-normalization to derive better embeddings for isloated nodes. MaskGAE [17] pre-masked a portion of edges and aimed to reconstruct the missing part. Different from the above models reconstructing the adjacency matrix, GALA [23] reconstructed the node feature matrix with a Laplacian smoothing-sharpening graph autoencoder. GraphMAE [10] focused on reconstructing node feature matrix with re-masking the hidden embeddings of masked nodes before the decoding process.

2.2   Graph Contrastive Learning

The graph contrastive learning takes inspiration from contrastive learning in computer vision which builds on maximizing mutual information between two augmentation views of the same image. However, unlike images, augmentation views of the graph-structured data can not been obtain simply. Augmentations on graphs can been categorized into two types: feature-space augmentations and structure-space augmentations. For feature-space augmentations, it can be masking or shuffling node features. For structure-space augmentations, it can be adding or removing some edges, sub-sampling, or generating global views.

Recently, there are more and more graph contrastive models proposed. MVGRL [9] achieved great performance on both node and graph classification tasks by maximizing MI between node representations of one view and graph representations of another view. GRACE [32] utilized node feature masking and edge dropping to obtian two augmented views, then focused on contrasting embeddings at node level. BGRL [27] was inspired from BYOL [7] and alleviated the reliance on negative sampling strategies. MERIT [11] deployed a self-distillation framework to enrich the supervision signals with multi-scale contrastive learning. AD-GCL [26] enabled GNNs avoid capturing redundant node features and allowed the encoder to capture the minimal sufficient feature information. There is no diffcult to find that the above models almost are trained for node and graph classification tasks and they are either sensitive to the choice of negative samples or need expensive memory. Moreover, they always just have two views to contrast with each other.

2.3   Barlow Twins

Contrast to previous self-supervised learning methods, Barlow Twins [31] utilized a symmetric framework without momentum, predictor, or stop-grad blocks. Meanwhile, Barlow Twins proposed a novel loss function having an invariance term and a redundancy reduction term. The invariance term can encourage the learned representations of the distorted versions of a sample to be similar, while the redundancy reduction term can encourage the diversity of learned representations. The key to the loss function is calculating the cross-correlation matrix between two learned representations of a pair of distorted inputs. Actually, Barlow Twins can be part of contrastive learning just contrasting on feature aspect to make the cross-correlation matrix close to the identity.

3   The Proposed Model

Let assume an undirected graph $\mathcal{G} = (\mathcal{V}, \mathcal{E})$, with $| \mathcal{V} | = n$ nodes and $| \mathcal{E} | = m$ edges, and denote $\mathbf{A} \in \mathbb{R}^{n \times n}$ as the adjacency matrix of $\mathcal{G}$, $\mathbf{X} \in \mathbb{R}^{n \times d}$ is the node features matrix. Specifically, $\mathbf{A}_{ij} = 1$ represents there is an edge between nodes i and j, otherwise, $\mathbf{A}_{ij} = 0$. $\mathbf{D}$ is the diagonal degree matrix of $\mathbf{A}$. Meanwhile, we define the latent variables $\mathbf{z_i}$, which is summarized in the matrix $\mathbf{Z} \in \mathbb{R}^{n \times d'}$.

3.1   Overall Framework

We propose a novel graph autoencoder named Core Barlow Graph Autoencoder(CBGAE). As illustrated in Fig. 1, our proposed model mainly consists of three components: data augmentations, a graph convolutional encoder, and an inner product decoder. And the original data $(\mathbf{A}, \mathbf{X})$ as core view, two augmented views as auxiliary views.

3.2   Data Augmentations

We consider two data augmentations on graph: feature augmentation and structural augmentation. For structural augmentation, considering that edge information plays an important role in link prediction, so we do not make edge modification, e.g. dropping and inserting a portion of edges. We acquire the diffusion

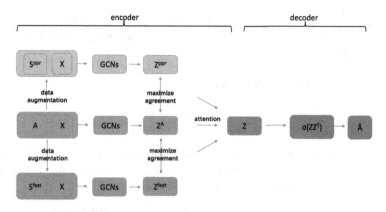

Fig. 1. The framework of CBGAE. $(\mathbf{A}, \mathbf{X})$ is the orginal data, $\mathbf{A}$ is the adjacency matrix, $\mathbf{X}$ is the node feature matrix. $(\mathbf{S}^{\text{ppr}}, \mathbf{X})$ and $(\mathbf{S}^{\text{feat}}, \mathbf{X})$ are augmented from the original view. The final embedding $\mathbf{Z}$ is fused by three specific embeddings from the above views.

matrix by PPR [21] to supply global topological information:

$$\mathbf{S}^{\text{ppr}} = \alpha(\mathbf{I_n} - (1-\alpha)\widetilde{\mathbf{D}}^{-\frac{1}{2}}\widetilde{\mathbf{A}}\widetilde{\mathbf{D}}^{-\frac{1}{2}})^{-1} \tag{1}$$

where α denotes the probability of random walk, $\mathbf{I_n} \in \mathbb{R}^{n \times n}$ is an identity matrix and $\widetilde{\mathbf{A}} = \widetilde{\mathbf{D}}^{-\frac{1}{2}}\hat{\mathbf{A}}\widetilde{\mathbf{D}}^{-\frac{1}{2}}$, $\hat{\mathbf{A}} = \mathbf{A} + \mathbf{I_n}$. For feature augmentation, we construct a k-nearest neighbor(KNN) graph based on node feature matrix $\mathbf{X}$:

$$\mathbf{S}_{ij}^{\text{feat}} = \frac{\exp(\cos(x_i, x_j))}{\sum_{k=1}^{n} \exp(\cos(x_i, x_k))} \tag{2}$$

where $\cos(x_i, x_j)$ measures the cosine similarity between two nodes.

3.3 Multi-view Graph Auto-Encoder

Now, we have obtained three views: $(\mathbf{A}, \mathbf{X})$, $(\mathbf{S}^{\text{ppr}}, \mathbf{X})$, and $(\mathbf{S}^{\text{feat}}, \mathbf{X})$. Then, we feed them into a GCN encoder stacked two layers separately, as follows:

$$\mathbf{Z}^{\mathbf{A}} = \text{ReLu}(\widetilde{\mathbf{A}}\text{ReLu}(\widetilde{\mathbf{A}}\mathbf{X}\mathbf{W}^0)\mathbf{W}^1) \tag{3}$$

$$\mathbf{Z}^{\text{feat}} = \text{ReLu}(\mathbf{S}^{\text{feat}}\text{ReLu}(\mathbf{S}^{\text{feat}}\mathbf{X}\mathbf{W}^0)\mathbf{W}^1) \tag{4}$$

$$\mathbf{Z}^{\text{ppr}} = \text{ReLu}(\mathbf{S}^{\text{ppr}}\text{ReLu}(\mathbf{S}^{\text{ppr}}\mathbf{X}\mathbf{W}^0)\mathbf{W}^1) \tag{5}$$

where $\widetilde{\mathbf{A}} = \widetilde{\mathbf{D}}^{-\frac{1}{2}}\hat{\mathbf{A}}\widetilde{\mathbf{D}}^{-\frac{1}{2}}$, $\hat{\mathbf{A}} = \mathbf{A} + \mathbf{I_n}$, $\mathbf{W}^0$ and $\mathbf{W}^1$ are weight matrices. Next, considering the importance of each specific learned embeddings from each view, we utilize the attention mechanism to fuse the above embeddings to obtain the final embeddings. For example, for the original view $(\mathbf{A}, \mathbf{X})$:

$$\mathbf{w}_{\mathbf{A}}^i = \mathbf{q}^{\mathbf{T}} \cdot \tanh(\mathbf{W} \cdot (\mathbf{z}_{\mathbf{A}}^i)^{\mathbf{T}} + \mathbf{b}) \tag{6}$$

where $\mathbf{W} \in \mathbb{R}^{h' \times h}$ is the weight matrix and $\mathbf{b} \in \mathbb{R}^{h' \times 1}$ is the bias vector. We get the attention values $\mathbf{w}_{\text{feat}}^i$ and $\mathbf{w}_{\text{ppr}}^i$ through the same way. Then we get the last attention weight:

$$\mathbf{a}_{\mathbf{A}}^i = \text{softmax}(\mathbf{a}_{\mathbf{A}}^i) \tag{7}$$

$$= \frac{\exp(\mathbf{w}_{\mathbf{A}}^i)}{\exp(\mathbf{w}_{\text{ppr}}^i) + \exp(\mathbf{w}_{\text{feat}}^i) + \exp(\mathbf{w}_{\mathbf{A}}^i)} \tag{8}$$

The attention weight $\mathbf{a}_{\mathbf{A}}^i$ implies the importance for relative learned representation. Similarly, $\mathbf{a}_{\text{feat}}^i = \text{softmax}(\mathbf{a}_{\text{feat}}^i)$ and $\mathbf{a}_{\text{ppr}}^i = \text{softmax}(\mathbf{a}_{\text{ppr}}^i)$. Finally, we fuse the above representation to obtain the final learned $\mathbf{Z}$:

$$\mathbf{Z} = \mathbf{a_A} \cdot \mathbf{Z^A} + \mathbf{a_{ppr}} \cdot \mathbf{Z^{ppr}} + \mathbf{a_{feat}} \cdot \mathbf{Z^{feat}} \tag{9}$$

Finally, we feed the final embeddings into the inner product decoder to reconstruct the original adjacency matrix:

$$\hat{\mathbf{A}} = \sigma(\mathbf{Z}\mathbf{Z^T}), \tag{10}$$

where $\mathbf{Z} = q(\mathbf{Z}|\mathbf{X}, \mathbf{A})$ is the final graph representation, $\sigma(\cdot)$ is a logistc sigmoid function.

3.4   Loss Function

Barlow Twins Loss Function Barlow Twins [31] loss function includes two terms: an invariance term and a redundancy reduction term. Details as follows:

$$\mathcal{L}_{\text{bt}} \triangleq \sum_{i=1}^{n} \left(1 - \mathbf{C}_{\text{ii}}\right)^2 + \lambda \sum_{i=1}^{n} \sum_{j \neq i}^{n} \mathbf{C}_{\text{ij}}^{\;2} \tag{11}$$

where λ is a positive constant trading off the importance of the first and second terms of the loss, and where $\mathbf{C}$ is the cross-correlation matrix calculated between the embeddings of two augmented views:

$$\mathbf{C}_{\text{ij}} \triangleq \frac{\sum_b z_{\text{b,i}}^{\mathbf{A}} z_{\text{b,j}}^{\mathbf{B}}}{\sqrt{\sum_b \left(z_{\text{b,i}}^{\mathbf{A}}\right)^2} \sqrt{\sum_b \left(z_{\text{b,j}}^{\mathbf{B}}\right)^2}} \tag{12}$$

where b indexes batch samples and i, j index the vector dimension of the networks' outputs. $\mathbf{C}$ is a square matrix with size the dimensionality of the network's output. We hope that the on diagonal elements $\mathbf{C}_{\text{ii}}$ to be equal to 1 and the off-diagonal elements $\mathbf{C}_{\text{ij}}$ to be equal to 0. Instead of setting batch size, we directly feed full size into the proposed model for link prediction.

In our model, we set the original data as the core view, so we can obtain two cross-correlation matrices. One is calculated by $\mathbf{Z^A}$ and $\mathbf{Z^{feat}}$, another one is calculated by $\mathbf{Z^A}$ and $\mathbf{Z^{ppr}}$. Details as follows:

$$\mathcal{L}_{bt}^{A,ppr} \triangleq \sum_{i=1}^{n} \left(1 - C_{ii}^{A,ppr}\right)^2 + \lambda^{A,ppr} \sum_{i=1}^{n} \sum_{j \neq i}^{n} C_{ij}^{A,ppr^2} \tag{13}$$

$$\mathcal{L}_{bt}^{A,feat} \triangleq \sum_{i=1}^{n} \left(1 - C_{ii}^{A,feat}\right)^2 + \lambda^{A,feat} \sum_{i=1}^{n} \sum_{j \neq i}^{n} C_{ij}^{A,feat^2} \tag{14}$$

Therefore, the total loss function can be presented as follows:

$$\mathcal{L} = \mathbb{E}_{q(\mathbf{Z}|\mathbf{X},\mathbf{A})}[\log p(\mathbf{A} \mid \mathbf{Z})] + \mathcal{L}_{bt}^{A,ppr} + \mathcal{L}_{bt}^{A,feat} \tag{15}$$

where the first term is the reconstruction loss and the left terms are Barlow Twins loss function.

4   Experiment

4.1   Datasets

To verify the performance of the proposed method on link prediction task, we carry on experiments on four popular citation datasets. In citation datasets, a publication as a node and a connection as an edge, meanwhile, the unique words in each publication as node feature. Each dataset has been summaried in Table 1.

Table 1. Dataset Statistics

Dataset	Nodes	Edges	Features	Labels	T/V/T
Cora	2708	5429	1433	7	140/500/1000
Citeseer	3327	4732	3703	6	120/500/1000
Pubmed	19717	44338	500	3	60/500/1000
Acm	3025	13128	1870	3	200/300/700

4.2   Implementation

All experiments are implemented in Tensorflow [1] and all parameters are initialized by Glorot scheme [5] and optimized with the Adam algorithm [13]. For Cora, for the optimizer, we set the learning rate as 0.001. What is more, the dropout rate equals 0.5 and epoch equals 200. Besides, the number of neurons in each GCNs is set to "1433-256-128–1433". Like Cora, for other datasets, the number of neurons in hidden GCN layers is set to "256-128". And $\lambda^{A,ppr}$ and $\lambda^{A,feat}$ are trade-off parameter, and we find that for Cora and Citeseer $\lambda^{A,ppr} = \lambda^{A,feat} = 0.5$ works the best. For Pubmed, epoch equals 300, $\lambda^{A,ppr} = \lambda^{A,feat} = 0.5$. For Acm, epoch equals 500, $\lambda^{A,ppr} = \lambda^{A,feat} = 0.1$.

4.3   Comparison Methods

The following state-of-the-art baseline methods are chosen for comparison.

- GAE and GVAE [14] contain an encoder and a decoder. GAE reconstructs directly the adjacency matrix while GVAE can learn an embedding whose distribution can match the distribution of samples by learning mean and standard deviation.

- ARGE and ARVGE [22] use an adversarial mechanism during the training process to keep the original graph topology information and node feature information as much as possible.
- sGraphite-VAE [4] can enlarge the normal neighborhood in the aggregation of GNNs, which aims at maximizing mutual information.
- SIGVAE [8] expands the flexibility of VGAE and replaces the inner product decoder with a Bernoulli-Poisson relative decoder.
- EVGAE [12] consists of multiple sparse GVAE models, which can aid in mitigating the over-pruning problem and boosting the generative ability of GVAE.
- FastGAE [24] can scale GAE and GVAE to large graphs with millions of nodes and edges based on an effective stochastic subgraph decoding scheme.

4.4   Experimental Results

Link Prediction Table 2 summarises AUC and AP scores on four graph benchmark datasets. As shown in Table 2, it is clear that for Cora, Citeseer, and Pubmed, CBGAE outperforms other models based on graph autoencoder, and all AUC and AP scores on four datasets are higher than 97%, especially the AUC and AP scores on Citeseer are 99.1% and 98.9%, which have increased the AUC and AP scores from 9.6% and 9% compared with GAE. Compared with GVAE, CBGAE improves by 8.3% and 6.9%, respectively. For Cora, CBGAE has increased AUC and AP scores from 7.8% and 6.7% compared with GAE. Meanwhile, compared with FastGAE, CBGAE has increased the AUC and AP scores from 7.1% and 6.4%. For Acm, we can see that each method can achieve good performance and ARGE's performance is the best. The performance of CBGAE is second only to ARGE. We think that the reason why the above methods can obtain good performance on Acm maybe is that there are a great number of edges in this data, which supplied rich connection information. Totally, we think that CBGAE aggregates comprehensive topology and node feature information by optimizing the Barlow Twins loss function by setting a core view way that can maximize the agreement feature information between different views. To easy to read, all the highest results of each following table are in bold.

Furthermore, to verify the effectiveness of core Barlow Twins loss function, we compared the proposed model with its variant called Full Barlow Graph Auto-Encoder(FBGAE). For CBGAE, the original data as the core view. Two augmented views calculate their specific cross-correlation matrices with the core view, individually. For FBGAE, there is no core view and each view will obtain its specific cross-correlation matrices calculated with each other, individually. At the bottom of Table 2 shows that setting the core view rather than the full view can achieve better performance on each dataset. For Pubmed, FBGAE even obtains the worst performance.

Table 2. AUC and AP for Link Prediction

Dataset	Cora		Pubmed		Citeseer		Acm	
Method	AUC	AP	AUC	AP	AUC	AP	AUC	AP
GAE [14]	0.910	0.920	0.964	0.965	0.895	0.899	0.955	0.955
GVAE [14]	0.914	0.926	0.944	0.947	0.908	0.920	0.960	0.960
ARGE [22]	0.924	0.932	0.968	0.971	0.919	0.930	**0.982**	**0.985**
ARVGE [22]	0.924	0.926	0.965	0.968	0.924	0.930	0.974	0.978
EVGAE [12]	0.929	0.938	0.968	0.969	0.915	0.932	–	–
FastGAE [24]	0.917	0.923	0.961	0.963	0.902	0.901	–	–
sGraphite-VAE [4]	0.937	0.935	0.948	0.963	0.941	0.954	–	–
SIGVAE [8]	0.960	0.968	0.970	0.971	0.964	0.963	–	–
CBGAE(ours)	**0.988**	**0.987**	**0.974**	**0.971**	**0.991**	**0.989**	0.978	0.972
FBGAE(ours)	0.978	0.975	0.903	0.899	0.957	0.948	0.957	0.948

4.5 Random Attacks on Edges

To investigate the robustness of our proposed model, we carry on experiments about random attacks on edges. We reduce the total number of edge sets in the training set on Cora and Citeseer: 85%, 75%, 65%, 55%, and 45%. Figures 2a and 2b show that as the number of edges in the training set decreases, CBGAE

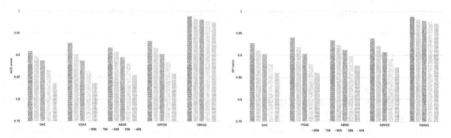

(a) AUC value of random attack on Cora. (b) AP value of random attack on Cora.

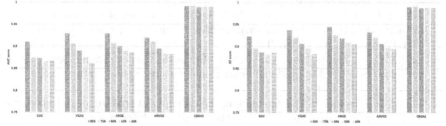

(c) AUC value of random attack on Cite- (d) AP value of random attack on Citeseer.   seer.

Fig. 2. Random attack on four datasets.

can always keep the best performance and the overall trend of CBGAE keep a slight downward trend, while trends of other baselines keep always a stronger downward. For Citeseer, the same case happens illustrated in Figs. 2c and 2d. The other models' performance is significantly affected by the number of edge sets in the training set, however, CBGAE has hardly been affected by reducing the edges of the training set.

5   Conclusion

In this paper, we propose a novel graph autoencoder with a core view to optimize the Barlow Twins and reconstruction loss functions together. First, we obtain two auxiliary views through data augmentations. Then, we feed all views into the graph convolutional encoder and obtain three specific hidden embeddings. Meanwhile, we calculate cross-correlation matrices between them to reduce the feature redundancy and promise feature agreement between different views. Experiment results that CBGAE can achieve competitive performance. Especially, CBGAE achieves the best performance in link prediction compared with some state-of-the-art models on three datasets.

Acknowledgment. The work is supported partly by National Natural Science Foundation of China (No. 62166003), the Project of Guangxi Science and Technology (GuiKeAD20159041), Intelligent Processing and the Research Fund of Guangxi Key Lab of Multi-source Information Mining & Security (No.20-A-01-01, MIMS20-M-01), the Guangxi Collaborative Innovation Center of Multi-Source Information Integration and the Guangxi "Bagui" Teams for Innovation and Research, China.

References

1. Abadi, M., et al.: TensorFlow: a system for large-scale machine learning. In: 12th USENIX Symposium on Operating Systems Design and Implementation (OSDI 16), pp. 265–283 (2016)
2. Ahn, S.J., Kim, M.: Variational graph normalized autoencoders. In: Proceedings of the 30th ACM International Conference on Information & Knowledge Management, pp. 2827–2831 (2021)
3. Albawi, S., Mohammed, T.A., Al-Zawi, S.: Understanding of a convolutional neural network. In: 2017 International Conference on Engineering and Technology (ICET), pp. 1–6. IEEE (2017)
4. Di, X., Yu, P., Bu, R., Sun, M.: Mutual information maximization in graph neural networks. In: 2020 International Joint Conference on Neural Networks (IJCNN), pp. 1–7. IEEE (2020)
5. Glorot, X., Bengio, Y.: Understanding the difficulty of training deep feedforward neural networks. In: Proceedings of the Thirteenth International Conference on Artificial Intelligence and Statistics, pp. 249–256. JMLR Workshop and Conference Proceedings (2010)
6. Goodfellow, I., et al.: Generative adversarial networks. In: Advances in Neural Information Processing Systems 3 (2014). https://doi.org/10.1145/3422622

7. Grill, J.B., et al.: Bootstrap your own latent-a new approach to self-supervised learning. Adv. Neural. Inf. Process. Syst. **33**, 21271–21284 (2020)
8. Hasanzadeh, A., Hajiramezanali, E., Narayanan, K.R., Duffield, N., Zhou, M., Qian, X.: Semi-implicit graph variational auto-encoders. In: Wallach, H.M., (eds.) Advances in Neural Information Processing Systems 32: Annual Conference on Neural Information Processing Systems 2019, NeurIPS 2019, December 8–14, 2019, Vancouver, BC, Canada, pp. 10711–10722 (2019)
9. Hassani, K., Khasahmadi, A.H.: Contrastive multi-view representation learning on graphs. In: International Conference on Machine Learning, pp. 4116–4126. PMLR (2020)
10. Hou, Z., Liu, X., Dong, Y., Wang, C., Tang, J., et al.: GraphMAE: self-supervised masked graph autoencoders. arXiv preprint arXiv:2205.10803 (2022)
11. Jin, M., Zheng, Y., Li, Y.F., Gong, C., Zhou, C., Pan, S.: Multi-scale contrastive siamese networks for self-supervised graph representation learning. arXiv preprint arXiv:2105.05682 (2021)
12. Khan, R.A., Anwaar, M.U., Kleinsteuber, M.: Epitomic variational graph autoencoder. In: 2020 25th International Conference on Pattern Recognition (ICPR), pp. 7203–7210. IEEE (2021)
13. Kingma, D., Ba, J.: Adam: a method for stochastic optimization. Computer Science (2014)
14. Kipf, T.N., Welling, M.: Variational graph auto-encoders. In: NIPS Workshop on Bayesian Deep Learning (2016)
15. Kipf, T.N., Welling, M.: Semi-supervised classification with graph convolutional networks. In: International Conference on Learning Representations (ICLR) (2017)
16. Li, J., et al.: Dirichlet graph variational autoencoder. In: Larochelle, H., Ranzato, M., Hadsell, R., Balcan, M., Lin, H. (eds.) Advances in Neural Information Processing Systems. vol. 33, pp. 5274–5283. Curran Associates, Inc. (2020). https://proceedings.neurips.cc/paper/2020/file/38a77aa456fc813af07bb428f2363c8d-Paper.pdf
17. Li, J., et al.: MaskGAE: masked graph modeling meets graph autoencoders. arXiv preprint arXiv:2205.10053 (2022)
18. Liu, Y., et al.: Graph self-supervised learning: a survey. IEEE Trans. Knowl. Data Eng. (2022)
19. Mo, Y., Peng, L., Xu, J., Shi, X., Zhu, X.: Simple unsupervised graph representation learning. In: AAAI (2022)
20. Van den Oord, A., Li, Y., Vinyals, O.: Representation learning with contrastive predictive coding. arXiv e-prints pp. arXiv-1807 (2018)
21. Page, L., Brin, S., Motwani, R., Winograd, T.: The pagerank citation ranking: bringing order to the web. Tech. rep. (1999)
22. Pan, S., Hu, R., Long, G., Jiang, J., Yao, L., Zhang, C.: Adversarially regularized graph autoencoder for graph embedding. In: Lang, J. (ed.) Proceedings of the Twenty-Seventh International Joint Conference on Artificial Intelligence, IJCAI 2018, July 13–19, 2018, Stockholm, Sweden, pp. 2609–2615. ijcai.org (2018). https://doi.org/10.24963/ijcai.2018/362
23. Park, J., Lee, M., Chang, H.J., Lee, K., Choi, J.Y.: Symmetric graph convolutional autoencoder for unsupervised graph representation learning. In: Proceedings of the IEEE/CVF International Conference on Computer Vision, pp. 6519–6528 (2019)
24. Salha, G., Hennequin, R., Remy, J.B., Moussallam, M., Vazirgiannis, M.: FastGAE: scalable graph autoencoders with stochastic subgraph decoding. Neural Netw. **142**, 1–19 (2021)

25. Shi, H., Fan, H., Kwok, J.T.: Effective decoding in graph auto-encoder using triadic closure. In: Proceedings of the AAAI Conference on Artificial Intelligence, vol. 34, pp. 906–913 (2020)
26. Suresh, S., Li, P., Hao, C., Neville, J.: Adversarial graph augmentation to improve graph contrastive learning. In: Advances in Neural Information Processing Systems 34 (2021)
27. Thakoor, S., Tallec, C., Azar, M.G., Munos, R., Veličković, P., Valko, M.: Bootstrapped representation learning on graphs. In: ICLR 2021 Workshop on Geometrical and Topological Representation Learning (2021)
28. Tschannen, M., Djolonga, J., Rubenstein, P.K., Gelly, S., Lucic, M.: On mutual information maximization for representation learning. arXiv preprint arXiv:1907.13625 (2019)
29. Velickovic, P., Fedus, W., Hamilton, W.L., Liò, P., Bengio, Y., Hjelm, R.D.: Deep graph infomax. In: ICLR (Poster), vol. 2 , issue 3, p. 4 (2019)
30. Zaremba, W., Sutskever, I., Vinyals, O.: Recurrent neural network regularization. CoRR abs/1409.2329 (2014)
31. Zbontar, J., Jing, L., Misra, I., LeCun, Y., Deny, S.: Barlow Twins: self-supervised learning via redundancy reduction. In: International Conference on Machine Learning, pp. 12310–12320. PMLR (2021)
32. Zhu, Y., Xu, Y., Yu, F., Liu, Q., Wu, S., Wang, L.: Deep graph contrastive representation learning. arXiv preprint arXiv:2006.04131 (2020)

Few-Shot Image Classification Method Based on Fusion of Important Features of Different Scales

Wu Zeng[1(✉)], Hengliang Zhu[1,2], Linkai Chen[1], Guangda Xu[1], and Shihao Zhao[1]

[1] College of Computer Science and Mathematics, Fujian University of Technology, Fuzhou 350118, China
2201905122@smail.fjut.edu.cn
[2] Fujian Key Laboratory of Big Data Mining and Applications, Fuzhou 350118, China

Abstract. At present, most few-shot learning faces some difficulties. On the one hand, during feature extraction, the feature information extraction is insufficient due to the single extraction scale. Another problem is that it is difficult to accurately extract the important information content in the image. To this end, a few-shot learning method-MSIFA is proposed. In general, this strategy mainly utilizes the designed multi-scale feature generation module MSFGM to generate feature information about samples at multiple scales, so as to enrich the feature representation of samples. Next, the SAFAM module constructed by the self-attention mechanism extracts the important feature information of the samples at various scales. Afterwards, these important feature information is spliced and combined as a more accurate feature expression of the sample. Extensive experiments are performed on multiple standard datasets. Experimental results show that our method can not only greatly improve the classification performance of baseline methods, but also surpass most advanced few-shot learning methods.

Keywords: Few-shot learning · Multi-scale features · Feature representation enhancement · Self-attention mechanism

1 Introduction

In recent years, with the continuous development of technology, especially with the support of many constantly upgraded basic computing hardware. Many fields of deep learning [1, 2] have made great progress. In general, the success of deep learning is partly due to the collection of large datasets (such as Pascal VOC [3], ImageNet [4], etc.) and computationally powerful computing devices. A large amount of data helps the algorithm learn a high-performance model, because a large amount of data can cover most real-world sample distributions. However, not all deep learning tasks can obtain a large amount of data for model training.

© The Author(s), under exclusive license to Springer Nature Switzerland AG 2022
S. Khanna et al. (Eds.): PRICAI 2022, LNCS 13630, pp. 513–524, 2022.
https://doi.org/10.1007/978-3-031-20865-2_38

In most convolutional neural networks [5] (CNN) tasks, the smaller the number of training samples, the greater the risk of model overfitting. In contrast, humans can learn some important characteristics of new things with only a small number of samples. For example, a person only needs to see a few pictures of a giraffe, and then go to the zoo to quickly recognize that this animal with a long neck is a giraffe. Inspired by this, researchers propose few-shot learning (FSL) [6], which can achieve a high-performance classification model with only a small amount of data.

Currently, researchers propose a variety of methods to improve the difficulties encountered in few-shot learning. It can be mainly divided into two categories, one is metric learning [7], and the other is meta-learning [8]. Metric learning mainly completes few-shot classification by comparing the similarity between labeled samples and unknown samples. Meta-learning is suitable for cross-task learning. Depending on the task, the initial parameters suitable for the current task are given to start training. It only takes a few iterations to obtain a model with high classification accuracy [9]. To this end, Korch et al. [10] proposed a similarity measurement model called Siamese Neural Networks. The model has two identical CNN networks, and will perform feature extraction on the two incoming samples respectively. Then compare the similarity between them, so as to realize the classification of unknown samples. Snell et al. [7] proposed the Prototypical Network (ProtoNet). This method first obtains the feature vectors of all samples in each category of the query set, and then finds a class center point in each category. Then, the distance between the unknown sample and the center point of each class of the known sample is calculated by Euclidean distance. The smaller the distance difference, the closer the categories are, thus realizing the classification of images. The above methods have achieved certain results, but there are still some shortcomings. On the one hand, the feature scale extracted by such methods is relatively single, so the feature information contained is not rich enough. On the other hand, such methods simply perform indiscriminate global feature extraction on images. It does not give different weights to different regions according to the different regions. In an image, in addition to the target object representing the label, it will also be disturbed by its background clutter, the size of the target object and its different poses. For example, in an image labeled panda, there may be different distractors in the background of the panda and it may have different poses in different images. The undifferentiated feature information extraction will include these interfering information content. The feature information of these distractors is not only unnecessary, but also affects the calculation of the similarity between samples, resulting in bias.

In order to improve the above problems, this paper learns the important feature information of multiple scales in the image, rather than focusing on the feature information at a single scale. The feature information obtained by a single scale has a certain one-sidedness, while the features of different scales can contain richer and more detailed feature information. The feature resolution of the lower layer is higher, so it has more location and detail information (such as edge feature information and color feature information, etc.). However, due to the insufficient number of convolutional layers, it lacks semantic information and thus contains more noise. The high-level features have stronger semantic information, but the resolution is also relatively low, so the perception of local details is weak. Therefore, the feature information of different scales may form a good complementarity.

The contributions of this paper are: (1) In view of the one-sidedness of single-scale feature information, this paper designs a multi-scale feature generator to generate feature vectors of samples at different scales. (2) In order to express the information content of the samples more accurately, a self-attention feature aggregation module is designed. The important information content of samples at different scales is obtained through the self-attention feature aggregation module mainly constructed by the self-attention mechanism. And these features are spliced and aggregated in order to serve as a more accurate feature representation of the sample image at different scales. (3) Conduct a large number of image classification experiments on multiple datasets. Experimental results show that our method can not only effectively improve the classification performance of baseline methods, but also surpass most advanced few-shot learning methods.

2   Related Work

In the exploration of the few-shot learning method, the main purpose is to obtain a model that can achieve high classification accuracy using only a small amount of data. In recent years, most methods using convolutional networks have achieved good results in few-shot learning. The methods mainly include few-shot learning methods based on metric learning and few-shot learning methods based on meta-learning.

The method based on metric learning is to measure the similarity between the query set samples and the support set samples, so as to complete the classification of unknown samples. Vinyals et al. [11] proposed a matching network, whose main method is to add a long short term memory network (LSTM)to the metric learning model. The extracted features are further processed by the memory network, and then the similarity between samples is calculated through metric learning. The relation network proposed by Sung et al. [12]. Its strategy is to give a model that can determine the relationship between objects by building a completely end-to-end network. The main role of relational networks is to provide a learnable nonlinear classifier. Chen et al. [13] proposed a multi-scale adaptive task attention network (MATANet) for few-shot learning.

The main method based on meta-learning is to guide the training of new tasks from a better starting point by transferring existing knowledge or experience. With only a few iterations, the model can achieve good classification accuracy. Santoro et al. [14] proposed a memory-augmented neural network (MANN) architecture. It mainly uses the LSTM module to realize the combination of neural network with long-term memory ability, so as to realize small sample learning. Finn et al. [15] propose a model-agnostic meta-learning method that can help other methods to train from a good starting point. Ravi [16] et al. used an LSTM-based learner to train an additional optimizer, enabling the search for a starting point for better initial parameters. Zhang et al. [17] proposed the Episode-level Pretext Task (IEPT) framework, which more closely integrates self-supervised learning (SSL) into few-shot learning to improve the performance of small-shot learning. Shyam et al. [18] proposed a recurrent network based on attention mechanism for few-shot learning, and achieved good results.

Most of the above methods only perform feature extraction on a single scale. Compared with multi-scale feature information, the feature information obtained through a single scale will inevitably be one-sided. On the other hand, most methods in metric learning are indiscriminate extraction of global feature information. It is not considered that some important information in the image is the key to reflect the image label, so the important information about the target object in the image cannot be obtained well. Different from most methods, this paper designs a multi-scale generation module to generate feature information about samples at multiple scales. And use the self-attention module to aggregate important feature information in different scales, so as to complete the more accurate expression of image information.

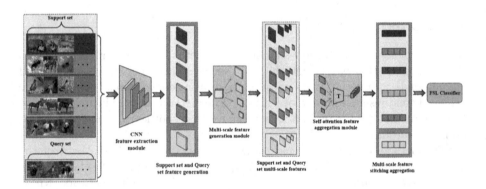

Fig. 1. Schematic diagram of the running process of the MSIFA model.

3   MSIFA Method

This section will introduce the MSIFA model architecture in detail. The overall architecture is shown in Fig. 1.

3.1   Problem Definition

Specifically, each meta-task T contains a support set S and a query set Q. N-way K-shot is expressed as extracting N categories from the training data set, and randomly extracting K samples from each category as the support set. Then continue to randomly select q samples from the remaining samples as the query set. Then there are:

$$S = \{(x_i, y_i) \,|\, i = 1, 2..., N \times K\} \tag{1}$$

$$Q = \{(x_i, y_i) \,|\, i = 1, 2..., N \times q\} \tag{2}$$

$$T = \{(S_i, Q_i)\}_{i=1}^{m} \tag{3}$$

where x_i and y_i represent samples and their labels, respectively, and m represents the number of meta-learning tasks.

3.2 Feature Extraction Module

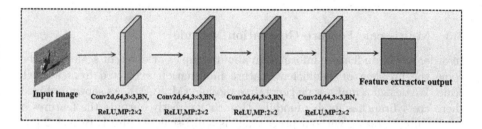

Fig. 2. Basic feature extractor based on 4-layer convolutional network.

In this paper, we choose ProtoNet [7] as the baseline model. And a CNN network with 4 layers of convolutional blocks is selected as the basic feature extraction network. The main structure of the network is shown in Fig. 2, in which each convolution block contains: 1 convolution layer (where the convolution kernel size is 3×3 and the number of channels is 64, BatchNorm layer, ReLU nonlinearity activation layer and max pooling layer of size 2×2. There is a non-parametric classifier in ProtoNet, whose main role is to update the parameters of the model through learning. Finally, a feature processor is used to calculate the feature embedding of each category, and the prototype v_k of the category is searched by the embedding function $f_\phi(\cdot)$:

$$v_k = \frac{1}{K} \sum_{(x_i, y_i) \in S} f_\phi(x_i) \tag{4}$$

Among them, ϕ represents the learned parameters, and x_i and y_i represent the samples and their labels, respectively.

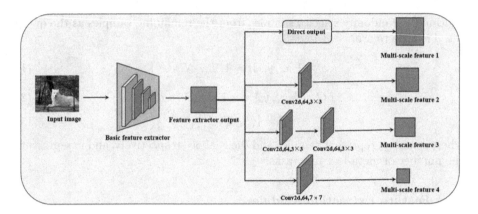

Fig. 3. Schematic diagram of the operation flow of the MSFGM module.

3.3   Multi-scale Feature Generation Module

In order to obtain feature information about samples at different scales, to over-come the problem of insufficient feature information extracted from a single scale. We design a multi-scale generative module (MSFGM). As shown in Fig. 3, there are 4 branches in this module. Branch 1 directly outputs the features of the feature extractor without processing, as multi-scale feature 1. Branch 2 pro-cesses the output of the feature extractor through a convolution block with a convolution kernel size of 3 × 3 and a channel number of 64, and then outputs it as multi-scale feature 2. Branch 3 processes the output of the feature processor with 2 convolutional layers (the kernel size is 3 × 3 and the number of channels is 64) as multi-scale feature 3. Through the convolution cascade of two 3 × 3 convolution kernels, the same receptive field as one 5 × 5 convolution kernel can be obtained, which improves the perception ability of global information, while the number of parameters is less. In the last branch, a 7 × 7 convolution kernel is added to obtain multi-scale feature 4. After each sample is processed by the multi-scale feature generation module, four sets of feature vectors at different scales can be obtained.

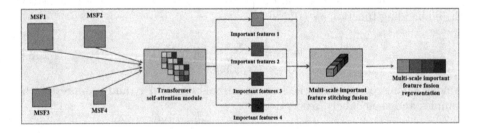

Fig. 4. Self-attention feature aggregation module.

3.4   Self-attention Feature Aggregation Module

The feature extractor only extracts the global feature information in the image indiscriminately, which may be affected by various image background interferers, and the size and posture of the target object. In order to better represent the important feature information in the image. As shown in Fig. 4, a Self-attention Feature Aggregation Module (SAFAM) is designed to extract important feature information in different scales. Then, through the self-attention feature aggregation module, four groups of important feature information in different scales are extracted respectively. Finally, these feature vectors are spliced and aggregated in order to generate a more accurate feature representation about the image. The fused feature representation enhances the details of the samples and the connection of the global features. Self-attention can not only obtain a larger receptive field and contextual information by capturing global information, but also reduce the dependence on external information and be better at capturing the internal correlation of data or features. Therefore, the self-attention mechanism can be used to better obtain important feature information in different scales. In general, based on $T_r = \{(x_i, y_i, r), r = 1, ..., R, i = 1, ..., l_k + l_q\}$, Where, l_k is the number of support samples, l_q is the number of query set samples, and r is the feature maps of different scales. For example, $(x_1, y_1, 4)$ represents the feature map of the fourth scale of the first sample. Construct feature tensor $F \in R^{(l_k + l_q) \times R \times d}$, where d is the feature dimension and R is the multiscale quantity. Then use the Transformer [19] to obtain the important feature codes. Multi-head attention in Transformer helps the model to capture rich feature information. The Transformer will receive a set of triples of input (F, F, F) as (Q, K, V), Among them, Q, K, and V are respectively represented as query, key, and value. $F^{(i)}$ and the attention module are defined as:

$$(F_Q^{(i)}, F_K^{(i)}, F_V^{(i)}) = (F^{(i)} W_Q, F^{(i)} W_K, F^{(i)} W_V) \tag{5}$$

$$F_{attn}^{(i)} = F^{(i)} + softmax(\frac{F_Q^{(i)} (F_K^{(i)})^T}{\sqrt{d_K}}) F_V^{(i)} \tag{6}$$

where d represents the feature dimension, and $d_K = d$. W_Q, W_K and W_V represent the parameters of the three fully connected layers, respectively. First, the features of the same image sample are generated by the multi-scale generation module to generate 4-scale feature maps. Then, the Transformer is used to extract the features of these four scales, and finally the key features of different scales are spliced and aggregated in order. And use this as the feature information representation of the sample, and the features of the splicing aggregation are represented as:

$$F_{all} = [F^S, F^Q] \in R^{(l_k + l_q) \times R \times d} \tag{7}$$

$$F_{all} = flatten(F_{attn}) \tag{8}$$

Among them, F^S and F^Q represent support set aggregation features and query set aggregation features, respectively. $flatten(\cdot)$ represents a flattening operation on the last two dimensions of F_{attn}. The loss of few-shot classification is shown in the following formula, where $h(\cdot)$ is the distance metric function.

$$L_{total} = -\frac{1}{l_q} \sum_{i=1}^{l_q} \log \frac{\exp(-h(F_i^Q, F_i^S))}{\sum_{n \in N} \exp(-h(F_i^Q, F_i^S))} \tag{9}$$

4 Experimental Analysis

4.1 Dataset and Evaluation Metrics

The experiments in this paper use four public datasets to verify the method proposed in this paper. The main indicators of the dataset are: the number of images in miniImageNet [11] is 60,000, the number of categories is 100, and the number of each category is 600. Among them, the number of training set classes is 64, the number of validation set classes is 16, and the number of test set classes is 20. There are 608 categories in tieredImageNet [20], with an average of 1282 images per category, where the number of training, validation, and test classes are 351, 97, and 160, respectively. The Stanford Dogs [21] dataset is a subclass of the large dataset ImageNet [4], which has 120 dog images, with 70, 20, and 30 training, validation, and test classes, respectively. CUB-200-2011 [22] contains 200 bird images, and the training set, validation set and test set have 130, 20 and 50 categories respectively. The experiment uses the Top-1 average accuracy to measure the performance of the model.

4.2 Experimental Setup and Comparison Methods

The MSIFA method is performed on the Pytorch framework and experiments are performed on 2 T-A100 (80G). The initial learning rate is 0.001, the weight decay is 0.00001, the momentum is 0.95, and the confidence interval is set to 95%. The backbone network selected for the experiment is conv4-64. In order to verify the effectiveness of the method in this paper, it is compared with a variety of advanced few-shot learning methods, namely: MatchingNet [11], RelationNet [12], ProtoNet [7], MAML [15], IMP [23], DN4 [24], DN PARN [25], DSN-MR [26], Neg-Cosine [27], BOIL [28].

4.3 Experimental Results and Analysis

Table 1 presents the experimental results on four datasets, miniImageNet, tiered-ImageNet, CUB-200-2011, and Standford Dogs. The experiments are mainly carried out under the settings of 5-way 1-shot and 5-way 5-shot. From Table 1, we can intuitively see that compared with other methods in the table, the method in this paper has achieved the best classification accuracy under various settings in the four datasets. In these datasets, in the experimental setting of 5-way 5-shot, compared to the baseline method ProtoNet, the classification accuracy is improved by 6.43%, 1.94%, 20.26% and 11.92%, respectively. Not only are they

Table 1. The experimental results on miniImageNet, tieredImageNet , Standford Dogs and CUB-200-2011(%).Among them, the bold font indicates the optimal result, and "-" indicates that the original paper did not give the experimental results.

Method	miniImageNet		tieredImageNet		Standford dogs		CUB-200-2011	
	5-way1-shot	5-way5-shot	5-way 1-shot	5-way5-shot	5-way1-shot	5-way5-shot	5-way1-shot	5-way5-shot
MatchingNet	43.56 ± 0.84	55.31 ± 0.73	–	–	35.80 ± 0.99	47.50 ± 1.03	55.92 ± 0.95	72.09 ± 0.76
ProtoNet	49.42 ± 0.78	68.20 ± 0.66	53.31 ± 0.89	72.69 ± 0.74	37.59 ± 1.00	48.19 ± 1.03	51.31 ± 0.91	70.77 ± 0.69
MAML	48.70 ± 1.84	63.10 ± 0.92	51.64 ± 1.81	70.30 ± 1.75	44.81 ± 0.34	58.68 ± 0.31	48.70 ± 1.84	63.11 ± 0.92
RelationNet	50.04 ± 0.80	65.30 ± 0.70	54.48 ± 0.93	71.32 ± 0.78	43.33 ± 0.42	55.23 ± 0.41	62.45 ± 0.98	76.11 ± 0.69
IMP	49.60 ± 0.80	68.10 ± 0.80	53.63 ± 0.51	71.89 ± 0.44	–	–	–	–
DN4	51.24 ± 0.74	71.02 ± 0.64	–		45.41 ± 0.76	63.51 ± 0.62	52.79 ± 0.86	81.45 ± 0.70
DN PARN	55.22 ± 0.84	71.55 ± 0.66	–	–	–	–	–	–
DSN-MR	55.88 ± 0.90	70.50 ± 0.68	–	–	–	–	–	–
Neg-Cosine	52.84 ± 0.76	70.41 ± 0.66	–	–	–	–	–	–
BOIL	49.61 ± 0.16	66.45 ± 0.37	–	–	–	–	–	–
MSIFA(ours)	**56.63 ± 0.80**	**74.63 ± 0.67**	**56.96 ± 0.94**	**74.63 ± 0.98**	**49.32 ± 0.91**	**68.45 ± 0.80**	**62.72 ± 0.78**	**82.69 ± 0.66**

improved, but the improvement is very obvious on individual datasets. The reason is that ProtoNet only performs feature extraction on images at a single scale, and the feature information contained is not sufficient. And it performs global feature extraction on the incoming image, and then outputs it directly. However, in an image sample with a label, the information representing the label of the image may only be a part of the area (target object area) in the image, and the feature information content of this part of the area is the key content of the image. Therefore, the feature information extracted by this method cannot better express the important feature information in the image. In order to improve the above problems, this paper designs a multi-scale generation module (MSFGM) to obtain rich image feature information about the original image. Then, the important feature information of the image at different scales is obtained by designing a module with a self-attention mechanism. This enhances the model's ability to capture important feature information in the image. Outperforming the baseline methods on multiple datasets not only proves the effectiveness of our method, but also shows that our method has good generalization.

Compared with the DN4 method which focuses on comparing the local details of the image for classification, the classification accuracy of this method on the Standford Dogs and CUB-200-2011 datasets exceeds that of the DN4 algorithm. Among them, there are 120 kinds of dog image samples in the Standford Dogs dataset, and 200 categories of bird data in the CUB-200-2011 dataset. What they have in common is that because the gap between categories is not only small, but also has many similar local details. This also just shows that the classification model that only focuses on the comparison between details may produce bias when the local details between categories are close. Moreover, the acquired feature information based only on a single scale is not comprehensive enough. The method in this paper relies on the multi-scale generation module to generate multiple sets of feature information about the sample. Then use the self-attention feature aggregation module to obtain important feature information at different scales, so as to complete the comprehensive feature learning.

Table 2. Experimental results of the impact of feature scale quantity classification performance.

Method	5-way 1-shot	5-way 5-shot
MSIFA^1(MS = 1)	54.71 ± 0.86	71.83 ± 0.73
MSIFA^2(MS = 2)	55.75 ± 0.87	73.45 ± 0.73
MSIFA^3(MS = 3)	56.38 ± 0.81	74.15 ± 0.66
MSIFA^4(MS = 4)	**56.63 ± 0.80**	**74.63 ± 0.67**

4.4 Ablation Experiment

In this section, four variant experiments are designed to verify the influence of the number of multi-scale features in the multi-scale generation module MSIFA on the model performance. In the miniImageNet dataset, the backbone network used is Conv4-64, and the experimental results are shown in Table 2. From the experimental results, we can know that: 1) The method MSIFA using 4 feature scales achieves the best classification accuracy. Compared with a single scale (MS = 1), four scales (MS = 4) have a more obvious performance improvement. The classification accuracy improves by 2.13% and 2.80% in the 5-way 1-shot and 5-way 5-shot settings, respectively. The reason is that a single-scale feature can only obtain feature information about an image at a single level, which is relatively one-sided. The features generated at multiple scales not only have more detailed image features, but also have global feature information of the image. Thus, more accurate information representation of images in multiple scales is achieved. 2) With the increasing number of scales, the classification accuracy is also increasing. But at the same time, we also found that with the continuous increase of the number of scales, the improvement of the classification accuracy is also smaller and smaller. In the final analysis, although features of different scales can enrich the feature expression of samples, the more scales, the more redundancy. In order to take into account the computational consumption of the model and the classification accuracy, this paper selects four scale features with high cost performance for experiments.

5   Conclusion

In this paper, we propose a few-shot learning method based on multi-scale important feature fusion MSIFA. The method firstly uses the multi-scale generation module MSFGM to generate the feature information of an image sample on 4 scales, so as to obtain the rich feature information of the sample. The feature information obtained in most few-shot learning strategies is relatively single. Then, the self-attention aggregation module SAFAM constructed by the self-attention mechanism extracts the important features of the same sample at four scales respectively. After that, they are spliced and aggregated together, and used as a more accurate feature information representation of the sample. Extensive experiments are carried out on 4 datasets for verification, and the experimental results show that the proposed method can significantly improve the classification accuracy of the baseline method.

References

1. Ji, X., Henriques, J.F., Vedaldi, A.: Invariant information clustering for unsupervised image classification and segmentation. In: Proceedings of the IEEE/CVF International Conference on Computer Vision, pp. 9865–9874 (2019)
2. Chen, L.C., Papandreou, G., Kokkinos, I., et al.: DeepLab: semantic image segmentation with deep convolutional nets, atrous convolution, and fully connected CRFs. IEEE Trans. Pattern Anal. Mach. Intell. 40(4), 834–848 (2017)
3. Everingham, M., Van Gool, L., Williams, C.K., Winn, J., et al.: The Pascal visual object classes (VOC) challenge. Int. J. Comput. Vision 88(2), 303–338 (2010)
4. Russakovsky, O., Deng, J., Su, H., et al.: Imagenet large scale visual recognition challenge. Int. J. Comput. Vision 115(3), 211–252 (2015)
5. Krizhevsky, A., Sutskever, I., Hinton, G.E.: Imagenet classification with deep convolutional neural networks. Commun. ACM 60(6), 84–90 (2017)
6. Fei-Fei, L., Fergus, R., Perona, P.: One-shot learning of object categories. IEEE Trans. Pattern Anal. Mach. Intell. 28(4), 594–611 (2006)
7. Snell, J., Swersky, K., Zemel, R.: Prototypical networks for few-shot learning. In: Advances in Neural Information Processing Systems, vol. 30 (2017)
8. Mishra, N., Rohaninejad, M., Chen, X., et al.: A simple neural attentive metalearner. arXiv preprint arXiv:1707.03141 (2017)
9. Nichol, A., Schulman, J.: Reptile: a scalable metalearning algorithm. arXiv preprint arXiv:1803.02999, 2(3), 4 (2018)
10. Koch, G., Zemel, R., Salakhutdinov, R.: Siamese neural networks for one-shot image recognition. In: ICML Deep Learning Workshop, vol. 2 (2015)
11. Vinyals, O., Blundell, C., Lillicrap, T., et al.: Matching networks for one shot learning. In: Advances in Neural Information Processing Systems, vol. 29 (2016)
12. Sung, F., Yang, Y., Zhang, L., Xiang, T., et al.: Learning to compare: Relation network for few-shot learning. In: Proceedings of the IEEE Conference on Computer Vision and Pattern Recognition, pp. 1199–1208 (2018)
13. Chen, H., Li, H., Li, Y.: Multi-scale adaptive task attention network for few-shot learning. arXiv preprint arXiv:2011.14479 (2020)
14. Santoro, A., Bartunov, S., Botvinick, M., et al.: Meta-learning with memory-augmented neural networks. In: International Conference on Machine Learning, pp. 1842–1850. PMLR (2016)
15. Finn, C., Abbeel, P., Levine, S.: Model-agnostic meta-learning for fast adaptation of deep networks. In: International Conference on Machine Learning, pp. 1126–1135. PMLR (2017)
16. Ravi, S., Larochelle, H.: Optimization as a model for few-shot learning (2016)
17. Zhang, M., Zhang, J., Lu, Z., et al.: IEPT: instance-level and episode-level pretext tasks for few-shot learning. In: International Conference on Learning Representations (2020)
18. Shyam, P., Gupta, S., Dukkipati, A.: Attentive recurrent comparators. In: International Conference on Machine Learning, pp. 3173–3181. PMLR (2017)
19. Vaswani, A., Shazeer, N., Parmar, N., et al.: Attention is all you need. In: Advances in Neural Information Processing Systems. vol. 30 (2017)

20. Ren, M., Triantafillou, E., Ravi, S., et al.: Meta-learning for semi-supervised few-shot classification. arXiv preprint arXiv:1803.00676 (2018)
21. Khosla, A., Jayadevaprakash, N., Yao, B., et al.: Novel dataset for fine-grained image categorization: Stanford dogs. In: Proceedings CVPR Workshop on Fine-Grained Visual Categorization (FGVC), vol. 2, no. 1. Citeseer (2011)
22. Wah, C., Branson, S., Welinder, P., et al.: The Caltech-UCSD birds-200-2011 dataset (2011)
23. Allen, K., Shelhamer, E., Shin, H., et al.: Infinite mixture prototypes for few-shot learning. In: International Conference on Machine Learning, pp. 232–241. PMLR (2019)
24. Li, W., Wang, L., Xu, J., et al.: Revisiting local descriptor based image-to-class measure for few-shot learning. In: Proceedings of the IEEE/CVF Conference on Computer Vision and Pattern Recognition, pp. 7260–7268 (2019)
25. Wu, Z., Li, Y., Guo, L., et al.: PARN: position-aware relation networks for few-shot learning. In: Proceedings of the IEEE/CVF International Conference on Computer Vision, pp. 6659–6667 (2019)
26. Simon, C., Koniusz, P., Nock, R., et al.: Adaptive subspaces for few-shot learning. In: Proceedings of the IEEE/CVF Conference on Computer Vision and Pattern Recognition, pp. 4136–4145 (2020)
27. Liu, B., et al.: Negative margin matters: understanding margin in few-shot classification. In: Vedaldi, A., Bischof, H., Brox, T., Frahm, J.-M. (eds.) ECCV 2020. LNCS, vol. 12349, pp. 438–455. Springer, Cham (2020). https://doi.org/10.1007/978-3-030-58548-8_26
28. Oh, J., Yoo, H., Kim, C., et al.: BOIL: towards representation change for few-shot learning. arXiv preprint arXiv:2008.08882 (2020)

Group Residual Dense Block for Key-Point Detector with One-Level Feature

Jianming Zhang⑩, Jia-Jun Tao, Li-Dan Kuang$^{(\boxtimes)}$⑩, and Yan Gui

School of Computer and Communication Engineering, Changsha University
of Science and Technology, Changsha 410114, China
kuangld@csust.edu.cn

Abstract. In this paper, we propose a novel key-point detector with only one-level feature with the stride of 8, which is 75.0% less than methods with the stride of 4. Due to the reduction of the feature layers, firstly we adopt a new key-point labeling method, which can make full use of the detection points on the feature map. Secondly, we propose a U-shaped feature fusion module with group residual dense blocks, which works together with grouped convolutional and re-parameterization methods to bring significant improvements while reducing parameters. Thirdly, we use a soft non-key-point branch to re-weight the classification score. Using NVIDIA GeForce 3060 GPU and based on the VOC dataset, the proposed model with RepVGG-A0 runs about 51.4% faster than Center-Net with ResNet-18, runs 261.3% faster, and achieves higher accuracy than CenterNet with ResNet-101 under the resolution of 512×512.

Keywords: Object detection · Key-point detector · One-level feature · Residual dense block · Re-parameterization

1 Introduction

Since deep learning has shaken up the traditional methods, convolutional neural networks (CNN) have indelible significance for object detection and show excellent performance. However, when considering precision, speed, and parameters, it is still an extremely complicated and challenging mission, due to the variety of shapes of objects and the complexity of the natural scene.

Anchor-free detectors address the problem of pre-defined anchor boxes, which are usually divided into two categories: pixel-wise prediction and key-point prediction. Pixel-wise detectors like FCOS [19] and FoveaBox [8] place positive samples in the ground truth, which are essentially a dense prediction. For one thing, some pixel-wise detectors use the re-weighting method to improve the detection quality. For another, the divide-and-conquer solution of feature pyramid networks (FPN) [12] using scales to manually specify that a bounding box falls in, can indeed help the detector to separate objects that are overlapped. During training, objects are designated to a certain layer, which is another form

© The Author(s), under exclusive license to Springer Nature Switzerland AG 2022
S. Khanna et al. (Eds.): PRICAI 2022, LNCS 13630, pp. 525–539, 2022.
https://doi.org/10.1007/978-3-031-20865-2_39

of anchor box, and every detection point of each layer has a fixed-size square anchor box. Although FSAF [26] dynamically assigns each object to the most suitable feature level, the detection heads at each layer bring heavy memory burden.

Key-point detectors such as CornerNet [11] and CenterNet [25] predict objects by using several key points or just one key point in the bounding box. These methods use feature map with stride of 2 or 4 because large feature map is not to have ambiguous samples. But such a large feature map also causes large memory burden, long training and inference time. For instance, the number of detection points in one feature map with stride of 4 is 4 times that with stride of 8. Besides, in the area where small targets gather, if only the center point is considered, it may lead to miss samples. In addition, since there are no pre-defined anchor boxes, anchor-free methods have higher requirements for feature ability especially in lightweight model.

Nowadays, most state-of-the-art models depend on the computer with extremely computation power. Complicated models need to be trained in powerful GPUs or distributed computing. Meanwhile, it is challenging to run a complex model in real-time. Therefore, it is difficult to be equipped in the industrial field and greatly limits the application and promotion. What if we propose a model that balances the precision, parameters, and runs on popularized GPU? This paper provides an idea. We propose a simple and lightweight anchor-free detector using the key-point method, a single-level feature map and group residual dense blocks. The main contributions of this paper are summarized as follows:

1. To avoid the limiting effect caused by invisible anchor boxes, we only use one feature map with the stride of 8 to predict all objects, and propose a new labeling method for key points. The number of detection points is reduced by 75% compared to the key-point method with the stride of 4, and 24.9% compared to multi-scale method which uses a feature pyramid with 6 levels.
2. We propose a novel U-shaped feature fusion module embedded group residual dense block (shorted as g-RDB) and use re-parameterization to merge the parameters, which can meet the satisfying performance and speed with only a few parameters.
3. We propose a soft non-key-point suppression (shorted as soft-NKS) branch to re-weight the classification scores of points which are far from key points.

The rest of this paper is arranged as follows. Section 2 describes the structure and missions of our proposed detector. In Sect. 3, we conduct experiments on the VOC and COCO datasets to verify the advantage of the proposed method. Finally, the conclusion of the paper is given in Sect. 4.

2   The Proposed Method

2.1   Backbone Network and Detection Head

The backbone of this paper uses the modified RepVGG-A0 [3] as the baseline. A two-layer image pyramid containing C_3 and C_4 with different sizes and channels from the backbone network is preserved, and the strides of each layer are 8 and 16, which is shown in Fig. 1.

For the detection head, we use several RepVGG blocks for P_3 layer. Then we decouple the network into two sub-networks, as independent branches can learn more features to suppress non-objects. Corresponding to the training missions, one sub-network is used for the classification branch, and another provides the share parameters for the localization branch and soft-NKS branch. Finally, we use a RepVGG block without BN [7] layer and ReLU [5] function to adjust the number of convolutional channels according to different tasks.

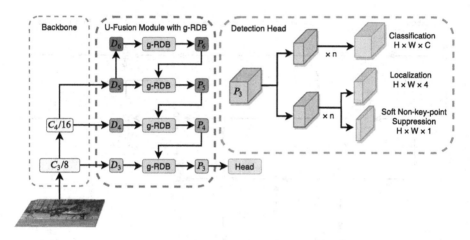

Fig. 1. The architecture of the proposed g-RDB for the key-point detector with one-level feature. 8 and 16 are the down-sampling ratios for each feature map layer. The detection head can be superimposed continuously, we only use one in our experiments unless specified otherwise.

2.2   U-Fusion Module with Proposed g-RDB

U-Shaped Feature Fusion Module. As shown in Fig. 2, we construct a four-layer structure in the fusion stage and make the original two-layer feature layer have a stronger expressive ability. we set the output channel number N to 128 as an example. First, we use two 3×3 RepVGG blocks with the stride of 2 to down-sample C_4 twice which are denoted as D_5 and D_6 respectively, and the channel number of D_5 and D_6 is half of N. The channel number of C_4 is reduced to half of N through a 1×1 convolution (denoted as D_4). If the channel number of C_3 is not the same as half of N, we add 1×1 convolution (denoted as D_3) to reduce the channels as well.

Secondly, D_6 is sent into g-RDB to generate P_6 for integrating and utilizing its internal feature information. Thirdly, we use bilinear interpolation to up-sample the feature map to the same size as the previous layer. If the channel number of feature layer that needs to be up-sampled is inconsistent with the previous one, we add a 1×1 convolution to adjust before up-sampling. Fourthly, the up-sampled map is merged with the corresponding feature map with the same size by concatenating operation. Finally, repeat the second to fourth steps until the four-layer features which generated in the first step. As a result, the feature layers P_3, P_4, P_5, and P_6 have strides 8, 16, 32, and 64, respectively. We use concatenation instead of element-wise addition. The element-wise addition focuses on reusing features, while the concatenation operation benefits from the discovery of new features [23].

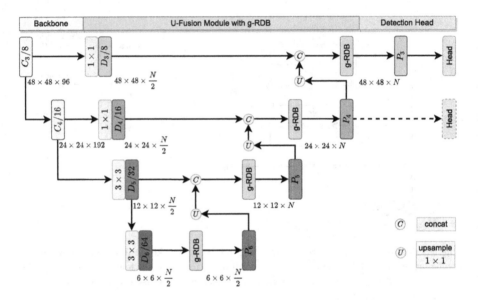

Fig. 2. The structure of the U-shaped feature fusion module with the proposed g-RDB. The detection head of the P_4 layer is represented by a dotted line, which means that it is deleted during the inference phase. We set N to 128 as the baseline. The 3×3 is composed of a RepVGG block, and 1×1 is composed of 1×1 convolution, residual, ReLU function, and BN layer.

However, when training, we only save the results of P_3 and P_4 as the input features for the next step. We retain the feature fusion and predict all targets on a feature map as much as possible. In inference, the branch of P_4 is deleted (as shown in Fig. 2), and all prediction results are obtained by P_3. We keep P_4 in training because the object in the P_4 layer can still be constrained by the loss function. Therefore, the part of information can be flowed from P_4 to P_3 and used when P_3 is fused, which further helps P_3 predict the correct object.

Proposed g-RDB. Figure 3 exhibits the structure of the proposed g-RDB. We first use three RepVGG blocks to preserve the information to access all the subsequent layers and pass on information [24]. Since the number of channels in the first three layers of convolution is the same, we add the original residual information and output from the previous convolutional layer (see the blue lines in Fig. 3) which can easily flow layer by layer. Each data after the three-branch block is skip-connected with the original input to minimize gradient explosion and gradient disappearance. Next, we concatenate the original input and all outputs from three convolution layers (see the green lines in Fig. 3), and the channel of the output feature is 4 times the original input. Then, we use a 1×1 convolutional layer to reduce the number of channels and add the original input for local feature fusion. To further reduce the number of parameters, we use grouped convolution [9] instead of the 3×3 convolution. The group residual dense block is defined as follows:

$$
\begin{cases}
F_{1_1} = \delta\left(\varphi_{3\times3}\left(F_0\right) + \varphi_{1\times1}\left(F_0\right) + F_0\right), \\
F_{1_2} = \delta\left(\varphi_{3\times3}\left(F_{1_1}\right) + \varphi_{1\times1}\left(F_{1_1}\right) + F_{1_1} + F_0\right), \\
F_{1_3} = \delta\left(\varphi_{3\times3}\left(F_{1_2}\right) + \varphi_{1\times1}\left(F_{1_2}\right) + F_{1_2} + F_0\right),
\end{cases}
\tag{1}
$$

$$
F_2 = \text{concat}\left(F_0, F_{1_1}, F_{1_2}, F_{1_3}\right), \tag{2}
$$

$$
F_3 = \delta\left(\varphi_{1\times1}\left(F_2\right) + F_0\right), \tag{3}
$$

Here F_0 is the original input, F_{1_1}–F_{1_3} are outputs of g-RDB, $\varphi_{1\times1}$ is 1×1 convolution, $\varphi_{3\times3}$ is 3×3 convolution, δ is ReLU function, and "concat" is concatenating operation.

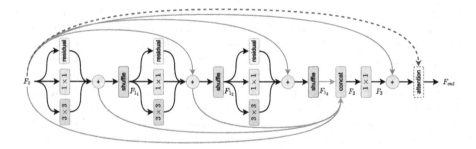

Fig. 3. The structure of proposed g-RDB [10]. (Color figure online)

However, grouped convolution brings another problem. Each group only convolutes on the feature map in its own group. In the residual dense block, information is continuously transmitted one by one. If the information is limited in each group, it could block the interaction between channels. Therefore, we appropriately use the method of disrupting the channel to help it carry out more information fusion. Grouped convolution allows the filter to learn in a sparse diagonal structure in the channel dimension, so parameters that do not need to be learned are no longer parameterized. In addition, grouped convolution can significantly reduce the number of network parameters while reducing the occurrence of network overfitting [21]. According to [16], in the g-RDB module, the feature information is shuffled and used as the input of the next convolution. In the meanwhile, the shuffled features are concatenated up and used as the input of the 1×1 convolution. Finally, we add original input features and output features together for another long local fusion. Our proposed g-RDB can also work well with attention modules, the attention modules can be used to further increase the feature extraction after long local fusion when necessary (see gray dotted line in Fig. 3). The attention modules are not used unless otherwise specified.

2.3   Detection Missions

Classification. The goal of the classification task is to predict the probability of the pixels on the feature map of each class. Since our purpose is to predict on a single feature map, we put the object on the P_3 layer as much as possible. The rules of labeling the key point of an object are listed as follows. Firstly, sort the area of the object from small to large. Secondly, mark the center point as a positive sample and ensure that the smallest object is placed on P_3. Thirdly, look for the second position if there is a conflict between the center point of the new object and the previous one. Expand outward from the center point to find the first non-conflicting position. The IoU value between this position and the ground truth bounding box must be greater than 0.7. Fourthly, look for the object on the P_4 layer by using steps 2–3 if still cannot find a position on the P_3 layer for the new object. Finally, give up labeling if there is still no position.

For any object which satisfies the conditions mentioned above, we calculate the position of a bounding box which is the only positive sample marked as (x^+, y^+), and other points in the bounding box become negative samples naturally marked as (x^-, y^-). We put the positive samples on the heat-map of each category, and let the positive sample prediction value $Y_{x,y,c}^{gt} = 1$. Following [25], we use a Gaussian kernel as background to soften the prediction value for negative samples. If two Gaussian values of the same class conflict in the same feature layer, the element-wise maximum is taken. Similar to [13], we train C binary classifiers instead of training a multi-class classifier, where C is the number of categories of natural scenes, which is 20 for the Pascal VOC dataset [4] and 80 for the COCO dataset [14].

Localization. For each positive sample, we use a 4-dimension vector $\mathbf{v}^{gt} = (d_l, d_t, d_r, d_b)$ for location regression. Here d_l, d_t, d_r, and d_b are the original image distances from the positive point to the four sides of the bounding box. Since we only use one feature map for detection, using the exponential function to map the distance may cause an overflow. We use ReLU function to map the point-to-boundary distances to $(0, +\infty)$.

Proposed Soft Non-Key-Point Suppression. Aggregated objects may cause a large number of prediction points with high scores to appear near the real key points, which is more obvious in lightweight detectors. It leads to redundant bounding boxes around the target and cannot be eliminated by NMS [17]. We proposed a simple and effective soft-NKS branch to predict the values for each point and soften the detected classification score of bounding boxes that are far away from the key point. We put the positive samples on a heat-map and let the soft-NKS prediction value $Q_{x,y}^{gt} = 1$. Then put a box with the same size as the ground truth bounding box in a negative position, and calculate the IoU value as the softened value for the negative sample. The score of the soft-NKS branch ranges from 0 to 1. The final classification score with soft-NKS is defined as:

$$p_{cls\_nks} = (p_{cls})^{(2-p_{nks}) \times \alpha},\qquad(4)$$

where p_{cls_nks} is score after suppression, p_{cls} is classification score, p_{nks} is soft-NKS score, and α is the inhibition ratio.

Loss Function. The loss for whole network defined as:

$$L = \frac{\lambda_1}{N^+} \sum_{x,y,c} \mathrm{FL}(Y_{x,y,c}^{gt}, Y_{x,y,c}^{pred}) + \frac{\lambda_2}{N^+} \sum_{x,y} \mathrm{IoU}(\mathbf{v}^{gt}, \mathbf{v}^{pred})$$
$$+ \frac{\lambda_3}{N} \sum_{x,y} \mathrm{BCE}(Q_{x,y}^{gt}, Q_{x,y}^{pred}).\qquad(5)$$

Here N^+ is the number of positive points and N denotes all detection points. $Y_{x,y,c}^{pred}$, $\mathbf{v}^{pred}$, and $Q_{x,y}^{pred}$ are the predicted values obtained from the network. We set "FL" denotes upgraded focal loss [25] for classification branch, "IoU" is IoU loss [22] for localization branch, and "BCE" denotes binary cross entropy loss for soft-NKS branch.

3   Experiments and Results

3.1   Training Details

In this paper, we build our experimental environments under Windows Server 2019 operating system, Intel(R) Core(TM) i7-10700 CPU, one NVIDIA GeForce 3060 GPU, PyTorch 1.9, CUDA 11.3.109, and cuDNN 8.2.1.32.

We train our model on the VOC 2007 and 2012 [4] which contains 16,551 training images and evaluate our performance on VOC 2007 test set which contains 4,952 testing images. All models are trained for 250 epochs. We use learning rate 10^{-5} to warm up at the first epoch [15], then go back to learning rate 10^{-3} and continue training for 99 epochs. Then we decay the learning rate to 10^{-4} with a cosine annealing for 100 epochs [6]. Finally, we decay the learning rate to 5^{-6} with a cosine annealing for 50 epochs.

We also train our model on COCO 2017 dataset [14], which contains 118k training images, and test on the test-dev set which contains 20k testing images. All models are trained for 110 epochs. We train 24 epochs with a learning rate

10^{-3}, then decay the learning rate to 10^{-4} with a cosine annealing for 64 epochs. Finally, we decay the learning rate to 5^{-6} with a cosine annealing for 22 epochs.

We use one GPU with 16 images per batch and initialize our backbone with the weights pre-trained on ImageNet. All models are trained with Adam optimizer. Data augmentation includes random expanding, random horizontal flipping, random cropping [18], and mosaic [1]. The mosaic is only used with a 50% probability for the VOC dataset when the learning rate is greater than 10^{-4}.

For the VOC dataset, we set the confidence threshold to 0.05, NMS with a threshold of 0.5, and report the mean average precision (mAP) at IoU thresholds 0.5 (AP_{50}) and balanced F_1 score with at IoU thresholds 0.5. We use the downloaded code[1] to evaluate the results of VOC2007. For the COCO 2017 dataset, we set the same confidence and NMS threshold, and report average precision (AP) overall IoU thresholds, AP at IoU thresholds 0.5 (AP_{50}), and 0.75 (AP_{75}). Frames per second (FPS) is tested on NVIDIA GeForce 3060 GPU with a batch size of 1 for each model on the same machine. The detection time includes the time-consuming of CPU and GPU, excluding the time when image data is transferred from CPU to GPU. Among them, the network inference and the soft-NKS are calculated by the GPU, and the NMS process is calculated by the CPU.

3.2   One-Level vs. Multi-Scale

Table 1 shows the effect of our proposed one-level method and the multi-scale method. Following other multi-scale key-point detector [10], we use the way of assigning the target samples to the corresponding feature layers. When the resolution is 384×384, the scale ranges of m_3 to m_6 are set to 48, 96, 192, and 384, respectively. When the resolution is 512×512, the scale ranges of m_3 to m_7 are set to 48, 96, 192, 384, and 768, respectively. So there are two models of different parameters for the multi-scale method. Since each layer requires a detection head, the parameters of the model at a resolution of 384×384 and 512×512 are 18.0% and 21.1% higher than the one-level method. Besides, the speed is reduced by 22.6% and 23.7%, respectively.

When the resolution is 512×512, the accuracy of the one-level and the multi-scale method is 84.47% and 87.51%, respectively. For the one-level method, the highest proportion of false positives occurs when the IoU threshold is lower than 0.5. The reason for this phenomenon is that multi-scale detection has more detection points than the one-level method. In addition, with soft-NKS, more detection points for suppression can be provided, so it is possible to eliminate duplicate objects and eliminate objects with lower IoU thresholds. The recall rates of the one-level and the multi-scale method is 73.93% and 62.59%, respectively, because the features richness increases from top to bottom in multi-scale prediction. Since the multi-scale method uses manually specifying a size for training, the semantic and spatial information required by different objects of the same size cannot be treated equally (such as a cat near and a tree far away).

---

[1] https://github.com/Cartucho/mAP/.

In the one-level method, all objects are predicted by the bottom feature map with the most abundant features, so the recall rate is higher than the multi-scale method.

The precision and recall have their own merits under those two methods, and the result of the F_1 score can better reflect the overall detection results of the model. Although the gap between the AP_{50} of the whole category is within 1%, the difference of the F_1 score is 6.2%. Therefore, the use of one-level method and multi-scale method needs to consider the actual application scenarios. If detecting scenes with pretty dramatic scale changes or pursuing a high recall, the one-level method is superior to the multi-scale method.

3.3   Grouped Convolution vs. Depth-Wise Separable Convolution

Table 2 compares our proposed g-RDB with a series of group numbers for normal 2D convolutions and depth-wise separable convolutions. When the group number is set to be 1, it means there is no grouping in g-RDB, but we still shuffle features for time-consuming. According to [16], the larger the number of groups, the slower the calculation. The group number is set to 4 and can still maintain a higher performance, and the parameters of inference are reduced by 58.7% compared to 1. When it is set to 8, the accuracy and speed decline.

Table 1. Ablation study for one-level and multi-scale method. "Params(M)" is parameters of the model when inference. We use RepVGG-A0 as the backbone and proposed a U-shaped feature fusion model. The output channels of all methods are set to 128.

Methods	Params(M)	Resolution	AP_{50}	F_1	FPS
Multi-scale methods	6.95	384×384	78.2	71.9	89.9
	7.13	512×512	79.0	72.5	85.3
Proposed one-level method	**5.89**	384×384	78.8	77.0	**115.8**
		512×512	**81.1**	**78.7**	111.8

While the depth-wise separable convolution method reduces the speed by 35.6% compared to the normal 2D convolution. For models that are run and tested on GPUs, using depth-wise separable convolutions which are designed for CPUs may cause less effectiveness. If the ordinary convolutions are replaced by depth-wise separable convolutions, the model size will indeed be significantly reduced, but the calculation speed of the model will be reduced because the original one-time calculation becomes two times.

Table 2. Ablation study for grouped convolution and depth-wise separable convolution. "DW Separable" is depth-wise separable convolution, and "Params(M)" is the parameters of the U-shaped module in millions after re-parameterized. We use RepVGG-A0 as the backbone, the output channel of g-RDB is set to 128. We observed up to 0.5 mAP jitter due to randomness in training.

Convolution type	Group numbers	Params(M)	AP_{50}	F_1	FPS
DW Separable	–	0.45	79.3	76.9	82.4
Grouped	1	1.84	80.7	77.8	114.6
	2	1.12	80.5	78.0	113.6
	4	0.76	81.1	78.7	111.8
	8	0.58	80.1	77.1	105.9

3.4   With or Without Soft-NKS

As shown in Fig. 4, we compare the proposed methods with and without soft-NKS. We set the NMS threshold as 0.5, and the confidence threshold as 0.2. Figure 4(b) displays two bounding boxes classified as car (vs. an extra bounding box with a confidence to 0.21 in Fig. 4(a)), and does not wrongly detect the graffiti as potted plants and a bicycle which are detected by Fig. 4(a). This is because the classification score is suppressed by the soft-NKS branch (i.e., (4)), and the score cannot reach the confidence threshold.

In addition, it can be observed that the car on the left side of the image is partially occluded. After the soft-NKS suppression, the score is reduced from 0.51 in Fig. 4.7a to 0.31 in Fig. 4.7b, which may be due to the small edge target

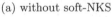

(a) without soft-NKS   (b) with soft-NKS

Fig. 4. Qualitative comparison results of the proposed methods without soft-NKS (a) and with soft-NKS (b).

Table 3. Ablation study for inhibitory factor in soft-NKS. We use RepVGG-A0 as the backbone. F_1 score takes into account the accuracy and recall of the model.

NKS	α	AP_{50}	F_1	FPS
–	–	80.9	77.7	**115.3**
$\checkmark$	1	79.4	75.6	111.9
$\checkmark$	0.9	79.9	76.5	111.2
$\checkmark$	0.75	80.6	77.7	111.8
$\checkmark$	0.6	**81.1**	**78.6**	111.8

leading to deviations in the prediction of key points. However, it can still be kept above the threshold. The person and bicycle in the center of the image can be maintained before and after using soft-NKS, indicating that the key point prediction is accurate.

To verify the influence as well as to find a proper value for the inhibitory factor, we set up some experiments on the VOC2007 test. The mAP, F_1 score, and FPS results with and without soft-NKS are detailed in Table 3. It can be concluded from Table 3 that the F_1 score of the proposed method with $\alpha = 0.6$ is 0.85 higher than without using soft-NKS. Meanwhile, only about 4 FPS are additionally calculated by soft-NKS (115.3 vs. 111.8).

3.5 Comparison Results on VOC2007

We compare our proposed detector with other state-of-the-art anchor-free detectors in the VOC2007 test in Table 4. We experiment proposed method with our modified RepVGG-A0, RepVGG-B0 [3], ResNet-18, and ResNet-50 [6] which only contains two layers. Therefore, the proposed method is much fewer parameters than other same backbone networks. Note that, the original FCOS [19] use the input images which are resized to have their shorter side being 384 or 512 and their longer side is scaled proportionally. In order to make the same comparison, we resize images to the same length and width.

Our proposed method with modified ResNet-18 achieves higher AP and FPS values than CenterNet with the same backbone, and parameters down by as much as 71.5%. Besides, our proposed detector with the modified ResNet-50 surpasses the CenterNet with ResNet-101 and obtains higher AP and FPS values, and cut its parameters by nearly 67.0%. Compared to FCOS with ResNet-50, the modified ResNet-50 achieves higher accuracy and shows 2.66 times higher FPS. Moreover, our proposed method with RepVGG-A0 reports better AP and FPS values than MSKPD [10] with ResNet-18 and about 48.9% drops in the number of parameters. In addition, our proposed method with RepVGG-B0 at a resolution of 512×512 achieves AP and FPS at 83.1 and 107 respectively, which is 0.9% higher and 1.37 times faster than MSKPD with ResNet-50.

Table 4. All models are tested in our experimental environments. "AP_{50}" with superscript * is copied from the original publications. Backbone with superscript † is the modified network that only contains two layers.

Methods	Backbone	Params(M)	Size	AP_{50}	FPS
CenterNet [25]	ResNet-18	13.78	384×384	72.6*	86
			512×512	75.7*	74
	ResNet-101	30.86	384×384	77.6*	34
			512×512	78.7*	31
MSKPD [10]	ResNet-18	11.37	384×384	77.3*	87
		11.52	512×512	79.3*	77
	ResNet-50	23.45	384×384	80.5*	65
		23.60	512×512	82.2*	60
FCOS [19]	ResNet-50	30.86	384×384	74.6	27
			512×512	76.6	25
	ResNet-101	48.31	384×384	81.1	17
			512×512	82.4	14
Proposed	ResNet-18†	3.93	384×384	76.2	99
			512×512	77.1	96
	ResNet-50†	10.18	384×384	80.9	82
			512×512	81.4	78
	RepVGG-A0†	5.89	384×384	78.8	115
			512×512	81.1	112
	RepVGG-B0†	11.23	384×384	81.6	109
			512×512	83.1	107

3.6 Comparison Results on COCO2017

We compare our proposed method with other anchor-based and anchor-free detectors on COCO val2017 in Table 5. We experiment proposed method with our modified RepVGG-A0 [3] which contains two layers. The CBAM [20] module is embedded in the end of the g-RDB of P_3 layer. Note that, RetinaNet [13], FCOS [19], YOLOF [2] use the input images which are resized to have their shorter side being 512 and their longer side is scaled proportionally. In order to make the same comparison, we resize images to the same length and width.

The proposed method with modified RepVGG-A0 and four-layer detection head has the highest AP over all IoU thresholds, AP at IoU thresholds 0.5 and 0.75. Compared to the CenterNet with ResNet-18 obtains an improvement of 2.8% AP over all IoU thresholds, 4.7% AP at IoU threshold 0.5, and 3.1% AP at IoU threshold 0.75. It even reduces the number of parameters by about 42.7%. Through experiments, our proposed method has advantages in small object detection (see AP_S). We speculate that this is because the g-RDB enhances the network's ability to retain detailed information and integrates the location information of shallow features. The proposed model with RepVGG-A0 and a four-convolution-layer head achieves real-time detection in natural scenes.

Table 5. The proposed method vs. other detectors on COCO val2017. Backbone with superscript † is the modified network which only contains two layers. Proposed method with superscript "h1" means that we use one convolution layer for detection head and "h4" means four. All models are tested under GeForce 3060 with a batch-size of 1.

Methods	Backbone	Params(M)	FPS	AP	AP_{50}	AP_{75}	AP_S	AP_M	AP_L
RetinaNet [13]	ResNet-18	18.91	38	24.8	40.6	26.0	8.5	26.4	39.6
FCOS [19]	ResNet-18	36.62	43	27.6	43.4	29.1	9.5	30.0	43.7
CenterNet [25]	ResNet-18	13.78	67	27.8	44.8	28.7	8.5	29.2	45.5
CenterNet [25]	ResNet-101	47.50	31	33.2	51.6	35	11.6	36.8	52.9
YOLO-Tiny [1]	CSPDarkNet-Tiny	7.53	79	28.0	47.8	28.5	12.7	32.6	37.5
YOLOF [2]	ResNet-18	29.64	87	25.9	41.6	27.0	5.8	27.4	45.3
Proposed^{h1}	RepVGG-A0†	7.44	88	29.5	48.5	30.2	12.4	31.1	43.8
Proposed^{h4}	RepVGG-A0†	7.89	86	30.6	49.5	31.8	13.2	32.5	45.3

4   Conclusion

In this paper, we proposed a novel key-point detector that relies on only one feature layer with g-RDB. First of all, we use grouped convolutions, multi-branch structures, and the shuffle method to obtain a powerful g-RDB module, which significantly improved feature extraction capability and reduced the number of parameters. Secondly, for avoiding the occurrence of ambiguous detection points due to the reduction of feature layers, we proposed a new sample labeling method. Thirdly, we proposed a soft-NKS branch to re-weight the classification score for points that are far away from the key point. We only use the regular image augmentation and the mosiac method as tricks, and experiment results demonstrate the advantage of our proposed method. Our proposed methods with RepVGG-A0 achieve 81.1 mAP and run at 112 FPS on NVIDIA GeForce 3060 which is about 51.4% faster than CenterNet with ResNet-18 and 261.3% faster than CenterNet with ResNet-101 on the VOC2007 test under the resolution of 512×512. Code is available at https://github.com/Tao-JiaJun/g-RDB.

Acknowledgments. This work was supported by National Natural Science Foundation of China under Grants 61972056, 61901061, Natural Science Foundation of Hunan Province under Grant 2020JJ5603, the Scientific Research Fund of Hunan Provincial Education Department under Grant 19C0031, 19C0028, the Young Teachers' Growth Plan of Changsha University of Science and Technology under Grant 2019QJCZ011.

References

1. Bochkovskiy, A., Wang, C.Y., Liao, H.Y.: YOLOv4: optimal speed and accuracy of object detection. ArXiv: abs/2004.10934, pp. 1–17 (2020)
2. Chen, Q., Wang, Y., Yang, T., Zhang, X., Cheng, J., Sun, J.: You only look one-level feature, pp. 13034–13043 (2021). https://doi.org/10.1109/CVPR46437.2021.01284
3. Ding, X., Zhang, X., Ma, N., et al.: RepVGG: making VGG-Style convnets great again. In: 2021 IEEE/CVF CVPR, pp. 13728–13737 (2021). https://doi.org/10.1109/CVPR46437.2021.01352
4. Everingham, M., Gool, L.V., Williams, C.K.I., et al.: The pascal visual object classes (VOC) challenge. Int. J. Comput. Vision **88**, 303–338 (2009)
5. Glorot, X., Bordes, A., Bengio, Y.: Deep sparse rectifier neural networks. J. Mach. Learn. Res. **15**, 315–323 (2011)
6. He, K., Zhang, X., Ren, S., Sun, J.: Deep residual learning for image recognition. In: 2016 IEEE/CVF CVPR, pp. 770–778 (2016)
7. Ioffe, S., Szegedy, C.: Batch normalization: accelerating deep network training by reducing internal covariate shift. JMLR.org (2015)
8. Kong, T., Sun, F., Liu, H., et al.: FoveaBox: beyound anchor-based object detection. IEEE TIP **29**, 7389–7398 (2020). https://doi.org/10.1109/TIP.2020.3002345
9. Krizhevsky, A., Sutskever, I., Hinton, G.E.: ImageNet classification with deep convolutional neural networks. Commun. ACM **60**, 84–90 (2012)
10. Kuang, L.D., Tao, J.J., Zhang, J., et al.: A novel multi-scale key-point detector using residual dense block and coordinate attention. In: 28th ICONIP 2021, pp. 235–246 (2021)
11. Law, H., Deng, J.: CornerNet: detecting objects as paired keypoints. Int. J. Comput. Vis. **128**(3), 642–656 (2020)
12. Lin, T.Y., Dollár, P., Girshick, R.B., et al.: Feature pyramid networks for object detection. In: 2017 IEEE/CVF CVPR, pp. 936–944 (2017)
13. Lin, T.Y., Goyal, P., Girshick, R., et al.: Focal loss for dense object detection. In: 2017 IEEE ICCV, pp. 2999–3007 (2017). https://doi.org/10.1109/ICCV.2017.324
14. Lin, T.-Y., et al.: Microsoft COCO: common objects in context. In: Fleet, D., Pajdla, T., Schiele, B., Tuytelaars, T. (eds.) ECCV 2014. LNCS, vol. 8693, pp. 740–755. Springer, Cham (2014). https://doi.org/10.1007/978-3-319-10602-1_48
15. Loshchilov, I., Hutter, F.: SGDR: stochastic gradient descent with warm restarts. In: 5th ICLR, pp. 1–16 (2017)
16. Ma, N., Zhang, X., et al.: ShuffleNet V2: practical guidelines for efficient CNN architecture design. ArXiv: abs/1807.11164, pp. 1–19 (2018)
17. Rothe, R., Guillaumin, M., Van Gool, L.: Non-maximum suppression for object detection by passing messages between windows. In: Cremers, D., Reid, I., Saito, H., Yang, M.-H. (eds.) ACCV 2014. LNCS, vol. 9003, pp. 290–306. Springer, Cham (2015). https://doi.org/10.1007/978-3-319-16865-4_19
18. Shorten, C., Khoshgoftaar, T.M.: A survey on image data augmentation for deep learning. J. Big Data **6**, 1–48 (2019)
19. Tian, Z., Shen, C., Chen, H., et al.: FCOS: fully convolutional one-stage object detection. In: 2019 IEEE/CVF ICCV, pp. 9626–9635 (2019). https://doi.org/10.1109/ICCV.2019.00972
20. Woo, S., Park, J., Lee, J.-Y., Kweon, I.S.: CBAM: convolutional block attention module. In: Ferrari, V., Hebert, M., Sminchisescu, C., Weiss, Y. (eds.) ECCV 2018. LNCS, vol. 11211, pp. 3–19. Springer, Cham (2018). https://doi.org/10.1007/978-3-030-01234-2_1

21. Ioannou, Y.: A tutorial on filter groups (grouped convolution) (2016). https://blog. yani.ai/filter-group-tutorial/
22. Yu, J., Jiang, Y., Wang, Z., et al.: UnitBox: an advanced object detection network. In: Proceedings of the 24th ACM MM, pp. 516–520 (2016)
23. Zhang, L., Wang, Q., Lu, H., et al.: End-to-end learning of multi-scale convolutional neural network for stereo matching. In: 2018 ACML, vol. 80, pp. 1–16 (2018)
24. Zhang, Y., Tian, Y., Kong, Y., et al.: Residual dense network for image super-resolution. In: 2018 IEEE/CVF CVPR, pp. 2472–2481 (2018). https://doi.org/10. 1109/CVPR.2018.00262
25. Zhou, X., Wang, D., Krähenbühl, P.: CenterNet: objects as points. ArXiv: abs/1904.07850, pp. 1–12 (2019)
26. Zhu, C., He, Y., Savvides, M.: Feature selective anchor-free module for single-shot object detection, pp. 840–849 (2019). https://doi.org/10.1109/CVPR.2019.00093

Author Index

Printed in the United States
by Baker & Taylor Publisher Services